HAZEL C. MATHEWS

Oakville AND THE SIXTEEN

the History of an Ontario Port

UNIVERSITY OF TORONTO PRESS

Reprinted in 2018
University of Toronto Press Incorporated
Toronto and Buffalo
Reprinted in Canada with corrections 1971, 1994
ISBN 0-8020-1820-3
ISBN 978-1-4875-7905-0 (paper)
Printed on acid-free paper

LINE DRAWINGS BY JULIET CHISHOLM, M.D.

TO MY SISTER JULIET

Let me express deep gratitude to the Friends of the Oakville Historical Society for the reprinting of this book. It was one of the first histories of small town Ontario at the time my mother penned it.

Oakville and the Sixteen has become the major reference for authors and Oakville readers alike. It spans the years from the early 1800's to post World War 2, and records the transition from a mainly market and shipping port to the present-day residential, commercial and industrial community.

An integral part of this book, and, the only change to it, is the Addendum prepared by Mrs. Frances (Robin) Ahern for the 1971 edition. Amalgamation of the Town of Oakville and the Township of Trafalgar necessitated street name and number changes. I am indebted to Frances for undertaking this onerous and difficult task.

It is my hope that this third edition, which I understand has been long anticipated, will be an interesting and informative addition to the bookshelves of all its readers.

Nancy Hart
Shelburne, Nova Scotia
July 18, 1994.

FOREWORD

IN HER PREFACE to the history of the Town of Oakville Mrs. Mathews has been good enough to mention some assistance I was able to give in its planning and preparation. From childhood I had the good fortune to spend summers on the shore of Lake Ontario not far from the town itself, and to watch the "small sleepy town" develop into a residential area and an industrial centre. As I became interested in Canadian history I began to see the significance of the old lake port as typical of the story of much of Southern Ontario.

The old custom house in which Mrs. Mathews wrote this book was the nerve centre both of the port and for the plans of economic development which William Chisholm, the author's great-grandfather, made for the town and for the district attached to it. More than a century later those plans came to fruition in greater amplitude than even that enthusiast can have dreamed.

Of the many approaches to the history of a country, that of the local historian is as difficult as it can be rewarding. It calls for a nice balance between a detailed examination of the community itself and a realization that its story has little meaning unless seen in the context of the larger whole. The smaller and the larger unit constantly react on each other. To study the former in the knowledge of this allows for a picture both of a community interesting in itself and yet of one typical, in varying degrees, of a country spreading beyond it. Mrs. Mathews has faced the fundamental problem of the local historian with skill and success. Those of her readers who know Oakville will be able to trace with a special interest the story of the people, houses, shops, churches, industries, social and political life of a town with which their personal association has aroused both affection and curisoity. Other readers of Canadian history will see this history as a microcosm. The general historian has, perforce, to trace the development of major themes; and, in doing so, is in danger of giving too much weight to the vocal leaders in thought and action. The corrective to this is to know the life of at least some of the areas, urban and rural, in which the varied and complicated life of groups of people can be seen at close hand and in all its human reality.

Mrs. Mathews was fortunate in having at her disposal family letters and papers of great interest. With the true spirit of the researcher she added to the nucleus information taken from official and unofficial records, from newspapers, letters, and diaries, and from the recollections of fellow residents of Oakville. This book is a triumph of industry and enthusiasm. It is good reading for the trained historian or the general reader; and the attractive illustrations complete a work which will, I hope, encourage the writing of similar studies of other communities in Ontario.

G. de T. Glazebrook

Ottawa, August 10, 1953

PREFACE

WHEN SOME YEARS AGO the suggestion was made that I compile a history of the Town of Oakville the prospect had a singular fascination. Taking stock of my qualifications for the task I arrived at the conclusion that if an insatiable curiosity, an obsession for the factual, and the persistence of a termite were assets, I possessed some of the requirements of a researcher. But the amber was not without its fly. To marshal a heterogeneous collection of facts into an orderly procession and march them between the covers of a book I considered outside the scope of my capabilities, and this task would have to be left to the pen of a more ready writer. Unaware of having entered a fool's paradise, I scurried about, happily engaged in searching for answers to an imposing array of questions. A quantity of family papers, untouched for half a century, formed the nucleus of this local history. Authentic data relative to Oakville's early period would be virtually non-existent had not the founder held posts in the government of Upper Canada. At the outset William Chisholm was merely a name, a grey form silhouetted against a background of oak staves and Scottish tartan. Very gradually he came into focus, and as his character became apparent he grew in stature; but only a few months ago, when his portrait was discovered tucked away in a warehouse, did he acquire a face.

Once begun, the story of Oakville unfolded in a most unexpected and gratifying manner. Several years had slipped by when I consulted a friend who is an historian of wide experience. He advised broadening the outlook of the history, and stated firmly that lack of experience notwithstanding, the writing of the book was up to me. I was dismayed, but being committed to the undertaking there was no turning back.

What was intended to be a little book grew into a big one. Since the aim was to record the history of the town as completely as possible, I could not omit important details. I have tried meticulously to eliminate errors and to draw only warranted conclusions. The facts have been recorded as found, and when I have disproved any time-honoured and beloved legends, I have regretted this as much as anyone.

Many friends have given me valuable assistance during the preparation of the manuscript. For aid in a variety of matters a very special debt of gratitude is owing to Mr. George P. de T. Glazebrook, formerly Professor of History in the University of Toronto. Under his encouragement and patient guidance the obstacles of many arduous tasks were surmounted. My thanks are due to Dr. George Spragge, Archivist of Ontario, for reading Part I with an eye for errors in history; to Mr. Ross Ryrie for searching legal documents; to Mr. P. W. Thompson of the *Oakville-Trafalgar Journal* for help in matters of style. I am grateful to the late Dr. Percy J. Robinson for giving generously of his knowledge of early French maps and Indian languages; to Mr. C. H. J. Snider, author of "Schooner Days," for initiation into the mysteries of the building of wooden ships; to the officers of the Lorne Scots (Peel, Halton & Dufferin Regiment) for access to the regimental archives; to Mr. George C. Atkins for access to files of the *Record-Star*; to Mr. Paul Hahn for a gift copy of Margaret Mitchell's *The Passenger Pigeon in Ontario*; to Mr. William J. Fleuty for data relative to Oakville's newspapers; for the aid of Dr. J. J. Talman and Miss Lillian Benson of Lawson Memorial Library, and of the staffs of the Toronto Public Library and the Legislative Library. I am indebted to Miss Helen McClung, the former Archivist of Ontario, for an interest which led to a friendship, and to Mr. George Power for enthusiastic assistance in tracing records and exploring the mill site on The Sixteen. To the innumerable persons who accorded me their friendly co-operation I extend my thanks.

Among those who provided me with valuable data either from personal recollection or from family records are Mrs. J. S. W. Williams, Mrs. M. C. Irvine, Miss Louisa Street, Misses Helen and Elizabeth Smith, the Misses Wilson of Toronto, Miss Jean Moore of Rochester, Mr. and Mrs. Charles Doty, and Messrs. Lorne Ashbury, Nelson King, Frank McCraney, R. F. Sanderson, Reginald M. Smith, W. J. Sumner, and Hugh S. Wilson.

Acknowledgment must also be made to several persons no longer living. Foremost among these is John A. Williams, whose full reminiscences shed light on many an obscure circumstance. For granting privilege of access to his writings I am obliged to Mrs. Sydney Williams of Eberts, Ontario. And there are George J. Sumner, whose forty-odd diaries, seen through the courtesy of Mr. George Doty, have been so valuable a source of happenings in the town; W. S. Savage, whose series of articles entitled "The Early Days" were made available to me by Miss Ellena Savage; R. K. Chisholm, whose carefully preserved papers are mentioned above; Mrs. Lillian Bell, who turned over to me what material she had gathered. There are also the individuals who delighted in keeping scrap-books: Mrs. Alfred Hillmer, Mrs. Mary Dill, William H. Young, whose "Serpent's Trail" was possessed by the late Mrs. John Byers, and Mrs. Cynthia Hinton whose daughter, Mrs. George Harker, kindly allowed me the use of those scrap-books in her possession. While using these sources I found pleasure in the thought that what had been so well begun by those of an earlier generation was being carried to completion and placed on record for those who follow.

The deepest debt of gratitude of all I have reserved to the last. In willingly giving so freely of her talent for illustrating this volume my sister, Dr. Juliet Chisholm, has both beautified it and enhanced its value as a record. Thirty-six of the line drawings were done by her, with remarkable accuracy and detail from old maps, prints, faded photographs, woodcuts in rare gazetteers and newspapers, actual objects and places. The remaining seven drawings are reproductions of woodblocks appearing in early newspapers. I cannot forbear to mention our most enthusiastic collaborators: five Siamese cats who with unfailing energy conducted their own research amongst drawing gear, card files, and other tools of industry. This activity was conducive to neither peace nor quiet, but any disputes arising out of a conflict in aims were readily forgiven because of their charming companionship in the old Custom House which is our home.

H. C. M.

Oakville, December, 1952

NOTE TO THE SECOND PRINTING

The changes in this second printing have been confined to corrections of minor errors, mainly typographical. Since the first printing, the boundaries of Oakville have been greatly extended (see caption to Plate 8, facing p. 103), and street names and house numbers in the old town have been altered. It is perhaps sufficient to mention here the following changes in street names that affect this work: Colborne Street, East and West, the main street of the old town, is now Lakeshore Road, East and West; and Dundas Street is now Trafalgar Road.

Two corrections require special mention. In the first printing, the drawing of the mill on page 23 faced the wrong way, probably having been reversed in the course of redrawing; this error has been rectified. The other correction concerns the birth date of George Chisholm given on page 133. As I explained in *The Mark of Honour* (University of Toronto Press, 1965, pp. 168–9 and note), family tradition had it that George Chisholm was born in the year of the Rebellion of '45, and that date was considered authentic at the time *Oakville and the Sixteen* was published. Since then a perplexing variety of birth dates has come to light, but the date of July 19, 1752, given in the Dalcross section of the Parochial Register of Croy and Dalcross at New Register House, Edinburgh, is of course unquestionable.

H.C.M.

Shelburne, Nova Scotia, September, 1971

CONTENTS

PART TWO. WHEAT

PLATES

IN COLOUR

IN BLACK AND WHITE

Between pages 102 and 103

Between pages 294 and 295

Between pages 406 and 407

Illustrations 24 to 43 inclusive are taken from the booklet, *Beautiful Oakville*, by courtesy of Mrs. J. S. W. Williams.

Photographic copies of the originals of nos. 1, 3, 4, 9, 11 to 15, 17 to 43, 47, and 50 were made by Frederick Crouch; of nos. 44, 45, and 46, by Nancy Hart.

LINE DRAWINGS

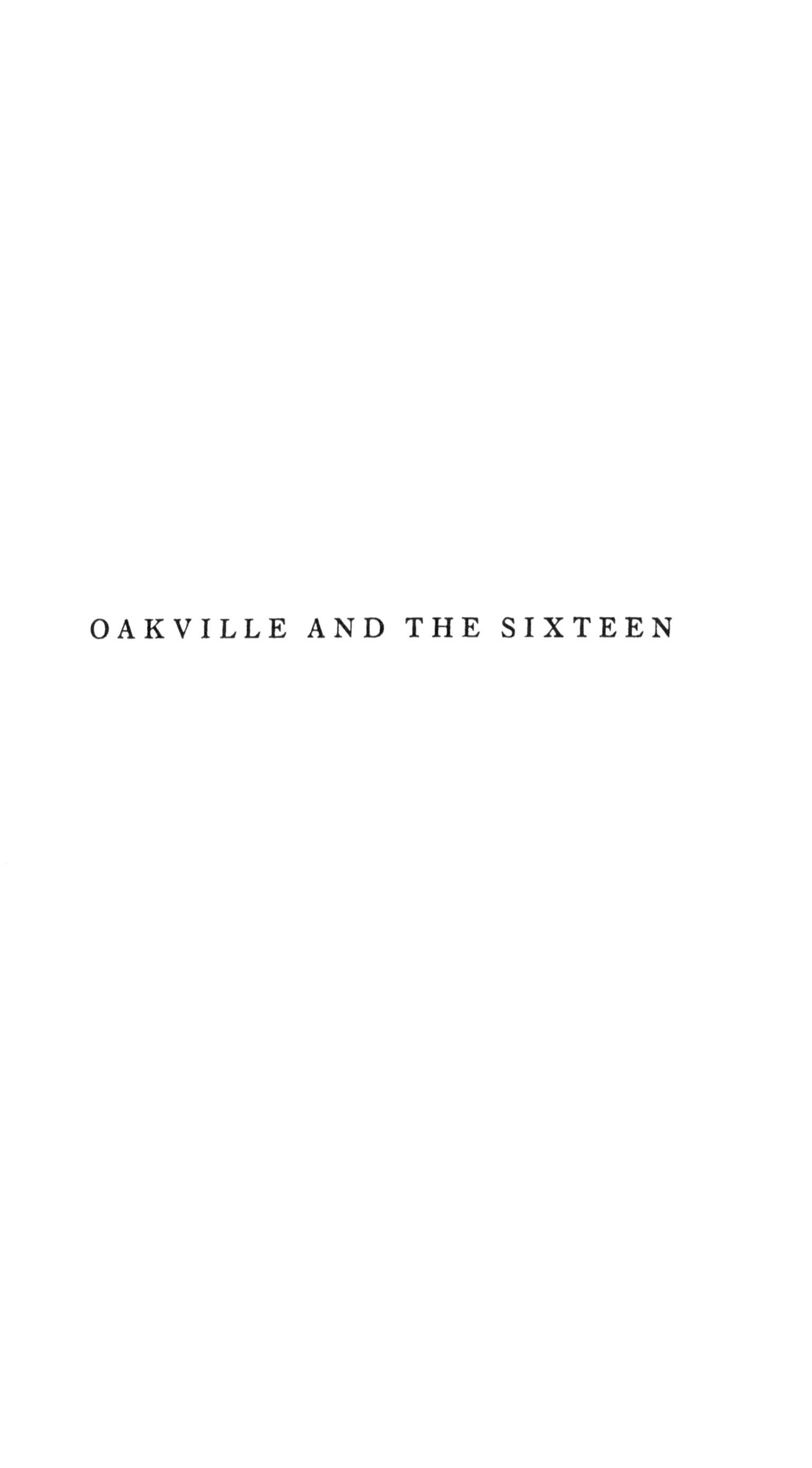

OAKVILLE AND THE SIXTEEN

PROLOGUE

Oakville is pleasantly and advantageously situated at the mouth of the Sixteen-mile Creek on the North shore of Lake Ontario on the new Lake Road from York to Hamilton; 22 miles from York, 10 miles from Wellington Square, or Burlington Beach, and 18 miles from Hamilton. It is the centre of the front of Trafalgar Township, has a rich and densely settled back country for 40 miles, of which Oakville must always be the market and shipping port. . . .[1]

WRITTEN in 1833 by the founder of the town, this description of its location includes the essential features of the present time. Now the largest town in the county of Halton, Oakville, from the time of its founding, has also been considered exceptional for its charm and beauty.

Trafalgar is one of four townships forming the rectangle of Halton County, which extends north-west from the curving shore of the head of the lake. However, the early simpler terms "north" meaning away from, and "south" toward the lake, continue in common usage and are adopted throughout this history. Accordingly, Trafalgar is bordered on the west by Nelson, on the north by Esquesing. In its north-western corner, which touches the fourth sister township, Nassagaweya, is the county town of Milton.

The smallest county but one in the province of Ontario, Halton presents sharp contrasts in its topography. The farm land rolling back from the lake through Trafalgar and Nelson rises gradually to the foot of the Niagara escarpment which extends through Nelson, a corner of Nassagaweya, and Esquesing. In formation and beauty the wilder terrain on the escarpment is comparable to the lake district of northern Ontario. From springs and cedar swamps in these upper reaches of the county rise the headwaters of two rivers which find their way through Trafalgar to the lake. The Twelve Mile Creek and the Sixteen Mile Creek farther east are similar in character, and since the times of the early British traders, several decades before settlement, have been called The Twelve and The Sixteen.

From the point where it enters Trafalgar Township the course of The Sixteen is winding and tortuous. As it meanders through the agricultural district, the lush growth in its valley providing excellent grazing for cattle, the banks rise higher and steeper in hills of red clay and shale which were great hazards to transportation until conquered by modern methods of engineering. Flowing over a rocky bed to within a mile from its mouth the river suddenly becomes deep and navigable. Fruits of a peculiar excellence grow in the sandy soil along the lake shore, and in the centre of this section is situated the town of Oakville.

The main thoroughfare of the town is one of the principal arteries in the province, the Lake Shore Road. A mile to the north is the railway and a second provincial highway of recent origin, the Queen Elizabeth Way. Three miles farther north is the oldest highway in the province, the Dundas Street. These roads together with the railway run parallel to the lake shore between the cities of Toronto and Hamilton, and midway lies Oakville.

Its situation would lead to the belief that like most villages Oakville had grown up gradually around a mill, a store, and a few houses which multiplied as the population rose. This, however, is not the case. Oakville was the result of foresight and planning on the part of its founder who was aware of the commercial possibilities of a harbour at the mouth of The Sixteen and the value of the river's water-power for manufacturing. For some years William Chisholm shipped oak staves and timber from the river, thus becoming thoroughly familiar with the district, and in 1827 he succeeded in buying the piece of forest which formed a part of the Crown Reserve surrounding The Sixteen. The 1,120 acres of this reserve, bordered by the partially cleared farms of settlers, had stood relatively untouched. How this valuable block of land with such obvious potentialities had escaped the settler's axe to come into the possession of one man is explained by events which took place in the earlier days of the province of Upper Canada.

With the increasing influx of those who fled the revolution in the southern colonies of British North America the British government negotiated with the Indians for the sale of land upon which these people could settle. In this new province without roads, only the land bordering water-ways was accessible for settlement. Townships stretched along the north shore of Lake Ontario from two directions. On the east the continuation of settlement in Lower Canada followed the St. Lawrence up and round the lake, and on the west the townships spread from the Niagara frontier, each, as it was added, forming a new link in a broken chain. Gradually all the land in Upper Canada situated on Lake Ontario was laid out in townships, until only the tract which lay between Burlington Bay and the Etobicoke River remained in possession of the Indians.

In securing this tract, the link which would complete the chain of townships bordering the lake, the British government encountered some delay. It was not until August 2, 1805, that the Missisauga Purchase was effected, whereby the Missisauga Indians surrendered to the Crown the land between Burlington Bay and the Etobicoke. For fishing and hunting preserves, blocks of land at the mouths of three rivers, including Sixteen Mile Creek, were retained by the Indians. To them the treaty reserved the "sole right of Fisheries . . . together with the flats and low grounds . . . which we have heretofore cultivated and where we have our camps."[2]

Since the interior of the tract was unexplored, only the shore line was known, and on early maps merely the outlets of rivers are indicated. These show that in its natural state the channel of The Sixteen was far different from what it is now. Two French maps, one dated *circa* 1756 and the other 1760, show an island at the mouth of the river which appears on the later map as "R. de Gravois [pebbly or gravelly]: deux Sorties."[3] The Indian name is given on a list of rivers and creeks on the north shore of Lake Ontario compiled by the early surveyor, Augustus Jones. Being married to the daughter of a Missisauga chief and familiar with the Missisauga language, Jones gave the names in translation,[4] and those in the district with which we are now concerned he listed as

Es qui sink   12 mile Creek N.S. [North Shore]   last out Creek
Ne sauga y onk   16 from B. Bay [Burlington Bay]   Having two outlets*

The primeval forest which grew thick and tall upon the land bordering the lake was the last of the great hardwood forest on the north shore of Lake Ontario. The region round the head of the lake supported a rich hardwood forest, an extension of the hardwood flora to the south. In this area grew oak, ash, hickory, walnut, butternut, elm,

*The author is indebted to Dr. Percy J. Robinson for calling attention to this list. Dr. Robinson separates Nesaugayonk into the following words: Ne = two; sauga = outlets; y = there are; onk = there, and points to the occurrence of "sauga" in such names as Missisauga, Saugeen, and Saguenay.

and maple, with only here and there an admixture of conifers. Because of the milder climate along the shore of the lake the growth was more luxurious than in any other area in all of Canada, with the possible exception of the shores of Lake Erie. The trees that grew here attained enormous height and girth.

In June, 1806, the land, apart from that reserved for the Indians, was surveyed by Deputy Provincial Surveyor Samuel S. Wilmot into three townships. To township no. 1 on the east was given the Indian name of Toronto. No. 2 was named Alexander and no. 3, Grant, in honour of the President and Administrator of the Government of Upper Canada, the Honourable Alexander Grant.[5] Only a few weeks after the negotiation of the Missisauga Purchase, however, the combined French and Spanish fleets were defeated off the coast of Spain in the Battle of Trafalgar, and while the world was still ringing with the news of this famous victory the name of township no. 1 was changed to Nelson in honour of Britain's great hero, and to commemorate the battle in which he lost his life the name of township no. 2 was changed to Trafalgar.

The delay in effecting the Missisauga Purchase had retarded the construction of the Dundas Street after its survey in 1793. Intended as a military road between the seat of the provincial government at York and the frontier at the head of Lake Erie, the Dundas Street had been conceived by Upper Canada's first Lieutenant-Governor, Colonel John Graves Simcoe, and named after the Right Honourable Henry Dundas, Secretary of State for the Colonies in the home government, soon to become Viscount Melville. In Britain the term "street" had been used for centuries to denote the military ways of the Romans, and it was in this sense that Simcoe used it in Upper Canada.[6] Though surveyed through the Missisauga territory the Dundas Street could not be completed while the tract remained in Indian hands.

Using the survey line of the Dundas Street as a base-line, Wilmot laid out two concessions to the north and four concessions to the south of "the Street." The exact boundaries of the Missisauga Indian Reserve at Sixteen Mile Creek not having been specified in the treaty, Wilmot was forced to hold up his work until the matter could be clarified with the help of the interpreter, "Mr. St. John."[7] This was St. Jean Rousseau, a trader who had settled at the Humber River during the French régime, and who, as he remained there after the British conquest, has been called "the last citizen of Old French Toronto and the first of new York."[8]

The Missisauga Indian Reserve lay on each side of the mouth of

Sixteen Mile Creek in the 3rd and 4th concessions of the new township of Trafalgar, occupying all of lots 13, 14, and 15. On the east it extended over into lot 12, and on the west into lot 16, taking a small strip from both these lots. Though the "flats and low grounds" along the river in the 2nd concession referred to in the treaty were included also, the reserve did not extend to the arable land on the banks above. To mark the south-eastern limits of the reserve Wilmot planted "a large squared White Oak post marked 'M.I.R.–No. 45W' " at a distance of "forty chains northeasterly from the centre of said creek." At the same distance on the west he marked in like manner "a large black ash tree (two trunks issuing from one root)."[9] It was the section of the reserve lying within the 3rd and 4th concessions that was the future townsite of Oakville.

In the southern section of Trafalgar Township development was considerably retarded by the manner in which the Dundas Street was constructed. In a country as extensive and thinly populated as Upper Canada the need for roads of communication was urgent. That the section of the street lying within the township might be speedily connected with the sections already in use, measures differing somewhat from the usual procedure were adopted. The lots bordering the Dundas Street were the first to be granted, and locations were drawn by lottery. The period within which settlement duties were to be completed was reduced from two years to eighteen months. Not until half of the road adjacent to their lots had been cleared, five acres cleared and fenced, and a house approximately sixteen by twenty feet built, could settlers secure a patent to their land.[10] Another contributing factor to the concentration of settlement along the Dundas Street was the placing of reserves, which was also contrary to general procedure. In these new townships one-seventh of the total acreage was held for Crown and another seventh for Clergy Reserves to be leased over a long period of years. The opening of roads being conditional upon the performance by settlers of their settlement duties, no continued line of communication could take place where there were reserves. Therefore, the Surveyor-General was instructed "to remove the Reserves . . . on each side of Dundas Street . . . and disperse them among the other lots."[11] Thus the greater proportion of Crown and Clergy Reserves were concentrated in the southern section where two Indian reserves already occupied 2,540 acres of Trafalgar Township. The result was that here settlers' clearings were isolated by long stretches of uncleared road allowance upon which the forest was likely to stand for a long time to come. By 1812 there were only twenty-six settlers on the twenty miles of lake shore between Burlington Bay and the River Credit,[12] and many more years were to pass before the front of Trafalgar Township would be accessible except by water. In consequence, development was seriously retarded on the lake shore while the section in the north along the Dundas Street throve.

In 1816 the Gore District was established and named for the Lieutenant-Governor, Sir Francis Gore. Two counties constituted this new district, Wentworth and Halton, the name borne by the latter being that of Major Matthew Halton, secretary to Sir Francis Gore. After another purchase of land from the Missisaugas in 1818 the townships of Nelson and Trafalgar were extended by the addition of New Surveys, in rear of which more townships were laid out. The Lieutenant-Governor directed that "the following names shall be given to the three Townships in the Mississagua Tract now under survey—namely to the Western Township in rear of Nelson, that of Nasagiweya. To the centre Township (in rear of Trafalgar) the name of Esquesing. And to the Eastern Township (in rear of Toronto) that of Chinguacousy being the Indian names of the principal rivers in each respectively."[13] The Indian name for The Sixteen survives to the present time, the west branch near its source being known locally as Nassagaweya River. But giving the name of the eastern township that of the Indian name for the Twelve Mile Creek appears to have been an error, as no branches of this river flow through Esquesing Township.

Inevitably, as settlement increased, the way was opened for the greater development of the southern section of Trafalgar. The Missisauga reserves lost much of their value as hunting grounds, and on February 28, 1820 "the five Principal Chiefs of the Mississagas" surrendered to the Crown their reserves at the Twelve and Sixteen Mile creeks.[14]

It was about this time that William Chisholm began buying timber and white oak staves throughout the district between Burlington Bay and the Credit River. William Chisholm was the son of George Chisholm, a Scottish emigrant who had settled in Tryon County, New York, in 1774 but had joined the British Army in 1777 and moved to Nova Scotia at the end of the Revolutionary War. Here William was born in 1788. When he was six years old the family moved to Upper Canada, where George Chisholm purchased a tract of land on the north shore of Burlington Bay. William and his brothers grew up here, and received their education at the common school in East Flamborough.

Chisholm fought through the War of 1812, and in 1816 settled on a farm on the Dundas Street in Nelson Township. He began buying wheat, timber, and oak staves, and established a general store. His business prospered, and he soon became a leading merchant in the district. An agreement exists between Chisholm and one David McDougall of the town of Niagara dated 1822, whereby Chisholm contracted to supply fifty thousand gross of white oak staves at £13.15 per thousand. The staves were "to be piled on the Lake Shore between the River Credit and . . . the outlet of the Little Lake [Burlington Bay]" at Burlington Beach. Chisholm was to pay hands for piling and culling, and McDougall was responsible for loading them onto sailing vessels.[15]

The larger merchants of Chisholm's day were both exporters and importers, handling practically every variety of goods produced or required in the settlements. From the ceaseless turnover, going both ways, they extracted a two-way profit. They also performed most of the functions of a bank. The calling of "storekeeper" was thus highly lucrative. But there were few ships at the head of Lake Ontario to transport their commodities and stocks to and from the points of transshipment on the St. Lawrence, and Chisholm soon became a shipowner, building his own ships on the shore of Burlington Bay, and engaged in the forwarding business. By 1827 his fleet of five "swift sailing Schooners" included the *Mohawk Chief*, Daniel Campbell, master; the *Telegraph*, Philo Bates, master; the *General Brock*, William Kerr, master; and the *Rebecca and Eliza* under command of Captain Edward Zealand, all built after 1822.[16]

In addition to his prosperous private concerns, Chisholm took an active part in public affairs. From 1820 to 1824 he was Member of the House of Assembly for the East Riding of Halton, and in 1823 was appointed one of the parliamentary commissioners to supervise the building of the Burlington Bay Canal, the first canal project attempted in the province of Upper Canada. He was one of a group which petitioned the government for the construction of a canal to connect Lake Ontario with Lake Erie, and when the Welland Canal became a reality he was appointed a commissioner. He was also on the board of directors. All this experience stood him in good stead later on, when he became concerned in the development of the tract at the mouth of The Sixteen.

A letter addressed in 1824 to the Lieutenant-Governor by Chisholm conveys the fact of his interest in The Sixteen. He states that "having learned that an application has been some time before the Executive Government of this Province for the grant of a portion" of the Crown Reserve on Sixteen Mile Creek, he wishes to point out that "from here is shipped a considerable proportion of the Staves made in the adjacent country and no doubt [this] in time will become a place from which much of the surplus produce in the rear will be shipped." Therefore, he continues, any person "coming into possession should be obliged to build a good and sufficient storehouse for the reception of goods and property which may be here landed."[17]

Again, in 1826, Chisholm expressed an interest in the advantages of The Sixteen. At this time there was considerable agitation to make Dundas instead of Hamilton the Gore District town, and a parliamentary committee was appointed to investigate and take evidence from leading merchants in the district. Chisholm gave as his considered opinion that because of its mill seat, Dundas would flourish. "But for the present and all time to come . . . a harbour at the mouth of the Sixteen would serve a greater proportion of the settlements."[18]

He was also aware of growing dissatisfaction among the settlers that the excellent water-power of The Sixteen remained undeveloped. This discontent is expressed in several petitions to the Lieutenant-Governor, Sir Peregrine Maitland, a singular solution being offered in the petition of John C. Harris who lived a short distance east of The Sixteen on lot 7 of the 3rd concession. In his petition Harris states: "Having some two or three years since observed in the papers an advertisement of the Agricultural Society of England promising a reward of fifty guineas or a gold medal to any person who could invent the best method of extracting stumps from off new land . . . your petitioner was instigated thereby to make an attempt towards inventing a Machine for that purpose and after much study and perseverance was successful in constructing one which has upon trial been thought well adapted to the purpose." Disappointed in his hopes of obtaining the reward, "as the medal was awarded to a gentleman in Nova Scotia," Harris had intended applying for a patent. But, he continues in all seriousness, he would prefer a grant of land in lieu thereof, "i.e., a situation on the 16 mile creek if the same should be at your Excellency's disposal. That creek affords excellent mill seats and situations for machinery which your petitioner is desirous of putting in operation should he be so fortunate as to obtain a spot thereon."[19] Harris secured the signatures of above a hundred settlers in the township and reiterated his appeal, directing Maitland's attention to the privations they were forced to endure for the lack of facilities such as mills would provide. And there were others who requested grants within the two Crown Reserves in the township.

Aside from providing a source of revenue for the provincial government, and of timber and masts for ships of the Royal Navy, Crown Reserves existed for the purpose of preventing the exploitation of natural resources. Though unwilling to make a grant of water privileges on the reserves at The Twelve and The Sixteen, Maitland was agreeable to selling these reserves, and the application addressed to his secretary by William Chisholm apparently brought the matter to a head.

York 2 May 1827

Sir—Being desirous to purchase the Tract of Land situated on the 16 Mile Creek . . . called the Indian Reserve, for the purpose of Building and improving thereon, should it be the intention of the Government to dispose of the same, I beg permission to request that you would be pleased to bring the subject under the consideration of His Excellency the Lieutenant Governor For His Excellency's pleasure thereon.

I have the honor to be
Sir
Your most obedient
Humble Servant
W. CHISHOLM.[20]

Sir Peregrine Maitland expressed the opinion that these valuable lands should be offered to "public competition, in the same manner as those lately sold at the Credit—the proceeds of which sale have not sufficed to meet the expense of the Indian Huts and the lands now applied for appearing . . . to be applicable to the same object." In this the Executive Council concurred.[21] Accordingly the reserve at The Sixteen, exclusive of the river flats in the 2nd concession, was placed on sale. On July 17, 1827, the following advertisement appeared in the *Upper Canada Gazette*:

Government Sale.—Public Notice is hereby given, that the Tract of Land in the 3d and 4th concessions, South of Dundas Street, fronting on Lake Ontario and situated on the 16-mile Creek, in the Township of Trafalgar, being composed of the West part of Lot no. 12, Lots no. 13, 14 and 15, and the East part of Lot no. 16, in the said 3d and 4th concessions—containing together 968 Acres—will be sold together or separate (to suit purchasers), at Public Auction, on Thursday the 16th. August next at 12 o'clock noon, at Mr. Crooks' mill, on the 12-mile Creek [at the Dundas Street]. . . . Terms of Payment—25 per cent to be paid down at the time of the Sale, and the remaining sum in three yearly installments bearing interest.

THOMAS RIDOUT, Surveyor General.[22]

In his report to the Surveyor-General, John Radenhurst, who conducted the sale, states that the "960 acres were sold to William Chisholm Esquire for 21/3 per acre . . . who paid 25 p cent on the purchase money, and executed the Bond."[23] This price, as are all prices in this history, was quoted according to the value it bore at Halifax, where the pound rated $4.00 and the shilling 20¢ in New York currency. Therefore the price Chisholm paid per acre was $4.25 and not the sixpence or 12½¢ which has been repeatedly asserted, a fallacy kept alive by those who have transcribed it unquestioningly. When Chisholm paid the final instalment on the purchase price to Receiver-General J. H. Dunn on March 24, 1831, he had paid a total of £1,029, or $4,116.[24]

The money from the sale of these lands was held in trust by the Commissioner of Crown Lands, Peter Robinson, for the benefit of the Missisauga Indians at the Credit River and used to complete the building of their village of log houses at New Credit about a mile from the lake. At the present time the Missisauga Golf Club stands on this site.

William Chisholm's primary reason for purchasing the Crown Reserve was the shipping out of timber, staves, and other products of the district. Because of the shallowness of The Sixteen at its mouth this could be accomplished only by building a harbour, which required the permission of the government. To the House of Assembly of Upper Canada Chisholm therefore addressed a petition "praying for provision to construct a harbour" and pointing to the fact of there being none between Burlington Bay and York where schooners could find refuge.[25] The petition was referred to a select committee whose sitting Chisholm attended. He informed the committee that he proposed to carry a pier into twelve feet of water which would "occasion it to extend not less than 200 feet," and desired authority "to levy tolls for reimbursing the charge there," i.e. the cost of construction. Along with a table of rates he submitted the suggestion that the period during which he be permitted to levy tolls should be not less than fifty years, "as a shorter term would not warrant the expenditure of so large a sum of money in the construction of works at all times of a very hazardous description and necessarily built of perishable material." Chisholm also explained that he intended to dredge across the bar at the entrance of the harbour to a depth of not less than eight feet of water, which was sufficient for vessels of the period.[26]

In March, 1828, the committee reported: ". . . there appears good reason to believe that such an improvement . . . will tend much to the convenience of navigation and the benefits of trade in the surrounding country."[27] On March 25 Parliament passed an Act to which the royal assent was soon given. It was enacted "that it may be lawful for William Chisholm, his heirs . . . etc. to within five years from the passing of the Act to . . . erect moles, piers . . . and edifices . . . for the protection of the said harbour and to collect tolls." The legislature might, after the passage of thirty years, purchase the entire estate in the harbour, upon estimation of its value to be arbitrated by three persons. Tolls in excess of 20 per cent on the capital investment should be regarded as a sinking fund, to accumulate for the purpose of purchasing the harbour for public use. The Act was "to be in force for 50 years at the end of which period the Harbour and all right to tolls . . . shall vest in His Majesty."[28] In short, Chisholm, in the expectation that over a fifty-year period the receipt of tolls would suffice to cover the initial expenditure, would bear the entire cost of construction. Notwithstanding the fact that time after time during the building of the Burlington Bay Canal he had witnessed the labour of months, sometimes of an entire season, swept away by a single storm, he was optimistic.

The name White Oak, given to Chisholm by the Indians, is said to have originated from his being so extensive a dealer in oak staves. His intimate friend, Robert Baldwin Sullivan, referred to him as "William Chisholm, whom we used to call White Oak, for his truth and honesty of character, and genuine soundness of heart."[29] According to one source[30] it was Sullivan who suggested the name of Oakville for the new village which took shape round the harbour of The Sixteen. On the other hand it is curious to find the names of Springfield (modern Erindale), Oakville, Burlington, Hamilton, and Newark (modern Niagara-on-the-Lake) duplicated in the names of towns and villages south of Lake Ontario in western New York State. Here they appear in the same sequence as the Canadian towns, along a road which early in the nineteenth century was already well travelled, leading over steep hills and through deep valleys into the heart of the Catskill Mountains to communities which bordered the western frontier of settlement before the Revolutionary War. It so happens that among a band of immigrant Scots from Inverness-shire who settled in this section of the Province of New York were the father and uncle of William Chisholm. In after years the father journeyed from his home on Burlington Bay in Upper Canada to revisit the community he had been forced to leave because of the war.[31] He could hardly have failed to recognize that his son's new village and the Oaksville situated on Oaks Creek south of Otsego Lake had much in common. They are similarly located in relation to their respective neighbours; Springfield on the north-east, and to the west Burlington, Hamilton, and, at some distance, Newark. Furthermore the early industries of both villages derived from the white oaks which flourished upon their townsites.

Be this as it may, we have in outline the circumstances essential to setting the scene in the Township of Trafalgar, Halton County, District of Gore, Upper Canada, for the founding of the Village of Oakville.

I

THE BEGINNING

CHAPTER ONE

THE PORT TAKES FORM

THE PROGRAMME of construction begun at the mouth of The Sixteen in the autumn of 1827 included several projects which were carried forward rapidly and simultaneously. As the plan unfolds it appears rather extensive for a time when conditions in the western section of the province were primitive and the distances by water so great. Where the purchase lay in the wilderness there was only a scattering of settlers' clearings. Being almost entirely surrounded by Crown and Clergy Reserves, the former Missisauga Indian Reserve was indistinguishable from the rest of the forest which stretched west and north for some distance before clearings were encountered. On the east in the 3rd concession, settlers' lands bordered it, but in this vast forest clearings were visible only from a short distance, "cut out of the wilderness, as stones hewn out of quarries, insignificant indentures apparently in the boundless forest."[1] The banks of the river were hidden by trees of an even greater height than those which grew on the higher land, and a temporary shanty standing on the beach furnished the only shelter.[2] Above the loop in the river, on the flats at the foot of the west bank, was a natural clearing where the Indians continued to cultivate their corn fields. To reach their camp the Indians crossed the river in canoes, ascended the curve of the east bank, and followed a trail which led directly to the lake shore, where at the eastern boundary of their reserve they had established a summer encampment. Wilmot's plan of survey shows cornfields and trail, as may be seen in the above detail of the reserve drawn from this plan. The Missisaugas were a migratory people, and this group continued to return each summer to their camp on the lake for years after the land had passed out of their possession.[3]

Aside from small boats and Indian canoes which could be dragged across the gravel bar clogging its mouth, no vessels could enter The Sixteen except when the water was high in spring. The first concern of William Chisholm therefore was the building of a harbour. Though many of the required materials lay at hand, all iron, machinery, tools, and other equipment, as well as provisions, had to be brought in. His second concern was that of turning the white oak and white pine, whose timber was the most valuable for commercial uses, into marketable products, and of building ships in which they could be transported. The water-power in The Sixteen was to be harnessed for the production of sawn lumber, and the prime requisite of a pioneer community, flour. Surrounding the harbour a townsite would be cleared and laid out, and, that the farmers might bring their produce to the port and their grain to the mill, the village had to be connected with the agricultural district by roads. It was only to be expected that Oakville, being so centrally located, and the only port between the seat of the government at York and the Gore District town of Hamilton, would soon attract many merchants and artisans. The commerce of this thriving community would, in turn, bring men with capital, and the water-power within the limits of the village would be developed for the purposes of manufacturing, which at this period was virtually non-existent in the province. The fact that neither York nor Hamilton showed any signs of industrial activity was a circumstance auspicious for Oakville's future. Labour recruited from immigrants arriving every spring at Montreal would be brought up the lake, housed, and provided for. All this work of laying out the new community was placed under the supervision of Merrick Thomas, Chisholm's brother-in-law and general manager of his enterprises at Burlington Bay.

The village which rapidly materialized became the focal point for the commerce of the district. What was taking place at Oakville was typical of what was happening throughout the province wherever rivers enter the lower lakes. The Oakville harbour, however, was one of the first improved harbours in the province, that at Kettle Creek (now Port Stanley) having been begun the previous year; other ports along the lake such as York and Kingston had large natural harbours which required no immediate major improvements. It was, moreover, the only case in the province of Upper Canada in which the development of a harbour was carried out by a private individual. And for fifty years it remained a private harbour, notwithstanding the disinclination of later owners to be burdened with it. William Chisholm also promoted the first joint-stock company incorporated for the development of water-power in the province. The purpose was to put the water-power in The Sixteen to use for industrial purposes.[4] Though the project failed and Chisholm's career was cut short soon afterwards, he died firmly convinced that nothing could stop the ultimate progress of the community he had founded. This optimism he expressed in the following terms: "The advantages of a fine back country of sixty miles having no other outlet, of an excellent harbour, and of water power now being made in the centre of the Town, are so obvious that they need only to be noticed to show that Oakville will soon be one of the principal Towns of the Province."[5]

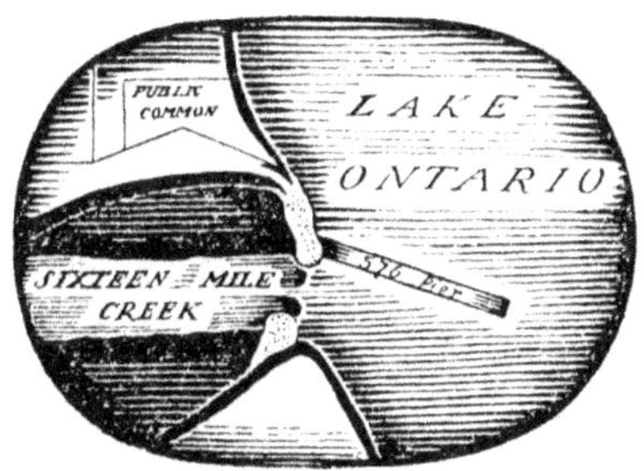

I

When work on the harbour was begun in the spring of 1828 there was great activity along The Sixteen. It was a most favourable circumstance that the preceding and succeeding winters were mild, dry, and open, with so little snow that the level of the lake was very low.[6] There is no record of an engineer having been employed, although it is reasonable to suppose that one of the engineers who planned either the Burlington Bay or Welland canals was consulted. Certainly much of the skilled labour was drawn from the construction work that was coming to an end at the Bay. During the winter many farmers in the township were available, and there was no difficulty in procuring the teams of oxen required to do the hauling.

It was planned to form the harbour by running parallel piers into deep water on cribs or frames of timber loaded with stone and sunk on the lake bottom, "the usual mode of forming piers in the province," according to Sir Richard Bonnycastle, the engineer.[7] Construction on the east pier began with the driving of a row of large piles in a line which extended from the shore into the lake for a distance of 576 feet.[8] The piles, each costing on an average 23¢, were driven into the bed of the lake by a piling machine mounted on a scow. The "floating pile engine" could be used in winter on the ice or at other seasons of the year on the water, according to Chisholm's description.[9] It was equipped with a weight of slightly under a ton[10] which was drawn up with block and tackle by man power. When it had attained a height sufficient to give it considerable force it was dropped on the pile.[11] The same principle was used after the introduction of steam but the invention of the jack-hammer at a later date was a great improvement. For the cribs which were to form the foundations of the pier large timbers, after being squared by lumbermen and secured by logging chains, were drawn by a yoke of oxen to the flats of The Sixteen. Here were constructed fifteen cribs, each approximately forty feet square. The first cribs built at the Burlington Bay Canal had been constructed without bottoms, and soon washed out.[12] Profiting by this experience Chisholm had his cribs built with bottoms. The timbers varied in price from 8¢ to 11¢ per foot, depending upon the size, and the spikes with which they were held together were made by journeymen blacksmiths for 8¢ a pound. As they were completed, the cribs were floated down stream to the harbour, fitted between the piles, and after being filled with many cords of stone varying in price from 10*s*. to 15*s*. per cord, were sunk. Upon the cribs timbers were then placed lengthwise one atop another until the pier was six feet above the water line. The planking which formed the walking surface of the pier cost 7*s*. 6*d*. per hundred feet. An item equally essential appears in the accounts for 1829: "for whiskey furnished at work, $70."[13] The east pier was not finished until the end of the second winter, and by then the west pier was under construction.

There was (and still is) a ledge of rock at the end of the east pier which forms a natural barrier to lake gravel and the silt washed down by the river, and to remove this bar and to deepen the channel required the services of a dredge. In May, 1830, Chisholm addressed a letter to Sir John Colborne, the Lieutenant-Governor, in which he requested permission to use the machine that had been built by the province for work on the Burlington Bay Canal, stating that the use of this machine would obviate the necessity of building one himself. Through his secretary Sir John replied that the request should be addressed to the commissioners of the canal; that he had no objection "if no inconvenience will be felt by his being allowed the use of it." Colborne added that he would be "glad to hear that it has been used in forming the harbour of the 16 Mile Creek."[14] The matter was satisfactorily arranged and a few months later the dredge started work.

The type of dredging machine employed at this period had long since superseded the scraper for deepening harbours and rivers. Mounted upon the hulk of an old sloop or scow, the machine consisted of two endless chains of buckets placed within frames of heavy timber, one on each side of the scow. One end of each frame was fixed to the stern of the scow, and the other end was suspended from the bow by chains and pulleys by which the frames could be raised or lowered. The operation of the dredge is described in a mechanical encyclopaedia of the period as follows: "When ready to work the chain frames are lowered until the buckets drag sufficiently upon the bottom to become filled with ballast and come up along the top of the frames by the motion of the chains, till they turn over and discharge their contents into large hoppers or troughs which conduct the gravel into barges moored beneath."[15]

The dredging was carried out by the system known as "trench-cutting." The dredge, moored by cables, moved forward in a straight line, digging a trench the width of the buckets and for the distance specified, then dropped back to the place of beginning to dig another trench parallel to the first. The machine left a ridge some two feet in width between the trenches. When the channel had been "fluted" by trench-cutting the intermediate ridges were removed. As can be imagined, this method left the bottom of the channel "like the teeth of a saw," and it was not until some twenty years later with the introduction of the system of "radius-cutting" that a smooth bottom was obtained. For this method the dredge was moored by many lines, much like a turtle that had been chained by its head, tail, and four feet. By letting out and drawing in the various hawsers the dredge was moved in a circle and deepened a wide area.[16] Underwater excavating by horsepower cost on an average of 2*s.* per square yard, compared with 1*s.* after the introduction of steam.[17] In the 1880's the cost of removing silt from the Oakville harbour was 25¢ per cubic yard[18] and in the 1940's it was 83¢ for the same amount. The modern dredge can scoop three cubic yards weighing over four tons.

In 1831 Chisholm found that he was unable to finance the completion of the harbour, and applied to the House of Assembly for a loan of £2,500. Upon the "furnishing of good security" the loan was granted at 6 per cent interest.[19] The townsite was then mortgaged to Receiver-General John Henry Dunn for £2,500.[20]

William Lyon Mackenzie used this loan as the subject of a diatribe against Chisholm, alleging that he had other motives for securing it: "Namely, to place it at his credit with William Allan & Co. for carrying on his mercantile business. . . . It certainly was not to improve the Oakville harbour, for nothing has been done during the present year, and all it had ever cost its proprietor will scarcely exceed £1000." Because Chisholm refused to sell any water lots Mackenzie claimed: "He monopolizes the whole harbour, charging his neighbors 2 pence half penny per bushel for storage and weighing, and civilly assuring those who grudge the imposition that they may buy lots in his village and build there."[21] This detraction caused several men to investigate for themselves and in a flurry of letters to the newspapers Mackenzie's assertions were labelled "a chapter devoted exclusively to scandal and falsity," "a tirade of ribaldry and falsehood," and the like. Wrote the editor of the *Western Mercury*: "Mr. Chisholm's acts are the best commentary on his professions and we believe there are few with whom he had ever had a transaction, but will bear witness to his perfect truth, strict integrity and what is more still, nobleminded liberality."[22]

The letters written in denial of Mackenzie's accusations give descriptions of the harbour and village in 1831 which would otherwise not have been available for this record. One correspondent asks: "Did he get his information from the half dozen ignoramuses who attend his meetings? . . . few of them possess sufficient sense to calculate how many pence there are in a York shilling. . . . Last season no laden vessel could pass into or out of the harbour whereas the largest ones on the Lake have passed in and out this season without the slightest difficulty."[23] Another visitor noted schooners drawing ten feet of water in the habour: "If these can pass through the channel, deeply laden, which was the case at this time, the harbour must be nearly completed: the piers are undoubtedly well secured, having withstood several heavy storms, while in an unfinished state, without injury. . . . The country surrounding this situation is also improving fast . . . and as this will continue to be a place from which large quantities of surplus products will be sent off, and where the supplies required for the increasing population will arrive, there can be no doubt that the indefatigable exertions of the enterprising proprietor (Col. Wm. Chisholm) will ere long, meet with well earned reward."[24]

The total cost of building the harbour up to the year 1840 was £9,620 ($38,480).[25] It is to be regretted that the sparse and scattered records reveal nothing of the great difficulties that must have been encountered. In all probability these in themselves would have formed a chronicle, as anyone familiar with the tremendous power of the water of Lake Ontario will fully appreciate.

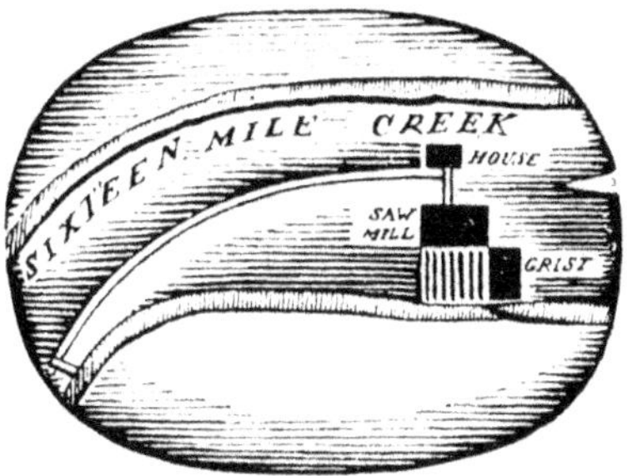

II

The building of the grist and sawmill was also undertaken during the winter of 1827-8. The location chosen for the mill site was the head of navigation on The Sixteen, where the rapids end and the water runs deep for about a mile before entering Lake Ontario. Though the banks rise high and steep the river curves conveniently, and its flat shale bed supplies a firm foundation for a dam. The detail of Castle's plan of Oakville showing both mills is reproduced above. To attempt a conclusion concerning the mills from this sketch is unwise, as the margin of error is too great, therefore the interpretation is left to the reader. (See Note to the Second Printing, p. xi.)

The dam was a vital part of the mill and great care was given to its construction. The best time to build a dam was in winter, when the water was low, and we know from Pickering that in this year the low water in creeks throughout the region forced many mills to cease grinding.[26] Besides, the oxen's task of drawing the huge logs required for the dam and buildings was lightened by snow and ice. In all probability the dam was built in the usual manner, which Mactaggart, writing in this same year, calls the American manner and describes thus: "Formed of round logs notched into one another: its shape is the long wedge: the trees are laid by one another slanting to the rapid, well bedded in the cross leaders: the lower tier is the shortest and thickest: the upper, longer and smaller. This outer slope is generally laid at an angle of thirty degrees with the rapid. Floods seldom are able to wash these dams away and they answer the intended end very well."[27]

The law required that all dams be equipped with an apron on an inclined plane "to facilitate the descent of lumber and the ascent of fish." In the above sketch one point is clear: logs floated in at the upper end of the mill pond were taken directly down to the sawmill, generally a structure of a temporary nature and little more than a frame shed over the machinery. By winch and chain the logs were drawn up a ramp and onto a horizontal carriage mounted on a track.

As the carriage progressed along the track a long saw, working perpendicularly, cut through the log. The day of the circular saw was not yet.

Authentic sources tell us that the sawmill on The Sixteen which went into production in 1830 was well equipped with two sets of saws. From its location it would seem that the lumber was transported to the harbour by raft or barge. At this period the average price of sawn lumber secured at a mill ran between 20*s.* and 35*s.* per thousand feet, "superficial measure,"[28] the sawyer taking in payment a percentage of the lumber. In June, 1833, Chisholm advised the public: "At the head of the navigable water of the Creek there is a superior Set of Saw-Mills that will cut forty thousand feet of boards per week; and an excellent Grist Mill for the accommodation of the country."[29]

The grist mill had just got into production. Its machinery being considerably more complicated than that of a sawmill, the services of expert millwrights, at wages ranging from 7*s.* 6*d.* to 10*s.* per day, were required.[30] Though most materials lay at hand, the iron, millstones, and such machine parts as could not be made on the spot had to be brought in by vessel. The three-storey building was built of stone from the bed of the river.[31] Further details are lacking, but it is evident from descriptions of mills found in contemporary writings that in Upper Canada one differed little from another. The machinery underwent constant improvement, but in all mills "wrought by water" the principle was the same. The average water-wheel was about twenty-four feet in height, and was made to revolve by the weight of the water falling upon it from above. Geared to the wheel was a revolving shaft which extended to the top of the building. All the machinery in the three-storey mill was run by attaching it by leather belts to this shaft.

Upon its arrival at the mill grain was dumped into a hopper and hoisted by an endless chain equipped with buckets to the top storey, where it went through a cleaning process. By means of another hopper it then descended to the millstones in the second storey. Placed one above the other, the stones were not close enough to touch. The lower stone was immovable, and through its centre rose a spindle on which the upper stone rested and revolved. The grain was admitted through a funnel into the hole or "eye" in the centre of the upper stone, and the quantity was regulated so that an even flow was continually supplied. After being pulverized the flour was forced out on all sides through shallow V-shaped furrows cut in the faces of the stones. While grinding was in progress the stones were covered by a wooden case, and as this became full the flour fell through an opening in the floor into a bin on the first floor of the building. From there long shutes carried it to where it was bagged.[32]

The stone best adapted for milling grain was the French burr, a stone of exceptional hardness imported from France. For proper shearing of the grain it was essential that the edges of the stones be sharp, and to "dress" them was the work of an expert. The V-shaped furrows running to the outer edges needed to be dressed every 140 hours or "a flour-mill week." Using a mill bill or pick, the stone dresser needed a day of ten and a half hours to dress one wheat stone. It was arduous work requiring great skill.

When it went into production in 1833[33] Chisholm's mill greatly benefited the settlers in all the country round. Charles Sovereign, a farmer on the lake shore at the Twelve Mile Creek, entered in his account book the following: "11 March 1834—I went to the Oakville mill. Paid or gave Old Ward one bushel of buckwheat. Had 6 bushels floured; 4½ of rye, 2 wheat, ½ corn."[34] From this amount of grain Sovereign obtained thirty-two pounds of flour, ten pounds of bran (this by-product, considered useless, he probably did not bother to take away), and thirty-two pounds of shorts. A year's supply for a family of six or eight persons was about twenty-five bags of wheat, a large load for a two-wheeled ox-cart. As to the rate for grinding Pickering has this to say: "Millers are allowed by law, for grinding, one twelfth, it has been one tenth I am told; but some wiseacres who thought it was not enough petitioned for one-twelfth."[35]

The stone mill soon became snowy white, as a flour mill should be, and the rattle of its ponderous wheel, the steady roar and thunder of the waste water as it fell over the dam, resounded from the surrounding forest.

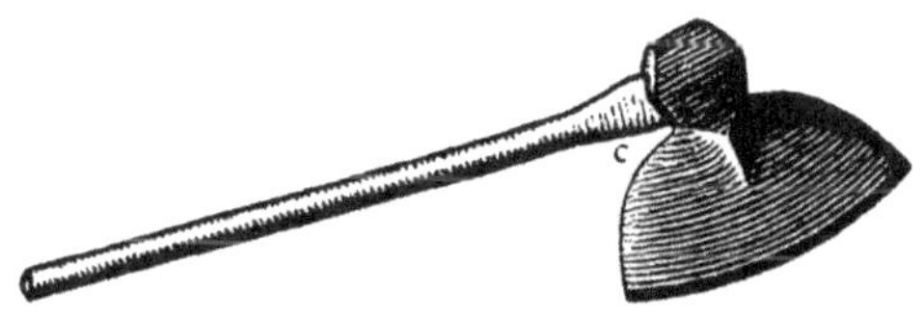

III

A few days after the sale of the Missisauga Indian Reserve, a warning began to appear in the *Gore Gazette*.

All persons are strictly cautioned not to cut or carry away timber on the new tract of land lately purchased by the subscriber from the Gov't, lying on the Lakeshore at the mouth of the Sixteen Mile Creek, in the Township of Trafalgar, County of Halton, District of Gore.

Any person or persons who may be found trespassing on said land after this notice will be prosecuted to the utmost rigour of the law.

Nelson, Aug. 18, 1827 WILLIAM CHISHOLM.[36]

The size of the trees that grew in former times is difficult to imagine in comparison with those growing on the same land today. In the primeval forest stood magnificent oaks, in particular white oaks, and pines rose for two hundred feet, the first hundred clear of branches. A few miles east of The Sixteen stood a pine tree of which we have this contemporary account: "Wonderful Tree—In Toronto Township near the Centre Road there is a pine tree of immense size—perhaps the largest in this quarter of the country. About a yard from the ground it is, by actual measurement twenty and one half feet in circumference and it appears to be little less for sixty or seventy feet up. Its height, as near as can be judged, is about two hundred feet. . . . It is called Johnnie Martin's Pine Tree because he never passed without stopping to admire it."[37]

From the time of earliest settlement the forests of British North America had supplied pine for masts and spars in ships of the Royal Navy. Marked with a "broad arrow" by agents for the Crown these trees were known as the "King's Pines." The Revolution put an end to the supply from New England, but with the opening of the province of Upper Canada a new source in addition to Nova Scotia was made available. Pine masts and oak timbers from the Canadas played an important part in maintaining the supremacy of the British Navy during the Napoleonic wars in which the French and Spanish fleets were swept from the seas at the great victory of Trafalgar. In the township named in honour of this battle parchment deeds and leases referring to Crown lands contain a clause which reserved to King George III "all White Pine Trees, that shall or may now, or hereafter grow, or be growing on any part of said parcel or tract of land hereby granted. . . ."[38] When the wars with Napoleon closed the Baltic ports from which Britain also obtained timber, fresh impetus was given to the Canadian trade.

By the time the clearing of the townsite of Oakville was begun the timber trade of Upper Canada had become closely allied to the flow of immigration. Previously, vessels carrying heavy outgoing cargoes of timber to Britain had returned to Canada with light cargoes or under ballast. Then it was found profitable to pack immigrants into the space this ballast formerly occupied. The upheaval caused by economic, political, and social forces in Britain after the close of the Napoleonic Wars, and the rapid growth of the industrial revolution, proved a stimulus to the emigration of many classes of people, especially farmers. The propaganda put forth attracted many thousands of the agricultural labouring class to Upper Canada, and it so happened that the tide of immigration was reaching its peak at the time Oakville was being settled. In 1827 over twelve thousand crossed the water to Upper and Lower Canada; by 1831 the annual total had risen to over fifteen thousand, and by far the largest proportion of immigrants found their way to the upper province.[39] From Quebec the vessels were towed up the St. Lawrence to Montreal, where passengers disembarked. Those bound for Upper Canada travelled by land to Lachine and from there by steamer. To recruit the labour he required, Chisholm made periodic trips to Lower Canada to meet incoming parties of immigrants. His schooners sailed down the St. Lawrence as far as Prescott, and many of the newly arrived immigrants he induced to come to work for him continued their journey on fresh water in vessels which had recently unloaded cargoes of wood and wheat. Upon their arrival at Oakville these people were temporarily housed in log houses and shanties, and the men were set to work cutting the timber from the townsite.

The timber most commonly used for mercantile purposes was white pine, which grew in "pineries," and this comprised nearly two-thirds of all timber that went to market.[40] But the most valuable wood for export was the white oak, the only kind of oak that was considered "merchantable." It was best adapted to shipbuilding and heavy construction work, particularly under water.

Then as now timber was cut in winter. After the trees had been felled and the branches removed, the logs were squared by lumbermen. For this process the log was placed knee-high and marked with a straight line by a chalked cord. A lumberman then proceeded to "hew the line" evenly and smoothly with a hewing axe. The handles of axes were made both right- and left-handed and if a left-handed hewer could be found the log was worked from both ends at the same time. When squared, the timber was easier to raft, and as it fitted snugly together in the holds did not shift with the rolling of ships on the Atlantic. As the discarded slabs were one-quarter of the logs, the waste of wood resulting from squaring was excessive, but the practice was continued until the disappearance of large timber made it unprofitable. The largest white oak squared to thirty inches, and the medium to about eighteen inches, both being some fifty feet in length. At Quebec white oak brought 10*d.* currency per cubic foot. Next in value to the white oak was white pine, which was cut in sticks from twenty inches (medium) to thirty-six inches square and sixty feet long. This timber brought 5*d*. per cubic foot.[41]

After being squared the sticks of timber were drawn to the top of the bank and rolled down into The Sixteen, where they were either loaded onto schooners or assembled into immense rafts. Millions of feet of squared timber were going down Lake Ontario to the St. Lawrence in raft-tows. The rafts were made by constructing cribs of timber measuring about 60 by 40 feet, upon which other sticks were laid crosswise and secured by chains. A number of these 60-foot cribs chained together made a dram of 200 feet in length containing, at this period, some 8,000 cubic feet of timber, or 120 or 130 sticks, depending upon the size.[42] As white oak was so dense that it would not float, enough cross-bars of pine were bound with it to give it buoyancy. When the raft was being towed down the lake by steamer, close watch was kept to see that it remained intact, and usually a crew of French-Canadian or Indian raftsmen lived aboard. For shelter a small shanty was built of slabs, containing bunks and a bench table. The cook and his helper laid their fire on a deep bed of sand, suspending their cooking pots above. Travellers during the twenties and thirties have left descriptions of these timber rafts gliding at night down the waters of Lake Ontario and the St. Lawrence. They tell of the red glow of fires reflected in black water, and the songs of raftsmen heard for long distances in the darkness. Bonnycastle wrote: "A raft a quarter of a mile long—I hope I do not exaggerate, for it may be half a mile, never having measured one but by the eye—with its little huts of boards, its apologies for flags and streamers, its numerous little masts and sails, its cooking caboose, and its contrivances for anchoring . . . with the men who appear on its surface as if they were walking on the lake, is curious enough; but to see it in drams, or detached portions, sent down foaming and darting along the timber slides . . . is still more so."[43]

Rafting timber down the rivers of the province was the only means by which it could be transported to ports on the St. Lawrence. Considerable skill was required on swift rivers, but the open waters of Lake Ontario were especially hazardous. Quick storms that arose without warning frequently caused rafts to break up, and in this event the white oak immediately sank of its own weight and the pine was scattered up and down the lake, at great loss to the owner. According to Bonnycastle the "hardships of rafting" were overcome during the forties by the conversion of old steamers into timber carriers. Adapted by being cut down and lengthened, they were masted and rigged as barques or sloops and treated in every respect like Atlantic timber-vessels. Into "these Leviathans of Lake Ontario," the timber, boards, staves, handspikes, etc., from the interior were shipped to Quebec. In fact, one of these vessels named the *Goliath*, as large as a frigate, was loaded at Toronto for a voyage direct to the West Indies.[44]

Some timber, and the lumber from Chisholm's sawmill on The Sixteen and other mills situated on lesser streams in the vicinity, went no farther than York. About 1832 at the foot of Bay Street at York, Richard Tinning established a timber and lumber business for which the stock was obtained primarily at Oakville and the Credit River. Tinning moved to the foot of York Street in the forties, where he erected the steam sawmill reputed to be the first in York.[45]

The smaller white oak was made into staves, for which there was great demand in both England and the United States for the manufacture of barrels of all sizes and shapes. Those sent to England were destined for the West India sugar trade and one writer tells us: "From England they are shipped to the West Indies, from the West Indies they return to England in the shape of sugar hogsheads and rum puncheons; and from thence they are again sent out to Canada, to be knocked to pieces and consumed on the very ground that gave them birth."[46] In making staves squared white oak was cut into blocks 5½ and 3 feet long. With wedge and beetle or wooden mallet a six-inch block could be split into four staves. The sizes most in demand were the extra heavy pipe staves and the somewhat lighter standard staves which measured 5½ feet in length, 5 inches in breadth, and 1½ inches in thickness. The shorter West India staves measured 3½ feet long, and were slightly narrower and thinner.[47] The longer lengths brought a price of $95 per thousand and the shorter $65,[48] and each stave was marked, as was the usual custom, with a hammer bearing Chisholm's initials.[49] On the east bank of The Sixteen at the curve south of the mills a wooden slide was built, down which staves were slid one by one onto the decks of schooners.[50]

Farmers make good lumbermen, and those in the rear of the township, being old hands at this work, kept up a steady flow of staves from that quarter. Made in the bush during the winter the staves were corded up on the banks of The Sixteen to await the breaking up of the ice in the spring. By then the banks for miles back into the country were piled high with corded staves, each bearing the mark of the owner. A settler who engaged in the industry wrote: "Before the spring freshet cullers were sent to throw out the culls and, as soon as the floods came, other men were hired to throw the selected staves into the Creek and pilot them down the swollen stream. These cullers were abundantly supplied with 'oh be joyful' and in the exuberance of the loyalty to employers thus created, it is said that everything went in, culls as well as selected."[51]

Carried down by the high water, the staves rushed down The Sixteen to the harbour where a boom kept them from being swept into the lake. Chisholm is quoted as saying that at times the water was so thick with staves that a man could walk on them from the harbour to the dam, a distance of about a mile.[52] Transient lumberjacks lived in shanties on the flats, and many were the tales told of brawls and carousals heard at night in these camps along The Sixteen.

IV

Upper Canada, the only British colony not situated on tidewater, was nearly a thousand miles from the sea. It was reached by the great water-way, the St. Lawrence River, and much of the trade of the province passed through the river cities of Montreal and Quebec. During the long period when the severity of the climate locked rivers and harbours in ice, the Canadas were quite isolated from the mother country. With the opening of navigation in the spring, schooners collected their cargoes of staves, timber, lumber, and wheat, and steamers their raft-tows, to sail down Lake Ontario to points of trans-shipment, Garden Island off Kingston, or Prescott farther down the St. Lawrence.

The commerce of Oakville was founded upon the two staple products of the province, wood and wheat. At the time the produce began to flow out of the harbour, Oakville was one of the farthest inland ports, and few schooners plied as far as the head of the lake. To transport the growing quantities of staves, timber, and wheat to markets on Lake Ontario and to points of trans-shipment on the St. Lawrence required the use of a number of vessels, and William Chisholm lost no time in establishing a shipyard on The Sixteen. For some years he had engaged in shipbuilding on the shore of Burlington Bay,[53] and the speed with which the new shipyard began to function points to the transference of equipment to the new location before navigation was closed in 1827. Among the shipwrights then employed by Chisholm were Jacob Randall, David Patterson, and possibly John Potter.

The size of sailing ships was limited by the shallowness of rivers and harbours, and those built in The Sixteen during the early years ranged from 50 to 100 tons' burthen, carrying capacity. Taking fewer hands to operate, the schooner rig held preference over the square rig. Schooners carrying 50 tons could be manned by three or four hands. Those of the 75 to 100 ton class required a crew of five or six hands at wages ranging from £3 10*s*. to £5 per month during the period of navigation. By comparison shipwrights commanded a wage of 7*s*. 6*d*. to 10*s*. per day, depending upon their skill.

Chisholm's shipyard was situated above the last sweeping curve of The Sixteen on the south bank (now the north end of Navy Street) where the water is deep close to the shore.[54] Here was laid down a 50-ton schooner on the same plan as the *Mohawk Chief*, one of five vessels then owned by Chisholm.[55] Being the first ship to be built and launched in the township this schooner was appropriately christened *Trafalgar*. In August, 1828, she was advertised as being "ready for business," and under the command of Captain John Eno plied the waters between the head of the lake, Rochester, and Oswego.[56] The following year Captain Nicholas Boylan became master of the *Trafalgar*.[57]

The second ship built at Oakville was ready for the water in the spring of 1830, and it may be that by then the sawmill was in operation. On May 19 the launch took place "in the presence of a large concourse of people, and never did a vessel glide more elegantly into her destined element, than did this, the *Lady Colborne*."[58] In less than a month this schooner was ready for service, and loaded with her first cargo. Among the accounts of the store at Burlington Beach run by Joel Smith in partnership with William Chisholm appears the following entry: "7th June 1830—Received on Board the Schooner *Lady Colborne* Thirteen Hundred and thirty four Bushels and fifty two pounds of Merchantable Wheat consigned to Forsyth Richardson & Co. Montreal signed by Robert Wilson, Master."[59]

During the winter another ship was laid down, and the launch in May, 1831, was attended by a visitor who described it in these terms: "On the 14th. a new schooner was launched at the 16 Mile Creek, named Mississauga Chief, the property of Wm. Chisholm, M.P. . . . There were in port, at the time of the launch four schooners, a drudging [*sic*] machine, and several small craft added much to the beauty and importance of the scene. . . . There were not less than 300 persons to witness the scene where a few years ago stood a pathless wilderness. The vessel being rigged and ready for sea, Col. Chisholm and a number of spectators made a short excursion on the Lake. At the 16 Mile Creek to all appearances there will be a handsome and extensive village in the course of a very few years."[60] It was not unusual at this period to launch a ship fully rigged. There is a case on record of a vessel that stuck fast on the ways, and the wind being favourable, her sails were hoisted and she was sailed off the ways into the water. On the flats along the east bank of The Sixteen was a tow path along which oxen towed vessels up from the harbour. Lake sailors called towing by oxen the "horned breeze," and when they bent their backs to the oars of sloops to row them up the river they provided the "ash breeze."[61]

One by one as they were made ready for service the new schooners joined the fleet of carriers bound for the markets in Lower Canada. Of the exports going to Britain from Upper and Lower Canada during the early 1830's, wood products made up nearly two-thirds.[62] At Quebec the white oak was judged for soundness, colour, and squaring, and stamped according to grade. Timber labelled merchantable was bought by factors of British firms, and great quantities of rejected timber which should have been cut into lumber rather than squared were allowed to rot.

The majority of schooners that sailed out of The Sixteen after the harvest with wheat beneath their hatches were bound for the St. Lawrence, but some crossed the lake to the United States. In 1830, while the harbour was still under construction, the exports of wheat amounted to 6,250 bushels. The exports also included 1,189 barrels of flour from mills on The Sixteen in the rear of the township, 5 barrels of tallow, and 109 barrels of potash.[63] Leached from the ashes of hardwood trees, potash was one of the chief sources of ready money for backwoods settlers. Before it was replaced by chemicals, potash was much in demand in Britain for the manufacture of glass and soap, and most merchants in the township ran asheries in connection with their stores.

On the return trip up the lake the schooners brought salt, which from the earliest times it had been necessary to import, and other merchandise, and immigrants. The *Mohawk Chief* carried freight from

Prescott to York for "6*d*. Halifax Currency per Cwt."[64] When landed at Oakville the merchandise was used to stock the shop Chisholm had established there. This merchant's shop and ship chandlery, which was doing business in 1828, was built on the side of the hill near the river[65] and stands today as the rear section of the house that is no. 5 William Street. Referred to both as the "Oakville Establishment" and the "Oakville Shop," it was a branch of the general store at Burlington Beach run in partnership by Chisholm and Joel Smith, who dealt direct with firms in Lower Canada, in particular Forsyth, Richardson & Company of Montreal.[66] Farmers in the township traded wheat and staves, and workers employed on the various construction projects in connection with the townsite gave their labour, in exchange for supplies. Current rates of pay were 2*s*. 6*d*. per diem cash or 3*s*. "store," i.e. by an order for provisions.[67]

Chisholm also carried on a forwarding business. On the river at the foot of the hill on William Street he built a warehouse where grain belonging to other buyers in the township was stored. As previously shown, Mackenzie, in his editorial in the *Colonial Advocate*, made an issue of the fact that at this time Chisholm refused to sell any water lots, "charging his neighbours 2 pence half penny per bushel for storage and weighing. . . ."[68]

The extent of the commerce that was moving outwards by the time the harbour was nearing completion in 1831 may be judged from the following description which appeared in a letter to the *Western Mercury* dated from Nelson Township late in the summer:

SIR: Having had occasion a few days ago to visit Oakville, the Village, (or rather the harbour) now forming at the mouth of the Sixteen Mile Creek, in Trafalgar, I was much gratified in witnessing the great improvement recently made. . . . What drew my attention more particularly was the number of vessels and craft of different descriptions in the Harbour, eleven of which sailed out together when I was there, and on enquiry I learned their names and destinations, which as nearly as I can recollect, were as follows:—

Schr.	*Rebecca and Eliza*	Staves	French Creek
do.	*Telegraph*	do.	do.
do.	*George the 4th*	do.	do.
do.	*John McGill*	do.	do.
do.	*William the 4th*	Wood	York
do.	*Erin*	do.	do.
do.	*Humber*	do.	do.
Packet	*Zephyr*	do.	do.
Wood boats	*Betsy, Defiance* and *Pirate*	do.	do.

I have been informed that there has been shipped this season upward of 165,000 bu. of wheat beside a quantity of pearl ashes, etc.—and that nearly 3,000 cords of Wood are in progress of being shipped, a part having already gone; I should think that if our good friends at the Capital, during the ensuing fall and winter, have to endure the inconvenience of *muddy streets*, they will not have so much reason to complain of the scarcity of firewood.[69]

At York householders were paying 10*s*. per cord for firewood,[70] and only the week prior to the publication of the above letter Chisholm had advertised, "eight good choppers wanted to whom employment will be given until November."[71] If correct, and not a printer's error, the 165,000 bushels of wheat quoted above as having been shipped in 1831 was not to be equalled for another twenty years. French Creek, also referred to above, was situated on the St. Lawrence in New York State opposite Gananoque; soon after the name was changed to Clayton.

By 1831 the deepening of the channel by dredging allowed vessels of greater draught to pass inward and outward. The fourth schooner built in the shipyard had double the capacity of her predecessors, being of 120 tons' burthen. This vessel was given the name of the Receiver-General of Upper Canada through whom had been made the government loan which had so infuriated Mackenzie and enabled Chisholm to finish the harbour. The launch took place on December 5, 1831, and was described by a witness: "While she glided into her destined element, hailed by the joyous cheers of the spectators, she was baptized the *John Henry Dunn* with the ceremony usual on such occasions. This, which is the fourth vessel built at the new harbour at Oakville presents proof of the prosperity of the vicinity, and of the incendiary intentions of Mackenzie. . . ."[72]

Not long after the sawmill went into production the United States began to absorb sawn lumber in ever increasing quantity. There is mention of a schooner, name unknown, which sailed out of Oakville heavily laden with a consignment of lumber for Lewiston, New York. Late at night when about three miles off the Niagara River she met disaster. According to the *Niagara Reporter* the vessel was "completely water-logged in a tremendous gale of wind; the rudder was quite unmanageable and the crew [of five] were for two hours standing up to their breasts in water, whilst the heavy waves were continually breaking over their heads." The schooner providentially drifted toward the river where she became stranded on a sand bar and the cries of the crew brought rescue. Most of the deck lading was lost, "but we are glad to hear the disaster extended no further," concluded the *Reporter*.[73]

Misfortune also overtook the first schooner to be built at Oakville. When on her way from Oswego to Cobourg heavily laden with merchandise and salt, the *Trafalgar* was badly damaged in a November storm which took a heavy toll on the lake.[74] After being rebuilt, however, she became a vessel of some importance and for a time belonged to William Marsh, magnate of Port Britain.[75]

The schooner in the facsimile of a daguerrotype shown in plate 1 has been identified as the *Britannia*, whose home port in the thirties was Oakville. Her master, Captain Nicholas Boylan, "was among the first who settled in Oakville" and was for twelve years in Chisholm's employ.[76] Alexander Muir who succeeded Boylan as master of the *Britannia* in 1840 described her as "an old vessel." After stating that his wages were $40 a month Muir continues: "She sailed fast as she had a standing keel and great dead rise in her floor timbers. She carried topsail and being very stiff when light she would work up the lake against a moderate gale of wind. We were freighting staves from the head of Lake Ontario to Garden Island. Her cargo was 7,000 pipe staves. She drew seven feet aft."[77]

The fleet of schooners engaged in Oakville's commerce increased apace, as a visitor reported who stopped there in 1834.

While dinner was preparing curiosity led me to examine the shipping in the harbour . . . and really I was much surprised to learn that three years ago, the mouth of the Creek, that would only admit an Indian Canoe, now contained sixteen vessels of the following burthens:

Schooners	Tons	No. of Men
J. M'Kenzie	180	8
Telegraph	120	6
Rebec [*sic*—undoubtedly *Rebecca and Eliza*]	120	6
J. H. Dunn	120	6
Lady Colborne	75	5
Mississauga Chief	85	5
Farmer's Daughter	85	5
Matilda	50	4
Ann and Susan	50	4
Dolphin	45	4
Rambler	30	4
Perseverance	50	4
Wm. IV	30	4
Swiftsure	20	3
Zephyr	15	3
Sarah Ann	40	4
Total	1,105	75[78]

V

By 1834 the harbour was indeed a busy place. Around it the wilderness was disappearing and the village was taking shape. Shanties and log cabins were being replaced by "a number of houses (some very good ones, two stories high) all occupied, in one of which a very commodious inn is kept, provided with most of the comforts and many of the luxuries of the present day."[79] Only fourteen months had elapsed since the holding of the first public sale of lots and it will be seen by the announcement that building was restricted, to the exclusion of primitive log houses:

Town Lots in Oakville
for Sale at Public Auction
on Tuesday the 10th. July next at 12 O'clock
at the Oakville House

The Town Plot of this thriving Village and Shipping Port being now regularly laid out in Streets, Town Lots and Water Lots, the Public are notified that Fifty of these Lots will be disposed of, at the time and place above stated, without reserve, to the Highest Bidder.

The Terms upon which these Lots will be sold are, One-half the Purchase Money to be paid at the time of Sale, and the other Half in Twelve Months—subject to condition of Building a Stone, Brick or Frame House, not less than 24 feet by 18 to be completed within eighteen Months from the day of Sale.

The Proprietor to give Bonds to the Purchaser, to give Deeds to the Lots upon the Conditions being complied with; or, in case the Purchaser prefers it, he may have a Deed at once, by paying the whole money down, or giving good endorsed notes for the latter half; the Proprietor taking the Bond from the Purchaser to erect a house on his Lot, agreeable to the conditions of Sale.

The Fifty Lots to be sold upon this occasion include all the most valuable Water Lots and Building Lots in the Town, or which can ever be obtained therein thereafter. Merchants and Farmers therefore, who wish to obtain situations for erecting Stores or Public Warehouses, for storing and shipping Produce, will have an opportunity of doing so at this sale.

Oakville is pleasantly and advantageously situated at the mouth of the Sixteen-Mile Creek . . . on the new Lake Road from York to Hamilton. . . .

The Harbour answers every purpose for vessels navigating Lake Ontario. At the head of the navigable water of the Creek there is a superior Set of Sawmills that will cut forty thousand feet of boards per week; and an excellent Grist Mill for the accommodation of the country.

WILLIAM CHISHOLM, Nelson.[80]

Oakville, June 24, 1833

Laying out the townsite had been a matter of no urgency, as no lots could be sold until the final payment on the purchase was made on March 21, 1831, and the patent secured from the Crown. Also, negotiations were in progress for obtaining more land along the borders of the purchase. Though some quarter-acre lots were laid out by 1830[81] the survey and its accompanying plan were not completed until just prior to the sale.

By that time the addition of land on both east and west along the lake shore in the 4th concession extended the village somewhat beyond the limits of the Missisauga Reserve. In 1833, for his services as a volunteer in a flank company in the War of 1812, Chisholm received a grant of lot 12 of the 4th concession. A wedge-shaped piece of this land he added to the town lot on the east. Bordering the village north of the concession road was the farm of Joseph Brant Anderson of Grimsby Township who had taken up this land about 1826.

Along the Missisauga Reserve on the west lay a narrow strip of land running through the 3rd and 4th concessions, the residue of lot 16 after the boundaries of the reserve had been established. In 1812 this land had been granted to James Brock, and in 1833 Chisholm succeeded in buying it from his widow Susannah.[82] Part of this land was added to the town plot, and the balance Chisholm traded to his brother-in-law, John Terry, for a farm at York. Terry gave the name of "Brock Lands" to his new farm.[83]

When first laid out the town plot was rectangular in shape and bounded on the west by Brock Street, on the north by Rebecca Street, which after crossing The Sixteen became Randall Street, and on the east by Allan Street. The survey was made by Deputy Surveyor H. J. Castle whose plan dated July 20, 1833, shows the shipyard with two unfinished vessels in the river, Chisholm's grain warehouse and merchant's shop, and the detail of the mills.[84] Usually surveyors worked in winter when the trees were without leaves, in a party which besides the instrument man included axemen, picket men, and chain-bearers. As the place of beginning Castle chose a spot not far from the lake on top of the east bank of The Sixteen. From here he took bearings on the land end of the east pier, on the opposite side of the river (the west pier not then being built), and on a corner of the warehouse on the river above, and established the line for a street paralleling the lake which became Front Street. A trail was blazed, lined out approximately by picket men, and axemen followed to "bush out the line." The surveyor then produced his true line and chain-bearers stretched their chains to gauge the distance. For measuring out the land Castle used the Gunter's chain of heavy metal containing 100 links of 7.92 inches each. The chain measured 66 feet in length, ten square chains equalling one acre, and the surveyor recorded his findings in "chains" and "links" instead of in "feet" and "inches."

Using Front Street as a base-line Castle laid out other streets parallel and perpendicular to it which squared out the land in a "checker board" plan of blocks. Most of the streets were made the usual width of one chain, but the main thoroughfare was given the width of eighty feet. On the east side of The Sixteen the blocks were fifteen square chains in area, i.e., 1½ acres. These blocks were divided into six quarter-acre lots lettered alphabetically from A to F inclusive. Though the same plan was followed on the west side of the river it was later altered to better suit the contours of the land. Thus the lots varied considerably in size and shape and instead of being lettered were numbered.

Castle's attractive water-colour plan of Oakville proves him to have been something of an artist. In fact, among canvases of Paul Kane, Captain Richard Bonnycastle, John G. Howard, and others which were shown in the first exhibition of the Society of Artists and Amateurs of York held in July, 1834, hung Castle's landscape of Muskoka, "Bala Lakes." According to one critic this painting was "a pleasing Scene but this gentleman wants breadth of light throughout all his work to give them vigour."[85]

For the accommodation of prospective buyers Chisholm commissioned S. O. Tazewell to make copies of Castle's plan of Oakville. Shortly before, Tazewell had moved from Kingston to York, where he set up the York Lithographic Press, the "only one in the North American Colony." He announced that "everything relating to Art can be done on the shortest notice. This office affords very great advantages to those Persons who have large tracts of Land for Sale as the Diagrams can be printed on the heading of Handbills which will immediately show the exact situation of every lot etc."[86]Using Canadian stone and

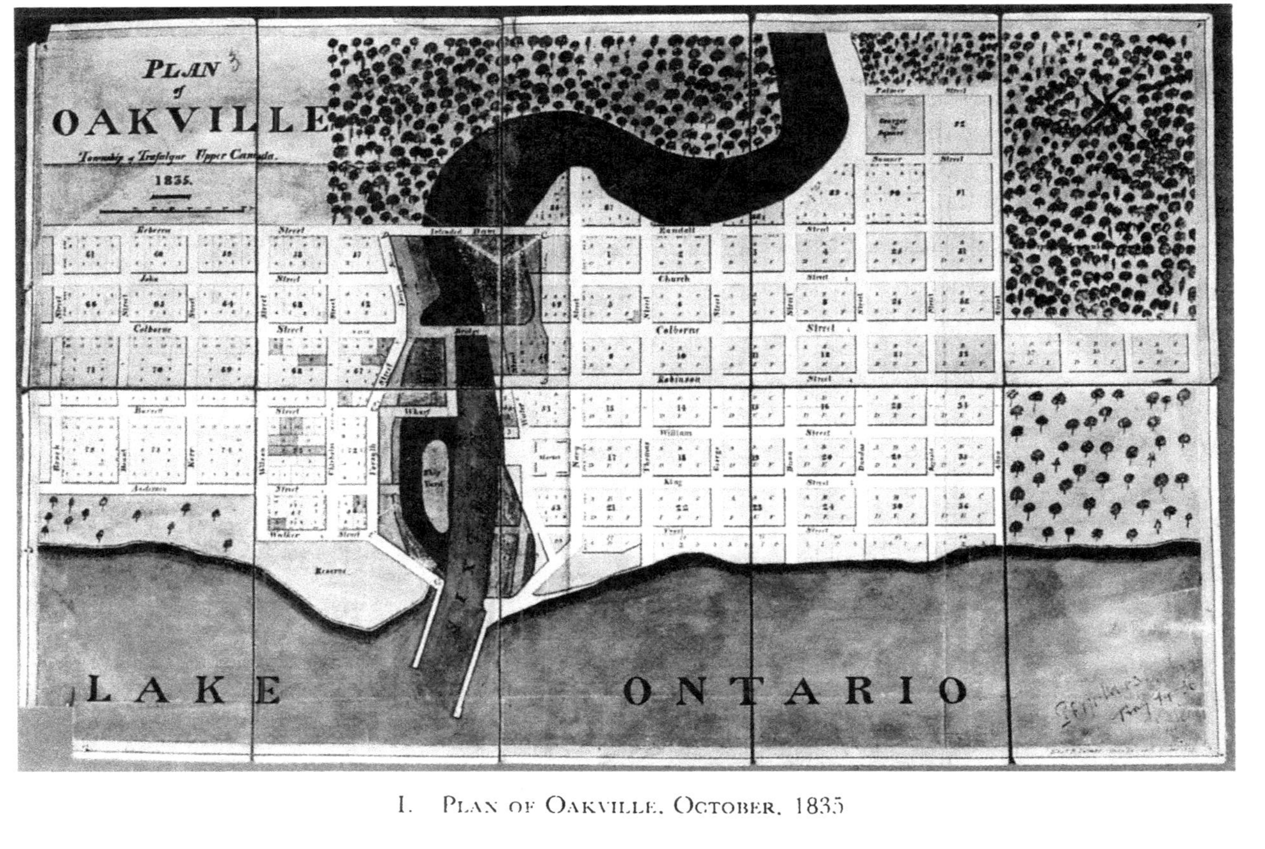

I. Plan of Oakville, October, 1835

paper made in Canada Tazewell produced lithographs of the falls of Niagara and Chaudière which at the time were considered very fine.[87] A copy of his lithograph of the plan of Oakville, 1833, at present hangs in the Old Post Office Museum.

Having made a heavy investment in the development of the harbour and wishing to show his holdings Chisholm commissioned from Edward Palmer the charming plan dated 1835 that is reproduced opposite page 38 of this history.[88] It will be seen that the harbour limits are well defined, and that several blocks had been added to the town plot. Those set aside for public purposes were the Market Block on Navy Street and a park, George's Square. Though unmarked, block no. 56 at Navy and Randall had been designated for the meeting-house and public burial ground, and both had been in use for some years.

The "Map of the Town of Oakville" dated August 1, 1836, and drawn by Robert W. Kerr, Deputy Provincial Surveyor, is the official plan used today at the Registry Office for Halton County. At this period "town" referred to area, whereas later a "town" implied a certain population. In the latter sense Oakville was not a town but a village, and so it would remain for another quarter of a century.

Kerr's plan shows the addition of several streets and fifteen "park" lots (larger than "town" lots and not necessarily of equal size) along the river to the north and on the lake shore west of The Sixteen. On this plan, unlike Castle's, the names of the streets appear, some of which had long since become established through usage. They fall into three categories: those of members of the Government of Upper Canada, those of early settlers, and the names of Chisholm's family and friends. Today, many streets in the old section of Oakville bear the names of friends and contemporaries of William Chisholm who were men of importance in the early days of the province.

Not long after Oakville was founded Sir John Colborne was appointed Lieutenant-Governor of Upper Canada. Owing to this appointment and his interest in improving the road from York to the head of the lake, the main thoroughfare of the village, which was a part of this road, was given the name Colborne Street. Sir John Colborne was one of the most notable generals in the Peninsular War. At Waterloo where he commanded the 52nd Regiment he was chiefly responsible for the defeat of Napoleon's Old Guard. Except that he was much taller, he was the counterpart in appearance of the Duke of Wellington. He exhibited great simplicity of character and a dislike for ostentation, and made an able governor.

When Colborne went to Lower Canada as commander-in-chief of

the British forces in Canada, he was succeeded as Lieutenant-Governor of Upper Canada by Sir Francis Bond Head. In January, 1836, Sir Francis and his retinue landed at New York and journeyed by sleigh to York, stopping to dine at Oakville. The streets named Francis, Bond, and Head make their initial appearance on the village plan of that year, and commemorate the visit of the new Lieutenant-Governor of the province. Francis Street, laid out along the flats on the west side of The Sixteen, is no longer used and appears only on deeds of land.

In the case of Robinson Street it is difficult to choose between two brothers, Chief Justice John Beverley Robinson and the first Commissioner of Crown Lands, Peter Robinson. Chisholm's contacts with the former dated back to the War of 1812, and his arrangements for purchasing the Missisauga Reserve were made with the latter. With only these meagre facts at hand it is impossible to determine who was honoured, but unquestionably it was one or the other, John Beverley Robinson being the likelier.

The Honourable John Henry Dunn, an Englishman who in 1820 was appointed to the post of Receiver-General of Upper Canada, bought lots in the village, and a street as well as a schooner was named after him. He held other important offices, and between him and William Chisholm there were various points of contact. One of the principal subscribers to the Welland Canal, he was made president of the board of directors (of which Chisholm was one), and it was for him that the town situated on the canal was called Dunnville. His wife is said to have been "one of the graceful lady-chiefs in the high life at York."[89] After resigning his posts Dunn returned to London. His son Alexander Roberts Dunn was in the famous charge of the Light Brigade at the battle of Balaclava. Of all the six hundred he won the highest award, the only cavalry officer in the Crimean War to win the Victoria Cross.[90] His sword and medals are now in the possession of Upper Canada College, where he was a student in his youth.

The Honourable William Allan was at this period the representative at York of the Montreal firm of Forsyth, Richardson & Company. Upon his arrival at Montreal about 1787 Allan had been employed by the company as junior clerk. About 1796 he moved to York, where he opened a general store and built the earliest landing place for larger lake craft, the Merchant's Wharf at the foot of Frederick Street. Allan acted as forwarding agent between merchants and traders in the western section of Upper Canada and the commercial firms at Montreal, and over a period of years Chisholm did considerable business with him. In 1800 Allan was appointed the first postmaster and customs collector at York; he was the first president of the Bank of Upper Canada, a member of the Legislative and Executive councils of the province, and held many other offices besides. In the early days a man of more than ordinary aptitude for affairs was required to act in many capacities. In connection with one of these offices Allan received a grant of land west of the Twelve Mile Creek in Trafalgar Township which he sold in 1810 to Phillip Sovereign, whose son Charles has been and will be quoted in this history from time to time. It is of interest to note that Allan was one of the militia officers who with the Reverend John Strachan negotiated favourable terms with the general of the invading American forces and saved the town of York from destruction during the War of 1812.

Of the barrister Edward Palmer, little is known other than that he drew the plan of Oakville shown opposite page 38 and made periodic trips to England. In 1838 he advertised in the *Christian Guardian*: "Old Country Agency—the subscriber intending to leave Canada in April next . . . on his second Tour in the Old Country, visiting London, Birmingham, Liverpool, Hull and Norwich again offers reasonable terms to take charge of Powers of Attorney, and to transact such Law Business and other reputable Commissions as may be entrusted to him. . . . Oakville, Gore District, U. C."[91] Nor is anything known of Thomas Sheddon, who died in 1836 and lies buried in the Town Cemetery.

Division Street, which runs on the line separating the north from the south half of lot 13 in the 3rd concession, formed the northern boundary of the village, dividing it from the wilderness. But it was not long before the land on the north was cleared for a farm by John A. Chisholm, second son of Oakville's founder.

Water Street ran along the marsh at the foot of the east bank from the harbour to Colborne Street and the derivation of its name is self-evident, but Front Street signifies more than is at first apparent. When the only means of approach to Upper Canada was by water, townships were first laid out along the St. Lawrence and Niagara rivers and Lake Ontario. Running their lines parallel to the shore, surveyors worked inland; therefore the shore line was the "front" of a township. Not until all the land along the water-ways had been laid out were the sections "in rear of the front" opened for settlement. In most older towns the street that runs nearest to the water is Front Street.

The reason behind the naming of Church Street defies discovery. As originally laid out this street ran to the top of the east bank of The

Sixteen, passing in front of the meeting-house. Though the primary function of a meeting-house in any community was that of a mission the building could not accurately be called a church.

The name "Navy Street" can be traced to the tremendous enthusiasm felt at this period for the British Navy. At all functions toasts were drunk to "Wellington and the Army" and to the "British Navy, three times three." After thirty years the Battle of Trafalgar was still green in the memories of the many settlers who had fought in the Napoleonic Wars. Other reminders of England's great admiral, Lord Nelson, are the names of Bronte and Palermo, which were conferred on villages in the township about the same time as the name Navy was given to the street in Oakville.

Thomas Street refers, of course, to Merrick Thomas whose large frame house stood on the south-east corner at Colborne Street. Merrick was born in Vermont, a son of Seneca Thomas whose forebears had migrated to the American colonies during the seventeenth century. Seneca Thomas brought his family to Canada in 1810, and when war broke out he was working on the fortifications at Queenston. Leaving his wife and children in Canada, he fled across the Niagara River and joined the American forces. When wounded and taken prisoner the British officers claimed that inasmuch as he had been working on the British fortifications, he was either a deserter or a spy. Nevertheless, when his wife died he was permitted to attend her funeral under guard. Seneca Thomas later escaped, and though he lived to a great age he never dared to return to Canada. Three of his children were taken by relatives, but Merrick, aged nine, preferred to fend for himself, and among his earliest recollections was that of driving an army cart to Burlington Heights in the rear of the British Army. Merrick found employment and a home with the owner of a store in Saltfleet Township who gradually acquired a sawmill, salt works, and sailing ships. From sawyer, sailor, and clerk Thomas worked up to the position of general manager of these various enterprises.[92] When he entered the employment of William Chisholm it was in the capacity of general manager in charge of the shipyard and the line of sailing ships engaged in the forwarding business on Lake Ontario. In 1827, a few months before Chisholm purchased the reserve at The Sixteen, Thomas married Esther Silverthorn, a sister of Mrs. William Chisholm. Thomas was well equipped with experience to oversee the development of the townsite of Oakville and was placed in charge as general superintendent. In 1833 he bought lot A in block 10 and built the house referred to above, but he also had a farm. In 1829 he leased the Crown Reserve, lot 17 of the 3rd concession (which he purchased ten years later) and calling it "Murray Hill Farm" he built the house which stands upon it today. When he took up permanent residence in Oakville in 1838, William Chisholm leased for his family the house at Thomas and Colborne streets.

There is but little doubt that King Street commemorates the name of Lieutenant George King, who died during the War of 1812. After his marriage to Chisholm's sister, Barbara, he had enrolled in the 1st Flank Company, 2nd Regiment, York Militia. Not long after, King died "on the Niagara frontier while doing duty with his Co. near Fort Erie," his death having been caused by an illness "contracted on said service," and William Chisholm served in his place in the flank company. Soon Barbara King died also, leaving two children whom Chisholm brought up as his wards.[93] After an adventurous youth one of these children, William McKenzie King, came to Oakville to build a house on the 6th Line that is still called "King's Castle."

Brock Street also takes us back to the War of 1812, and tracing the ownership of the land upon which it runs brings an interesting fragment of history into focus. James Brock, a relative of General Isaac Brock, came to Upper Canada as paymaster of the 49th Regiment. At that time war was brewing, and General Brock was administering the government. Paymaster Brock became his private secretary at a considerable reduction in pay; "indeed the salary is a mere pittance," wrote the General.[94] At this period civil servants were given land in part payment of their services, the home government being either unwilling or unable to expend much money on maintaining a provincial civil list. Accordingly James Brock petitioned the government for "a grant of the Waste Lands of the Crown; having learnt that his predecessors in office have uniformly obtained that indulgence."[95] The Executive Council granted him 1,200 acres, part of which was located in Trafalgar Township: the narrow strip of land west of the Missisauga Reserve previously referred to. This grant is dated 1812.[96] The year following, after General Brock was killed at Queenston Heights, James Brock took charge of all the General's possessions and boarded the schooner *Elizabeth* at York for Kingston.[97] The vessel was captured by the Americans and all on board were brought before Commodore Chauncey, U.S.N. Upon learning his identity and his mission, Chauncey granted Brock parole after he had pledged "his word to return to this place immediately" should the Secretary of the United States Navy disapprove. (The apologetic letters Chauncey wrote in explanation to his superior are rather entertaining.)[98] After this incident we lose track of James Brock, as his relationship to the General is uncertain. General Brock had several brothers and cousins in the British Army and to complicate matters further there were two James Brocks, both paymasters of the same regiment at different times. Whether the brother or the "near relative" owned the land on the border of Oakville has not been determined.

A reminder of early Irish settlers is found in the name given to a little hill north of John Street that forms a bank of the stream running between Chisholm and Kerr streets. Several generations of residents on the west side of the village knew it as Vinegar Hill, a sad reminder of the Irish Rebellion. The Battle of Vinegar Hill was fought in 1789 at the town of Wexford in the south of Ireland between Catholic "rebels" and the royalist forces of King George III, resulting in great slaughter. Examination of an old print of this battle[99] shows that a distinct resemblance exists between the original hill and its namesake in Oakville. Apparently this was recognized by an early resident who gave to the little hill a name that is yet remembered with hatred in Ireland.

The names John, William, and George recur so regularly in several generations of the Chisholm family that it is impossible to know who was indicated in the street names. It may well be that they were named for the three Scottish brothers who migrated from Inverness-shire to the Province of New York before the Revolution and came to Canada as Loyalists. George Chisholm settled at Burlington Bay on land adjoining that of the famous Mohawk warrior and chief of the Six Nations Indians, Thayendanegea, better known to the British as Joseph Brant. The street names of Brant and Kerr recall friends and neighbours in the wilderness on the north shore of Burlington Bay. Brant was related by marriage to the eminent military surgeon, Dr. Robert Kerr of Niagara, whose sons were contemporaries and intimate friends of William Chisholm. Besides being closely associated with him in the affairs of the government, the "hero of Beaver Dams," William Johnson Kerr, was Chisholm's neighbour on the Bay. Robert William Kerr, Deputy Provincial Surveyor, who made the official map of Oakville, was a friend for whom Chisholm named one of his sons. Again the question arises as to which Kerr is indicated in the name of the street but the weight of evidence seems in favour of the surveyor.

"Being desirous of setting apart a plot of ground for a public free park for the use of the citizens of the . . . town for purposes of recreation" Chisholm set aside the block on the bank of The Sixteen, "calling the same 'George's Square.' "[100] The most plausible suggestion for the source of this name is that it was the founder's father, the pioneer settler of Burlington Bay.

As this record progresses, other persons from whom streets in the village take their names will be encountered, and the tracing of some will take us even further afield in the early history of the province.

VI

The roads surveyed in the township in 1806 did not traverse the Missisauga Indian Reserve. At the time it was laid out the town plot was connected with the surrounding territory only by trails made by the Indians, and that farmers might have access to the port it was of paramount importance that the village should be joined to the agricultural district.

The concession roads of the 1806 survey, and the line roads running perpendicular to them, blocked out the township in areas a mile and a quarter square with five 200-acre lots to a square; between every five lots ran a line road. The 7th Line situated between lots 12 and 13 does not, therefore, appear on the survey and was a "given road" opened at a later date upon petition of freeholders. With the laying out of the New Survey of Trafalgar Township in 1819 on a different plan from that of the Old Survey, the road between the 7th and 8th concessions of the former connected with no corresponding road in the latter. Nor was there any reason that it should have done so prior to the founding of Oakville. By then, however, settlement was pushing many miles inland with the opening of new townships, and to continue this road through the Old Survey would enable settlers from the rear townships to travel directly to the mills and harbour at Oakville. The £25 appropriated in 1831 by the House of Assembly for the road "from

Post's Inn in Trafalgar to Oakville"[101] might be considered evidence of the 7th Line being a new road. The sum to be expended on the 6th Line to the west "from Mrs. Munn's to Oakville," an equal distance, was only £12 10*s*.[102] Also, it is at this time that Post's tavern first makes its appearance on the south-west corner of the 7th Line at the Dundas Street four miles to the north.

The construction of roads within the townsite would seem to have been the responsibility of the owner, William Chisholm. Had the 7th Line been continued south in a straight line it would have entered the village inconveniently along its eastern border, Allan Street. By the simple expedient of running the 6th and 7th lines to converge at the upper curve of The Sixteen the traffic was brought to the mills and the harbour by the shortest route. Within the limits of the village the 7th Line became Dundas Street. It may have been so called because it connects with the old Dundas Street on the north, but it was also the most direct route to the thriving town of Dundas, which at this date was being opened to the commerce of the lake by the building of the Desjardins Canal. Chisholm, being a director, was much interested in this project. As it follows the curves of the river in a manner more suggestive of an old Indian trail than a surveyor's road, Oakville's Dundas Street gives the impression of having been in use long before there was a village.

The moist and swampy land, of which there were large areas in the district, was made passable by causewaying. This type of road construction was also known as "corduroy," a term which obviously originated from its resemblance to the ridged cloth of that name. It consisted of placing round logs side by side, and tremendous quantities of small logs which would otherwise have been burned were utilized. Since the round logs were of various sizes and no attempt was made to fill in the spaces between, horses and cows passing over them were in continual danger of breaking their legs. On this subject one traveller commented: "Fewer accidents, however, occur in this way, than might be expected. Cattle of all kinds in this country are so accustomed thus to dance upon beech and maple, that, before they attain their second year, they acquire such proficiency in the art of log-walking, that I should not be at all surprised to hear of an American horse or bull becoming a rope-dancer."[103] Another wrote that the corduroy road "should have been included by Dante as the proper road to Pandemonium, for none can be more decidedly infernal."[104] At 10*s*. per rod causewaying was a very expensive part of road making, but under existing circumstances it was the best possible. Large sections of corduroy were to be found in every highway in the province, and the 1833 plan of Oakville clearly shows that the gully at the junction of Dundas Street and the 6th Line was spanned by a log causeway.

The roads required enormous upkeep. When wet the clay soil made heavy going, and since lofty trees bordering both sides of the roads excluded sun and wind, the deep mudholes took long to dry. The system of statute labour by which they were maintained was inadequate to their requirements, with the result that the roads were frequently impassable. Under this system each freeholder was required to spend a given number of days, based on the value of his assessment, on road work. The picks and shovels wielded by man-power were supplemented by horse-drawn scrapers. When the state of the roads became such as to require more attention than statute labour would produce, a petition to the House of Assembly sometimes brought financial assistance.

"Roads of communication," however, were the concern of the government, which undertook the construction of the Lake Shore Road from York to the head of Lake Ontario during the summer of 1832. This was the surveyor's road running in front of the 3rd concessions of the townships along the lake. But it was not the first Lake Shore Road. About a mile farther inland was an earlier road which had been used for ages by the Indians. It was a link in the long trail leading from Quebec on the St. Lawrence River to New Orleans at the mouth of the Mississippi River. In the vicinity of Oakville the trail ran at the foot of the low ridge a mile from the lake. Known locally as the Red Hill this ridge is the shore cliff of Lake Ontario's predecessor known to geologists as Lake Iroquois. The land south of the ridge was gravelly, level, and dry, and wherever practicable the Indians made use of this prehistoric shore line. This was also the route taken by couriers of the French régime and later by the British during winter when navigation on the lake was closed. It is shown on numerous early maps. Though it was little more than a horse trail, the government spent large sums in spanning the creeks and rivers along its route with bridges, which were often washed away by spring freshets.[105] This road is described in detail by William Allan, who as one of three road commissioners submitted to the government a report in 1804 when the tract of land between the Humber and the head of the lake was still in possession of the Missisauga Indians. After stating the amount of causewaying required "to make the Road perfectly good," Allan continues: "A Ridge begins, and runs closs to the present Road all along to the 16 Mile Creek—Most of all the bad places can be avoided, by cutting the Road along the Ridge. . . . The Hill at the 16 Mile Creek is cappable of being much improved at no great expense on both sides . . . there is a place, we mark't much better for carrying the Road along down the Hill, and nearly opposite, to where it assends on the other side. . . ."[106]

The commissioners' recommendations were never carried out, for soon afterwards the Missisauga Tract was purchased by the government and surveyed into townships. Wilmot on the plan of his survey made in 1806 shows quite clearly how what he called the "Old Road from York to the Head of the Lake" swung south from the ridge to cross The Sixteen a little to the north of where he ran the concession road (now the Queen Elizabeth Way). Here is the only remaining section of this old road in the township. It so happened that the new concession road descended the east bank at the very place the commissioners marked as "much better for carrying the Road along down the Hill." When the region became farm land many settlers continued to use the old road, notwithstanding that the concession roads were supposed to replace it. John Lucas, through whose farm on the Town Line in Nelson it ran, preferred the old road when teaming lumber to Hamilton, and upon returning one day he was much annoyed to find the road commissioner had had all the bridges removed.[107] The farmers were thus forced to use the concession or Lower Middle Road, and soon all traces of the old road were effaced where it ran through the farms.

The mathematical precision with which the land was surveyed into farms ignored the laws of nature and the topography of the country. In a land of boundless forests it was the simplest approach for the surveyor, but many generations of the rural population were forced to struggle up and down dangerous hills, through swamps and bogs which could have been avoided had earlier trails been made use of.

As has already been pointed out, the clearing of the road in front of the 3rd concession was greatly retarded by the paucity of settlers and the large number of reserves, both Crown and Clergy, facing it on both sides. A meeting was held in 1827 of the "Inhabitants of Nelson and Trafalgar on the Lake Road leading from the Burlington Bay Canal to the 16 Mile Creek" at which the following resolution was adopted: "That the road from Burlington Bay to the Capital of Upper Canada ought to be improved for Post Coaches to travel with ease and safety upon . . . by which road the distance is now seven miles shorter than the Dundas Street, and dangerous hills are avoided."[108] It was also agreed that funds be solicited among the settlers and that a petition requesting financial aid in building bridges and causeways be sent to the Lieutenant-Governor.[109] However, it was not until Colborne became Lieutenant-Governor that action was taken.

Sir John Colborne was much interested in promoting emigration, particularly among the poorer classes, and when he became Upper Canada's Lieutenant-Governor he grasped the opportunity of putting some of his ideas into effect. During the first difficult years immigrants were forced to maintain themselves and their families by hiring themselves for wages, and in many cases it was some time before they could become established on their own land. Colborne planned to use immigrant labour paid with government funds to clear land and open roads. In this way districts would be rendered more desirable to those who could afford to buy improved land, the poorer immigrants would receive assistance, and colonization would be accelerated. Government assistance was decidedly an innovation at this period.

Included in Colborne's scheme was the improvement of the Lake Shore Road. To oversee the work and handle government funds, the two Members of Parliament through whose constituencies the road passed were appointed commissioners. These were William Chisholm of Nelson and William Gamble of Mimico who built the stone grist mill on the Humber River which now stands as a ruin beside the Old Mill Tearoom. Those named in Oakville to oversee the work on the section of road east of The Sixteen, for which the appropriation was £60, were Merrick Thomas, Jacob Randall, and William Young, proprietor of the Oakville House. An additional sum of £187 10*s*. was set aside for "levelling the hills and making a mound across the flats of said Creek,"[110] and for building a "good draw-bridge."[111] The following letter dated from Nelson, April 9, 1832, was written to Colborne's secretary by William Chisholm:

When in York last, I had the honour of an interview with his Excellency the Lieutenant Governor, and in the course of our conversation we spoke of the Lake Road from York to the head of the Lake, particularly the Bridge on the Humber and river Credit, and I mentioned that it would cost more to make such Bridges in the summer than in the winter season, on account of driving the piles, which could be done at less expense on the ice etc.

But since that time, by an examination into my business of the kind at Oakville I have ascertained that it can be done as cheap after the ice is gone, as it could in the winter.

I have the Machine all ready which I used for driving the piles on the ice and find, on examination, that I have also a scow, which I used for making the Harbour, that will answer to put the piling machine into, with very little expense. I will furnish all those articles and will not charge for the use of them for the erection of the Bridges above mentioned. The Emigrants that his Excellency spoke of, would answer, as labourers for mostly all the work, it would only require a capable person to supervise it. If his Excellency would think proper to make this great improvement, I would be most happy to do all in my power to forward his views, which, I think would be the means of assisting a number of the poorer class of Emigrants, and at the same time, be of great advantage to the Public. . . .

WILLIAM CHISHOLM.[112]

The work was begun shortly thereafter and in August a traveller wrote to a news sheet:

I have visited the Lake road, and was much pleased with the improvement made upon it. In the course of next month, I think it may be travelled; and when it is completed, it will make one of the finest roads in the province. From York to Burlington Bay, it lies near the Lake; and there are no hills of consequence. There is a fine bridge building across the Humber, near James Stewart's under the direction of W. Chisholm, Esq. of Nelson, and another at the Credit. When these are completed, the road will be passable from York to Hamilton. The entire line of roads has been made under the superintendence of Messrs. Chisholm and Gamble, who have spared no pains upon it. The work has given employment to many needy emigrants, until they found employment in the adjoining neighbourhood; and will be of more service to the country than all the grievance-mongering prate, writings and petitions of the whole province. The Lt. Gov. deserves much praise for suggesting the idea of employing the poorer description of emigrants in this manner.[113]

As we know it today the Lake Shore Road is a surveyor's road to the 4th Line west of Oakville. There it escaped the survey to follow an older road running closer to the lake which had been kept open by use, and this at the present time is one of the prettiest sections of the Lake Shore Road in the township. Until 1858 it crossed the Twelve Mile Creek at its mouth, but erosion made it necessary to move the road back from the lake shore to pass through Triller Street in the village of Bronte.[114]

With a provincial highway second only to the old Dundas Street running through its centre Oakville showed every promise of becoming a place of importance. Numerous shops and houses were rising as the port attracted more and more people. In 1836 Dr. Thomas Rolph estimated the number of inhabitants at above three hundred, and wrote that "the village has increased so rapidly that it now extends across the Creek—it was formerly only on the left bank."[115]

CHAPTER TWO

"A PLACE OF SOME IMPORTANCE"

THE FIRST RESIDENTS of the newly established Village of Oakville were general merchants, artisans—shoemakers, blacksmiths, cabinet-makers, carpenters, and shipwrights—and tavern keepers who depended for their livelihood upon the trade of the port. Their wares and skill were exchanged for the produce of settlers who had succeeded, after years of back-breaking labour, in raising a surplus over and above their own requirements. Though primitive, the life of the villagers was comparatively free from the privations endured by settlers in the agricultural district. Communities such as this were springing up all over Upper Canada. Where there was a tavern and a store, blacksmiths and other craftsmen were not long in setting up shop. But unlike most of the small communities of Upper Canada, Oakville was a village planned and sponsored by its founder.

Probably the first project of a public nature undertaken by Chisholm was the erection of a meeting-house. The land north of Colborne Street on the east side of Navy (block 56) was set aside for the use of the inhabitants, and there, close to the edge of the bank of The Sixteen, a frame meeting-house was built in 1827.[1] At the rear lay the public cemetery, in earlier times an Indian burying ground, according to tradition.

By the time stores and dwelling-houses were being built by resident freeholders lumber was readily obtainable at the sawmill on The Sixteen. Scores of these structures still stand, though their original exteriors of clapboard or board and batten are hidden by stucco of a later period. The appearance of many has been altered by the raising of the roof to allow for a full upper storey or by enlargement in other ways. The strictly utilitarian storey-and-a-half houses with gable roofs are extremely simple in design, and rely for their architectural character upon the proportions of walls and roof, and the placement of windows and doors. They are small, with low ceilings, and most of the early windows set with small panes have been replaced with the double panes in vogue during the seventies or the one large pane of the nineties. In several instances on the interiors hang hand-planed doors whose two small panels set above two larger ones so that the centre stile and rails form a vertical cross identify them as Christian doors. With few exceptions the steep enclosed stairways with narrow winders have been replaced, during the course of enlargement, by open staircases.

That the streets nearest the harbour and along the river were the first to be built up was only natural. Among the first purchasers of land was the shipwright Jacob Randall, who in 1831 secured four lots on the east side of Navy between Church Street and the street that bears his name. One of ten sons born to Jacob Randall senior, a Loyalist who had migrated in 1783 from the Province of New York, Jacob junior was born in Nova Scotia. In 1822 he accompanied his father and five brothers to Upper Canada where all secured grants of land.[2] He found employment in William Chisholm's shipyard at Burlington Bay, later moving to Oakville to superintend the building of the piers. At some time in the late 1830's Randall and his brother-in-law John Jeffery took over from Chisholm the shipyard on The Sixteen. Randall's name is perpetuated in the name of the street but his house which faced upon it has long since been destroyed by fire. On the east side of Navy Street at the bank of the river is the house built by William Baker, butcher. He brought his wife, Phoebe, and eight children from Ireland in 1834 and two years later bought the land and erected the dwelling that is now no. 55 Navy Street North. Of this section of Oakville John A. Williams wrote in his memoirs: "All the back streets along the river were called French Village. Many French Canadians were employed in the ship-yard below the hill and in loading staves and timber onto vessels which came through the swing bridge and up the river almost to the mills. They appeared to be a hot-headed lot and when primed with whiskey went off very easily, swearing and jabbering in French. But although they fought savagely, jumping on a man when he was down with their heavy boots I don't remember anybody being killed but lawsuits for assault were a weekly occurrence." Philip Bisnois (also spelled Besnah and Bisnagh) and his large family who spoke little English lived here, and land records disclose the names of Precoure, Boudron (Baudron), Londree (Londray), and other French names. Though mostly rebuilt at various periods, a majority of the houses found in this section date from the thirties or early forties.

Several carpenters and joiners who had come to Oakville to work on the piers contracted to build houses at wages ranging from 5*s*. to 6s. 3*d*. per day. The house of John Potter, carpenter, on Dundas Street north of Sheddon was destroyed by fire, but that of David Patterson, who chose the south end of Navy Street, stands today. Born in Ballymena, County Antrim, Northern Ireland, and of Scottish Protestant descent, Patterson was apprenticed at an early age to learn the trade of carpenter and shipwright at Belfast. He came to Canada about 1826, and was employed in Chisholm's shipyard. Upon his marriage to Agnes, daughter of George Griggs, an early settler on the lake shore east of Oakville, he built the house which is now no. 63 Navy Street South. Originally frame, this house underwent several stages of enlargement and was veneered with brick in the eighties, but the two large fireplaces are good examples of the period in which they were built. James McDonald, native of Aberlour, Banff, Scotland, chose to live on the lake shore, and in 1837 bought land at the foot of Thomas Street and built the house that is now no. 54 Front Street. At that time there was land enough in rear of the house to permit of the planting of a fair-sized orchard beween it and the lake. The house of Robert Leach, carpenter, now The Shuttle at no. 15 Dundas Street South, is relatively unchanged, though it has been moved twice since it was built on the south-east corner of Dundas and Colborne streets. Robert and his brothers, Ransom and William, learned the trade of carpenter from their father, Joshua Leach, a cabinet-maker who set up an early sawmill east of Oakville.

The clay in the vicinity being well suited to the making of brick, some houses were of this construction. They are difficult to trace, but we may be certain of Samuel Lawson's house on Dundas Street. Desiring to build a dwelling for his family, but being unable to finance both its construction and the purchase of the land, Lawson obtained from Chisholm title to park lot K, for which he was to pay when he was able. Here he erected a one-and-half storey house of hand-made brick, planting an orchard around it. The well close to the front door was soon hidden by lilacs. The Lawsons were probably the first family to settle so far north of the village proper, and doubtless no other houses existed between theirs and Potter's at Sheddon Street. The street bordering the property on the north became known as Lawson Street. As it happened Lawson never succeeded in paying for the land, and knowing this, his last descendant willed the property to a grandson of William Chisholm, it having only two owners over the space of more than a hundred years. The house stood vacant for some time and there was little left but the brick shell to use in the present structure, no. 12 Lawson Street. Now the huge lilacs are gone, and five houses occupy the site of the orchard.

By the time these and the many other early buildings of Oakville were being built stoves for both heating and cooking were coming into general use. The square box heating stoves were of all sizes, from the very smallest to those which admitted several large unsplit sticks of wood at one time. However, the transition from fireplace to stove for cooking purposes involved somewhat different kind of equipment, and in some houses such as Potter's and Justus Williams' the fireplace continued to be used. Of his home on Colborne Street, John A. Williams tells us: "We used to have a fireplace and a round flat iron kettle about twelve inches high for making bread. A bed of hot coals was made in the corner of the fireplace on which the pot full of dough was placed. The coals were gathered around the sides and on the iron cover and in about an hour a fine loaf of bread would be turned out. Biscuits were baked in a tin baker in the front of the fire and the bright tin reflected the heat down until the cakes and biscuits were done." This utensil, called a "reflector," was much used during the pioneer period. Made of bright tin, it was rectangular in shape and enclosed on all sides but one, the open side being placed next to the heat, which was evenly reflected by the tin.

In the basement of David Patterson's house stood a large stone oven which was used for the family baking until about the 1860's. A wood fire was built inside it and when the oven was hot the coals were raked out and replaced by pans of dough. Wood was the only fuel used at this period; "coals from Ohio," brought by vessel through the Welland Canal and selling for 1*s*. 6*d*. per bushel,[3] were used only by blacksmiths.

The majority of householders built barns in which an assortment of domestic animals were housed. To preserve meat for winter use carcasses of mutton were hung up and frozen, beef and pork were salted down in tubs or barrels. Should supplies run short a 200-pound barrel of pork could be bought for £3 5*s*. An advantage of living in a village was that fresh meat was obtainable from a butcher throughout the year. The rangy bush cattle provided beef notorious for its toughness, but hogs fattened on the Indian corn so extensively grown in the township made excellent pork. At a butcher's stall fresh pork, beef, veal, or mutton retailed at 3*d.* to 5*d.* per pound and venison at 3*d.* Turkeys and geese ranged in price from 2*s.* 6*d.*—"half a dollar"—to 5*s.*, depending upon the size, and ducks "wild or tame" and fowls, always sold in pairs, brought 1*s.* 3*d.* a pair. When packed in snow poultry could be kept from the middle of December to the first of April. Eggs sold at 7*d.* a dozen, butter at 7½*d.* a pound, salt at 7*d.* a pound or 5*s.* a bushel, and potatoes at 1*s.* 8*d.* per bushel. Every house had its garden and a frost-proof cellar or root-house where vegetables could be wintered. The excise tax made the price of tea very high, the average being 5*s.* a pound with the result that the greater proportion of tea sold in the province had been smuggled in from the United States. At the Port of Toronto alone it was estimated that some three thousand chests of contraband tea were sold annually.[4] The above prices, quoted from the accounts of Smith & Chisholm, are slightly higher than those charged by merchants at York owing to extra carrying charges, for example:

14th May 1830—	Oakville Establishment Dr.	
	To 80 Bush. potatoes @ ⅛ pr. Bill	£6.13.4
	To Boat a/c pr Boating Potatoes to 16 mile per Bill	1.10.0[5]

With only slight variation the prices quoted above prevailed until the 1860's.

The high price of cane sugar made preferable maple sugar at 7½*d.* per pound. The Reverend G. W. Warr, resident at Oakville, commented on the amount of preserves that "in some shape or other" were introduced at each of the four meals eaten daily in Upper Canada: "To the uninitiated reader this may appear gross extravagance; but it is to be remembered that the greater part of such delicacies are formed from maple sugar. Very large quantities are manufactured."[6] In one year the farmers of Trafalgar Township made over twelve thousand pounds of maple sugar[7] which sold for between 6*d.* and 1*s.* a pound.

To a young Irish servant girl the making of maple sugar from sap was so curious that she described it to her "dear fellow Servant, and fellow school-fellow" at home as follows:

> But what flogged anything I ever seen was making sugar out of a tree, Mary—not a word of a lie do I tell you—: You take a big gimlet and make a hole in the tree—(the *maypole,* I think they call it) and out

comes the shuggar, like sweet water thick like, and you boil it, and you—but where's the use of my telling you anything about it, as you have no sugar trees at home.

I remember when you and I thought a shuggar stick, a mighty good sort of a thing, never thinking I'd lay my eyes upon a *sugar-tree*.[8]

She gave Mary an "aisy" recipe for "bumkin pie":

You takes and slices it like apples, and gives it plenty of maypole, and a pinch or two of cloves, and a glass of whiskey, which is like ditch-water here, and it's mighty good eating.[9]

This young woman regarded Indians with suspicion. She wrote:

Some of them without any manner of doubtification, are very fine Ingines, but . . . they say they won't mix, and may be all for the better, for I'd rather die an old maid than be called a squawl, and have a porpus tied on my back, rolled up like a salmon in a hay-rope, on the Wexford Coach; and more than that, to be made to do all the druggery by land and water, in the shanty and kinnoo, gutting all the fish, and dressing all the birds and beasts, for never a hand's turn will them fine haroes do, but hunt, and shoot, and fish, and eat plenty, and drink hearty, like any gentlemen. Fond as I am of cooking, Mary, this would be beyand the beyands, (as the saying is). . . .[10]

Life in these pioneer times was hard but simple, and the individual had to learn to contrive. A wide variety of household necessities were made at home from raw materials supplied by the general merchant. Yeast, vinegar, cider, candles, soap, and a great many other commodities were the products of home labour.

Wild meat was used extensively, as game of all kinds abounded in the immediate neighbourhood. A favourite method of hunting deer was on horseback accompanied by dogs. After a deer had been raised the horsemen kept it headed for the lake and forced it to take to the water. It was then a simple matter to row out in a boat, rope the animal by the horns, and drown it. The sight of deer running through the village pursued by dogs was a familiar one until the fifties.

In the spring The Sixteen abounded with Atlantic salmon; in fact, one eighteenth-century French map shows it as "Riviere au Saumon." The fish ran up the St. Lawrence into Lake Ontario in great numbers to spawn in rivers and creeks, where they were taken in large quantities. Weighing from fifteen to eighteen pounds, the salmon were easily caught, a night's catch sometimes filling eight or ten barrels. When salted down the 200-pound barrels sold for 30*s*. or 35*s*. each. Fishing in The Sixteen is thus described by Mr. Warr:

The mode of fishing practised by the Indians is exceedingly interesting. The operation is carried on at night; two men generally steal along with the utmost caution in their canoe; the one uses the paddle, the other the spear; the former sits in the stern, the latter stands at the bow of the boat; they invariably carry a large piece of pine lighting in a grate which is so arranged at to cast a strong glare upon the water and enable the spearman to see the fish, which he strikes with his harpoon with an unerring aim, and instantly throws it into the boat. In this way they continue night after night. . . . It need scarcely be observed that it requires both the eye and aim of an Indian to be a successful angler after this manner; and yet the author has met with gentlemen who were not only quite captivated with, but generally successful in these nocturnal sports of the native tribes.[11]

At times the salmon were so plentiful where The Sixteen was shallow that settlers heaved them on shore with pitchforks. In after years William Howes who lived about nine miles north on the 7th Line stated that he had seen "waggon loads of beautiful salmon taken out there" and pointed to a spot where the east branch of The Sixteen runs through his farm. "They were speared with pitchforks, but the dam spoiled all that," said Howes.[12] John A. Williams remembered the time when salmon "as long as a man's arm" sold for a shilling, but when they became more scarce the price rose to 3*d.* a pound at the local merchants.[13]

The salmon stopped running during the 1840's and were never again seen in Lake Ontario, perhaps because of reckless slaughter and the contamination of the water of streams by sawdust from sawmills. Several attempts were made by the government to conserve the salmon, but the measures were apparently taken too late, and proved difficult to enforce.

The wolves that were so plentiful in the back country frequently followed the valley of The Sixteen almost down to the village, and could be heard howling at night in the vicinity of the mill.

This northern section of the village was a favourite resting place for the myriads of wild pigeons that came every spring from the south. Wrote Mr. Warr: "The author himself has seen countless thousands flying over his house in an immense black cloud; they fall easy prey to sportsmen, and are captured by the hundreds in their nets."[14] These birds were noted in flocks a mile wide, which took as long as four hours to pass, and a single flock was estimated at over two million birds. They migrated to Canada for the nesting season, and in the more heavily wooded sections of Halton County where supplies of berries, seed, and grain were most plentiful they were considered a great nuisance. There was a distinct resemblance between the passenger pigeon and the mourning dove, to which it was closely related, but the pigeon was larger in size and more definite and brighter in colour. Being noisy and loud, the passenger pigeon was not at all dovelike in its actions. When huge flocks settled for the night, trees broke under their weight and countless birds, injured by the fall, could be picked up from the ground. In some pigeon-roosts the cooing and whirring of wings were so loud that the report of a gun could not be heard, and several inches of dung was left on the ground. The section of Oakville along Dundas Street between George's Square and the mill, and east through Anderson's bush, is described by Williams as "the place where we gathered in the spring and fall with our old flint-lock muskets and shotguns, to fire at the millions of wild pigeons which used to fly over the town." The birds were also knocked from their nests with long poles, or caught in the net traps. Their breasts were salted down in barrels and the other parts reserved for immediate use or, as is more likely, thrown away. The *Streetsville Review* reported that "a singular feature of the present season [1851] is the large flights of wild pigeons now roaming about this country." A native of the township recalled that "the sky was full of birds for an hour or two, but none were shot . . . though the guns were all out," as the flocks flew too high.[15] Not long afterwards the games committee of the Ohio legislature reported that the passenger pigeon needed no protection; "wonderfully prolific, having the vast forest of the North as its breeding grounds, travelling hundreds of miles in the search of food . . . no ordinary destruction can lessen them. . . ."[16] None the less the passenger pigeon became extinct. In the vicinity of Oakville the last were seen in the seventies, and today they exist only as stuffed specimens in museums.*

Books written by travellers from the old country are a productive source of information concerning the country of Upper Canada. It was the fashion to put such experiences into print, often for the information of possible emigrants, and these books were in great demand in Britain, where little was known about the colonies. They make most interesting reading, but the pitfalls of inaccuracies and personal prejudice must be avoided. Occasionally one encounters arresting statements. E. A. Talbot in his *Five Years' Residence in the Canadas* gave a superior snigger at an earlier writer who unwittingly asserted: "Wolves are scarce in Canada; but they afford the finest furs in the country. Their flesh is white and good to eat; and they pursue their prey to the tops of the tallest trees."[17]

*Owing to the interest and activity of Mr. Paul Hahn the Royal Ontario Museum has an outstanding collection of passenger pigeons. See Margaret Mitchell, *The Passenger Pigeon in Ontario* (Toronto, 1935). Mr. Hahn informed the writer that some specimens, the work of a local taxidermist, had been obtained not far from Oakville.

Upon turning a few pages we find Talbot, in all seriousness, had written: "The Red Squirrel . . . possesses a singular address in crossing rivers, and small lakes. On arriving at a piece of water, which they wish to cross, a large party of red squirrels assemble together, and constructing a raft of sufficient size, which they launch without difficulty, embark, fearless of shipwreck; and turning up their spreading tails to the propitious breeze, are speedily wafted across to the opposite side."[18]

Anna Jameson, who stopped to dine at an inn at Oakvile in the winter of 1837, was a traveller who gave the village more than merely casual mention. Her husband, Robert Sympson Jameson, had come to the province as Attorney-General for Upper Canada, but they were not on congenial terms and Mrs. Jameson allowed three years to elapse before joining him. She was already a writer of some reputation, having begun her literary career with an account of her travels in Italy, and her book on Canada was only one of many on various subjects. A group of essays on the women in Shakespeare's plays, dedicated to her friend Fanny Kemble the actress, is still read today. Coming as she did from the sophisticated atmosphere of London drawing-rooms, Mrs. Jameson found Toronto society and the annoyances of housekeeping almost beyond her powers of endurance. She welcomed every opportunity of escaping for a few days into the Canadian countryside, and noted much that has since been of value to succeeding generations. Her first trip with a friend by sleigh brought her through Oakville, which she described in the following words:

> Oakville stands close upon the lake, at the mouth of a little river called Sixteen Mile Creek; it owes its existence to a gentleman by the name of Chisholm, and, from its situation and other local circumstances, bids fair to become a place of some importance. In the summer it is a frequented harbour, and carries on a considerable trade in lumber, for so they characteristically call timber in this country. From its dock-yards I am told that a fine steam boat and a dozen schooners have already been launched.
>
> In summer, the country round is rich and beautiful, with a number of farms all in high state of cultivation; but Canada in winter and in summer must be like two different regions. At present the mouth of the creek is frozen up; all trade, all shipbuilding suspended. Oakville presents the appearance of a straggling hamlet, containing a few frame and log houses; one brick house, (the grocery store or general shop, which in a new Canadian village is always the best house in the place), a little Methodist church painted green and white, but as yet no resident preacher; and an inn dignified by the name of the "Oakville House

Hotel." . . . Oakville contains at present more than three hundred inhabitants, who are now subscribing among themselves for a school-master and a resident clergyman.[19]

Within the next three years the resident population of Oakville reached a total of 450. Of this number more than half were Canadian-born of British origin. The next largest groups were the Irish, who comprised 26 per cent, and the English, 13½ per cent. There were sprinklings of Scots (3½ per cent), Americans (3), and French Canadians (2 per cent) but no Europeans or Negroes whatsoever. Of the seventy occupied premises in the village, forty-four were inhabited by "proprietors of real property," and thirty-six by tenants. Besides numerous shipwrights, mariners, and labourers there were many workmen skilled in other trades: John Laskey, the cooper; two William Bakers, the wheelwright and the butcher; three blacksmiths, three shoemakers, and two cabinetmakers, two saddlers and two tailors. There was John Terry the watchmaker, John Urquhart the apothecary, William Kirkwood, medical doctor, and Amelia Sovereign, milliner. Three of the eleven carpenters had work-shops. In addition to seven merchants and five tavern keepers, fifteen separate trades were represented.[20]

II

In all communities the general merchant, a trader in the widest sense, was of first importance. He bought and sold practically everything, and in a small way acted as banker for his customers. He traded his merchandise to farmers who paid for it after the harvest in wheat, staves, and other produce, according to the standard value of the country's staple, wheat. The merchant extended long credit to the farmers but in turn obtained at least six months' credit from importers, whom he paid the following year. Trade was conducted under the system of barter, each party trying to beat the other down in an attempt to make the best bargain. Virtually anything could be traded for something else; one merchant offered men's hats "very cheap for cash, or sheared lamb's wool, or lambskins with the wool on. . . . Hats exchanged for lumber."[21] In an account book of Smith & Chisholm we find:

10 July 1830 Isaac Corning Dr. pr self & daughter
To 14 yds calico @ 1/8, £1.3.4
Cr. 5s., the Balance to be pd. in Butter.[22]

The merchant's prices being scaled according to the price of wheat, the farmer often felt he had been cheated when the price of grain dropped. Knowing little of economics, he failed to understand why it took more produce to buy three yards of cloth one week than it had the previous week. Since there was no set price for merchandise, it was the merchant who generally came out on top, and the farmer, being almost permanently in debt, barely contrived to make a living.

The system of barter had arisen out of the great scarcity of fractional currency in the country. No workable plan had been evolved for the establishment of a uniform currency throughout the British Empire, and in Upper Canada a jumble of coins from many countries circulated as legal tender. From France came louis, double louis, napoleons, and double napoleons; from Spain, Mexico, and Colombia came pistoles and doubloons, and from Portugal and Brazil coins called dobraons, moidores, and crusados. English money included a seven shilling piece as well as the usual sovereign, half guinea, and guinea.[23] According to law the money was equal to the value it bore at Halifax, but this was merely a bookkeeping standard, without actual coins to correspond. In the section of Upper Canada that bordered upon New York State the currency circulating in that state was passed in considerable quantities. Consequently there were two standards of exchange: Halifax currency and New York currency. Halifax currency rated five shillings to the United States dollar, and the pound at four dollars. New York currency was valued at eight shillings to the dollar, a fraction of this dollar (12½¢) being known as a "York shilling."[24] All prices quoted in this history are in Halifax currency at five shillings to the dollar.

At the time merchants were setting up shop in the new village of Oakville merchandising methods were undergoing a change. Kingston and York were becoming secondary centres of importation of goods from Britain, and imports from the United States were increasing rapidly. The "foreign" goods were cheaper, and were being sold at York at prices 35 per cent lower than the British merchandise. The Americans sold cheaper for cash, whereas the importers in Lower Canada still scaled their prices according to the long-term credit system.[25] However, in buying merchandise from the United States it was wise to be on guard against fraud. There was no redress from misrepresentation of the type outlined in the sprightly account which appeared in the *Kingston Chronicle* in 1833.

> A novel importation from the land of wooden nutmegs, bass-wood pumpkin seeds, oak-leaf cigars, and pine hams, has excited the curiosity of our inhabitants for the past two or three days, in the shape of several kegs of butter (or rather buttered kegs), which, if their true character had been undiscovered, would have furnished a fine "chance for speculation." These kegs, which were supposed to be filled with the fat of the earth, were found, upon the suspicions of an individual who had come from the wrong side of the Tweed to be easily duped by the ingenuity of even a Yankee, to contain, in 44 lbs. weight, 20 lbs. butter, and 24 lbs. excellent limestone—the stratum of stone being very geologically placed under the stratum of butter. Conjecture has been extensively excited to know the benevolent individual who has thus furnished us with this granatical donation—some supposing that the donor, with prudent foresight, had intended it to form part of the walls of the Penitentiary, while others have presumed it as designed to assist in the macadamization of our streets, in consequence of the great scarcity of stone in Kingston; but our opinion on the subject is, that it was put in the kegs, to make them weigh a "leetle more." A wag at our elbow declares, that *hard* as the case may seem, we were not so *soft* as to be *taken in* along with the butter. It is an act of justice to state that the persons who sold the butter, after it arrived at Kingston, are by no means chargeable with the fraud, they having purchased it without knowledge that any existed.[26]

The small merchant devoted the winter season to disposing of his merchandise and to collecting produce which was easily transported when snow was on the ground. Trade in the village depended upon a good fall of snow, and an open winter was disastrous to merchants and farmers alike. When spring brought the opening of navigation on the lake, the collected produce was taken to market by schooner and during summer and autumn goods for the coming winter were laid in. Those who dealt in wheat and staves contracted with Chisholm or other forwarders to transport them down the lake to Montreal or across to the United States. According to custom those merchants who had shop licences for selling liquors kept on hand an open barrel of whiskey, with a tin cup handy, for the convenience of their customers. The liquor was free to all, but it was assumed that only regular customers would avail themselves of the privilege.

The earliest merchants to choose Oakville as the place in which to make their start in mercantile trade were Charles Reynolds, James Reid, William Hatton, Robert Young, John L. Bigger, Justus W. Williams, and William Creighton. Reynolds had migrated from Ireland in 1827 and come to Oakville in 1833 to set up shop on the south-west corner of Colborne and the street that bears his name. James Reid, a Scotsman, had come the previous year, and Young and Bigger were natives of the township. Creighton came out from Ireland in the late thirties and established a general store in the building which still stands between Dunn and George streets as No. 81 Colborne Street East. Hatton bought the lot on the south-west corner of Colborne at Thomas Street in 1832. Of him little is known, other than it was his success which influenced Williams to choose Oakville instead of Hamilton as a place to set up in business.

In 1819, when a young man, Justus Wright Williams had come from Vermont to settle with his family on the plains near Burlington Bay, where he engaged in the business of contracting to build houses and bridges. He married Nancy Aikman, daughter of Captain John Aikman and Hannah Showers Aikman, members of old Loyalist families.[27] Another daughter was the wife of Egerton Ryerson, a young Methodist missionary whose first station was among the Missisauga Indians at their reserve on the Credit River. After some years Williams concluded that the life of a merchant was preferable to that of a contractor and started looking about for a suitable location for a shop. The news that Hatton was doing well at Oakville, combined with the potentialities of the new harbour, led him to buy two lots for £100 in 1831.[28] Installing his family temporarily in a small rented house, Williams proceeded to build a dwelling, with a general store to the east of it, on the south side of Colborne between Dunn and Dundas streets (block 12, lots B and E). The shop is shown in the drawing on page 60. In 1833 Williams advertised: "New Store in the village of Oakville—The subscriber, having commenced a mercantile business intends to keep on hand a general assortment of dry goods and Hardware, also a few groceries and medicines."[29]

John A. Williams, who has been and will be frequently quoted during the course of this history, was a son of this family, and was three years of age when he came to live at Oakville. He spent the greater part of his life there, and being greatly interested in its growth as a community he spent much of his later life in writing his reminiscences. Because of the accuracy of its material his manuscript has been invaluable to this record.

As a small boy John A. Williams was impressed with the Indians who continued to return each summer to their old camping ground near the lake on the border of the village east of Allan Street. "Along to 1836 and after the Indians camped in a beautiful second growth grove opposite Anderson's farm. Their encampment was a clearing surrounded by pine, wild cherry and maple. They made baskets, moccasins, bows and arrows, axe handles, ox yokes, brooms and mats to be traded in Oakville. Small Indian boys amused the white boys by shooting coppers out of a stick split so as to hold a copper while the sharp end was pushed into the ground. Old George Crookfinger was one of their leaders."

Merchants in the rear of the township carried on trade with the Oakville merchants. After establishing a grist mill on the west branch of The Sixteen in the northern section of the New Survey, Jasper Martin started a store and an ashery. The potash was traded at Oakville, the returning waggons bringing such necessaries as were demanded by his customers.[30] For the village that grew up around Martin's mill the name of Milton was chosen. Three dealers in wheat and staves who, with Chisholm, were the most important in the district, built grain warehouses at Oakville and two of them opened branch stores there.[31] George Chalmers, whose village in the Sixteen Hollow at the Dundas Street was beginning to flourish, built a storehouse on the bank of the river at the foot of King Street just south of Chisholm's. Alexander Proudfoot erected a warehouse on the north side at the foot of Robinson Street, and a store on the north side of Colborne Street midway between Navy and Thomas streets. George Brown, merchant at Milton, built a frame store on the south side of Colborne Street in the centre of the block between Thomas and George streets which stands today as nos. 56 and 60 Colborne Street East. The fifty-foot hand-hewn beams fourteen inches square running the length of the building, and the round cross-beams still wearing their bark, bear witness to the age of this building, erected in 1836. Except for his store Brown had little connection with Oakville. Proudfoot, on the other hand, an influential man in the township, had close contact with the village.

George Chalmers and Alexander Proudfoot, the first merchants to become established in Trafalgar Township, had set up shop about 1820. Proudfoot located his business at the south-west corner of the 9th Line at the Dundas Street. He married Amelia Jarvis whose father, Stephen Jarvis, of the Loyalist family of York, had settled a few miles east of Oakville in Toronto Township. Her mother belonged to a neighbouring family, the Merigolds of Merigold Point. After Amelia married Proudfoot, her younger brother Peter was employed as clerk in the store on the 9th Line, of which he wrote as follows:

> As our family was large it was thought time for me to begin life on my own account, and it had been arranged that I should enter the employment of my brother-in-law, Alexander Proudfoot, who was engaged in an extensive and varied business at Trafalgar and Oakville. He kept a general store and bought farmers' produce of all kinds, in addition to staves and timber. The wheat was hauled to Oakville, some of it coming from as far back as Georgetown and Esquesing. From Oakville it was shipped in our own vessels to Kingston and then forwarded to England. The staves and oak timber were shipped in the same manner. . . . We also kept an ashery. Out of ashes which came from the burned logs of the settlers, we manufactured large quantities of potash, which we shipped to England. . . . I had a great desire for life at sea and readily devoured any story of the the sea that I could get into my possession. This desire was increased by a trip I made to Kingston one fall in one of our vessels. On the return voyage in November, an Easterly snow storm came upon us during our trip up the lake and we were nearly driven ashore on Burlington Beach, but escaped by passing through the canal into Burlington Bay.[32]

The two-masted, 105-ton Schooner *Amelia,* built for Proudfoot at Oakville in 1836 by Jacob Randall,[33] may well have been the vessel in which Peter Jarvis first experienced navigation. He was a seaman for several years, sailing to China and other countries of the Orient.

In 1836 Proudfoot bought lot 1 in block 54 at the foot of Robinson Street for £60. The deed gives the grantor, Chisholm, the right "to erect and to continue erected a Towing path not more than Ten feet wide along the limits of said lot abutting upon said Creek for the purpose of towing Vessels, Boats, and Rafts in and out of the said Creek and to said path Alexander Proudfoot, his heirs . . . etc. . . . shall have the right to use and enjoyment at all time in common with other persons but no erection of any other kind or description shall be made between the said land and premises."[34] On this lot Proudfoot built a warehouse which he owned and used until he left the province and moved to Montreal in the 1850's.

The third grain buyer to establish a branch store at Oakville was James Gage, an active, intelligent business man who came from the western section of the county. When a youth he migrated about 1780 with his widowed mother, a sister of Augustus Jones the surveyor, from the State of New York to settle on a grant of land south of Burlington Bay at Stoney Creek. James, who carried much of the family responsibility upon his shoulders, became a merchant and opened a log store opposite his home. He married Mary Davis, daughter of another Loyalist family who had settled across the bay near the Brants and Chisholms. In 1810 Gage purchased from Catherine Brant over three hundred acres of the land situated in Nelson Township on the north shore of the bay which had been granted to her deceased husband for his services to the Crown. Upon this land James Gage laid out a village which he called Wellington Square. This was the name of the home of Joseph Brant, who had made the acquaintance of the Iron Duke when on a visit to England. The Battle of Stoney Creek was fought over the Gage farm during the War of 1812, and the farm house is now an historical site, Battlefield House, where relics of the Gage family, including portraits of James and Mary Gage, are on public view. Close by on the hill stands the monument commemorating this British victory.[35]

Being related to the Chisholms by marriage (his wife's sister, Sarah, had married William Chisholm's brother John, Collector of Customs at the Burlington Bay Canal), James Gage was well aware of the developments at Oakville. He and his son, James Philipse Gage, were heavily engaged in lumbering and flour-milling in the country round Wellington Square, and upon coming to Oakville he leased a frame store on the south-west corner of Navy and Colborne streets.[36] Soon after, we find him associated with Benjamin Hagaman, an American with affiliations at Oswego, New York. Gage & Hagaman operated a branch store at Bronte,[37] the village laid out in 1834 by the government on part of the Missisauga Reserve at the Twelve Mile Creek.

The commerce of Oakville being aligned to water transportation, its business section centred around Navy Street, the thoroughfare communicating with the harbour, and here was set up a weighing machine for grain. The machine in general use at this time, consisting of a platform resting upon levers, could weigh a waggon containing a load of over a ton. Could it have been a "Fairbanks Platform Scales, Portable or Stationary" which the blacksmith Joseph Janes was manufacturing in Hamilton at this time?[38] In the spring of 1836 the *Observer* commented: "The weighing Machine, erected in Navy Street, although not a conspicuous object, has nevertheless been a great convenience to the town, and advantageous to the neighbourhood."[39]

In those days an expert blacksmith was an important person and an asset to any community. A mechanic capable of forging iron into many shapes and forms, from the thinnest hinges to the heaviest farm implements, the skilled smith could also improvise with great facility. He charged according to the amount of iron used, a commodity that was extremely scarce, usually about 1*s*.3*d*. per pound. If the iron was found, the charges averaged 7½*d*. per pound. He was more frequently called upon to shoe oxen than horses, as the strong deliberate ox was better suited to the rough work on a pioneer farm than the more impatient horse. Because of its weight and short legs the ox cannot stand on three legs and must be lifted free of the ground while being shod. Every blacksmith had an ox-shoeing stall equipped with a heavy oak frame on pulleys in which the ox could be suspended in the air while the shoes were hammered on. When horses were rare and valuable they were used only for riding purposes, but by the thirties they had become sufficiently common to be used for long distance hauling. In 1835 Charles Sovereign of Twelve Mile Creek entered in his journal, "Joe the French smith at Oakville shod my horses before and found one shoe for which he charged 3*s*.1½*d*. to be paid in lumber." The other blacksmiths in Oakville were Lorenzo Hammond and William Norton.

In the Canadas young men learned trades under the ancient system of apprenticeship employed for centuries by the guilds of Britain and Europe. Until they became of age they were bound to a master by indenture. The articles of agreement quoted below are representative of the terms of apprenticeship at the period and were drawn between Pierre Romain and one William Ayres, painter and glazier, both of Montreal. The apprentice, William Francis Romain, came at a later date to Oakville as grain merchant, eventually to become a leading citizen of the town.

When bound to Ayres in 1829 he was only eleven years of age. It was agreed that the boy should remain until he attained the age of twenty-one years.

The apprentice his said Master will and faithfully shall serve, his secrets keep, his lawful commands at all times willingly obey, do and perform, hurt to him he shall not do nor knowingly suffer to be done by others, the goods of his said Master he shall not embezzle or waste, nor lend them without his consent to any, he shall not haunt taverns, or playhouses, from the said service he shall not at any time depart or absent himself without leave, but in all things shall and will demean and behave himself faithfully, soberly and honestly during the said term.

And the said William Ayres . . . doth hereby bind and oblige himself to teach and instruct or cause the said apprentice to be taught and instructed in the trade and business of Painter and Glazier with all things thereto belonging, and will furnish him with board and lodging, washing and mending and all other necessaries both in sickness and in health during his apprenticeship as is fit and usual for such an apprentice, and allow him to attend evening school during six months of the term of his apprenticeship which schooling the said William Ayres hereby promises to pay and defray at his own costs;—and the said William Ayres doth further bind and oblige himself to pay or cause to be paid to his said apprentice at the end of these presents the sum of Ten pounds current money of the said Province provided the said William Romain behaved himself faithfully during the whole term of his apprenticeship.[40]

James Steele, saddler and harness maker, brought his family to Oakville in 1833, six years later building a shop on the south side of Colborne Street near Dunn. A second saddler, Henry Gulledge, arrived from Somersetshire, England, in 1835. When faced with deciding on a corner lot at Temperance and Yonge streets at Toronto or a lot on Colborne Street in Oakville, the new harbour at the latter place proved the factor that determined his choice.[41] From him a set of harness could be purchased for £3.5*s.* on six months' credit.[42] It would be interesting to know if Steele or Gulledge shared the same prejudice against American leather as the Englishman at Toronto who announced that he woud make "Saddles, Harness, etc. of Canadian Leather only, as cheap and good as anybody, but never will he, under prospect of gain, stoop to the soul-degrading practise of working up the contraband trash of the FOREIGNER along with a splendid hardware of England, and then selling the compound product under the name of BRITISH SADDLERY."[43]

Prior to the advent of resident shoemakers and tailors, the inhabitants had had to depend upon itinerant craftsmen who visited the village periodically. They set up their tools in the kitchen and boarded with the family until the work was finished. Some settlers, however, preferred to cobble their own boots. Sovereign, for instance, during the winter made up a year's supply for his family from leather he himself had tanned. One of the first shoemakers to come to Oakville was Charles Davis, who set up shop in the building he erected at the northwest corner of George and Colborne streets. Here he made boots and shoes to measure in return for extra leather or farm produce. If bought at a shop a pair of "coarse boots" cost £1 10*s.*[44]

The procuring of woollen clothing was becoming less of a problem than during the twenties. To raise enough sheep to provide the wool required for the family's clothing was part of every farmer's work, but it was no longer necessary for the women folk to weave all of the cloth. Mechanization of the woollen industry in Britain had led many skilled hand weavers to migrate to the colonies, and custom weaving had become common in Trafalgar Township. By the early thirties there were several weavers in the vicinity who would make a yard of cloth from every two and one-half pounds of wool furnished, accepting in payment one-half of the total amount of wool used. One weaver went so far as to guarantee cloth "to be finished in a complete manner . . . from Sheep shears to Tailor's shears."[45] This included the process of "fulling," whereby the cloth was well soaked and worked in water to shrink and tighten the weave. The price current among itinerant tailors for fashioning a man's coat was £1, and for every vest or pair of trousers 5*s*., less board at 5*d*. per day and lodging. After one visit Sovereign entered in his accounts, "Paid Andrew the tailor 400 feet of siding at 3/9 per foot for the making of a coat which was four dollars." Doubtless Joshua Van Allen, the first tailor to settle in Oakville, conducted his business in like manner. He located on the north-east corner of George Street across from Davis where he remained until his death in the forties. Van Allen sewed by hand, but it was not many years before sewing machines became available in Canada.

As well as making furniture, Oakville's two cabinet-makers fashioned coffins for the dead as is still the custom in small communities in Britain. Lawrence Culloden came from Ireland in 1833 and David Duff from Scotland in 1840. The year following his arrival Duff purchased the store of George Brown, where he remained in business for over two decades.

On the western outskirts of the village was John Terry, to whom watches and clocks were sent for repairs from Toronto, Dundas, and Hamilton. A native of London, Terry had learned the trade of watchmaking and engraving before migrating to Upper Canada to settle at York. He married a sister of Mrs. William Chisholm, Elizabeth Silverthorn, and it is their names coupled together that were given to the schooner *Rebecca and Eliza*. Having traded his farm at York for land at Oakville, Terry brought his family by sailing vessel, landing at the foot of his new property. The four small Terrys were carried ashore by sailors over a huge oak that had fallen into the lake. Terry made regular trips home to England and from time to time Eliza's father, John Silverthorn, would ride from Etobicoke Township to see how the family fared. In winter he frequently found the cabin buried to the eaves in snow, but as he approached he could hear the mother and her children singing hymns within. The little log cabin of the Terrys was across the Lake Shore Road from that of another

Silverthorn sister, Mrs. Merrick Thomas, and was incorporated in the house which today stands on the south-west corner of Brookfield Road.[46]

OAKVILLE HOUSE,

BY W. J. SUMNER, (late of Grove Inn, Nelson,) Village of Oakville, on the Lake and 12 miles from Toronto—18 from Hamilton.
Noember 12, 1834. 104 ts

III

A tavern for the accommodation of travellers was looked upon as essential to all pioneer communities. According to law a tavern was required to have three bedrooms besides those of the tavern keeper and his family and stabling for at least four horses. Before a licence could be obtained from the Court of Quarter Sessions, certificates had to be presented bearing the signatures of "respectable persons" in the neighbourhood who stated that a tavern was needed in the "situation applied for."[47] Of the five taverns in the village, the Oakville House was the earliest; it was, in fact, one of the first buildings to be erected during the winter of 1827–8, when the forest still stood thick upon the townsite. Under its original name and in the same building at Navy and Colborne streets this tavern still does business at the present time. William Young, who became the first proprietor of the Oakville House, was placed in charge of its construction by the owner, William Chisholm, and the raising of the frame was marked by an incident recalled by a settler nearly a century later. "On the day of the raising," he wrote, "one beam had been raised and securely stayed, the event being celebrated by a drink of whiskey all round, costing at that time 20 cents a gallon. Word was brought to the crowd by a man on horseback that a large bear had been treed by dogs where the residence of James Ryrie now stands. The raising was at once informally adjourned, the whole crowd joining in the hunt, when with axes, crowbars and hand spikes the bear was soon dispatched. His hide for years lay before the open fireplace in the large sitting-room, where travellers rejoiced in the roaring fire and drank their grog in comfort."[48]

William Young was a son of Jacob Young, Loyalist from Sussex County, New Jersey, who had been present at Yorktown to see Cornwallis surrender his sword to Washington. After fleeing to Upper

Canada to settle for a time at Forty Mile Creek (now Grimsby), Jacob and his son William fought in the battles of Queenston Heights, Lundy's Lane, and Stoney Creek. When the War of 1812 came to an end Jacob traded a team of horses and a waggon for a farm west of the Twelve Mile Creek, and William married Elizabeth, daughter of the owner of the sawmill on the creek, Joseph Hixon. About 1825 William Young leased the Dundas Street tavern of Millicent Munn, widow of Daniel Munn. Situated at the south-east corner of the 6th Line, known as Munn's Corners, this tavern and stage-house was the first in Trafalgar Township.[49] After two years Young removed to the Oakville House which a traveller in 1831 described as being "two stories high" and "very commodious . . . being provided with most of the comforts and many of the luxuries of the present day; to which is attached a most excellent garden of an acre and a half."[50] Unfortunately, Young died at an early age in that year and his wife was forced to sell all the inn's equipment. The sale was called a "vendue," and the terms stated in the announcement were as follows:

> To be sold at PUBLIC VENDUE . . . on the premises of Elizabeth Young, Oakville, Trafalgar Twp., the following articles
> One pair excellent Horses
> One set double Harness
> One good double Waggon
> Two cows
> Three sleighs
> Large quantity household furniture including beds and bedding. Terms—Twelve months credit will be given for all over 15*s.* by giving appropriate security; below 15*s.* cur'y must be paid down. Sale 18 Oct. 1831.[51]

Elizabeth Young continued to reside in Oakville, and her son, William Hixon Young, whom she apprenticed to Duff the cabinet-maker, we shall meet with later in this work.

The Oakville House was leased by William Chisholm to his friend and neighbour, William Johnson Sumner, who since the early 1820's had been proprietor of the Grove Inn at Hannahsville (modern Nelson) on the Dundas Street in Nelson Township. He was a son of Thomas Sumner, a soldier who had fought under Wolfe at the taking of Quebec in 1759, and whose story is found in one of the hundreds of memorials that passed through the office of the lieutenant-governors. Thomas Sumner experienced the sufferings that were the common lot of thousands of Loyalists who fled the Revolution, and his account, so simply told, is herewith presented in full.

To his Excellency Sir Peregrine Maitland Esquire Knight Commander of the Most Honorable Military order of the Bath Lieutenant Governor of the Province of Upper Canada and commanding His Majesty's Forces within said Province & & &

The Petition of Thomas Sumner, of Clinton, Esq., Humbly Sheweth
That your Petitioner was born in Hebron in the then Colony of Connecticut, that he was in his Majesty's Service at the taking of Quebec under the Command of General Wolf that after the close of the war by the Governor of New York appointed one of the Judges of the County of Glocester which Commission he held until the year 1775 when he was drove from his Home and from his family and was obliged to flee to the British army for safety and Protection, by the Rebels, who seized all his property which they afterwards confiscated and sold for the benefit of what is now the Government of the United States as will appear by the annexed Statement and certificates regularly authenticated that your petitioner continued with the British army until the end of the war when he went to New Brunswick with the American Loyalists in the year 1783—
That on the arrival of the Commissioners in that province to ascertain the just claims of the Loyalists, Your petitioner was under the necessity of returning to the United States in order to establish his claim and after much Difficulty obtained vouchers of a small proportion of the property he possessed before the Rebellion, as the principle part of his landed property to the amount of £2000 lawful money dollars at 6/ your petitioner could not obtain certificates for
That from the severity of the Season and ill health your petitioner did not reach the Province of New Brunswick again until the Commissioners had left the Province and in Consequence of his Indigent situation he was not able to follow them, and therefore was deprived of the opportunity of laying his Claims before Government, and renewing [receiving?] a remuneration for his losses and sufferings.
That your petitioner applied to the Government of Upper Canada and on the 22ᵈ of July 1818 obtained an order of Council for two hundred acres of Land under the then existing Regulations.
That your petitioner is now Eighty five Years of Age reduced to the most indigent circumstances, that he has no means of support, is past labour and not able to perform the Settlement Duty.
Your petitioner therefore humbly prays that Your Excellency will take his melancholy situation into your serious consideration and grant him such relief as your Excellency in Your wisdom May seem meet
and your petitioner as in duty Bound will ever pray

York Upper Canada THOS SUMNER[52]
11th October 1819

This petition was granted, the Lieutenant-Governor relinquishing his share of land fees and seven civil servants following suit,[53] but the next year Thomas Sumner died, aged eighty-six. Not long after we find his son proprietor of the Grove Inn. William Johnson Sumner was an ironclad Tory who was closely associated with Chisholm.

It is a happy circumstance that having at one time been a printer, Sumner delighted in advertising. Periodically he burst into print, and his announcements, which use the full range of printer's type, show him to have been something of a wag. At the time of his removal to Oakville the following appeared in the *Hamilton Free Press*: "The Proprietor of the Grove Inn, Nelson, takes this method of announcing to the public that he intends leaving the above establishment on the first of December next, and requests all those who have favoured him with some of their TRUST CUSTOM, to pay him before that time, or expect trouble in the wigwam, by an invasion of a battalion of the LAW*!* . . . P. S.—I want all Editors to insert this to oblige an old Printer, alias Tavern Lord—gratis, mind ye."[54] Upon another occasion he "very earnestly requests" that his patrons "will be as polite in handing in the *few* dollars, shillings and sixpences to pay their Tavern debts as they were in contracting them."[55]

Sumner bought park lots on Dundas Street at Oakville, and it is for him that Sumner Avenue is named. In 1831 for £20 he bought the adjoining lots at the north-east corner of Navy and William streets (lots D and E, block 13) and built the houses that are today no. 27 Navy Street South and no. 33 William Street. He sold both houses for £100 eight years later.[56]

Gradually the British term "inn" was giving way to the American term "hotel," and Sumner called his establishment the Oakville House Hotel. A traveller who passed in 1831 noted in his journal that for bed and breakfast he paid 7*d*. and 9*d*. respectively, and for dinner and supper a total of 1*s*.2*d*. Before retiring he "had two glasses, 6*d*."[57] During the twenties, thirties, and forties the price of whiskey across the bar remained at 3½*d*. per gill: a 500 per cent profit, according to Pickering.[58]

Sumner bought the Oakville House from Chisholm in 1834. Two years later the *Observer* commented upon "the erection of several new houses, and additions to others. Among the latter we cannot but particularly mention the additions to appearance and comfort of the Oakville House."[59] Upon completion of these alterations Sumner announced:

> The Subscriber informs the Public that . . . during the past summer, he has improved and enlarged his Home "internally and externally." A large commodious Gallery has been attached, from which the Town of Niagara, Brock's Monument, Spray of Niagara Falls, and some of the Villages on the borders of Ontario are distinctly seen. Two stages arrive daily to dine. His beds are clean and comfortable—Larder as well stored as the market will admit—Good Liquors, purified by an addition of Ontario's beautiful waters—good fires to cheer the minds of his guests

and warm their cold fingers—good Stables—good Hay and Oats—attentive Ostlers to comfort the noble steed—and his charges are NOT "locked" up in the "chase" of Oppression. Call and see an old Tavernkeeper. W. J. SUMNER.[60]

It was about this time that Sumner was host to Sir Francis Bond Head who stopped to dine at the Oakville House when on his way to take up his duties at Toronto. It is to be regretted that in his *Narrative*, a detailed account of his term as Lieutenant-Governor of Upper Canada, Sir Francis made no mention of this episode. Therefore, nothing may be added to the fragment found in the *Observer*. "Of this house his Excellency, we understand, was pleased during his short stay in the town, to observe that it was the best tavern he had been in since he left Albany."[61]

Only a few weeks later Mrs. Jameson stopped at the Oakville House and wrote of her visit:

> I stood conversing in the porch, and looking about me, till I found it necessary to seek shelter in the house, before my nose was absolutely taken off by the ice-blast. The little parlour was solitary, and heated like an oven. Against the wall were stuck a few vile prints, taken out of old American magazines; there was the Duchess of Berri in her wedding-dress, and as a pendant, the Modes de Paris—"Robe de tulle garnie de fleurs—coiffure nouvelle, inventée par Mons. Plaisir." The incongruity was laughable! I looked round me for some amusement or occupation, and at last spied a book open and turned down upon its face. I pounced upon it as a prize, and what do you think it was? "Devinez, madame! Je vous le donne en trois, je vous le donne en quatre!" It was—*Don Juan*! And so, while looking from the window on a scene which realised all you can imagine of the desolation of savage life, mixed with just so much of the commonplace vulgarity of civilised life as sufficed to spoil it, I amused myself reading of the Lady Adeline Ammundeville and her precious coterie. . . .[62]

Mrs. Jameson had apparently failed to meet her host, William Sumner, for had she done so she would have shown less surprise at finding in the parlour a copy of Lord Byron's poetry. Unless we have seriously misjudged him, Sumner would have greeted with enthusiasm the opportunity of relating for her entertainment some singular and rather highly coloured tales which would have delighted her sense of humour and enriched her narrative considerably.

The Oakville House continued under the management of William J. Sumner until his untimely death at the age of forty-one years on September 18, 1841.

Near the bank of The Sixteen, underground springs fed a stream that ran to the lake through George Street, and south of Colborne Street the land fell away into a depression called the "hollow." In 1831 William Uptegrave bought the lot on the south-east corner and in the hollow built a tavern which came to be called the Royal Exchange Hotel. After a few years Uptegrave leased his hostelry to John Diamond and moved across Colborne Street to open another tavern on the west side of Davis, the shoemaker.[63] Uptegrave was a "botanic doctor" as well as tavern keeper and did good business in both capacities. He lived in a house at the north-east corner of Reynolds and Colborne streets which at a later date was divided into two houses, and today these stand as nos. 153 and 157 Colborne Street East. The stairway in the latter is said to be that of the original house.

The second proprietor of the Royal Exchange, John Segur Diamond, was a native of Red Castle, County Clonenagh, Ireland, and before migrating to Upper Canada in 1831 he had belonged to the Irish Constabulary.[64] He married a daughter of another tavern keeper at Oakville, William Dolmage, who later was attached to His Majesty's Commissary General at Toronto. John Segur Diamond junior, born in 1836 at Oakville, became a surgeon in the Canadian Artillery. The Diamonds lived in the small dwelling that is now no. 69 Robinson Street, and here John Diamond senior, a citizen much respected in the community, died in 1848.

The tavern of William O'Reilly stood on the south-east corner of Dunn and Colborne streets, and after passing out of his hands it became a rather notorious establishment. John A. Williams who lived next door remembered it well as a child and wrote the following description: "It was a rough-cast and quite noted building. Thomas Lloyd, Esq., an Old Country gentleman, kept a hotel here and in the yard a black bear chained to a pole. It ran around the pole backwards and forwards and made the most horrible noises while being fed, specially when a live pig was given to it, a man holding the pig's hind legs while it was torn to pieces. It was awful to hear the growls and squeals but it drew a crowd of whiskey suckers and loafers. Lloyd kept raccoons and other animals, a regular zoo." With scenes such as this being enacted so close to his home it is not surprising to find Justus Williams the moving spirit in the cause of temperance in Oakville.

The inn of John Forman, farmer on the Lake Shore Road East, was the only temperance house in the village. In 1833 Forman bought the lot on the south-west corner of Dundas and Randall streets, and there built an inn which he ran without licence. The following year part of this building was leased to Joseph Mackinder, recently arrived in Oakville by ox-cart, who started the first bakery in the community.[65]

A large percentage of the Irish who settled in Oakville and the surrounding district had come from Northern Ireland, and in consequence were Orangemen. An Orange Lodge was formed very early in Oakville, but the date remains obscure. According to John A. Williams their favourite rendezvous was Paddy Smithwick's tavern, situated on the north-west corner of Reynolds and Colborne streets across from Uptegrave's; "a rum place it was, too," wrote Williams, who continues: "On the 12th of July the Orangemen gathered in the Town from all the country Lodges within a circle of eight or ten miles, and they would march around town from Paddy Smithwick's where a pail and cup or glasses were passed around. Then the Fife and Drum started again, halting at Diamond's in the centre of the town, then up to the Oakville House where dinner was prepared and all enjoyed a feast once a year at least. . . . The 12th was a great day, the Catholics took it good naturedly and enjoyed the music, dancing, etc. with the Orangemen, and likely it is the same yet."

In a grain-producing district such as that surrounding Oakville a grist mill was soon followed by a brewery and distillery. Whiskey and beer, being by-products of the grain business, were manufactured in large quantities and sold cheaply in Upper Canada. Grain that was otherwise useless from having been frozen or rusted could be disposed of at the distillery, the farmer often taking its products which he sold to taverns. With the influx of Scottish settlers came an increase in the number of distilleries and breweries in the province and it is therefore not surprising to find two Scotsmen, Messrs. Hopkirk and Watson, establishing the Oakville Brewing and Distilling Company. The frame building they erected on Walker Street overlooking the harbour (block 106) was nearing completion in the spring of 1836,[66] and assessment rolls show that shortly afterwards the distillery went into production. Three or three and one-half gallons of whiskey could be made from a bushel of wheat, and the average daily output of a distillery at this date was between forty and sixty gallons. The prices of whiskey and beer at the local distillery are not available, but the bill of a merchant shows that by the gallon whiskey retailed at 2*s*. 6*d*. and by the barrel at £2 13*s*. Beer sold for 1*d*. the quart.[67] The Oakville Brewing and Distilling Company flourished to the extent of becoming Oakville's leading industry.[68] James Hopkirk, "L L D and Advocate," lived on the lake shore nearby at the foot of Wilson Street (park lot K) which he called "Rowmore," and this was his place of residence until his appointment to a post in the government took him to Toronto in 1839. The distillery was then leased to the local merchant, John L. Bigger, who at once started a steam grist mill in conjunction with the business.[69]

Being both plentiful and cheap, liquor was consumed in large quantities by all classes of people. Life in the bush tended to have a demoralizing effect upon settlers who more and more learned to depend upon whiskey as a reinforcement for their physical energies. Being exceedingly prevalent, drunkenness was more or less accepted as a necessary evil about which little could be done. Eventually, however, reaction set in, and a temperance reform movement spread from the United States to Canada, where the first society was organized at Montreal in 1828. In 1830 a society was formed in the Township of Trafalgar.[70]

The Temperance Hall at Oakville was the first to be erected in the province,[71] and therefore it is only fitting that some space should be devoted to the cause for which it has stood for more than a century. By 1834 the Oakville Temperance Reformation Society had been formed, its meetings being held in the store of the president, Justus Williams. Joshua Van Allen was secretary, and the members of the committee were Thomas Leach, carpenter; Robert Wilson, mariner; John Potter, carpenter; and John A. Chisholm, farmer.[72] Emphasis was placed on temperance rather than on total abstinence and only whiskey, brandy, and rum were attacked. At a later date cider and beer were added to the proscribed list and the societies ("damned cold water societies," some called them) preached total abstinence.

The year the Oakville society was being formed the editor of the *Patriot* who became quite incensed over the methods of temperance advocates offered another solution. Pointing to the gardens of Birmingham, England he wrote:

> These gardens were owned by what may be emphatically called the *working* people, who with such pleasing cares upon their hands needed no admonishing of *Temperance*. No temptation could lure to the Tavern, while the prize cauliflower, the giant asparagus, the huge gooseberry, the gay tulip or fragrant carnation demanded attention. . . . It is all fal lal, to preach abstinence from this and abstinence from that. Man is never satisfied but with full employment of head and hand. . . . Perhaps no place in the world is worse supplied than this with vegetables. . . . When the Temperance papers preach up this kind of improving industry we shall have more confidence in their sincerity than we now have. We would rather see the *Guardian* calling to a show of early Cabbages than to Camp meetings. . . .[73]

The Reverend Robert Murray, Scottish Presbyterian minister stationed at Oakville, also held that temperance people adopted the wrong approach. In his forthright manner he said as much in a series of lectures "exposing the Tendency and Efforts of Temperance Societies" which, according to the announcement in September, 1839, were "published at the request of his congregation."[74] Immediately the wrath of Dr. Egerton Ryerson, editor of the *Christian Guardian*, descended upon his head, and the public was invited to attend a temperance meeting at Oakville when "the Rev. Murray's lectures will form a basis of the remarks to be made."[75]

The building of a hall in which the temperance society could hold meetings was undertaken by Justus Williams and Thomas Leach. They procured the lot on the south-east corner of Dundas and Randall streets and provided much of the materials, and other members gave liberally of their time and labour. John Potter framed the building of timber drawn from Anderson's bush, and made joists by ripping large timbers in half, placing them only two or three feet apart across the width of the building. The window sash was made by Joshua Leach, and it is probable that much of the lumber was from his mill. When working on the building the men took their dinner at Forman's inn across the way.

The hall was finished in 1843, and for the official opening the secretary of the Montreal Society, R. D. Wadsworth, was brought to Oakville to respond to another pamphlet against temperance which had recently appeared in print. He was met by a large assembly of people as he descended from the stage-coach, and was driven to the hall in a carriage drawn by four horses. Over 150 persons attended the meeting and it was a great success.[76]

Within a short time after his visit to Oakville, Wadsworth published *The Temperance Manual* in which the aims of the movement are outlined and suggestions given for the forming and carrying on of temperance societies. He suggested pledges of three kinds: society, person, and juvenile. Emphasis was placed upon the forming of a juvenile society or "Cold Water Army." He recommended that children march to church with badges, banners, and music. Wadsworth included a number of short stories for children in which Death and the Devil figure prominently; each story ended with a summary under the heading of "Moral." There were also many temperance hymns. One entitled "The Water King" runs as follows:

We're soldiers of the Water-King,
His laws we will obey;
Virtue and health are his reward—

We want no better pay.
(*Chorus*)
Then, let us sing the Water-King,
Good soldiers, one and all—
Our banners to the breeze we'll fling,
And *down* with *alcohol.*

Others were the "Old Oaken Bucket," "Try, Try Again," and the "Cold Water Army," the chorus of which runs:

We love the clear Cold Water Springs,
Supplied by gentle showers:
We feel the strength cold water brings,—
"The Victory is Ours."

Wadsworth concludes his *Manual* with an eloquent plea: "To those who have not aided the enterprise, we say, join the cause while it requires some moral courage to do so. It will soon be little credit to you to enter its ranks. How will your cheeks crimson, as your grandchildren shall gather round you, and ask you the history of the reformation, if obliged to tell them that it went on without you—that you withheld from it your co-operation! . . . Let there be a long pull, a strong pull, and a pull together! Glorious result—Intemperance fallen, and sobriety universally prevalent. Amen!"[77]

IV

Within the first decade of its existence Oakville suffered two serious setbacks, both of which were shared in common with other communities of Upper Canada: the epidemic of Asiatic cholera which swept the country, and economic depression.

Hardly had Oakville become established when the dreaded cholera, brought from Britain by immigrants, struck the Canadas. In 1832 the disease spread from Europe to Britain, where the number of cases reached the total of twelve thousand, with a very high mortality.[78] Inevitably it spread to the colonies, starting in the cities along the St. Lawrence where the "coffin ships" landed their passengers.

Without adequate accommodation or proper ventilation, those timber ships were a nightmare of privation to the poor passengers. The British government failed to control the traffic, and the emigrants were "prodigious sufferers from the want of some regulations to protect them."[79] The law specified that each vessel should carry one person per ton burthen, but almost all carried more than was allowed. One way of circumventing the regulations was to list each child under fourteen as one-half and those under seven as one-quarter of a passenger.[80] Paid in advance, the whole expense for an adult was about £10, and for a child, £6.[81] The filthy conditions may be imagined when we read that the harbour master's boatmen had no difficulty in distinguishing by the odour alone a crowded immigrant ship at the distance of a gun shot.[82] In the ships' holds where timber had so recently lain, as many as forty berths were ranged along the sides, each built to hold six adults. In these crowded quarters, so highly favourable for the spread of disease and lice, the immigrants cooked and ate their meals, slept, and passed the time during the six weeks to two months that it took to make the passage to Quebec. Their food, provided in minimum quantities by themselves, consisted principally of salt pork and beef, rice, oatmeal, ship's biscuit, tea, and sugar. The provisions rarely lasted the voyage, and the immigrants, wasted by starvation, died by hundreds. The Gulf of St. Lawrence was strewn for miles with the bedding of those who had been buried at sea. The ships' captains took every opportunity of fleecing the passengers of their money and many of those who reached their destination were quite penniless. A medical officer at Quebec who served the immigrants in the thirties called the ships "itinerant pest houses" and continued:

> These poor creatures, on landing, creep into any hovel they can with all their foul things about them. When they are so numerous as to figure in the streets, they are put, I believe by the Colonial Government, into dilapidated houses, with something like rations, of which latter the worthier portion of the emigrants are apt to see little: they are clutched by the clamorous.
>
> The filthy and crowded state of the houses . . . can only be guessed by a very bold imagination. . . .
>
> After starving about Quebec for months, the helpless Irishman and his

family begin to creep up the country on charity or government aid, and thus strew the colony with beggary and disease.[83]

On Grosse Isle in the St. Lawrence near Quebec a quarantine station was hastily established, but the immigrants were required to stay there only three days. The quarantine sheds and the hospital stood close together, and inadequate disposal of human waste gave infection every opportunity to flourish and spread. Due allowance must be made for the lack of knowledge of the cause of cholera at this period, but nevertheless the blame for the epidemic in the Canadas cannot be laid upon the shoulders of the colonial government. It rests squarely upon members of the home government who allowed the relaxing of passenger-vessel laws.[84]

When cholera reached Upper Canada Governor Colborne took immediate action to establish boards of health at every landing-place of ships on the route westward. The Gore District received a grant of £500, and late in June, upon recommendation of the Lieutenant-Governor, a meeting of magistrates in the district was called "to take into consideration and adopt such measures for the prevention and cure of the Cholera, as may seem advisable." Boards of health were appointed, that for Oakville being composed of William Chisholm, Merrick Thomas, William Butts, William O'Reilly, and William Uptegrave.[85] A young doctor who had recently established his practice on the Dundas Street in Nelson Township, Dr. Daniel Black, was appointed health inspector for all vessels carrying immigrants arriving at Oakville and Burlington Bay.[86] The following August Dr. Black was dead of cholera.[87]

To what extent Oakville suffered at this time goes almost unrecorded. A man who with two companions came to Oakville the following year in search of employment stated in his journal that they were engaged by Chisholm at the wage of 3*s*.6*d*. per day, type of work unspecified. But "we heard it was a very unhealthy place, many having died there . . . we therefore determined on declining and to go further in the country."[88]

During the winter of 1832-3 the epidemic on both sides of the Atlantic gradually subsided until it was supposed that cholera had been wiped out, and a day in April, 1833, was set aside for general thanksgiving throughout the British Empire.[89] But in the summer of 1834 the disease reappeared. This was the year of the largest migration from southern Ireland that had yet taken place, and vessels sailing from Irish ports were the worst offenders in overcrowding and filthy conditions.

Oakville was badly affected by this second epidemic. The results of a meeting of the inhabitants of the village held "for the purpose of taking into consideration the most effectual means for prevention of Cholera" are recorded in a letter addressed to Sir John Colborne by William Chisholm, written by William J. Sumner as secretary and dated from Oakville, August 2, 1834:

> . . . it was unanimously resolved—
>
> 1st That a committee of nine persons resident in the village be appointed to examine all houses, outhouses, cellars, etc.
>
> 2nd That this committee consist of Jacob Randall, George Brown, William Chisholm, Esquire, Wm. Hatton, Wm. Butts, James Steele, Wm. Uptegrave, Justus Williams and Merrick Thomas—Whose duty it will be to recommend to the occupier of any house in the village to cleanse and fumigate their houses, outhouses, etc. and whitewash the same with lime.
>
> 3rd That this committee is authorized to adopt any measure they may deem prudent and essential for the health of the village or the purchase of necessary medicines.[90]

On August 18 Lieutenant Colonel Rowan, Chairman of the Board of Health at York, replied from Government House:

> SIR:—I am directed by the Lt. Governor to acquaint you that from the general prevalence of the cholera in the province, and the peculiar difficulties that the townships may experience in procuring medical aid, His Excellency will place at the disposal of every board of health, established in the province, such a sum as the members of the board may consider indispensably necessary, to enable aid medical to be offered to persons who have no means of procuring it, and to towns or villages in which the disease may appear to render the aid of the board requisite.[91]

The following day Colborne declared Oakville a Port of Entry and appointed William Chisholm Collector of Customs.[92] This was an important step in controlling the epidemic for at all ports in the province it was the Customs Collector who was responsible for the entrance of immigrant ships. Before permitting passengers to land he investigated the state of their health, and if any contagious disease was found the vessel was quarantined. Arrangements were made for the stricken to be cared for in isolation camps until the danger of epidemic had passed. Colborne also appointed Justus Williams "to form a Board of Health in and for the Village of Oakville and Vicinity" and Williams named the men chosen at the public meeting.[93] On August 28 another meeting was held and reported through Sumner, secretary of the board of health, that within only a few weeks' time twenty-five cases of cholera had developed, seven resulting in death, six in recovery, and the others being as yet in the balance. The committee also reported that a sum of £10 had been raised "to defray expenses attending cholera cases of indigent persons, and finding their means not sufficient for the number beg leave to ask your Excellency for an appropriation of money which may be in your power to grant us."[94] Accordingly Colborne authorized the Bank of Upper Canada to advance to the board of health at Oakville the sum of £30.[95]

A curious remedy for cholera used at this time, according to John A. Williams, was a teaspoonful of charcoal in a glass of water. He also remembered his father and James Steele treating a woman who had been given up as hopeless with a solution of smart weed. This remedy was applied externally to the abdomen and internally by mouth, with successful results. Appendix B gives other remedies of Justus Williams.

According to tradition a hospital was set up by the board of health on the west side of The Sixteen, and a young man named John Urquhart was placed in charge. Born in Scotland, Urquhart had worked as a lad on the estate of the Duke of Sutherland, but he had great ambitions to become a teacher and studied far into the night by rushlight. In 1830 he migrated to New York, but finding life in the republic not to his liking he came to Upper Canada and taught school for a time near Lake Simcoe in West Gwillimbury Township. When the cholera struck York he gave up his school to assist in the hospital at York.[96] In those days a young man wishing to practise medicine apprenticed himself to a licensed medical practitioner. He studied the doctor's books and accompanied him on his rounds of hospitals and private homes. Trips on horseback or by buggy gave ample opportunity for discussion, and the medical student acquired knowledge by practical experience and by personal contact with the doctor. Thus, after two years' experience among cholera victims both at York and Oakville, John Urquhart was considered qualified to practise medicine. When the epidemic subsided he remained at Oakville, and built a combined apothecary's shop, surgery, and dwelling which he opened under the name of "Medical Hall," a popular term at this period, on the south side of Colborne Street between Thomas and George streets. In this building which is now no. 62 Colborne Street East, his son, also named John, was born in 1844.

No sooner had the cholera subsided than Oakville began to feel the effects of an economic depression. For some time the province of Upper Canada had been approaching financial breakdown, and economic difficulties were aggravated by political unrest. In 1837 the province was overtaken by commercial collapse and political crisis.

During the year following the Rebellion the commerce of the province came virtually to a standstill.

The suspension by banks of specie payments in 1837 caused great hardship throughout the country. Fractional currency, always limited, disappeared almost entirely. As the law permitted the issuing of bank notes for less than 5*s*., merchants began to issue their own paper notes in small denomination, 7½*d*., 1*s*.3*d*., and 2*s*.6*d*. When signed by the merchants who issued them these small bills passed as currency. They were bound in book form similar to the cheque book of today, and bore the merchant's name printed upon the face.[97] Though good only in the neighbourhood in which the merchant was known, they served their purpose temporarily. In French Canada and adjoining sections of the upper province these merchants' notes were called "bons," (from "bon pour") while in the western section they were called by the American term of "shin plasters." The original shin plaster, a remedy for curing a sore shin, was made of brown paper covered with tar and vinegar, and the name had facetiously been applied to the worthless currency in circulation after the Revolutionary War. When banks resumed specie payments in 1840 the shin plaster disappeared.

The village of Oakville experienced its share of the country's "hard times," and its trade and commerce were badly hit, particularly the stave industry, although no figures exist to show to what extent. Since Chisholm and his deputy were "absent on government business" during 1838, no returns from the Custom House were made to the government.[98] The only source of information relative to this phase of Oakville's history is the reminiscences of John A. Williams. The economic setback the village suffered must have been serious indeed to have impressed itself upon the mind of a lad so forcibly as it did. Apparently some villagers attempted to solve their difficulties by engaging in a little smuggling of merchandise from the United States.

The Port of Oakville is conspicuous by its absence from government lists of contraband goods seized over several decades. The only reference to smuggling appears in the commission drawn up in March, 1838, by William Chisholm appointing his son Deputy Customs Collector. It reads:

> Whereas information hath been given me that sundry Goods, Wares, and Merchandise have been and are now being brought into the Province from the United States, without the duties having been paid and contrary to Law
>
> Now KNOW YE that by virtue of the power and authority in me vested, I have authorized, and by these presents do authorize Robert Kerr Chis-

holm of the Town of Oakville my lawful deputy for me and in my name to seize and detain all goods, etc. coming from the United States into this Province without the Duties having been paid. . . . WILLIAM CHISHOLM Collector.[99]

As the harbour served all the district between Toronto and Hamilton it was expected that the volume of imports would increase at a steady pace after Oakville became a Port of Entry. The bulk of customs duties on merchandise coming from Britain was collected in Lower Canada, and Oakville, therefore, was forced to depend upon duties collected on imports from the United States. But instead of buying direct the merchants continued to buy their goods from importers at Toronto and Hamilton. As late as 1842 the Customs Inspector found that virtually no imports came through the Port of Oakville.[100] Not until the middle 1840's was the first shipment brought in from New York by Justus Williams and gradually other merchants followed his lead.[101]

It was on the export trade that the commerce of the village throve, but whether recovery from the depression was swift or protracted has not been determined. In Upper Canada as a whole conditions did not improve until after its union with Lower Canada into one province. However, it is probable that, being dependent upon the two staple products of the country, wood and wheat, the trade and commerce of Oakville recovered somewhat more rapidly.

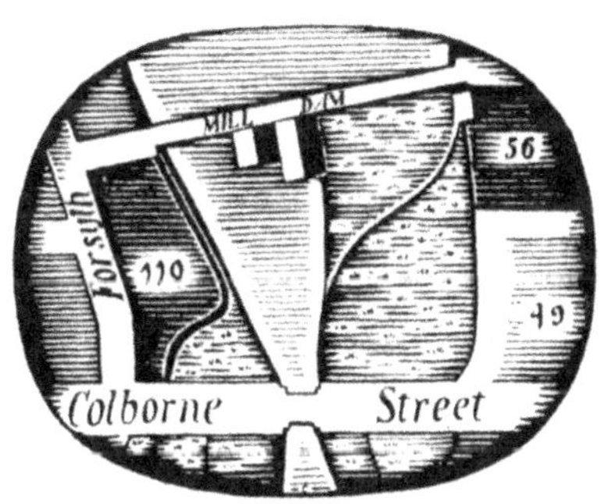

V

It was not until all the essentials of an outport had been developed that the plan was advanced for harnessing the water-power of The Sixteen for industrial purposes. It is abundantly clear that William

Chisholm broadened his original plan for Oakville and endeavoured to make it a manufacturing village. The potential water-power which lay within the limits of Oakville was an asset possessed by neither Toronto nor Hamilton. Toronto was a commercial centre and market, which also depended largely on revenue derived from the garrison and from governmental institutions, while Hamilton was a banking centre. In the head-of-the-lake area it was Dundas that flourished because of its excellent water-power.[102]

Owing to its small population, Upper Canada had by the 1830's made little progress industrially, and for manufactured goods of all kinds depended almost entirely upon Britain and the United States. What industrial activity there was in this agricultural country was confined principally to the processing of products of the farm. The commodities thus produced were for purely local consumption only and their supply was governed by the needs of the district immediately surrounding the factory. Skilled mechanics required by the more specialized industries were procured mostly from the United States where manufacturing of all kinds was going forward at a rapid pace.

For some time paper made from rags had been produced in small quantities in Upper Canada, and stoves manufactured from bog iron were making their appearance. Men of enterprise were also aware of the new methods of textile manufacture which had been and were being introduced in Britain and the United States. But until the 1830's there were neither raw materials nor labour enough for the operation of more than a few woollen mills in Upper Canada. By then wool was being produced in larger quantities; mechanization of the textile industry in the British Isles was driving many thousands of workers to the province. Thus sufficient labour and raw materials were available for industry on a larger scale.

By 1836, when William Chisholm was appointed to the parliamentary committee for the improvement of trade and manufacture in the province because of his interest in industrialization,[103] the first power looms were making their appearance in Upper Canada. Of the type of industry Chisholm intended to establish at Oakville documentary proof is lacking, but the weight of evidence is heavily in favour of the manufacture on power looms of woollen cloth, its processing and finishing. The 1841 census shows that there were no woollen mills in the township. The only "manufacturies containing machinery moved by wind, water, steam or animal power" were Flick's chair factory at Palermo, Joseph Hixon's "shingle mill moved by animal power" at Bronte, and the Oakville distillery, where steam was used.[104]

In March, 1836, the *Observer* gave a forecast of Oakville's new industry. "Although the intended Dam across the creek is not yet in progress, creditable report induces us to believe, that ere long we shall have the satisfaction of announcing, that this vast improvement to our town is in progress. When this undertaking, with the Mills to be erected upon it, is completed, it will impart fresh impulse to our advancement, and of which the intended improvement of our excellent harbour will enable the town to reap the full benefits."[105] When this plan was initiated it has proved difficult to determine, but the evidence presents itself in the following sequence. Subsequent to the government loan of £2,500 to William Chisholm, the large Montreal mercantile firm of Forsyth, Richardson & Company took a second mortgage for £6,500 on the townsite and Chisholm's farm in Nelson Township.[106] In 1835 and again in 1836 Chisholm and Forsyth, Richardson & Company held joint sales at which 150 building lots and some choice water lots were placed on the market. In the announcement of the latter sale reference is made to "the advantages . . . of water power now being made in the centre of the Town."[107] Another of Palmer's plans, drawn in 1837 for the purpose of showing the divisions of the townsite under mortgage, designates as "The Joint Property" of Chisholm and the Forsyths that section of The Sixteen and the land bordering upon it which is outlined in pink on the plan that appears opposite page 38 of this volume. Also the mills are identical with the detail of Kerr's plan as shown on page 85.[108]

That the firm of Forsyth, Richardson & Company was involved in the project is an indication of its importance. This influential firm had widespread connections and invested in large-scale enterprises. Established in 1790, Forsyth, Richardson & Company early engaged in the fur trade. Shortly after the British conquest of Canada, four brothers Forsyth had migrated from Scotland, two to settle at Montreal, another at Cataraqui (Kingston), and the fourth at Niagara, and all became prominent merchants. Thomas Forsyth became a partner in Robert Ellice & Company of Montreal, which engaged in the fur trade through Detroit and Michilimackinac. Reorganized in 1790 by Thomas and John Forsyth and their cousin, John Richardson, under the name of Forsyth, Richardson & Company, this firm of general merchants and fur-traders speedily secured a leading position in the commercial life of Montreal, becoming associated with the North West Company.

When the fur trade began to decline, Forsyth and Richardson built up a general trading and forwarding business, and among their customers were many colonists along the shores of Lake Ontario. The company traded in wood, wheat, lumber, and tea (they were agents for the "Honourable East India Company," which had a monopoly on all tea coming into the colony), and engaged in banking, canal building, land companies, and in fact every sphere of Canadian business, and on a very large scale. Richardson was a principal organizer and Forsyth a director, in 1817, of the first chartered bank in the Canadas, the Bank of Montreal, and both men were members of the Legislative Council of Lower Canada.[109]

The representative at York of Forsyth, Richardson & Company was the Honourable William Allan, whose name has already been mentioned in connection with Allan Street, and the names of members of the firm which appear on so many deeds of land on the west side of Oakville also survive in the names of streets in this section of the town. There is William Walker, head of their Quebec branch and later chairman of the board of trade at that city, who was also member of the House of Assembly of Lower Canada. There is James Bell Forsyth, Chisholm's good friend, for whom he named not only a street but one of his sons. Forsyth was later a lumber merchant on his own in the city of Quebec, an astute business man and an author of no mean ability. His pamphlet, *Brief Remarks on the Waste Lands of the Crown in the Canadas with Reference to Emigration and Colonization*, published at Quebec in 1847, is a competent piece of work, advancing many ideas which may seem obvious today but which were new at the time. Forsyth, an extensive traveller, also wrote a book entitled *A few months in the east; or a glimpse of the Red, Dead and Black Seas.*[110] Others who gave their names to Oakville streets were David Burnet, a merchant of the city of Quebec, who, though not a member of the firm, had business connections with them, and Thomas Brown Anderson, head of Forsyth, Richardson & Company's Montreal branch. When the firm was dissolved in 1847,[111] Anderson and others carried it on under several changes of name until 1861.

The detail of Kerr's plan of Oakville reproduced on page 85 of this volume shows the dam and mills which were to be constructed on the flats of The Sixteen north of Colborne Street at the foot of the east bank. Above on the hill were the meeting-house and cemetery situated on block 56, which had been given for public use. Chisholm now gave block 43 on Reynolds Street in exchange for block 56, and it was to record this exchange that he commissioned Kerr to draw the plan referred to above. The interments in the "old cemetery" were gradually moved to the new[112] but the meeting-house remained undisturbed. It will be seen that the dam was to extend from the head of Randall

Street to approximately the foot of Rebecca Street, and to accomplish this it was necessary to fill in the marsh on the east side of the river. The largest of three buildings was to stand at the head of Randall Street. Two smaller structures were to be placed directly over the water on the south side of the dam, possibly a further indication that they were to be woollen mills, as large quantities of water were used in the processes of scouring, fulling, and dyeing.

As originally laid out, the town lots west of The Sixteen were in blocks of six, each on a quarter of an acre, as were those on the east side of the river. Kerr's plan shows that before the sale in 1836 these lots had been re-surveyed and considerably reduced in size, Forsyth, Richardson & Company taking over large numbers of them. These lots were obviously intended for workingmen's dwellings. Thus the idea which has persisted until recent times, that those who lived "over the creek" belonged principally to the working classes, seems to have originated with this power project.

In 1839 further mortgages placed on the townsite raised the total of its encumbrances to £10,625 ($52,125).[113] This was a large debt, considering the greater value of money at that time. Early in 1840 Chisholm and nine other townsmen petitioned the Lieutenant-Governor "for the Incorporation of a Company to be called the Oakville Hydraulic Company . . . for constructing a dam within the bounds of the Village, producing water power sufficient to propel all description of machinery, and to which vessels . . . may ascend safely."[114] The co-signers with Chisholm were Edward Palmer, James Hopkirk, William J. Sumner, James Reid, Andrew Wilson jr., Merrick Thomas, James Arnott, J. L. Bigger, and John S. Diamond. An Act was drawn up and passed by Parliament to which the royal assent was given on February 10. It was enacted that stock to the limit of £20,000, eight hundred shares at £25 each, could be sold.[115] Judging from the number of mortgages placed at this time on village lots it would seem that many townspeople invested in this company.

Unequivocally it may be stated that the Oakville Hydraulic Company was the first company incorporated in the province of Upper Canada for the purpose of developing water power for manufacturing.[116] Unfortunately, the papers in connection with the incorporation were in the files of the Legislative Assembly of Upper Canada, and were lost in the fire which consumed the Parliament Buildings at Montreal during the riot of 1849. These documents would have revealed many details of the project; possibly the purpose for which the mills were designed.

The plan of making Oakville an industrial centre was, however, doomed to failure. According to tradition the depth of The Sixteen south of the loop made the building of a dam impossible, and after large amounts of money and some years of labour had been sunk in the enterprise it had to be abandoned. Those who had invested in the attempt lost heavily.

Toward the end of 1841 the banks foreclosed. Through January and February, 1842, the *Journal Express* at Hamilton ran an advertisement of a sheriff's sale. The Bank of Upper Canada, the Gore Bank, the Commercial Bank of the Midland District, and sundry individuals had brought suit against William Chisholm, Merrick Thomas, and John Moore. The list of lands "taken in execution of several writs of *fieri facias*," which included Chisholm's interest in the harbour and the townsite of Oakville, stretch down a long column. The sale was scheduled to take place at the court house in Hamilton on March 2, 1842, and two days later William Chisholm was dead.

All he had believed in and worked for he lost in the crash. The extent of his insolvency has not been determined, but besides his interest in the town several farms in Trafalgar Township and his old farm in Nelson Township went to his creditors. George Chisholm had pledged the property on Burlington Bay in East Flamborough Township as security for his brother, and he lost the homestead.

The sole remaining physical evidence of the undertaking is the finger of land reaching out from the foot of the east bank to the edge of the water of The Sixteen, still called the "old dam" in the eighties. Once easily discernible where it ran through the marsh, it is less so since the marsh to the south has been filled in. But this finger of land may yet be distinguished by its higher level and the trees that grow upon it where it runs parallel to the south side of the radial bridge. The marsh, always a hazard to health, was filled in by being used as the town dump after the turn of the century. Within the past few years it has been covered with soil and is now Busby Park where the softball teams play.

Had Chisholm's plan been effectually carried to completion and the hydraulic company successful, Oakville might well have become, as he and others hoped, "one of the principal Towns in the Province." It is ironic that after the passage of more than a century, changes in the industrial pattern are bringing manufacturing plants from Toronto and Hamilton to Oakville, the town which might well have been their industrial forerunner.

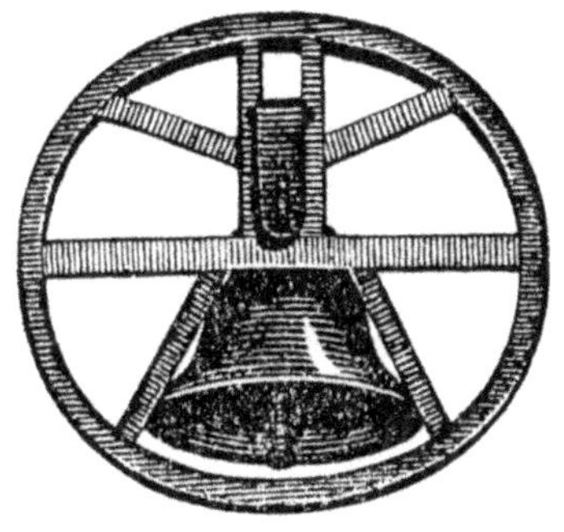

CHAPTER THREE

THE MISSIONS AND THE SCHOOL

FROM THE TIME of its founding Oakville had had the benefit of the religious teachings of missionaries who had laboured for years among the settlers in Trafalgar Township. Whatever their creed, these missionaries, travelling on horseback throughout extensive territories, encountered primitive conditions and experienced great hardship. To quote the Reverend Anson Green, Methodist: "I had no place which I called my home; and yet I found a home whenever night overtook me. My saddle was my study, saddle bags my wardrobe and my Bible and hymn book my select library. . . . My needs were all supplied and I wanted nothing but more grace."[1] The Reverend Thomas Greene, missionary of the Church of England, wrote: "Thank God I am still strong, though I have worn out one horse; plunging over deep mud-holes day after day is trying to the best of horses—I might add to the best constitution. . . . Who, O Lord, being in the flesh, is sufficient for these things? No one; all strength and sufficiency must be from on high."[2]

Because of the familiarity of the Methodist organization with the problems and techniques of frontier settlement, the evangelical religious movement of Methodism which had come by the way of the United States was particularly successful in the settlements of Upper Canada. The reliance of the Methodist Church upon a "call" to the ministry rather than upon educational qualifications greatly facilitated the enlistment of itinerant preachers. The Methodist circuit preachers came from the ranks of the people among whom they laboured, and were well equipped to withstand a life of privation and hardship. The Roman Catholic Church also, whose work in the Canadian wilderness reached back for centuries, provided for its priests the necessary training. The Church of England and Presbyterian Church, on the other hand, lacked both funds and ministers willing to leave their homelands, and the men who did come were ill equipped for colonial conditions. The clergy from England, Ireland, and Scotland, reared in an upper or middle class environment and educated in a theological school, lacked the appreciation of the problems and manner of life of a pioneer farm population.

Numerically the Methodists predominated in Trafalgar Township. Before the migrations from overseas the population of the township, being largely of Loyalist descent, was predominantly of American origin, and the close American connection of the Methodist Church gave it a great advantage in winning their support. Moreover the Methodist missionaries were the first to enter the township; by 1817 two itinerant saddlebag preachers were at work.[3] Some years later a circuit was formed which extended from the Credit River to the swamps of the Grand River. Two preachers, each having thirty appointments in the four weeks it took to cover the territory, had under their pastoral care some four hundred persons.[4]

The earliest chapel in the township was the Trafalgar Chapel on the Dundas Street around which the village of Palermo sprang up. According to the Reverend Anson Green, who preached there in 1826-8, the church was small but well filled; the class lively, and its leader, Brother Lawrence Hagar, "stirs them up as an eagle stirs up her nest."[5] At Munn's Corners at the 6th Line a congregation met in the schoolhouse, and at the Twelve Mile Creek a group met regularly at the home of Mahlon Bray near the Lake Shore Road.[6] However, the Church of England clergy alone were authorized to perform the marriage ceremony, so that settlers were obliged either to await the arrival in their district of a Church of England missionary or to travel long distances to his headquarters. Only after a long and bitter struggle was the privilege of performing marriages extended in 1831 to ministers of other denominations.

Little is known of Methodism in Oakville until 1832 when the union of Canadian and English Methodism was effected and the name of Wesleyan Church in Canada adopted. A small minority broke away to establish the Methodist Episcopal Church in Canada, but in its early period this church failed to gain support in Oakville.

It was to the Wesleyan Church that Oakville's Methodists adhered. At this time, 1832, the Nelson Circuit of the Wesleyan Church was formed. This new circuit embraced the territory that approximates Halton County today, and extended north into Erin and east into Toronto townships. The missionaries "in charge" were the Reverends Franklin Metcalfe and Samuel Belton, and Justus Williams was appointed Recording Secretary, an office he was to hold some thirty years. In the Minutes of the Nelson Circuit appear accounts which show £50 per annum to be the salary of a circuit preacher with wife and family. In addition to horse-shoeing, allowances were made for other items such as:

Table expenses	£29.10.0
Horse Keep	5.0.0
Fuel	2.10.0
Each child under 7	7.0.0[7]

The preacher's salary was supplemented by contributions of various kinds of produce from members of the congregations on the circuit.

Each missionary preached fourteen times in eight days over the twenty-five regular appointments on the Nelson Circuit. Oakville was within the district of the senior preacher, Franklin Metcalfe. He had been studying medicine in his native state of New York when he made the decision to become a Methodist missionary. Obtaining a release from his indentures he came to Canada in 1811 at the age of twenty-one. Metcalfe was a handsome man with "a fine discriminating judgement, a logical mind, well stored with facts and ideas, a remarkably clear and methodical way of arranging his subject."[8] A contemporary asserted metaphorically that Metcalfe made the log piles and Waldron set them on fire.

At the first quarterly meeting of the Nelson Circuit "holden at Nelson Chapel" near Hannahsville, October 13–14, 1832, it was decided to locate a parsonage at Oakville, and a house was procured for the annual rental of £11.11.3. The Recording Secretary, an indefatigable worker, told in after years the circumstances under which the Wesleyan Methodists at Oakville built their first chapel. He wrote:

> In March, 1833, I moved to Oakville. At that time there was no place set apart for the worship of Almighty God but the school-house [which] . . . was used for that purpose by all Christian denominations who desired it.
>
> In 1835, the late lamented Wm. Chisholm, then well-known as generous and philanthropic, kindly said that he would give an acre of land, then considered worth $400, and $50 cash, to assist in building the first church

which should be erected in Oakville. The subject was mentioned to the late beloved and lamented Rev. Wm. Case, then presiding elder of the District, and to several other members of the Wesleyan Church, who all approved of building immediately, as it appeared to be a favourable opportunity.[9]

Writing from memory after the passage of more than thirty years Williams made an error in the date—it was at the quarterly meeting of the Nelson Circuit held at the Trafalgar Chapel on May 24, 1834, that the project was approved:

Resolved: This conference approve of building a chapel at Oakville and that the following persons be appointed Trustees for the purpose of securing land for the same.

Charles Sovereign
William Hatton
Elijah Dexter
Justus Williams
Robert Leach[10]

Of this committee Hatton and Williams lived at Oakville, Sovereign (as we know) at the Twelve Mile Creek, and Dexter and Leach a short distance east of Oakville on the Lake Shore Road.

Despite the early optimism, it soon became apparent that the financing of the project would be difficult. Indeed, Hatton and Leach, Williams relates, "when they saw the small amount of subscriptions obtained, and the difficulty likely to ensue to the committee, declined to take any responsibility in regard to debts which might be incurred in the building. In this, perhaps, they acted wisely." Williams, therefore, assumed responsibility and himself carried the greater portion of the financial burden of building the chapel. To resume his narrative: "By the advice of the Rev. Wm. Case and the consent of Col. Wm. Chisholm, it was agreed that we should buy a site in the centre of the town, from the late James Gage, Esq., of the City of Hamilton, at sum of $500, and in order to secure me in the purchase of the lot and building, it was agreed that the lot purchased from Mr. Gage and the acre given by Col. Chisholm, should both be deeded to me, which was accordingly done, and the building commenced."[11] The situation chosen for the chapel was the north-west corner of Colborne and Thomas streets (block 5, lot C). The subscribers to the building fund paid little in cash, giving the equivalent in lumber, stone, carpentry work, cartage, and the like. Copies of some of Williams' accounts show that the system worked somewhat as follows:

A was a merchant from whom B, the owner of a sawmill, had bought merchandise on credit. C was a farmer and the owner of a good stand of pine who had also bought goods on credit from A, and

D was another merchant appointed to the subscription committee. A agreed to furnish the amount of his subscription in pine lumber and at once ordered a number of pine logs from C, crediting them to C's account with his store. C teamed the logs to B's sawmill where they were cut into lumber, the cost of the operation being credited to B's account with A. C delivered the lumber to D who gave him a receipt for "lumber, being £5.10.2½. on . . . [A's] subscription towards the building of the Meeting-house."[12] Over and above the subscriptions the sum of £300 was borrowed in England.[13]

At the laying of the corner-stone on August 12, 1835, a considerable number of persons assembled to hear the address delivered "in his usual and impressive style" by the Reverend William Case. William Chisholm then laid the corner-stone under which was deposited a lead case containing several coins of the reign of William IV and three newspapers: the *Christian Guardian*, the Dundas *Weekly Post*, and the *Toronto Courier*. Included also was a written document certifying, "This stone was laid August 12th, 1835 by William Chisholm, Esq., founder of the town of Oakville, aged 47 years."[14]

It is immensely gratifying to find the Reverend William Case officiating upon this occasion. One of the early founders of Methodism in Canada, he lived a long and useful life, holding many high offices in the Church. So much has been written about the "Father of Canadian missions" that to enlarge upon his work is quite superfluous.

The building of the chapel was commenced at once. It was the second Methodist chapel in Upper Canada to be provided with steeple and bell, the chapel at Belleville being the first.[15] The tinned spire surmounting the frame building rose 100 feet into the air.[16] From the photograph (plate 3) it may be seen that architecturally the chapel was Colonial in style, closely resembling St. Andrew's Church, built a few years later, which still stands in Oakville today. Painted white with green trim, the Methodist chapel measured approximately 36 by 60 feet, had "a good stone basement,"[17] and was capable of holding 300 people.[18] The pride of the community was expressed by the editor of the *Oakville Observer* when he wrote in March, 1836: "The past six months has witnessed the erection of a very handsome Methodist Church to which the addition of a spire not only adds to the elegance of the building but makes it an ornament to the town. Indeed, we have frequently anticipated the pleasure of viewing from the deck of the *Oakville*, on her way to Toronto, the vast improvement to the interesting appearance of the town, which the Church and spire must create."[19]

On February 3, 1836, a few months after the laying of the cornerstone, the Oakville Branch of the Wesleyan Missionary Society was formed by the Reverend William Lord who was on a tour of the province for the purpose of founding such societies. His account of this two months' journey is herewith quoted in part:

Since the 19th. of January I have travelled about one thousand miles; as far west as London, and east as Brockville, including several visits to places at a considerable distance from the principal roads. I have experienced all the variety of weather a Canadian winter affords. On some days I have passed along canopied with a blue and cloudless sky, the sun shining in his splendour; on others, the clouds have poured upon me their contents of rain, or the wind has driven against me the snow from morning to night. There has not been, during this winter, more than one stormy day on which I have not been travelling for several hours. The roads have been as various as the weather. Sometimes the frost has rendered them as hard as flint, and rugged as confused heaps of stones, or smooth as glass; at others, the rain has made them soft as the clay of the potter, and as adhesive, too; and then again, they have been thickly covered with their mantle of snow. Of course my mode of travelling has been accommodated to the state of the weather and roads. So, Mr. Editor, if variety be the charm of life, my life recently has abounded with charms. And I can assure you I have often been often charmed after a stormy and fatiguing ride to be met with smiling faces, who have given me a hearty welcome to their hospitable habitations; and I have been more than charmed in having the opportunity of closing the day in laying before attentive and crowded congregations the state and claims of a perishing world, and in witnessing their ardor and zeal in the cause of Christ.[20]

The purposes of missionary societies are set forth in a letter dated from Oakville September 29, 1835, written by the minister recently appointed to the Nelson Circuit, the Reverend James Norris. He wrote: "The prospects of the Circuit are very encouraging; a considerable reformation has taken place at several of our appointments . . . the attention of our friends here is of late particularly directed [to] our missionary undertakings. The claims of the Indian tribes, and destitute settlers, . . . [are] regarded by them with lively interest. . . . At present there are three Branch Missionary Societies organized on this circuit, the Oakville Branch, the Trafalgar Branch and the Nelson Branch, from which we expect considerable sums towards the support of your missions."[21]

A native of Ireland, Norris had gone to the United States, where he was solicited to join the Pittsburgh Conference, but instead he offered himself to the Canadian Conference. Notwithstanding his family of small children (for unmarried men with few responsibilities were preferred) "his abilities and desirability for the work were thought to counterbalance any objections arising from that source," and he was accordingly received in 1827.[22] At the time the Oakville chapel was under construction Norris was appointed to the Nelson Circuit, remaining for three years.

The chapel was not yet finished and services continued to be held in the meeting-house when the following resolution was passed at a quarterly meeting in 1837: "That the parsonage house be located at Oakville, and that the subscription be circulated by the Superintendent of the circuit immediately after the conference and as soon as there shall be enough subscribed to pay for the lot and the building of the house the committee proceed to build."[23] These plans failed to materialize, however, and during the succeeding five years we find the preachers on the circuit living in various sections of the village.

Notwithstanding the splendid beginning and the efforts of Justus Williams the Wesleyan Methodists encountered serious financial difficulties in building the chapel. According to his own statement Williams "had obtained and collected most of the subscriptions, procured the lumber, timber, stone, and other materials and superintended the work gratuitously, without expectation of any reward save that of an approving conscience."[24] The funds were found to be insufficient to finish the interior of the chapel and when the Reverend Samuel C. Philp was stationed on the Nelson Circuit in 1839 the congregation was still holding services in the old meeting-house. During his period of service the chapel was at last completed. He wrote:

> The first year I was there, the Rev. H[amilton] Bigger was superintendent; he resided in Oakville, I in Palermo. The next year the Rev. R[owland] Heyland was superintendent. On account of family afflictions he could not remove onto the circuit, but resided in Streetsville. It was thought best for me to reside in Oakville; I did so, I then set to work to get the church finished. Some part of the Centenary subscriptions were to be applied to the building of churches. I spoke to Dr. Green, Chairman of the District, and he brought it before the committee, and they consented to my collecting what I could on the circuit for that purpose. . . . We got the floor laid, the pews put in, walls plastered and gallery built. The church was finished without additional debt.[25]

The Wesleyan Methodist chapel was dedicated on October 18, 1840, by the Reverend Anson Green, assisted by the Reverend Peter Jones. A son of the provincial surveyor, Augustus Jones, and his Indian wife, Reverend Peter Jones was missionary to the Missisauga

Indians at their village on the Credit River. Previous to the dedication of Oakville's chapel he had been in England where he was presented to King William IV and, in 1838, to Queen Victoria.

The Methodists, who regularly held services on Sunday morning and evening, invited the Presbyterians and Anglicans to share their chapel on alternate Sunday afternoons. But the Methodists soon found that they had assumed too great a financial burden, and after using their chapel for somewhat under a year they sold it for the amount of the debt to the Anglican Bishop of Toronto.[26] The Methodists thereupon returned to their former place of worship, the meeting-house, where their services were held for another ten years. The Reverend Samuel Philp wrote that about 1845, when he visited his brother who was stationed on the circuit, "I went to Oakville, and to my great mortification had to preach in the old schoolhouse again. The Episcopalians had possession of the church, and they would not extend the kindness we had extended to them."[27] Soon after Mr. Philp's visit arrangements were made for the use of the Temperance Hall.[28]

The minister who succeeded Philp, unwilling to brave the fever and ague which were so prevalent, had refused to live at Oakville. A parsonage was built on the Dundas Street,[29] and for some years few ministers on the Nelson Circuit resided at Oakville. However, this was not true of the following decade when a number of ministers while stationed on the Nelson Circuit made Oakville their home. Among them are several names familiar in the history of Canadian Methodism: the Reverends Hamilton Bigger, Matthew Whiting, James Norris, William Willoughby, and Thomas Spencer. At the time Spencer resided in the village he was editor of the Methodist Church newspaper, the *Christian Guardian*. And there were Edwy and John Ryerson, two of the five brothers who entered the ministry of the Methodist Church.[30]

Presbyterian missionaries from the United States followed the Methodists to Oakville. The earliest record of services are those organized by an American minister, the Reverend Samuel Sessions, of the Niagara Presbytery. A number of ministers from Upper New York State had joined together and in 1833 formed the Niagara Presbytery which had no connection with any synod. Of the various branches of Presbyterianism the American Presbyterian Church was the most evangelical, and its ministers in Canada adopted revivalist methods. A narrative was published in 1834 by a committee which stated that in describing the congregations under their care they "were forcibly reminded of the faithfulness of God's promise—'The desert shall rejoice and blossom like a rose.' " The section dealing with services held at Oakville is here given in full:

The church at Oakville was organized in April, 1833, consisting of eleven members. They had but very little preaching until December, when Mr. Sessions came to the place. Since then five have united with the church, and more are expected to unite soon. The congregation attending worship in this village is large, and for some time more than ordinary seriousness prevails generally. Weekly prayer meetings, with an interesting female prayer meeting and monthly concert, were well attended. A Bible class has lately been organized which promises much. There is also a temperance society in this place. It is in contemplation to build a meeting-house to cost $2,000 and to be completed at the close of next autumn. The Sabbath school, which is connected with the Methodists, consists of about eighty scholars and is in a flourishing condition. With God's professing people the state of religion is interesting at the present time.[31]

The meeting-house alluded to was not, however, built at this time, and we hear no more of the ministers of the Niagara Presbytery at Oakville.

At this period Protestants from the North of Ireland and Scotland were coming into Oakville in increasing numbers. These people, bound together by strong national attachments and denominational loyalties, had little in common with the American Presbyterians, and the American ministers apparently met with little encouragement. As soon as they were able the immigrants secured the services of one of their own countrymen, and in March, 1836, the *Oakville Observer* reported: "A very considerable subscription has been entered into towards the salary of a Presbyterian Clergyman to officiate in this town and neighbourhood. We trust . . . this will occasion the erection of a Presbyterian Church, to add to the number of public buildings."[32] Kerr's plan of Oakville shows that the land situated on the south-east corner of Anderson and Kerr streets had recently been set aside for a "Scotch Church" (block 71, lot A, now part of the town reservoir). In April of the same year the *Toronto Albion* announced: "We have received a very interesting communication from Oakville . . . of the ordination of the Rev. Mr. Murray as Pastor of the new Scotch Kirk there and it is highly gratifying to discover the rapid progress of that flourishing and delightful place."[33]

The Reverend Robert Murray would appear to have been the third son of John Murray, merchant in the Parish of Bannbridge, County Down. This village on the River Bann in Northern Ireland is south-west of Belfast. Robert Murray attended the University of Glasgow, where he matriculated in 1809.[34] The following year at a meeting of the Presbytery of Armagh he was "examined on Greek and Logic, previous to his going to College the second time, and gave satisfactory proof of his diligence and attention."[35] Upon returning from the University in 1811 he was again examined and "considered as having made considerable proficiency in his studies."[36] Of Robert Murray's whereabouts thereafter or the circumstances surrounding his ordination and appointment by the Toronto Presbytery to the congregation at Oakville nothing has been discovered. However, a man reared in Ireland and educatèd in Scotland must have been most acceptable to these Scottish and Irish Protestants. During their residence in the village Mr. and Mrs. Murray occupied a house on the lake shore at the foot of Brant Street (park lot B). It is in relation to education, with which he was to be identified, that the Reverend Robert Murray emerges in clearer perspective.

During Oakville's early years members of the Roman Catholic Church attended services held by Father Gordon, who worked among the Irish settlers along the 9th Line in the New Survey of the township some ten miles to the north. His headquarters were at York, and his territory was so extensive as to enable him to visit this congregation only once in five weeks. His pastoral charges, called "Stations," were some fifteen miles apart, and the priest covered his district on foot or horseback, saying mass, hearing confessions, preaching the word of God, and administering sacraments in log huts and barns. To follow the blazed trees marking the route to a clearing in the dusk of evening was difficult, and at times the weary priest wandered for hours in the dense forest. In a letter to the Bishop of Kingston, Father O'Grady, his superior, wrote of Father Gordon: "He is a sensible, modest unassuming man, and very willing to promote the cause in which he is engaged to the utmost extent of his ability, but then his means are limited and must continue to be so, as long as he is under the necessity of carrying a large trunk with his vestments, a large folio Missal, (etc.) . . . on the pommel of his saddle from Twp. to Twp. I feel this is more than we have a right to expect of him."[37]

Edward John Gordon was born in Dublin, Ireland, and reared in the Church of England. He was educated in England, and through the efforts of his elder brother was converted to the Roman Catholic faith. After emigrating to Canada he prepared himself for the priesthood at Quebec Seminary and at the Iona Seminary at St. Raphael, Glengarry County, and laboured in adjoining missions after being ordained.[38] In 1830 Father Gordon was transferred to the district surrounding the town of York. A "Register of Baptisms performed by the Rev. Edward Gordon in the Townships above York during his mission of three years five months" shows that during a four-month period he performed 306 baptisms in his district.[39]

It was the result of his efforts that a mission was built in Trafalgar Township. Early in 1831 Father O'Grady reported to his bishop: "Mr. Gordon too is doing well. He has under my direction opened a Subscription list in Trafalgar and we have very nearly funds enough to build a good frame church in the township. We want only the land. . . ."[40] Soon this was forthcoming, and in 1835 the mission was being attended by 150 persons,[41] some of whom undoubtedly were from Oakville. The following year a mission was established at Oakville by Father W. P. McDonough (McDonagh), also from Toronto, who said the first mass.[42] Father McDonough has been described as a man "of commanding presence, and familiar with the language and habits of the Irish immigrant."[43] Within two years of the saying of the first mass in 1836 preparations began for the building of a church, and for this purpose land at the corner of King and Reynolds streets (block 35, lot D) was given by William Chisholm. During the years 1838 to 1840 when funds were being raised by subscription, the congregation was attended by Father Eugene O'Reilly. The families principally responsible for erecting the church were those of Thomas and John Sweeney, Patrick Rigney, Patrick O'Shaughnessy, John Caven, Captain Nicholas Boylan, the O'Boyles, and the McDermotts. John Caven, carpenter, gave freely of his time and labour. According to an anecdote, one day he was working high up on the belfry when the rope by which he had ascended was let loose by an incompetent workman and slipped through its pulley. The wind caught the rope and blew it toward Allan Street and Caven was marooned on the tower at the dinner hour. Taking off his stocking he unravelled it and let it down to the ground, where someone soon tied another rope to the woollen yarn. "Would the yarn today lift a rope up?" asked the writer of this anecdote some forty years ago.[44]

Tradition says that it was because of the assistance received from Scottish Presbyterians that the mission was named in honour of the patron saint of Scotland, St. Andrew. The burying ground was situated on the north side of the church. The first mass in the finished church was said by Father Eugene O'Reilly late in October, 1840.[45] During succeeding years St. Andrew's Mission was attended by various priests from the town of Dundas, whose territory was still so extensive that they continued to visit each mission only once in five weeks. In

1842 the territory was divided and Father James O'Flynn was appointed to "Dundas and the neighbouring missions of Oakville, Wellington Square, Trafalgar, Etc."[46] "But how can this priest reach these stations without horse or carriage?" asked Vicar-General MacDonald of Bishop Gaullin.[47] It would seem that Father O'Flynn was provided with a horse. Some of the male members of the Oakville congregation who wished to attend mass more often travelled on foot to Dundas. They journeyed the twenty-odd miles on Saturday, returning after the Sunday service, and this they continued to do for a number of years.

Though the stucco which covers the original frame building is of a later date, St. Andrew's Church has been little altered from the time it was built. It is the only church in Oakville which survives in its original form, and is a charming example of the churches of Colonial design which were built in the western section of the province.

The Church of England in Canada, whose missionary work was financed from the parent country, found greater difficulty than other denominations in providing missionaries to work in the colony. An appeal for funds made by Charles Stewart, Bishop of Quebec, when visiting England, brought about the formation of the Upper Canada Travelling Mission Fund, called the "Stewart Missions" in honour of the Bishop. To provide information on the state of religion in the mission fields, and to encourage subscription to the funds, reports were published which included letters from missionaries in Canada. Among these are the letters written by the Reverend Thomas Greene, whose headquarters were at Wellington Square. Mr. Greene had begun work in the section between Toronto and Hamilton in 1836, but it was not until three years later that he came to Oakville. The first communion to be held in the village by a missionary of the Church of England is thus described by Mr. Greene:

Aug. 12th. [1839] On Wednesday last I went by appointment to the Town of Oakville, where I found a very large and respectable Congregation assembled, although the harvest had commenced. The singing was excellent, and all the responses were made with fervour and devotion. An unction from on high seemed indeed to pervade the whole assembly. It was really a very striking and impressive sight. Everything around us seemed calculated to produce solemnity of feeling, a bright blue sky over our heads—the Lake with its placid waters, brightened by the summer sun, lay spread out before us—at a little distance behind us was an intensive wood, waving ever and anon its shadowy branches, in all their beautiful variety of foliage, as each succeeding breeze sighed gently among the leaves. . . . From all I could learn, I have reason to believe that there is scarcely a single member of the Church in this place who has had an

1. The *Britannia*

2. Gable of the Temperance Hall

3. The Methodist Chapel, later St. Jude's Church

4. Dr. William Tassie

5. Reverend George Winter Warr

6. A Weller stage-coach

7. Colonel William Chisholm

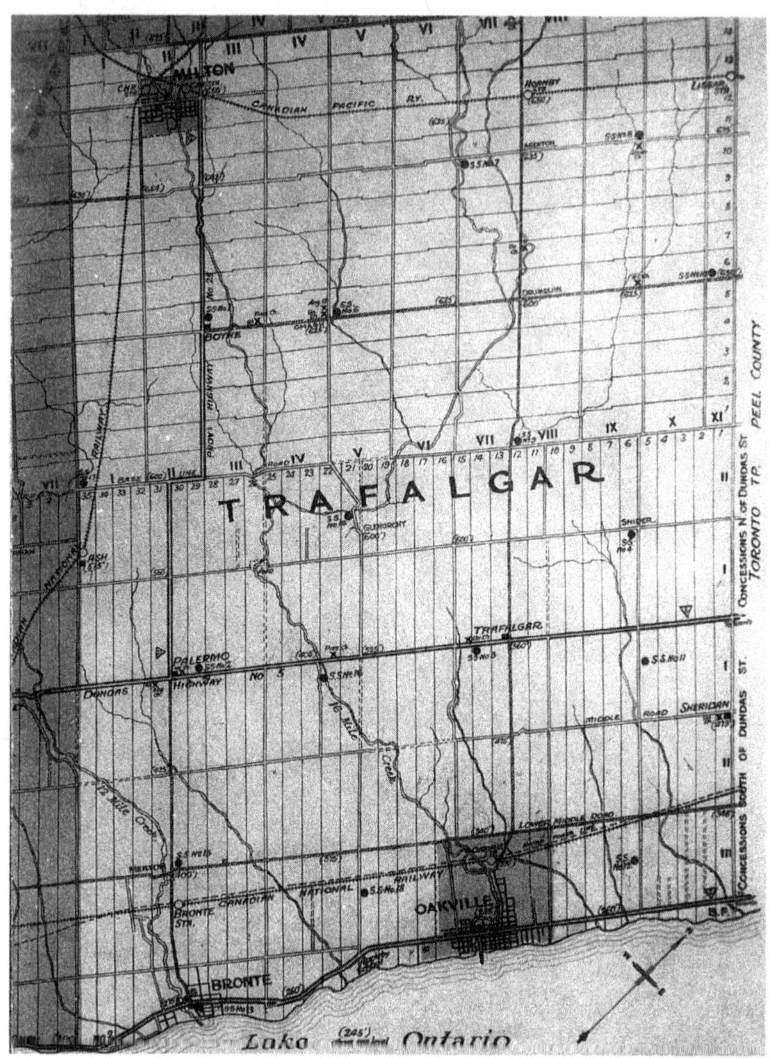

8. Map of Trafalgar Township, Halton County. Oakville now extends over all of Trafalgar Township (including Bronte but not including Milton), an area of 10 miles by 15 miles. Toronto Township on the east and Nelson Township on the west have suffered the same fate, the former having lost its identity in the newly formed Mississauga and the latter in Burlington. The old names now appear only in land records.

opportunity, since their arrival in the country, of partaking of the Lord's Supper; although many had been resident from three to six years, and some of them from ten to twelve.[48]

Subsequently Mr. Greene learned that he was the first missionary of his denomination "who had ever administered the Holy Sacrament in that vicinity."[49] On September 8, after holding a service "at the Square," Mr. Greene again visited Oakville, "and found a very large congregation assembled in the Methodist Church, which was kindly offered by a Canadian Wesleyan. After Service I administered the Sacrament, my communicants were all females—a circumstance which I attribute to their extreme ignorance (the result of their neglected condition) which everywhere prevails in the bush."[50]

The Reverend Thomas Greene was the first of a long line of graduates of Trinity College, Dublin, who were to become rectors of the Church of England at Oakville. Sent out under the Travelling Mission Fund he reached Quebec late in 1835, where he was the guest of Bishop Stewart. After being ordained by the Bishop he came to Upper Canada, where he travelled widely through the Gore District. He settled at Port Nelson after his marriage to a sister of the Honourable Robert Killaly of the Royal Engineers. His wife, who had come to Canada with her brother, was fortunate in having the means to acquire a large property on the lake shore at Port Nelson. Her fondness for the wild briar indigenous to the country led her to plant many of these pink roses around her house, which was called "Roseland."[51]

St. Luke's Church at Wellington Square was opened for services in 1839, and for forty years Mr. Greene was its rector. Indians in the neighbourhood applied to him their usual term for missionaries, "the Black Coat." Mr. Greene always called himself a Stewart Missionary.

Immigration was bringing to Oakville many English and North of Ireland families who were members of the Established Church. Realizing that the village was well situated and would grow into an important centre, Bishop Strachan seized the opportunity to secure the attractive little Methodist chapel for the Church of England. In 1841 the chapel became the Oakville Mission of the United Church of England and Ireland in Canada. The land in the rear of the church (east half of lot C, block 5) was purchased "for the site of a Burial Ground." The deed is of interest because of its wording. After describing the land, it continues "Together with All and Singular the Houses Outhouses Churches Buildings Woods Watercourses Easements Privileges Profits Hereditaments and Appurtenanes whatsoever to the said parcel or tract of Land."[52] Bishop Strachan appointed a resident clergyman to the Oakville Mission, the Reverend George Winter Warr, an Irishman and former Methodist preacher who came from Dublin to Canada in 1842.[53] Ordained by Bishop Strachan, he studied for priest's orders under Mr. Greene at Port Nelson while ministering to the congregation at Oakville. At this period the Church was ready to enlist the services of a man willing to undertake missionary work no matter how unprepared he might be. Mr. Warr, who began his ministry in the summer of 1842, was tall, personable, and well knit. It was through his efforts that missions were established at Palermo on the Dundas Street to the west, and at Hornby on the 7th Line to the north of Oakville.[54]

The Anglican Church throve and prospered. Indeed it seems to have been the only denomination in Oakville which succeeded in avoiding any serious financial difficulties.

By the 1840's the Congregationalists were gathering strength in Oakville. Their pastor, the Reverend Ireland Denney, who had come from England in 1835, preferred to use the term Independent.[55] Congregationalism had sprung from the Independent Puritan sect during Cromwell's time. In Canada Congregationalists had close American affiliations.

In 1842 the Congregationalists in Oakville were in circumstances to maintain a chapel. The trustees—Absolom Smith, Jacob Snider, Peter Kenney (all of American origin), John Roach, James and Joseph Clark, and Hiram Denney[56]—purchased from William Walker and the Forsyths the land on the north-west corner of Wilson and John streets (lot 1, block 59) on the west side of the village. Here a frame building "capable of holding one hundred and fifty persons"[57] was constructed by John Potter.[58] The interior of the chapel was never completed, however, and the members of the congregation became involved in financial difficulties which resulted in the sale of the chapel to the Methodist Episcopal Church. The Reverend Ireland Denney moved to the northern section of the township, and was replaced as minister by his relative, Hiram Denney. Thereafter the sect fell into oblivion in Oakville so completely that its existence in the town would have remained unsuspected were it not for references in sundry early records.

The spreading influence of the Sabbath School movement was early felt in Oakville. The school served the useful purpose of bringing together on terms of equality children of all classes, and of kindling an interest in such elementary subjects as reading and writing. Moreover, being non-sectarian and open to all, the Sabbath School promoted the idea of free education. Justus Williams and his wife had established the first Sabbath School in the vicinity of Burlington Plains (modern Aldershot), and set to work to organize a school as soon as they settled in Oakville.[59] Thus the Union Sabbath School, founded in 1833, was connected with the Methodists and was conducted in the meeting-house. According to the report of the Presbyterian minister (see page 99) the school had eighty pupils and was in a flourishing condition by 1834. As early as 1839, notices were appearing in the Methodist newspaper, the *Christian Guardian*, of Sabbath School excursions by steamer to Niagara Falls. The classes of the non-sectarian Union Sabbath School continued to be held in the meeting-house until the congregations, as they acquired places of worship, took over the support of a school as a denominational activity. By 1870 they were being called Sunday Schools.[60]

In Oakville the religious organizations under American influence were unable to withstand the pressure of the unsympathetic viewpoint of immigrants from Britain. The Methodists, the largest body in Oakville in the early years, had close connections with American Methodism, and with few exceptions the first members of the Methodist congregation at Oakville were of American origin: Justus Williams, the McCraneys, Leaches, Sovereigns, Andersons, Youngs, Labarres, Kenneys, and others.[61] The position of the Methodists was greatly weakened by conflict which split the congregation into Canadian and American *versus* English Wesleyans even before the dissolution in 1840 of the union of 1832. By 1840 Methodism had ceased to be the predominating religious influence in the village that it had been formerly, and that it continued to be in the township. Immigration had strengthened the Roman Catholic and Scottish Presbyterian congregations at Oakville and had made the Church of England the strongest denomination in the village. The immigrants of the upper classes from Northern Ireland were predominantly members of the Church of England. The Denominational Census shows that by 1840 the resident population of Oakvile was about 34 per cent Church of England, 20 per cent Church of Scotland, and 15 per cent Roman Catholic, the remaining 30 per cent consisting of Methodists, Congregationalists, and "no denomination."[62] Though the last to organize, the Anglicans had contrived to secure and maintain a place of worship and a resident clergyman, both within two years of the first visit of a missionary of the Church of England. There is reason to believe that a good proportion of the residents were so-called "old country gentlemen" of some means and education. As in the province of Upper Canada as a whole, the Church of England gained the support of and became identified with the upper class colonial society. It would therefore seem that the Toryism and set class distinctions, so characteristic of Oakville at a later date, which segregated it from the surrounding district, existed almost from the beginning.

II

In Upper Canada secular education depended upon the willingness and co-operation of the members of each community, and again we find Justus Williams taking the lead in Oakville. Although some headway had been made in obtaining government assistance, the educational system was weighted heavily in favour of the affluent. Under the legislation in force when Oakville was founded, townships, towns, or villages whose inhabitants united to build a schoolhouse and pay part of a teacher's salary, and could show a minimum attendance of twenty pupils, were eligible for a grant from the government. The inhabitants could elect three trustees who were authorized to examine the teacher's qualifications, engage or dismiss him, lay out the course of study, select textbooks, and draw up rules for regulating the conduct of the pupils. Since there was no provision for a school tax the money required for maintenance, apart from the small government grant, was met by fees. The rate, fixed by the trustees, customarily ranged between 7*s*.6*d*. and 10*s*. per quarter for each scholar. Schoolmasters received a salary of from £15 to £20 per year. They "boarded round" a week or so at a time with the patrons of the school in proportion to the number of pupils they sent, and often helped with morning and evening chores. Because of the pitifully small salaries, the instructors usually were men who were incapacitated or too old to do any other type of work. A broken-down pensioner, "ancient tippler," or, in fact, anyone who could satisfy the trustees as to his learning could become a schoolmaster.[63]

Secondary schools had long received government assistance. Each district had its grammar school, under government direction, which offered advanced courses. They were essentially classical schools for the well-to-do, and Latin and Greek took precedence over other subjects. At the Gore District Grammar School at Hamilton there were in attendance in 1828 sixty-five pupils ranging in age up to thirty years.[64] This number may seem small when the size of the Gore District is considered, but it becomes less surprising when we learn that a decade later the proportion of children in Upper Canada who received an elementary education was about one in twenty-four. This average was worse than Ireland's with one in eighteen, or of the slave state of Kentucky, with one in twenty-one.[65]

The record of Oakville's first school, the Oakville Common School, begins in 1836. Indications are that conditions in it were far better than those of rural log schools. For one thing, the trustees, of whom Justus Williams was one, engaged as the first schoolmaster William Tassie, a man subsequently to be renowned as an educator. He was of Scottish descent, but had been born in Dublin and educated there. When he migrated to Upper Canada in 1834 he went to Nelson Township where he may have gained his first experience as a teacher. When engaged by the trustees at Oakville, Tassie was a tall handsome man twenty-one years of age, who "believed in the rod as did all Old Country teachers."[66] Moreover the neat frame building of the meeting-house, which was used as a schoolhouse, was an advantage over the structure of rough logs usual for schools at the period. Under the low windows on three sides of the room were ranged desks of slanted boards suspended on hinges which could be let down when religious services were held. (During the week the pulpit was relegated to a corner of the room.) Only those who were being taught penmanship used the desks. For other lessons children sat on long benches facing the master's desk, each pupil's equipment consisting of a slate, pencil, and the odd book.

The schoolmaster's work was confined to the teaching of the three R's to three grades of students: those who were learning the alphabet, those who could read the primer, and those who had progressed as far as the Bible. As the teaching aimed at giving the pupils the skills of literacy, the appeal was essentially to the memory. In arithmetic the pupils memorized number combinations, tables, and rules, and later solved problems by their mechanical application. Lessons were accompanied by little if any explanation, and mostly recited in unison. At least two hours daily were devoted to writing, and much of the schoolmaster's time was spent in preparing quill pens, ruling loose sheets of paper, and "setting copies." The instructor was actually more school-keeper than schoolmaster. The trustees drew up the rules of conduct for the school:

1 School to be opened at 9 o'clock A.M. and an intermission for fifteen minutes at ½ past Ten, and to be dismissed at 12 o'clock noon—to be called in at 2 o'clock P.M. an intermission for fifteen minutes at ½ past 3 P.M. and dismissed at 5 o'clock P.M.

2 Due regard to cleanliness, and the avoiding of all infectious diseases among the children in School such as the Itch and Whouping Cough &c—

3^d^ The Pupils to be strictly required to observe good order at the intermission and noon hours, to avoid all screaming and useless noises, quarelling &c—

4th Good fires to be kept during all wet and damp days—

5 As all children from their cradle are possessed by enquiring minds, that proper attention be given to all enquiries they may make relative to education in mildness, with an approbation of their conduct in so doing.

6 That swearing, calling of bad names be strictly forbidden.

7 That punctuality in attendance on the regular School hours be particularly required by the Teacher, and also that his example in so doing be a sufficient warning to them—

8th That all pupils in the School do not be allowed to whisper and laugh during the School hours, and but one allowed to be out of School at a time, and not then without the consent of the Teacher

9th That the Teacher be required to take a parental as well as pedagogical care over all pupils placed under his tuition.

10th That the teacher require each subscriber to the School to furnish his quota of firewood for the season and have it cut and properly piled for the use of the Stove in said School room.

Some other minor laws are actually necessary which should be discretionary with the Teacher by and with the advice and consent of the Trustees.

The original transcription of these rules and regulations made by Justus Williams, together with the first desk which stood in the schoolhouse and Tassie's "Quarterly report of the Oakville common school from Decr 12th 1836 to March 12th 1837; shewing the progress, attendance, &c of the pupils receiving instructions therein" are on exhibit at the Old Post Office Museum.

It is reasonable to suppose that the pupils of the Oakville Common School used books that were in general use throughout the township: Mavor's Spelling Book, Morse's Geography, and either Dabol's or Walkingame's Arithmetic.[67] *The American Geography* by Jedediah Morse (father of Samuel F. B. Morse, inventor of a telegraph and the

Morse Code) was first published in 1794 and revised in 1825. Its maps are exquisitely engraved, but almost no space is devoted to the Canadas, and the work was severely criticized as being anti-British. In fact, the majority of textbooks were American, and in sentiment and idiom, anti-British. Critics claimed that in history children were being taught false accounts of the late war, in geography that cities of the United States were represented as the largest and the finest in the world, and so on. The use of American spellers, grammars, and dictionaries undoubtedly accounts for the large number of American terms which were replacing British terms in general usage: druggist for apothecary; store for shop; hotel for inn; railroad for railway; shipbuilder for shipwright; teacher for schoolmaster; and principal for headmaster, a few examples among many.

Francis Walkingame's *The Tutor's Assistant, a practical Arithmetic,* published in London, contains a familiar verse:

> The days are thirty in September,
> In April, June and November,
> Twenty-eight in February alone,
> But every leap year we assign
> To February twenty-nine.

One of the exciting school events of the period was the spelling-match. On the day appointed many parents and spectators gathered, bringing apples, doughnuts, or maybe a barrel of cider. The most rigid silence was observed as words were pronounced and spelled alternately by the two teams. Sometimes after the vocabulary of the spelling book was exhausted recourse would be had to dictionary or Bible, and any differences of opinion as to the victor were settled later, with fists, behind the schoolhouse.

A favourite pastime with several generations of children who attended the school was excavating in the playground, frequently with excellent results, for Indian bones and artifacts. Another was digging under the foundations of the building which stood so close to the top of the bank that there was always the hope that it might be pushed over into the marsh.[68]

The community looked to the schoolmaster for leadership in adult forms of education, and judging from the *Observer*'s report Tassie would seem to have lost little time in taking a leading place in the life of the village. "For months a debating society has afforded amusement to many persons during the winter evenings, and in the establishment of a Public Reading-room, which we hope will lead to the formation of a Public Library. We feel satisfied that we may conclude

. . . by pronouncing that both Oakville and its inhabitants are 'going ahead.' "[69]

The library when it finally did materialize was given by a Wesleyan Methodist organization which had seriously undertaken to provide libraries for Sabbath Schools. Twenty-four libraries, each containing one hundred books, were ordered from the London Religious Tract Society; the first ten arrived in 1839. The society's report shows that one of these libraries was sent "to form a Village Library at Oakville." In his biography of Jesse Ketchum, who was much interested in this project, E. J. Hathaway remarks that the library "for the village of Oakville was probably the first public library in Upper Canada."[70] All researches directed towards learning more of this matter have proved fruitless.

After about three years at Oakville, William Tassie went to Hamilton where he taught for fourteen years, at the same time studying for a master's degree at the University of Toronto. He was appointed in 1853 headmaster of the Gore District Grammar School at Galt, which thereafter was popularly known as Dr. Tassie's Grammar School. This was the second grammar school to be established in the Gore District. It was founded about 1844 at Palermo, Trafalgar Township, and Andrew Hall was headmaster. For some reason, probably the decline rather than the increase in population, and regardless of numerous petitions of protest addressed to the Lieutenant-Governor, it was "decided to remove the Palermo Grammar School to Galt" in 1850.[71] Next to Upper Canada College Dr. Tassie's was considered the best secondary school in the province. To it came boys from all parts of Canada and from distant places in the United States; it was thus more than merely a local institution.[72] In 1871 William Tassie was made an LL.D. of Queen's University, Kingston. After twenty-eight years at Galt he resigned his position and became headmaster of the Collegiate Institute at Peterborough where he died in 1886.

Tassie's successor at Oakville was a stout genial gentleman who was well liked by both parents and pupils, C. G. Friend, who lived east of the 8th Line of the Lake Shore Road (lot 9, 4th concession). That is the extent of our knowledge of Mr. Friend. Nor have we any knowledge of the next schoolmaster, John Cook, except that there were under his care in 1841, "seven males and eleven females."[73]

By this time the Reverend Robert Murray and his intimate friends were becoming influential in the educational affairs of the province. Mr. Murray was much interested in social and educational problems, and having attended the University of Glasgow he found much to criticize in the system then existing in the province. He must frequently have discussed the subject with his friends, Dr. James Hopkirk, his next-door neighbour on the lake shore at Oakville, and Samuel Bealey Harrison. Hopkirk was a Scottish advocate who had come to Oakville about the same time as Murray, and with one Watson established the brewery and distillery. Harrison was well known in England as barrister and jurist. He had come to Upper Canada with the intention of farming, and in 1837 bought a section of the former Missisauga Indian Reserve at the Twelve Mile Creek north of Bronte. Here he built a grist and sawmill.[74] Harrison had been in the province only a short time before he began to interest himself in educational matters. His talents were enlisted by the government when he was appointed secretary to the Lieutenant-Governor, Sir George Arthur, and he was one of three commissioners appointed in 1839 to enquire into the state of education in Upper Canada with a view to improvement and extension of educational facilities. Hopkirk received the appointment of secretary to the commission. Seeking the opinions of men of experience, the commission circulated a questionnaire, to which some of the answers were severe in their criticism of the backward state of education in the province. Of those published, the letter of Robert Murray contains the severest evaluation, and it stands alone in setting forth suggestions as to how the situation may be remedied.[75] Murray wrote that he did not consider "the present provision for Education in the Province at all adequate to its wants." He continues:

> I consider it to be deficient in toto; but more particularly—
> 1st. The manner of electing Teachers to Common Schools appears to be an insult to common sense. Three individuals as trustees or superintendents, are appointed by the people in the neighbourhood of the school house, without regard to their education; these three men . . . have the sole power to judge of the qualifications of candidates for the school, and to appoint and eject the Teacher, while they themselves may not have received even the first rudiments of a plain English Education. Such men are . . . unfit to judge either the qualifications of a schoolmaster or of the progress of the pupils.
> 2nd. The power of ejecting schoolmasters vested in three trustees . . . the teacher is thus left at the mercy of the public, who proverbially have no conscience, and his situation is rendered more precarious and degraded than that of a shoeblack.[76]

Murray believed in an idea not generally acceptable at the period: that "the number of schools should be adequate to the accommodation of the entire youth of the Province" from six to fifteen years of age.

He advocated a more adequate Board of Education, uniform textbooks picked by the board, that each district determine the rate of pay of schoolmasters, and that provision be made in each school for a few free pupils. These and many more were his suggestions, made in the closing weeks of 1839. Two years later Upper and Lower Canada were united into the Province of Canada, and the former became Canada West. Lord Sydenham chose S. B. Harrison as his Provincial Secretary in Canada West (popularly known as "Mr. Secretary, West") and Hopkirk as his assistant ("Assistant, Secretary West"). Both removed to the seat of the government at Kingston. Within a few months' time Harrison put a motion to the House of Assembly "to make provision for the Establishment and Maintenance of Common Schools throughout the Province," and a few months later the Common School Act of 1841, sponsored by him, was passed.

There is no place in this history for a discussion of Murray's recommendations as related to the numerous provisions of the Common School Act. Suffice it to say that the influence of his opinions is reflected in this legislation. The statute created a storm of protest in the House, was called "liberal without precedent" and labelled republican and democratic, but it fell far short of what Murray could have wished. Nevertheless, the new Common School Act was an important milestone in the history of education in Canada. It was the first attempt to introduce a uniform system for all elementary schools in the province, and to shift their financing from private to public responsibility. A permanent school fund was established in each township, and the Trafalgar Township Council was made responsible for raising through taxation a sum of money equivalent to the government grant (considerably increased) for the support of its schools. In addition to the assessment a school fee of 1*s*.3*d*. per month was levied on each child of school age irrespective of school attendance. For the first time schools in the township had a permanent source of income. Each school received a number; the Oakville Common School became School Section No. 14, Trafalgar Township.[77]

The post of Superintendent of Education for Upper Canada had been held for many years by Bishop Strachan. Upon the union of the provinces this office was held by the respective provincial secretaries, and thus the Honourable S. B. Harrison became Superintendent of Education for Canada West. The actual work, however, was handled by an assistant, and to fill this position the Reverend Robert Murray was sponsored by William Chisholm. Representations were made to the Lieutenant-Governor in favour of Murray by his sponsor, who forwarded testimonials signed by Sir Allan MacNab, Dr. Hopkirk, and a number of prominent residents of the Gore District.[78] In May, 1842, Murray was appointed Chief Superintendent or, as he was officially designated, Assistant Superintendent of Education for Canada West.[79]

Upon the announcement of this appointment the inhabitants of Oakville held a public meeting at which resolutions were passed and an address outlined. It had been intended to invite Murray to a public dinner previous to his departure to Kingston, but "the gloom spread over the inhabitants, by the death of Col. William Chisholm afterwards caused the resolution to be abandoned."[80] The address was presented to Mr. and Mrs. Murray by George Chalmers, a prominent member of the Presbyterian congregation at the Sixteen Village, accompanied by a large deputation. Murray replied at length, saying in conclusion:

> Your approval of my ministerial character and labours at Oakville, I value next to my own conscience; and although my sphere of labour is now extended, and the nature of my duties greatly changed, yet I sincerely trust that my exertions to promote the best interests of all, will be found beneficial to you.
>
> With every kind wish for the prosperity of Oakville, and its vicinity, in which I shall ever feel a deep interest, I fervently commend you to His protection, who can shield you in every danger, and comfort you in every trial.[81]

Soon after the Murrays moved to Kingston.

Murray's task as Superintendent of Education was not light, and it soon became apparent that many features of the School Act were unworkable. In its framing, too little consideration had been given to racial and religious differences of the people in the reunited provinces. Authority was vested in District Boards of Education whose members, elected yearly, were more proficient in politics than in learning and Murray's authority was restricted to the making of recommendations The discouragement he felt is evident in his first report to the government. He wrote: "All hope of establishing any uniform system of education is utterly vain. By the present method, more than three hundred different systems of education might be in operation in Canada West, changing every year, and how these can be harmonized, and reduced into one uniform system by the suggestion of an individual who has no power to enforce improvement . . . is altogether unintelligible. To bring about the result desirable, would not only require a person of judgement and discretion, but also that his hands should be strengthened by the strong arm of the law."[82]

Murray's letters show that he hoped that new legislation passed in 1843 would enable him to carry out more extensive improvements; instead of this the Act abolished the office of Assistant Superintendent and the duties relating thereto were transferred to the Provincial Secretary. Murray continued as the Secretary's representative with authority to handle all matters pertaining to education. However, no provision was made for him to have even a clerk, and he was forced to attend personally to all correspondence, submitting drafts of letters to the Provincial Secretary for his approval. At the end of two years Murray resigned his office to which Dr. Egerton Ryerson succeeded, and accepted the Chair of Mathematics and Natural Philosophy at King's College[83] which had opened the previous year, 1843. Six years later King's College became the University of Toronto.

Robert Murray has been described as "a gentle-spirited scholar who was out of place in this period of storm and stress in Canadian education."[84] R. B. Sullivan, in a letter to his friend, William Chisholm, emphasized another angle when he wrote: "A new Scotch teacher and minister is not the most likely to carry on a harmonious system of general education for Episcopalians, Catholics, Methodists, etc."[85] What Sullivan probably had in mind but hesitated to express was that Murray had become embroiled with the Methodists, especially Dr. Ryerson, on the subject of temperance when his lectures appeared in print. A fondness for good living is suggested in the couplet current among Murray's students at the University:

> Here's to the professor of dull mathematics
> He knows more about steaks than he does about statics.[86]

The work of Robert Murray as Superintendent of Education for Canada West has not been accorded the recognition it merits. Ryerson's reputation in the field of education completely overshadowed that of his predecessor. Esteemed as the "founder of the elementary school system of the province," Ryerson is generally considered to have been the first to hold the office of Superintendent of Education. While no comparison between the two men is intended, the fact remains that the contributions made by Murray before Ryerson stepped into his place deserve more than the indifferent treatment they have received in works on education in Canada. The time was not ripe for the adoption of Murray's advanced ideas. Though it may not truthfully be said that he "paved the way," the row of solid stepping stones Murray set was used to advantage by his successor, who had excellent opportunity to view from afar the mistakes that had been and were being made. Ryerson demanded and was given full authority, together with two years in which to travel extensively to study educational systems in twenty countries. Upon returning home he had a hand in framing the legislation which assisted him to set up in the province the system which to the present day has proved an outstanding success.

During the years at the University Murray returned frequently to Oakville to perform marriages and baptisms, and his name was given to several children born at that period. One of his namesakes is well remembered by persons living today. Robert Murray Thomas, son of Merrick Thomas, born in 1846, had the misfortune to be a deaf mute, but overcame his handicap sufficiently to become a teacher of deaf mutes. Murray Thomas was an exceptionally cheerful man who lived a very active life in the community until his death in 1931 at the age of eighty-five.

Of Murray's friend, Dr. Hopkirk, we lose trace after he left Oakville in the forties. S. B. Harrison resigned from the government when elevated to the Bench in 1843 and moved from Bronte to Dundas Street, Toronto. Where Harrison and Foxley streets now run was a cedar swamp which he drained and among full grown cedars he created a beautiful natural garden, calling it Foxley Grove.[87] Of this ruddy jovial man Dr. Scadding wrote: "The memory of Judge Harrison as an English Gentleman, genial, frank, straightforward, is cherished among his surviving contemporaries."[88]

The Reverend Robert Murray continued as professor at the University of Toronto until his health declined and in the spring of 1853 he died at Port Albert on Lake Huron north of Goderich.

CHAPTER FOUR

CONTACTS WITH THE WORLD BEYOND

FOR SIX YEARS after its founding Oakville was as isolated as most Upper Canadian villages of the time. But this isolation ended abruptly in the spring of 1833 with the inauguration of regular transportation services on both land and water. With the establishment of a post office two and one-half years later, the village had mail service the year round. And to these attributes of progress a fourth was soon added: Oakville's first newspaper, the *Observer*.

The earliest steamer to ply the head of Lake Ontario regularly between Hamilton, York, and ports on the south shore in the United States was the *Constitution*, built and launched in The Sixteen. The true forerunner of the steamship was the horseboat of which several were in operation on the Niagara River at Queenston and Fort Erie as early as 1793. After the steam engine was combined with the paddle-wheel the first vessel of the new type to be built in the Canadas was the *Accommodation*, launched at Montreal by John Molson in 1809, three years after Fulton's experiment on the Hudson River. The *Accommodation*'s engines, generating six horse-power, propelled her at a speed of five miles an hour. A steamer launched on the American shore of Lake Erie two years later was given the charming name of *Walk-in-the-Water* in honour of an Indian chief. When she entered the Detroit River on her first voyage a French farmer on the Canadian shore rushed out of his house crying, "Look at the river! What are these Yankees sending us now but a sawmill!"[1] The first steamship to make the Atlantic crossing was the *Royal William*, built at Quebec and manned by Canadians. In 1833 she sailed from Halifax, and nineteen days later steamed triumphantly into the Thames. And the same year which marked this historic event saw the launch at Oakville of the *Constitution* in the waters of The Sixteen.

The lack of steamer service to and from the head of the lake had been the subject of a public meeting called at Hamilton in 1831 "to consult on the expediency of building a Steam vessel to ply between Burlington Bay, York and Niagara, the Genessee and the Oswego Rivers, the last two named places being the entrance to the Erie Canal and the city of Rochester." At the meeting, of which William Chisholm was chairman, it was decided that "more speedy intercourse was needed to be established between Burlington Bay and the Capital of the Province"; and that therefore a vessel of sufficient dimensions to carry both passengers and freight should be constructed.[2] The joint stock company formed to carry out the project offered shares at £25 each to the public. Tenders were invited, and the contract for building the steamship was awarded to Chisholm. Under the supervision of a master builder named Hathaway the work progressed in the shipyard at Oakville, and the principal frames were raised in August of 1832.[3]

The vessel, outfitted with the latest equipment, was one of the largest steamboats on the lake at this period. She was of 150 tons burthen, 133 feet in length, and across the beam measured 23 feet. Her bilge timbers were of "Tumeric" (tamarac), half the top timbers of red cedar, and "the body of the best white oak and pine."[4] Her engines of eighty horsepower, obtained at Montreal and brought in by water, were more powerful than usual; most lake steamers were propelled by engines of only about fifty horsepower. The ladies' cabin on deck, rather an innovation, contained thirteen berths and was "furnished in the most superb style." The mens' cabin accommodated twenty-four, with extra cabins in the bow for another fourteen. Furnishings such as chairs and settees were made and upholstered "by Rainey and Schofield of Oakville . . . , and are equal to those manufactured at Buffalo or any other chair manufacturing places."[5] At the outset it had been estimated that £6,000 currency would cover the cost of construction, but this amount proved insufficient, and some delay was caused by the need of raising more funds. However, the vessel was finished within the time specified in the contract, and the launch, of which we unfortunately have no description, took place "at noon precisely" on January 19, 1833.[6]

The name chosen for the steamship was one of particular significance at this time. The clamourings of William Lyon Mackenzie and his followers for governmental reform were regarded by the Tories as an attempt to overthrow constituted authority in Upper Canada. They considered themselves as "devoted to the interest of the Provincial Constitution," and referred to those of their number who were members of the provincial legislature as "the Constitutional Members of the House." The board of directors of the Hamilton Joint Stock Company, all prominent Tories, availed themselves of the opportunity of demonstrating in the name of this steamship their stand on the side of the Government.

Under command of Captain William Critchell, R.N., retired, the *Constitution* made her trial run from Oakville to York in two hours, averaging twelve miles per hour.[7] Not many weeks later the *Montreal Gazette* reported: "On Sunday noon, the new steamboat *Constitution*, lately built at Oakville, made her first appearance in Kingston Harbour on her way to Prescott. She is apparently a very fine vessel, not quite as large as the *St. George* but is supplied with an engine of the same power. She promises to be a useful addition to the number of the Lake boats."[8] During the winter of 1834 various changes were made in the steamer's construction. When ready for service she ran on the following schedule: "She will ply daily between Hamilton and York, touching at Oakville, and divide her time so that persons residing at Hamilton or Oakville may leave home in the morning and return the same day, having at least five hours time to transact business at York. Should sufficient encouragement be given she will continue on the above mentioned route during the season; but if not, when sufficient trial has been made, will change for some other."[9] Apparently the arrangement did prove unsatisfactory for the steamer soon began running to Cobourg and Rochester as well.

For several years the *Constitution*, under the command of Captain Edward Zealand, was the only steamboat plying between Rochester and the head of Lake Ontario. Twice a week, weather permitting, she called at Oakville in the morning on her way to Toronto and in the afternoon on the return trip up the lake to the Port of Hamilton where a carriage waited "in readiness to convey passengers and luggage to any part of the Town of Hamilton."[10] Press notices of this "Splendid Low Pressure Steam Boat" advised that "Emigrants and others, destined for the Western Part of Upper Canada will find it to their advantage to come by way of Rochester and proceed by the *Constitu-*

tion."[11] Goods from the United States could also be forwarded by way of Rochester directly to the head of the lake; among the steamship's many agents was Merrick Thomas at Oakville. Captain Zealand, who had at one stage in his career been master of an ocean-going ship, was formerly master of the schooner *Rebecca and Eliza* and other vessels owned by William Chisholm.

The *Constitution* was sold in 1835 to Captain Hugh Richardson, a well-known pioneer of steam navigation, who promptly changed her name to the *Transit*.[12] Captain Richardson was a colourful personality. The son of a West India merchant, he had gone to sea when fourteen years of age. In 1810 he was captured in the English Channel by a French privateer, and thereafter spent several years in a French prison. Following his release, Richardson migrated to Canada in 1821, and became master of the steam packet *Canada*. In *Toronto of Old* Dr. Scadding tells of Captain Richardson's being accused of refusing other passengers when the Lieutenant-Governor, Sir Peregrine Maitland, engaged passage on the *Canada* between Niagara and York in 1828. "I have to declare the same to be an impudent lie," he wrote indignantly to the *U. E. Loyalist*, concluding with the pronouncement: "Born and bred under a Monarchial Government, educated in the discipline of a British seaman, I have not yet learned the insolence of elbowing a desire (in right, an order) of the Representative of my Sovereign, by an impertinent wish of my own. I have only to say that as long as I command the *Canada*, and have a rag of colour to hoist, my proudest day will be when it floats at her mast-head indicative of the presence and commands of the Representative of my King. Hugh Richardson, Master and Managing owner of the *Canada Steam Packet*." Captain Richardson was most particular, Dr. Scadding continues, that at all times the "established distinctions in society" be observed. "This brought him into collision occasionally with democratically disposed spirits, especially from the opposite side of the Lake; but he did not scruple to maintain his rules by main force when extreme measures were necessary, calling to his aid the stout arms of a trusty crew."[13] Upon retirement Captain Richardson was appointed harbourmaster at Toronto, and when he offered a silk hat to the master who brought the first cargo into the harbour each spring he established a custom which is still followed in the lake ports of Canada.[14]

The *Constitution*, travelling under her new name of *Transit*, became a famous steamer and plied the lake for many years. Sir Richard

Bonnycastle, after asserting that "nothing can exceed the comfort and style" of many of the lake steamers, mentions the *Transit* as being "fitted out with a service of plate and china."

> They very often have music aboard, and in the ladies cabin is a piano. A respectable stewardess waits on the female cabin passengers, who are ushered to dinner etc. by the captain, and take the head of the table.
> In short, everything is very orderly, and very well conducted on board the British steam-boats and, I have no doubt, it is the same on board the Americans, which are very splendid.[15]

Bonnycastle, however, deplored the American custom of mixing alcoholic beverages and calling them by such absurd names as "cocktails," "gin slings," and "mint juleps."

The year following the launch of the first steamer in The Sixteen saw the laying down of another, the 150-ton *Oakville*, which slid into the water at 2 P.M. on May 7, 1834.[16] In August under command of Captain John Mills she "commenced her regular trips from Hamilton to Toronto, touching at Oakville and the Burlington Bay Canal each way."[17] Two years later when Nathaniel Hughson of Hamilton purchased the *Oakville* her name was changed to the *Hamilton*. Still under the command of Captain Mills this steamer continued to ply the lake, touching at Oakville on the way up and down. At a later date she was renamed the *Union*. During the forties her engines were removed and the *Union* ended her days under sail as a barque.[18]

In the winter of 1835-6 the shipyard on The Sixteen was devoted to a project which was to be of importance in improving and maintaining the Oakville harbour. Here was built the first piece of heavy construction machinery driven by steam-power to be used in Upper Canada: the Provincial Steam Dredge or, as it was more generally called, the "P.S.D." During the building of the Welland Canal the dredging equipment was found to be inadequate and American engineers who had worked on the Erie Canal advised the purchase of a steam dredge of the type which had proved successful in that work. For this purpose the House of Assembly appropriated the sum of £1,400 and appointed a commission of three to investigate the matter. A survey disclosed the fact that equipment of such a size was not available in the Canadas and one of the commissioners, Dr. Charles Duncombe, Member for Middlesex, while on an extensive tour of the United States, made inquiries about securing a dredge there. Finding the appropriation insufficient to purchase the complete equipment, he arranged with Lyon and Howard of Albany, New York, to buy the machinery "without either paddle-wheels or lighter for the money named." To speed construction and reduce costs the commissioners decided to have the barge upon which the machinery was to be mounted and six lighters built at Oakville. "Col. Chisholm very generously gave permission for the contractors to use his premises, buildings and timber free of charge, and to afford them opportunity of purchasing sawn and other lumber as they might require at reasonable prices."[19] Accordingly, the machinery was loaded on a barge at Albany and started through the Erie Canal. But winter set in unusually early that year and the barge was frozen in. It therefore became necessary to unload the machinery, transport it 150 miles overland to Oswego, and load it on a lake vessel which brought it to Oakville. It was entered free of import duties, Colonel Chisholm "relinquishing his share of the tolls," and the work of constructing scow and lighters proceeded. Early in March the *Observer* reported: "The Government Steam Dredging Machine is building in our shipyard, under the contract of D. S. Howard, Esquire from the States. This employs many hands during the winter, and if prompt, weekly payment of the men makes no slight addition to our circulating medium."[20]

Mechanically, the performance of this dredging machine was the same as that used in building the harbour, already described, with the exception that the capstan and horses were replaced by a steam engine mounted upon a foundation of brick. In conjunction with the dredge were six lighters, "two to dump from the centre bottom for deep water and four to dump from the sides for shoal water."[21] The final cost amounted to more than twice the original appropriation, but after much heated debate a further sum of £2,000 was voted by the House of Assembly[22] to meet the total amount of £3,400.[23] By the middle of June the P.S.D. was ready for action, and during the try-out on the Oakville harbour it "operated well" and was "found successful."[24] Some weeks later "through the obliging intervention" of Colonel Chisholm, arrangements were made to have the dredge proceed to the Desjardins Canal and complete the terminal basin of this waterway which had been cut through the marshes from the Burlington Bay Canal to the town of Dundas, five miles distant. Shortly after, the Desjardins Canal had its formal opening.[25] Though it fell into disuse after the advent of the railway, the piles outlining it may still be seen in the northern section of Burlington Bay.

The Provincial Steam Dredge was used in constructing other canals and ports along the lake, returning each winter to lay up for repairs at Oakville and to deepen the harbour in the spring. In May of 1838, for instance, the dredge worked twenty-one days on the Oakville harbour before proceeding to other harbours on Lake Ontario.[26] Thus the first piece of heavy construction machinery using steam-power to be employed in Upper Canada was built in The Sixteen and was first used to dredge its harbour. Also, its master for a few years was Jacob Randall of Oakville.

After the completion of the P.S.D., a 150-ton steamer was constructed at the cost of £4,000; when launched in 1837 she was christened the *Burlington*.[27] She ran between Hamilton, Dundas, and Toronto, calling at Oakville three times a week.[28] Her first master was John Gordon, but the year following his place was taken by Robert Kerr, the same who at an earlier date had commanded several of Chisholm's vessels. Kerr was a giant of a man, six foot five in height, and built in proportion, with enormous strength but a quiet disposition. Because of his courtesy he was popular with the travelling public, but on duty he was a strict disciplinarian, allowing no undue familiarity from his chief officer or crew.[29] In the spring of 1840 the *Burlington* was lying at the Government (later the Queen's) Wharf at the foot of Bathurst Street, Toronto, when she caught fire. A rumour was circulated that on board were two barrels of gunpowder. This caused quite a sensation until it was found that the explosive had already been delivered. Before the blaze was conquered by the fire brigade the steamer's decks were destroyed and her engines badly damaged. Eventually, as was true of so many steamships during the nineteenth century, this vessel was completely destroyed by fire.[30]

The *Burlington* was the last steamboat on record built at Oakville by William Chisholm. Shortly after, Jacob Randall in partnership with his brother-in-law, John Jeffery, took over the shipyard on The Sixteen.

Passenger fare for the two-hour run between Oakville and either Toronto or Hamilton was the same: 6*s*.3*d*. cabin class and 3*s*. for deck passengers.[31] The trip from Hamilton to Toronto, taking four hours, cost 10*s*. cabin and 5*s*. deck.[32] The little steamers, all side-wheelers, continued to be equipped with masts and sails so that full advantage could be taken of a favourable wind, the engines being used only to sail against the wind. They consumed enormous quantities of hardwood, which was taken on at every port, piled on the decks, in the engine room, and every available spot on board until the steamers looked like "floating wood piles." All that could be taken aboard sufficed for only a short distance—the fact that the firemen's pay included wood ashes which they sold to potash makers may partly account for the large amounts consumed. Like bunker coal at the present day, wood was taken aboard at every port of call. At Oakville it was piled along the lake bank between Navy and Thomas streets. Every autumn several thousand cords were contracted for with farmers in the district, who brought it in during the winter and stacked it row upon row, making the lake bank a favourite place for the village children's game of hide and seek.

"Wooding up" was a lively business. At the wharf the incoming vessels were met by labourers who stood in wait with loaded wheelbarrows, and the wood, dumped upon the deck, was quickly stowed away. The putting down and taking up of passengers was also accomplished with much bustle and dispatch. When ready to depart the steamer's cannon thundered a salute (a practice which was continued until the advent in the middle forties of the steam whistle upon the lakes) and, chuffing up a column of wood smoke, the steamer was off to her next port of call. Usually the steamboats were owned in part if not entirely by their masters, and competition was severe among vessels engaged in traffic on the lake, increasing in proportion to their numbers. As the first ship in port took on all passengers and freight, the race to outstrip each other at times grew frantic, and some captains showed little regard for the safety of either vessel or passengers.

A speedy steamer of the same tonnage as the *Constitution* was the *Traveller*, which was built on the Clyde, shipped to Canada in sections, and assembled at Montreal.[33] Her master, Captain James Sutherland, had navigated the first steamship to cross the Atlantic from Britain to Quebec, the *Unicorn*. After spending some time in the Hudson's Bay service he was placed in command of the new steamship *Traveller* which called regularly at Oakville.[34] In April, 1836, when his ship was the first to venture out into Lake Ontario, Sutherland and his passengers had a unique experience. Starting from Niagara, the *Traveller* forced her way through fifteen miles of ice two inches thick. "When about the middle of the Lake," reported the Toronto *Courier*, "it was considered necessary to examine the vessel, to ascertain if she was sustaining any damage. During the stop . . . the passengers and Captain left the boat and went upon the ice," where they walked around for half an hour. "We understand this to be an unprecedented circumstance," continues the *Courier*, "as far as has been ascertained as to the state of our Lake in winter." And the editor adds that were it not for the integrity of Captain Sutherland the story would not have been credited.[35]

By 1836 the volume of marine traffic between the piers had become so great as to render essential the services of a lighthouse at Oakville. A petition to which ninety-six names were affixed was addressed to the

House of Assembly, praying for financial aid in its construction. A loan of £500 was granted by the House to William Chisholm[36] and on April 6 of the following year the *Upper Canada Gazette* announced that his Excellency the Lieutenant-Governor had been pleased to appoint Chisholm, George Chalmers, and Merrick Thomas commissioners for the erection of a lighthouse at Oakville.[37] Soon these commissioners reported that they had "advised with several of the Masters of Vessels, respecting the proper place to erect a Lighthouse, and after due consideration, the end of the Pier was decided upon. To make the foundation sufficient it was found necessary to sink three additional cribs."[38]

The work was started in August, 1836, and by November, 1837, the lighthouse was completed at a total cost of £852; the amount in excess of the government loan (£352) was met by Chisholm.[39] Built of wood, the lighthouse was octagonal in shape, and stood thirty-six feet from the level of the pier to its top. The height from the level of the water is specified as having been forty-two feet, which shows the pier, when built, to have been six feet above the water line. The light was a fixed oil lamp with colourless glass and reflector on the "catoptric principle," having the visibility of "eleven miles in clear weather."[40] (Over a hundred years later, in 1947, the Department of Transport reported the Oakville light as being "visible for eleven miles in clear weather.") In their final report to the government the commissioners stated in conclusion: "The Commissioners would respectfully beg leave to state, that having thus closed their proceedings, are of the opinion, that the Light-house at Oakville is inferior to none on Lake Ontario, and trust that the duty assigned to them has been discharged in a manner that may be found satisfactory."[41]

About this time two new steamers made their appearance in the harbour: the 150-ton *Experiment* and the *Gore*, which called at Oakville three times a week.[42] For many years the master of the *Experiment* was Captain Thomas Dick who, upon retirement, built and owned that landmark in Toronto, the Queen's Hotel. In 1840 the *Burlington, Gore*, and *Britannia* formed a line running between Rochester and ports on the north shore of Lake Ontario,[43] and another steamer, the *Eclipse*, was built especially for the Toronto-Hamilton route. When launched in 1842 she had been christened the *Commerce*, but having succeeded in bettering the time of the steamer holding the speed record on the lake, she was renamed *Eclipse*.[44] It was at this period that the new screw propeller which was eventually to replace the paddle-wheels made its appearance on the lakes.

HAMILTON AND YORK
STAGES.

II

The roads in Upper Canada being what they were, they could be travelled for any distance only in winter. Wrote Joseph Pickering: "The winter is the most lively part of the year: when there is about four inches of snow with frost, sleighing is universal, for business and pleasure, from one end of the Province to the other. A span of good horses conveys two or three persons in a sleigh forty or fifty miles a day, with ease and they often go sixty and seventy. With warm clothing, a fur cap, and a bear or buffalo skin over the back and feet, it is a pleasant way of travelling, enlivened by the numerous sleighs and the jingling of bells which the horses are required to wear; in this season many of the Canadians have quite a military appearance."[45]

During the 1820's stage lines were run by various proprietors along the Dundas Street between York and Hamilton. In 1831 a line was operated on this route by the innkeeper at the Etobicoke Creek, James Boyce. His stage-coaches halted at Philip Buck's tavern in Trafalgar Township and at the Grove Inn of W. J. Sumner in Nelson.[46] Boyce informed the public that he expected the lake road to be open soon; he hoped that a sufficient proportion of the funds recently appropriated by the House of Assembly would be allotted "to the great road leading from the Head of the Lake to York, rendering it one of the pleasantest stage routes in the Canadas."[47] From this announcement we learn that the fare of 13*s*.9*d*. currency allowed each passenger thirty-six pounds of luggage. However, it was not until the spring of 1833 that Boyce's Telegraph Coach began running along the Lake Shore Road. Scheduled to leave Hamilton or York on alternate days at 8 A.M. it arrived at Oakville around 2 P.M. and at its final destination of York or Hamilton at 8 P.M.[48] The woodcut heading Boyce's schedules is shown above. In 1835 we find the Telegraph Line being operated by William Weller, who later became the well-known proprietor of extensive stage-coach lines. Weller contracted to carry passengers and freight "through in daylight, on the Lake Road, during the winter season."[49] At Toronto the headquarters were situated in the gore at the junction of Front, Wellington, and Church streets known as the "Coffin Block." The corner entrance was accessible from three streets, and it was a busy place with stages continually arriving and departing.[50] The stages, mounted on runners and drawn by four horses, held about nine passengers. Along the sides, to keep out the weather, hung leather curtains which were rolled up and strapped to the roof when not in use. "The old Canadian coach," wrote Bonnycastle in 1846, "has not yet quite vanished before modern improvement. It is a mighty clumsy conveniency, hung on leather springs, and looking for all the world as if elephants alone could move it along."[51] Passengers were frequently called upon to walk up hills to ease the horses, or to assist in extricating the coach from deep mud-holes with poles borrowed from snake (or zigzag) fences along the road. Horses were changed at Half-way House, about a mile east of Oakville, the inn of Barnet Griggs, where relays of horses were kept.

Barnet Griggs and his brother George, residents of New Jersey, had been pursuaded to follow many of their Loyalist friends to Upper Canada in 1811. Barnet and his wife Nancy made the journey on horseback, a grandfather's clock strapped to the side of one of their horses. He bought from the Loyalist grantee, Joseph Bradt junior, lot 6 of the 3rd concession of Trafalgar Township. While their house was building he lived with his wife in a log house they found there, whose doorway was flanked by two young pear trees, and which overlooked the stream that passes through the south-west corner of the land. George Griggs settled on lot 10 of the 4th concession, where he built the house now owned by J. Douglas Peck.

When the states of Michigan and Illinois were being settled many migrating families from New York passed this way, and found a night's lodging with Barnet Griggs. The word that he had accommodation for travellers soon spread, with the result that the number of travellers knocking at his door induced him to enlarge his house into an inn.[52] Assessed for a one-storey frame house with one fireplace in 1828, a few years later Griggs was assessed for a two-storey house with three fireplaces, and shortly thereafter was listed as "innkeeper."[53] Though moved back from the Lake Shore Road and thoroughly renovated some years ago by its recent owner, Harry Ryrie, the Half-way House still faces its contemporaries, the two ancient pear trees.

Upon the occasion of her first journey into the Canadian countryside Anna Jameson passed along the Lake Shore Road in a sleigh, and her description of what she saw in January, 1837, is so vivid and agreeable as to demand inclusion in full.

At half past eight Mr. Campbell was at the door in a very pretty commodious sleigh, in form like a barouche, with the head up. I was absolutely buried in furs; a blanket, knitted for me by the kindest hands, of the finest lamb's wool, rich in colour, and as light and elastic as it was deliciously warm, was folded round my limbs; buffalo and bear skins were heaped over all, and every breath of the external air excluded by every possible device. Mr. Campbell drove his own gray horses; and thus fortified and accoutred, off we flew, literally "urged by storms along the slippery way" for the weather was terrific.

I think that but for this journey I never could have imagined the sublime desolation of a northern winter, and it has impressed me strongly. In the first place, the whole atmosphere appeared as if converted into snow, which fell in thick, tiny, starry flakes, till the buffalo robes and furs about us appeared like swansdown, and the harness on the horses of the same delicate material. The whole earth was a white waste; the road, on which the sleigh track was only just perceptible, ran for miles in a straight line; on each side rose the melancholy pine forest, slumbering drearily in the hazy air.

Between us and the edge of the forest were frequent spaces of cleared or half-cleared land, spotted over with the black charred stumps and blasted trunks of once magnificent trees, projecting from the snowdrift. These, which are perpetually recurring objects in a Canadian landscape, have a most melancholy appearance. Sometimes wide openings occurred to the left, bringing us in sight of Lake Ontario, and even in some places down upon the edge of it: in this part of the lake the enormous body of the water and its incessant movement prevents it from freezing, and the dark waves rolled in, heavily plunging on the icy shore with a sullen booming sound.

A few roods from the land, the cold gray waters, and the cold, gray, snow-encumbered atmosphere, were mingled with each other, and each seemed either. The only living thing I saw in a space of about twenty miles was a magnificent bald-headed eagle, which, after sailing a few turns in advance of us, alighted on the topmost bough of a blasted pine, and slowly folding his great wide wings, looked down upon us as we glided beneath him.

Upon arriving at Oakville Mrs. Jameson and her escort alighted at the Oakville House, in reference to which her comments have already been quoted. Here passengers on the stage-coach customarily took dinner. Mrs. Jameson continues her narrative with a description of the stage-coach:

While I was reading, the mail-coach between Hamilton and Toronto drove up to the door; and because you shall understand what sort of a thing a Canadian mail is, and thereupon sympathize in my irrepressible wonder and amusement, I must sketch it for you. It was a heavy wooden edifice, about the size and form of an old-fashioned lord mayor's coach, placed on runners, and raised about a foot from the ground; the whole was painted a bright red, and long icicles hung from the roof.

This monstrous machine disgorged from its portal eight men-creatures, all enveloped in bear-skins and shaggy dreadnoughts, and pea-jackets, and fur caps down upon their noses, looking like a procession of bears on their hind legs, tumbling out of a showman's caravan. They proved, however, when undisguised, to be gentlemen, most of them going up to Toronto to attend their duties in the House of Assembly.[54]

Mrs. Jameson was apparently under the impression that the stage-coach running along the Lake Shore Road carried the Royal Mail, but records of the Postmaster General's Department show this not to have been the case. The mail was transported along the Dundas Street upon which the post offices were located. The Trafalgar Post Office, opened about 1822, was the first post office established between the provincial capital and the town of Dundas. The second was the Nelson Post Office at Hannahsville, established 1825, of which William Chisholm was postmaster. When Oakville secured a post office it was a "bye route" of the Trafalgar Post Office, and the mail bags were transported to and fro on horseback. The Trafalgar Post Office served a large area which included all the southern section of the township as well as thirty miles north into Erin Township. It was located in the general store of the postmaster, Alexander Proudfoot, on the west corner of the Dundas Street and the 9th Line.[55] Jacob Cook, who from an early date had been under contract with the government, transported the mail along the street, travelling by waggon, sleigh, or on horseback, depending upon the state of the roads. It is for this man that Cooksville was named. Proudfoot's young brother-in-law, Peter Jarvis, recorded the following anecdote in his memoirs:

We kept the Post Office as well as a General Store. The postage in those days was very high, ranging from four and half pence to three shillings in Canada, according to the distance; to the Old Country it was as high as six shillings and seven shillings. On one occasion a letter came from Ireland for one Wm. Armstrong, Trafalgar, the postage on which was seven shillings. One day when I had been left alone, I saw a rough looking Irishman coming down the concession on a white horse. He drew up at the door and asked, "Is there ever a letter for Wm. Armstrong?" I replied in the affirmative and he said, "Let me say it." I brought it out and handed it to him and told him the amount of the postage to be paid. He asked if I thought it was for him, and I said, "Certainly if your name's Wm. Armstrong." He replied, "That's my name, open it." I told him he must open it. This he did and asked me to "rade" it. I read it over and where I could not make out the names, he would pronounce them for me, as many of them were new and outlandish to me. After I read it once, he said, "Rade it again." This I proceeded to do and when I had finished he said, "That letter isn't for me at all. You must put it back in the office." And to my amazement he strolled off leaving the postage of seven shillings unpaid.[56]

When the volume of mail for the southern section of the township handled through this post office became heavy enough to warrant a separate office, the Oakville Post Office was established.[57] Because of William Chisholm's ten years' experience as postmaster at Nelson he was appointed to that office at Oakville under a commission dated October 6, 1835, issued by Thomas A. Stayner, Postmaster General.[58] Some time later Chisholm appointed as his deputy his son, R. K. Chisholm, who then moved from Nelson Township to live permanently at Oakville.

The site chosen for the little frame post office was the top of the east bank of The Sixteen on the south side of Colborne Street west of Navy Street. During the course of its removal in 1950 to the lake front at the foot of Thomas Street and its restoration as the Old Post Office Museum this twenty-foot square building was found to have always stood on the same site. As it was situated high on the hill above the road it was approached by a flight of square timber steps; the front entrance, protected by a narrow porch, faced upon the river. The building is constructed of twelve-inch planks four inches thick and twenty feet long which were cut at the sawmill. Running horizontally and dovetailed at the corners, the planks are held together by a spline or loose-tongue joint, the edges of the boards having been grooved and a separate thin piece of wood inserted in the grooves. The slabs that were by-products of cutting the lumber were used as overhead beams. The building sat on timbers a foot square, and the only iron used in its construction is in the spikes and bolts which held it to its foundation. Shingles of a later date hide a covering of tin. Since the building was used as a storage warehouse (in the sixties when a second storey, since removed, was added and the windows closed up), a blacksmith's shop, a stable, and a welder's shop, nothing is left of interior partitions. It was restored with a minimum of new material; the floor of the porch, its pillars copied from those of Justus Williams' shop built in 1833, and window and door frames are all that is new. The entrance door and window sash are those of the Trafalgar Township Hall, a contemporary building recently demolished. The Old Post Office Museum is now the repository of many documents referred to in this history.

At the time this building came into use as the Oakville Post Office the provincial postal service under the control of the British government was not remarkable for its efficiency. The high rates of postage, payable in currency only, were a hardship to a majority of the settlers. The number of sheets of paper a letter contained determined the rate of postage charged. A single sheet rated single postage, but a second sheet or enclosure, however small, constituted a double letter. A sheet of paper, written on one side only, could be made to serve the purpose of two when "crossed" with writing. No envelopes were used; the sheet was folded in such a manner that it could be secured by a bit of sealing wax and addressed on the blank side. Nor were stamps used at this period. On each letter was written the date of mailing and the amount of postage; if this was prepaid, red ink was used, but if the letter went postage collect the amount was written in black ink.[59] Money was often enclosed in letters and if they failed to reach their destination the honesty of the postmaster or his clerk was brought into question. Only men of integrity were appointed to the office of postmaster.

The rate of postage between Oakville and Toronto was 4½*d.* At Oakville the mails were received and dispatched twice a week, on Mondays and Thursdays.[60] D. Snider (possibly David Snider of Snider's Corners on the 9th Line) was under contract with the Post Office Department at £13 per annum to transport mail to and from the Trafalgar Post Office. The contracts specified that the return trip be made in one and one-half hours. During the first few years Snider was obliged to pay the following penalties:

Leaving behind mail bag, accidental	$4.00
Ditto, willful	8.00
Omitting service to a P.O.	4.00
Ditto, second offence	8.00
General penalty for breach of contract	16.00
Total	$40.00[61]

The commission issued by the Postmaster General indicates the extent of remuneration to the postmaster:

> William Chisholm is hereby authorized to keep and retain Twenty per Centum out of the produce arising by the Post of Letters received by him, in recompense for his care and trouble in the performance and execution of the trusts reposed in him, so long as he shall continue to be employed by me as my Deputy.
>
> (signed) T. A. Stayner.[62]

The revenue of the Oakville Post Office during the year 1838 amounted to £55.4.9 of which Chisholm retained £13.12.6¾. Owing to misdirected, forwarded, and uncalled for letters there was a loss of £5.13.10.[63]

The establishment of a post office gave an impulse to Oakville's progress. As the editor of the *Observer* commented, it "has conferred upon the town the means of holding communication with the world, without which no place can prosper."[64]

The founding of its first newspaper, in February, 1836, was equally important to the village. At a time when books were few, expensive, and difficult to come by, the majority of literate persons, particularly in the agricultural districts, were forced to depend on religious and agricultural journals and newspapers for reading matter. Collecting subscriptions was a matter of grave concern to newspaper editors. In the early days of the *Gore Gazette*, published at Ancaster, the editor announced "wood, butter, hams taken in payment—also feathers of good quality."[65] But he soon found that the principle of barter could not successfully be applied to the publication of a newspaper. In the first issue of the *Oakville Observer* (*Observer* was a name popular throughout the province for newspapers), which appeared February 8, 1836, the "proprietor" stated: "It being the universal complaint of our brother editors that their subscribers will not punctually pay their subscriptions, we intend preventing our having to make similar complaints by publishing one copy and paying for it ourselves."[66] Considering the amount of information concerning Oakville that was provided by the editor of the *Observer*, it is a matter of regret that no clue exists to his identity. The length of the existence of this newspaper is also clouded in mystery. So far no issues have been discovered and the quotations used in this volume appeared as reprints in the Upper Canada column of the *Montreal Gazette*.

The Canadian news sheets of the eighteen twenties and thirties are as interesting to read as those of the forties and fifties, with long-winded, involved political harangues, are tiresome. However, there is little local news. Adopting the principle that happenings in the community were known to all, editors placed emphasis on news from outside. They devoted much space to events that took place in Britain, and the proceedings of Parliament in London were followed quite as closely as those of the House of Assembly at Toronto. News was collected by a system of wide exchange with other newspapers in the provinces and in the United States. It was indeed a dull issue that did not contain under the caption "Melancholy Circumstance" or "Fatal Affray" the description of at least one murder or sudden death. After stating that the affair is too "dreadful to relate" the editor proceeds to give details in full. Tiny cuts and ornaments were used to prefix advertisements: a house for the sale or lease of real estate, a steamer or a stage-coach, such as those reproduced in this chapter, for transportation schedules, and a prancing horse for stray animals. Patent medicines were guaranteed to cure quite as many diseases as those of a later date, and some unpronounceable maladies listed would confound the medical profession of the present day. The small type, almost microscopic in size, was made necessary by the scarcity of paper, but the print is very legible. Journeymen printers who laboriously set it by hand and redistributed it into their cases must have found it tedious to handle. The surprising durability of the rag paper largely accounts for the number of newspapers which have survived the interval of time. Ink was so difficult to secure that during one winter publication of the *Gore Balance* at Hamilton was suspended "for want of Printer's Ink, which could be procured only by making a journey to York, over one of the most frightful roads that disgrace the face of our country."[67]

Within the space of three years Oakville had thus achieved the full complement of contacts with the outside world. At this time, just before its ninth birthday, it was a community of close to four hundred people. Though set in beautiful surroundings, it was an ugly village. Its aspect was that of all Canadian frontier villages, raw and crude; even the most travelled thoroughfares were full of stumps which were not to disappear for some time to come. The area between Colborne Street and the lake must have been almost bare of trees, or William Sumner could not have claimed that a view of the opposite shore was to be had from the new gallery of the Oakville House. The trees of the primeval forest, having for so long been interdependent, could not stand alone, so clearing had necessarily been thorough. But the crudeness was much softened by the waters of Lake Ontario, which was visible from almost any part of the village.

Oakville had developed according to the plans of its founder, we have stressed. At this point in the narrative it seems best to look more closely at the varied undertakings of the man in order to bring the activities of the time into focus.

W. Chisholm.

CHAPTER FIVE

A MERCHANT POLITICIAN

WILLIAM CHISHOLM is representative of the type of man who was active in the affairs of Upper Canada during the pioneer period. A farmer and merchant engaged in various commercial enterprises, like so many of his contemporaries who were also merchants, he rose to become a central figure in the politics of his county. But he probably had a better understanding of the country than a large proportion of his political associates who, having come as immigrants, had the cultural background of the British Isles. He was reared in the district at the head of Lake Ontario where his father, George Chisholm, a Loyalist Highland Scot, was one of the earliest settlers.

Of all the immigrants from Britain, the Scot, and in particular the Highland Scot, is conceded to have made the most successful settler. The rigorous struggle for existence he encountered in Canada was in many ways similar to the hard life to which he had been accustomed in his homeland. This class of agriculturalist formed the backbone of the Loyalist population which spread from Niagara round the head of the lake and into the townships of Nelson and Trafalgar. To follow the fortunes and misfortunes of one of these families gives some comprehension of the Loyalist background which is the heritage of this section of Canada.

Born in 1752,* George Chisholm migrated in 1773 from Springton on the Leys (a farm situated high on the moorland above the City of Inverness) in company with his brother John and others from the Presbyterian Parish of Croy, and settled deep in the heart

*Not 1745 as family tradition had it. See Note to the Second Printing, p. xi.

of the Catskills on the frontier of the Province of New York. During the Revolution the brothers joined the Royal Standard. John fought in the Indian Department under Captain Joseph Brant; George served in the army of General Burgoyne and was taken prisoner at Saratoga. At the end of the war George was transported with the army to Nova Scotia and settled on a farm near Shelburne, where his son William was born. Like many others who settled here he found difficulty in subsisting on the land, and after seven years abandoned it. Accompanied by his wife and six children he made the long journey from Shelburne to join his brother John on the Niagara peninsula in Upper Canada. For sixteen years George Chisholm, as he himself stated, had "met with a continued Series of Losses and Disappointments."[1] Upon proving his claim as a United Empire Loyalist he was granted land in the new province, which however he did not retain, having already selected a tract, lying on the north shore of Burlington Bay, which bears so striking a resemblance to his birthplace in the Highlands of Scotland that it is almost a replica in miniature.

In 1793 George Chisholm purchased jointly with Charles King upwards of 900 acres of the tract of land situated in East Flamborough Township which had been granted to Dr. Robert Kerr, military surgeon, for his services during the war.[2] This tract borders the grant of Captain Joseph Brant on the south-west, being divided from Brant's Block by the Purchase Line which set off territory ceded to the Crown from that remaining in possession of the Indians. The first survey line run in Upper Canada, the Purchase Line now forms the western boundary of Halton County.

George Chisholm was one of the earliest settlers on the shore of Burlington Bay. As commissioner on behalf of the British Government he negotiated treaties with the Indians,[3] took the initiative in petitioning the provincial Government for new roads, and supervised the building of the first roads at the head of the lake.[4] Regardless of his age of sixty-seven, he served with his three sons in the War of 1812.[5] This hardy Highlander, who three times had pioneered in different sections of British North America, lived to attain the great age of ninety-eight. He exemplifies innumerable Loyalists whose progeny spread from the old townships to the new Township of Trafalgar and the newer village of Oakville. His son William, too, is a representative figure: the man of enterprise who, despite the handicap of little education, competed successfully with educated immigrants and rose to leadership in his district.

William Chisholm and his brothers John and George junior (the regularity with which the names John, William, George, and Janet appear among descendants of the two immigrant brothers is confounding to the genealogist) grew up in the wilderness. They associated with few white children, and being thrown in close contact with the Indians, particularly their neighbours, the Brant family, the young Chisholms spoke their language. George junior became proficient in several Indian dialects.[6] Not far away in the forest was a place they called Fort Stanwix[7] where they and their companions re-fought battles in which their fathers, Indian and white, had engaged the Continentals.

In 1812 William Chisholm married Rebecca Silverthorn, daughter of John Silverthorn, a Loyalist from the Niagara district who had settled in Etobicoke Township, York County. He fought through the War of 1812 as a "flanker." When war with the United States loomed, Britain was still fighting Napoleon; in fact his invasion of Russia and retreat from Moscow, and the later campaigns of the Peninsular War were fought during that year. There were few regular troops in the province, and on the advice of General Brock two companies were selected from each regiment of militia to serve as flank companies. Though these volunteers were asked to drill six days each month without pay and find their uniforms and muskets, the flank companies were filled almost instantly. Many settlers in Trafalgar Township fought through the campaign of 1812-14 as "flankers" of the York Militia.[8]

The first action in which these men engaged was the capture of the fort at Detroit. Three regiments of York Militia and the 5th Lincoln Regiment accompanied General Brock to the western district in August, 1812. William Chisholm served as ensign in the first flank company of the latter regiment under Captain Samuel Hatt. The hardships of this journey in open boats are described in the diary of William McCay,[9] later a business associate of William Chisholm. Brock's small force was ill equipped and sadly outnumbered, but he demanded that the Americans across the river at Detroit surrender. To his amazement they did so within twenty-four hours. Thirty-five hundred Americans were taken prisoner by a force of some three hundred regulars, four hundred militiamen, and about six hundred Indians. The British entered the fort in triumph, as is described at a later date by Major John Richardson: "A guard of honour consisting of an officer and forty men were immediately formed to take possession of the fort . . . and among those of the militia who . . . had first the honour of entering the fortress were the present Chief Justice Robinson, Samuel Jarvis, Esquire . . . and Colonel William Chisholm of Oakville. The American flag was lowered, and a Union Jack, which a blue jacket had brought with him, hoisted in its place."[10]

Two months later, on the day the Battle of Queenston Heights was fought, the forces assembled by General Brock numbered somewhat over two thousand men, more than half composed of militia and Indians. The superior military resources of the Americans approached seventeen thousand. It was his fearless and defiant way of maintaining confidence in the face of enormous odds that so endeared Brock to the militia who fought under him. This engagement was fought over the farm of William Chisholm's uncle John, who is referred to as "old Chisholm" in documents relating the day's events.[11] The battle ended in a spectacular victory for the British, though they lost their brilliant leader, General Brock, who as he died is said to have urged on his men, "Push on the brave York volunteers." There are those who have maintained that the wounded general was carried to the shelter of John Chisholm's house. Having been transferred to one of the flank companies of the 2nd Regiment of York, Ensign William Chisholm fought in this action and his gallantry drew special mention in the dispatches of General Sheaffe.[12] Two months later he was promoted to lieutenant.[13]

The Battle of Lundy's Lane, fought in the summer of 1814, was the last action in which Chisholm (and the men of Trafalgar) participated. Again the British forces were inferior, but from the standpoint of military tactics this was the best-fought battle of the whole campaign. The War of 1812-14 did much to convince the American invaders that Canadians had no desire to change their allegiance, and that British North America could not easily be annexed by the United States.

II

In 1816 William Chisholm moved to a farm on the Dundas Street in Nelson Township, only a short distance from his old home. The year following saw the beginning of a series of events which undoubtedly contributed to his popularity in the district, and caused William Lyon Mackenzie later to refer to Chisholm as a "Gourlayite." This assertion combines with documents found among Chisholm's papers to throw light upon his interests and activities at this period.

Robert Gourlay, a Scotsman concerned in stimulating emigration from Britain, began the preparation of a statistical account of Upper Canada. In 1817, through the medium of a Niagara newspaper, he addressed to resident landowners in all townships a questionnaire by which, as he stated, he hoped "to gain the most authentic intelligence concerning this country for the information of our fellow subjects and Government at home."[14] Question 31 aroused the attention of the authorities; "What, in your opinion, most retards the Improvement of your Township in particular, of the Province in general; and what would most contribute to the same?" The majority of landowners gave in effect the same answer as those in Trafalgar Township, who stated:

> What in our opinion would most contribute to the improvement of our Township and the Province at large would be to encourage men of property into the Country to purchase the waste lands of our Province which, if sold even at a moderate price, would introduce such a flow of Capital into our Province as would not only encourage a respectable race of settlers of every description to come in and cultivate the face of the country, and turn the wilderness into fruitful fields, but it would also make trade and manufacturing of all kinds flourish. Then would our Province no longer remain poor, neglected and unknown to the rest of the world, but she would add a large revenue to the British Crown and her redundances would contribute to feed the hungry and clothe the poor of other nations.[15]

In the eyes of the provincial Government this and other similar statements amounted to criticism, and in those days criticism was synonymous with disloyalty to the Crown. To make bad matters worse, Gourlay held a convention to which representatives of the townships were invited to discuss remedies for the backward state of the province. By then Gourlay had come to be regarded as a dangerous agitator. He was sent to prison and eventually banished from the country. Among those in Nelson Township who drew up and signed answers to Gourlay's questionnaire and who attended the convention was William Chisholm.

At this same time the Government passed a long-delayed bill providing for land grants, known as the Prince Regent's Land Bounty, to those "flankers" who had served during the war. Infuriated by Gourlay's convention, the Lieutenant-Governor, Sir Peregrine Maitland, attached a rider to the bill in which those who had attended the meeting were disqualified from receiving the Bounty. Seven years passed before Maitland was instructed to allow grants to those disqualified "as soon as they severally assure you of their deep contrition for having belonged to an assembly which was highly derogatory and repugnant to the spirit of the Constitution of the province and tended greatly to disturb the public tranquility."[16] Among Chisholm's papers are two letters which prove that he was under the constraint of making this declaration before receiving his grant of five hundred acres.[17] Part of his Prince Regent's Land Bounty, as has already been shown, was located in Trafalgar Township on lot 12 of the 4th concession, the section of Oakville that lies south of Colborne Street between Allan Street and the 8th Line.

Meanwhile Chisholm embarked on his career as a merchant, establishing a general store and buying wheat, timber, and oak staves. In this new country two classes of men predominated, the farmer and the merchant. The majority of farmers possessed considerable property in land and cattle, but it was only men engaged in commerce who accumulated any measure of wealth and influence. At this period trade was relatively simple, and it was possible for a merchant to know and understand, through the conduct of his own business, the commercial system of the country as a whole. The merchant who showed particular enterprise in the field of commerce was almost invariably the one chosen to represent his district and look to its interests in Parliament during a period when finances played an important role in the affairs of the government. It was in 1820 that William Chisholm was elected Member for the East Riding of Halton County in the House of Assembly.[18] This was the eighth Parliament of Upper Canada, and the second in which the county was represented. Apparently Chisholm's liberal tendencies, which had placed him in bad grace with the Tory Government, had increased his popularity with the Tories of the county.

At this period Halton County was very much more extensive than it is today. When formed, it was comprised of the townships of Trafalgar, Nelson, East and West Flamborough, Dumfries, Waterloo, Woolwich, and Nichol, "with the reserved lands in the rear of the townships of Blenheim and Blandford."[19] Gradually these reserved lands were surveyed into new townships, and others to the north-west were annexed, until by the 1820's there were thirteen, and by 1831 eighteen, townships within Halton County. Those added gradually were the townships of Beverley, Esquesing, Erin, Eramosa, Garafraxa, Guelph, Nassageweya, Puslinch, and Wilmot. By 1840 Halton County extended over an area of 1622 square miles,[20] and its population totalled 35,216.[21] In terms of today this extensive territory is bounded on the north-east by Orangeville, on the north-west by Arthur, on the south-west (roughly) by Paris, and on the south-east by Dundas. As a result of some further division of townships there are at present twenty townships in what was at one time Halton County. Within the area are now the cities and towns of Guelph, Galt, Paris, Preston, Hespeler, Kitchener, Waterloo, Elmira, Elora, and Fergus, as well as those mentioned above. Because of its extent the county was originally divided into two ridings, the East Riding covering 666 square miles with a steadily rising population which, by 1840, exceeded eighteen thousand.[22] As the population rose with settlement new districts were formed and townships rearranged into new and smaller counties, until in 1852 Halton County was reduced to its present size of four townships, its area of 363 square miles making it the smallest county but one in the province of Ontario.

The business of William Chisholm prospered, and he soon became a leading merchant in the district. Dealing in timber lead easily to ship building. By 1822 Chisholm was building at least one vessel yearly on Burlington Bay until he owned and operated a fleet of five schooners. Transportation of his commodities to and from Lower Canada was slow and expensive. Sailing ships loaded at the head of the lake could go no farther down the St. Lawrence than Prescott, where their cargoes were transferred to flat-bottomed Durham boats and batteaux for trans-shipment to Montreal and Quebec.[23] But to go down the river was quite different from coming up. Craft loaded with from four to ten tons of merchandise were slowly and laboriously poled up the long miles by bargemen, and at rapids they had to be assisted by animal power. At one place the boats could be worked upstream only "by cattle viz. from 4 to 5 yoke of oxen."[24] Freight crossed the Atlantic from Liverpool to Montreal at £1 per ton, but it travelled the one hundred miles from Montreal to Prescott at £2.10 per ton.[25] In advertising his ships engaged in the carrying trade Chisholm stated "that he has taken every precaution in selecting sober and industrious men to be masters and crews of said vessels," and that they were all "well furnished" with anchors, cables, rigging, etc. This is a revealing commentary on the irresponsibility of masters and the inadequacy of equipment so common on the lake at the period. He adds that his schooners are of the "first class on Lake Ontario both for safety and fast sailing."[26]

While Member for East Halton, Chisholm was appointed one of

the government commissioners to supervise the building of the canal at Burlington Bay. The inlet from Lake Ontario was so shallow that it was necessary to trans-ship goods destined for the villages of Dundas and Hamilton into shallow barges; William Chisholm's elder brother, John, for many years Customs Collector at Burlington Beach, was engaged in this local forwarding business. In 1823 the Government decided to expedite transportation by constructing a canal,[27] the first attempted in the province of Upper Canada, and although it was on a small scale much first-hand knowledge was acquired of the tremendously destructive forces of Lake Ontario which proved valuable in building larger canals. Engineers and contractors were employed who had previously worked on the Erie Canal in the United States.

Upon the occasion of the opening of the canal by the Lieutenant-Governor, Sir Peregrine Maitland, in the summer of 1826, the first vessels to pass through the canal were the schooners *Rebecca and Eliza* and *General Brock* belonging to Chisholm. The *Rebecca*, under the command of Captain Edward Zealand, was the first lake vessel to deliver a cargo at the new Port of Hamilton.[28]

For some years Chisholm was a partner in McCay, Smith & Company (William McCay and Joel Smith) whose store was situated on the beach near the canal. Here was sold "merchandise received direct from Quebec and Montreal which were carefully selected by William Chisholm" in exchange for the usual "wheat, flour, Indian corn, Rye, Pork, Pot and Pearl Ashes, Pipe staves, Etc."[29] When the second post office between York and Dundas, Nelson Post Office, was established in 1825, Chisholm was commissioned postmaster[30] and the office was located in his general store. His eldest son, George King Chisholm, assisted in the post office after returning from Upper Canada College, where he was among the earliest pupils.[31] Having himself been forced to do without the advantages of higher education, Chisholm saw that his sons attended the Gore District Grammar School at Hamilton, and sent the eldest on to Upper Canada College.

The election of 1824 had not returned Chisholm to Parliament, nor was he returned in 1828 when the Reform candidate, Caleb Hopkins, a merchant at Hannahsville and Chisholm's neighbour, won in the East Riding of Halton County. Hopkins was one of the earliest organizers of the Reform party in the Gore District; because of his affiliation with the "Ryerson faction" the Tory press delighted in referring to him as the "saddlebag candidate." Being at this juncture free of political and governmental responsibilities, Chisholm was able to devote all his energies to his new project, the village of Oakville.

Upon the death of George IV and the accession to the throne of William IV in 1830 an election was called, and Chisholm again stood for Parliament. At that time any British subject, by birth or oath of allegiance, who owned property, even wild land, to the value of £5 could qualify as a candidate simply by announcing his intention to do so. William J. Sumner, proprietor of the Grove Inn, Nelson (prior to his taking over the Oakville House), proposed to stand in this election as Conservative candidate, wording his intention to do so as follows: "To the Electors of the County of Halton, Gentlemen—As the death of our much lamented Sovereign George the Fourth, has caused a dissolution of our Provincial Parliament, you are again called upon to exercise the Elective Franchise. I take this method of announcing to you that I am an *unsolicited* Candidate at the approaching Election, and should I be elected one of your Representatives, I shall do all the good I can—in the meantime (according to Custom) do good for MYSELF. I am, Gentlemen, WM. J. SUMNER."[32] Within a week, however, Sumner announced a change of plans.

Freeholders of Halton, Gentlemen—It was my serious intention some few days ago to have been a Candidate at your election, but upon mature deliberation I find *six* reasons why I should decline the honor.

1st—My purse is too empty to carry it on "according to custom."
2nd—My creditors have a better claim on my loose *cash* than my VANITY.
3rd—My Wife, my Children and my Tavern could not be wanting me.
4th—My talents and local knowledge of my country, are not sufficient to qualify me for a legislator.
5th—I am a stranger to History, (and like some candidates) my politics never soared above the Bar-Room fireplace.
6th—I have not the *impudence* nor the hypocrisy enough for that HONORABLE situation, and not only so, *I have my doubts of being elected.*

Now, gentlemen, upon these considerations I hope you will excuse me, but should you at any further period require my services only let me know it.

I am, Gentlemen,
Grove Inn, Nelson. W. J. SUMNER.[33]

Chisholm won the election in his riding, and to him and the successful candidate in the West Riding Sumner addressed an open letter. He asked them to give their attention to road improvement in the province, and to remember the freeholders in the county "when you are sitting on your cushioned chairs in the House of Assembly, and consider who put you there, and to what purpose."[34] To some degree this admonition seems to have been heeded, because it was during this session that Parliament appropriated funds for improving the principal roads in the province, including the Lake Shore Road. It would be interesting to know what else might have taken place that year which led Sumner to christen his son, a future citizen of Oakville, William Chisholm Sumner.

Many turbulent scenes were enacted in the House during the ensuing sessions of Parliament. William Lyon Mackenzie was expelled from the House no less than five times for publishing libellous articles in his newspaper, the *Colonial Advocate.* At first Chisholm voted for expulsion, but on other occasions thereafter he was conveniently absent.

In general the Reformers did not trouble to make fine distinctions, as Egerton Ryerson pointed out when he wrote: "In Upper Canada, every man that supports the Constitution, however active and even Ultra-Liberal he may be in his views and measures of practical reform, is, by the Anti-Constitutional party, called a 'Tory.' "[35] That Chisholm was not an extreme Tory as were so many of his friends and associates may best be proved by the inclusion of his name in a list of "Moderate Tories" published by Mackenzie himself.[36] None the less, Chisholm came in for a full share of Mackenzie's acidulous criticism. One attack, labelled by a correspondent as "perhaps as mean as contemptible and as unjust as ever Mackenzie published or uttered in the whole of his reprobate career,"[37] was somewhat softened by the closing paragraph: "There are others whom we would much rather have made the subject of these remarks than Col. Chisholm whose great good nature and pleasant manner we greatly admire; but the day approaches when these qualities will not be passports to popular approbation under similar circumstances, and the press must do its duty fearlessly, please or displease whom it may."[38]

During this session of Parliament Chisholm served on a committee whose lengthy recommendations, if and when adopted, would affect every property owner in the province, the committee for the revision of the assessment laws of Upper Canada.[39] He was also appointed to the Upper Canada Finance Committee[40] and to other committees concerned either directly or indirectly with financial questions; he was also chosen director of the Gore Bank pursuant of charter.[41]

In the general election of 1834 Chisholm stood for re-election, but regardless of red ribbons bearing the inscription "Chisholm forever, Hopkins never"[42] worn by Tories in the East Riding he went down in defeat before a Reform victory. This was the day of the open vote.

It was the custom to hold the elections in one of the larger towns in the county, and under the Election Act polling continued for six days, Monday through Saturday. Early on Monday morning candidates and their henchmen set up their respective headquarters in a nearby tavern or tent, and by one o'clock when polling began electors were pouring in from all the eastern section of the county. A platform known as the "husting" was erected in front of a window, inside of which sat the returning officer and poll clerks. Each elector ascended the husting and through the half-open window gave his name, address, occupation, and the name of the candidate for whom he cast his vote. This information was given in a voice loud enough for all to hear, and the crowd could thus follow the progress of the election from day to day. Political feelings and animosities, easily aroused by this practice, were intensified by the free distribution of liquor by both candidates, and the pressure of intimidation was openly applied. Riotous conditions were prevalent, and in the brawling and fighting each party was called upon to protect its voters. Towards the end of an election it was usual for the followers of the losing candidate to exert themselves to prevent electors of the opposing party from voting. All in all, election week was such a lively time that few shirked their political responsibilities.

The attempts of Mackenzie and his Reformers to stir up popular sentiment by agitation and "grievance meetings" met with little success in either Oakville or the surrounding township, especially the southern section. British immigration contributed a conservative influence, and Oakville, being largely populated with merchants, small tradesmen, and newly arrived immigrants, of whom many were Orangemen, bore a distinctly Tory aspect. As Dr. Masters points out in *The Rise of Toronto*, Orangeism and Toryism went hand in hand. "The North of Ireland Irish transplanted the same attitudes which had flourished at home."[43] Fervent loyalty to British institutions and to the Empire made Orangemen sworn enemies of the Reformers, and they shared with the Tories a dislike of Americans. Mackenzie's reforms, modelled on the republican principles of the United States, had no appeal for them. Undoubtedly some settlers of American origin, who had been exposed to southern republicanism, lent an ear to Mackenzie, but the political climate of Oakville was not favourable to the cultivation of Reform principles. Almost solidly the village was ranged on the side of the "Constitutional Party."

Trafalgar, according to Mackenzie, was "a hot bed of Orangeism."[44] Following a meeting held in Esquesing he wrote: "It is provoking to see Storekeepers continually against Reform. . . . Who were more indefatigable in raising recruits to put down the voice of the town[ship] and its 5000 inhabitants than Squires O'Reilly, Brown, Chalmers and Chisholm . . . all merchants."[45] He referred to George Brown of Milton, George Chalmers of the Sixteen Village, and, of course, William Chisholm, all prominent Tories. (Peter Jarvis recalled that Mackenzie delighted in labelling the senior class of Upper Canada College the "Prepare-a-Tory Form.")

Those who subscribed to Tory principles and supported the King's representative welcomed every opportunity to express their loyalty to the Government and the Crown. The accepted form was for the inhabitants of villages, towns, and townships to present the lieutenant-governors with addresses of welcome upon their arrival in, and farewell upon their departure from, the province. This was also a convenient means of placing on record their names as loyal Tories. Upon the appointment of Sir John Colborne to the post of Governor-General of both provinces the "Inhabitants of Oakville and the Township of Trafalgar" presented him with a farewell address in which was expressed their satisfaction with his administration and regret at his departure. Colborne's reply, treasured by Chisholm, turned up a century later among his papers. It reads:

Head Quarters
Montreal 24th March 1836

Gentlemen

I have the honor to receive your Address which you have had the goodness to forward to me at Montreal.

It is most gratifying to me to receive from you this expression of your opinion of my proceedings, during my Administration of the Government of Upper Canada, and of the results of my exertions.

I beg you will accept my sincere thanks for your kind wishes for Lady Colborne and my family, and be assured that I shall ever take a most lively interest in the welfare and prosperity of the Province.

I have the honor to be
Your faithful servant
J. COLBORNE[46]

As Lieutenant-Governor, Colborne had been popular, and his journey with Lady Colborne to Lower Canada during the winter of 1836 was in the nature of a royal progress.[47]

Within a few days of Colborne's departure the new Lieutenant-Governor, Sir Francis Bond Head, passed through Oakville on his way to take up his duties at Government House in Toronto. To him fell the task of rallying the "loyal elements in the province against American democracy." Almost immediately he and the Reformers came to grips, and an impasse ensued. Sir Francis dissolved Parliament and called for an election. At a meeting in Trafalgar, "numerously attended," the Tories unanimously agreed to present an address to Sir Francis, declaring loyalty to the constitution and the Crown. The address was drawn up, "numerously signed by all classes in this Township" and a deputation headed by Dr. James Hopkirk proceeded on May 10 to Toronto "to await His Excellency, to present the address."[48] Convinced that self-government in Upper Canada was an innovation inconsistent with British institutions, the local Tories were determined to fight resolutely against it to the end.

The election held a few weeks later was an outstanding victory for the Tories, and Chisholm was returned to Parliament by the "Glorious Majority of Conservatives" in East Halton. The returns as given in the *Patriot* were impressively headed "For British Supremacy and Sir Francis Bond Head" and "For Democracy or Elective Institutions and Responsibility."[49] In honour of the new members for Halton a "Grand Constitutional Dinner" was given by the "loyal and patriotic village of Guelph." The ballroom of Morgan's Hotel was "tastefully decorated" with boughs, banners, artificial flowers, and "transparencies with appropriate devices." Over the head of the chairman hung a large transparency bearing the inscription, "Sir Francis Bond Head, the pilot who has weathered the storm." At each end of the room hung banners inscribed, "Fear God and honour the King" and "The loyal men of Gore." After a sumptuous dinner the M.P.P.'s were formally introduced to the assembly.

Col. Chisholm then rose [continues the *Patriot*], and was received with loud cheering.—He said, "Gentlemen, most heartily do I thank you—most sensibly do I feel this unexpected honour. However, I congratulate you on the triumph the Constitution has met with. We met as men who love justice, and whose motto is Principle. We met as British subjects who love liberty, whose banner is the British Constitution. We met as Canadians who love the country of our birth; we met as Canadians who love the country of their adoption whose best prayers are for good government and prosperous times;—and lastly, though not least, we met as British freemen, whose password is, the 'Constitution of the Province shall be firmly upheld.' Gentlemen, we are embarked upon a sea of rational freedom, we have taken the principles such as those contained in Lord Glenelg's Despatch, for our vessel; the British rights for our rigging; integrity and perseverance for our flag; British subjects for our crew, and Sir Francis Bond Head for our pilot;—Therefore we must, we will have a prosperous voyage and a safe anchorage. Gentlemen, in conclusion (he said) you have nobly and generously supported me. Be assured I will never desert or betray you!" (Loud and enthusiastic cheers.)[50]

Toronto, the seat of the government in Chisholm's time, was a city of six streets about two miles in length running parallel to the lake, and less than a mile in depth, about the size of Oakville at the present day. King Street, the main thoroughfare running east and west, stopped at Peter Street on the west, and the eastern boundary was the Don River. Lot Street, now Queen Street, the surveyor's base line, was the northern boundary, and the land which stretched north to the concession road, now Bloor Street, though laid out in township lots, was mostly open fields and bush. Prominent citizens chose to live on Front Street which ran along the top of the bank close to the shore-line of the bay. From their windows could be seen the broad sweep of the bay, the lazy vessels and busy steamers of Lake Ontario coming and going against the background of the peninsula beyond. Where ships then sailed is now dry land, hundreds of acres covered by a large industrial development having been added by several extensions of the waterfront. And where ships now sail was once dry land, for the peninsula did not become an island until after a storm in 1858. At the north-east corner of Front at York Street, where the Royal York Hotel stands today, was the home of Dr. John Strachan, rector of St. James' Anglican Church. This was the first house in York to be built (1818) of locally made instead of Oswego brick. Of "capacious dimensions and good design with extensive appurtenances" it was finished throughout in black walnut. After the elevation of Dr. Strachan to the Bishopric of Toronto it was called "The Palace." In the block west of York Street at Simcoe Place, now occupied by railway tracks and freight sheds, stood the Houses of Parliament, in the rear of which, on rising ground and facing Wellington Street, stood Government House. At the head of John Street was "The Grange," the home of D'Arcy Boulton which today is part of the Toronto Art Gallery. In the eastern section of the town on Duke Street was the house built by Sir William Campbell, a soldier who became Chief Justice of Upper Canada. Its situation at the head of Frederick Street gave this house a fine view of the bay and its resemblance to the long vanished Bishop's Palace is striking. With "The Grange" it survives as an example of the charming town houses of the period when York was capital of the province.

In winter and summer the bay was the recreation centre of the city, and the peninsula was a popular playground. As early as 1833 "the new Boat, Sir John of the Peninsula, propelled by four horses . . . Commodious, and safe for Parties of Pleasure" ran to and from "The Retreat on the Peninsula . . . opposite the town."[51] The proprietor of both, Michael O'Connor, had obviously fought under Sir John Moore. He announced: "He will be ready to accommodate sportsmen, Parties of pleasure and individuals who may wish to inhale the Lake breeze, with every kind of refreshments. . . . He trusts that from long experience, and strict attention to business, to merit a share of Public favor, and that the Retreat on the Peninsula, will be patronized by those whose recollections of the Spanish Peninsula, will ever be dear to their memories as recorded in the pages of British History."[52]

When York was incorporated as a city and its name changed to Toronto in 1834, William Lyon Mackenzie, who had emerged from his controversies with the Assembly a popular hero, was elected Toronto's first mayor. For a city whose social life was pervaded by the influence of the official and military classes this seems a strange choice. The *Patriot*'s editor commented acidly that in signing official documents " 'Mackenzie' 'Mayor'!!! just in the fashion of the Lords Ascendant in the purlieus of St. James' London he assumes the style never assumed by the higher Aristocracy."[53]

In the quantity and quality of its mud the city stood supreme in the province, and one of Mackenzie's accomplishments was to provide the first sidewalk. A resident states that "soundings" taken in the centre of King Street established a depth of twelve inches of mud. This estimate could be considered conservative, judging from an anecdote current at the period as recounted by C. C. Taylor:

> A Gentleman, walking on the loose planks forming a sidewalk on King Street espied a good-looking hat in the middle of the street. Curious to see and pick up the hat, he managed to reach it, and on removing it, discovered to his surprise the head of a man underneath.
>
> This individual at once appealed for help and deliverance, urging, as a special plea, that if prompt assistance was not rendered, his horse which was underneath, would surely perish.
>
> The usual method of extraction by the use of shovels and oxen was applied, and the man and horse excavated.[54]

As mayor of Toronto Mackenzie was succeeded by Robert Baldwin Sullivan, to whom Oakville is said to be indebted for its name.

The marriage of Queen Victoria to Albert, prince of Saxe-Coburg and Gotha, was celebrated by a "Grande Fete and Illumination." The public was informed that "One Ox—to be roasted, in the vacant space next to the Post Office. . . While the band plays the Roast Beef of Old England the Bill of Fare served to the Public by the City Authorities" would include "boiled beef, vegetables, Plum Pudding and Strong Beer. Every man, woman and child who intends to partake of this Banquet will be expected to come neatly attired, each with a *Knife, Fork and Plate*."[55]

During its last years at Toronto, the government of Upper Canada met in the new Parliament Buildings on Front Street, first used in 1832. As seen in reproductions the simplicity and dignified proportions of these Georgian buildings, with their high pedimented windows and doorways, are very pleasing. The interior appointments were plain but massive, and the lofty rooms were heated by a central heating plant constructed on the same principle as hot air furnaces in use today. Sir Richard Bonnycastle describes the building of this heating system. A space in the cellar was enclosed with masonry in which the required number of holes were left for stove pipes running to various floors. A large stove was placed in the centre and the wall in front filled in, leaving only the openings needed for firing and removing ashes. Though probably not very efficient, as later photographs show stoves in some rooms, this heating plant was in use as early as the 1830's.[56]

The salaries of members of the House of Assembly were levied by special rate and paid by their respective constituencies rather than by the government. Pickering states that they had voted themselves 9*s*. per day during the time the House was in session.[57] Chisholm's stipend as Member for East Halton for the year 1837-8 was £60.10.0.[58] Some members travelled long distances on foot to attend the sessions of Parliament, but Chisholm travelled mostly on horseback. Most of them took lodgings, obtaining rooms and board for between 13*s*.6*d*. and 18*s*. per week.[59] Many attended the assemblies held regularly at the British Coffee House (admission tickets, 7*s*.6*d*.).[60] On Sunday nonconformists as well as conformists attended the morning service at St. James' Church on King Street round which the fashionable life of the city centred. "St. James, of a Sunday morning," writes Dr. Masters, "presented the spectacle of the Tory party at prayer."[61] At the south end of the church was the canopied pew of the Lieutenant-Governor and on the west the pew allotted to the military. East of the Governor's pew was the parliamentary pew where William Chisholm sat when in Toronto for the session. Dr. Scadding stated that Chisholm, being a Scottish Presbyterian, used "facetiously to object to the clause in the Litany where 'heresy and schism' are deprecated, it so happening that the last term was, by a Scottism, read 'Chisholm.' "[62]

The entrance of the Lieutenant-Governor attended by all his retinue was an impressive sight, with the officers in full regimentals heavily braided in gold, accompanied by all the clanking accoutrements of sword, spurs, and decorations. Many venerable gentlemen of the earlier generation who had founded York still wore the powdered wigs, buckled shoes, and knee breeches to which they had always been accustomed. The ladies' costumes, usually obtained in London, were charming and flattering: wide skirted cloaks, tiny fur muffs, and feather-trimmed bonnets framing short curls. As advertised in the *Patriot*, "Gentlemen's silk and fur hats" ranged in price from $1.50 to $4.50, and dragoon and cloth travelling caps from $1.50 to $3.00: "Latest improved Oval-shaped extra-light Ventilating Water-proof Superfine Beaver LONDON HATS."[63] The same paper claimed that Rowland's Macassar oil (which kept ladies busy making "anti-macassars" for the backs of chairs and settees) "makes hair soft, curly and glossy . . . keeps it firm in curl, uninjured by damp weather, crowded rooms, the dance or in the exercise of riding."[64]

Early in the winter of the second year of William Chisholm's return to Parliament, 1837, the peace and tranquility of the city were interrupted by the Rebellion. A "battle" was fought on north Yonge Street, the "Patriots" were repulsed by provincial militia, and a number of their leaders, including Mackenzie, fled the country. Of Chisholm's reaction to this event which had so profound an effect upon the political and economic status of the province we know nothing. Nor have we the impressions of any of Oakville's citizens. As we shall see in a later section, however, the large turnout of militia indicates the collective reaction to have been that of all good Tory towns, and there were no arrests of persons residing in or near Oakville for "High Treason." Disturbances resulting from the Rebellion continued along the border, and to avoid a rupture between the United States and Great Britain and, if possible, to restore peace to the peoples of Canada, Lord Durham was sent out by the British Government in 1838. At the time of his visit to Toronto he held a levee at Government House, and among those presented to his Lordship was Colonel William Chisholm.[65]

The epoch-making *Report on the Affairs of British North America* which Lord Durham upon his return to England submitted to Queen Victoria created a great stir and much opposition in Upper Canada. The radicals were quick to appropriate "Durham" as a synonym for reform, and the Tories accordingly classed as disloyal any of their own number who favoured Durham's principles. The "Durham Meetings" held throughout the province during the summer and autumn of 1839 were characterized not only by opposition but also by some violence. Those called at Dundas and Hamilton, though held during the hay harvest, were numerously attended. At Dundas the two members for Halton were present. Chisholm addressed the meeting and spoke in favour of the practical reforms embodied in the

Report but "he was interrupted in the course of his speech, which he in consequence soon brought to a close."[66] At Hamilton the day following, the meeting was preceded by a parade of thirty well-filled waggons bearing flags inscribed "Durham and Reform" and "Durham and Responsibility." According to the *British Colonist* "both Sir Allan MacNab and Col. Wm. Chisholm of Oakville, M.P. spoke manfully their sentiments, and each had a patient hearing."[67] A Tory of the deepest dye, MacNab spoke long in denunciation of Durham's *Report*, and upon his resorting to personalities the meeting became lively. Referring to Aikman, M.P. for Wentworth, MacNab stated, "he is a dirty bird indeed who dirties his own nest." Whereupon the assembly adjourned in disorder.[68]

The session of 1840 was the last meeting of the House of Assembly of Upper Canada. When Parliament was dissolved at Toronto the Parliament Buildings would not again be used as such. The two provinces were united into the Province of Canada, and the seat of the government was moved to Kingston. It was also the end of William Chisholm's political career. Before the election in March, 1840, he addressed the electors of the East Riding of Halton County as follows:

The day having now been fixed, and being close at hand, when you will be called upon to exercise the elective franchise, in sending a Representative to the Parliament of Canada, I beg to return to you my best thanks for the cordial and courteous manner in which I have been received by You, during the progress of my canvass, and to remind such of you as mean to afford me your support of the necessity of meeting me at the hustings on the earliest day of the election.

Having so long had the honour of serving you in Parliament, it seems unnecessary for me to give any exposition of my political principles which are already well known to you, and have been I trust, sufficiently set forth by my public conduct.

The re-union of the provinces, having, however, made great changes in our political situation, I may perhaps be excused for saying a few words in reference to that measure which, you are aware, I have always advocated, and which I have long been, and still am, convinced, will, if we are true to our best interests, be found of the most benefit to the Province at large; and particularly to that part of it which formerly constituted Upper Canada.

On ourselves the Governor General has truly said, depend our future prospects; and if we can only forget the subjects of dissention and join together like brothers, in promoting and furthering such measures as are for the general advantage of this great and splendid Country, we have no reason to fear the result.

I have been a supporter of Lord Sydenham's measures because I conceive they are calculated, and intended to be, and are *likely to prove* conducive to the general interests of the inhabitants of this Province, and so long as they are so, I shall ever be found ready and willing to afford them my most strenuous support.

From my long familiarity both with commercial and farming occupations, I think I have acquired some experience of the true interests of this country; that experience I trust I have hitherto used for your benefit, and if I shall be returned by your suffrages to the Parliament of Canada, you will ever find me in it as in that of Upper Canada, a supporter of all liberal and enlightened measures; anxiously alive to your real interests, and watching over and advocating every plan calculated to promote the general good of the Province, as well as at all times a determined supporter of our permanent connection with that mighty empire, of which we are so fortunate as to form a part.

I am, Gentlemen,
Your faithful servant,
WILLIAM CHISHOLM.[69]

Oakville, March 1, 1841.

The election was a riotous one. "Tories, Liberals, Unionists, Anti-Unionists, Conservatives and Reformers" struggled at the polls, putting the finishing touches to the events of the day by fighting in the evening. When the returns were in it was found that Caleb Hopkins, the Reform candidate, had won by sixty-eight votes,[70] and when the government of the new Province of Canada met at Kingston it was he who took the seat of the member for Halton.

During his twelve years in Parliament Chisholm had taken "a prominent part in the educational legislation of the House"[71] and had voted in favour of the Clergy Reserve Bill which authorized the sale of the remainder of reserves and the distribution of income among all recognized denominations. This bill settled for some time an issue which had been troublesome for many years. As a general rule Chisholm rarely entered the debates, and when he did he showed some reticence, preferring the use of a casually dropped remark to gain a point. For example, when the report of an inquiry into suspected irregularities of an officer of the Crown was under discussion, he observed that in his opinion "the report of the Commission is like the handle of a jug, all on one side."[72] His appeals to the voters were in accordance with the fashion of the times, but his letters are much to the point, with never a word too many. In the record of his political activities there are ample indications that William Chisholm possessed a liberality and tolerance of spirit far from usual in politicians of his time.

III

Like many of his political contemporaries William Chisholm was prominent in the provincial militia. The appointment of officers in the 1830's not being contingent upon former military service, few officers of the militia had seen active service, whereas Chisholm, who had fought through the War of 1812 "was, in every sense of the word, a military man and occupied high positions in the force in Canada."[73] The first regiments of militia in Upper Canada were formed of disbanded soldiers of British regiments who were granted lands as settlers. Not intended to operate alone, the militia was an adjunct to the regular troops. Service was compulsory and unpaid, the law being based upon the broad principle that every man of fighting age would do his duty to the state without pay. The rank and file were busy civilians who had to devote some of their time to soldiering. Every man between the ages of sixteen and sixty was required to attend the annual training day which was set by the Militia Act of 1808 as the birthday of King George III, June 4. Each militiaman was required to provide himself with "a sufficient musket, fusil, rifle, or gun, and at lease six rounds of powder and ball."[74] As previously pointed out, the Trafalgar Township settlers were enrolled in the 2nd Regiment of York Militia but with the setting apart in 1816 of the Gore District the Gore Militia was organized and the men within the district transferred to its regiments. At this earlier period officers were chosen from those men who had seen active service, and William Chisholm was gazetted captain in the 2nd Regiment of Gore Militia.[75] In 1824 he was promoted to lieutenant colonel of the 4th Regiment, of which his brother John was colonel.[76]

Two months later, on October 13, 1824, the anniversary of the Battle of Queenston Heights, Chisholm attended a gathering of militia officers on the occasion of the removal of the remains of Major-

General Sir Isaac Brock and Colonel Macdonell to the vault beneath the monument then in course of construction on the heights. This beautiful column, erected by the people of Upper Canada, stood high on a rocky promontory above the Niagara River on the edge of the farm of John Chisholm, uncle of William.[77] All militia regiments in the province were represented in the military escort which accompanied the remains of the General and his aide from Fort George to Queenston Heights. A traveller described the Tuscan column as being built of the "coarse gray limestone . . . of which the hill is formed." It rose to a height of 126 feet from a base which stood 350 feet above the river. This traveller was impressed by the "very fine and extensive" view from the top of the monument; the Canadian towns of Queenston and Newark, York harbour in the distance, and "a vast level tract of country covered with a uniform forest, and the horizon, formed by the lake itself."[78]

Probably typical of the activities of the provincial militia is a muster of the Trafalgar Squad in 1830: "New Year's Day being the Annual Drill of the Trafalgar Squad, Second Gore Militia they paraded at the Twelve Mile Creek, Nelson to perform Manual, Platoon and Light Infantry exercise. . . . At four o'clock they commenced street firing, advancing led by the instructor of the drill . . . after which they fired three volleys at Mr. Chisholm's Tavern and retired to a sumptuous dinner. . . . After the cloth was removed Lt. Chalmers was appointed to preside over the festivities of the board when the King, the Duke of Clarence and the Navy, Wellington and the Army, Sir John Colborne etc. were drunk with warmth." The occasion was impressively climaxed with, "To British America, the right arm of Mother Britain—palsied the hand that would sever it from its noble trunk."[79]

By 1831 there were enough men in Trafalgar Township to make up a regiment. The 2nd Regiment of Gore Militia was reorganized, its limits were set as the Township of Trafalgar,[80] and William Chisholm was appointed its colonel.[81] During time of peace only a nominal organization was maintained, and records were kept of officers only. A pay list of the 2nd Gore shows that when it was formed the second in command was Lieutenant-Colonel Charles Bigger, a Loyalist grantee who had lived on the Dundas Street near The Sixteen from the opening of the township. Alexander Proudfoot was major, and among the Oakville men were Captain William Hatton, merchant; Captain John Diamond, tavernkeeper, whose son John S. Diamond was adjutant; and Lieutenant Thomas Lloyd, tavernkeeper.[82] An old soldier of the regular army was drill sergeant.

By 1831 captains were obliged to call out their companies for parade at least twice during the year. From the military standpoint the militia system left much to be desired, as one critic, who wished to see training extended to the District Grammar Schools, pointed out to Sir John Colborne: "Our Militia," he wrote, "are obliged to train, punctually and on stated days. The trainings expose them to ridicule; and yet afford no public advantage whatever! When the Infantry move, it is a *horse*-march—not a *man*-march; for to the eye of a Disciplinarian the movement of their legs looks like the confusion apparent among the legs of a number of *horses*, than that regularity of step, which ought ever to distinguish disciplined men."[83]

That Mackenzie and his "Patriots" were preparing for armed insurrection was no secret in government circles in 1837, and during the autumn Colonel Chisholm called out the 2nd Gore for extra drill. The parades, musters, and exercises with which the militia was kept busy proved most diverting to the younger generation, according to John A. Williams. "Us boys used to see the soldiers riding and marching through town and going through the drill down on the lake bank and after they came to present arms they would fire a volley over to the Yankees. We had our drill too and rode sticks for horses and got sharp points of tin on the end of sticks for lances." Williams explains that the tin points were obtained at the tinsmith's who had opened a shop on Colborne Street next to the Methodist chapel. For the making of wooden muskets the boys arranged with Tom Noles, a blind man who lived in a log house on the bank of The Sixteen at George Street and whittled axe handles, etc. for a living. Each musket cost 7½*d*., to be paid a penny at a time. But the plan fell through and, continues Williams, "the rebels might have taken the town had it depended upon our company."

The first week of December was full of alarums and excursions. News was received at Oakville that Mackenzie was marching down Yonge Street towards Toronto with an army. The first accounts were greatly exaggerated by the time they reached the villages on the lake shore, and excitement and activity prevailed. The militia was called out and guards were stationed along the lake shore day and night.[84] As the weather was exceptionally mild for December, steamers still ran on the lake[85] and on Wednesday, December 6, the Trafalgar men boarded one (some say the *Burlington*) and within a few hours arrived at Toronto. Colonel Allan MacNab, Speaker of the House of Assembly, with about sixty "men of Gore" whom he had assembled at an hour's notice, arrived about the same time on the steamer *Traveller*.[86] Rebellion had broken out some weeks previously in Lower Canada, and all regular troops had been dispatched there by Sir Francis Bond Head. Therefore, it was left to the militia and volunteers to defend the city of Toronto against Mackenzie's rebel forces. Commanded by officers in dark green uniforms, the militia marched to the city hall on Front Street "in which 4,000 stand of arms and accoutrements had been deposited, all that were left in the province."[87] On the morning following their arrival the militia assembled for action. Colonel MacNab headed the principal body, the right wing being commanded by Colonel Samuel Jarvis and the left wing by Colonel Chisholm assisted by former Speaker of the House, Justice McLean.[88] The plan was to approach Mackenzie's headquarters at Montgomery's tavern on the hill on north Yonge Street (above what is now Eglinton Avenue) in three divisions from three directions, converging near the tavern. Chisholm marched his men of the 2nd Gore through College Avenue, now University Avenue, west of Yonge Street,[89] and arrived to find the action already commenced. Lacking a concerted plan on the part of their leaders, the odds were against the rebels. They were soon routed, and the "battle" of Montgomery's tavern ended almost before it had begun. The leaders scattered to the United States, their followers went into hiding, and the search for them was continued for many months.

The persistent and conflicting legends in connection with Mackenzie's flight need not be seriously regarded. It has been said that he was hidden close to Oakville and while having his horse shod by a local blacksmith was recognized by many, including a constable. Or again, the tale has it that he rode through Oakville dressed in women's clothing. Because of his unwillingness to involve those who had assisted him, Mackenzie's own narrative, the only reliable record, is incomplete as to detail. We can only assume that with a price of £1,000 on his head he would have been foolhardy to dally in a Tory stronghold such as Oakville. It may be that he has become confused with another leader, Dr. John Rolph, who was taken at Oakville. In the diary of an unknown Loyalist, which has recently come to light, the following extract appears: "Wed. 6th Dec. 1837—The volunteers from Hamilton, Niagara, Oakville and Toronto began pouring in. Dr. Morrison taken, Rolph gone the night before, decamping with all speed, taken prisoner at Oakville, let go by saying his sister was sick at Long Point, escaped to the United States."[90] Dr. John Rolph, son of Dr. Thomas Rolph of Ancaster, returned after the amnesty to found the Rolph School of Medicine at Toronto.

According to Mackenzie's narrative, he and a companion arrived at Streetsville at about three o'clock on Friday, the day after the battle. There they learned that "Col. Chisholm and 300 of the hottest

Orangemen, and other most violent partisans were divided into parties searching for us."[91] They dined with a sympathizer who hitched up a waggon and drove the fugitives along the Dundas Street. "Though known to everybody, we proceeded a long way west before danger approached. At length, however we were hotly pursued by a party of mounted troops . . . and when near the Sixteen Mile Creek we ascertained that my countryman, Col. Chalmers, had a party guarding the bridge." Mackenzie and his companion hurriedly left the waggon and disappeared into the forest. "The men in chase came up with our driver almost immediately after we left, took him prisoner, seized his team, gave the alarm to all the Tories and Orangemen in that part of Trafalgar, and in an hour or thereabouts, we were annoyed by reports of rifles and the barking of dogs near by the place where we were hidden."

Meanwhile the driver of the waggon was arrested and sent back to Toronto by Chisholm and Chalmers, but without guard and with a pass. Upon arriving at the Credit River bridge he was again arrested by James Magrath, an ironclad Tory. When shown Chisholm's pass "Magrath swore Chisholm was the biggest rebel in the province." Colonel Starr Jarvis who examined the pass said it should be respected, but Magrath placed the man under guard for the rest of his journey.

"Trafalgar," continues Mackenzie, "was a hot bed of Orangeism, and as I had always set my face against it, and British Nativism, I could hope for no friendship or favour, if here apprehended. There was but one chance of escape, however, surrounded as we were—for the young man had refused to leave me—and that was to stem the stream, and cross the swollen creek. We accordingly stripped ourselves naked, and in a bitter cold December night, buffeted the current, and were soon up to our necks." The crossing was apparently made at the dam of Chalmers' grist mill in the Sixteen Village, but the fugitives soon gained shelter nearby, and after a change of clothing set out once more. That night, the second day of his flight, Mackenzie crossed the Twelve Mile Creek "about midnight" and continued to the head of the lake.[92] On Monday morning he crossed the Niagara River into the United States.

Thus, between the hours of three in the afternoon and midnight of the same day Mackenzie travelled along the Dundas Street from Streetsville to The Twelve, a distance of about sixteen miles, with frequent interrupting incidents—a time-table which would hardly permit of any deviation to Oakville.

Mackenzie established his headquarters on Navy Island in the

Niagara River; from here he recruited sympathizers, and here he was joined by many who had escaped from Canada, together with a large assortment of Americans. However, the call for volunteers to guard the Niagara frontier did not go out until the last week in December. Dispatches were issued to officers of the 2nd Regiment of Gore Militia by Colonel Chisholm, who addressed to one the following orders:

Head Quarters Oakville
23d Decr 1837

Captain Hiram Smith
Wellington Square
Sir

You are directed to ascertain without delay what number of Volunteers you can raise to meet at Wellington Square by 7 o'clock on the morning of the 25th instant to proceed under the command of Capt Chalmers to join the detachment proceeding with Colonel McNab to the Lines—It is expected that such only as are active efficient men, and can leave home without great inconvenience are to go—Such as have Queens Arms and Accoutrements and do not go are to deliver them to those who do—You will also provide teams to carry such as go who will be paid at Twenty Shillings pr diem—

W. Chisholm
Col 2d R G M[93]

The Oakville Company left home on Christmas day, reaching Lundy's Lane the following day and moving to Chippawa, a mile above the falls, on December 27. The 2nd Regiment of Gore Militia's muster rolls show the rates of pay per diem of men on active service to have been: privates 1*s*., lieutenants 6*s*.6*d*., captains 11*s*.7*d*., majors 16*s*., the lieutenant-colonel 17*s*., and the colonel £1.1.[94] Captain Hiram Smith, who was "put in charge of the Oakville & Wellington Square Company" until his transfer to the Quarter Master General's Office, kept his wife, Hannah, informed on the news. On December 28 he wrote:

The Rebels made several shots of Cannon on our shore yesterday and last night but did no harm to any one. Our forces have been making batteries to erect their cannon and will probably make heavy fire in the course of a day or two. . . . We are now waiting for the arrival of the Lt. Governor, to decide what shall be done—The Colonel commanding reviewed the whole of the Regiments this afternoon, after our arrival today from Lundy's Lane, and is said to consist of from 2 to 4000 men, all equipt with arms &c—which having been drilled for some few days made a splendid appearance. . . . It is said that McKenzie and his party are still recruiting, and are about 600 or 900 men, with about 20 pieces of cannon . . . mostly of small size. Yesterday two of our boats went up the River a little above the Island on which McKenzie is and then put out to the middle of the Channel and so down to this place. McK. fired several shots of cannon at them but did not hit any one. They also fired with Rifle and Muskets and planted one ball in the stern of the boat, but no damage.[95]

Replying to this letter of her husband's Hannah Smith wrote: "I was glad you mentioned J[ock] in your last letter he was delighted to get a letter from his papa, you know how he can read, he often says mama do not cry and I will go fetch him home, and then away he rides at full speed on the broom and vows he will kill all the rebels."[96]

As the rebel forces continued to grow there was considerable cross-firing between them and the government forces under Colonel MacNab stationed on the Canadian shore. On the evening of December 29 the little forty-ton steamer *Caroline* was seen plying between Fort Schlosser on the American side and Navy Island. Colonel MacNab conferred with Captain Drew, R.N. retired, and they decided to attempt the destruction of this means of transporting men and arms to the rebels. Under cover of darkness the *Caroline* would be "cut out" and set afire. Captain Smith reported to Hannah: ". . . last evening a party of about 50 men with boats, armed with pistols and cutlasses, set out for Navy Island in search of the Steam Boat which for some days has been employed in their service carrying men, provisions &c between the American shore and the Island. They went round the Island, found the Boat was at Fort Slougher. . . . When they reached her the word was On Board. All hands followed, and took the boat, killed some of the persons on Board. They then fired the Boat and towed her out in the River and in a few minutes she was in flames, and so down the River until at last down the falls she went."[97] Captain Drew's version of the *Caroline's* fate is more detailed:

When free from the wharf at Fort Schlosser, her natural course would have been to follow the stream which would have taken her along the American shore and over the American Falls; but she acted as if she was aware she had changed owners, and navigated herself right across the river, clearing the Rapids above Goat Island, and went surely over the centre of the British Falls of Niagara as if she had been placed there on purpose.

There were hundreds of people on the banks of the river to witness the splendid sight, for it was perfectly beautiful, and the descent took place within a quarter of an hour after our landing; and no human ingenuity could have accomplished what the vessel had so easily done for herself.[98]

It is a well-known fact that a number of Oakville men took part in the "cutting out of the *Caroline*," but with the following exceptions names and details are wanting. It was Captain Edward Zealand who cut the steamer from her moorings and superintended the firing,[99] and John Moore (not the tinsmith but another) is said to have stayed aboard to rescue a cat, being taken off by his companions only in the nick of time. Upon returning home, Moore found it prudent to disappear into the north country with a surveying party until the excitement created by the episode had blown over. Captain Robert Wilson had in his possession a cutlass marked with the cipher of King George, which was undoubtedly Navy issue. He was said to have obtained it on this expedition, but when questioned in later years "he would not talk." The cutlass is still retained by his descendants.

The militia continued to strengthen their position on the Canadian shore of the Niagara River. On January 4 Captain Smith wrote to his wife:

I have nothing very particular to communicate to you respecting the progress of the wars here. Every moment of the time since I last wrote you has been occupied in making ready every thing for attacking the rebels on Navy Island. We have made eight batteries on our shore, and now have guns to each all placed ready for operations, and understand tomorrow morning at nine o'clock it is intended to open fire on the Rebels—The Americans have sent over to us, several communications on the subject of the *Troubles.* They say they have no wish nor inclination to participate with the *Rebels* and that all will be left to be settled by us and them—We have now mounted at the Batteries two 24 pounders, two 18 pounders, 2 Mortars, 2 Howitzers—and Rockets &c—with which we intend hammering away for perhaps 24 hours, before attempting to cross to the Island. I fear McK. will again make an escape from the Island, but we cannot yet tell—some say that the Rebels are leaving—others say not. . . . there are still some on the Island to be seen, nearly as many at any time heretofore. Yesterday they fired several shots over on this shore with their cannon, but as yet they have done no damage to any of our men. . . . I enclose you the countersign for this night—You will perceive it is a compliment to the Men of Gore. They stand higher in the estimation of the Governor and other commanding officers, than any other men here, both for sobriety, loyalty and being brave men—The Lincoln Militia are a considerable number turned out here but a great many of them are apparently a very careless and drunken, noisy set of fellows. . . . Should the wars continue much longer, and if my father has not made market for his oxen, I think it would be well for him to bring the beef down here to the public market. . . . The roads all about this quarter . . . are in a most dreadful state, just like travelling through *batter*. . . . I never enjoyed better health than since I left home, and have been up nearly every night to 12 o'clock, and till 2 or 4 in the morning, and then every night except two, laid on the floor, and part of the time with only my clothes on me, and some times with a block of wood for a pillow. . . .[100]

The burning of the *Caroline*, though it marked the end of Mackenzie's "Provisional Government," caused an international incident which very nearly led to war. However, the British Government stood behind Colonel MacNab, and knighthood was conferred upon him by the Queen. Parliament passed a bill, in favour of which Colonel Chisholm cast his vote, granting "100 guineas to enable Her Majesty to cause to be presented to the Honourable Allan McNab, the Speaker of this House . . . a suitable Sword" for services on the frontier. Seventy-five guineas were also voted for a sword to be presented to Andrew Drew, retired Commander of the Royal Navy "for the capture and destruction of the piratical Steamer *Caroline*, while employed in supplying a banditti of pirates, rebels and incendiaries then in occupation of Navy Island."[101]

In celebration of the successful outcome of the Rebellion a dance was held at the home of William Baker which now stands as no. 55 Navy Street North. A rebel flag showing two stars representing the two Canadas obtained at Chippawa was contemptuously nailed to the floor for staunch Oakville Tories to dance upon.

A song popular throughout Canada after the Rebellion reveals the sentiments of a large percentage of the people. It was set to the tune of the "Soldier's Return" and some verses ran as follows:

When McKenzie's rebel band was beat
Away from Gallows Hill, Sir,
To Buffalo he did retreat, and said
We had used him ill, Sir.

The Buffalonians did sympathize
And soon began to roar, Sir,
They kicked up such a tarnation noise
It reached the British Shore, Sir. . . .

Now Uncle Jonathan be wise
And of yourselves take care, Sir,
For each Canadian loudly cries
"Invade us if you dare," Sir. . . .

The Spirits of our Wolfe and Brock
Do still around us hover,
And still we stand on Queenston's Rock
To drive those Yankees over.

No slave shall ever breathe our air,
No Lynch Law e'er shall bind us,
So keep your Yankee mobs at Home,
For Britons still you'll find us.[102]

The hunt for rebels lasted throughout the following year. Many a poor yeoman and mechanic was arrested for "High Treason" and thrown into gaol. Those judged guilty were transported to Van Dieman's Land (now Tasmania) or banished from the colony. Among those men awaiting trial were a number with whom Colonel Chisholm was well acquainted, and upon several occasions he visited the gaol at York. Charles Durand, who was confined there for some time, recorded in his memoirs: "Col. William Chisholm . . . came in and we had a long conversation. He said, 'Well, Mr. Durand, this is all the fate of war; we are up, you are down. It might well have been otherwise.' "[103] Possibly Chisholm was also acquainted with Joseph Milbourne, who was detained in York Gaol at this time and who, not long after, was to come to Oakville as Deputy Customs Collector.

In December, 1838, Chisholm made a tour of the rear townships in Halton County to feel out the political situation. In this district, now the counties of Waterloo and Wellington, Mackenzie had a strong following. Chisholm reported to Chief Justice John Macaulay that he had encountered intense hostility; that several militia officers including Colonel MacNab, Captain Chalmers, his two brothers, and himself were "likely to be murdered." Chalmers and George Chisholm had "been shot at lately." He goes on to say that day or night he never travelled unaccompanied, "as I do not like to be killed in this way. If they meet me and give me a chance I do not fear them."[104]

It was shortly after returning home from this tour of the county that Chisholm took up his residence in Oakville. He moved his family into a large frame house on the south-east corner of Thomas and Colborne streets which he leased from Merrick Thomas. On January 17, 1839, however, the house caught fire from a defective stove pipe and "by the vigorous exertions of the inhabitants of the beautiful village of Oakville" the furniture was principally saved, but the house was destroyed.[105] Thereafter, according to John A. Williams, the family lived at the foot of Navy Street, on the harbour. The census of 1841 shows that Chisholm carried on farming activities in the surrounding township, raising the same crops as the other farmers. Of the 1,100 acres he had under cultivation 200 were sown in oats, 100 in Indian corn, and 700 in potatoes. Farm animals included eleven cows, ten hogs, six horses and thirty sheep from which were procured seventy-five pounds of wool for the twenty-five yards of wool cloth "produced by the family" that year. By then the family consisted of his wife, six sons, and four daughters, ranging in age from two to twenty-eight years. To these and all of his other activities were the added responsibilities of the offices of Justice of the Peace, coroner, and "Issuer of Marriage Licenses."[106]

The unrest resulting from the Rebellion seethed for some time. Feuds were kept alive by such accusations as "you are a rebel" or "the son of a rebel." Periodically "sympathizers" from the United States crossed the border to set fire to churches and houses. The *Transit*, like most steamers on Lake Ontario, carried racks of pikes and muskets on her deck. Land in Upper Canada, particularly in the western district, was unsalable at almost any price, and the atmosphere of suspicion and uncertainty led many to leave the province. The more settled conditions in the United States were preferable to immigrants, and emigration to Canada came virtually to a standstill.

In the spring of 1839 Chisholm again addressed Macaulay, stating that he had learned on good authority "that there are many stand of arms in possession of persons who took them from the owners on suspicion of the parties not being loyal, and they still hold the same. As I think such proceedings injurious to the country, I would be glad to receive some advice from His Excellency the Lieutenant Governor, to know what course I should take . . . to restore to the owners their property."[107] Through Macaulay His Excellency replied: "The station and influence which you hold among the inhabitants of the Gore District, afford you the means of doing much good; and in no respect can you more beneficially exert yourself, than endeavoring to persuade those persons who . . . have seized, and who still keep in their hands the guns or other arms of their neighbors, to restore them openly and fully to their rightful owners. . . . In this way, you will render an important service to the country."[108]

The newspaper editor who published this correspondence stated that the disarming of suspected persons, "that is, persons differing in politics from the parties employed, or allowed to ransack their neighbor's houses" had been almost incredibly extensive, and that Colonel Chisholm had "exerted himself in several back townships of the Gore District with the most praiseworthy humanity putting a stop to this pernicious proceedure, and in getting the fire-arms which had been seized restored to their rightful owners."[109]

The frustration resulting from the failure of the reform movement is manifest in the pages of the Denominational Census of 1840, the first to be taken in the province. It was closely related to the burning question of Clergy Reserves, a principal grievance of the Reformers. The returns show many singular entries under the heading of "Other Denominations" such as "Non-professors and Honest men," "God save the Rest," "Tremendous Lucky," and the like. It was the opinion of many persons interviewed that to inquire into their religious persuasion was not the right of the Government, and a committee appointed by the House of Assembly to investigate the matter "strongly suspected that these names were introduced in derision and insult to the authorities."[110]

Another aftermath of the Rebellion was the destruction of Brock's monument on Queenston Heights by an act of vandalism. On Good Friday, 1840, a charge of gunpowder was placed at the base of the shaft by an Irish Canadian who had been banished from the country after participating in the Rebellion. Badly shattered, the column lay in ruins. The indignation felt at this act was general, and three months later Sir Allan MacNab organized a "Public Meeting of Militia and Inhabitants of Upper Canada" for the purpose of establishing a fund for the erection of a new column. This function, held on Queenston Heights, was largely attended by people coming by steamer from all parts of the province. Tickets of admission included transportation and three meals, breakfast and supper aboard a steamer and the banquet on the heights. Cabin passage cost 15*s*. and deck passage, 7*s*.6*d*. At 7 A.M. on the day appointed an assembly of members of the government and militia officers, among whom was Colonel Chisholm, boarded the *Traveller*, *Transit*, and *Burlington* at Toronto. Since Sir George Arthur, Upper Canada's last Lieutenant-Governor, was aboard the *Traveller*, she flew at her mast-head the Royal Standard. Captain Richardson's *Transit* (named *Constitution* when launched at Oakville) was so thickly decorated from bow to stern with evergreens as to be likened by the editor of the *Patriot* to Birnam Wood. The three steamers were met at Fort Niagara by five others from different points around the lake, and a special flourish was added to the occasion when all these paddle-wheelers, bright with standards of national societies and the colours of England, Scotland, and Ireland, steamed abreast up the Niagara River. Reported the *Patriot*: "Eight fine vessels, streaming with ensigns . . . all breasting together the cataract-fed current of the rushing river, the numbers of brave men on board of them, all united in one common purpose, and the martial strains which floated on the breeze, all contributed to the effect."[111]

Near the spot on the heights where General Brock had fallen a pavilion had been erected in which six hundred sat down to dinner. Toasts were drunk in champagne and some forty speeches were heard during the afternoon. The assembly passed a resolution that "a general committee be appointed to carry into effect the object of the meeting, namely the reconstruction of Brock's monument." Colonel William Chisholm, representative of the 2nd Gore Militia, was appointed to the committee of sixteen which met the following week.[112]

That day a band of men, expatriated after the Rebellion for having been followers of Mackenzie, gathered on the American shore of the river and raised the British flag in tribute to General Brock.

The dinner on Queenston Heights set in motion the campaign which culminated in the erection of the shaft whose colossal surmounting statue stands nearly a thousand feet above the Niagara River as a reminder of Canada's great hero. "Erected," reads the plaque, "chiefly by the Voluntary contributions of the Militia and Indian Warriors of the Province aided by a grant from the Legislature." A rate according to rank was asked, but not required, of all men in the militia. Of the total of some two hundred and fifty names on the subscription list of the 2nd Regiment of Gore Militia forty or more are those of Oakville men who contributed in a descending scale from the £1.5 of their commanding officer to the 1*s*.3*d*. of privates.[113] But on the October day in 1853 when the corner-stone was set Colonel Chisholm was not among those who assembled to witness the ceremony.

SALE OF

CROWN LANDS.

IV

The settling of the country, particularly the waste lands of the Crown, was a favorite scheme of long standing with William Chisholm. By the middle thirties the last remaining section in the province where good land was to be had lay to the north-west between Garafraxa Township and Lake Huron. When the Saugeen Tract around Georgian Bay was surrendered by the Indians to the Crown in 1836, Oakville was well established, and Chisholm was quick to recognize a fact of considerable importance; should this region be made accessible its produce would flow south through the nearest port on Lake Ontario, Oakville.

As we have already seen, the main concession roads in the province were constructed by settlers as part of their settlement duties, and the secondary roads were opened by statute labour; in addition main arteries, such as the Lake Shore Road, were built by the Government. As settlement spread to the more remote sections of the province, colonization roads were built to open new tracts of land. The road running north from Oakville, called the 7th Line in Trafalgar Township, was open for some forty miles into Garafraxa Township in the north-western section of Halton County. From Oakville it ran straight to the northern boundary of Esquesing Township where the village of Ballinafad later sprang up, and there it turned west to run for a short distance along the base-line, then north-west through Erin Township. At the northern boundary of Erin it took a westerly direction, crossing the triangular township of Garafraxa to end at its north-western angle.

In March, 1837, following the acquisition by the Government of the Saugeen Tract, Chisholm petitioned Sir Francis Bond Head for the continuation of this road to Owen Sound on Georgian Bay. The petition reads:

Oakville a convenient Port situate on the North Side of Lake Ontario . . . is, I am told about 75 miles from Owen Sound or Big Bay on Lake Huron and a road from these two points would be a very great accommodation to the public, particularly the numerous settlers living in the neighbourhood of the intended road. It would in addition open a beautiful tract of country. . . . From these and other advantages . . . I am induced respectfully to request that His Excellency will be pleased to direct that a Survey be made which . . . will produce advantages equal to the expense of opening the same. I beg leave to state that there is now Forty miles of this road travelled thro' the Twps of Trafalgar, Erin and Garafraxa.

WM. CHISHOLM.[114]

A few weeks thereafter Sir Francis directed that the survey be made at once, and the instructions of the Surveyor-General to Deputy Surveyor Charles Rankin read in part: "It will be your duty to explore the country between Garafraxa and Owen Sound. . . . You will commence your work at Oakville and will call on William Chisholm, Esquire, who has promised to render you valuable aid in engaging men, supplying provisions and obtaining preliminary information respecting the interior from Indians and others."[115]

From Rankin's journal we learn that he was delayed for two days at Toronto by an east blow. The following entries then appear:

May 17th—To Oakville by steamer with the men [6] engaged . . . to the 20th inclusive spent in procuring flour and pork in which we met some delay.

May 21st—Engaged the following additional men as pack carriers and axe men for service, viz. Joseph and Philip Bisnois, George Burt, and Edward Baker, a boy.

May 21 & 22nd—Mr. Chisholm having supplied us with two teams at—per day for hauling provisions and luggage—set off. . . .[116]

Rankin began the survey at the north-west corner of Garafraxa Township, but being unable to obtain supplies locally he was forced to return to Toronto within a few weeks' time. With him he took Philip Bisnois "who has attack of pleurisy and is desirous of returning to his home at Oakville" and Baker, who proved too inexperienced for the rough work of surveying bush land. The party returned by way of Yonge Street. Bisnois was so ill that he was unable to bear the jolting of the stage-coach and was left at an inn at Richmond Hill, while Rankin and Baker continued the journey to Toronto. After arranging for supplies they returned the following day to find Bisnois already in the stage. "Was glad to find poor Philip in it though still very ill having been bled and blistered," wrote Rankin. At Toronto he put Bisnois and the lad aboard the steamer *Brittania* for Oakville.[117]

Notwithstanding this and other delays, Rankin continued his survey northward. Upon reaching the enormous swamp, the source of tributaries of the Grand River, he merely ran his lines around it, and reported it "all swamp." At a later date this section was surveyed into the townships of Luther and Melancthon. It is said that one of the surveyors, a Roman Catholic, became so wrathful while surveying this bog that he gave the townships over which it extended the names of the leaders of the Reformation.[118] As late as 1850 no white man was known to have traversed Luther Township from border to border.[119]

On the shore of the Sound, where the Sydenham River enters the bay, Rankin surveyed a concession or two contiguous to the road and a portion of the town plot of the village to be named Sydenham. Though officially the road was named the Owen Sound Road, several generations of people living along it knew it as Rankin's Road or the Garafraxa Road.

For several years the road remained only a blazed trail through the bush. During the financial depression following the Rebellion all public works in the province were suspended. In 1839 William J. Sumner and other overly optimistic men of the Gore District petitioned the Government "for a loan of money to plank the road from Oakville, on

Lake Ontario to Owen's Sound, on Lake Huron," a distance of 130-odd miles. The investigating committee recommended "that the prayer of the petition be complied with so far as to enable the Petitioners to plank said road from Oakville to Post's Corners on Dundas Street," a distance of *four* miles.[120] Nothing more was heard of the matter for the time being.

But the problem of settlement was to receive more attention from the Government after the arrival of the new Governor-General, Charles Poulett Thomson (soon to become Lord Sydenham). Before the opening of the Legislature at Toronto in 1840 he made a tour of Upper Canada, and his impressions of the western section of the province he thus described in a private letter:

> This tour has indeed been a triumph—a series of ovations. You can conceive of nothing more gratifying than my progress through Upper Canada, especially in the west. . . . I am delighted to have seen this part of the country; I mean the great district, nearly as large as Ireland, placed between three lakes—Erie, Ontario and Huron. You can conceive of nothing finer! The most magnificent soil in the world—four feet of vegetable mould—climate certainly the best in North America—the greater part of it admirably watered. In a word, there is land enough and capabilities enough for millions of people, and for one of the finest provinces in the world; the most perfect contrast to that miserable strip of land along the St. Lawrence, called Lower Canada, which has given so much trouble.[121]

Returning from London by the Dundas Street His Excellency was entertained all along the way to Oakville. He embarked upon the *Traveller*, which early the following morning steamed out of the Oakville Harbour for Toronto.[122]

When the union of the provinces became a reality Lord Sydenham embarked upon a "great programme of reconstruction" which included the completion of the Owen Sound Road. The inhabitants of Oakville presented him with an address dated September 10, 1840, in which, after the usual formalities, congratulations, etc. had been observed, the following sentiments were expressed:

> We have viewed with great satisfaction the successful result of your Excellency's administration of the Government of this important portion of the dominions of our most gracious Sovereign, and we confidently trust to the wise and vigorous policy of your Excellency, for the completion of our Public Works; for the encouragement of emigration from the Mother Country, and the settlement of those extensive tracts of fertile land—which, particularly in the rear of this section of the Country require only to be rendered accessible by the opening of Roads, to afford

a happy and comfortable maintenance to thousands of our fellow subjects who now languish from want of a field for their exertion.

In avoiding those extremes of party politics, and that violence of party strife, which has heretofore been so prejudicial to the best interests of the Country, we feel assured that we shall be rendering the most valuable aid to that system of the administration which your Excellency has declared to be your object to establish; an administration in harmony with the well understood wishes of the people, to whom peace is necessary for the restoration of their commercial and agricultural prosperity, and for the full enjoyment of those natural advantages with which Providence has blessed this highly favoured Country.[123]

To which Lord Sydenham replied:

Gentlemen:

I thank you for your kind address, and I observe with great pleasure the sentiments which you express in it.

I assure you that my best efforts will be directed to whatever may conduce to the improvement of this Province, and the prosperity of its Inhabitants.[124]

A month later, Dr. Thomas Rolph of Ancaster was honoured by a dinner at Hamilton on the occasion of his return from Britain, where he had gone in the interests of immigration. Dr. Rolph, who has been called the "champion of British immigration," stated in his speech: "Owing to the zeal and talent of the Hon. Mr. Sullivan, to the unremitting assiduity of Col. Chisholm . . . a large portion of the public domain has been now assigned for settlement. . . . The tract of land to which I refer . . . extends from Garafraxa on the South to Owen's Bay on the North. At its Southern extremity it will connect with the fertile lands of the Canada Company, with the townships of Nicol, Woolwich, and Guelph, and with Lake Ontario through Oakville."[125] Dr. Rolph then summed up the principle which from the earliest times had been accepted as the basis upon which the development of the province rested: "Any man who substitutes a bushel of corn for a tree is a benefactor to his country."

When Colonel Chisholm's health was proposed "the toast was received with rapturous applause." "Col. Chisholm returned thanks in a very feeling and efficient speech, congratulating the Country that the efforts which he had long been making to obtain a free communication from Oakville to Owen's Bay had proved successful, and that free grants of land were now provided for actual settlers that would prove eminently serviceable in developing and extending the resources of the country. (Loud cheers.)"[126]

It was at this time that the following verse was addressed to Dr. Rolph by a correspondent of the *Patriot*.

Sir,
Since you've busied yourself to promote immigration,
Tis *sartin* we owe you some *re come pence ation*,
Bring the *Bulls* and the *Scots* and the *Paddies* from Cork,
And we'll find them with *Praties* and plenty of Pork,
But if John Bull still grumbles nor thinks it relief,
Tell him four pence per pound will supply him with beef.[127]

In November, 1840, twelve men were employed along Rankin's survey in clearing a "winter road," i.e. removing trees and bushes from a space the width of a waggon track which, not being chopped or underbrushed, could be travelled only when covered with snow. Meanwhile John Telfer, Crown Lands Agent at Owen Sound, was engaged in building a Government House for the reception of immigrants. This log house, a combination storehouse and dormitory, was "fitted up with tiers of bunks around the walls like the steerage of a ship. In the centre stood a large VanNorman stove, with some ordinary appliances for cooking."[128] In response to handbills circulated and posted up at Ports of Entry by the Department of Crown Lands, the first group of immigrants arrived in the spring of 1841. They had been advised that 50 acres of land would be granted to actual settlers, and an extra 50 acres would in each case be reserved for purchase. If one-third of the grant was placed under cultivation within four years, patents would issue free of expense. Like Colborne before him, Lord Sydenham believed that immigrants were entitled to government assistance during the first difficult years.

The settlement was six months old when William Chisholm was commissioned to visit and report on the progress of the inhabitants. The Owen Sound Settlement was planned to border both sides of the Garafraxa Road from Arthur ("the southern division") to Owen Sound ("the northern division of the Road"), but even at this date settlers in the latter were isolated as the road was "open for oxcarts" for only five miles north of Arthur, and merely chopped out for another sixteen miles.[129] Chisholm travelled this rugged country on horseback. In a letter dated Kingston, September 15, 1841, he tells of a conversation with Lord Sydenham on the subject of settlement.

When in Montreal early in May last, I had an interview with His Excellency the Governor General . . . who stated to me that he was sure I could be of service to the Gov't in assisting to carry out the plan adopted for settling the waste lands of the Crown. Nothing further took place at this time in consequence of His Excellency having been taken ill a day or two afterwards.

The Honble Mr. Sullivan was anxious that I should immediately proceed to the Owen Sound settlement at Garafraxa and see that the settlers were provided with provisions, and seed for their spring crops, stating at the same time that I would render much service in looking over and reporting upon the state of the settlement and new Roads which the Government had undertaken. . . .[130]

On the 12th of May I left Montreal, and proceeded to Garafraxa, making a minute examination of the roads and settlement. My report on this subject is now in possession of the Government. After which I was called to report on the country in rear of Kingston and was then directed . . . to go to Garafraxa to put Captain Dunsford in charge of that station in place of James McNab, at which time I inspected the whole line of road to Owen Sound, the mill privilege and country around it, all of which was most satisfactory.

Having had long experience in making roads and settling a new country, as also in building mills etc. I am induced to believe that I could save the Gov't in prosecuting these settlements and improvements a sufficient sum to give me a fair remuneration for my constant employment.

The settling of the country on the North side of Lake Ontario to Lake Huron in the manner at present adopted, has been a favourite scheme of mine for many years, as well as in getting the waste lands of the Crown generally settled, in which I believe I have not been unsuccessful—The present prosperous state of the Garafraxa settlement, which was only commenced last fall, can only be ascribed to the manner in which it has been carried out, and it is now of the greatest importance that the road should be opened as soon as possible through to Owen Sound, which if completed will soon make one of the best settlements in the Province. The mill at Owen Sound may I think be built by private individuals, thereby relieving the Gov't from a heavy expense, at the same time be of the greatest service to the settlers.

Should my services be required . . . I will keep an office at Oakville where all Immigrants can during my absence get every information and advice without any expense. I have the honour to be, sir, your obedient Servant

W. Chisholm[131]

In his report to the Government, referred to in the above letter and published in the *Journals of the Legislative Assembly, Province of Canada*, 1841, Appendix, volume I (M.M.), Chisholm states that "reports became afloat" that nothing more was to be done towards finishing the road and granting more land, "consequently great despondency prevailed, and many were on the eve of abandoning any further efforts. But on the appearance of a person from the Commissioner of Crown Lands amongst them, confidence became again restored, and one and all resumed their labour with fresh alacrity." He found many lacking potato seed and provisions; these he arranged to be delivered to the agent and their cost was to be repaid by the settlers in labour on the roads. He continues his report: "I look upon it as no sacrifice at all on the part of the Government to complete the opening of this Road, nor yet the continuance for a time of the grants to actual settlers; so extensive a body of land so remotely situated, were it the property of an individual it would be the most effectual scheme he could devise to open it for the market; such as can afford it will almost in all cases purchase in addition to their grants, and this must be encouraged, for the inducement of capitalists to come into the Settlement, as otherwise none can be expected to come." Chisholm recommended that the frontage of the lots be widened, that the line of road be straightened, "wherever natural obstructions do not mitigate against doing so," that swamps be crosswayed, etc. All of these projects were eventually carried out by the Government.

The furthering of the colonization schemes of Lord Sydenham, to which Chisholm devoted his energies, involved long journeys on horseback, by stage-coach, and by steamer. His papers reveal that during eighteen months he took 353 days and travelled more than a thousand miles to supervise the building of roads and attending to the needs of settlers. When lodging at Francis Martin's tavern in Arthur Township he paid 1*s*.7*d*. for bed and breakfast and 1*s*.6*d*. for supper. The charge for whiskey toddy was 3½*d*. per gill and for plain whiskey in like amount, 2*d*.[132]

On one of these tours of inspection he was accompanied by his good friend, Robert Baldwin Sullivan, Commissioner of Crown Lands. Sullivan was born of Irish parents who had emigrated to York, where his father opened a general store. He studied law in the office of his uncle, Dr. Warren Baldwin, and was admitted to the bar. In 1835 Sullivan held his first public office when he opposed William Lyon Mackenzie and was elected Toronto's second mayor. The following year he was appointed Commissioner of Crown Lands and was soon called to the Executive and Legislative Councils of the province. R. B. Sullivan is said to have possessed "very high intellectual powers. As an orator he certainly had no rival among his contemporaries. He had a brilliant imagination, and a wonderful power of expression."[133] And again: "This was truly one of the greatest statesmen, politicians and lawyers Canada could reckon among her . . . sons."[134] Sullivan spoke with a strong Irish accent, and having himself come as an immigrant he desired to see his countrymen better themselves. He did what he could to stimulate the flow of immigration from Ireland. In a lecture delivered before the Mechanics' Institute at Hamilton he stressed government assistance to immigrants, and in passing told the following anecdote. He was one day riding out towards the Owen Sound Settlement with William Chisholm, "whom we used to call White Oak, for his truth and honesty of character, and genuine soundness of heart." In Garafraxa Township, "after getting over a detestable road, and having been long without seeing a house," the two men came to a hundred acre clearing, with herds of cattle grazing in the fields, sheep clustered in the shade of fences, wheat ripening in the fields, and apples reddening in the orchard. There was a good log house and a better barn and stable. The settler, his wife, and several grown-up daughters fared well. They had books which they could read, and were engaged in spinning, churning, knitting, etc. After leaving the farm Sullivan turned to Chisholm and exclaimed, "I do envy you your countrymen!" Upon being told that the settler was the first in that section of the country; that when he came there was no white man between him and Lake Huron; that he was very poor, had educated his children himself, and had done all the work himself, employing no labourers, Sullivan repeated his envy of "This Scotch prudence, Scotch energy, Scotch courage." "Well," replied Chisholm, "It may be all just as Scotch as you like to make it, but after all the man is an Irishman."[135]

At Oakville, the debarkation point for immigrants travelling to this new tract, Chisholm was always ready to assist in securing transportation and supplies for the arduous journey inland, and though immigration was at a low ebb during the early forties many settlers undoubtedly came through. In the spring of 1842 the Scotsmen who founded Durham on the Garafraxa Road passed through Oakville.[136] The same spring three and possibly more Oakville men moved to the colony on Owen Sound: John Doyle, William Hatton the merchant, and Francis Arnott, near whose grant grew up the village of Arnott.[137] The following year the population of the village of Sydenham (today the city of Owen Sound) stood at about forty.

This colonization project was of no immediate benefit to Oakville. Delays resulting from various causes retarded the completion of the Garafraxa Road, and it was not until the summer of 1845 that the first horse team got through to Sydenham. The boggy section through the swamp, some forty miles in length, was left unfinished because the Government, regardless of promises to build bridges and causeways, could not induce settlers to come in. One drawback was the distance to shipping ports. Some settlers, finding it impossible to farm the swampy land, turned to lumbering, and great quantities of cedar logs were floated down the rivers to sawmills. Deforestation of this swamp is considered today as a contributing factor to the disastrous floods which occur periodically in the valley of the Grand River, necessitating an extensive programme of flood control.[138] To prove the fallacy of the principle that "a man who substitutes a bushel of corn for a tree is a benefactor to his country" took nearly a century. Eventually, however, the townships filled up. In this remote region communication was better with Lake Ontario than with Lake Huron, and farmers were able to command fairer prices for their produce in markets to the south.[139] In increasing abundance the golden harvest poured in, filling warehouses and holds of the grain fleet of the port. Warehousemen made fortunes, and a grain schooner could earn her cost in a single season. The towns in the path of the widening stream became covered with gold, and Oakville, "the wheat market for the Country of Halton,"[140] rose to prosperity on the tide of wheat.

But William Chisholm did not live to see all this come to pass. On May 4, 1842, he died very suddenly, as William Miller (who was to be the first reeve and in 1861 mayor of Owen Sound) advised his brother at Sydenham:

> Dear Brother
>
> I send you a few lines to let you know that we are all well but alas, the father, protector, and friend of Owen Sound Settlement is no more. I mean Colonel Chisholm—he died a week ago today with a fit of apoplexy in a very few hours sickness. Let the inhabitants go in mourning from Arthur to Owen Sound for never will another man do what Colonel Chisholm would have done. It was his intention to go down to Kingston in a few days. . . . don't forget to write to
>
> WILLIAM MILLER[141]

The remains of William Chisholm were buried in the village cemetery on Reynolds Street, and the following obituary notice appeared in the *British Colonist*:

> It is with feelings of the deepest regret, that I convey to you the painful intelligence of the death of Colonel William Chisholm, of this place. He expired at his residence here, of inflammation of the brain, after an illness of thirty-six hours, on Wednesday evening last, and has left a blank, not in the hearts of his own family alone, but of all who knew him. From the moment that his death was known in Oakville, till his remains were consigned to the dust, business was suspended at the stores, and other places of resort, and one sensation of gloom and sorrow seemed to pervade all the inhabitants of this neighbourhood. Colonel Chisholm was the founder of this place; and the deep interest he took in it, and all connected with it—the kindness of his disposition—but most of all, the warmth of his heart, had endeared him to all who were acquainted with him. On Friday, last his body was borne to the grave by a number of Masonic Brethren, with the officers of his Regiment as pall-bearers—followed by many hundreds of mourning relatives and friends.[142]

If not actually insolvent at the time of his death, William Chisholm was not far from bankruptcy because of the crushing load of debt incurred in his attempt to industrialize Oakville. As mentioned in connection with the Oakville Hydraulic Company, foreclosure proceedings had already been instituted by his principal creditors, and his interest in the townsite of Oakville had been seized by the Sheriff of the Gore District. The Sheriff's sale was advertised to take place only two days before Chisholm's death. Under the terms of his short concise will, drawn the previous year, two-thirds of his property was applied to the payment of his debts and the maintenance of his family. The remaining third was left to his wife until such time as the youngest child should come of age.[143] The seized lands, sold by the Sheriff of the Gore District to the highest bidder on November 12, 1844, were bought in by the executors of William Chisholm, his three eldest sons. The deeds poll are dated April 22, 1845.[144] These instruments do not disclose the nature of the business transactions behind the legal documents, nor have any papers relating to Chisholm's affairs prior to or following upon his death come to light. What happened remains obscure.

With the untimely removal by death, at the age of fifty-four, of William Chisholm, the village of Oakville lost the guiding spirit of a man of wide experience who had been vitally concerned with its welfare. The numerous activities in which he alone had engaged were carried on by others, but there was no one immediately to fill the place he had held in the community. His eldest son, George King Chisholm, having been appointed Serjeant-at-Arms in the Parliament of the Province of Canada, carried on in the sphere of public affairs. He bought the land in the south half of the 3rd concession bounded on the south by Rebecca Street, which included some town lots but was mostly bush. John Alexander, the second son, was a farmer in Nelson Township until he took possession of the north-eastern section of the townsite where the mills were situated. He ran the mills, and clearing the land east of The Sixteen gradually converted it into a farm. Robert Kerr, the third son, who had been his father's deputy in the Custom House and post office at Oakville for some years, was appointed to succeed him in both capacities. He seems to have been interested mainly in town lots. William Chisholm's place in the community was largely taken by one of Oakville's most active and progressive citizens, Justus Wright Williams. It was he who assumed the responsibility of leadership in the affairs of the village.

The death of William Chisholm marks, as it were, the end of the beginning. The first period of Oakville's history was now completed.

WHEAT

CHAPTER SIX

THE RISING TIDE

As a market Oakville grew rapidly in importance. The commerce of the port was augmented by produce drawn from a steadily expanding area as the frontier pushed farther to the north-west. While still in its natural state during the 1820's the Sixteen Mile Creek had been the way by which staples flowed out of the township. By the time vessels could enter the harbour the little port was contributing substantially to the supplies of timber, lumber, staves, wheat, and flour passing through the St. Lawrence on the way to Great Britain. And the shipyard was turning out sloops and schooners which every spring sailed out to join the fleet of carriers bound for the St. Lawrence.

In the Canadas, where commerce was entirely dependent upon the waters of lakes and rivers, the great water-way of the St. Lawrence was a factor of supreme importance. This enormous water system, extending for fifteen hundred miles from the centre of the North American continent to the sea, was the highway of the trade with Great Britain. All things came by it; all things went by it. A staple-producing commercial state, Canada exchanged her raw materials for the manufactures of Great Britain and Europe. Furs, which had formed the basis of the economic system during the French régime, continued as the first staple after the British conquest. In canoes, batteaux, and Durham boats peltries poured down the waters of the lakes and rivers in what seemed a never ending stream. But the spreading civilization invaded the forest to drive the fur trade westward away from the St.

Lawrence and Lake Ontario. The old economy based upon a hunting society gave way to an agricultural economy, and gradually the old staple, fur, was replaced by the products of settlement—wood and wheat. Through the lake and down the St. Lawrence the produce of Upper Canada was floated to the warehouses of British merchants at Montreal, the river city, and Quebec, the ocean port. To meet the changing economy the British merchants in French Canada reorganized their business methods. As has already been shown in the case of Forsyth, Richardson & Company, of Montreal, they became promoters and money-lenders in the development of the agricultural province.

The trading system between Canada and Great Britain included natural products of the United States. As both Canada and the republic produced the same staples there was little trade before 1830 between the two countries, and such natural products as wheat, timber, lumber, potash, and (after 1830) flour entered Canada free of duty. In the eyes of the British, anything that touched colonial soil became colonial, so that upon entering Canada these products from the United States were considered to be of British origin, and entered British ports under the colonial system of preferential duties. Thus the natural products of the whole northern interior passed through the great water system of the St. Lawrence, to the increase of the trade of Upper and Lower Canada.

By the time Oakville became established as a port the Erie Canal in the United States was bringing about changes in the trade routes of the Great Lakes. It had opened the port of New York as a shipping point for the produce from the western section of Upper Canada. Being free from ice during the winter, this port could be used throughout the months that the St. Lawrence was closed to navigation. Also, to ship by this route was cheaper than by the northern route, where expenses of transportation were increased by the frequent trans-shipment made necessary by rapids in the St. Lawrence. Though the Assembly of Upper Canada was enthusiastic about building more canals to bypass the rapids, the province could ill afford to finance these projects, and the French in Lower Canada, being suspicious of British commercial enterprises, were unsympathetic towards spending large sums on public works. In consequence, with the opening of the Erie Canal, much of the trade which, having no other outlet, had formerly converged in the St. Lawrence, became diverted through the United States. The programme of canal building in Canada that was carried forward after the union of the provinces came too late to regain the trade which had slipped away through the neighbouring country.

I

The United States appeared as Upper Canada's first foreign market in the 1830's. As her population increased and her forests diminished the republic looked across the border for supplies of wood and food. About 1834 the United States began to absorb large quantities of the secondary product of the timber industry, sawn lumber. That sawmill operators in and around Oakville were in the forefront to take advantage of this new market is evidenced by the fact that lumber was shipped in the summer of 1835 to Lewiston, New York.[1] The demand created by the United States markets stimulated mills already in operation to raise their output and proved an incentive for the erection of new ones. Another factor in the increase in the number of sawmills was the decline, in the forties, of the trade in squared timber.

In the township of Trafalgar the large timber was coming to an end, and with it the stave industry. In 1840 more than 31,000 cubic feet of pine and oak timber went out of the Port of Oakville, but five years later only a little above 3,000 feet was exported. Thereafter none went out.[2] Over 27,000 pipe staves came down The Sixteen in 1840 but within two years the number and decreased to somewhat over 5,000, although the smaller West India staves straggled out a little longer. With the exhaustion of the large timber in the region, the timber trade went the way of the fur trade, to the upper lakes. On the other hand, the smaller second-growth timber was being shipped in ever increasing quantities as sawn lumber. Export lists of the Custom House show that between 1840 and 1850 nearly fifteen million feet of pine boards went out from the township.[3]

As it follows its winding course in sharp curves to the lake the Sixteen Mile Creek is admirably suited to mill-races and water-wheels. Between the Dundas Street and the head of navigation, a distance of less than three miles, the river bed drops about 125 feet. In this section there were, exclusive of the mill at Oakville, four mills evenly spaced along The Sixteen by the late thirties; wherever a meandering stream could be made to turn a water-wheel, a sawmill soon appeared. The lumber cut by these mills passed out through the harbour in vessels belonging to the port.

The first mill in the township was built on The Sixteen by Phillip Triller, a Loyalist who in 1806 had brought his wife and ten children from New Jersey to Upper Canada. Upon receiving a grant of land, Triller drew lot 20 of the 1st concession south of Dundas Street, through which The Sixteen runs. Two years later he addressed to the Lieutenant-Governor a petition in which he stated, relative to his grant:

> . . . although the Lot contains but very few acres fit for cultivation Your Petitioner has performed the settlement duty thereon and has received the Patent.
>
> That Your Petitioner has purchased, for £1,000 Prov. cy. the broken front Lots no. 1 and 2 upon Lake Ontario in Nelson whereon he lives, and has cleared about twenty acres and built two houses.
>
> That as the streams called the 16 and 12 Mile Creeks, in the Township of Trafalgar from the Lake to Dundas Street have been reserved by the Indians—it is with much difficulty that mill sites are to be found on the south side of Dundas Street.

To get a mill site Triller requested lot 32 on the lake shore in Trafalgar Township, not far from his home. This land, he explained, "has a small stream of water upon it on which a sawmill might be erected."[4] But lot 32, which bordered the western limits of the Missisauga Reserve at the Twelve Mile Creek, already belonged to William Allan (for whom Allan Street in Oakville was named), and it was Charles Sovereign who later secured it and built a sawmill on the stream. When nothing came of his petition Triller proceeded with the work of establishing a mill at Dundas Street.

To harness The Sixteen and gain access to the flats from Dundas Street demanded considerable ingenuity. For the site of his "mill, grist and saw, one run of stones, wrought by water"[5] Triller chose a level spot below the loop in the river about a mile south of the Dundas Street, and not far from the Upper Middle Road. Here the bed of The Sixteen drops twenty-five feet within a short distance. He ran the mill-race from the head of the curve close along the bottom of the east bank. After passing over the mill-wheel the water poured out through a natural tail race cut out by a stream descending a ravine south of the mill. Triller opened a road to the mill from the Dundas Street through his farm, "Hickory Grove." The road ran for some distance through the bush and descended steeply into the flats at the head of the mill-race. A contemporary outline of conditions as they existed in 1817, drawn up and signed by a number of settlers in the township, states that "the rate of sawing is one half when the sawlogs are carried to the mill."[6] This first mill in the township ground grain and cut logs for the settlers until some time in the 1830's.[7] It has long since sunk into oblivion and were it not for authentic records its existence would be completely forgotten. Only the old road through the bush and the mill-race still lead explorers to the site.

It is highly probable that after 1827 the trade of this rather inaccessible mill suffered from the competition of Chalmers' mill which stood on "the great high road from Toronto to the Western District," the Dundas Street. George Chalmers, a Lowland Scot, had started as a general merchant at Munn's Corners about 1820.[8] Having money to invest he began in 1826 to buy up land along The Sixteen where it crosses the Dundas Street. On the south side of the hazardous road abruptly descending the steep banks of red clay, Chalmers built a saw and grist mill with one run of stones to which he brought the water through a mill-race from some two hundred yards upstream. This mill went into operation in the year that Oakville was founded, 1827,[9] and with a store, an ashery, and the mills as a nucleus, a village known as Sixteen Village or Sixteen Hollow[10] soon spread down the valley. Its products of flour, potash, timber, lumber, and staves combined with those of Triller's mill to form the first exports that passed through Oakville while the harbour was still under construction. The people in the village were largely Scottish Presbyterians, and the Reverend Robert Murray visited them periodically, establishing a connection with the Oakville Presbyterians which was to continue for fifty years.

Chalmers lived in a frame house in the village he had founded. It has been said of him that he had "business ability, a natural Scottish shrewdness, a military training and bearing . . . that made him both respected and admired."[11] As colonel of the 5th Regiment of Gore Militia he took an active part against the Rebellion. By 1840, however, he was beset by financial difficulties, and in that year Forsyth, Richardson & Company announced the sale of "the Grist and Sawmills at the Sixteen-mile Creek known as Chalmers' Mills." The property included "a Distillery, Dwelling-house, Tavern Stand, with Barns, Blacksmith Shop and other buildings suitable for a large establishment of the kind. The Land attached to the mill comprises 400 acres of good Land . . . [where stands] a great deal of Valuable Timber."[12] The mill property passed into the hands of John Proudfoot under the name of the Trafalgar Mills[13] and the village became known as Proudfoot's Hollow.

At the Dundas Street the red clay banks of The Sixteen rise to their highest point of 125 feet. From the earliest times, in petitions for government assistance in improving the road, land holders stressed the numerous accidents caused by the steep incline of the road. As late as 1847 a petition stated that many persons had "narrowly escaped with their lives, and that of their teams, in passing said dangerous hills" and that frequently the Royal Mail was seriously delayed.[14] A parliamentary committee described the hills at The Sixteen and The Twelve as the "steepest and worst, in every respect, of any to be found between Quebec and Sandwich."[15] Upon one occasion a farmer was putting drags on his heavily loaded sleigh when it suddenly "moved forward with great velocity, forcing the horses to the mill-race upon the spikes of which they were both precipitated and suddenly mangled."[16] In his journal Charles Sovereign noted that he had been "providentially preserved at the Sixteen Hill."

In spite of its unfavourable location, however, Sixteen Village grew, and during its most prosperous period boasted a three-storey hotel, a tannery, a carding mill, a distillery, a steam stave mill, and the shops of many small tradesmen and artisans such as blacksmiths, weavers, shoemakers, and a tailor. The head distiller, Donald MacKay, had come from Thurso, Caithness, in the northernmost section of Scotland. Within a few years he was joined by his brothers, John and William, who engaged in teaming barrels of whiskey from the Hollow to Oakville for shipment. John and William MacKay soon settled on farms situated in the 2nd concession west of The Sixteen on the Lower Middle Road where, on part of this land, their descendants live today.

On the east bank of The Sixteen overlooking a little ravine stood Proudfoot's home, "Park Hall." On the west bank was situated the steam stave mill "complete with all requisite machinery . . . with proper management capable of turning out 1,800 staves per hour and the same readily sold for $5 to $6 per thousand."[17] One year, according to an anecdote, John Proudfoot contracted with a man named Forbes for the delivery at Oakville of a large quantity of oak staves for shipment. That they might be floated quickly down the river Forbes applied to one of the Chisholm brothers for permission to open their dam but the request was refused. Proudfoot instructed Forbes to open the dam anyhow, promising that he would handle any legal complications which might arise. One morning before daylight Forbes and his eight stalwart sons removed about twelve feet of the Chisholms' dam, floated the staves down to the harbour, and loaded them onto a vessel that was under charter to the Chisholms. As Forbes possessed nothing there was little point in bringing suit against him, and the Chisholms therefore had no redress.

A youth who was reared in the village went far in the affairs of the province. Adam Wilson was born in Edinburgh, a son of George Chalmers' sister. He had accompanied his mother and uncle to Upper Canada and worked as a clerk in Chalmers' general store. Desiring to become a barrister, he entered the Toronto law office of Robert Baldwin in 1834, and five years later was called to the bar. After serving as mayor of Toronto and Solicitor-General in the cabinet of Sandfield Macdonald, Sir Adam Wilson was appointed Chief Justice of the Court of Common Pleas.[18]

Eventually the village in the Hollow disappeared. Some claim that its decline dated from the unfortunate end of Colonel Chalmers. A strong Tory, Chalmers was elected Member for East Halton in 1844, filling the seat vacated by Caleb Hopkins who in the previous election had defeated William Chisholm. Four years later Hopkins defeated Chalmers, who very soon after committed suicide by shooting himself. His action, according to some, was the result of his defeat in Parliament, but others said that while under the influence of liquor he had signed a note for £2,500 which he could not meet.

The decline of the Sixteen Village seems to have been caused by the exhaustion of the wood upon which its industries depended, and the disappearance of the stage-coaches which brought it trade. Proudfoot sold out in the 1860's and went to Cleveland, Ohio,[19] and the people in the village gradually moved elsewhere. By the time the three-storey mill closed down in the eighties, only two dwelling-houses remained occupied. As time passed the spring floods erased the signs of human habitation, and the building of the high-level bridge which now spans the valley completed the obliteration. But the mill-race still winds along the flats of The Sixteen, and every spring the apple, pear, and cherry trees which have long run wild fill the valley with their blossoms.

To us who live in the age of motor transportation the view of the Sixteen Mile Creek from the high-level bridge is probably the most familiar, and it is impressive. As one stands on the north side of the bridge one sees the wide valley spreading out more than a hundred feet below. The west bank is thickly wooded and in the distance the river sweeps from the west to skirt the bare red shale of the west bank and flow in an S curve around a lone and ancient elm which has withstood the battering ice and rushing waters of many springs. The greater part of what is seen to the north was the settler's grant of

William McCraney who preferred, however, to live on the lake shore where he became one of the earliest settlers west of Oakville. Though he made no attempt to develop the water-power, McCraney realized its potential value and held his grant for twenty years, when Chalmers took up the project of its development. McCraney saw the mill-pond spread across the flats, and the great trees fall one by one, either to disappear into the sawmill or to float down the river to the harbour. But he never saw the village growing in his valley, as he died in 1829. It was his son Hiram who built a sawmill lower down on The Sixteen near Oakville's northern boundary.

A blacksmith by trade, William McCraney had come from the United States to Upper Canada in 1801, and with his wife and three children settled at the Grand River.[20] That same year Hiram was born. With the opening of Trafalgar Township McCraney petitioned for land, drawing lot 23 on the north side of the Dundas Street, as mentioned above. Choosing to live near the lake he leased the Clergy Reserve, lot 19 of the 4th concession, in 1807, and the year following bought from the grantee the 200-acre lot 20 of the 3rd concession bordering the 4th Line. The junction of the road and the Lake Shore Road became known as McCraney's Corners. From the Crown McCraney leased the adjoining Clergy Reserve, lot 18, 3rd concession, and the lease, drawn when George III was King of England and Sir Francis Gore Lieutenant-Governor of Upper Canada, shows the terms to have been as follows:

> William McCraney, his Executors, Administrators and Assigns from the Twenty-Ninth Day of September, One Thousand Eight Hundred and Seven for during and unto the full end and term of twenty-one years, . . . the Rent or Sum of Ten Shillings of Lawful Money of our said Province or Three Bushels of good sweet clean Merchantable Wheat. . . . During the second seven years . . . the yearly Rent or sum of One Pound or Like Lawful Money or Six bushels of like Wheat . . . and paying during the third seven years residue of the said Term of Twenty-one years . . . the yearly Rent or Sum of One Pound Ten Shillings . . . or Nine Bushels of Like Wheat . . . all the aforesaid payments to be respectively made on . . . the Twenty-fifth day of March and the Twenty-ninth day of September every year by even and equal portions at such place and in such manner within the Home District [as shall be designated].[21]

When he grew to be a lad, Hiram McCraney travelled as far as the village of Dundas to have his father's grain ground into flour. With the bags strapped to the neck of his horse he rode through the forest, returning the following day, a journey of forty miles. Wishing to plant an orchard, William and Hiram carried the young fruit trees on their backs from Dundas.[22] When at the age of sixty-seven William Mc-

Craney died he was buried beside his wife, Eunice, who had died in 1812, two daughters, and Rachel, his step-mother, in the family burial plot situated in the east corner of the farm. In 1876 Hiram had the remains transferred to St. Jude's Cemetery.[23] When Sir Edmund Walker, wishing to further education in Canada, founded Appleby School for boys in 1911 he chose part of this farm. The McCraney homestead, now the property of the school, still stands on the north side of the Lake Shore Road near McCraney's Corners.

Hiram McCraney settled north of the Lower Middle Road on lot 17 of the 2nd concession, now the property of Colonel L. H. Nelles. Since the "flats and low grounds" along The Sixteen reserved to the Missisauga Indians were located here the water privileges were not available until after the cession of the reserve to the Crown. Hiram McCraney then erected a sawmill which went into operation in the 1830's.[24] By 1851 it was "capable of sawing 350,000 feet of lumber yearly and about two hundred and fifty pounds currency are invested in the establishment."[25] The mill was approached from the Lower Middle Road by a road leading through "Mount Farm," as McCraney called his land, to the flats of the river. The road is still there but nothing remains of the mill but the stonework of the mill-race. Hiram's son William became an extensive lumber dealer who was closely associated with Oakville.

About three-quarters of a mile north of Hiram McCraney's mill, on lot 18 of the 2nd concession (now owned in part by the Jesuit Association), was a sawmill established by Thompson Smith, a native of the district who became an important man in Oakville. Smith was a farmer who learned the trade of cabinet-making, and is said to have got his start by teaming the products of his skill to Toronto for sale. He built his mill below the curve in the river, bringing the water to it from some two hundred yards upstream through a mill-race close to the east bank, in the usual manner. On a level stretch of ground situated midway between the top of the bank and the mill on the flats he built a frame dwelling-house. The mill was reached by a road running north through Smith's farm for about half a mile to connect with the Upper Middle Road west of the 6th Line not far from the river. Because of the steep banks the Upper Middle Road did not cross The Sixteen nor has the wide valley since been bridged. Smith's mill began cutting logs in 1838[26] and gradually he expanded his business throughout the township, and ultimately throughout the county, until by the time he went to live at Oakville in the forties he was one of the largest lumber dealers in the district.

Thompson Smith and the brothers Charles and John Culham,

having married into the Post family, were related by marriage. In 1844 the Culhams bought the north half of the lots surrounding the mill, and the mill was taken over by Charles Culham, who then occupied the dwelling-house in the valley. Smith retained an interest in the mill, and as he was an energetic business man, many hot arguments are said to have taken place between him and Culham, a strict Methodist, relative to operating the mill on Sunday. Gradually all the pine along the 6th Line was turned into lumber at this mill. The Culhams bought up the surrounding Clergy and Crown Reserves, dividing the whole into two large farms, and each built a spacious brick house facing the 6th Line. Both houses are still standing.

To those who are familiar with it, the site of Culham's mill is a favourite spot in the afternoon when the sun drops behind the trees crowning the red shale bank which rises almost perpendicularly from the bed of The Sixteen. The foundations of the house and its well are hidden by lilacs and snowberries, and tall elms grow upon the banks of the mill-race, which has withstood the passage of time and the ravage of floods.

On the Lake Shore Road within a short distance east and west of Oakville were a number of sawmills powered by the waters of lesser streams. The mills of John Hinton and Joshua Leach had been cutting logs into lumber for some years before the village was founded, and after the opening of the harbour sawmills sprang up on streams all over the southern section of the township.

A mile and a half west of Oakville, only a short distance beyond the 4th Line, runs the Little Sixteen, in most respects a replica in miniature of its namesake. At its mouth the intervale and banks are similar to those of The Sixteen, and there is about the same proportion of navigable water forming a tiny harbour. Here on lot 21 John Hinton erected his sawmill. He and his eldest son James came from the United States to Upper Canada in 1806 with the intention of becoming permanent settlers. At that time he stated that he was an "old servant of the Crown, having served His Majesty on Board the *Kent*, man-of-war of 74 arms."[27] The Hintons seem to have come to the township through an arrangement James Hinton made with Quetton St. George whereby he was to perform the settlement duties on St. George's grant, lot 21 (now the estate of Lady Baillie) and lot 22 of the 4th concession.

Laurent Quetton, who upon his escape to England on St. George's day during the French Revolution had assumed the name of St. George, was the only French *émigré* to receive land in the township of

Trafalgar. As an officer who had fought in the British Legion of the royalist army he was granted 5,000 acres in Upper Canada which, as he stated, was a "Grant of Lands equal to [grants to] persons of the same rank who had served in the American Corps of Loyalists."[28] Unlike General de Puisaye, Count and Viscount de Chalus, and other royalist *émigrés*, who became discouraged with the difficulties they encountered and returned to France, the Chevalier de St. George established himself as a merchant at York. In 1807, with brick brought from across the lake, St. George built at the north-east corner of King and Frederick streets the first brick building in the town of York.[29] He carried on trade with the Indians round Lake Simcoe, and the little French-Missisauga dictionary he compiled for his own use has survived to the present time.[30] He realized, however, that a man not brought up to the heavy labour of clearing land was more likely to break his back than to make a fortune.

Having performed the settlement duties on the 108 acres in Trafalgar Township, James Hinton bought or traded this land from St. George, and with his father erected on the Little Sixteen a sawmill described as "wrought by water, on the lake."[31] Since the earliest township assessment roll is that of 1823, it is impossible to know just when this and other early mills first went into production, but Hinton's mill continued in operation as long as there was sufficient water-power in the Little Sixteen. In 1851 three sawyers were employed, and 75,000 feet of lumber was being cut annually.[32] The Hintons lived here until the eighties, and a seventy-five-year-old map shows a house surrounded by an orchard standing where the tennis court is located in the rear of the house now owned by William Sterling. Many Hintons became sailors and masters of vessels out of Oakville, and their descendants still live in the town.

After the opening of the Oakville harbour two more sawmills appeared on the Little Sixteen. Much of the lumber used in the construction of the Methodist chapel at Oakville was supplied by that of Robert Smith.[33] He was the son of Joel Smith, the merchant of Nelson Township who was William Chisholm's partner at the time Oakville was founded. When Joel married Margaret Campbell he was a millwright in the nearby township of Thorold. Margaret was a daughter of Robert Campbell, former sergeant-major of Butler's Rangers,[34] and as daughter of a Loyalist she was granted lot 22 of the 3rd concession, Trafalgar Township. In 1833 her son Robert became owner of this land, through which the Little Sixteen finds its way, and built his sawmill. Five years later Joel Smith bought from King's College the adjoining Crown Reserve, lot 23, and above, on the same stream, he also built a sawmill. It stopped running after his death in 1845. However, Robert's mill flourished, and in 1851 it was cutting 100,000 feet of lumber annually and employing eight men.[35] Hiram, another son of Joel and Margaret Smith, bought from King's College in 1840 lot 21 bordering the 4th Line where today his descendants live in the house he built of brick hand-made in the vicinity. A section of this farm has lately been developed as Maple Hurst Gardens.

Along the Lake Shore Road east of The Sixteen other sawmills stood on lesser streams. The earliest was that of Joshua Leach who supplied much of the lumber, and made the window frames, sash, and possibly much of the interior woodwork, for the Temperance Hall at Oakville. A carpenter by trade, Leach had come in 1797 to the new town of York, where he was "engaged in the King's work."[36] In 1806 Leach was granted town lot no. 1 on the north-west corner of what were then Hospital and Toronto streets, and are now Richmond and Yonge streets where the store of the Robert Simpson Company stands today. However, Leach preferred to build his dwelling-house facing upon Hospital Street in the centre of the block that is now bounded by Queen, Yonge, Victoria, and Richmond streets,[37] and this building, erected prior to 1812, became the first court house of the town of York.[38] In 1803 Leach made a chair for the Legislative Council, and the £7 he received in payment points to its having been a fine piece of furniture.[39] This chair was lost when the Parliament Buildings were burned by the Americans during the War of 1812. We find Leach making repairs to the gaol in 1807, and again in 1813, when "he laid before the court [of Quarter Sessions] two accounts for Work done by him by Order counting together to £11.0.0 New York Currency equal to £6.17.0 Pro: Curr'y."[40]

It was in 1822 that Joshua Leach bought lot 3 of the 3rd concession two miles east of the future townsite of Oakville, and within a few years he had a sawmill working on the stream that passes through his land. His sons, Ransom, William, and Robert, became carpenters and joiners who built many houses in Oakville and the vicinity. In 1844 the mill was taken over by William, and in the fifties by Robert. The road leading north from the Lake Shore Road through the 200-acre farm to the mill is today known as Still's Lane. At the point where it meets the stream the explorer may find the foundations of Joshua Leach's home and the perfectly preserved stoned well hidden by cedars and overgrown with lilacs and snowberries. The house overlooked the mill-pond, and directly below among the cedars in the ravine are to be found the shoulders of the dam. The workmanship in two handsome sideboards that are now in possession of a descendant show Leach to have been a fine craftsman. Born in 1776, Joshua Leach lived to the age of eighty-six, and lies buried in the Oakville cemetery.

Along the streams in the vicinity of the Town Line sawmills multiplied. The haulage of their output was reduced by "lake shore loading." Lumber and timber hauled by oxen to the foot of the 9th Line were piled to await a spell of calm weather, when several Oakville schooners would "drop down" to collect it. In winter, pines suitable for masts in ocean-going ships were hauled to the lake shore on a kind of sleigh pulled by six or eight yoke of oxen. The butt end of the timber rested upon a hollow bunk with which the sleigh was fitted, and being attached to it by a heavy chain containing a swivel link, the stick revolved without injury when it struck a tree or a stump. These masts, measuring seventy to eighty feet in length and from three to four feet in diameter after the removal of their bark, brought high prices on the English market.[41]

The technique of loading in the open lake where vessels were without protection was difficult and hazardous. Long "lake shore lines" were run from vessel to beach. Timber-men slipped lumber down a slide and rolled squared timber into the water where it was built into temporary rafts by vessel-men. The raft was floated alongside the vessel by men who stood or sat on the raft and hauled on the "lake shore line." Those engaged in this long slow work were often soaking wet all day. From the time it went into the water the lumber and timber became the responsibility of the vessel's captain, who continually kept a close eye on the weather.[42]

Some conception of the rapidity with which the land was being denuded of its trees may be gained from the following isolated example. In 1848 on lot 2, which adjoined on the east Leach's farm in the 3rd concession, stood "25 acres of clear fine pine timber; 2,000,000 feet of pine boards can be cut off this lot and the rear is expected to yield 50 cords of hardwood per acre, beech, maple, hickory, etc."[43] Thompson Smith, lumber dealer at Oakville, secured this land, and the trees, felled by the timber cutter's axe, were hauled off to one of his sawmills. John Alton, the new owner, engaged the escaped slave, James Wesley Hill, to remove the stumps and clear away the underbrush. Within a decade the trees that stood on these two hundred acres were mostly confined to a small woodlot.

With the deforestation of the heavily wooded areas, the water in the streams began to diminish. The destruction of the trees by the axe, and of the plant cover by the plough, allowed the water to drain off too rapidly, causing floods and soil erosion. Streams that had once run clear now ran red with irreplaceable top soil and during the spring thaw or a heavy rain The Sixteen spread a muddy swath in the blue waters of Lake Ontario. By the 1850's there was not enough water during the dry season to turn the water-wheels, and many sawmills resorted to steam during part of the year. When the water was high their machinery worked night and day to cut the logs that had accumulated during the winter.

As long as the timber resources lasted those mills which had converted to steam continued in operation, a large majority of them being taken over under lease or sale by Thompson Smith. But after Smith established his mill at Oakville these old water sawmills fell gradually into disuse.

GREAT WESTERN RAILWAY.

Opening of the Hamilton & Toronto Branch!

II

As the forest disappeared and the acreage of land under cultivation increased, the production of grain mounted steadily. With the settling of all the fertile land in the province there was no longer a frontier, and backwoods settlements were becoming a part of the commercial agricultural society. The pioneer period was rapidly passing away, and with it the democracy of the frontier.

Britain was calling for more and more wheat. When the amount grown at home was decreased by industrialization, she looked to Canada and the United States for supplies. Until the beginning of the nineteenth century the working people had known only dark bread, and the white bread made from wheat flour was eaten only by the ruling classes. But the adage "the whiter the bread, the nobler the eater" no longer held true after the victory of the masses during the French Revolution. Rye, oats, barley, and (for domestic consumption) Indian corn were widely grown in Canada, but preference was given to wheat, the grain for which there was the most demand in Britain and Europe.[44]

Canadian grain was also being absorbed by the United States. There are indications that before 1837 schooners were delivering wheat across the border at the Oswego branch of the Erie Canal. Called Chouégan by the French, Oswego had been the first British port on Lake Ontario. Here the shipping of the lake met the canal barges, and as time passed Oswego continued more and more to tap the commerce of Lake Ontario.

As in biblical times, men sowed and harvested the grain by hand, using farm tools that had remained substantially the same for many centuries. The first combine among agricultural implements, the cradle, was an improvement over the plain scythe used in the British Isles. "This generally used implement," wrote the Anglican clergyman at Oakville, the Reverend G. W. Warr, "is formed by the scythe being affixed to a cradle, or a number of wooden prongs, upon which the wheat falls; so that it is literally mown down with as much rapidity as grass is converted into hay."[45] A row of cradlers striding across a field at harvest time, cutting wide swaths in the standing grain, was a splendid sight. But the work of cradling and binding was slow and required many hands at the wage of 5*s.* or its equivalent in wheat and board per diem. Threshing was accomplished by the ancient method of treading out the grain on the barn floor, the oxen walking around in it "up to their bellies," or by the use of the flail. With this short wooden beater attached by leather thongs to the end of a long handle the farmer beat loose the kernels of wheat from the straw. Gradually threshing mills operated by horses or by water-power were set up on many farms. By 1841 there were thirty-three in Trafalgar Township.[46] Joseph B. Anderson on the eastern and Merrick Thomas on the western border of Oakville had threshing mills, and those of Joshua Leach, Richard Coates, and others along the Lake Shore Road were undoubtedly operated in conjunction with their sawmills. The mill to which Charles Sovereign took his grain threshed twenty-five hundred sheaves a day. When the increasing scarcity of labour forced the farmers to use horse-drawn machinery, the self-rakes, reapers, separators, horsepowers, and other agricultural implements manufactured by Jacob Lawrence in his foundry at Palermo were employed extensively throughout Halton County.

The commerce between Canada and Britain suffered a severe blow when the mother country abolished the corn laws in 1846. With the termination of the system of colonial preference Canadian wheat was no longer admitted on favourable terms. It is a notable fact, however, that although the province suffered as a whole, the commerce of Oakville was not seriously affected since the greater proportion of the exported grain went to the United States. During 1846 and 1847 only a slight drop occurred in the amount shipped, and a sharp rise in the export of whiskey indicated that some of the grain destined for the British market was being diverted to neighbouring distilleries.

By then Oakville was beginning to reap the benefits of colonization in the district to the north-west. The 7th Line, which was the southern section of the road leading from Owen Sound, was well travelled by farmers bringing their wheat and other produce to market. A tavern and a blacksmith's shop were to be found at many cross-roads, and every few miles villages had sprung up. One of the oldest and most famous of the taverns on the 7th Line was Post's Inn four miles north of Oakville, and at the time of writing this building still stands on the south-west corner of the Dundas Street.

The several Posts who settled in Trafalgar Township were sons and daughters of Jordan Post, "late Loyalist," who had come to York from New England in 1802. According to his own statement, Jordan Post "was born in the late Province, now State, of Connecticut, in the now United States of America, in the Year 1744 during the Reign of His Majesty George the Second, and has always been a good Subject to the British Government . . . all his Children—8 in number—followed him into the Province, and . . . he has, in the Province, 40 Grand Children, and 20 Great Grand Children, all, excepting 5, born therein."[47] Four of the eight children mention settled in Trafalgar Township, the earliest being Ezekiel, born at Hebron, Massachusetts, and Millicent, wife of Daniel Munn. Ezekiel Post drew lot 7 on the north side of the Dundas Street west of the 9th Line, and opened a tavern there in 1816.[48] He was appointed the first constable (in 1809) and elected the first Town Warden (1814) in the township of Trafalgar.[49]

Daniel Munn drew Lot 16 on the south-east corner of the 6th Line where he also opened a tavern some time prior to 1814,[50] and this cross-roads soon became known as Munn's Corners. Munn was the first settler in the township to hold the office of Town Clerk (1813).[51] After his death his widow Millicent continued for many years to run the tavern. Evidently her brother Ephraim came later to the province. He bought Lot 12 on the north side of the Dundas Street, and occupied as well lot 13 on the south side. With the opening, after the founding of Oakville, of the 7th Line between these two lots, Ephraim Post took advantage of his location and opened a tavern on the south-west corner of the cross-roads which soon became known as Post's Corners. When it was taken over in 1841 by Ephraim's son, Hiram, the tavern was considerably enlarged by the erection of a two-storey addition across the front of the building. The establishment then had the unusual number of five fireplaces. The Corners was a busy spot for Post's Inn was a change-house for stages running along the Dundas Street, and across from and a short distance west of the tavern, on the north-west corner, was the general store of Squire (James) Appelbe, where the Trafalgar Post Office was now located. Upon the resignation of Alexander Proudfoot (probably in the 1840's), Appelbe had been appointed postmaster and thereupon the post office was moved into the store where it remains at the present time.[52]

By the forties the traffic coming down to the port from the north was so heavy that it was decided to improve the 7th Line. In Canada, where resources of timber seemed so abundant, the surfacing of roads with planking was becoming extensive. The first plank road on the continent had been built out from Toronto in 1836, and thereafter this type of road, constructed mostly by joint-stock companies, spread rapidly. In ease of draught and speed, and in comfort to passengers, planks roads promised to be superior to macadamized roads. Heavier loads could be drawn in all kinds of weather, and when it was too wet to work in the fields farmers could do their hauling. For the purpose of constructing a plank road from Oakville to Fergus, a distance of sixty miles, the Trafalgar, Esquesing and Erin Road Company, a joint-stock company, was formed in 1846.[53] About half of the directors were Oakville men; Squire Appelbe was appointed president and R. K. Chisholm secretary-treasurer, and the company's headquarters were located in the Oakville Post Office.[54] Stock in £20 shares was subscribed to the amount of £2,000 in the townships through which the road was to pass, the Trafalgar Township Council subscribed another £2,000,[55] and the County Council assisted with a loan of £3,000,[56] a total of £7,000.[57] The Gore District Surveyor, Robert W. Kerr (who in 1836 had drawn the official plan of Oakville), submitted an estimate of costs and materials. Stating that "timber and lumber may be procured at hand for low prices," Kerr gave £14,411.14.0 as his estimate for a road graded twenty feet wide with a plank way of eight feet for the nineteen miles which lay between Oakville and "Stewart's Town" in Esquesing Township. Kerr based his estimate upon grading at 8*d.* per cubic yard, ditching at £80 per mile, and three-inch planking at £336 per mile. In addition, eighty-one culverts ranging in width up to thirty-two feet were required to bridge the streams and swamps which the road encountered.[58] By erecting its own sawmill, the company was able to reduce the costs of these items below Kerr's estimate.[59]

Although the building of the plank road was not begun until April, 1850, once it was started no time was lost in completing it. The road bed was sloped for drainage, and upon it were laid lengthwise four-inch square sills or sleepers which were packed in earth to prevent decay. Upon these sleepers the three-inch planks were laid crosswise, their weight being sufficient to keep them in place without nails. The nineteen-mile stretch was finished within seven months, and the new road was officially opened early in December with a public dinner held at Stewarttown. On this occasion the Hamilton *Spectator* pointed out that as the planking would enable farmers to bring their produce to market when prices were good, instead of having to wait as formerly until such time as the road was passable, it would be a great boon to all in the district. "We may observe," continued the *Spectator,* "that the Trafalgar, Esquesing, and Erin Road Company owes its organization to three or four enterprising men, conspicuous among whom is the reeve of Trafalgar, George K. Chisholm, Esq. We do that gentleman's colleagues no injustice in stating that he has been most active and persevering, and that he has succeeded amidst an opposition sufficient to deter men of ordinary spirit and capacity. The grant from the County Council was obtained entirely through his exertions, and during the construction of the work nearly his whole time was devoted to it. He had valuable assistance, however, as the fact we have mentioned, that eighteen miles of road were constructed in seven months, abundantly testifies."[60] The *Spectator* concludes with the comment that, as the most difficult part of public improvements is to make a good beginning, it now seemed certain that the original plan of constructing a plank road from Lake Ontario to Fergus would be carried out.

To obtain revenue for maintenance and repairs, toll-gates were placed every few miles along the plank road. In Oakville the planking extended down Dundas Street to Colborne Street, and at the junction of the 6th and 7th Lines was situated a toll-gate where Donald Campbell was employed as gate-keeper. Campbell had come to Canada with the Imperial forces at the time of the Rebellion, and on being discharged from the Argyle and Sutherland Highlanders in 1842 he settled at Oakville. After his marriage to a sister of Mrs. John Urquhart he bought the lot on the north-west corner of Reynolds and Division streets from John A. Chisholm in 1856. Here Campbell erected the brick house, no. 34 Division Street, in which his descendants live at the present time.

The quantity of wheat shipped out of the port of Oakville mounted steadily. The 11,243 bushels exported in 1840 rose to 165,839 bushels in 1850.[61] The farmers in the county were putting a large acreage into wheat, and they were getting a very high return for it. According to the agricultural census of 1851 the highest average of wheat per acre in the whole province was raised in Halton County, "the township of Esquesing having taken off the Palm."[62] After the harvest a continual stream of grain-loaded vehicles passed down the 7th Line from the north. Business literally came knocking at the doors of taverns, filling their bars, dining rooms, and drive sheds. Supper could be had for a York shilling, and bed and breakfast for three York shillings. The largest percentage of business was, of course, done in the bar. Drinks cost 4¢ a mug, with a liberal reduction when it came to treating the crowd of "thirsty loafers." Teamsters who stopped to water their horses were expected to spend money over the bar and failure to do so met with much resentment.

The outbreak of the Crimean War in 1854 brought an urgent demand for provisions which absorbed all the produce farmers could raise. The rise in price of wheat at Toronto to the unprecedented height of $2.50 per bushel spurred farmers to mortgage their land to buy more in an effort to increase their output. The volume of traffic along the plank road, coming from as far away as the Owen Sound district, was enormous.[63] On the strength of this traffic, Arthur Verner laid out a village three-quarters of a mile north of Oakville.

A younger son of Sir William Verner, Bart., of County Armagh, Ireland, who was related to the Duke of Wellington, Arthur Cole Verner was a graduate of Trinity College, Dublin. We first encounter him in 1837 when he applied to purchase the north half of the Clergy Reserve on the east side of the 7th Line, south of the Upper Middle Road. Through a pretty ravine on this land runs the stream which furnished the power for Coates's sawmill farther south near the lake. William Chisholm was not favourably impressed with this land, and reported to the Department of Crown Lands: "At the request of Arthur Verner, Trafalgar, I have examined the north half of lot 12 in the 2nd concession South of Dundas Street, and find it a very poor lot, part of it is quite unfit for cultivation and I consider it not worth more than 15 shillings."[64] That was the price per acre that Verner paid when he purchased the lot—£75 for the hundred acres.[65] On the north-east corner near the Middle Road facing upon the 7th Line, he built the frame house which the census enumerator described as "ruffcast." For a time Verner was headmaster of the Wellington Grammar School and lived at Guelph[66] but he returned to Trafalgar Township when engaged as master of the Oakville Common School in the 1840's.

The village that Verner planned, to be called Vernerville, lay south of his home and consisted of about 30 lots charmingly situated on streets running between the ravine and the 7th Line. It was to have a church, a school, and, in the manner of the old country, a village green. It was to be populated by immigrants, and authentic records show that Michael Lannagan, shoemaker, Robert Harper, tailor, D. B. Smith, Negro rope-maker, and other unnamed artisans built dwellings there. A number of Oakville grain merchants owned lots, and it was their intention to establish branch stores in the village though they may not actually have done so.[67]

At the time Robert Harper, the tailor, moved from Munn's Corners he considered Vernerville to be a village with a future. His daughter, Martha Matilda, who was then only a few months old, grew up to found in 1888 a world-renowned treatment for the hair, the Harper Method. Many will recall the photographs of Miss Harper used in her advertising which show the phenomenal length of her hair in her youth. At the time of writing she lives in retirement at Rochester, and the house in which she lived as a child, the sole survivor of Vernerville, is owned by David Hawley.

The 7th Line plank road was not the success that had been expected. In general, plank roads did not prove durable, and needed to be resurfaced every five years. A plank road full of holes was a public menace, and had either to be repaired or removed. Most companies elected to take out dividends in order to regain part of their investment, as did the Trafalgar, Esquesing and Erin Road Company, and gave up all thought of replacing the planking. A contributing factor to the rapid deterioration of the planking on the 7th Line was the transportation over this road of heavy machinery and materials used in constructing the Grand Trunk Railway through the northern section of Halton County. The equipment, brought by water to Oakville, was teamed from there to Georgetown by way of the 7th Line.

But in spite of the condition of the road the number of toll-gates, which were considered to be almost "too much either for the pockets or patience of Her Majesty's subjects," in no way diminished for a time. The story is told of one irate farmer who, after fortifying his courage at a nearby distillery, tore up a sizable portion of the planking of the 7th Line. And there were other road companies in the province which suffered the dissatisfaction of the public. In a Cobourg newssheet a sarcastic advertisement invited tenders for one hundred mud scows, as it was felt that this "new mode of conveyance is necessary, as the loss of horses, wagons, and valuable lives in the fathomless abyss of mud . . . was fearfully alarming. Until the completion of the said mud scows the company will continue to exact toll from those who may be so fortunate as to escape alive through the gates."[68]

Four years and four months after the opening of the 7th Line plank road the president of the company finally announced that the directors had found themselves without funds to repair the road. He gave public notice that after April 12, 1856, "no toll will be collected at the several gates on the Road, in the Township of Trafalgar."[69] In 1858 the road company petitioned the County Council to relinquish its claim on the loan of £3,000, stating that because of the perishable material of which the road was constructed it had become almost unserviceable and that the company was unable to reconstruct it.[70] The planking was finally removed and mud and deep holes returned once more to the 7th Line. As a result, before it had become well established Vernerville declined, and all that remains as a reminder of its founder are the lilacs and rose bushes growing over the foundations of his house and the ancient willows which he planted before his door not far from the Upper Middle Road.

As the railways took over long-distance traffic, most plank roads were disappearing. Canada had entered upon the railway era and the fever was at its height. It was popularly believed that a railway would bring prosperity to any district or community. The first railways in Canada had been constructed to connect water-ways. In the 1830's a charter was granted for a railway to be called the Great Western Railway to run between the Burlington Bay Canal and London. Eventually it would be extended east to Niagara and west to Detroit. However, more than fifteen years passed before construction was begun, and then, as a result of the exertions of Sir Allan MacNab, the railway passed through Hamilton instead of by the canal.

In the early days each company decided the width of the gauge of its railway, with the consequence that there were as many as twenty-three different gauges in the United States alone. To guard against possible invasion by the United States, the British War Office insisted that a gauge not in use across the border be used in Canada, and the five-foot six-inch gauge was therefore adopted. The Standard Gauge, measuring four feet eight and one-half inches in width, had been fixed in 1840 by the British Parliament. This gauge had been determined largely by chance, as the first tramways built in English coal districts were made to conform to the gauge common to road waggons which in turn had to some extent been determined by Roman chariot builders and roadmakers. It was not until transportation had been seriously hampered by reloading during the Civil War that the United States adopted the Standard Gauge, and Canada soon followed suit.

The greater proportion of Canadian railway stock was subscribed in Britain, and the Hamilton and Toronto Railway, incorporated in 1852, was no exception.[71] The following year arrangements were made to lease the new railway upon its completion to the Great Western,[72] and it then became the Hamilton and Northwestern Branch of the Great Western Railway.[73] (It is said that railway men still refer to the C.N.R railway from Hamilton and Toronto as the Toronto branch of the Hamilton railway, much to the delight of citizens of the "Ambitious City.") All the towns between Hamilton and Toronto wanted the railway to pass through or close by them and controversy waxed bitter. The *Streetsville Review* stated: "Without hesitation we affirm that the route should be struck so as to intersect Milton in Trafalgar and Streetsville in the Township of Toronto. A straight line between Hamilton and the City of Toronto, as everybody knows, runs through one of the most indifferent portions of Western Canada, whether considered in an agricultural, commercial or manufacturing point of view. Marshes, sand plains, quagmires, and sour sterile soil are the leading features of that region. On the other hand the Milton route exhibits a tract of country unrivalled in the Province for richness and fertility, and replete with manufacturing establishments, the feeders of a railway."[74]

None the less, the directors chose to run their railway in a straight line between the two cities. They proposed that it should pass near the mouth of the Sixteen Mile Creek, a route which would avoid the necessity of bridging the deep ravine higher up. For the privilege of running the railway through the centre of Oakville, George K. Chisholm asked the sum of $50,000 but this the company was not prepared to pay. The line was therefore run through the northern boundary of the village.[75] To have a railway in the centre of a town was considered a great asset and that Oakville should have been deprived of this "great benefit" was the subject of loud complaint lasting over a period of many years.

Farmers who sold the right of way through their land were allowed to keep the timber they cleared away. Teams and scrapers for grading the road bed and labour for laying the tracks and building the brick piers for the timber trestle across the Sixteen were hired locally. The iron rails in the shape of an inverted V and less than four inches high were brought in by water and laid in a single track, with the exception of a short section of double track beside the Oakville station where trains could be switched for passing.[76]

On December 3, 1855, a great crowd assembled to see the first train pass through Oakville and the "Railway Celebration" held at Toronto on the 20th was well attended by Oakville's citizens, judging by the local press. Free invitation tickets for the "Dejeuner and Ball" passed out on trains were duly honoured when presented in advance "to the Conductors of Cars" and on the afternoon of the great day a special train ran from Hamilton to Toronto, stopping at Oakville.[77]

Although devoted to the interests of the agrarian population of Canada West, the Toronto *Globe* was thoroughly railway minded and reported the event in the following significant terms: "The mercantile community of Toronto and those who will share in their prosperity consider that the construction of the Toronto and Hamilton Railway is to be to them a great benefit, and they desire to mark their sense of it in a way which will . . . serve as a memorial."[78] At a similar celebration elsewhere William Weller, who had become the largest stage-coach proprietor in Canada West, contributed to the gaiety of the occasion in a speech: "I know why you have called upon me for a speech,—it is to hurt my feelings; for you know I get my living by running stages, and you are taking the BIT out of my mouth at the same time as you take it out of my horses' mouths. You are comparing in your minds the present time with the past when you had to carry a RAIL, instead of riding one, in order to help my coaches out of the mud. But after all I am rejoiced to see old things passing away and conditions becoming WELLER."[79]

"Going by the cars" was a great experience which was missed by few. Rocking over loose-ended rails, swaying over wooden trestles in the little trains at a speed hitherto unknown, was thrilling. Six trains, three going east and three going west, stopped daily at Oakville. According to the schedule a fast train made the journey from Toronto to Oakville in thirty-eight minutes, and from there to Hamilton in another thirty-two minutes.[80] The fare was the same as by stage or steamer, 2*s*.6*d*. unless a passenger boarded a train without a ticket, when an extra charge of a York shilling was collected.[81] Daily stages carrying passengers and the mails connected northern sections of the county with the railway. All trains carried two classes of cars, first and second class "Passenger Emigrant Cars." According to travellers, the wood stoves with which the cars were heated were kept going full blast regardless of the enormous fur coats worn in winter by most men passengers.

Some of the "iron horses" came from the United States but the majority were built in England and each had its name, Ontario, Kent, Gazelle Samson, etc., and its permanent engineer. They were attractively painted a dark green and were heavily banded with highly polished brass. There was no bell but they were equipped with a satisfactory whistle. The funnel-shaped smokestack was designed to keep down the shower of sparks from the wood fuel. For "wooding up" the tenders' piles of cordwood similar to those kept on hand for the steamers lined the tracks at every station. At Oakville the wood was cut by circular steam saw located on the 7th Line near the tracks and was stacked along the road to the toll-gate at the junction of the 6th Line. The station master and his family lived in the station. Matthew McMurtrie was the first to occupy this post at Oakville.[82] Upon his death, Walter Laidlaw was appointed stationmaster,[83] and the conservatory he tended in his living quarters was much admired. Miss Laidlaw, his daughter, gave music lessons, "at the Oakville Station" as late as the nineties.[84] At various periods the station was rebuilt, but the beams and foundation upon which the present building rests are those of the original station which stood at the time the railway was opened.

In the spring of 1857 the province suffered its first major railway accident, which occurred east of Hamilton at the Desjardins Canal. When the afternoon train stopped at Oakville on March 12 there stepped aboard two sisters, Mary and Ellen Divine, aged fifteen and twenty. The train, made up of the engine "Oxford," a baggage car, and two first-class cars carrying ninety-five passengers, was travelling between six and ten miles an hour as it approached the swing bridge across the canal. The trestle gave way, the engine, tender, and one passenger car plunged forty feet through two feet of ice into the canal, and the third car lay on its side on top of the ice. Among the sixty dead were the Divine sisters and Captain James Sutherland of the steamboats *Traveller* and *Magnet*. The *Streetsville Review* reported: "The two sisters were found together and not separated. Their brother, ignorant of the catastrophe, came to meet them, and his anguish at the unexpected sight of corpses was very great."[85] Mary and Ellen Divine are buried in the St. Andrew's section of the Oakville Cemetery.

The Desjardins Canal Catastrophe proved the greatest news item of the fifties in Canada; six thousand copies of the Hamilton *Spectator* were dispatched to England alone. For a long time thereafter all trains were required to come to a full stop before crossing the canal, and many passengers crossed the bridge on foot.

The inhabitants of Oakville showed the greatest enthusiasm for the railway. With more rapid transportation running east and west it needed only a railway running north from Oakville to ensure permanently the commerce of the port. This project was launched by twenty-eight merchants and hotel proprietors in the village who applied to Parliament, and in 1855 were granted the charter for a railway to be constructed from Oakville to Arthur in Wellington County. This village, in the establishment of which William Chisholm had played so important a part, was situated only twelve miles north of Fergus, the initial objective of the plank road. The railway was incorporated under the name of the Oakville and Arthur Railway.[86] That Oakville's future depended upon its being situated on railways was a belief firmly held. As a visitor expressed it in a letter to the local press: "The Lake's on one side of you, the Railway's on the other; a great country in your rear; Mills, Foundries, Shipbuilding, Cabinet-making &c, &c, in your midst; what in the world is to prevent this place growing to be an important City? It must, there is no preventing it. No doubt your leading Merchants will soon take steps to organize your Railway to the interior, for which a charter was granted last year; when that is done and the Railway commenced, there can hardly be a limit assigned to the increase in the value of property."[87]

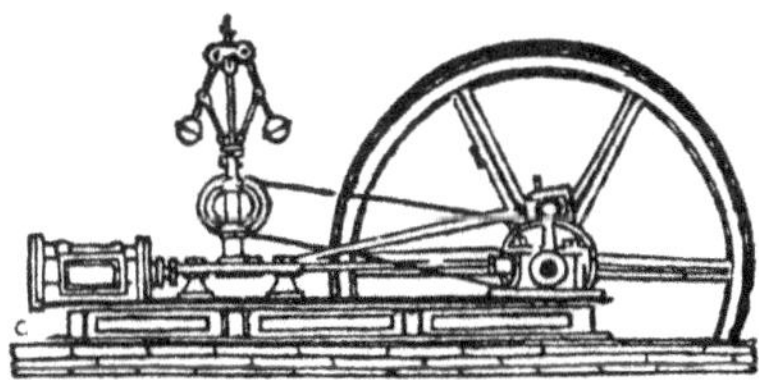

III

By the 1850's the manufacturing which, because of the unsuccessful attempt of William Chisholm to harness the water-power in The Sixteen, had failed to materialize was made possible by the use of steam-power. The new industries established at this time, a foundry, a tannery, and a sawmill, were to prove of considerable importance to

Oakville. There is little question that they were attracted not by the railway but by the expansion of the facilities of the harbour carried out in 1850.

The Oakville harbour was the only "private harbour" in Canada West[88] and its maintenance was an expensive undertaking. After the death of William Chisholm his eldest sons, as executors, had petitioned Sir Charles Bagot, Governor-General of the province, to authorize the taking over of the harbour by the newly formed Board of Works. However, the committee of investigation reported that they "did not know of any reason to induce the Government to comply with this request."[89] In an effort to spread the liability the Chisholm brothers then formed the Oakville Harbour Company[90] and in 1846 proposed to the government that surplus tolls accruing during the past year be used to dredge the channel and extend the pier, the work to be under the supervision of the Board of Works. To this proposal the Executive Council agreed. When the work was completed the cost exceeded the amount of the accrued tolls and the Oakville Harbour Company was reimbursed by the government to the extent of £359.[91] Again in 1849 the harbour company "in consequence of the receding waters of the Lake was desirous of extending the pier 60 feet for the purpose of seeking deep water" and requested authority to retain £452 in accrued tolls to cover the cost. As has been previously pointed out, the province depended for its revenue partly upon its ports, and Oakville's commerce was on a steady upward curve. The collections, totalling £762.18.11 in 1846, had risen within three years to £1,300[92] and "as the proposed improvement will increase the business and the revenue of the harbour the application is recommended for favourable consideration."[93] The work was authorized and in the spring of 1850 the *Oakville Sun* commented: "We are pleased to see the extension of the East Pier of our Harbour is nearly completed, which improvement will render Oakville Harbour inferior to none on the Lake as a Harbour of Refuge."[94]

In April, 1850, in response to a petition to the government by "a number of merchants and other inhabitants," Oakville was declared a Warehousing Port[95] at which foreign goods in transit between the Americas and Europe could be landed without payment of duty. R. K. Chisholm, Collector of Customs, then built a warehouse on the land end of the east pier where goods for trans-shipment might be protected from the weather. To supervise the large volume of goods passing through the port the Collector of Customs had been provided by the government with an assistant in 1845 when Anthony Dixon was appointed "Landing Waiter and Surveyor." Upon the death of Dixon, Joseph Milbourne was appointed to the office on March 10, 1851.[96]

During the winter of 1852–3 the harbour underwent repairs to the extent of £147.7.5, and as the accounts are extant we can ascertain the costs to have been as follows: Square timber cost 20*s.*, and "flatted timber" 17*s.*6*d.* per thousand feet; "ties" cost 1*s.* apiece and a cord of stone 10*s.* The planking was bought from Thompson Smith at 30*s.* per thousand feet and transportation was 3*s.*4*d.* per team per day.[97]

In the late fifties or early sixties the area of the south end of the east pier was increased to the extent that waggons with double teams could drive around the lighthouse. Though the lighthouse stood on a pier that was privately owned, it had been built at public expense, and was maintained by the Department of Public Works. On the other hand, R. K. Chisholm acting for the proprietors of the harbour, engaged and paid the keeper of the light. For some unexplained reason this arrangement was continued after Confederation when the control of Canadian lights, marks, buoys, fog warnings, and storm signals was taken over by the federal government and placed under the administration of a Minister of Marine.

After the failure in the forties of the Oakville Hydraulic Company to develop water-power from the Sixteen Mile Creek within the village, there seems to have been no further attempt at manufacturing until Doty and Hibberd established their foundry. John Doty was a machinist who came to Oakville from Lewiston, New York; Abiather Ashley Hibberd was also a machinist and the inventor of a conveyor for supplying steam-boilers with water. In 1851 these men went into partnership[98] and on the west side of The Sixteen immediately north of the Colborne Street bridge east of Forsyth Street (block 110) they built a foundry for the manufacture of steam-engines of all descriptions. In the spring of 1854 Doty and Hibberd had the misfortune to have their building "totally destroyed by fire, the loss being estimated at $10,000, there having been only $1,000 of insurance."[99] The foundry was immediately rebuilt, but the year following the partnership was dissolved. Doty then took as partner R. K. Chisholm and under the name of John Doty & Company advertised as follows: "Oakville Steam Engine and Machine Works, John Doty & Co. situated on the water's edge of the harbour at Oakville, Canada West. They are large and commodious, and supplied with the best description of Machinery for executing both Heavy and Light work. Steam Engines, Circular Sawmills, Boilers, Mill gearing. Every description of machinery for making lumber and flour, also fittings for vessels. Special attention given to the overhauling of Steamboat and Propeller engines."[100]

The company prospered, and in the winter of 1856–7 erected "a large and commodious stone building" constructed of limestone brought from Kingston as ballast in grain vessels.[101] According to the assertion of a visitor to Hamilton about this time, steam engines and flour-mill machinery could not be made fast enough to meet the demand.[102] Soon Doty & Co. were doing $10,000 worth of business annually.[103]

In 1863, when the discovery of petroleum in the western district round Bothwell was causing great excitement, Doty dissolved his partnership with R. K. Chisholm.[104] Removing to Hamilton, he went into the manufacture of machinery for oil and salt wells, and for some time the foundry at Oakville stood idle. But the interest in oil soon subsided, and Doty resumed business at Oakville, adding to the products of his foundry an axle of his own invention for which he held patents. However, the chief work of the foundry continued to be the making of sawmill equipment and marine engines, in the manufacture of which about one thousand tons of iron brought in by water was used yearly.[105]

The other industries that came to Oakville in the fifties, the tannery and the sawmill, were both established on the west side of The Sixteen by Thompson Smith. In 1854 Smith purchased from James Hopkirk "and others" of the Oakville Brewing and Distilling Company the distillery which since 1836 had been running steadily. After converting the building into a tannery, Smith placed the business in charge of Joseph Milbourne to whom he was related by marriage into the Post family.

Joseph Milbourne was a Quaker who had had a rather eventful career before coming to Oakville to work in the Custom House. With his father, James, and two brothers, he had migrated from England to Upper Canada in 1819.[106] Shortly afterwards Joseph married Desdemona, daughter of Jordan Post, "the younger, watchmaker at York"[107] and one of the "40 Grand Children" referred to by Jordan "the elder" on page 192. With his father, brothers, and sisters, the younger Jordan had come to the province in 1802 to settle at York, and when Ezekiel and Millicent moved into Trafalgar Township he remained at York where he acquired considerable property. It is of interest to note that in 1815 he bought the acre lot now bounded by King, Yonge, Melinda, and Jordan streets for £875 sterling. He laid out Melinda and Jordan streets, naming the one for his wife and the other for himself. In the late twenties and early thirties some of these lots were bought by his son-in-law, Joseph Milbourne. In the year York became incorporated as the City of Toronto, Jordan Post, watchmaker and jeweller, accommodated a prominent citizen with a set of false teeth—so that he might better enjoy his Christmas dinner.

In 1831 Joseph Milbourne purchased land on the east side of Yonge Street in Markham Township (lot 30, concession 1) where the village of Thornhill grew up.[108] Here he earned a living for his wife, Desdemona, and nine children by farming and running a tavern. Nearby were extensive tanneries where his sons, Jordan, William, and possibly Woodruff, were apprenticed to learn the trade of tanner. Milbourne joined Mackenzie's Patriots, but being a Quaker did not actively engage in the fighting at the time of the Rebellion. None the less he was arrested for "High Treason" and during the eight months he lay in York Gaol[109] he whiled away the time by making little boxes of inlaid wood, one of which was preserved by the family. Milbourne "confessed his guilt by petition to the grand jury"[110] and when brought to trial in August was sentenced for life to Van Dieman's Land (now Tasmania).[111] However, he was among those fortunate prisoners who were pardoned by Queen Victoria in commemoration of her coronation on condition that within three days of their liberation from prison they banish themselves for life and remain absent from the country.[112] After some three months Sir George Arthur granted Milbourne permission to return to Canada[113] and he applied for a licence to re-open his tavern on lot 30. But before long he advertised in the Toronto *Examiner* that his "House and Premises on Yonge St., situated within 11 miles of the city, known as Milbourne's Tavern" were for sale as he was "compelled to leave the Province not being able to obtain a license to keep a tavern." The editor of the *Examiner* commented that he regretted to publish this announcement "which will explain that Mr. Milbourne, after having received the pardon of the Crown is driven by Tory persecution from the Prov. . . . The Tories will live to repent the diabolical policy they are pursuing."[114] However, it was not for another four years that Milbourne began selling off his property to Benjamin Thorne and others.

When the Baldwin Government came to power Milbourne was given an appointment in the Custom House at Toronto. In 1851 he was transfered to Oakville, and until his death twenty-three years later, worked amicably side by side with that ironclad Tory, R. K. Chisholm. Upon moving to Oakville the Milbourne family lived in the large house on the north-east corner of Reynolds and Colborne streets formerly occupied by William Uptegrave and later divided into the two houses which now stand as nos. 167 and 171 Colborne Street East.

When Thompson Smith established the tannery, Milbourne was able to combine its management with his duties at the Custom House by taking his three sons, Jordan, William, and Woodruff, into the business. The tannery first opened under name of Joseph Milbourne & Co. in 1856. The following year Charles Sovereign, who was still making his own and his children's shoes, had hides tanned on shares for $4 per hundredweight. From bills receipted by Joseph Milbourne to William Walsh, shoemaker at Oakville, we find that in 1857 sides of sole leather sold for 36¢ a pound, sides of upper leather for 47¢, and splits for 40¢ a pound. Tanned calf skins cost the shoemaker 90¢ a pound. During 1861 some three thousand hides were turned into six thousand sides of "Patent sole and upper leather," in the processing of which three hundred cords of tanbark were used by the tannery.[115] Steam-power was employed, and the property and machinery were valued at $3,200.[116]

Just when the sawmill in connection with the grist mill built on The Sixteen by William Chisholm stopped cutting lumber has not been determined, nor has the date of the setting up by Thompson Smith of his steam mill near the harbour. It would seem that Smith erected his sawmill at the time the Chisholm brothers converted their mill to a flouring mill exclusively. When Smith located his mill below the Colborne Street bridge the whine of its saw was heard within the heart of the village, and along the flats on the west side of the river rose piles of seasoning lumber and dunes of sweet-smelling sawdust. Along the east bank of The Sixteen on Randall Street, up Dunn and Dundas streets, stood piles of sawlogs teamed in during the winter. When the ice was gone in the spring the logs were rolled down the bank into the river and floated to the mill below the bridge. Among the vessels which came to dock at the lumber yard were some built for and owned by Smith: the *Europe*, the *Smith and Post*, and those bearing the names of his daughters, *Elizabeth, Almina,* and *Ardelia*. As the wife of Henry Howland, brother of Sir William Howland, Ardelia Smith, in the sixties, was mistress of Sherbourne House at Toronto, which is now a club for self-supporting business and professional women. Thompson Smith employed as machinist a brother of the owner of the foundry across the way, Pharis Doty, who soon became manager of the sawmill.[117]

When he moved to Oakville, Thompson Smith remodelled and considerably enlarged the house reputed to have been built by George

Griggs, which now stands on the south-west corner of Second Street as no. 226 Colborne Street East.[118] Smith owned or had a financial interest in numerous sawmills and large timber workings in the vicinity of Oakville, at Campbellville, and in other sections of the county. His interest and talent lay in buying up small businesses of various kinds and building them into important concerns. He had his finger in many financial pies and his name appears on all manner of documents relating to Oakville. Though his connection with the village is long since forgotten, Thompson Smith greatly influenced its industrial development before moving to other fields where his abilities had wider scope.

At the time Smith and Doty were becoming established, the Chisholm brothers' grist mill on The Sixteen underwent extensive alterations which substantially expanded its output. The increasing demand for flour which could have absorbed many times over the mill's former output called for an enlarged capacity. John A. Chisholm, who had run the mill since the death of his father, took into partnership his brother, George K., and from 1853 to 1855 the alterations went forward. Because of the deforestation of the land, the water in the river had decreased in volume to the degree that by 1851 the mill was listed as "discontinued,"[119] and to obtain a continued rather than a seasonal flow, the water was brought from farther upstream. Above the mill the river curves back upon itself, forming a finger of land with steep banks known as the "hog's back" and at the beginning of the curve an island had formed in the river. Here the river runs from west to east and between this point and the mill there is a drop of about thirty feet in the river bed. A new dam was built from the island to the south bank, and the water from the dam was brought down in an open mill-race, then by means of a tunnel through the hog's back in a direct course to the mill. The 350-foot tunnel is said to have been constructed by two Irishmen. With pick and shovel one man started on the west side to dig a tunnel about four feet wide and five feet high through the bottom of the hill, removing the dirt in a wheelbarrow. The land being composed of alternate layers of limestone and shale it was possible to clear a space under a stratum of stone which served as a ceiling for the tunnel. The other Irishman, beginning on the east side of the hog's back, worked in a similar manner and after several months the two men came within four feet of meeting in the centre of the hill. This miscalculation is supposed to account for the jog which is found in the tunnel. The walls are lined with masonry of creek stone reinforced at a later date with brick. At both entrance and exit the ceiling is man-made for some fifty feet; huge slabs of stone over three inches thick and approximately three feet square are supported by the stonework lining the walls of the tunnel. Since the disappearance of the iron screen at the entrance, mud and debris have collected in the tunnel, making it very shallow, but the interior masonry is still intact.

From the dam the water ran through some 1,485 feet of open mill-race to the entrance of the tunnel[120] and upon leaving the tunnel was carried down to the mill by a closed mill-race. The pipe or tube crossed the river under the railway bridge, following close to the bottom of the east bank. In length the tube was approximately the same as the open mill-race, and about eight times the length of the tunnel. It was constructed of the largest size of white oak staves, pipe staves, which had gone out in great quantities from the district in earlier times. These staves, measuring some seventeen or more feet in length, four inches broad and two and one-half inches thick, were bound together by hand-forged iron bands secured with bolts. The bands, three and one-half feet in diameter and three and one-half inches broad, were spaced about a foot apart. Though tradition says these iron bands were made of discarded waggon tires, the import list of 1854 shows that a large quantity of "hoop iron" from Scotland passed through the Custom House. Where it runs along the ground the oak of the pipe has rotted away, but it was preserved where it crosses the bed of The Sixteen and some has survived to the present day. By the time the diverted water reached the mill from the dam it had run through 3,300 feet of open mill-race, tunnel, and pipe.

At the same time that the water-power was being increased the buildings of the mill were enlarged. To take full advantage of the water-power the old overshot wheel was replaced by a turbine wheel and the original run of millstones was increased to five. On the hill above, a brick house of a storey and a half was built for the miller, James Crozier. In 1855 the following announcement appeared in the Oakville *Sentinel*: "Chisholm Bros. new mill at Oakville. The subscribers beg to inform the public that they have nearly completed the new flouring mill at the Head of Navigation in the village of Oakville and will be open for business April 2nd., 1856."[121] When complete the mill property was valued at $30,000 and the five runs of stones had a production capacity of 6,000 barrels of flour per year.[122]

In general the barrels of flour were loaded directly on to schooners which sailed up The Sixteen to the mill. However, there were times when the harbour was in such a poor state of repair that it became necessary to bring the flour to the harbour by other means. For this purpose a large scow about forty-five feet wide and some sixty feet long, built of white oak, was used; it could transport as many as two hundred barrels at a time. This scow is known to have sunk near the east bank of the river south of the Colborne Street bridge where, it is claimed, it still rests in the mud.

We are fortunate in having a painting of the mill dated the year of its reopening, 1856. It is said to be the first work in oils of a young man who later became a famous artist, Sir Frederick Verner. The painting, reproduced as plate 14, shows the mill as viewed from the top of the east bank of The Sixteen on Dundas Street south of the 6th Line. As it was painted in the autumn the trees are bright shades of yellow, red, and brown. The water is shown as it gushed from the turbine wheel into the tail race, and in the background a train is passing over the wooden trestle of the railway. In the foreground is Snake Island which has long since disappeared; at the time, so John A. Williams tells us, it was the haunt of black water-snakes six feet long and mud turtles large enough to carry a man standing on their backs.

Frederick Verner, son of Arthur C. Verner, was born in the house on the 7th Line and received his schooling at the Guelph Grammar School.[123] He made a facsimile of a United States bill which his father was proud of exhibiting to his friends as it was very nearly impossible to detect the difference between it and a real bill. Fred Verner presented his painting of the mill to George K. Chisholm, in whose family it still remains. In 1859 Verner and other Oakville boys (whose names do not appear) went to England, joined the British Legion, and served under Garibaldi during the Italian campaign.[124] After studying in England Verner returned to Canada in 1862 to make an extensive tour through the West, and his paintings of Canadian prairie life gained him much fame. His work was exhibited at the Royal Academy in London, at world fairs in the United States, and throughout Canada. Scenes of the camp life of the Indians, and the animals they hunted, particularly bison, are famous. During the latter half of his life Sir Frederick Verner lived in England. He returned to Oakville, where he had many friends, for the last time in 1909.

During the 1850's the three industries situated along The Sixteen made great headway. Although accurate statistics are not available, many men were employed. In summer, the slack season at the foundry, fifty-five men were given employment and during the busy season the machine shop and axle works alone required sixty men.[125] Thus to the commerce in grain, flour, and lumber were added the manufactures of heavy industrial machinery, marine engines, and leather for wide distribution.

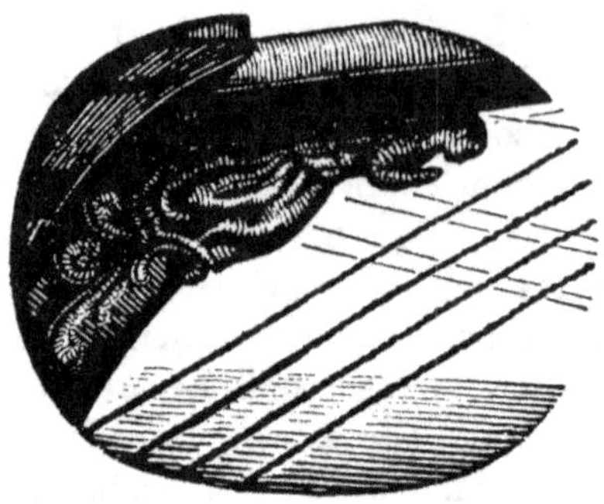

IV

Inevitably, certain features in the history of a community cling to the minds of the older generation, and through continued repetition become local legends. One of Oakville's hardiest perennials concerns the length of the waggon train standing in the streets, and the large number of ships loading simultaneously in The Sixteen during the period when the commerce in grain was at its height. The line of waggons is said to have extended from William Street along Navy and Colborne to end in the neighborhood of George's Square and spill into adjoining streets. Tradition states that it was not unusual for a teamster to wait in line from dawn to dark before his turn came for unloading.

The facilities for storing the grain had been considerably expanded by the fifties. To the warehouses built by William Chisholm (in 1828), Proudfoot (in 1836), and Chalmers (in the early forties) had been added those of Romain & MacDougald and of Gage & Hagaman. These five warehouses standing along the east bank of The Sixteen between King Street and the Colborne Street bridge were approached by Water Street. When a waggon arrived at a warehouse the bags of grain were weighed (at times by Chief Sumner, as this was one of his supplementary occupations) and dumped into a little hopper car running into the top of the warehouse on the rails of a trestle. From the storage bins of the warehouse the grain was loaded on to schooners lying below in The Sixteen. At times a dozen schooners moored along the east bank were taking on cargoes. Carried in bulk, the grain was handled by manpower, and several days were required to load a vessel. Under supervision of the mate, the crews, who did the work of both sailors and longshoremen, carried the grain in wheelbarrows from warehouse to hatch.

There were many grain dealers in Oakville, but five in particular did the greatest percentage of business: James Reid, W. F. Romain, P. A. MacDougald, John Barclay, and the largest of all, the firm of Gage & Hagaman.

James Reid, who migrated from Scotland in 1832, came to Oakville and in the forties bought the branch store of Alexander Proudfoot which he built into a large concern. The storage warehouse he purchased in 1846 from George Chalmers stood on the river bank at the head of King Street.

Another extensive grain buyer was William Francis Romain, who was born in Quebec. It is from the articles of agreement between his father, Pierre, and a painter and glazier of Quebec that the quotation on page 67 was taken. The gravestone of Pierre Romain in the Oakville Cemetery bears the earliest date but one to be found there, 1779, the earliest being Joshua Leach's, 1776. W. F. Romain, known as Frank, entered the service of the grain merchant, W. P. Howland, and within two years became manager of Howland's store at Brampton where he was appointed the first postmaster.[126] Romain became established at Oakville, married Esther Ann, eldest daughter of William Chisholm, and in 1854 took into partnership Peter A. MacDougald, who within a year became his brother-in-law. As near as can be determined it was Romain and MacDougald who built the stone warehouse that stands today at the head of Robinson Street on The Sixteen.

Peter Archibald MacDougald was born in the western district where his parents, John and Sarah MacDougald, had migrated in 1817 with a party of Scots to settle on the lands of Colonel Talbot in Aldborough Township. Singularly enough, the stream that ran near their farm was called Sixteen Mile Creek.[127] Though reared in Upper Canada, Peter MacDougald had Scots Gaelic, and succeeded in qualifying as a teacher of the language. After serving his time as clerk in a mercantile firm he came to Oakville in 1844 to work for four years in Alexander Proudfoot's store. He then spent some time in Georgetown, and returned to Oakville to enter into partnership with Romain. After marrying Mary Jane, second eldest daughter of William Chisholm, Peter MacDougald struck out for himself.

Matthew Barclay, father of John, had brought his family from Paisley, Scotland, in 1832, about the time that another Scotsman, James Arnott, and his family migrated also. Both men became farmers in the vicinity of Oakville, though Arnott soon turned to the business of general merchant. Upon removing to Oakville in 1841 Arnott put up for sale his farm north of the Lower Middle Road (now the Queen

Elizabeth Way) on the west side of the 8th Line, lot 2 of the 2nd concession. The stream running through what was then Verner's land farther north passes through Arnott's, and in the vicinity of the Lake Shore Road it was known as Coates' Creek. Arnott advertised that on his land this stream was "capable of driving machinery in the spring and fall."[128] In Oakville the Arnotts lived in the house on the north-east corner of William and George streets that is now no. 81 William Street.

Young John Barclay became assistant in the Oakville Post Office where he remained from 1847 to 1849.[129] He then acted as clerk for Romain for four years, and in 1853 embarked upon his career as general merchant and grain buyer. He married Jean Scotland Arnott.

It was Gage & Hagaman, however, who developed the buying and shipping of grain into big business in Oakville. Benjamin Hagaman, an American with affiliations with relatives of the same name at Oswego, formed a partnership with James Gage, one of Oakville's early merchants. This firm became established early at Bronte; in 1842 Charles Sovereign noted in his journal, "Gage and Hagaman is still receiving goods for shipping and putting up a fine store." At Oakville their frame store stood east of the post office on the south-west corner of Colborne and Navy streets. Benjamin Hagaman turned over the Oakville business to his cousin, Worthington Ely Hagaman, in 1852, thereafter devoting his time to the Bronte store.[130] Two years later, upon the death of James Gage, his interest in the business was carried on by his son, James Philipse Gage. Gage & Hagaman had many ships under charter carrying their grain across Lake Ontario to Oswego.

The fleet of sailing vessels engaged in the carrying trade of lumber and grain were, for the most part, built in the shipyards on The Sixteen, and commanded by Oakville captains. Many of these ships became famous on the lakes, but of those that came from the shipyard during Jacob Randall's time the record is a blank. John A. Williams tells us that during the forties whipsawyers worked on the common between the school and the Oakville House. Of top- and under-sawyers he wrote: "There were often several whipsawyers, one standing on the timber about eight feet high supported on trestles and the other below with a veil over his face to keep out the sawdust while they cut timber into plank for the ship-builders to spike into the frame-work of strong oak, shaped and ready for planking." For sawing pine into planking three or more inches thick, whipsawyers were paid at the rate of 7*s*.6*d*. per hundred feet. But oak, being more dense and far more difficult to cut, commanded the higher wage of 10*s*. per hundred feet.[131]

The contracts for building ships were based upon the schooners' carrying capacity. As cargoes carried in the lake bottoms out of Oakville were predominantly grain, the capacity was estimated in bushels, and the average price for building a schooner was about a dollar a bushel. The tonnage of a vessel of this type refers, therefore, to her carrying capacity rather than to her displacement.

For hundreds of years the methods employed in the building of wooden ships had altered little. A ship's hull, having no straight sides, required greater skill than the building of a house. The shipwright needed a steady eye, skill in the use of edged tools, and great patience in fitting the heavy pieces of oak into the frame. The narrowness of The Sixteen made necessary the broadside launch, and the ways of oak timber were laid at right angles to the stream and their top surfaces planed very smooth to form the "butterboard." Upon blocks placed on the ways the keel was laid, into each end of which the stem and stern posts were set, well shored to keep them in position. Then came the construction of the many frames made from wood chosen with a natural crook approximating the shape of the hull, and each complete in itself. As they were finished, the frames were raised upon the keel to form ribs into which the planks were spiked. Temporarily the frames were held in place by ribbands, which came off when planking began. In order to make the wood of the three- to six-inch planks pliable enough to fit the contours of the frames, they were placed in a steam chest, a long box of rough wood, open at each end and connected by a pipe to a boiler. After five or six planks had been laid within and well packed round with pea straw they were subjected to steam for some twenty-four hours. While still hot each plank was held in place on the frames with clamps, shores, wedges, chains, and almost superhuman effort while it was tailored to fit into its particular position. The bevelled edge of each plank met that of the next in a V-shaped seam to take the caulking, and the planks were fastened to the frames by spikes driven in with a heavy spike maul. Inside the hull the same process was repeated (this was the ceiling) except for the underside of the deck. The seams of the hull were caulked with oakum (old hemp shredded and soaked in pine tar) which came in huge bales. To horse up the oakum with a caulking iron took great strength, the planks squealing in resistance. Seams above the water-line were payed with tar while those under water were similarly treated with tallow. A ship was then ready for the water, and not until after launching was she rigged.

In a shipbuilding town a launch was an important event. Williams continues: "When the boat was ready all the people for miles around gathered to see it launched and to cheer lustily when it struck the water without mishap. The day was a holiday and quite a bit of whiskey was launched down the necks of those who came to town for amusement." For days the neighborhood had been scoured for all the soft soap that could be obtained, and hours were spent in making sure that the ways were well "buttered." From the day of the first launch in 1828 the official time for a ship to take the water at Oakville was twelve o'clock noon. When the hour arrived the dog-shores were knocked away from under the vessel, wedges were driven in from the land side, and within a few moments, if all went well, the ship slipped down the ways into The Sixteen to the cheers of the assembled crowd.

In the late forties Captain Randall and his brother-in-law and partner, Captain John Jeffery, sold their shipyard to the Simpson brothers, and with Randall in command went sailing in their schooner the *John Jeffery* to trade on the upper lakes. It was in 1856 that the vessel with all hands was lost in a gale on Lake Huron and the frozen body of Captain Randall, lashed to the mainmast, was found where it had washed up on a beach.

The vessels built by John and Melancthon Simpson at Oakville and other ports close by were considered among the finest of the day. These ships carried more brightly coloured stripes along the rail than those built in other ports, and they were noted for their beautifully carved and painted figure-heads, the work of a local wood-carver. Most of the Simpsons' vessels, ranging from the 141-ton *Lily* to the 238-ton *Sea Gull,* were schooner rigged. [132] The average was between 150 and 175 tons and during 1853 a total of five vessels, aggregating 630 tons, slipped into The Sixteen. That year fourteen ships belonged to the port.[133] One of the schooners to come from the Simpsons' yard was the *Royal Oak,* launched in 1852. When rebuilt some years later at Kingston she was renamed the *Fabiola,* and she sailed the lakes until after the turn of the century, the white oak of Halton County in her bottom having lasted well over fifty years. The *Champion, Coquette,* and *Royal Albert* were among those schooners to which the Simpsons gave particularly attractive figure-heads and trailboards. Launched in 1852 and first commanded by Francis Jackman, the *Champion* came to grief eight years later, wrecked in a storm. At Bronte the Simpsons built the *Flying Cloud,* and the largest schooner built in Twelve Mile Creek, the *Peerless.*[134] The *Coquette,* a schooner of 175-tons register built by Melancthon Simpson for Captain George Brock Chisholm in 1857, was much admired around the lakes. She was the pride of the port and some thought her the prettiest model that ever sailed out of Oakville. From her prow leaned a figure-head maiden dressed in white with long flowing hair. Her feet disappeared into a cluster of red and green vine leaves, and across the bosom of her dress two ribbons crossed, a red and a green. This colour scheme was carried further in the many stripes along the rail of the white hull, and an extra flourish was added in topping the masts with gold balls. From the mainmast flew the Chisholm house flag, a red C on a white ground edged with blue.[135]

Captain G. B. Chisholm's brother Duncan (sons of William Chisholm's brother, George) was also a shipbuilder at Oakville. Duncan Chisholm was born in the old homestead at BurlingtonBay, and after the Rebellion served in the provincial navy under Captain Drew of burning-of-the-*Caroline* fame. In 1848 he established an iron and tin business at Oakville, and in the late fifties began building ships on The Sixteen at the head of William Street. He built the *Victoria,* the three-masted *Monarch* of 348-tons' register, and the *White Oak,* launched on the first Dominion Day for his brother, Captain George. The *Monarch,* built under the personal supervision of a young master mariner, Maurice Felan, was one of the largest schooners on the lakes. Felan sailed many ships during his time but the *Monarch* always remained his favourite. As well as being builder and owner of various schooners, Duncan Chisholm was master of the *Oddfellow, Royal Oak, Three Bells,* and other vessels.

Another shipbuilder, John Potter, a native of Nova Scotia, had come to Oakville to work as carpenter on the piers when the harbour was under construction. He became a contractor in the village, and many houses he built are standing today. When Potter began building ships he established his yards on the flats of The Sixteen in the reaches above the curve at Dundas Street. Here he built the *Smith and Post* for Thompson Smith and in 1866 a 100-ton schooner with a gilded figure-head for Captain George Chisholm, who named it *Kate* in honour of his nine-year-old daughter. On May 13 the year following, Potter launched the 175-ton *Dauntless* which was first commanded by one of Oakville's early master mariners, Captain Hiram Williams. At this period all of the twenty vessels registered at the Port of Oakville, with the exception of the two previously mentioned as having been built at Bronte, were built in the shipyards on The Sixteen. For a fuller list of vessels and masters see Appendix D.

Besides the larger shipbuilders there were shipwrights who now and again built vessels, among them several Cronkrites, sons of the owner of an early sawmill. It was probably Hiram Cronkrite who built for Alexander Proudfoot the *Arabian* launched in 1853.

John Potter and Melancthon Simpson lived side by side on Dundas Street, close to the former's yards. Simpson and his wife, Esther Louisa, daughter of John Terry, lived in the little cottage that is now no. 113 Dundas Street North, and Potter occupied a frame house on the north side. We learn from Sumner's diary that this and other houses close by were destroyed by fire in 1869 and it would seem that it was some time thereafter that Potter built the brick house, now no. 119 Dundas Street North which townspeople dubbed "Potter's Folly." One man commented that it was "built more like a railway station" than any house he had ever seen. When Potter died at the age of ninety-seven he was the oldest man in Oakville.

For fifty years the wind-driven fleets carried the heavy freight, their white sails dotting the open waters of the lakes, and the volume of sail-borne cargoes that came and went at Oakville was enormous. A forest of masts extended from the harbour to the bridge, and the shipping crowding The Sixteen filled the river and town with busy life. In the spring the first cargoes to go out were made up of lumber. The crews of the ships, bending their backs to the halyards, raised their voices together in the songs of the lakes.

In a handy three-master I once took a trip
Hurrah, boys, heave 'er down!
And I thought that I was aboard a good ship
Way down, laddies, down![136]

With tall sails filling, the trim schooners one by one passed the Oakville light, to begin a run which might be long or short, depending upon wind and weather. After the harvest, hatches were battened down on cargoes of grain and high prices were paid those captains who would chance a late run. The average wage paid a master mariner during the period of navigation was £10 per month and a man before the mast drew about £6 per month.[137] By November the vessels were usually all back in port and their crews went about the work of laying them up for the winter. During the months that the river was locked in ice the ships underwent a thorough overhauling. Rigging was renewed, sails were mended with palm and needle, and the winter air rang with the sound of the adze, the scrape of the saw, and the ring of the caulking iron laid to many a hull. The Sixteen was a veritable hive of industry. Small boys who infested the area were recruited for giving a hand with a hawser or swinging aloft to replace a halyard, thus learning much about a schooner rig that was to prove valuable to those of them who later went out on the lakes as fresh-water sailors. As spring approached, the vessels, all fitted out, stood ready in their new paint for the day when the rotting ice would give way to the spring flood.

The breaking up of the ice in The Sixteen occasioned much general interest as many exciting things could happen and frequently did. Every year when the report was circulated that the ice was going out, the bridge at Colborne Street was jammed for hours with spectators. Many interesting objects came down on the crest of the flood: cattle, sheep, whole trees and logs, and on occasions a bridge or two from the rear of the township would round the curve in The Sixteen to sweep majestically out into the lake. There was always the danger that vessels lying in the river would be damaged or sunk, and one year the old *Rebecca and Eliza,* which for years had lain submerged, went out on the freshet.[138] On April 4, 1850, occurred unusually high floods. At an emergency meeting of the township council it was found that several bridges had disappeared completely, and that at least a dozen more had been denuded of their flooring. The Oakville bridge underwent extensive repairs, but within four years was found to be so dilapidated as to be beyond repair. The council appropriated £100 and planned to build a new bridge "during this winter while the travel can pass on the ice."[139]

It was not uncommon for a ship to sail out of the harbour into oblivion. In 1857 the schooner *Amelia,* built twenty years before by Jacob Randall, was setting out on a voyage when an argument arose between her captain and a seaman, Joseph Mackinder. Mackinder claimed that the vessel was too deeply laden with wheat, and that being down at the head, heavy work was promised for the man at the wheel. So Mackinder did not go in her. The *Amelia* sailed out of The Sixteen to vanish after rounding Merigold's Point a few miles east of Oakville. Mackinder then shipped aboard the *Tempest* bound for Australia; in her crew besides himself as first mate were other Oakville men. The *Tempest* was never heard of again, and all hands were lost.[140] And there was the "staunch little vessel calculated for the grain trade" mentioned by Williams. When she sailed out under the command of Captain William Lawson she was noticed to be a "little heavy in the bow." She also disappeared without trace. Quite probably this ship was the *Sultan* which was recorded as "lost." John Potter scorned the superstition that Friday was an unlucky day. On a Friday he laid down a schooner for which the plans had been drawn on a Friday, launched her on a Friday, and she sailed out for Hamilton on a Friday. She was never heard of again.

The year the *Tempest* went to the bottom of the Atlantic the *Son and Heir,* built for Gooderham and Worts, distillers of Toronto, by Melancthon Simpson, collided with an excursion steamer. It was a warm summer evening, and the *Forest Queen* was returning to Detroit from Belle Isle. In the saloon hundreds were dancing when suddenly in their midst appeared the jib boom of a schooner. The *Forest Queen* had run afoul of the *Son and Heir,* and although there were no casualties both ships were badly damaged.[141] In 1862 Captain Thomas Hinton of Oakville became master of the *Forest Queen.*

The voyage of the *Sea Gull* to South Africa and back all in one season has been called "probably the most noteworthy . . . of any lake sailing ship."[142] Built in 1864 by John Simpson, the little 238-ton schooner *Sea Gull* was 105 feet in length with a 22-foot beam, and drew only ten feet of water. Some of her planking was four inches and some six inches thick. Her carrying capacity of about 10,000 bushels made her one of the medium-sized lake vessels. She was re-rigged as a brigantine the same year she was built, and was chartered by Messrs. Davids & Co. of Toronto for the voyage to Africa. Packed "full as an egg" with farming machinery, buggies, and lumber, and with numbers of knocked-down houses for settlers on her decks she set sail for the Atlantic. Her master and owner, Captain Francis Jackman, and her first mate, John Murray, were both citizens of Oakville, and in voyaging three thousand miles to Durban the *Sea Gull* inaugurated trade between Canada and South Africa. After loading a cargo of tropical products the brigantine returned by way of the island of St. Helena, where the crew visited the grave of Napoleon Bonaparte. Two years later, under the caption of "Marine Novelty," the *Milwaukee News* carried the following account of this sea-going lake ship:

> We notice in our harbour yesterday the brig *Sea Gull,* Captain Jackman from Toronto, with a cargo of pig iron and salt, consigned to R. G. Clarkson of this city. Though only 220 tons burthen, this little brig has quite an interesting history. About two years ago Capt. Jackman took on a cargo of lumber, and made the trip from Montreal to Port Natal, South Africa, some 900 miles east of the Cape of Good Hope. Here he disposed of his cargo at the modest figure of 8 pence sterling per foot. . . . Return-

II. THE *Sea Gull*

ing, he brought from the African coast not less than 27 passengers, and with a cargo of molasses, sugar, wool, ivory, red pepper, oil root, etc. arrived safely at Boston after a trip of about 13 months.[143]

R. G. Clarkson, referred to in this news item, had gone to Milwaukee from Clarksons in Toronto Township a few miles east of Oakville. But the *Sea Gull* never again returned to salt water. For twenty-three years she remained in the lake service and ended her days as a tow barge. In 1888 she was destroyed by fire at East Tawas, Michigan.[144]

Bound together by the hazards of life on the lakes the crews of the sailing fleet developed a lore of narratives and traditions which in the main went unrecorded. These men were proud of their craft and contemptuous of the steamers and barges which eventually were to carry the commerce of the lakes. But tales of exploits and experiences of crews and captains once told by former generations died with them, and few have survived the interval of time. To posterity most of Oakville's old master mariners must remain names only, although a few facts relative to some have been assembled.

Captain Nicholas Boylan, an Irishman who migrated to Upper Canada in 1821, was one of the earliest to settle at Oakville. Boylan entered the employ of William Chisholm in 1830 as master of the *Telegraph* and during the following twelve years commanded many of his vessels including the *Britannia*. After Chisholm's death Boylan owned and sailed the vessels *Enterprise, Princess Royal,* and *Merry Trances*. He lived on the south-east corner of Robinson and Navy streets and was active in St. Andrew's congregation at the time the church was built. Upon his death in 1852 the Hamilton *Spectator* stated that Captain Boylan "was respected by all for the true characteristics of a sailor. . . . There are but few of the class of old sailors now left to which he belongs."[145]

The three Wilson brothers, Robert, William, and George, had also come early to Oakville. These sons of John Wilson, linen manufacturer in Belfast, Ireland, came to Canada after the death of their father when Mrs. Wilson brought her ten children to settle at Perth in 1817.[146] Three years later Robert began his career as a sailor at the head of Lake Ontario, his two brothers following soon after. It may be recalled that in 1830 he was the first master of the second schooner built at Oakville, the *Lady Colborne*. The Wilson brothers were large, well set up men, and Robert and William married sisters from Port Nelson. In 1832 Robert bought the lot on the north-east corner of Navy and King streets from William Chisholm, building the little house that to-day is no. 23 King Street. He is said to have brought the first coal-oil lamp to be used in Oakville from Tonawanda, New York. Captain Wilson frequently had trouble with his crew because of his disregard of the Friday superstition. However, nothing could induce him to break sail on the Sabbath. Captain Robert, as he was known to all, bought park lot L in 1837 but it was not until about 1862 that he built the brick house that is no. 187 Dundas Street North. This became known as "Mariner's Home" because of his custom of bringing ill and homeless sailors to live with him during the winter. For many years Captain Robert sailed the *Baltic,* built in 1854 at Wellington Square, and once crossed the Atlantic to Liverpool with a cargo of flour from Chisholm Brothers' mill. The gold-headed cane presented to Captain Robert upon the occasion of his golden wedding anniversary inscribed, "presented by his Sailor Friends, 1881," is now a proud possession of his descendants.

For a time Captain William Wilson lived next door to his brother at no. 41 Navy Street South in one of the oldest houses in the town, said to have been built by William Chisholm. This house originally stood at the top of the east bank of The Sixteen at the head of Front Street, and was moved to its present location about 1859. About the time that Captain Robert built his house on Dundas Street, Captain William also built a brick house on the south-east corner of First and Colborne streets, now no. 204 Colborne Street East. When Captain Robert returned from the lakes one season he found that the hardware he had secured in Oswego for his own house had been installed by mistake in Captain William's.

For some years John Moore sailed out of Oakville. He had been educated for the Presbyterian ministry in County Armagh, Ireland, but on a voyage across the Atlantic about 1820 his career was changed when the captain of the vessel taught him navigation. After coming to Oakville Moore kept the books at Richard Coates's sawmill, and when Coates said he could save shipping charges and make more money by owning his own vessel Moore contracted to have one built. The *John Mackenzie,* a four-masted schooner of 180 tons, was ready in 1833, and is listed as loading in the Oakville Harbour the following spring (see page 35). John Moore and his wife, Sally, daughter of Barnet Griggs, lived in the house that is now no. 9 Thomas Street South at the north-east corner of William Street where in 1839 their son, Barnet Griggs Moore (or Barnie Moore) was born. The part John Moore played in the *Caroline* affair has already been mentioned, and the record of trips he made during the forties to the United States through the Erie Canal and "by the cars" is still in the possession of his descendants.[147]

The four McCorquodales, father and sons, were all mariners. Peter McCorquodale, a native of Scotland, had migrated in 1830, and two years later he bought a lot on Front Street between Navy and Thomas streets. Here he built the house which faces the lake, no. 31 Front Street, where his family lived until the 1890's. Peter McCorquodole commanded the *Royal Tar* of which he was part owner. Upon the occasion of his death in 1850 the *Oakville Sun* in what was probably typical of its obituaries, said of him that "after sailing through this tempestuous world with ardour and integrity, he has cast anchor in that haven from whence no traveller returneth."[148] His sons, Duncan and Robert, became masters of sailing vessels, but James was a steamer captain. The row of poplars which stood before their home was a landmark that several generations of sailors steered by when swinging in to make the Oakville channel. All of these tall poplars have long since disappeared.

Hiram Williams, who succeeded McCorquodale as commander of the *Royal Tar,* was another early comer. He bought the lot on the north-west corner of George and King streets at the foot of the hill and built a brick house which still occupies this site as no. 46 George Street South. Here his son was born, named Murray after a former first mate of the *Sea Gull,* Captain John Murray. When he grew to manhood, Murray Williams became an innkeeper and a prominent citizen who is well remembered by many of Oakville's residents. For many years Captain Hiram Williams commanded the *Dauntless* out of Oakville.

In an era of unmarked reefs and channels and unreported weather, these and other captains of the port sailed the intricate waterways of the lakes. Lights at harbour mouths were infrequent, and no Coast Guard Service existed. In fighting fierce gales and the hazards of rocky shores, these masters and their crews developed a skill, resourcefulness, and hardihood equal to that of any salt-water sailors. Some lived to retire, others to go into business in the town, but many did not survive. That they may not be forgotten, their names are recorded with those of the schooners launched in The Sixteen at a time when the village at its mouth was, in name and fact, the Port of Oakville.

The commerce through this busy port reached its highest point during the Crimean War when the price of wheat soared to $2.50 per bushel. To those who grew and harvested it, dealt in it or transported it, the grain brought gold. The wheat poured in an avalanche through the port, and Oakville rose high on the wave of prosperity.

CHAPTER SEVEN

PROSPERITY

OAKVILLE had entered upon its golden age. From "a place of considerable business for its size" with some five hundred and fifty inhabitants in 1846[1] it had very nearly doubled in population by 1851.[2] Three years later the number of inhabitants reached one thousand, and when the railway became a reality more people poured in, causing a rise in population from one to two thousand within the space of three years, 1854–7.[3] To established merchants it seemed that Oakville was on the way to becoming a city, and they expanded their business accordingly. Impetus was given to small industries and the building trades, property values advanced about 400 per cent within two years,[4] and with the opening of new residential surveys the eastern boundary of the village was extended. It was at this point that Oakville was incorporated as a town, thereby attaining the status of a separate municipality.

In this rapid transition from village to urban centre the multitude of changes wrought in the physical, social, and cultural aspects of the town sharpened the division between it and the surrounding district. As life in this expanding commercial centre became more complex it was attended by those attributes to success, increased gentility and the tightening of social distinctions. The large stores and private residences which suddenly sprang up in the community symbolized the affluence of those who dealt in grain.

Prior to the railway era Oakville was a village of wooden buildings centring at the western end of Colborne Street and along Navy Street, the main thoroughfare to the harbour. Standing near the post office beside the store of Gage, Hagaman & Company, a passerby looking along the broad expanse of Colborne Street would have seen shops of one and two storeys, each with its porch to protect the entrance from the weather. The spaces between and in the rear of the little buildings were planted in gardens shut off from the street by board fences. The plank sidewalks running close to the entrances of the shops were unprotected by trees; in fact every street in the village was quite devoid of shade. Between the sidewalk and the road ran a deep drainage ditch across which plank crossways at each corner led to the walk on the opposite side. The outstanding feature of the sky line of Colborne Street was the tin spire of St. Jude's Church at Thomas Street glistening above the buildings as it caught the sunlight. To the north behind George Baker's livery stable, was to be seen the new brick schoolhouse, a rectangular building some forty by twenty-five feet, of good proportions and with large windows, a new departure. The entrance of the schoolhouse, surmounted by a bell cupola, faced east upon Navy Street. The Oakville House across the way stood little changed since Sumner's time though its garden no longer occupied the entire block. Directly in front of the hotel on the south-east corner of Navy and Colborne streets stood a log house and beyond at the south-west corner of Thomas Street were two more, reminders of the recent pioneer period. Log structures were disappearing or being incorporated in barns and other outbuildings, but seven log houses and four log shanties were still to be seen within the village. In rear of the log house on Navy Street, at the corner of Robinson Street, stood one of the four brick dwellings in the community, the home of G. K. Chisholm, which today is no. 13 Navy Street South. Perhaps the same passerby might have seen Chisholm's pleasure carriage which was valued at £20, as were those owned by James Reid and W. F. Hagaman. Navy Street was now free of stumps but they were still to be found in outlying streets. At this time lots on Colborne Street could be bought for between six and eight hundred dollars, and farms within a mile of the village could be had on liberal terms of payment for from twenty to fifty dollars per acre.[5]

This was Oakville as first visited by an unknown traveller in 1853. Upon returning after a lapse of two years he was so impressed by the changes in so short a time that he wrote to the editor of the *Sentinel*:

> To say that I was astonished at the growth of the place during the interval is to say no more than the truth. At my first visit—as you know—

I was casting about for a location; an eligible place to establish myself in business and this was the place I selected, because I was satisfied in my own mind that, at no distant day, this village from its position—half way between Hamilton and Toronto—and natural advantages would become a place of considerable commercial importance. . . . I was, however, I must confess, hardly prepared to expect in so short a time the improvements and developments, which have already been made in the village and neighbourhood. Most of the private dwellings I am told, as well as some of the stores and manufacturies have been built this year. Property has advanced in price at least four hundred per cent since I was first here. . . . I notice that there is a good sprinkling of Yankees here now, which is certainly an earnest for the go-a-headitiveness of the place, so long as there is material to work with.

This unsigned letter embodied the popular attitude toward the great advantages afforded by railways, which largely accounts for the influx into Oakville of new tradesmen, mechanics, manufacturers, and professional men. The writer continued, in a passage already quoted: "The Lake's on one side of you, the Railway's on the other; a great country in your rear; Mills, Foundries, Shipbuilding, Cabinet-making &c. &c. in your midst; what in the world is to prevent this place growing to be an important City? It must, there is no preventing it."[6]

A passerby returning to the vantage point near the old post office would have found the face of Oakville changed indeed, and the new aspect that it wore was to remain essentially the same down to recent times. St. Jude's spire was no longer the dominating feature of Colborne Street. At Navy and Colborne now stood the handsome four-storey building of Gage & Hagaman. The brick schoolhouse had been enlarged to the west and its main entrance now faced upon Colborne Street. In place of the log house on the opposite corner was the three-storey Navy Block of W. F. Romain. Built of brick it contained four stores and occupied a third of the block on the south side of Colborne Street between Navy and Thomas streets. On the north side, east of the Oakville House, James Reid had replaced his frame store with a three-storey brick building and further along at the north-east corner of Thomas Street stood the twin brick buildings of James Arnott and his son-in-law, John Barclay. In the centre of the block beyond Thomas Street was the new frame post office, and east of George Street the large brick store of a newcomer in the grain business, Obadiah Marlatt. Oakville was spreading east along Colborne Street; Duncan Chisholm had built his new tinshop on the south-west corner of Dunn Street and next door on the east was another large store. These brick buildings, now nos. 94 and 98, together with those of Marlatt (no. 77) and

Reid (no. 37) are still conspicuous on Oakville's main street, Colborne Street East. Gage & Hagaman's building was destroyed by fire only as recently as 1948. In the decade 1851–61 the number of brick structures in Oakville increased from four to forty-five.[7]

With the expansion of business the village was fast becoming built up. This led to the opening of two residential surveys lying side by side east of Allan Street between the lake and the Lake Shore Road. The land, not long since a favourite camping ground of the Indians, was part of the Prince Regent's Land Bounty granted to William Chisholm for his services in the War of 1812 (lot 12, 4th concession of Trafalgar Township). In 1855 W. F. Romain bought from G. K. Chisholm the strip bordering Allan Street; retaining the lake frontage for his own use he laid out the balance in building lots as the Romain Survey. On the adjoining land to the east Thompson Smith laid out Smith's Survey. First Street divided the two developments; the lots running between Allan and First Street comprised the Romain Survey and those along the east side of First Street and on both sides of Second Street belonged to Smith's Survey. The two new streets were connected by Union Street.

Thompson Smith's frame residence of a storey and a half with a long verandah extending across the front was representative of the large dwelling of the period in Canada West. It stands on the southwest corner of Colborne and Second streets. The drawing (plate 13) shows it as it looked in 1863 after it had passed into the hands of Dr. D. D. Wright. The doctor's buggy stands in front of his surgery. About twenty-five years later this house was divided and the rear section moved back to where it now stands as no. 14 Second Street. The front section, no. 266 Colborne Street East, was remodelled, the verandah removed, the roof raised, and the frame covered with stucco. Though it is difficult to find much resemblance between the house as illustrated and that which we see at the present time they are, none the less, one and the same.

Dundas Street, in the early days called the River Road, was not popular as a residential section until after the advent of the railway. Frame dwellings then began to appear and, because of the number of Englishmen who built there, the section became known as English Town. The land east of Dundas Street and north of Division Street was the farm of John A. Chisholm, manager of the flour mill, whose farm house sat back from Dundas Street at the end of a long lane. This farm house, moved close to the road and considerably remodelled after the turn of the century, now stands as no. 277 Dundas Street

North. When the town spread north, Chisholm employed Henry Winter, Provincial Land Surveyor and county engineer, to lay out a survey along the southern boundary of his farm. The John Chisholm Survey, comprising two blocks bounded by Dundas, Division, Allan, and a new street named Spruce Street, was opened in 1861. The plan of the survey shows Reynolds Street running between these two blocks, but this throughfare was not cut through until a later date.

Of the new stores that of Gage, Hagaman & Company was the most impressive architecturally. Also it was the only building entirely devoted to commercial uses; the upper floors of the others were used as living quarters by owners or tenants. This building was equally divided into two stores, each with its own entrance flanked by show windows and on the south side was a small addition called the "iron" shop. The show windows, divided by slender columns ending in capitals with delicately curling acanthus leaves, were surmounted by a cornice; all were cast in iron. Each of the four windows was fitted with iron shutters, which in the English custom were lowered against the uncertainties of the night. When raised on chains the shutters rolled up to disappear into the tops of the windows. Even the glazing bars between the six large window lights were of iron, and the windows of the upper floors were topped by curved iron mouldings and had iron sills. Made by D. D. Badger, New York, and brought from Oswego in lake schooners, this cast iron was classical in design and the acanthus leaf motif was carried out in the carving of four large wood supports which decorated the top of the building below the overhanging roof. Inside, heavily moulded cornices of wood and plaster more than six feet in width curved from the sidewalls onto the high ceilings. Rows of little iron stools covered in red plush stood in front of the heavy panelled counters, which possibly were of either mahogany or walnut, as were those in the new Custom House. At the rear of each floor wide doors opened to admit crates of merchandise brought up by a hoist on the top of the building.

The Navy Block built in 1854 by Romain on the opposite corner is said to have been almost identical to Gage & Hagaman's building, and the others along Colborne Street, although executed in a less costly manner, followed much the same pattern. Limestone from Kingston for the foundations and brick from Oswego were carried as ballast in returning grain vessels. The bricks cost $4.50 per thousand delivered at the pier,[8] and the brickwork shows a distinct preference for American bond, that is, one course of headers for each five or six courses of stretchers. The price of squared timber is not recorded but there is reference to a stick which measured seventeen by eighteen inches and twenty-eight feet long selling for 18*s.*[9] Held together by wooden pegs, the hand-hewn beams in the attic of the Canadian Hotel (now Hotel Murray) run straight as a die the full length of the sixty-foot building. Masons and builders received the wage of 1*s.*3*d.* per hour, carpenters and joiners were paid two York shillings per hour or 5*s.* for a ten-hour day, and labourers one York shilling (12½¢) per hour. For "three coats" work plastering cost 10½*d.* per square yard, for two coats 7½*d.*, and for one coat, 4*d.* Iron casting such as that for door frames for vaults, etc. came tc 5*d.* a pound.[10]

The working drawings for the buildings of Gage & Hagaman and Duncan Chisholm are said to have come from the same "architect and surveyor" (terms yet current in Scotland) but his name is lost. Nor do we know much about the local master builders and contractors. Samuel Jull, who in partnership with William Moulds built the schoolhouse, came from Kent County in the thirties to lot 5 of the 2nd concession of Trafalgar Township where he ran a sawmill. The Boon brothers, Isaac and Joseph, were stone-masons and brick-layers from North Devonshire, who came to Oakville about 1849. There were the older established house carpenters such as David Patterson, John Potter, James McDonald, and the brothers Leach. More recent arrivals included James O'Connor, house carpenter from Wexford, Ireland, who lived at no. 17 Reynolds Street South at Robinson, and John MacLean, also an Irishman. John Gallie, carpenter and joiner from Stirling, Scotland, came in 1853 and the following year built for his family the frame cottage that is now no. 145 William Street at the north-west corner of Reynolds. His sons and grandsons became medical practitioners at Toronto and have made the name of Gallie famous in the medical profession in Canada. Will Carson, who worked on the building of Gage, Hagaman & Company, was born of Irish parentage in New Brunswick, and served as a carpenter's apprentice for seven years before coming to Canada West.

The money that had been made in grain was also being spent on the erection of new houses which in 1855 were appearing all over Oakville. The handsome house of W. F. Romain at the foot of First Street was long the home of W. S. Davis in recent times. William Robertson, hardware merchant, built what is now no. 63 First Street, across the way. To the north the house of W. E. Hagaman appeared, no. 10 First Street (in the recent past the Oakville Temporary Hospital). In anticipation of his coming marriage R. K. Chisholm built an addition across the front of his house overlooking the harbour (no. 66

Navy Street South) which doubled its size. He gave it the name of the seat of the Chisholm clan in Inverness-shire, "Erchless". Close beside this residence was the new office building, now no. 70 Navy Street South, where the Custom House was located. On his farm on the west side of The Sixteen at the north end of Forsyth Street G. K. Chisholm built a new home which he called "The Retreat," and John Doty built next door (nos. 15 and 43 Bond Street respectively). On the lake at Brant Street William Cantley, retired bank director and native of Aberdeenshire, Scotland, added a second storey to his brick cottage which may have stood there some years earlier when the Reverend Robert Murray lived on this property. Robert Balmer built "Ferniehirst" (no. 60 Church Street) at this time.

There is a striking similarity between the residences built in Oakville between the years 1855 and 1857 and their Scottish contemporaries in and around the city of Inverness. In both appears the same adaptation of the Georgian style of architecture, and were it not for the substitution of brick for the famous pink granite of Inverness one might suppose that the Oakville houses had been transplanted from the "Rose of the North." The resemblance, encountered nowhere else, is unmistakable. From the broad aspect of the Georgian lines and proportions this similarity continues down through the lesser details of decoration and mouldings. The new departure of larger windows and higher ceilings evident in the brick buildings and cottages of the later forties and early fifties (for example the school, no. 63 Church Street, and no. 18 Dundas Street North) was carried even farther in those erected a few years later. In them the ceilings are as high again, the windows more than twice the size of pioneer houses built in the thirties, and the airy spacious rooms are in great contrast to the cramped quarters of the early dwellings. The contrast is particularly noticeable in the houses of Cantley, R. K. and G. K. Chisholm, and Romain where earlier two-storey brick houses complete within themselves (the last two with basement kitchens) were enlarged by the building of impressive additions across their fronts. Thus rooms which had formerly served as parlours and bedrooms degenerated into kitchens, service quarters, etc.

The largest and most elegent was the house of W. F. Romain. Double parlours which extend across the south side overlooking the lake, each with its carved marble fireplace, the spacious sweeping stairway, and heavy elaborate plaster-work on ceilings and cornices (said to have been the work of men from Glasgow) are characteristic of the period. In Romain's time the windows were hung with silk damask, the floor was heavily carpeted, and the rooms were furnished with "mahogany and black walnut furniture in complete sets in parlour and bedrooms . . . and all other necessary furniture for a genteel residence."[11] It is quite probable that the bathroom with its lead piping and twelve-foot copper "bathing tub" was installed at or soon after the time the new section of the house was constructed. According to *The Carpenter's Assistant* (1848) by William Brown, large houses of this period were equipped with "water works" consisting of a brick cistern situated in the cellar and another holding up two five hundred gallons placed high up in the bathroom. The water was drawn from the cellar by a force pump which also supplied the bathtub with hot water from the kitchen boiler. On the lead-lined sink stood two copper pumps, one for soft and the other for hard water; Brown recommends "sinks which may be in the form of furniture." John Moore, tinsmith at Oakville, was agent for Richard Perry & Son, "wholesale manufacturers of Block Tin and Japanned Ware" of Wolverhampton, England. His illustrated catalogue of 1853, now in the Old Post Office Museum, shows six types of shower baths of grained oak with oiled curtains costing from £2.16.0 to £5.8.0. which he advertised in the *Sentinel.*[12]

Romain was a lover of trees, and surrounded his house with all the varieties indigenous to Canada, one specimen of each. Oakville is indebted to him for the trees which line its streets, as will be seen in due time.

Other residences built at this period, although smaller in size and simpler in architectural design and appointments, were still amply "commodious." Chapters could be written on the gracious living in Canadian homes when the reign of Queen Victoria was at its height, and there is every indication that Oakville's gentry adopted to a large extent the urban tone and living pattern of upper-class society at Toronto and Hamilton. This was the era of ornamental wax, bead, and hair flowers, and of a general clutter of knick-knacks; of mutton-shop whiskers and congress boots, Paisley shawls, beaded mantles, snoods, and exceptionally wide hoop skirts. We read of a walnut shell mounted in silver containing a pair of ladies' Irish lace gloves which was obtained at Toronto for a gift. In delicacy the ladies compared favourably with the ornaments of alabaster and shell by which they were surrounded. Susanna Moodie who with her sister, Catharine Traill, pioneered in the north woods, and who therefore had little patience with feminine frailty, observed: "The term *delicate*, be it known to my readers, is a favourite one with young ladies here, but its general application would lead you to imagine it another term for *laziness*. It is quite the fashion to be *delicate* but horribly vulgar to be considered capable of enjoying such a useless blessing as good health."[13]

The glimpse of the Victorian bride given by Mrs. Moodie may well describe the experience of Flora Matilda Lewis from New York State who came to "Erchless" in 1858 as the bride of R. K. Chisholm. Mrs. Moodie wrote:

> The Monday after the bride and bridegroom make their first appearance at church, every person in the same class prepares to pay them a visit of congratulation, and if . . . the parties are well known, the making of visits to the bride lasts to the end of the week. The bride, who is often a young girl from sixteen to twenty years of age, is doomed for this period to sit upon a sofa, or reclined in an easy-chair dressed in the most expensive manner, to receive her guests.
>
> Well she knows that herself, her dress, the furniture of her room, even her cake and wine, will undergo the most minute scrutiny, and be the theme of conversation among all the gossips of the place for the next nine days.[14]

(Elsewhere Mrs. Moodie describes a wooden doll which cries out at the touch of a spring and comments on the "chewing gum" so popular in the United States.)

The lace curtains and heavy draperies with which the Victorian housewife covered windows and doors were well calculated to keep out both draughts and sun. Dark wall papers were greatly favoured, particularly tones of brown, and in the deep ochre of the woodwork the grain of wood was simulated. "Woods and marbles neatly imitated," announced John Cowton, "Grainer, Glazier, and Paper Hanger" who lived in the house that is now no. 28 Chisholm Street at the corner of Rebecca. "The Subscriber having had many years experience in London and New York, is prepared to execute work in the above branches according to the best styles of the above named cities."[15] Those who preferred marble imported from the United States patronized the Oakville Marble Works of the Tiers Brothers, "manufacturers of Hearths, Mantles, Table Tops, Monuments, Tablets, Tombstones and Paint stones."[16]

In the small iron baskets of the fireplaces was burned grate coal at three tons for £7.15.6, but for general heating purposes there were wood-burning stoves with pipes to the chimneys above. According to the *Oakville Weekly Sun* the Phoenix Foundry at Toronto carried a varied assortment of these: "Cooking, parlour, box and coal stoves. Vulcan air-tight cooking stoves, having a very high oven, requiring a very small amount of wood. This stove is arranged so that meat may be roasted on a Spit in front of the Fire. Also, Summer arrangement attached, to burn Charcoal or Chips, without using the other part of the Stove."[17] Coal imported from the United States was used primarily by the foundry, tannery, and blacksmiths until the first experimental shipment of anthracite was brought in bags on the deck of a schooner about 1870.

As ice was being used for the preservation of food ice houses had come to be regarded as almost a necessity by the middle fifties. It was bought from ice harvesters, who cut it in The Sixteen near the bridge, and was stored by householders in their own ice houses. When, because of a mild winter, the ice was not thick enough to harvest, it was brought from across the lake by schooner.

With gentler living came a preference for trained servants, who were difficult indeed to find in Canada West. Immigrants who had been in domestic service in the homeland did not continue for long as servants in a country where independence was so easily secured. Negroes trained in the south, who had escaped from slavery in the United States, were employed in the larger establishments. For many years Christopher Columbus Lee served as butler at "Erchless" and several owners of carriages had negro coachmen. In conjunction with his livery stable George Baker ran the "Oakville General Registry Office, opposite the Oakville House. All persons wanting situations can call and leave their names, and parties wanting Servants can do the same, by paying 7½*d.* each."[18]

Not until young ladies had become proficient in needlework, drawing, music, French, and other accomplishments were they regarded as "finished." Rather than send their children to the common school some families placed them in the charge of a governess. Elizabeth Delamore, governess to the Romain children, taught also a number of their little cousins: MacDougalds, Chisholms, Balmers, and others. In the large dining-room dancing classes were held, which were attended by many children in the town.

And there was the "Ladies' Select Academy" of Miss Sarah Hewson, whose prospectus for 1857 is given in full:

OAKVILLE LADIES' ACADEMY

MISS HEWSON

WOULD intimate to Parents and Guardians, that the Oakville Ladies' Academy will re-open on Monday, August 17th.

Miss H. by devoting herself to the instruction and improvement of her

pupils, hopes to give satisfaction to those who may entrust children to her charge, and deserve a continuation of the liberal support she has hitherto received.
Instruction given in the English Branches, Music, French, Drawing, Needle-work, &c.

TERMS:

Under 8 years of age	$3.00	per Term.
Over that age	4.00	"
Music	6.00	"
French	3.00	"
Drawing	3.00	"
Board, (without tuition)	28.00	"

Boarders to supply themselves with Bedding, and Towels.
Washing an extra.

The School is divided into four terms commencing August 17th, November 3rd, February 3rd, April 26th, terminating July 12th. No deduction for absences of less than four weeks' duration.
Pupils joining the School in the middle of a Term will be charged from the day they enter.
Two weeks holidays will be given at Christmas and one at Easter.
Five shillings will be charged during winter to each pupil, for fuel.

MISS HEWSON WILL BE ASSISTED BY COMPETENT TEACHERS.

Oakville, 5th. August, 1857.[19]

There was much entertaining in the new houses, and the Christmas ball at "The Retreat" was anticipated with great pleasure each year. Public entertainments were always well attended. Summer brought circuses which since the 1830's had travelled along the Dundas Street from the United States. Charles Sovereign and his family of four attended a circus at Oakville in 1845, which cost him 5*s*.8½*d*. By the fifties circuses were almost annual events. Lady performers were elegantly styled "Mademoiselle." Pentland & Company's Circus and Minstrels had two side-shows which exhibited such marvels as "the Horned Horse, the last of its race."[20] Robinson & Lake emphasized the fact that their "Great Combined Menagerie" was all under one tent.[21] Each year the Queen's Birthday was celebrated "with the usual demonstration of loyalty, that has so long characterized our noble Town," in which firearms played an important part. From his home at Bronte Sovereign heard quite clearly the celebration at Wellington Square and at Hamilton. There was always a parade of gaily decorated waggons, competitive races, and a game between the Oakville baseball club and a visiting club.[22] Elections brought torchlight processions through the streets; in fact torches were carried at all nocturnal celebrations.[23]

The "True Blues" continued to celebrate the Twelfth of July. Wearing blue ribbons and orange lilies on their coat lapels the men of Orange Lodge no. 272 commemorated the victory of William of Orange at the Battle of the Boyne which had assured in Great Britain the ascendancy of Protestantism. The lodge, founded prior to 1850, met the first Wednesday in each month.[24]

The Temperance Hall was used for public meetings until Lewis Hall, "the only public hall in the village," was opened on the second floor of the Navy Block. Then with the erection in 1862 of the Market Building or, as it soon came to be called, the Town Hall, public functions such as professional entertainments and exhibitions, balls, church tea-meetings, and strawberry teas took place in its larger auditorium. But the sporadic attempts to hold fairs were none too successful until a later date.

It was during this period that a group of boys and girls engaged in a furtive hunt for buried treasure. According to a legend passed by word of mouth for half a century, the treasure was the wages of the British soldiery which had been buried at Coates' Creek during the War of 1812. It appears that a company of soldiers were proceeding by boat to Burlington Bay when in the offing they espied what was thought to be an American gunboat. Fearful that should they be overpowered the gold they carried would become a prize of war, they turned off their course, slipped into a creek, and buried a chest of gold and silver under a tree. Joel Mackinder, one of Oakville's old-timers, told of how he and a half-dozen boys and girls from the town held nightly hunts for this treasure. After hearing the tale from an old man they approached a fortune teller who, for fifty cents, told them that the chest would be found beneath three oak stumps near a creek. "We'd mostly dig by night in relays . . . but we never found it," wrote Mackinder. After the Coates moved away to the western district the sawmill was run by an Irishman from County Limerick. "At first," says Mackinder, "he could scarcely scrape up enough to pay the rent. Then a metamorphosis—he was rolling in wealth and lending money, at 20 per cent interest, to his neighbours. He may have found the treasure, but if he didn't, I know where it still may be." Mackinder concludes that being the only one left who knew the supposed location of the treasure, he intended leaving in his will instructions to his descendants.[25]

In September, 1857, the Royal Canadian Yacht Club, then three years old, ran a yacht race from Toronto to Oakville. Because of rough weather and heavy squalls only four entries covered the course, the yachts *Prima Donna, Canada, Cygnet,* and *Queen*. The race was won by the *Prima Donna* in four hours, forty-nine minutes, and twenty seconds.[26]

That same September a "Monster Pic-nic" was held at Beardsley's Grove, on the lake shore east of the 8th Line, where were erected "swings and the usual etceteras attendant upon a camping out in the wild wood." The three hundred persons who assembled danced to the music of a band and were served refreshments on rustic tables. At six o'clock the crowd dispersed to attend the cotillion held at Lewis Hall, and that evening seventy couples "stood out on the floor." The day was such a huge success that it was planned to hold similar events in the future.[27] But all the citizens did not approve of the entertainment. Two young girls who were members of the Methodist choir and who participated in the dancing were soon informed that their services in the choir were no longer required.[28]

The band that played for the dancing at the Monster Pic-nic was a visiting band. That an attempt was made at an earlier date to form an Oakville band is seen by the report of a Soiree given in March, 1851, by the Sons of Temperance (Lodge no. 61 formed February 11, 1850, Robert Balmer, W.P.): "From what we can learn there has been nothing got up to aid the temperance cause during the year equal to the Oakville Soiree. There was a public procession of the Sons, in full regalia, in the streets. Between two and three hundred Sons marched from the Temperance Hall to the Lake shore, and then back to the Hall where tea and choice refreshments were served to an overflowing house. The house contained about 500 persons, and hundreds could not enter it for want of room. . . . The nett receipts of this Soiree were about $125.00 which sum is to be expended in the buying of instruments for an Oakville band. The house was tastefully ornamented and everything conducted to the satisfaction of all."[29] This effort to organize a band apparently came to nothing, as the next we hear of an Oakville band is in connection with the militia.

The owner of Beardsley's Grove was one of the earliest practicing lawyers in Upper Canada. Bartholomew Crannell Beardsley was the youngest son of John Beardsley, chaplain in His Majesty's forces during the American Revolution. A native of the Province of Connecticut, John Beardsley had been educated at Yale College and King's College (now Columbia University) at New York City. In 1762 he had gone to England for his ordination and upon returning to the Province of New York he officiated in the Church of England at Poughkeepsie and at Fishkill on the Hudson River where his son was born. He refused to take the oath of allegiance to the Continental Congress, and was appointed chaplain to the Loyal American Regiment commanded by the chief supporter of the Fishkill Church, Beverley Robinson.[30] Accompanying his regiment to Nova Scotia, Beardsley settled on the St. John River. His son Bartholomew, who was educated as a barrister, came in 1797 to Upper Canada where large grants of land were being offered as inducements to professional men to settle in the new province. He was granted 1200 acres and several town lots at Newark (the first capital of the province, now Niagara-on-the-Lake) and at York.[31] Within two years B. C. Beardsley was appointed to the bench.[32] After serving as Member for the Niagara District in the House of Assembly he returned to New Brunswick where in 1837 he was elected Member for Carleton County,[33] and later was appointed Chief Judge of the Court of Common Pleas. In 1847 he bought lot 10 of the 4th concession "one mile below Oakville on the Lake Shore Road,"[34] where he and his family lived in the house built by George Griggs. The house, so long the home of W. D. Gregory, is now owned by J. Douglas Peck. Because of the large number of chestnut trees growing on his land Beardsley named it "Chestnut Grove" but the bush, a fine place for picnics, was more usually referred to as "Beardsley's Grove."

Though in his seventies when he came to live at Oakville the old Judge still practised law. As a lad John A. Williams frequently accompanied him on long drives into the country to see his clients. Williams wrote that the Judge, who had a "fine knowledge of men and events," had told him many interesting stories of earlier days in the province which he regretted having neglected to record. According to Williams, Judge Beardsley "had some peculiar ideas which were too advanced for his time to which his family did not take" and he was fond of repeating that one day his land would be worth $30,000 as a summer resort. The old Judge died in 1855. His farmer son, James J. Beardsley, lived at "Chestnut Grove" until his death nearly a quarter of a century later. He sold the east part of the property to Alexander Robertson, a son of Andrew and brother of William Robertson who had come to Oakville in the forties from Stirling, Scotland. Some of the bush has been preserved and in the spacious house which Alexander Robertson built and called "The Grove" his descendants live at the present time.

Men of other professions, particularly medical practitioners, were choosing Oakville as a place of residence. Since there was great prejudice in rural districts against the medical profession, doctors gravitated toward towns and cities, and by 1855 at least five physicians and surgeons were practising at Oakville. Dr. William G. Gunn, a Scotsman, had been in the village since the early 1840's. Next to his residence he had built a "doctor shop." Within a few years Dr. Christopher Flock, "surgeon and accoucheur" and son of William Flock, local merchant, established his office "three doors East of the Plank Road" at the corner of Reynolds and Colborne where Paddy Smithwick had formerly conducted his tavern. Dr. David Dolmage Wright, son of a Wesleyan minister and "Graduate of the Whittakerian School of Medicine and Surgery, New York, of the University of Jefferson Medical College, Philadelphia, and Licentiate of the Medical Board of Western Canada,"[35] began his practice at Post's Corners in 1851. Three years later he moved "opposite the Custom House where he will be found always ready to attend promptly and diligently all cases entrusted to his care. Dr. W. is also prepared to execute orders in Dentistry."[36] In 1854 Dr. Wright went into partnership with Dr. Edwy J. Ogden who remained in practice in Oakville for some twenty years. Dr. Ogden built the house at the north-east corner of Thomas and Robinson streets, now no. 49 Robinson Street South. John Urquhart's Medical Hall supplied doctors with "English, French, American drugs and chemicals and live leaches."[37] The Halton School of Medicine was instituted at Oakville by Dr. Van Norman of Bronte and young Dr. Anson Buck of Palermo, with Dr. Flock as registrar, and announced "regular lectures in all courses in connection with the Profession."[38] When Dr. Flock was appointed coroner for Halton County he moved to the county town of Milton.

In his journal Charles Sovereign gives us an insight into the system of apprenticeship by which young men were trained. Johnson Simmerman was a dentist who visited the Oakville House on the first Wednesday of each month, and on April 10, 1855, Sovereign noted concerning his son: "Homer leaves home and goes with Johnson Simmerman to learn to be a dentist. Is to have his board but finds his travelling expenses and pays $60.00 in all; $30.00 in advance and the balance after learning." Dentists at this period were concerned principally with pulling teeth to relieve pain. Evidently Homer "learned" with alacrity, because his father was able to write only two months later: "Homer left home this morning in capacity of Dentist. Went to Paris, Canada West. Was well provided in his line, I hope he may do well."

As a port through which immigrants continually passed, Oakville suffered from the epidemics which periodically swept the country. After the great scourge of cholera in the thirties came respite until typhus, then known as "ship's fever," spread in 1847. The danger of disease was increasingly fearful because of the large numbers now crossing the ocean to escape the wretchedness caused by the industrial revolution. One-tenth of Manchester's population was living in cellars and some eight hundred thousand handloom weavers scattered over England were receiving a wage of 2½*d.* per day. To five million Irish who had been reduced to a diet of potatoes, crop failure brought ruin and desolation. During the summers of 1844 and 1845 blight turned the green potato plants to withered stalks, and untold thousands died of starvation. The thousands who fled from the famine-stricken land had to spend many days in ships made by fever into "floating coffins" before they reached their new country.

In the summer of 1847 the quarantine station on Grosse Isle in the St. Lawrence was filled to overflowing. The immigrants died at an average rate of fifty per day, and it became impossible to care adequately for the large numbers still arriving. Those who were pronounced well after a cursory examination were permitted to resume their journey westward, and to spread the dread disease through the upper province. On July 27 George Chalmers, Member for East Halton, requested that the Lieutenant-Governor establish a Board of Health at Oakville, suggesting as chairman G. K. Chisholm and as members of the board the township clerk, Thomas C. Harris, and John Urquhart.[39] These appointments were made, and in August the board sent to the government a bill for £30.7.5. for "Expenses incurred by the Immigrants, no. 13"; £22.17.0 was specified "For Hospital." In attempting to account for so large an expenditure in so short a period a government official surmised that this "must include furniture for the hospital."[40] Full payment was refused, but the Oakville Board of Health was allowed £20 to assist in defraying its expenses.[41] In 1854 the cholera returned to take its toll in Canada West, but although Oakville suffered much distress, details are lacking. At Bronte, Sovereign noted that "The Cholera is now in our village and neighbourhood" and that many deaths had resulted.

Apart from the periodic country-wide epidemics, other diseases took their toll. The burial registers of the Oakville churches show that infant mortality was very high, particularly among children under two years of age. Over a forty-year period beginning in the 1840's fourteen out of every thirty deaths were of children under ten years of age. New-born infants, whose deaths are too numerous to estimate, are excluded from these figures. The names of some maladies listed as the cause of death may sound curious: "purple disease," "infant inflammation," and "spotted fever." "Malignant throat," which we know to be diphtheria, in a few days wiped out a family of six between the ages of two months and nineteen years. The illnesses of adults were given such diagnoses as "bloody flux," "red gums," and "overgirth of the heart." If a vermiform appendix ruptured this was diagnosed as "inflammation of the bowels" and the patient was usually doomed. The fever known as "ague," "ager," and "malaria," which was the scourge of early settlers in Canada, was very prevalent in Oakville. The disease was associated with swamps and marshes, although it was not then known to be carried by mosquitoes. Since no screening was used it was just as well that night air was believed injurious and all outside air best left outside.

The incidence of disease was undoubtedly increased by overcrowding resulting from the rapid growth of Oakville's resident population. Prosperity, which had enabled many to raise their standards of living, drew in its wake numerous social problems. The new aspect of opulence that was spreading over the community could hardly have concealed deficiencies in sanitation and other conditions badly in need of regulation and control.

II

The increase during the flourishing fifties of shopkeepers and tradesmen in Oakville is striking; general merchants alone increased from six to ten. With prosperous times merchandising methods were undergoing changes which are readily traced in newspaper advertising of the period. Storekeepers no longer confined their stocks to merchandise of a utilitarian nature such as crockery, staple goods, and plain clothing. The reader's attention was now directed to commodities which until recently could be obtained only in the larger centres. The accent was placed on style rather than quality, and the word "fancy" was applied to a wide variety of clothing, groceries, and other types of merchandise. James Arnott offered a large assortment of "Paisley and Indian Filled Shawls—plain and filled centres, four sides. The variety of his goods is extensive and the styles cannot be surpassed in this village." The advertisement drew attention also to robes of "no. 1 buffalo skins" and to "French merino, German plaids, Delaines, Cashmeres and Coburgs." Charles Reynolds whose store was "directly opposite the English Church" announced a new line of millinery "under the special direction of Miss R., viz. Silk, Satin, Plush Bonnets, Fancy Straw, Tuscan and Dunstable do. Brocaded Silk and Satin Visettes, Silk Satin Plain do. of the Latest Styles and Fashions. Gloves, Hosiery, Head Dresses, Shawls, &c. in quantities which would be rather perilous to believe without seeing."[42] There were mantillas, cloaks, ribbons, laces, and edgings; with each issue the advertisements became longer. And many refinements were to be had. At Mrs. Martyn's millinery, straw-bonnet, and dressmaking establishment could be obtained "Berlin wools, every description of Fancy Goods in connection with Ladies' Needle work constantly kept on hand." Duff the cabinet-maker was now able to provide "Drawing Room, Parlour, Dining Room and Bedroom Setts and Window and Bedroom Drapery." R. W. Coote, bookseller, could supply magazines and the latest books including Harriet Beecher Stowe's *Uncle Tom's Cabin.* Before Christmas in 1855 John Urquhart received a "fresh supply of fruit direct from Marseilles." He regularly kept on hand raisins, currants, soft-shelled almonds, and "Cross and Blackwell's Genuine Sauces, Pickles, Sardines, Anchovy Paste, Yarmouth Herrings, Lobsters hermetically sealed."

These items call to our attention the fact that tinned foods had been available in Canada for a number of years. Cooked food placed in air-tight glass bottles and processed in boiling water had been produced in France by Nicholas Appert for the armies of Napoleon. Appert's book in English translation on the art of food preservation had marked the beginning of home canning in the United States and Canada. By 1840 the hand-made "tin cannister" was being used as a commercial food container for lobster and salmon in the Maritime Provinces and along the New England coast. The first gold to reach Boston from California in 1849 was brought in a can of Underwood & Co., the earliest canning company in the United States, founded by an Englishman, William Underwood.[43]

Gage, Hagaman & Co. made special mention of their "ready pay store." "We pay no rent, employ no extra clerks to keep books, make out accounts &c., and make NO BAD DEBTS. With our system of READY

PAY, we are enabled to sell at all times at lower prices than the CHEAPEST CITY HOUSES." This statement, which appeared in the Oakville *Sentinel*, April 7, 1854, is of more than ordinary interest. Timothy Eaton who established his store at Toronto in the late sixties has been credited with having introduced epoch-making ideas in business when he adopted the principles of selling goods for a set price and for cash only. Eaton's biographer affirms that when made public in 1868 these principles were considered so "startling," "revolutionary," and "amazing," that they "caused profound astonishment" and were generally looked upon as "the hallucinations of a madman."[44] Whether the policy of Gage & Hagaman included a fixed price is not indicated, but their advertising proves that in the early fifties they were selling merchandise for cash only, a practice which fifteen years later was considered such a "radical measure" by Toronto merchants.

A subsidiary of an American firm, Gage & Hagaman laded their grain vessels with American merchandise at Oswego, and were the largest importers at Oakville of goods from the United States. Far in advance of Canadians, the Americans were manufacturing ready-made clothing of many kinds. The prejudice against "foreign" goods of inferior quality was strong in Canada, but, since this type of merchandise was obtainable at Oakville rather earlier than farther inland, the prejudice was sooner overcome there, and by the middle fifties a variety of American goods was making great inroads on domestic and British manufactures.

The importation of ready-made men's clothing was affecting the business of local tailors. Of the four tailors who were in Oakville in 1846, only two remained by 1851. George Addison added ready-to-wear suits to his custom tailoring, calling himself "merchant tailor"; a facsimile of the little woodcut which prefixed his business card in the *Oakville Weekly Sun* of 1850 is shown on page 238. Upon its construction in 1852 Addison occupied the brick cottage at the north-west corner of Church Street and the plank road (now no. 18 Dundas Street North, the Gilbrea Dairy).

Those who preferred the homespun to which they had always been accustomed took their wool to Nancy and Thomas Thomas, custom weavers from South Wales, who wove cloth of neat patterns. At their home on Church Street (now no. 84) equipment such as spinning-wheels, heads, reeds, etc., was kept on hand. In the seventies Nancy Thomas still operated her loom for custom work.

During the fifties wool figured in larger quantities among the items of produce farmers traded to the merchants. The district surrounding

Oakville was a fine grazing country, and the flocks of sheep increased as more land was cleared. Farmers brought their surplus wool from great distances to obtain the higher prices that Oakville buyers were able to offer because of their facilities for shipping. Wool makes its first appearance as an export in 1859. Oakville soon became important as a wool market, the four principal buyers (Hagaman, MacDougald, Barclay, and Cyrus Moore) handling twenty thousand pounds of fleeces per season.[45] Hagaman converted the little building in rear of his store, which until recently had been the post office, into a storehouse for baled wool, doubling its capacity by adding a storage loft. The census shows that in 1861 the three farms within the boundaries of Oakville belonging to John Terry, George K. Chisholm, and his brother John A., totalling some four hundred and sixty-five acres of which half was under cultivation, were producing between 120 and 160 lbs. of wool each. In frontier areas sheep occupied a position of first importance, supplying wool for clothing and meat for food. With the disappearance of the frontier the raising of sheep declined, and a drop in the price of wool during the late sixties caused large numbers of farmers to turn to dairying.

Shoemakers did a thriving business at this period. Ready-made footwear manufactured in Canada was to be had, but the large proportion was coarse and of inferior quality, being the product of convict labour at Kingston Penitentiary. Between 1846 and 1851 the number of shoemakers in Oakville increased from twelve to twenty, four of whom had shops. The enterprising shoemaker who formerly had attended to all the work himself began to employ journeymen shoemakers and to produce shoes in large quantities, becoming a "shoe merchant." He also imported shoes from the United States. (Samuel S.) Kenney and Howes employed many shoemakers in their factory on Navy Street (now no. 12 South) and when the business was taken over in the sixties by Michael Robinson it was valued at $12,000.[46] On the next corner (no. 18 Navy Street South) was the shop of William Sherburne, a native of the township, who moved to the premises about 1850, adding the little wing on the south side for his shop. In an announcement of 1854 there is no mention of his carrying ready-made shoes: "The Subscriber, although not speculating on the prospects of enlarged capabilities is, nevertheless, giving his whole attention to the manufacturing of Boots and Shoes."[47] Two years later in a jubilant advertisement he states that although he is continuing his "home made work, as usual in great abundance" he also carries ready-made shoes, having just received a shipment of one thousand pairs of boots and shoes from New York: "GREAT EXPLOSION!! First Selling at Cost, and Cheaper than ever! Jerusalem!!!"[48]

The increase in the amount of flour, whiskey, planks and boards, and grain shipped to the United States swelled the business of the Custom House. The gross revenue obtained from Customs collections rose from £410.12.5½ in 1846 to £1,472 in 1850.[49] As already mentioned, Oakville was declared a Warehousing Port in 1850.[50] The Collector of Customs, R. K. Chisholm, had been provided with an assistant in 1845, Anthony Dixon, at a salary of £15.6.9[51] When in 1851 Joseph Milbourne succeeded Dixon, his salary was £75 per annum[52] and in 1855 it was increased to £100.[53] Chisholm's salary at this time was £175 per annum.[54] As the salaries of Customs officers were based on the amount of the port's collections together with length of service and the importance of the port, these figures are an indication of the state of Oakville's commerce.

Chisholm provided the building for the Custom House, the government paying £15 rental per year.[55] It stood near the harbour at the foot of Navy Street. William Chisholm had deeded this property (block 83) to his son, R. K. Chisholm, the year he appointed him Deputy Customs Collector. The location of the Custom House at this period has not been definitely established, but it may have been the north part of the brick building now no. 66 Navy Street South, which seems to have been built about this time and which in its original form would have been well suited to a Custom House. According to John A. Williams the Chisholms "moved to Navy Street" after their house on Colborne Street was destroyed by fire, and it is highly probable that the Custom House was moved to an adjacent frame building and that the brick building, enlarged by the addition on the south side, was converted into a dwelling. Whether or not this was originally the Custom House it was here that the family lived after the death of William Chisholm.

In 1855 R. K. Chisholm began a third addition across the south side of the house, erecting at the same time a new office building close by on the east. This two-storey brick building of simple Georgian architecture was planned to contain two offices, one for the Custom House and one for a bank. The former opened on the lake side and the bank faced east on Navy Street. About one-third of the space on the ground floor was devoted to two vaults, one for each office, with walls, floor, and circular ceiling constructed of brick two and one-half feet thick, and with double iron doors made by the famous Taylor Safe Works of Toronto. In the Custom House the long panelled counter supported by heavy S-shaped pedestals was of solid mahogany, and that in the bank, of simpler design, was of black walnut. Each counter held many ample drawers, and at one end was a teller's cage of delicately turned spindles. On the back wall of the Custom House was a large mahogany dresser with drawers and cupboards below, and above, extending almost to the ceiling, dozens of pigeon holes. Behind the exterior wall which connected this building with the residence were situated the "offices," as privies were discreetly termed.

The new Custom House, now no. 70 Navy Street South, was opened for business in 1856 at an annual rental to the government of £22.10.[56] The rear office was occupied by the first branch of the Bank of Toronto,[57] founded the previous year, 1855. Under the heading of "Bank of Toronto Agency" the manager, John T. M. Burnside, informed the public on July 20, 1857, that "This institution has now commenced business, and will allow interest at the rate of 3 per cent on current accounts, and the rate of 4 per cent on permanent accounts."[58] The funds of the municipalities of Trafalgar Township, Halton County, and the Town of Oakville were deposited with this bank.[59] The manager lived in the apartment above, where his sister kept house for him.

The transaction of banking and business became less involved with the adoption in 1858 of the decimal system of currency throughout the province. To replace the English pounds, shillings, and pence Canada issued her own currency in dollars and cents, and the miscellaneous coins which had proved such a nuisance gradually disappeared from circulation.

As in earlier times merchants still depended upon winter roads to bring customers from long distances to trade at their counters. C. C. Taylor, who laid claim to being the first commercial traveller in Canada West, wrote: "The thermometer is . . . a sure indication of the state of trade which rises and falls according to whether we are favoured with a good fall of snow or otherwise, its absence being regarded as a great calamity by all business men."[60] Shopkeepers were inclined to stay open until a late hour but in 1855 we find twenty of them agreeing "to close their respective places of business at 7 o'clock P.M. between October and April."[61] There was such a great diversity of opinion on this subject that it was continually under discussion for a long period of years.

A butcher business was started in the fifties by a lad named Edward Hillmer who had come to Canada at the age of eleven. Upon arriving in Oakville he went into partnership with a young man who promptly disappeared with the assets, and Hillmer was reduced to one English penny. The following day he told his story to a farmer, who let him have a calf on credit. Hillmer obtained permission to butcher the animal in a shed adjoining a hotel, and then peddled the veal through the town. After selling all of the meat he walked out into the country to pay the farmer who, struck by the lad's honesty and determination, offered him a pair of fat ewes upon the same terms. Before long some townsmen took an interest in Edward Hillmer. One provided him with an old horse and another with a rickety waggon, and thus he got his start as a butcher in Oakville.[62]

In the eastern section of Colborne Street were located two bakeries. On the north side between George and Dunn streets was Ann Butler, "baker and confectioner," who also kept a boarding house. For many years her husband, Michael Butler, Irish shipwright, had worked for William Chisholm and Jacob Randall in the shipyard on The Sixteen. In the east half of a large frame building on the south side at the corner of Dunn Street was the bakery of Mrs. Mary Wilson, wife of Captain George and a lady who was famous for her tarts and cakes. Mrs. Wilson sold her business to John Ferrah and his son, Robert, bakers and confectioners by trade, soon after they arrived from Scotland.

According to family tradition the Ferrahs came to Canada from Berwick-on-Tweed the same year that Timothy Eaton crossed the Atlantic, about 1854. Not long after they bought Mrs. Wilson's business the building they occupied was moved across to the north side of the street, where it was set lengthwise on the lot and remodelled into one shop which stood until lately as Guild's bookshop. The Ferrahs lived in a new house leased from Ransom Leach, which he built about 1854 at the south-east corner of Dunn and King streets (now no. 49 Dunn Street South and the home for so many years of the late Mr. E. T. Lighbourn and his family). In 1868 upon the removal of David Duff, the cabinet-maker, to London, the Ferrahs bought his shop and from the large brick ovens they installed in the rear of this building came to the community and district supplies of baked goods. At four o'clock in the morning John Ferrah could be seen working in the bakery even when he was well past eighty years of age, and the business he and his son founded was continued by their family for three-quarters of a century.

Cabinet-makers who in earlier times had made only furniture and coffins had by the fifties added the complete business of undertaking. We find Duff announcing along with "a large assortment of hair, cotton and straw mattresses" that "a hearse will attend funerals on short notice and with punctuality."[63] It had been customary for burials to take place within twenty-four hours of death, but with the advent of the art of undertaking the time between death and burial was extended to two days. To wait three days for a funeral did not become the custom in Oakville until the 1880's.

When a boy, William Hixon Young, son of the Oakville House's first proprietor, bound himself to Duff as apprentice. He was born at Munn's Corners, where his father had leased the tavern of Millicent Munn prior to the building of the Oakville House. After the death of his father his mother's health failed and the family was broken up. For a while William lived with his grandfather, Jacob Young, near Wellington Square, then with J. B. Anderson at Oakville and Phillip Triller on the Dundas Street. But he ran away from Triller's to his cousin, William Young Pettit, whose farm was close by. In 1840 at the age of fifteen Young bound himself to Duff and, to use his own words, "put in my full time. . . . I entered into partnership with Mr. Duff who afterwards entered into partnership with my sister Mary by marrying her."[64] In 1848 he set up in business for himself, combining undertaking with cabinet-making; he was the local agent for Fiske's Metallic Coffins. As pictured on Young's and other undertakers' business cards, the hearses were elaborate, with black ostrich plumes which also crowned the horses' heads. "Shrouds, scarfs, crape and gloves supplied on short notice," reads an advertisement.

George Ziller, a cabinet-maker of French extraction, started his business in Oakville at about the same time as Young. The brick cottage where Ziller lived for many years (now no. 63 Church Street), is, except for the fretwork ornamentation added at a later date, one of the few remaining examples of the type commonly built in the early fifties. John A. Williams was employed by Ziller and Young to cut inscriptions on name-plates for coffins. A large number of dates of birth and death as recorded in his reminiscences, he tells us, were obtained in the exercise of these duties.

The death of James Steele left Henry Gulledge the only saddler and harness-maker in the town, but Urquhart was not long the only druggist. He encountered the competition of J(ames) B(ell) F(orsyth) Chisholm, youngest son of William Chisholm, a druggist who occupied a store in the Navy Block. Chisholm also conducted a soap and patent medicine factory, where he manufactured "essences" of various kinds. The factory was located on the lake shore on the east side of the harbour near the large oak tree which stood at the foot of the hill until its removal as recently as 1949. After the proprietor's death in 1868 the building fell into disuse and was washed away by the lake. The drug store was taken over by C. W. Pearce.

In Lewis Hall, on the second floor of the Navy Block, William Wass conducted his Auction Mart where "town lots, cleared farms and wild lands, mercantile goods" were sold at auction. A native of County Lincoln, England, Wass had established himself in 1852 as auctioneer at Snider's Corners. Moving to Oakville a few years later he became also land and estate agent, conveyancer, stock and money broker, etc., and with the rise in property values in town and district did well in his business. After he secured the east strip of J. B. Anderson's land Wass went into farming and erected, at a time when others were building with brick, a large frame residence facing upon the Lake Shore Road. When Wass gave up farming in the early seventies he sold off the east section of lot 11, 3rd concession, and opened a street called Centre Avenue. Moving the house built in the fifties to the north, Wass built a new residence on Colborne Street, in recent times occupied by C. W. Freer who called it "Balsam Lawn." Centre Avenue was renamed Balsam Drive not long ago. The original frame house now stands on Balsam Drive, the property of the late Gordon H. Watts.

There were three dealers in tin, iron, and copper. John Moore was probably the first of them to settle at Oakville. He had come from England in 1847 and taken over the shop on the north-east corner of George and Colborne streets (nos. 75A, B, C) after the death of Joshua Van Allen. He travelled about the country bartering his skill and his tin, announcing to patrons:

> "Down with your RAGS and I'll down with my TIN!" John Moore would remind his old friends that he intends visiting them, when he will be prepared as usual to barter TINWARE for Sheep-skins, Rags, Wool, Feathers, Furs, Copper, Brass, Pewter, etc.
>
> Beware of Counterfeits, and recollect that J. Moore is the person to Exchange with to profit and advantage for any kind of the above Plunder. Stoves of all sizes and patterns kept constantly on hand for Sale Cheap.[65]

In 1849 he stopped at the farm of Sovereign who noted in his account book that Moore had had "one bushel of oats, horses to hay, supper and lodging and breakfast; say 4s.4½d. By repair of boiler, 4s.4½d." Moore also sold gunpowder, to obtain which farmers came from as far away as Orangeville. But very soon the itinerant tinsmith became the "hardware merchant" with a shop, and no longer made trips with his horse and waggon far into the country.

As we have already seen, Duncan Chisholm was "dealer and manufacturer of tinwear, iron, copper and stoves" as well as shipbuilder and master mariner. Until the erection of his large brick store which today stands on the south-west corner of Colborne and Dunn streets Chisholm occupied half of the frame building next to Mrs. Wilson's bakery.

The Scottish brothers William and Andrew Robertson were in partnership as hardware merchants in the Navy Block, and at a later date William Robertson took over the little "iron" building of Gage & Hagaman. Instead of the more usual greatcoat worn at this period the brothers always wore plaids thrown about their shoulders. Other Scotsmen commonly seen about the town wearing plaids with their grey stove-pipe hats were John Barclay, John Gallie, Robert Balmer, and R. K. Chisholm.

Facilities for keeping gentlemen's clothing in respectable condition were not lacking as several Negro barbers attended to "clothes cleaning in all its branches." Joe Wordsworth was the first Negro to set up in business in Oakville. He is said to have been much plagued by sailors, who threw all his barber's tools into The Sixteen, but Joe took it all in good grace, and remained to become a popular member of the community. His business card appeared as follows in the *Oakville Weekly Sun*:

> Joe Wordsworth—Barber, Hair-Dresser, Curler (at residences, if required), Clothes-Cleaner, Etc.:
>
> J. W. would respectfully acquaint his numerous customers that he will be found at his shaving-shop at regular hours, where they can be well accommodated with a comfortable shave, and Hair cut in the best style. Come one come all and all will go away well pleased. July, 1850.[66]

The Fugitive Slave Law of 1850 caused Negroes to leave the northern states in large numbers. Canada West was the promised land for runaway slaves, as once their feet touched Canadian soil they could no longer be pursued. After they crossed the Mason and Dixon Line there were numerous societies in the northern states to assist them, Fugitive Slave Laws notwithstanding. Travelling by night and following the North star, they made their way into one of the northern states, where they contacted the organization called the "underground railroad." Under cover of darkness the fugitives were forwarded from station to station, and by the thousands they tumbled across the border into British North America. The following verse is from a song they sang, in all probability to the tune of "O Susannah":

I'm on my way to Canada,
Where everyone is free,
So good-bye Ol' Massa,
Don't chase after me.

James Wesley Hill was one of those who followed the North star to Canada, across the Potomac River into Pennsylvania, and then, so it is said, across the border in a packing box. His first earnings he sent to his former owner as payment on his purchase price. Hill settled on a farm on the 9th Line south of the railway. His handsome daughter Ruth was born on the farm, living there and in the vicinity until her death in 1946 at the advanced age of eighty-seven.

Hill became an agent for the underground railroad, penetrating the deep south to assist many of his people to escape. He hid them in cornfields, and sometimes carried the women on his shoulders. After they reached Canada he gave them work on his farm, thus enabling them to repay their expenses. The Johnsons, Wallaces, William Holland, Benedict Duncan, and Lloyd Brown remained in the locality, but others who had been aided by Hill joined the Negro community at Dresden, near Chatham, where lived the Reverend Josiah Henson, the "Uncle Tom" of Harriet Beecher Stowe's famous novel.

Some slaves, assisted by lake captains, crossed the lake as stowaways in the holds of grain vessels. Captain Robert Wilson in particular rescued many Negroes in this manner. Two brothers, in expression of their gratitude, would slip into the captain's garden early in the morning to hoe his potatoes. After the Civil War was over, Negroes gathered annually on Emancipation Day from all over the western section of the province for an excursion to Oakville. They picnicked in George's Square, and those who had gained their freedom through the help of Captain Wilson always visited him at "Mariner's Home" on Dundas Street North. As the years passed the number of visitors dwindled until one year only one man climbed the steps to Captain Wilson's door. The following year none came.

The blacksmith, Samuel Adams, a free Negro from Baltimore, settled at Bronte in 1855, with his son Jeremiah then three years old. When he grew to manhood Jerry became teamster for the Chisholm brothers' mill, and was well known in the community of Oakville. He was to have a long experience of that community; in 1948, shortly before his death at the age of ninety-seven, this man who had attended the inauguration of General Grant as president of the United States celebrated with his wife, Eliza Butler, their sixty-fifth wedding anniversary.

As Oakville passed rapidly in the mid-century from rural to urban centre, many industries which had small beginnings in the shops of artisans blossomed into important enterprises. The jack-of-all-trades was being supplanted by specialized tradesmen, and this was particularly true in the case of blacksmiths. Out of their shops grew carriage works, and a foundry which manufactured stoves; one blacksmith of an inventive turn made stumping machines and pumps for ships and wells of his own design. Between 1846 and 1851 the number of blacksmiths in the town increased from five to ten, half of whom had their own shops. Blacksmiths were advised by Gage & Hagaman: "We buy our Iron from the manufacturer IN SCOTLAND and are, therefore enabled to sell at CITY WHOLESALE PRICES. Blacksmiths will always find our Stock large and well assorted, and for their accommodation we intend always to keep a stock of COALS suitable for their use."[67]

Jacob Barnes was a skilled blacksmith and mechanic who is reputed to have invented the stove damper in use today. In his shop near The Sixteen at the head of King Street, which faced upon the Market Square, he did "ship blacksmithing" and "general blacksmithing."[68] Barnes was born in the United States, a son of Jacob Barnes who settled on lot 9 of the 3rd concession on the Lake Shore Road east of the 8th Line. This was a Clergy Reserve and the lease of this land "appropriated for the support and maintenance of the Protestant Clergy within our said Province," dated August 12, 1818, and assigned to Barnes, contains a clause worth noting. It reserved to King George "all mines of Gold, Silver, Copper, Tin, Lead, Iron, and Coal . . . , and also all of the White Pines, that do now or may or shall hereafter grow or be growing" on the land.[69]

At the time Jacob senior came into the township he was obliged to go to York for supplies. In winter he made the journey by horseback along a blazed trail too narrow for a waggon, and in summer he voyaged by a small boat, marking well his landing-place on the lake shore. When very young, Jacob junior became a blacksmith, and by 1850 was manufacturing his own "Improved Stump Extractor, the most simple and powerful machine now in use . . . on a new plan." The first year three were in use: "J. B. Anderson's is the nearest, only a step from Oakville, which may be seen at any time."[70] Sovereign, who all his life had removed stumps with chain and oxen, bought half interest in one of these machines, and was much pleased with its performance.[71] Barnes exhibited his invention in 1854 at the Provincial Exhibition at Toronto.[72] He also exhibited the "Reciprocal Ship and Well Pump" of which he was patentee, and was awarded a prize of 10*s*. for "2nd. Best pump maker's work."[73] Water was conveyed by the well pump through pipes made of hollow logs bound with iron hoops to keep them from splitting, and fitted together in lengths, the number depending upon the depth of the well.

From the blacksmith shop on the north-east corner of Dundas and Colborne grew the foundry of Robert Leach & Co., "Iron founders and machinists." This business was purchased in the early fifties by the English iron moulders, James and Henry Sammers, who branched out into stoves and ploughs, for which they took old iron in exchange.[74] In 1854 the Sammers sold their foundry to James Walsh, waggon maker, who is said to have built "the best waggons in the province." He was superseded by the Excelsior Carriage Works of Harper & Helson. A facsimile of the drawing they used in their advertising is found on page 222.

The hardwoods of the district being well suited to the building of waggons and carriages, Oakville soon became a centre for this type of manufacturing. Waggon builders increased from two to four between 1846 and 1851, and thereafter several more appeared. The buggy, a light carriage with large wheels, drawn by one horse and seating two persons, was well adapted to the muddy, bumpy roads everywhere encountered. The three-seated democrat, a light spring waggon drawn by two horses, was very popular with the farmers. Ezra Hemphill, waggon maker, was located in a brick building on the west side of the plank road, between Colborne and Church streets. In 1855 this became the firm of Hemphill & Birge; but, when the latter soon afterwards dropped out, Hemphill continued as maker of carriages, waggons, and sleighs.[75] Within a few years James Fairfield, blacksmith, bought Hemphill's business, calling it the Halton Carriage Works.

James Kelley, who came to Oakville in the late forties, and his half-brother, Louis Kemp, a native of Ryckman's Corners on the mountain south of Hamilton who arrived somewhat later, kept to the trade of "smith and farrier." Kelley's shop and dwelling stood side by side on the south-west corner of Robinson and George streets until, in 1949, the shop was pulled down. The dwelling, now no. 70 Robinson Street, is representative of frame houses built in the fifties which, later, were covered with stucco. Kemp located his "West End Blacksmith Shop" on the south-west corner of Chisholm and Colborne streets, where he paid "particular attention to horses with contracted feet."[76] Although this shop has long since disappeared, Kemp's dwelling is now no. 60 Colborne Street West.

A carriage maker of distinction was Jeremiah Hagaman, who came in the early fifties to establish the Oakville Carriage Factory on Navy Street between Robinson and William streets on the hill that slopes down to Water Street. The double house that is now nos. 26 and 28 Navy Street South was originally Hagaman's dwelling. At once he began building waggons and carriages, for which he took three prizes at the Agricultural Exhibition at Toronto in 1856: for the "best two horse pleasure carriage, diploma and £2; for the best two horse pleasure sleigh, £2 and for the best two horse waggon £1."[77] Hagaman enlarged his factory the following year, announcing that he was "prepared to supply any amount of carriages, waggons, sleighs, etc. . . . turning them out in unequalled style, combining strength with beauty."[78] By 1870 Hagaman had a business which required the services of twelve men and was valued at $7,500.[79]

For many years, Hagaman employed a carriage painter by the name of William Whitaker who came to Oakville from England in the fifties. John A. Williams tells of how Whitaker, just recently arrived, came into his shop exclaiming, "This is a queer country where a man cannot buy hot water to wet his tea in." After some years Whitaker left Hagaman to paint carriages and waggons at the Halton Carriage Works. He later became a partner in that firm, whose vehicles were traded to farmers in exchange for wool, quarters of beef, sides of bacon, and other farm produce. Under the name of William Whitaker & Sons the business continues on the same site, although today it deals in automobiles in a new building which was erected after demolition of the old building in the 1930's.

The building boom of the fifties created considerable demand for the products of a planing mill. By then steam engines were being used to make finished wood products. Having a steam plant, Hagaman added a machine for making shingles. Window sash, doors, blinds, etc., which formerly carpenters had done entirely by hand, could be obtained made up at the planing mill on Dundas Street. It stood on the east bank of The Sixteen, south of Lawson Street (block 114) where no. 182 Dundas Street North is now located. This situation was chosen because of the presence of springs east of Reynolds Street from which water was piped to the mill for use in its boilers. This seems to have been another enterprise of Thompson Smith, who installed George Ewan as manager. In 1856 through the medium of the Hamilton *Spectator,* Smith addressed to his patrons a letter announcing that pine flooring was now available at the planing mill at Oakville. He recommended Ewan who, "it is allowed, makes as good dressing as any in the Province, being a practical man and attending punctually and personally to his business. What is of the most importance for flooring it is seasoned, being two years cut."[80] The following year William Litchfield, recently arrived from England, was employed as engineer in the planing mill;[81] Ewan was succeeded as manager by William Lee, builder and contractor. When Thompson Smith moved to Toronto he sold the planing mill to Richard Shaw Wood, Lee continuing as manager. In the late sixties to the products of shingles, sash, and doors R. S. Wood added the manufacture of "Superior Washing Machines."[82]

Wood, who came to Oakville in the late fifties, was essentially a promoter, and a man of many parts. His propensity for wearing a fur hat summer as well as winter has been attributed to a desire to show his affluence, rather than to the more probable reason of his feeling a change in climate, being a native of Bermuda. The discovery of oil around Petrolia in the western district of the province was causing much excitement at the period, and Wood was alert to it. On the bank of The Sixteen north of Lawson Street, he established the Oakville Oil Refinery which became one of the largest refineries of "coal oil" in Canada.[83] In 1867 he bought from George K. Chisholm the house that is now no. 13 Navy Street South and in the rear built a two-storey addition round which many legends have grown up. A trap door in the floor gave rise to romantic tales about a passage leading under the street to the Canadian Hotel, and it has been suggested that the building was used for the storing of contraband liquor, smuggled in from Bermuda. However, there are indications that Wood intended the building for a bank, and that the trap door, designed to go under the teller's cage, opened into a recess which could have served as a vault. The building, as far as is known, was never put to whatever use it was intended for.

Close to the river bank on Dundas Street at Division Street was the steam brewery, of which James Brown was proprietor in 1858. About 1863 Henry Hogben took over this business, which later became "Mr. Townsend's Brewery." When Francis J. Brown became proprietor, about 1870, he called it the Victoria Brewery.[84]

Innumerable small industries, shopkeepers, tradesmen of whom no mention has been made were doing business in Oakville at this period along with the larger enterprises already described. By the time the town had attained its thirtieth birthday, it was thus very nearly a self-contained community and was no longer dependent upon larger centres.

III

With the exception of sailors who visited distant ports around the lakes, few people in Oakville travelled very far from home in the days before the railway. Much of the social life of the village centred around the Royal Exchange, formerly Diamond's tavern, the change-house where fresh horses for the stage-coaches were kept. As one of the main lines of stages running along the lake from Montreal to the western district of the province and the United States passed through Oakville, the monotony of quiet village life was relieved by the bustle around the change-house and a small crowd of spectators was usually on hand to greet the dusty coach. When the road was dry the journey could be made from Toronto in five or six hours, the stage leaving at 9 A.M. and arriving about 2 P.M.[85] A new line of stages operated by Weeks & Co. with headquarters in Hamilton began running via the Lake Shore Road in the spring of 1854. Leaving Hamilton at 8:30 A.M. and 3 P.M. daily except Sunday the stage-coaches called at Oakville on their way to Toronto.[86] After a stop for refreshments, passengers again boarded the stage and, to the accompaniment of a blast on the horn, flourishings of the whip, and much hallooing to the horses on the part of the driver, the coach would depart. James Macreadie took over the tavern after the death of John S. Diamond in 1848 and gave to it a name popular for inns throughout the province, the Royal Exchange Hotel. But it was also frequently referred to as Macreadie's Hotel. In the sixties this hostelry was bought by Joseph Boon, bricklayer and contractor, who enlarged the building to almost twice its former size by building an addition on the west side, as may be seen in the photograph (illustration 35). As long as the stages ran along the Lake Shore Road the Royal Exchange remained their headquarters at Oakville.

Other inns and taverns in the village continued to prosper. The two-storey frame inn of John Forman, on Dundas Street at Randall, was taken over about 1850 by the shoemaker Charles Davis who continued it as the Oakville Temperance House. "Comfortable meals and beds furnished travellers. Good stabling for horses," he announced somewhat ambiguously the following year.[87] However, Davis became involved with the authorities for selling "spiritous liquors."[88] His establishment was taken over in 1859 by Jacob Barnes the blacksmith and was thereafter run under licence as the Halton County Hotel.[89]

A large new hotel, the Frontier House, known as the "steamboat hotel" because it catered to travellers by water, opened on Navy Street in 1853. The lot on which it stood on the south-east corner of Navy and King Streets had been bought in 1834 from William Chisholm by John Moore. Four years later it passed into the hands of Moore's father-in-law, Barnet Griggs, and the house which stood there was leased to various tenants, of whom the last were Robert Balmer and his wife, Elizabeth, daughter of John Terry. Balmer had succeeded John Barclay as assistant to the postmaster and there is reason to believe that for a time the post office was located here. Balmer was the last to occupy the house before Griggs remodelled it into a large hotel which Jesse Belyea of Bronte took under lease. To the public Belyea announced: "His hotel is the largest, and his accommodations the best in Oakville. He has spared no expense in fitting up his house for their reception. Coaches always in attendance to convey passengers to and from boats. Jesse Belyea. Oakville Dec. 23, 1853."[90] Opposite the hotel, south of King Street along Navy, stood long drive sheds where patrons could leave their teams for a day when making trips by steamer. In 1855 Reuben Brookes became proprietor of the Frontier House, but after 1860 the building ceased to be a hotel. It reverted to a private house, which it remains to the present time, as no. 51 Navy Street South.

What happened during the forties at the Oakville House is obscure. William J. Sumner died in 1843 at the early age of forty-four, and nine years later the inn was taken over by John Williams,[91] brother of Captain Hiram Williams and not to be confused with John A. Williams, merchant and writer of reminiscences. Having come to Oakville at an early date and in his youth sailed the lakes as mariner, Williams was popular with farmers and sailors alike. When he took over the Oakville House, he informed his customers that he would be happy to "cater to their appetites."[92] His money, mostly in silver, he kept in a pint measure behind the bar; as drivers of grain waggons were also accustomed to entrust to him large sums of grain money for safe keeping over night, Williams had a number of secret caches about the hotel.

Improved methods of transportation seem to have rendered Oakville's hotel facilities inadequate, for at the time of the opening of the railway in December, 1855, a traveller wrote to the *Sentinel*: "There is one thing much needed, which is, a good building for an Hotel."[93] John Williams forthwith supplied this need by building two hotels, one close to the railway and the other on Navy Street. The Railway Station Hotel, situated south-east of the station, was a type of building popular from early times for hotels and taverns in this section of the province. It was a roughcast building in the shape of a wedge, with the bar entrance on the east point of the wedge. When they went to the city, farmers could leave their teams in the long sheds adjoining the building on the west. Williams soon sold this establishment, and there followed a long line of proprietors, most of whom ran it in conjunction with other hotels in the town, until about 1923. After being closed for some years the building was used as a storage house by a wine factory. When it was demolished in 1935 the heavy timbers fastened with wooden pegs were used in the construction of another house.[94]

Following the trend toward large brick buildings, Williams erected the Canadian Hotel upon the site of Captain Boylan's dwelling at the south-east corner of Navy and Robinson streets. This hotel, which had twenty-one bedrooms, many of them only about six feet square, and four parlours, opened "to receive travellers" on December 15, 1857.[95] Williams had provided for the care of his patrons' valuables by building next to the cellar stairway a row of cupboards which were hidden by hollow panels and almost impossible to detect. He ran the Canadian Hotel until 1867 when he sold it to James Teetor for $2005.[96] Taking over the Oakville House once more, Williams remained there until he retired about 1875.

A dwelling-house on the north-west corner of Dunn and Colborne streets, said to have been built in the forties by a blacksmith named Howard, was converted into a hotel about 1860 by John Wray. The remodelling included the building of a verandah across the front. The establishment, named the Victoria House, passed into the hands of Arthur Goring some eight years later.

By the middle fifties the old post office had been replaced by the new, and R. K. Chisholm was no longer postmaster. In 1844 Chisholm had wished to resign, giving as his reason "the long absences getting out wood for the steamboats," and recommending in his place John Urquhart "as his store is in the most central part of the village." However, "not being certain of his permanency in Oakville," Urquhart declined and Chisholm, persuaded by his friends to reconsider, decided to continue as postmaster.[97] In 1847 he took as his assistant John Barclay, who was succeeded about 1850 by Robert Balmer. Chisholm continued as postmaster until 1856.

A radical change in postal communication came about when the control of the service passed from the Imperial to the provincial government in 1849. Thereafter, the system improved so greatly that the use of the mails increased about 50 per cent. Service was faster, and rates were reduced by one-third. In April, 1851, a uniform rate of three pence was adopted and Canada's first postage stamps were issued, but it was still permissible to send letters postage collect upon delivery. The same system of cancellation was used, the date of mailing being written by hand on the face of the stamp. Outgoing mail was impressed with a postmark of a crown encircled by the legend "Oakville, Upper Canada." The term Canada West received official sanction, but the old term, Upper Canada, lingered in popular usage until Confederation. Periodically the names of persons appearing on undelivered letters were advertised in the local press by the postmaster.[98] After the inauguration, in 1855, of the money order system, money could be sent through the mail with safety.

Until 1851, the Oakville Post Office was a "bye route" of the Trafalgar Post Office and, as formerly, the mails were brought down from the Dundas Street by waggon, sleigh, or on horseback, depending upon the state of the roads. After the establishment in that year of the Bronte Post Office, new arrangements were made. The contract for carrying the mails daily in winter between Toronto and Hamilton, along the Lake Shore Road, was given to Hiram Weeks, possibly of Weeks & Company, stage line operators. The contract specified "fifteen minutes allowed for changing horses at each stage, two teams to be regularly employed. Seven minutes allowed for changing mails at each Post Office."[99] For this service Weeks was paid £635 per season. In summer the steamer *Magnet* transported the mails, and at Oakville the contract "for carrying the mail on foot from Post Office to Wharf, Daily" went to the postmaster at £5 per season.[100]

The Great Western Railway took over the carrying of the mails in 1855, and the positions of the Trafalgar and Oakville Post Offices were reversed: the mail for Trafalgar and Bronte arrived at the Oakville depot, and was taken from there to these places by waggon.[101]

The Oakville mail was transported between the station and the post office by omnibus, a practice which was to continue as long as a bus service was in operation, above sixty years. The day the first train ran through on the railway, John Holden's bus began its route "to and from the cars for the accommodation of travellers and carrying the mail . . . calling at respective places of abode."[102] In a drawing of the Canadian Hotel made shortly after its opening the bus is shown awaiting passengers.[103] Holden's livery stable was situated in rear of his "saloon" (restaurant) on the north side of Colborne Street between Navy and Thomas, one door west of James Reid's store. Here an array of typically American dishes was served: "Keg, Can or shell Oysters, direct from New Haven, Lobsters, Pork and Beans, Pickled Tongue, Pigs' Feet, Sardines, Hot Coffee. Oysters served up in every style."[104] Oysters were "all the rage" and were handled by the bakers who advertised "Fresh Oysters always on Hand."

George Baker, whose livery stable was situated at the north-west corner of Navy and Colborne streets, upon what was later to become the playground of the school, ran an "Accommodation Carriage for the benefit of Oakville and the Travelling Public generally. In connection will be an Express Waggon to carry Baggage, Merchandise, Parcels, &c. &c."[105] The term "express" is here used to denote speed, but it was not long before Baker became agent for one of the private companies which at this period handled shipping by railway express, the American Merchants Express. Somewhat later, Ebenezer Hillmer, brother of Edward, was appointed agent for the Montreal Express, a Canadian company.

When R. K. Chisholm permanently resigned the office of postmaster, his deputy, Robert Balmer, was appointed his successor on May 15, 1856.[106] By then the facilities of the little post office had become quite inadequate, and it was necessary to seek larger quarters. On his land on the north side of Colborne Street in the centre of the block between Thomas and George streets, Balmer constructed a frame building[107] which was taken under lease by the government for the Oakville Post Office. As the rear door of this building opened into the garden of his home, "Ferniehirst," Balmer had a most convenient arrangement during the thirty-odd years he was postmaster.

The more rapid form of communication, the electric telegraph, had been inaugurated between Toronto and Hamilton in December, 1846. Though it would seem that an office was soon established at Oakville, the earliest proven date of the existence of one is 1850, at which time Charles Walker was telegraph operator.[108]

The telegraph was a boon to newspapers. No longer were they dependent solely upon the exchange of news with other newspapers, although the editors of smaller papers continued to give liberal space to reprints from British, American, and provincial newspapers. With the spread of literacy came a noticeable increase of newspapers in the province. There seems to have been no attempt to found a newspaper at Oakville until some years after the fleeting *Observer* had ceased publication, but when newspapers finally became established they apparently throve.

G. W. Hopkins came from Toronto to establish the *Oakville Weekly Sun*, and the first issue came off the press on July 20, 1850. The two copies which are extant, vol. I, nos. 5 and 7, show in the "banner" a fiercely glowing sun under which is the motto, "It shines for all." The subscription was $1.00 per year, in advance, and King Henry Munn, son of that early settler on the Dundas Street, Daniel Munn, told of bringing the first cord of wood chopped off his farm to pay for his subscription. He added that, after clearing, the yield of wheat had been thirty bushels to the acre and had sold at $1.00 a bushel.[109]

The *Oakville Weekly Sun* was printed in the stone building "next to the Royal Exchange" which is now no. 86 Colborne Street, and stands on the east side of the present post office. Printed on good rag paper in type known today as eight-point Cheltenham, the newspaper devoted one whole column to news from Britain and Europe, and another to the proceedings of the Legislative Assembly when in session at Toronto. Many Toronto and Hamilton firms were advertisers, and a company as far away as Cleveland, Ohio, requested furs and sheepskins. The largest percentage of advertising space was devoted to patent medicines, and the advertisements included testimonials of cures. The front page of one issue was given over to cooking recipes, a two-column account of a murder, and the announcement of the arrival at New York by steamer of the famous "nightingale," Jenny Lind. The little woodcut heading the advertisement of George Addison, the tailor, has already been shown on page 238. A form of advertising popular at the time was a narrative such as that used by the editor of the *Sun*:

SUBSCRIBE—by Telegraph! A subscriber tells a good tale of a young Farmer who was lately married in the neighborhood to a beautiful and highly intellectual lady, who was pained to observe that his wife looked thoughtful at times. He thought it was caused by the absence of female companions, and induced several young ladies, relations, to visit. His beloved, though apparently joyous and cheerful while conversing with him, as soon as the conversation lagged, relapsed into the melancholy mood. Surprised at this, he fell to pondering the cause, and came to the conclusion of buying a pianoforte. Well, the musical companion arrived, and then it discoursed such ravishing melody, as the snowy fingers of the bride pressed the keys. He was in raptures and thought he had solved the mystery, but he was mistaken. Though music hath charms, it is not the only desideratum in the world—for awhile it pleases the ear and touches the heart, but ministers not to the mind. He at last, to solve the riddle of his discontent, asked if she did not regret being married. Never, said she, for a moment, have I been other than your happy wife, but—SOMETIMES—

Well, said he, sometimes, what dearest?

If I must tell you, she answered—sometimes I regret that you do not take that little luminary the OAKVILLE WEEKLY SUN. Papa takes half a dozen![110]

An advertisement carried by the Hamilton *Spectator* in which the name of Jacob Barnes, blacksmith at Oakville, appears as reference must have entertained highly those farmers who chanced to read it.

GREAT HORSE TAMING SECRET

. . . Whereby any lady or gentleman, or any little girl or boy, can make the wildest, most ferocious, unmanageable horse perfectly tame, gentle and docile in a few minutes, so that he will remain perfectly tractable ever afterwards. The horse will be perfectly tame, draw wherever you wish and cheerfully do whatever you tell him.

By being aware of this secret you can tame any wild animal,—lion, tiger or elephant.

Any person enclosing the sum of $3.00 &c.[111]

In 1853 John C. Shea founded the *Sentinel* and nailed his colours to the mast in a prospectus which is herewith quoted in full:

Prospectus of the "OAKVILLE SENTINEL," a weekly journal, to be published in the village of Oakville, County of Halton. . . . The advantageous position which Oakville occupies, and the fertility of the adjacent country require to be widely made known, which can only be accomplished by the support of a local Press devoted to the welfare of this section of the country.

In Politics the "SENTINEL" will be Liberal and Independent, and will zealously strive to promote those measures which may seem to be for the good of the Province at large. Its columns will be open to all parties for the temperate expression of opinion.

The "SENTINEL" will contain a careful digest of the current events of the world, Scientific Discoveries, and the latest Foreign, Provincial, Commercial and Local intelligence, Reports of Markets, &c. To the Family Circle it will be rendered particularly interesting by the introduction of choice selections from the general literature of the day, useful Receipts, &c, &c.

The "SENTINEL" will be well printed, with new type, on good paper, at 10s. per annum, payable in advance.

Oakville Nov. 22, 1853 THE PUBLISHER[112]

Within two years this newspaper became the *Semi-Weekly Sentinel*, published on Tuesday and Friday mornings, "terms $2.00 in advance or $2.50 if not so paid." At this time the hand press was replaced by a steam power press, although type continued to be set by hand. We find the Hamilton *Spectator* complimenting "the gentlemanly proprietor . . . [who] spares no pains to give the earliest news on all occasions." The "*Oakville Sentinel* and its extras," continues the *Spectator*, "are now received in advance of the Hamilton and Toronto papers—having the Telegraph office close at hand he is of course placed on equality with his City contemporaries and nearer 'to home,' hence his facility for early communications."[113]

Notwithstanding his aim at "Liberal and Independent" politics, John Shea remained true to Oakville's Tory-Conservative tradition. The issues of the day involved principles which were of prime importance to national life, and it was natural that newspaper editors should become leaders in political battles. The subject of annexation with the United States was repeatedly under discussion, reciprocity was in the air, and sentiment in favour of Confederation was growing steadily. Constant vigilance was necessary if the country was to be kept free from republicanism. The fifties were noted for the bitterness which prevailed both between parties and between individuals. In violence of tone and "exuberance of expletive" newspaper editors vied with politicians. In the general election of 1854, Shea, after referring to the Reform candidate as "the plastic platform swallower," warned against misrepresentation and corruption, saying in conclusion: "Let the Electors of Halton not slumber in fancied security, for the enemy is at their doors. We promise them that the 'Sentinel' will not be found asleep at his post."[114]

Towards the end of 1855, John S. Diamond, son of the tavern keeper, bought the *Sentinel*. Within a short time, he took into partnership W. G. Culloden who, with his father Lawrence Culloden, had migrated from Ireland in 1833 and for a time had settled at Oakville. In the hands of Diamond and Culloden, the *Sentinel* ran continued stories, news of the Crimean War as gleaned from British newspapers brought across the Atlantic by the fast steamship *Baltic*, but little local news. As formerly, editors continued to assume that everyone knew what happened in his own community.

After remaining a short time with the *Sentinel*, Culloden moved to Milton to edit and publish the *Halton New Era*. Culloden appears to have been a progressive newspaper man, as he was among the few to attend the conference which resulted in the formation of the Canadian

Press Association, and for a number of years he continued to attend its meetings.[115]

Another Oakville newspaper in the fifties was the *Oakville Advertiser* published by William Mackenzie King, one of the few publishers of whom we have considerable information. It was his grandfather, Charles King, who in partnership with George Chisholm had bought upwards of 900 acres of land on the north shore of Burlington Bay in 1793. Charles's son George married Barbara, daughter of George Chisholm. With the advent of the War of 1812 George King joined the volunteers and was commissioned lieutenant in the 1st Flank Company of the 2nd Regiment of York Militia. While stationed near Fort Erie he contracted an illness to which he succumbed in December, 1812.[116] His widow survived him for some years but before her death, which occurred prior to 1822, placed her young sons, James and William Mackenzie, in the care of her brother, William Chisholm. As their guardian he attempted to secure for his nephews the Prince Regent's Land Bounty to which their father would have been entitled had he survived the war.[117] There is no record as to what provision was made for the rearing of the two boys. In 1845 William King wrote to a cousin at Oakville from New York City (postage 10¢) stating, "I am going very distant to spend the rest of my days."[118] But events turned out otherwise. After a varied career as a sailor during which he circled the globe three times and was shipwrecked twice, his wanderings ended when he struck gold in California. Returning to Oakville, King established the *Oakville Advertiser*, possibly the first Reform newspaper in the town. In 1854 he purchased the south half of lot 16, 2nd concession, bordering upon the northern limits of the town and remodelled the house which faced upon the 6th Line into the neo-Gothic residence with steeply pitched roof and numerous ornamental gables now owned by Arnold Banfield. Although King chose the name "Solitude" for his home, people persisted in calling it "King's Castle." The earliest copy of the *Oakville Advertiser* extant is dated 1855. In make-up it closely resembles the *Sentinel* and the Reform sympathies of its owner and publisher are very evident. Except for the fact that it was still appearing in 1860[119] little more can be said of this newspaper.

A little sheet of brief existence in the sixties, which cannot be ignored, was *The Bee*, whose editor and publisher was a Negro and possibly an escaped slave, John Cosley. According to his business card, Cosley engaged in the pursuits of "Barber, hairdresser, proprietor of Indian root shrub, toys, gunsmith, etc."[120] The "etc." included inventions, two of which had been patented at Ottawa: a breach loading rifle and a combination water and feed trough which folded up so that it could be packed underneath a buggy seat.[121] For printing *The Bee*, Cosley made a little hand press which printed both sides of the paper at once. By happy circumstance, the following paragraphs came to light in Milton's *Canadian Champion* of 1868:

> We have just received a number of a new newspaper called *The Bee*, published in Oakville by John Cosley, Barber, and why should not a barber turn editor and shave closely every time. . . . Mr. Cosley seems to be a genius in his way, and although like Napoleon, Artemus Ward, and other great men his orthography is not orthodox, he gets off some striking ideas. We cull the following from a bouquet of beauties in *The Bee* which is the successor of *The Wasp* whose "hot little feet" used to probe the good people of Hannahsville and vicinity:
>
> "The laterst news from british columbia gives the contray to what has long been thalked of as annexation with the states; the are now holding meetings through out the country to come in with the united kingdom of british north america; if the sucseed in joining the new deminion, it will be vary apt to take the annexation fever out of the oppersit party; the only way to Secour peace is to strengthen the country by loylty, if a man is disloyl to his country, he is also dis loyl to his family, and to his own soel, and the never see the truble untel two late."

"The Barber," comments the *Champion*'s editor, "is evidently 'loyl to the coar.' "

The *Little Wasp*, referred to above, was published weekly "in good style." It was a famous little sheet whose motto, "Aeeah! how hot his little feet is" was said to have been the remark of an ingenuous Irishman while stroking the back of a hornet that had lighted on his hand.[122]

On the subject of the railway gauge, Cosley produced the following: "The rail road safety has been debated on in meny towns in ontario and has not yet got through, it is everdent that the brord guage will be far the saf estand would cost a gratdal more then the narrow guage, but the narrow guage are certnly the lightest working road of the two and the more apt to capscise, and jest as much produce can be halld over a narrow guage road as a brord gauge." "Wood is very dear in Oakville," wrote the *Champion*'s editor, "so he advocates the following original way of making chips: 'Take a one horse wagon and go into the wood and get you sef a good size stum and hollow the top out like the inside of a wash bold, and put into the place a large chip the size of you hand, put the stump in the hen's house near the door, and take one of the hens off the rust; place the hen cairfully in the top of the stum so that you don't break the nest egg, and the next morning you will find she has hatched chips enough to last all day for your wife to cook with."[123]

The Bee reported the revival in 1868 of the temperance society, of which there would otherwise be no record: "March the 3, the re-organization meeting of the oakville temperance society was held in the temperance hall, and with grate success and quietness. after the minute was red, the foloing members was elected:—W. Williams, president; rev. Mr. Mickle, vice; Justus Williams, Sicotay; Dr. lusk, correspondint Secty; B. M. coote, tresure.—the rev. Mr. brown delivered a short lecttur on the good cause, with great deph, hwos words feel with such wait upon the ordeanc as to cause 33 to join."[124]

After committing the indiscretion of stinging persons of importance in the community, *The Bee* came to an abrupt end and Cosley sold his printing press for $35 to one Charles Conover.[125]

In the matter of water transportation, great strides had been made during the forties. The little side-wheelers with their low pressure engines were outclassed by steamers with screw propellers and high pressure engines, commonly called "puffers." They were remarkable for their vibration, the volume of their smoke, and the high-pitched, penetrating scream of the steamwhistles. Steamboats were depended upon for rapid communication whereas all bulk cargoes were carried by vessels under sail. Steamer runs varied each season; but we find such old friends as the *Transit, Eclipse, Britannia, Experiment*, and *Traveller* still calling at Oakville. In 1843 Captain Sutherland's *Traveller* had the distinction of carrying from Kingston to Oswego the remains of the Governor-General, Sir Charles Bagot. At New York, Lady Bagot and party were met by the British warship, *Warspite*, which transported them home to England.[126] During 1846, 946 steamboat calls were made at Oakville.[127]

Year by year the steamers were becoming larger and faster. The vibration caused by more powerful engines, which wood could not withstand, and the introduction of the screw propeller led to the increasing use of iron for hulls in shipbuilding centres on the Clyde. Captain Sutherland saw the possibilities of securing for Lake Ontario a larger, faster steamer built of iron. On a visit to England he obtained financial assistance from the British Government in return for which his steamboat was to be at the services of the Government whenever it was required. Iron secured in Scotland was shipped to the Niagara Dock Company which built a steamer of 500 tons' burthen. This steamer, the *Magnet*, launched in 1847, was the first iron steamboat in Canada West, and the largest on Lake Ontario. On her trial trip she crossed from Niagara to Toronto in two hours and twenty minutes. As one of the Royal Mail Line, she ran from Lachine to Hamilton, calling at Oakville.[128] For the 384-mile voyage from Lachine to Oakville, the fare for deck passengers was 25*s.* and for cabin class, 43*s.*[129] The fare between Oakville and either Toronto or Hamilton by this and other steamboats cost 2*s.*6*d.* for cabin and 1*s.*6*d.* for passengers who remained on deck, a considerable reduction from the 6*s.*3*d.* and 3*s.* for the same classes in the thirties. After Captain Sutherland lost his life in the Desjardins Canal Catastrophe, the *Magnet* continued to ply the waters of Lake Ontario for more than half a century, bringing many immigrants from Lower Canada to Oakville.

A trip by steamboat was full of exciting possibilities. Competition was even keener among the fast new vessels than it had been among the earlier steamers and racing between ports reached alarming proportions. In attempting to be the first to capture the waiting passengers and freight, captains and crews resorted to a variety of tricks which showed little regard for security. Safety valves were fastened down, oil was poured on the fuel, and once when a steamer left Hamilton without sufficient fuel, chairs, tables, and benches went into the furnace lest a competitor win the race to Bronte. On one occasion irate passengers aboard the *Magnet* made a public complaint against the captain of another steamboat. They reported that he kept his vessel weaving back and forth across the bow of the *Magnet* and that an accident was avoided only by Captain Sutherland's expert handling of his ship.

During 1853 passenger steamers made 1163 calls at Oakville.[130] From R. K. Chisholm's account book we learn the names of those that called regularly between 1852 and 1855 together with the kind and amount of wood supplied to each. There were the steamboats *City of Hamilton, Passport, Maple Leaf, England, New Era, Princess Royal, Arabian, Chief Justice Robinson, Magnet, Britannia,* and *Highlander.* The largest contracts for wood were made by the *Princess Royal* and *Magnet,* the former using 538 cords billed at £235.7.11 and the latter 432 cords at £196.13.4 during the season of 1852. Pine was priced at 8*s.*9*d.* and a mixture of pine and hardwood at 9*s.*6*d.* per cord, for the cutting of which Chisholm paid wood cutters 5*s.* per cord for pine and 7*s.*6*d.* per cord for hardwood.[131] The rise in price of pine to 12*s.*6*d.* and of hardwood to 16*s.*3*d.* per cord three years later shows that wood was becoming more scarce.[132] Supplies were taken aboard at other ports besides Oakville, and some steamers consumed more than five thousand cords during a season. It was said of one old side-wheeler, which had been converted to a "river steamer," that when she was taking a heavy tow up the swift current in the St. Lawrence "the charred dollars could be seen coming out of her funnels."[133]

Many old steamers, being too slow to compete with newer types, were used for towing timber rafts in the St. Lawrence. The *Traveller* ended her days as a "river steamer" of Calvin, Cook & Company of Garden Island near Kingston,[134] and the *Highlander* was bought by this company for the same purpose in 1865. When on the Toronto-Hamilton run the *Highlander* had had as master a most obliging man, Captain McBride; passengers residing upon the lake shore between Port Credit and Oakville could depend upon him to sound his whistle when opposite their homes so that a conveyance might be sent to meet them.[135] The *Highlander* towed rafts until she "burned to the water's edge " in 1871. After the machinery was removed from the charred hull the remains were left behind Garden Island where traces could be seen as recently as eight years ago.[136]

By 1856 Oakville had become one of the most important ports in Canada West and was fulfilling in some measure the expectations of its founder. With prosperity and growth in population came also the expansion of facilities for study and worship and to these aspects of the cultural development of Oakville we will now turn.

CHAPTER EIGHT

NEW CHURCHES AND SCHOOLS

The year 1850–51 was memorable for the erection in Oakville of a new brick schoolhouse to replace the old frame building, a Presbyterian Church, and a Wesleyan Methodist church. Until then the Presbyterian and Wesleyan Methodist congregations had met for services either in the old schoolhouse, the Temperance Hall, St. Jude's Church, or private homes.

Upon the appointment of the Reverend Robert Murray as Superintendent of Education for Canada West and his subsequent removal to Kingston in 1842, the Scottish Presbyterians at both Oakville and the Sixteen Village on the Dundas Street were left without a pastor. The Church of Scotland still found difficulty in persuading its young ministers to leave their homeland and take up the rigorous duties of a missionary in Canada. The shortage of missionaries therefore made it impossible for the Presbytery of Toronto to fill the vacancy. The Reverand Alexander Gale, one of the first missionaries to work in the Gore District, came intermittently from Hamilton to perform marriages and baptisms at Oakville. Mr. Murray, after he began teaching at King's College at Toronto, also visited his former congregation, and until his death in 1853 maintained his contact with Oakville.

In 1843 a large portion of the Presbyterian Church in Scotland seceded to form the Free Church. A few years later Sir Richard Bonnycastle wrote: "The Kirk is wofully divided in Canada by widespread dissent";[1] in fact, the adherents to the Old Kirk were far outnumbered by dissenters. The Presbyterians at Oakville and the Sixteen Village ranged themselves on the side of the Free Church or, to give it the official name, the Presbyterian Church of Canada. The new church was, of course, under the necessity of training its own missionaries, and in 1844 founded at Toronto a theological school, Knox College. At this period the college occupied a brick row on Front Street which was soon to be remodelled into the Queen's Hotel.[2] Meanwhile the Oakville-Trafalgar charge was still vacant, and the church at the former was carrying on under its elder, David Duff. In 1846 Mr. Gale was appointed Professor of Classical Literature at Knox College, but he continued his visits to Oakville, and also arranged for theological students to take services there. One of these students was a young Scotsman named James Nisbet.

The minutes of the united congregations of Oakville and Trafalgar show that the first joint Session was regularly organized in 1846. David Duff, cabinet-maker, was Elder for Oakville, and Matthew Barclay, yeoman, was Elder for Trafalgar; both were Scotsmen. With the exception of the Irishmen, William and Robert Wilson, all heads of families in the Oakville congregation were Scotsmen: John Urquhart, Peter McCorquodale, James Arnott, Donald Campbell, William Cantley, Robert Balmer, and Andrew Robertson. By 1849 the number of families had increased to twenty-eight and it was then decided to build a church. At this same time John Barclay became Superintendent of the Sabbath School, an office he was to hold for forty-five years.[3] He was also Elder and Session Clerk for over thirty years.[4]

The Canada Presbyterian Church, opened in 1850, was situated on the north side of William Street midway between Dundas and Reynolds streets (block 28, lot E), and was constructed by the veteran carpenter who had come twenty years earlier to work on the piers, James McDonald senior. The Scotch Kirk, as it was called, is described as a "neat plain building of nearly the same capacity" as St. Jude's Church, three hundred persons, "and worth about two thousand dollars."[5] Another account states that the building was valued at £430.[6] It was a white frame structure with high ceilings and arched windows glazed with frosted glass. The two aisles flanked by pews enclosed with little doors led to the high pulpit behind which stood the minister's chair covered in horse-hair. Above the entrance was the gallery where the primary class of the Sabbath School received instruction.

The Reverend James Nisbet was inducted into the charge at Oakville on January 11, 1850. Born in the Parish of Gorbals, James was a son of Thomas Nisbet, master shipbuilder of Rutherglen on the Clyde, now a suburb of Glasgow. At the age of thirteen he had taught a Sabbath school class and at fifteen was made superintendent of a mission school, possibly a record. James was apprenticed to learn the trade of carpenter. In 1841 he and his elder brother, Henry, travelled over four hunderd miles on foot from Glasgow to London, to offer themselves to the London Missionary Society for foreign service. James was refused because of his youth. Henry, being twenty-three, was accepted and went as an early missionary to the islands of Samoa in the South Seas.* In 1844 James Nisbet accompanied his family to Canada West where he entered the newly founded Knox College. After graduating he spent nine months in Montreal before coming to Oakville.[7] Included in the charge at Oakville, for which the stipend was £120 per annum,[8] was the "congregation at the Dundas Street" and on Sunday afternoons Nisbet rode on horseback to the church on the east bank of The Sixteen at Proudfoot's Hollow. During the winter he made excursions into the counties of Simcoe, Grey, and Bruce to conduct services among scattered settlements that had spread back from the Owen Sound Road. Assisting the young minister at this time as Elders of the Session were Captain Robert Wilson, Robert Balmer, Matthew Barclay, and John Barclay.

The Session of the Presbyterian Church was a parochial ecclesiastical court which kept a stern eye on the members of its congregation. Only after careful questioning on their "views of divine faith" were new members "received into the fellowship of the Church." The Session was also most vigilant in issuing certificates of membership. Upon one occasion a lady, after moving from Oakville to the United States, requested a certificate of membership. Four years passed before the Session replied that when this request "came before them . . . they were unable to grant it on account of current reports regarding her moral character, that nothing had been done since to explain . . . therefore they are unable to grant the letter she asks."[9] Any irregularity of conduct occasioned a visit to a member from an Elder of the Session and a notice to appear before the Session. Suspension not infrequently followed and not until the Session was convinced of a member's penitence was he or she restored to "good standing." Members were called to account for inattendance at church, "using spirituous liquors in large quantities," and numerous other forms of "improper

*In the Oakville Cemetary beside the grave of Thomas Nisbet is another with a headstone bearing the inscription, "In memory of Sarah, wife of Rev. Henry Nisbet of Samoa, Polynesia and daughter of the late Rev. W. P. Crook of Tahiti. She died at Oakville 15 Nov 1868 after 27 years service in the mission field."

conduct." Periodically the communion roll was scrutinized and revised to include only the names of "members in good standing." The Session set the Sabbath on which "to dispose the Lord's supper." On the preceding Friday communicants were examined and given tokens of stamped metal as vouchers of their fitness to be admitted to communion. The service itself began at 10 A.M. and lasted until 2 P.M. It was customary at the weekly service for the minister to preach a sermon lasting about two hours.

No provision had been made at Oakville for a manse, and Mr. Nisbet, who was a bachelor, and his father set to work to build for themselves a brick cottage with basement kitchen on the lake shore east of the town (lot 11, 4th concession, Trafalgar Township). Before the house, now no. 92 Park Avenue, was ready for occupancy in 1852 they had already planted around it a small orchard "of about twenty-five trees."[10] All the land between the Nisbets' and Allan Street was bush (John A. Williams tells of hunting game there in the early fifties) and until Romain's estate blocked the way the minister and his father followed a path along the lake shore to the village.

Among the visiting ministers at Oakville was Nisbet's old classmate at Knox College, the Reverend John Black, the first missionary to go out to the Scots at Kildonan, the settlement founded on the Red River by the Earl of Selkirk. In 1862 Mr. Nisbet was appointed to assist him. Being a missionary at heart, Mr. Nisbet welcomed this appointment in the far west, and leaving his comfortable charge at Oakville where he had laboured for twelve years, he journeyed to Fort Garry, a trading post of the Hudson's Bay Company. During the four years he remained there he travelled over a territory 120 miles square, and supervised the erection of many schoolhouses. He drafted the plans, superintended the construction, and with his own hands made most of the interior woodwork of the stone schoolhouse in which Manitoba College was founded. In 1867 he accepted an appointment to serve among the Cree Indians on the North Saskatchewan River, the first missionary to be sent by the Canada Presbyterian Church to the Indians of the North-West. Mr. Nisbet planned to show the Indians the advantages of a settled life by teaching them farming, trades, and hand-crafts, and for that purpose he founded an industrial mission which he named Prince Albert in honour of Queen Victoria's deceased husband. He and the missionaries of other denominations did valuable work among the Indians of the North-West, and contributed greatly to understanding and good relations between settlers and Indians. On the whole, settlement in the Canadian West was accomplished without the massacring of white settlers which characterized pioneering in the western United States.

By the summer of 1874 the health of both Mr. Nisbet and his wife had begun to show the effects of their strenuous toil. They journeyed back five hundred miles to Kildonan but died shortly after their arrival. Mr. Nisbet had founded not only a mission but a city on the North Saskatchewan. His son Thomas, born in 1870, was the first white child born in Prince Albert.[11]His children returned to Oakville to live with two aunts in the brick cottage by the lake and today descendants of the Reverend James Nisbet still live in the town.

Mr. Nisbet's successor at the Canada Presbyterian Church was the Reverend Robert Scott who arrived in May, 1863. He was followed five years later, in January, 1868, by the Reverend William Meikle. At this time the church was enlarged and while alterations were in progress services were held at the Temperance Hall.[12] A social was given in aid of the building fund by Mrs. Barnet Moore, a leading singer in the choir, and the affair was attended by over a hundred persons. "Wealth and position were wisely laid aside and all conventionalities lost sight of," reported the *Canadian Champion*. "Rev. Mr. Meikle . . . appeared to appreciate the good old games of our grandmothers' days, as highly as any of his flock, and participated in the sport of 'forfeits,' 'blind man's buff,' &c., without any ostensible compromise of his clerical dignity."[13] From this social $14 was realized by the building fund.

Two members of the Scotch Kirk were well remembered by the younger generation: John Gallie, who as precentor stood under the pulpit and with his tuning fork set the pitch for the choir and led the singing, and William Strothers, the sexton. Strothers, a liberated slave who made brooms for a living, attended the door on Sundays in his frock coat and received the worshippers with "the courtly manners of the southern gentleman."

In the same year in which the Presbyterians decided to erect their own church the Wesleyan Methodists raised a place of worship. After selling their chapel to the Anglicans in 1841 the Methodists had reverted to the custom of holding services in the schoolhouse but with the erection of the Temperance Hall arrangements were made for its use.[14] The Nelson Circuit, of which Oakville was still an appointment, reached north into Erin Township, and in 1844 had a membership of over eight hundred.[15] That year the circuit was divided and a parsonage for the use of the preacher on the eastern division of the circuit was built at Oakville.[16] During the years that followed so many new members were added to the circuit that a meeting held at the Brick Church, Palermo, on February 23, 1850, adopted a resolution acknowledging the necessity of building a church at Oakville. Trustees appointed to obtain a site and oversee construction were Joseph Kenney, Robert Leach, John Potter, Thomas Jull, Soloman Savage, Hiram McCraney, and David Lebarre.[17] The land on the south-east corner of Dunn and Randall streets (block 4, lot A) was purchased in 1851 and on it was erected a building similar in construction and capacity to the Presbyterian Church.[18] Not until December, 1857, was the gallery installed, in time for the reopening of the church five days before Christmas.[19] In 1856 the Methodists obtained the lot on the south side of the church on Dunn Street (lot D) and within a few years built the large brick parsonage which stands today as no. 14 Dunn Street North.

In the meantime, the membership throughout the district had increased, and the circuit had been divided in three: the Milton, Waterdown, and Nelson circuits. In 1858 the name of Nelson Circuit was changed to the Oakville Circuit.[20]

The split which in 1832 had divided the Methodist denomination into the Wesleyan Methodist and Episcopal Methodist churches left the latter very weak in Oakville. Forced to struggle along as best they could, the Episcopal Methodists were not numerous enough for some time to secure there own place of worship. However, in 1856 they succeeded in buying the Congregational chapel on the north-west corner of John and Wilson streets, the interior of which had never been finished. At this time the trustees of the Methodist Episcopal Church at Oakville were Nathaniel Carroll, Samuel Harris, James Mulholland, James Denman, and David Hammond.[21]

In both Methodist churches were often held protracted meetings lastings for weeks, when preachers from all over the country came to exhort the large crowds that assembled. During the summer camp meetings were held in the open, but this form of religious appeal was meeting with less favour than in earlier times, and was being gradually abandoned. As the Methodist ministry became more professional, preaching became more moderate and less evangelistic in character. One of the largest and possibly one of the last camp meetings to be held in the district was organized by the Reverend A. T. Green, Wesleyan minister stationed at Oakville. It took place in June, 1857, at Mulholland's bush, on the east bank of The Sixteen between Culham's sawmill and the site of Triller's grist mill, the approach being by the Upper Middle Road. Whole families coming from a radius of perhaps fifty miles were prepared to spend days if not weeks camping in the bush. Usually at such gatherings supplies were obtainable on the spot, but since Mulholland's bush was so close to Oakville it was announced that on this occasion "No Grocery or Provision Tent will be set out on the grounds."[22] For lighting the evening sessions, fires of pine roots were kept burning on a large platform covered with clay standing about ten feet off the ground. During the month that the camp meeting lasted, between twenty and thirty preachers attended in rotation; as soon as one became exhausted another would take his place on the speakers' platform. A number of people from Hamilton joined together to prepare "Hamilton tents," where one of the preachers, Dr. Palmer, and his wife remained for a fortnight.[23] Mr. Green has left the following description of the gathering: "About four thousand were on the camp-ground on Sunday and twelve to fifteen hundred on other days. As nearly as can be ascertained about two hundred were converted. The meeting was attended by the most extraordinary manifestations of divine power I ever witnessed: and the oldest ministers present declared they never before saw anything like it. An impulse has been given to the work of God which must result in much spiritual good."[24] Those acquainted with the beauty of the spot will readily appreciate how easily the minds of masses of people could be impressed whether consciously or unconsciously in such surroundings. Here the red shale banks of the winding Sixteen are high and steep, and a brook drops down to the river through the mossy bed of a deep ravine which penetrates the bush for half a mile, dark with hemlock and cedar.

Two of the preachers who lived at Oakville and attended this revival meeting were the Reverend George Washington and the Reverend T. M. Jefferis, both of whom had come to Canada West in the forties. Middle aged when he became a circuit rider in Canada, Mr. Washington, a Primitive Wesleyan, was soon superannuated, and then took up farming. In 1853 he purchased the south-east quarter of lot 19 of the 3rd concession, the Clergy Reserve on the outskirts of Oakville which William McCraney had leased in 1807 for twenty-one years at a rental of eighteen bushels of wheat.[25] Near the Lake Shore Road facing upon a little brook that runs through this land, Washington built a one-storey brick cottage which he called "Retreat."[26] After twenty years of farming he sold his land to a retired officer of the Royal Navy, Captain Hugh Pullen, who added a second storey with mansard roof to the cottage. A decade later this building became "Rosedale Villa," the boarding house of Thomas Walsh, and after the turn of the century it passed into the hands of Captain G. H. Morden. Today it is the property of A. H. Downey. The Reverend George Washington was almost ninety when he died, and his name survives in Washington Avenue in the small division off Kerr Street laid out by his daughter.

The Reverend T. M. Jefferis lived to an even greater age. He was born at Bath, Somersetshire, and he supported himself from the age of eight by working in a factory. When Victoria was crowned queen he was fifteen years old. Two years later he became a local preacher, and in 1847 he migrated to Canada. His ship was wrecked off Cape Breton, and after he became a saddle-bag preacher he made this experience the subject of his sermon on each anniversary of the shipwreck. His salary of £17 per annum was supplemented by donations of wheat, corn flour, beans, pork, venison, and other produce from members of the congregations to whom he ministered. He knew what it was to have clothes so shabby that a respectable appearance at the annual conference demanded that his wife should turn the old suit. But on one occasion the gift of wool which he had woven into fulled cloth made him an almost imperishable suit of clothes. For the consideration of 5*s.* he joined in marriage many couples in Oakville and the surrounding district whose marriage licence had cost the groom £1.10. When superannuated Mr. Jefferis took up fruit farming on lot 10 of the 3rd concession on the eastern outskirts of Oakville. A young minister who came to study with him and who became his son-in-law, J. W. Warne, went as a missionary to India where he was given charge of the only European Methodist Church in Calcutta, and was soon made a bishop. In the nineties Mr. Jefferis moved into the town and there enjoyed many more years of life. When he died in 1922 he had passed the century mark by one month.

The Roman Catholic "Missions of Dundas, Oakville and Trafalgar" were given in 1847 under the care of the Reverend John O'Reilly of the Parish of Dundas.[27] The land adjoining St. Andrew's Church on the north side (lots A and B, block 35) was purchased in 1855, and a one-storey brick presbytery with basement rooms[28] was built under the supervision of Father O'Reilly. The house was ready for occupancy in 1858 but the first resident priest, Father Fitzgerald, remained for only seven months. On September 15, 1859, the missions of Oakville, Trafalgar, Milton, and Wellington Square were given under the charge of the Reverend Jeremiah Ryan and during the seventeen years of Father Ryan's energetic service St. Andrew's grew and prospered. It was through his exertions that St. Mary's Separate School was established in 1860, and that the church was enlarged to the east some ten years later. A description given at this time presents the church as having seating capacity for three hundred persons and to be worth "about three thousand dollars."[29]

Under the guidance of the Reverend G. W. Warr, resident clergyman of the Parish of St. Jude's, the Oakville mission of the Anglican Church had continued to flourish. A clever man of commanding presence, Mr. Warr was specially interested in the young people of the parish, and at his first confirmation twenty-nine persons entered the Church. However, in the third year of his incumbency discord arose about payment of the rector's salary and his authority over the sexton, and these matters were submitted to Bishop Strachan for arbitration. The bishop ruled that "the sexton may be appointed by the Church Wardens acting for the Church and Congregation . . . yet they are under the Clergyman's directions . . . and it belongs to him to give directions when to ring the bell or otherwise."[30] Neither Mr. Warr nor his wife were happy in their situation or in Canada. The rector wished to return to England and gave as the reason for relinquishing his charge the effects of the Canadian climate upon the health of his wife. This was considered of insufficient importance by the Bishop, but when Mr. Warr produced two doctors' certificates in confirmation, his resignation was reluctantly accepted. He was appointed to a new church, St. Saviour's, on Upper Huskisson Street, Liverpool, in 1846, where he remained until 1870. Thereafter until his death twenty-five years later he was vicar of Childwall. In his memory the east window and reredos were placed in St. Saviour's Church and the accompanying brass plaque records the fact of his having been "a missionary in Canada for the Society for the Propagation of the Gospel in Foreign parts from 1841 to 1846." A son, George Charles Winter Warr, born at Oakville and educated at Trinity College, Cambridge, was for twenty years Professor of Classical Literature at King's College, London. St. Saviour's Church is a beautiful building, classical in architecture; it sustained bomb damage during World War II, as did the district surrounding it, but has since been repaired.

During the five years Mr. Warr spent in Oakville he became intensely interested in the rural district surrounding it. He had occasion to take frequent journeys to the missions at Palermo and Hornby which had been established through his efforts and he noted in detail his observations on agricultural practices and conditions generally in the township. Upon his return to England he published a book entitled

Canada as it is; or Emigrants' Friend and Guide to Upper Canada (London, 1847) in which he gives an excellent picture of Trafalgar Township though he does not refer to it by name. This rare little volume is a valuable source book for present-day historians.

When given his choice of two vacancies by Bishop Strachan, the Reverend Alexander Pyne chose Oakville rather than Kemptville, and in 1847 he became rector of St. Jude's Church. Mr. Pyne was a distinguished scholar and Gold Medallist of Trinity College, Dublin, which was to supply St. Jude's with so many of its rectors. At that period about twenty-seven of its graduates had served or were serving in Upper Canada.[31] In 1847 the first mention is made in the church records of the names of Churchwardens: Alexander Proudfoot and John L. Bigger. The baptismal record begun in 1842 is headed by the name of Elizabeth born to Alexander and Amelia Proudfoot in that year.

We have a first-hand description of St. Jude's Church at this time in the report to Bishop Strachan by Archdeacon A. N. Bethune (subsequently Bishop of Toronto) of his extensive tour of the parishes in the province in 1848. In March he wrote:

About 9 o'clock I left [Toronto] in the stage for Oakville. The day was mild and the roads a good deal improved, so that we reached the village about 2 o'clock. The Rev. A. Pyne was very kindly watching the passing of the stage, and requested me to alight at his dwelling, some little distance East of Oakville. I met one of the Churchwardens at dinner there; and at 6 o'clock, according to appointment, we proceeded to the Church.

St. Jude's Church originally belonged to, and was purchased from, the Methodists, and is more ecclesiastical in its appearance than the sacred edifices ordinarily erected by that body. It wants painting, however, both within and without; and in my address after the service, I took occasion to call the attention of the Churchwardens to that want. It is out of debt, with the exception of a claim made by Mr. Wm. Creighton, now of Toronto, for about £33, which has been the subject of much discussion and the cause of acrimony. . . .

The pews are let generally but at very disproportionate amounts for which there did not appear adequate reasons. I recommended, therefore, a re-consideration of this, as the standing revenue of the Church might be materially benefitted. The number of free-sittings is 120 in the Gallery, and the space of four pews below. The collections are weekly and average about £200 per annum. A Font and Bell have been provided; and a subscription is in circulation for procuring an organ. The Communion Plate is complete, but I advised the procuring of a surplice, as the one in use is the property of the clergyman.

There is no endowment of land attached to the Mission, and the spot

> upon which the Church is situated I represented as wholly insufficient,—being only a quarter of an acre. While land is comparatively cheap I advised their augmenting this quantity to what would be required for a Burial Ground, as well as for a Parsonage house,—about £70 per annum is given towards the support of the Clergyman.[32]

Archdeacon Bethune left Oakville on the steamer *Eclipse* the day following these active hours of observation.

By 1849 the church was out of debt and a petition "of the Missionary at Oakville and members of the United Church of England and Ireland" was sent to Bishop Strachan in which he was asked to consecrate the church "by name of St. Jude's." The petition was signed by Alexander Pyne and four church wardens, Charles Bigger, J. L. Bigger, William Langtry, and William Jarvis.[33] The dedication reads in part as follows:

> In the name of God. Amen.
>
> The Reverend Alexander Pyne and Mr. William Jarvis
>
> Forasmuch as the members of the Church of England in the Parish of Oakville and the Propagation Society have purchased a church in the village of Oakville . . . for the sole use of the inhabitants of Oakville village and neighborhood forever under the name of St. Jude's the measurement of which church is as follows; length 60 feet and breadth 25 feet or thereabouts, and have provided a pulpit, reading desk, communion table and altar and all things requisite for the decent performance of Divine Worship . . . the church wardens have humbly requested us, John, by Divine permission Bishop of Toronto . . . to dedicate the same as a church for the worship of God. Given under our hand this 1st. Day of July in the year of our Lord, one thousand eight hundred and forty-nine. . . .
>
> JOHN TORONTO.[34]

In 1852 the Reverend Robert Shanklin, formerly missionary at Fenelon Falls, became rector at St. Jude's, and it was during his incumbency that the recommendation of Archdeacon Bethune was adopted relative to a site for a rectory and a more suitably located burial ground. Lot no. 17 in the 4th concession on the lake shore west of the village was procured in 1853. This land had comprised part of the 600 acres granted by the Crown in 1806 to William Stanton of the Town of York. As an officer in the Royal Navy, Stanton had seen much service in the East and West Indies, in the Mediterranean, at the siege of Gibraltar, and on the coast of North America during the Revolutionary War. In 1786 he had entered public service in Lower Canada and served in several military and civil capacities in both provinces. In 1805 Stanton was chief clerk in the office of President Alexander Grant, who during a leave of absence of Sir Francis Gore was "administering the Government of U.C." It was the policy of the British government to remunerate civil servants in part by grants of land and Stanton received lots no. 17, 18, 19, and 23 in the 4th concession of Trafalgar Township. Between 1811 and 1815 he was Serjeant-at-Arms in the Parliament of Upper Canada, being succeeded by Allan (later Sir Allan) MacNab. It is rather remarkable that five sets of twins were born to Mrs. Stanton.[35] A son, Robert, King's Printer, published the handsome early volumes of the *Journals of the Assembly of Upper Canada.*

The land for the new rectory and cemetery is said to have been given to St. Jude's by Esther Thomas, wife of Merrick Thomas who lived opposite on the north side of the Lake Shore Road. She was the farmer of the family and pastured her cows on the sandy land of lot 17 across the way. She considered it of little use as farm land, and though one of the largest stands of white pine in the district covered the lot, she gave it to St. Jude's for a cemetery. Although Merrick Thomas does not appear as owner of this land it was assessed to him in 1850 and the year following it was assessed to the "Trustees of the English Church." The deed, as previously stated, is dated 1853.

In the spring of 1853 a two-day bazaar was held in Temperance Hall "for the purpose of creating a fund to assist the erection of a PARSONAGE HOUSE." This event was concluded by an amateur and professional concert.* The rectory was built near the southern end of the lot, and a wide swath was cleared to give a vista of Lake Ontario. The house was approached by a carriage road running through the bush. At the time of writing this bush, never having been timbered, still stands. Among the pines in the north-east corner of the lot was laid out St. Jude's Cemetery.

Mr. Shanklin was a man of musical talents, and he soon procured a harmonium for the church and placed a small orchestra in the gallery. This interest in music led to the installation about 1857 of a pipe organ built by a member of the congregation, Richard Coates.

Musician, painter, and one of the earliest builders of pipe organs in Upper Canada, Richard Coates had had a varied and interesting career. He was a Yorkshireman, born at Thornton near Pickering, the only son of Sir Richard Coates and Dorothy Reynolds, a near relative

*A wit wrote to the *Streetsville Review*: "I have learned that some of the finest looking girls of this vicinity are to visit Oakville in the steamboat excursion specially got up for the Bazaar. Four, at least, of these charmers have acquired the degree of Belle—and three out of the quartette possess a plethora of tin at their disposal. Your Bachelors, therefore, should call at the Bazaar and see and judge for themselves before popping the question elsewhere." *Streetsville Review*, April 9, 1853.

of England's great portrait painter, Sir Joshua Reynolds. As bandmaster in the British Army, Richard Coates led his band at the Battle of Waterloo. Upon migrating to York in 1817 he settled with his wife and two children on Duke Street not far from where it enters Parliament Street. When he petitioned for land as a settler in 1824 Coates described himself as a painter "executing his trade at York."[36] Dr. Scadding wrote of him: "An estimable and ingenious man, whose name is associated in our memory with the early dawn of the fine arts in York. Mr. Coates in a self-taught way, executed, not unsuccessfully, portraits in oil of some of our ancient worthies. Among things of a general or historical character, he painted also for David Willson, founder of the 'Children of Peace' the symbolical decorations of the interior of the Temple at Sharon. . . . He built an organ of some pretentions in his own house on which he performed. He built another for David Willson at Sharon."[37] As the first organist and choirmaster of the Children of Peace, Coates led the white-robed choir in the music which formed a large part of their services in the beautiful Temple at Sharon. The organ he built and two banners painted by him are to be seen today at the Temple, now the museum of the York Pioneer and Historical Society.

In 1831 Richard Coates moved to Trafalgar Township, buying lot 8 of the 3rd concession, which "sold for assessment" for 18*s*.9*d*. per acre.[38] This he called "Thornton Farm" after his birthplace. Soon he acquired the land on the south side of the Lake Shore Road and on the stream that came to be called Coates' Creek (where it now runs through the land of Colonel W. G. Mackendrick) he set up a sawmill. Coates did a thriving business; John A. Williams wrote that the honesty and pleasant banter of father and sons made dealing with them a pleasure. Richard junior was a farmer who in the early fifties received prizes at the Provincial Exhibition at Toronto. He was the proud exhibitor of the "3rd best Southdown ewe" and his three-year-old bull, the Duke of Devonshire, took first prize, £8, two years running.[39] The ceremony of his marriage to a daughter of his neighbour, Barnet Griggs, was performed by the Reverend James Norris, first resident Methodist minister at Oakville.[40] Perhaps with the family's musical connections in mind the eldest of their ten children was named Orpheus.

Richard Coates senior was seventy-nine years of age when he was commissioned to build a pipe organ for St. Jude's Church. His log workshop was situated not far from the sawmill. Some of his earlier organs had been barrel organs, a type in which a pin-studded revolving cylinder acted mechanically on the keys. Several barrels were used, each producing a number of tunes, and no skill was required of the player. However, the organ for St. Jude's was to be played by an organist, and, as described by a lady who was organist in later years, this instrument would seem to have been very similar to the one that Coates built some years earlier for the Davidite Temple at Sharon. Unlike modern church organs built into the wall it stood as a separate unit in the gallery of the church. Through pipes standing in the high case, air was pumped by interior bellows operated from behind by a handle similar in action and appearance to that of a well pump. The boy who bent his back to the pump handle was paid at the rate of ten cents an hour. The stops, placed in a recess above the keyboard, were enclosed when not in use by little sliding doors.

In 1862 the Reverend Robert Shanklin went to Thornhill, and the Reverend John Fletcher, graduate of Trinity College, Dublin, became rector of St. Jude's. He was succeeded in the spring of 1869 by Canon John Bell Worrell. Born near London and educated at King's College, Mr. Worrell had come to Canada in 1847. He studied theology at Trinity College, Toronto, and then was rector at Woodstock, Smith's Falls, and Oshawa. After these incumbencies he officiated at the cathedral at Kingston; there he was made a canon. From Kingston he came to Oakville where he was to be rector for over thirty-four years.

II

Many improvements had been made in the educational system of the province after Dr. Ryerson became Chief Superintendent of Education for Canada West. Under the Common School Act of 1846 the power to make regulations for the schools was withdrawn from the trustees and vested in the Chief Superintendent, although the monthly rate bill was continued. All schools were required to use the same textbooks, and for the first time teachers' certificates were divided into three classes, first, second, and third, according to the teacher's qualifications. Official visitors were clergymen of all denominations having pastoral charge over the district in which the school was located, justices of the peace, judges, and municipal councillors. They were given the right to attend examinations and to advise the teacher.

Just when Arthur C. Verner, whom we have already encountered in connection with Vernerville, was appointed master of the Oakville Common School is uncertain. Our sole authority, John A. Williams, does not make this clear but it would seem to have been in the late forties. Williams tells us that for years it had been the custom of pupils to lock the teacher out of the schoolhouse on the first day of each new quarter and not until gifts of candy, apples, etc. were forthcoming was he permitted to enter. On one occasion when he was refused entrance Verner turned away towards Colborne Street. When he was seen returning with a large bundle under his arm the pupils unlocked the door. As Verner walked to his desk one of the pupils poked a hole in the bundle; great was the disappointment when it was found to consist of a large roll of cotton batting. Williams also tells of the day when Philip Bisnois (who a few years before had accompanied Rankin's party on the survey of the Owen Sound Road) came to the schoolhouse swearing vengeance on Verner for "thrashing" his daughter. Bisnois was a burly French Canadian and a great fighter, but Verner spoke to him in French "and succeeded in talking him down." Because of a deformity of his right arm Verner had the use of his left hand only, but with it he was exceptionally deft. The children enjoyed his sleight-of-hand tricks, and his ability to punch a penny through his desk without a hole being discovered always caused great astonishment.

With the growing interest in education and the rapid growth in population the school facilities at Oakville were becoming inadequate. By 1850 the number of scholars attending the common school had increased to 140[41] and the necessity for larger quarters was urgent. The Trafalgar Township Council authorized the raising of £300 for the erection of a new building. Two hundred pounds was borrowed by issuing debentures and the balance raised by a special assessment on ratepayers in School Section no. 14 of ¾*d.* in the pound.[42] The new two-storey brick building was situated north of the old schoolhouse. It was constructed by Jull and Moulds, contractors, and was twenty-five feet wide by approximately forty feet in length. Surmounting the main entrance on Navy Street was a bell cupola with an arrow-shaped weather-vane. This building, which stands today as the middle section of Central School, was ready for occupancy early in 1850. Desks and other necessary furniture were obtained from the firm of Jaques and Hay, Toronto.[43] The school was open during twelve months of the year, and with an attendance of 190 scholars was the largest in the township. Extraordinary as it may seem, only one teacher was employed. His name is omitted from the educational reports, but as it is mentioned that he was educated at Knox College and the University of Toronto, he could not have been Arthur Verner. The schoolmaster's salary of £100 per annum was the highest paid in the township.[44] The old schoolhouse, built in 1828, was remodelled shortly after, and one end was used to house the newly acquired fire engine.[45]

For maintaining the common schools people in many parts of the province were showing preference for a tax on their property rather than on their children, and a law passed in 1850 gave them the option of abolishing or continuing the monthly attendance fee. The attitude of Halton County towards free schools was summed up by a local superintendent, who wrote: "Education has never engaged the attention of parents and landholders so much as it has done these four weeks past. Free Schoolism has fallen upon their slumber like a bomb. Meagre, stupid, lifeless school-meetings, have at once given way to full, animated and eloquent assemblies. What a storm there has been! The childless and the patriarch of grown-up families, who can sell wheat . . . without arithmetic, and find their way home without geography, together with those who have educated their own children and a few families whose sense of justice is excessive, have been expectorating large quantities of bile, and see, in the future, tax pile upon tax . . . till they are fairly crushed underneath."[46] A similar attitude prevailed apparently in Oakville, as the common school continued for some years under the old system of collecting 1*s*.3*d*. per month for each child.

New legislation passed in 1853 placed grammar schools, which until then had been the responsibility of the provincial government, in the hands of municipal councils. The councils were authorized to levy taxes for building, maintaining, and equipping grammar schools and the trustees were empowered to appoint masters who must be university graduates. Thereafter grammar schools were no longer merely boarding schools for the wealthy, but became an integral part of the educational system of the province. Immediately the Trafalgar Township Council availed themselves of this opportunity for securing advanced education for the children of the township, and we find the Local Superintendent reporting: "In Oakville they have made arrangements for establishing a grammar-school in connection with the common school, and which will go into operation immediately."[47]

The chairman of the Board of Education at Oakville, George K. Chisholm, hoped that the grammar school would become free. He wrote Dr. Ryerson at the close of 1853 for assistance in this cause: "A lecture by yourself . . . on the subject of Free Schools would be acceptable to a large portion of our population who will next year as I think adopt the principle in connection with our Grammar School to be established after the new year."[48] His optimism proved premature, however, as neither grammar nor common school became free for some years.

In February, 1854, the township council authorized the raising of £250 "to be expended in building an addition to the present School House, and in providing seats, desks, etc."[49] The school was enlarged by the addition on the west end of a thirty-five foot section containing in each storey one room lighted by two windows on the north and two on the south. These rooms were approached by a new entrance, hall, and stairway, and the building whose main entrance had formerly faced east upon Navy Street now faced Colborne Street on the south.[50] The grammar school was to be situated in the two rooms in the new section on the west and the common school continued to occupy the two rooms in the eastern section of the building. When the building was ready for use, a petition was dispatched to the government "on behalf of the Inhabitants of the Village of Oakville . . . representing that the building to be used as a Grammar School is now completed and requesting the establishment of said School."[51] There had been no grammar school in Halton County since the school at Palermo had been moved to Galt three years before, and the government therefore authorized the establishment of the school at Oakville as the County Grammar School.

With both common and grammar schools housed together, the building was often referred to as the Union School, and the headmaster of the grammar school was styled "head of the entire academy." In 1854 Arthur C. Verner, graduate of Trinity College, Dublin, formerly master of the Oakville Common School and headmaster of the Wellington Grammar School, was appointed first headmaster of the Halton County Grammar School at a salary of £197.10 per annum.[52] Daniel Benjamin Chisholm was placed in charge of the common school. No kin to the Oakville family, Chisholm, upon migrating from

Scotland, had taught school at Streetsville and Milton. The trustees of the grammar school at this time are not listed, but on February 3, 1855, the County Council appointed the Reverend Thomas Greene of Wellington Square, the Reverend Robert Shanklin, James Arnott, William Cantley, and George K. Chisholm as trustees.[53] Fees for the grammar school ranged from 7*s*.6*d*. to £1.2.6. per quarter, depending upon the number of subjects taken by a pupil. During the first year there were twenty pupils and within three years the number had quadrupled. In 1858 the total number of pupils in both common and grammar schools was three hundred and there were five teachers.[54]

Apparently the students of those days were not kept constantly at the three R's. Before Christmas, 1855, the children held a concert "accompanied by the Melodeon, proceeds to be appropriated to purchase a Melodeon to accompany children at their singing exercises." For adults admission was 2*s*.6*d*. and for children under twelve, 1*s*.3*d*., "the concert to commence at 7½ P.M."[55]

A pamphlet issued by the school board in 1857 entitled *Programme of Course of Instruction in the Oakville Grammar School—Rules and Regulations*[56] gives insight into the functioning of the school. G. K. Chisholm was still head of the school board, Justus W. Williams was secretary, and William Oliver, B.A., University of Toronto, had that year succeeded Verner as headmaster (salary, £200). D. B. Chisholm (at £150) was still in charge of the common school, Harriet Bowes (at £75) taught the junior department, and Elizabeth McDonald (£65.12.6) and Sarah Bedell (£63.15.0) conducted the primary classes. The treasurer attended on the first Monday of each month to collect the "Tuition Fee," which for the common school was 1*s*.3*d*. per month; for the grammar school 1*s*.3*d*. was collected for each branch of study "until the whole shall amount to 6*s*.3*d*. after which no further charges shall be made." The winter term commenced on January 7 and ran until five days before Easter, the spring term began the Wednesday after Easter and ended the middle of July, and the summer term ran from the second Monday in August to October 15. Then began the autumn term which ended December 22. Thus approximately two weeks' holiday was given at Christmas, a week at Easter, and one month in the summer, totalling seven weeks in the twelve months of the year.

The first bell in the morning rang at quarter before nine, the last at nine o'clock, and the times of dismissal were "twelve noon and four and a half P.M." The "Programme or Time Table" included reading and spelling, slate arithmetic, copying letters on slates, penmanship, mental arithmetic, drawing, and singing. The textbooks used in the grammar school were Bullion's *Latin Reader and Grammar*, Furton's and Eastman's *Bookkeeping*, and Colenso's *Mathematics, Trigonometry and Algebra*. In the common school Lambert's *Physiology* and Davies' and Colburn's mental arithmetic were used.

The report also dealt with discipline in the school. "Should a child be found truanting, he (or she) must be dealt with wholly at home," ruled the school board. "The Pupils are expected to conduct themselves towards each other in such a way as accords with a kind heart and good manners, and to their teachers they are required to be always respectful, and yield a just obedience, while improper language or conduct on any occasion shall subject the pupil to discipline."[57]

By 1858 it appeared that even the new school building was inadequate to accommodate the school population of Oakville. The chairman of the Board of Education wrote to the town council: "The subject of education is of the first and most imperative importance. When our present comfortable school house was erected, it was thought sufficient for many years, in two years it was found too small, and today it is quite insufficient for the wants of the people."[58] He then suggested that a larger school building be erected on Reynolds Street in the eastern section of the town, but the plan was never carried out. A decade later out of 452 pupils the average attendance was only 184, about 40 per cent, of which only 70 attended more than 200 days.[59]

The common school became free in 1860, and the Local Superintendent, the Reverend James Nisbet, remarked in his report to Dr. Ryerson: ". . . we have no complaints about the change."[60] The grammar school, however, continued to collect rates until about 1868, when it also became free.

It was not until 1861 that the first pupil matriculated from the Oakville school and entered the University of Toronto. Nisbet reported proudly to Ryerson, "You will observe that the Grammar School department has produced some gratifying fruits, as shown by the university examinations." He adds, "prizes given in the Union School consist of certificates and honor cards, which, in my opinion, are preferable to books: they excite emulation, and are not so productive of envy and strife as the giving of books."[61] The second pupil matriculated in 1868, and two more succeeded in passing the examinations in 1870, but twelve years passed before other matriculants were reported.

Dr. Ryerson exerted his influence to obtain libraries for all schools in the province. According to the Local Superintendent's report of 1861 a library established in connection with the Oakville school was "procured chiefly by the Grammar School Department from proceeds of public exhibitions, at which a small charge is made. The books are covered and the circulation is good. There are 462 books in the catalogue." A catalogue published in 1865 shows 620 books to the value of $1,060.[62]

William Oliver was succeeded as headmaster of the grammar school in 1864 by William Fleming of the University of Toronto who remained for only one year. James Choppin Morgan, double Gold Medallist of the University of Toronto, appointed in 1866, resigned after two years.[63] During 1869 John Pepper, also of the University of Toronto, acted as headmaster, but difficulties arose which caused the school board to request his resignation, and Morgan returned until the appointment in 1870 of the Reverend William Lumsden of Victoria College.[64]

In 1860 Oakville acquired another school, when Father Ryan established St. Mary's Separate School. A separate school is, of course, not necessarily Catholic, but may be formed by dissentients of any denomination. According to the School Act of 1841 "any number of Inhabitants of any Township or Parish professing a Religious Faith different from that of the majority of the Inhabitants" may form their own school, which shall be entitled to a share of all school moneys.[65] St. Mary's School was located in the rear of St. Andrew's Church and was in the hands of the Sisters of St. Joseph, an order newly come to Canada from the United States. Established in France in the seventeenth century, the order was employed in educating the young, visiting the poor, and attending to the needs of orphans, the sick, and the aged. A group of nuns were induced to come to Canada, and the separate schools of Toronto were entrusted to their care in 1852. Thereafter, wherever possible, separate schools were committed to the charge of the Sisters of St. Joseph. In 1860 there were three sisters of charity in Oakville,[66] two of whom taught the 107 pupils attending St. Mary's. Two years later there were 127 pupils enrolled in the separate school[67] but by 1870 the number had dropped to an average attendance of between 80 and 90.[68]

The property across from the church on the south-west corner of Reynolds Street was added to the church holdings and for some years three of the sisters conducted a convent in the brick house that is now no. 150 King Street. Children of all denominations were given instruction in music, drawing, sewing, etc. until the sisters left Oakville about 1890.

Besides the Union and Separate schools there were several private schools in Oakville. Indeed, private schools for younger children and for the tutoring of older boys in advanced subjects were by no means new in Oakville. As far back as the 1830's various clergymen stationed in the village or living in the vicinity had conducted small schools or prepared young men for the clergy. One of the earliest boys' schools was that of Isaac Whiting who lived on the south side of Colborne near Thomas Street. Son of a preacher on the Nelson Circuit, Whiting was an early graduate of Victoria College then situated at Cobourg, and one of the first Canadian-born teachers at Oakville. The small schools conducted by women "were more select but not as good for boys," according to John A. Williams. In 1858 forty pupils are listed as attending the four private schools and academies (including Miss Hewson's) which were conducted in the town.

In the absence of an Anglican school of divinity the Reverend Charles Dade, Fellow of Caius College, Cambridge, and teacher of mathematics at Upper Canada College at Toronto,[69] prepared young men for ordination. Two of his pupils who rode on horseback to his home on the Lake Shore Road East, Alexander Williams and John Langtry, later became prominent in the Anglican Church. They also attended the school of the rector of St. Jude's Church, the Reverend Alexander Pyne, who lived one mile east of Oakville Williams was the elder son of Justus W. Williams, and brother of John A. whose reminiscences have contributed so substantially to this history. John Langtry lived on a farm west of Oakville. The two friends went up to Trinity College, Toronto, on its opening day in January, 1852. After being ordained both served for some time as travelling missionaries in the western section of the province between Lake Erie and Georgian Bay, enduring many privations. For forty-seven years the Reverend Canon Alexander Williams was rector of the Church of St. John the Evangelist, Toronto, and his daughter, Mrs. E. T. Lightbourn, was a resident of long standing in Oakville. As well as founding St. Luke's Church, Toronto, of which he was rector for more than thirty years, the Reverend John Langtry succeeded in securing the establishment at Toronto of the Bishop Strachan School. With the exception of Roman Catholic convents there were at that time few schools where girls could obtain a thorough and well-rounded education under refining influences; the "select academies" for young ladies did not maintain a very high scholastic standard. Mr. Langtry was one of the chief movers in the small group of men who attempted to remedy the deficiency by starting the school which was named in honour of the Bishop of Toronto.[70]

Between 1863 and 1869 the Reverend John Fletcher, rector of St.

Jude's Church, Oakville, tutored young men who lived with him at the rectory during the summer months. In 1867 a son of the Anglican rector at Dundas, William Osler, came to read for matriculation examinations. Although several years his senior, "Jemmy" Morgan, headmaster of the Oakville grammar school, had known Willie Osler at Barrie. Together with several other young men they would sit up till midnight watching through a microscope the activities of fresh-water algae. In the autumn Osler went up to Trinity College with the intention of entering the ministry, but his interest in medicine which had begun with the study of protozoa in marshes and ponds soon led him to change his course.[71] In the field of medicine Sir William Osler was perhaps the most outstanding figure of his time.

A form of adult education which had become increasingly popular all over the province was that provided by the Mechanics' Institutes whose aim, according to the *Streetsville Review*, was "to make the man a better mechanic and the mechanic a better man." An act of Parliament passed in 1851 providing for the establishment and incorporation of Library Associations and Mechanics' Institutes gave great impetus to the movement. Since 1839, when the village had received the gift of 100 books, Oakville had had a small public library, but the Institutes were more than libraries, and provided facilities for lectures on a wide range of subjects. The Oakville Mechanics' Institute was established in January, 1852, and its object as stated in a pamphlet setting forth the constitution and regulations was "the diffusion of scientific and literary knowledge, by Library of reference and circulation; by the formation of a Museum of specimens of Zoology, Geology, or other subjects of Nature, Science, or Manufacture; by Conversation; or any other Method the Committee may judge necessary. . . . Entry money £1, annual contribution 5*s*. per year payable in advance."[72] Members were entitled to attend lectures and to receive a library ticket. Any person over eighteen was eligible to join. A member's right in the society was transferable upon his death to an heir, who was admitted to the privileges of the Institute upon payment of 2*s*.6*d*. There is little of interest in the list of books included in the pamphlet except that its printer had altered the heading "Belles Lettres" to read "Belle's Letters." Officers of the Institute were G. K. Chisholm, president; Justus W. Williams, vice-president; Robert Balmer, secretary; and James Reid, treasurer. The committee was made up of John Potter, Wm. N. Mills, James Arnott, Robert Leach, William Moulds, John Barclay, and William Flock, M.D.[73]

In a letter to Dr. Ryerson the following January the president stated:

"Our Institute has been in operation one year, consists of upwards of one hundred members with a library of five hundred volumes. Last year we had weekly lectures."[74] The lectures were given on subjects of a scientific nature, and classes formed for imparting practical knowledge were afforded facilities for studying "models and apparatus." During the first five years the Oakville Institute received a grant from the government of £50 yearly.[75] In the event that an Institute by discontinuing classes and lectures became merely a circulating library, the grant was withheld and in 1858 this happened in the case of the Oakville Institute. Like many other Institutes throughout the province the Oakville Institute languished through lack of support from those whom it was intended to benefit and there is reason to believe that eventually its library was pooled with that of the grammar school.

No further changes of interest or importance occurred in connection with the Oakville schools until the innovations instituted by the School Law Improvement Act of 1871, and consideration of its terms will be reserved for a later chapter. In the meantime the brick schoolhouse had been the scene of an important ceremony. The strong feeling of dissatisfaction with being governed by the township council had led to the application early in 1857 to the Government to make Oakville a separate municipality by raising it to the status of a town. In July, 1857, the first municipal council of the Town of Oakville took the oath of office.

CHAPTER NINE

A MUNICIPALITY IN CANADA WEST

THE PERIOD that ended in the establishment in Canada West of a system of rural self-government, which has remained almost unchanged for one hundred years, is well illustrated in the history of Trafalgar Township. This is also the history of Oakville's local government, as during the first thirty years of its existence as a village Oakville was an integral part of the township. We may be justly proud of the system adopted in this province, which served as a model for Canada's younger provinces. It evolved over a stormy half-century, and at the end of this time the powers of government had passed from officers appointed by the Crown into the hands of officers elected by the people.

Until the Act of Union in 1841, the system of local government was centred in the Court of Quarter Sessions of the Peace, an ancient institution of English origin. Composed of Justices of the Peace in the district, the court met four times a year to levy taxes and dispose of revenues, over which it had sole control. Their offices were in the gift of the government and the Justices were answerable for their actions to the Executive Council rather than to the people. They were called "Squires," and the use of "Esquire" following a man's name was much more restricted then than it has been since.

During the early period when Trafalgar Township was within the Home District, the local Justices attended the Court of Quarter

Sessions sitting at York. After the creation, in 1816, of the Gore District, formed of the counties of Wentworth and Halton, the Justices of Trafalgar Township met at Hamilton, the District Town. The Court of Quarter Sessions of the Gore District met the second Tuesday in January, April, July, and October.[1] This court declared the rate of taxation, determined the disposition of the tax money, and set rates for additional taxes to remunerate the local members of Parliament. The Justices in session regulated many of the duties of town officers, who were elected in town meeting, and confirmed them in their office.

The town meeting was an American institution introduced by Loyalists upon their arrival in the province. Though many British officials considered the practice republican and therefore dangerous, the Loyalists had insisted on holding town meetings in the manner to which they had become accustomed. At the annual town meeting, held the first week in January, the ratepayers in Trafalgar Township elected by popular vote a town warden, a town clerk, two assessors, a collector of taxes, a poundkeeper, and a number of overseers of highways and pathmasters. These town officers were allowed little initiative, and were accountable to the Justices rather than to the people who elected them. The positions were not sought after, and it became necessary to impose a fine of 40*s*. upon those who declined to serve after being elected.

The town clerk was required to make a list of inhabitants for the use of the Justices and assessors. Landowners paid a tax of 1*s*.5*d*. per acre on uncultivated land, and 1*d*. per acre on cultivated land. Houses were assessed according to size (decided by the number of fireplaces and the number of storeys) and type of construction (hewn log, frame, stone, or brick). Taxes were levied on shops, mills, industries, and items of property such as cattle, horses and oxen. Beginning in 1830, "gigs, curricles, and pleasure waggons" were subject to taxation. During the first thirty years, ratepayers in the village of Oakville were listed on the township assessment rolls, and paid their taxes to the township collector, who turned the money over to the district treasurer. The assessment rolls in themselves are of interest. Consisting of narrow sheets of paper, many yards in length, folded like an accordian, they are easily handled and quickly read. From the account book of Charles Sovereign, a Justice of the Peace, we learn that the paper was bought by the yard. As may be seen in the photograph (plate 18) the headings are handsomely engrossed; in several instances, they are so similar to Sovereign's engrossing that undoubtedly they are his work.

Rolls of this type were superseded in the thirties by large square sheets of paper, roughly stitched together into book form by the assessor and, in 1839, by properly bound books with printed headings. The Trafalgar Township assessment rolls that are extant begin in 1823 and with few exceptions are continuous down to the present time.

Much of the tax money was allocated by the Quarter Sessions to the construction and maintenance of secondary roads. Purely local roads were built and maintained by the labour tax, commonly known as statute labour. The assessed value of the landowner's property determined the amount of labour to be performed; men whose names did not appear on the rolls gave two days' labour. It was permissible, however, for those who so preferred to commute their statute labour by paying the prevailing wage for labourers, 2*s*.6*d*. per day. The work was directed by overseers of highways, who notified pathmasters as to what sections of roadway were to be repaired. It was the responsibility of pathmasters to assemble all men in their road divisions between the ages of twenty-one and sixty, and to obtain teams and waggons, scrapers, and other necessary equipment.

An early town meeting of Trafalgar Township fixed five and one-half feet as the height of fence necessary to protect crops from domestic animals allowed to run at large. It was the duty of fenceviewers to make regular inspections to see that this regulation was enforced, and to arbitrate disputes over fence lines, etc. Animals found trespassing upon fields enclosed according to law were impounded until the owner had paid for any damage they had caused; if not claimed after fifteen days, the animals were sold and damages paid out of the proceeds. Fees exacted by the poundkeeper were regulated by the Quarter Sessions of the Peace.

Not until after the Rebellion was provision made for a new form of government. Lord Sydenham believed that "the capital cause of misgovernment" in the province was "the absence of Local Government." The system he devised had as its unit the district. The District Councils Act of 1841 incorporated the districts as municipalities, and set up a body of councillors for these, elected by the ratepayers, which assumed many of the powers and functions of the Court of Quarter Sessions. The District Council had in its hands the power of taxation. Until then the greater part of the expenses of carrying public affairs had been borne by the provincial government. Sydenham claimed that only great works should be financed by provincial funds, and that purely local expenses should be voted on and borne by the localities themselves.

Though the right to appoint the warden and treasurer and to disallow by-laws was retained by the governor-in-council, these controls did not seriously hamper the District Councils.

The Journals of the Proceedings of the Municipal Council of the District of Gore show that the chief work of the council, which met at Hamilton, was the sifting and weighing of petitions relating to roads and bridges. The new law required that a qualified surveyor be employed to supervise all public works, and for many years Deputy Surveyor Robert W. Kerr, whom we have met before, held this post in the Gore District.

A by-law passed by the Gore District Council in 1843 authorized the expenditure of £54 on building a new bridge "with good approaches at the Town of Oakville."[2] Bridges were built so close to the water that they did not long survive the increasing violence of spring floods resulting from the deforestation of the land. The new bridge had only been built seven years when it and the bridge at Bronte were carried away by the "most disastrous freshet ever known in the vicinity." For several days all travel including transportation of the mails was suspended on the Lake Shore Road.[3] Again a new bridge was built, yet within four years it was found to be "in a dilapidated state." The commissioners appointed to administer the £100 required to rebuild it were Thompson Smith, Richard Coates, and R. K. Chisholm.[4]

Naturally these recurring alarms were responsible for anecdotes. When one flood rose dangerously close to the floor of the Colborne Street bridge, so the story goes, the village fathers held consultation. It was decided to reinforce the bridge by hitching stout ropes at each end and securing them to the land. By the time this was accomplished it was very late at night but all the workers went home convinced that the bridge would be saved. At daylight it was discovered that the bridge had disappeared without trace. Under cover of darkness someone had stolen the ropes.

It soon became evident that the districts were too large and the district town too remote from outlying townships for efficient administration. Provision was therefore made for Township Councils. A Trafalgar Township Council was elected at the "Twp. meeting of the Inhabitants, Freeholders and Householders of the Township of Trafalgar, pursuant to public notice, held at the Inn of Ephraim Post" in January, 1845; Justus W. Williams, of Oakville, was elected Town Warden, and he was re-elected each year until 1849.[5] Robert Balmer, also of Oakville, succeeded Thomas C. Harris in 1848 as Township Clerk at a salary of £25. per annum.[6]

The new system stimulated interest in township affairs among farmers and villagers alike. For holding elections, McGuffin's tavern on the Dundas Street, near the 6th Line, was most frequently chosen.[7] Here the magistrates periodically held court at which cases of assault and battery, cases involving small debts, and other trifling appeals to the law were settled. The fact that the Methodist Church and the school were situated on the north side of the Street across from McGuffin's gave rise to the popular saying, "the south for legislation and damnation, the north for education and salvation." Tradition has it that elections were also held in the little Post Office at Oakville, the voting taking place by a show of hands. Outside the building differences of opinion were settled by a show of fists.

Even at this period, the "Twp. Laws and Regulations" were concerned mostly with statute labour and the control of domestic animals. The overseers of highways appointed in 1844 for the Lake Shore Road in the vicinity of Oakville were Ransom Leach on the east, Thomas Lloyd within the village, and Hiram McCraney on the west. William Langtry and John Moore were appointed fenceviewers in Oakville.[8] They dealt with infractions of the ruling "that horses, colts, bulls, boars, rams, hogs under 40 lb. weight, or cattle that are in the practise of throwing fences, shall not be free commoners. That lawful fences shall be five and one-half feet in height and well put up. That any person riding or leading a horse on the plank or footways in Palermo shall be liable to a fine of five shillings for every such offence."[9] In the matter of plank sidewalks, Palermo was well in advance of Oakville, where none were laid until 1849.

That was the year in which the struggle for local government ended with the passing of the "Magna Charta of municipal government," the Municipal Act. Although the Act has been amended from time to time, the changes wrought have been chiefly in the nature of amplification; and, after the passage of a century, the main principles still stand. The districts were abolished (thus ended the Gore District) and the District Council was replaced by the County Council. The townships, incorporated as municipalities, were given considerable freedom and independance in handling their own affairs, including taxation. The continuance of the town meeting was authorized by the Act, but Trafalgar Township chose to adopt the new method of electing the members of its Council in rural wards. Every January its ratepayers elected five councillors who elected a Town Reeve and Deputy Reeve from among themselves and appointed a township clerk, a treasurer, assessors, and a tax collector. The council was empowered to enact a code of town-laws or by-laws. The latter word, so familiar a term in local government, comes from an old English word for town, "by" or "bye," which was derived from the Danish and which also survives in place-names given by the Danes such as Whitby, Grimsby, Appleby. By-laws related to the regulation of the duties of township officers and their remuneration, the erection and support of common schools, the purchase of such real property as might be necessary, the building of a town hall, the control of inns and taverns, and the regulation of shows and exhibitions. The council was responsible for constructing and maintaining highways, bridges, streets, etc., enforcing and applying statute labour, opening drains and watercourses, and destroying noxious weeds. And, of course, there were always the domestic animals to be controlled. Other local regulations could be enforced as needed and, under certain restrictions, money could be borrowed for municipal purposes. These powers, granted at this time to the Trafalgar Township Council, were later granted to the Town Council of Oakville when, after some years, Oakville became a separate municipality.

The first election of officers for the Municipality of the Township of Trafalgar took place early in 1850. For Ward 4, in which Oakville was situated, the "place of holding the election" was "the inn in the 16 Hollow, near the Trafalgar Mills."[10] Afterwards the annual election for the ward was held at the Oakville House.[11]

The first meeting of the Township Council was held January 21, 1850, in the Temperance Hall at Oakville. To this council the electors of Ward 4 sent George K. Chisholm of Oakville. The Oakville Temperance Reformation Society had agreed "to present the Councillors of the Township with the gratuitous use of the Temperance Hall" and it continued in use as the Township Hall during the six years that followed.[12] The requisite furniture of desk, table, and chairs was bought for £7 from David Duff, and a platform was erected (quite possibly the section on the east end found there until recently), the council paying £2.10 towards its cost to the society.[13] Taxes were levied during the first year under the new system at the rate of "One Penny and One Farthing on all land, and One Penny and One Farthing in the £, on all Ratable Property other than Land."[14] For every day's attendance, the councillors were paid 6*s*. 3*d*.[15]

In the Town Council of 1850 George K. Chisholm was unanimously elected Town Reeve by the councillors; he also represented Trafalgar

9. Sir Frederick Verner, 1869

10. Joseph Milbourne

11. Captain Robert Wilson

12. The Tannery, 1863

13. Thompson Smith's residence, 1863

14. THE MILL. PAINTING BY SIR FREDERICK VERNER, 1856

15. Choir of the Canada Presbyterian Church, *circa* 1870

Top row, Mrs. Watt (Miss Balmer), Mr. W. Laurie, Miss M. Scott

Middle row, Mr. McCorkindale, Miss Margaret Arnott, Mr. Newlands, Miss S. McCorquodale, Mr. R. Robertson

Bottom row, Miss J. Scott, Miss McCorquodale

16. A class of the Oakville Grammar School, *circa* 1868

17. MERIT CARDS GIVEN TO PUPILS OF THE OAKVILLE SCHOOLS

18. TRAFALGAR TOWNSHIP ASSESSMENT ROLL, 1828

19. Colonel George K. Chisholm

20. Chief Constable George J. Sumner

21. John Barclay

22. Justus W. Williams

23. The Market Building (Town Hall), 1863

Township on the Municipal Council of the United Counties of Wentworth and Halton. Robert Balmer, who for two years had served as township treasurer, was appointed township clerk, Justus Williams succeeding him as treasurer. After serving as town reeve for three years, G. K. Chisholm resigned at the end of 1852. He was followed by W. F. Romain for one year, and his brother R. K. Chisholm held office from 1854 to 1856. When Oakville withdrew from the township in 1857, all these men, having been schooled in municipal affairs, were elected to office and the councillor chosen to serve as Oakville's first mayor was G. K. Chisholm.

Although a prominent figure in the affairs of Halton County, having followed in his father's footsteps both as a Member of Parliament and lieutenant-colonel of the militia, George King Chisholm had little association with Oakville until the late forties and has, heretofore, entered only casually into this narrative. The eldest son of William Chisholm, he was born in Nelson Township in 1814, was educated at the common school, at the Gore District Grammar School at Hamilton, and at Upper Canada College, where he was one of the first pupils.[16] As long as his father was postmaster at Nelson, he assisted in the post office.[17] In 1830 he was commissioned captain in the 2nd Regiment of Gore Militia, and saw active service during the Rebellion.[18] What took him to Hamilton is obscure but in 1840 he is listed as "Paymaster, 1st Incorporated Battalion, Hamilton, U.C."[19] That year he married Isabella, daughter of Colonel Robert Land, and granddaughter of the founder of Hamilton. Chisholm thereafter lived for some years in that town. Upon the reuniting of the Canadas, he was appointed, June 21, 1841, to the office of Serjeant-at-Arms in the Legislative Assembly of the Province of Canada.[20]

The Serjeant-at-Arms, usually an officer in His Majesty's Forces, is appointed for life by letters patent under the Great Seal of the province. His duties are to attend the Speaker with the mace upon entering and leaving the House, and to take into custody "strangers" who have been irregularly admitted or who misconduct themselves and to remove them from the House. In Chisholm's time, the Serjeant-at-Arms was also official house-keeper, having the care and furnishing of all rooms and offices of the House of Parliament. The mace which he carried by virtue of his office is a symbol of authority of great antiquity. Originally made of iron or steel, it was a weapon used by the Serjeants-at-Arms who guarded the early kings of England. When the House of Parliament is in session, the mace rests on hangers under the clerk's desk and, at all times, the Serjeant-at-Arms is responsible for its safe keeping.

In 1845, a replica of the mace used in the British House of Commons was procured by the Speaker of the House, Sir Allan MacNab. This mace, measuring five feet in length, was of silver, richly gilded and elaborately chased. It was made by a silversmith in London, and cost £500. Four segments upheld by female figures bore the rose of England, the thistle of Scotland, the harp of Ireland, and the Prince of Wales' plume. The top, in the shape of an open crown, was surmounted by an orb and cross.

For a time Kingston was the seat of the Government of the united provinces; but after a few years Montreal became the capital. There, during the 1849 session of Parliament, a bill was passed which became a particular storm centre, and proved to be the acid test of responsible government. The Rebellion Losses Bill was designed to compensate claimants in Lower Canada, those in Upper Canada having previously received compensation. Discontent had been so widespread in Lower Canada that it was next to impossible to weed out loyalists from rebels. In consequence, no distinctions were drawn, and the bill made it possible for all to collect on their losses, money for payment being taken from the consolidated revenue of the united provinces.

Led by Sir Allan MacNab, the Tories of Canada West violently opposed the Rebellion Losses Bill, and the first to protest openly in public meeting were the Tories of Oakville and Trafalgar Township. Clarioned the *Hamilton Gazette* in its report of the meeting:

> Trafalgar is roused! Now the ministry propose . . . to allocate the amount to all, whether Rebel or Loyalist, and if the offender was as good a pedestrian as he was a villain, and was able to "Leave his country for his country's good," before conviction, then he is to be paid.
>
> The men of Trafalgar have spoken out and their denunciation of this iniquitous scheme will be followed by that of other townships.[21]

The gathering, called for March 8, took place at Rolston's Inn on the Dundas Street west of the 6th Line. William Y. Pettit was invited to occupy the chair, and Robert Balmer was appointed secretary. The *Gazette*'s account leaves no doubt of the liveliness of the proceedings.

"Resolved—that this meeting learns with feelings of indignation that the losses are to be paid out of the consolidated revenue of the Province." John Terry moved that it was a "great injustice"; William Hatton that the meeting "must protest. We will not consent to reward traitors, rebels and murderers." A resolution was unanimously adopted that a petition for refusal of the royal assent by the Governor-General be drafted, circulated for signatures, and dispatched at once to Lord Elgin. After giving three cheers for Her Majesty, Sir Allan MacNab, "and the glorious minority," the meeting separated, "much pleased to find that Trafalgar could not produce one man to defend the cause of payment to traitors."[22]

Notwithstanding the petitions calling for disallowance with which the "glorious minority" flooded his office, Lord Elgin gave the royal assent to the Rebellion Losses Bill. Not entirely satisfied with certain features of the bill himself, he nevertheless followed the recommendations of his cabinet ministers, thus upholding the principles of responsible government his father-in-law Lord Durham had worked so hard to attain for Canada. Riots broke out in Montreal, Lord Elgin was pelted with rotten eggs, and, during an evening session of Parliament, a mob was whipped into action.

The Serjeant-at-Arms recorded that his first intimation of the proceedings of the mob was the breaking of the windows of the House. After ordering that all doors be secured, he stood by the Bar. The narrative is continued in Chisholm's words:

> The mob entered the Chamber and commenced breaking the Desks, Gas standard, Speaker's Chair, Etc., and I think there were between thirty and forty of the rioters in the Chamber at the time. . . . Their commencing to break the railing near me with Clubs, I went partly up the steps leading to the Library and stood there. . . . A man took the Mace from under the Clerk's Table and came towards the door under me. I descended the stairs, and met him at the bottom, took the Mace from him and attempted to take it upstairs, when half way up, the same person seized hold of the small end of the Mace. I again drew it from him and, at that moment three or four men rushed in from the Lobby, one of whom struck me with a cane or club on the head which stunned me for a moment and the Mace was carried off. . . . One man . . . took the Speaker's Chair and declared Parliament dissolved—afterwards breaking all the ornaments near him with a large club. . . . When the cry of fire was raised the visitors left the Chamber, I remained until I believe every person had left with the exception of the two Reporters. . . .

The fire "entered the Chamber in the rear of the Speaker's Chair." Chisholm went to his room and gathered as many of his belongings as could be put in a trunk. When he came out of the door he found the fire in the Lobby. "I went down the stairs where I also found the lower passage which I had to cross full of blaze and smoke. Seeing no alternative I rushed through it and succeeded in reaching the Street in safety."[23]

The Parliamentary Library, said to have been the finest in America, together with great quantities of government records among which were the papers relating to the Oakville Hydraulic Company, were destroyed in this fire. As to the mace, Chisholm states that "after considerable search, the next morning in company with the Honble. Speaker we found the Mace in the Executive Council Office." This version of its fate differs somewhat from those that appear in memoirs of prominent Reformers who accused Sir Allan's "extreme Tory faction" of having perpetrated the outrage and claimed that he had held the mace as a trophy of victory in his room at Donegani's hotel. After surviving two other fires, the mace at the time of Confederation passed to the Dominion Parliament at Ottawa. A new one, more modest in appearance, was obtained for the opening of the Ontario Parliament. The old mace was finally lost in the fire which destroyed the Parliament Building during World War I. In the ruins was found a small mass of metal which was supposed to be all that remained of the mace that for seventy years had served the provincial and Dominion Parliaments of Canada.

The injuries he sustained in the riot of 1849 confined G. K. Chisholm for several months to his new home at Oakville (now no. 13 Navy Street South) where he had moved shortly before. During his absence, his duties as Serjeant-at-Arms were performed by a deputy.[24]

At this time provincial politics were enlivened by the emergence of the offshoot of the Reform party known as the Clear Grits, so called because of their slogan, "All sand, no dirt, clear grit all the way through." Two of the men instrumental in forming this faction we have met with before: Dr. John Rolph and Caleb Hopkins, that early organizer of the Reform party in the Gore District and political opponent of William Chisholm. The Clear Grits had a strong following, and the struggle with the Tories became fiercer than ever. In *Life in the Clearings versus the Bush* their contemporary Susannah Moodie wrote: "However moderate your views might be, to belong to the one was to incur the dislike and ill will of the other. . . . Even the women entered deeply into this party hostility, and those who, from their education and mental advantages, might have become friends and agreeable companions, kept aloof, rarely taking notice of each other, when accidentally thrown together."[25]

In Halton, political rivalry was increased in the fifties by a local issue. When the Gore District was abolished in 1849, the counties of Halton and Wentworth were united. It was at this time that Halton was reduced to its present size of four townships: Trafalgar, Nelson, Esquesing, and Nassagaweya. During his last term as Reeve of Trafalgar Township, G. K. Chisholm started proceedings which ended in the separation of Halton in 1853.[26] Halton County then established its own county town. The bill passed by Parliament which declared Milton the county seat had been introduced by the Liberal Member for Halton, John White, who then lived near Milton. Most villages in the county, particularly Bronte, aspired to this distinction and, because the matter had not been put to the vote of the ratepayers, there were loud outcries of indignation. Oakville's resentment was very bitter and the bitterness diminished little with the passage of time. This action of John White's spurred the Conservatives of Halton County to greater effort and, as the election of 1854 approached, they laid plans. The Hamilton *Spectator* commented: "The Family Compact, in its palmiest days, never robbed the Province to nearly the same extent as the brood of harpies who are now preying upon it. . . . The Conservatives are . . . determined that, whether willing or not, Mr. George K. Chisholm shall be their candidate, and successor to Mr. White. Mr. C. holds the office of Sergeant-at-Arms in the Legislative Assembly, but we trust he may be induced by his friends in Halton to resign, and take his place on the floor of the House as their Representative."[27] Their persuasions were effective for Chisholm resigned his post as Serjeant-at-Arms, which he had held for thirteen years, to stand for Parliament. Caleb Hopkins, by now an octogenarian, at first agreed to fight the election for the Reformers, but soon withdrew, explaining that he contemplated retiring from the political arena. As the election drew near, the editor of the Oakville *Sentinel* wrote:

> A single desire was manifested by all to ensure the defeat of the present Member, who has violated every pledge made to the electors who trusted him, and who has become a mere toady of the most corrupt and reckless Ministry that ever disgraced a country. . . .
>
> The true issue is now before the electors of Halton. Let them not be deceived by false promises. The time has arrived for energetic action. We have to contend with a man who will descend to misrepresentation and every baseness to secure a vote.[28]

Chisholm won a notable victory over John White. The personal enmity which was rife among political antagonists is evidenced in the following excerpt from a letter written by Chisholm to the *Spectator*: "To all who are cognizant of the policy adopted towards me during the late election in Halton, by Mr. White and his friends; to those who witnessed his wailing and gnashing of teeth towards me and all my connexions; to those who have since heard his threat that he would follow me and mine to the day of my death, for revenge; to all such it will be a matter of surprise that his *open* attacks have been so long deferred."[29] Details of these attacks are lacking except for an instance of a later date when relationship was claimed between G. K. and one William Chisholm who was convicted of horse stealing and other "numerous offences." G. K. Chisholm wrote that were he compelled to choose relationship between the parties he should "decidedly prefer that of the now convicted thief to the sneaking poltroon" who had circulated "the slander."[30]

It was in the fifth Parliament of the Province of Canada, meeting at Toronto in 1854, that G. K. Chisholm represented Halton County. During this time he received promotion in the militia. Under a commission dated December 11, 1856, he was gazetted lieutenant-colonel of the 1st Battalion of Halton, the new name for the 2nd Regiment of Gore Militia upon its reorganization after the Gore District was abolished.[31] However, John White was again Member for Halton during the years of the "Perambulating Parliament," so called because it alternated between Quebec and Toronto.

In addition to this, George K. Chisholm, like his father before him was genuinely interested in farming. His farm of some two hundred and sixty acres, about half of which he had under cultivation by 1860,[32] lay on the west side of Oakville, between The Sixteen and Kerr Street, the Lower Middle Road forming the northern and Bond Street the southern boundaries. Near the junction of Forsyth and Bond streets, where from the west bank of the river there was a fine view of the harbour, stood the house which Chisholm enlarged. The new residence, called "The Retreat," was ready for occupancy about 1857.

By then, Oakville had attained a population of two thousand, and application was made to the Government for incorporation (i.e. legal establishment) as a town. The petition "praying that Oakville might be erected into a separate municipality," dated March 2, 1857, was signed by John Barclay "and others."[33] On March 27, five months short of the thirtieth anniversary of the founding of the village, royal assent was given to a bill passed by the previous session of Parliament entitled An Act to Incorporate the Town of Oakville.

WHEREAS from the rapidly increasing population of the Village of Oakville, in the County of Halton, and from its being one of the principal Shipping Ports on Lake Ontario, it is necessary to confer upon the said Village the power of Municipal Government; Therefore, Her Majesty, by and with the advice and consent of the Legislative Council and Assembly of Canada, enacts as follows:

1. From and after the passing of this Act, the inhabitants of the Town of Oakville shall be a body corporate, apart from the Township of Trafalgar in which the said Town is situate, and as such shall have perpetual suc-

cession and a Common Seal with such powers as are now by law conferred upon Incorporated Towns in Upper Canada; and the powers of such Corporation shall be exercised by, through and in the name of the Municipality of the Town of Oakville.[34]

It was enacted that the Town be divided into three wards: "No. 1, all of the Town west of Navy Street, with the entire portion lying on the west side of the Sixteen Mile Creek," No. 2, all of the town east of Navy Street and south of Colborne Street, and No. 3, all the district north of Colborne Street on the east side of The Sixteen. It also was enacted that an election of councillors be held and that "the first meeting of the said Council shall be held in the School House in the said Town, at eleven o'clock on the first Saturday after the day on which the election of Councillors shall have been held."[35] A full transcription of this statute is in appendix F.

"In pursuance of the Act of Incorporation" the first meeting of the newly elected council was held in the brick schoolhouse on July 7. Justus Williams, who as Justice of the Peace "was requested to occupy the Chair until a Mayor was elected," announced the following gentlemen to have been returned for the several wards:

Ward No. 1—George K. Chisholm, Esq., M.P.P.
W. E. Hagaman
R. K. Chisholm
Ward No. 2—W. F. Romain
P. A. MacDougald
John Urquhart
Ward No. 3—James Reid
John Barclay
John Potter

A motion made by John Urquhart and seconded by James Reid that George K. Chisholm "be elected Mayor" was unanimously adopted. Thus in the usual manner the first mayor was elected from their number by the councillors, although an amendment to the Municipal Act the following year took from the council and entrusted to the ratepayers the right to elect the mayor. Reversed in 1866, this right again returned to the municipal electors where it has since remained. Mayor-elect G. K. Chisholm "took the oath of office before Justus W. Williams, Esq., J.P." A resolution was unanimously adopted that James Reid be elected reeve, and "the Mayor then administered the oaths of office to the Reeve and the Councillors."[36] Robert Balmer was appointed town clerk, an office he was to hold during the succeeding forty-five years. Justus Williams, who already acted as treasurer for various organizations in the town, was appointed treasurer of the municipality, and served in this capacity until his death eighteen years later. The town council began its work with the adoption of two resolutions, one to the effect that the mayor, reeve, and two councillors "be a committee to submit Rules for the guidance of the Council," and a second that "the Mayor do report the number of Standing Committees of this Council, and the names of the Members to compose the same." It was decided "that for the present the Corporation's Seal of the Town be a Crown with the word 'Oakville' thereon." Having thus concluded its ground work, the council adjourned to meet in the schoolhouse the following Thursday at 7 P.M.

At the second meeting, the mayor informed the council of his appointments to five Standing Committees: those on Finance, Streets and Sidewalks, Market and Buildings, Fire and Water, and Police and Public Order. He also introduced By-law no. 1, entitled "To provide a fund for the support of Education in the Town of Oakville." This after being read three times was passed by the council.[37] It was enacted that "all monies accruing to this Town from the Municipalities Fund of Upper Canada, shall be and the same is hereby set aside for the support of Education in the Town of Oakville."[38]

As the Trafalgar Township Council had made arrangements to hold its future meetings at Post's Inn on the Dundas Street,[39] the Town Council of Oakville was offered the use of the Temperance Hall. At the third meeting, this building was "declared the Town Hall for the time being."

The machinery for local government, which the council proceeded to set up, was essentially the same as that by which Oakville, as an integral part of Trafalgar Township, had been governed for the past seven years. The contract for publishing the council minutes and accounts was given to the *Sentinel.* Justus Williams, the treasurer, anticipated by four months the law of the province by adopting for his accounts the decimal system of dollars and cents, thereby reducing the *Sentinel's* printer to a state of utter confusion. The printer consistently used commas instead of a decimal point and, regardless of his efforts to eliminate the pound sign, it continued to creep into the accounts throughout the first year.

It was not until October that the salaries of municipal officers were fixed. Those of the town clerk and chief constable were set at $300 per annum and the treasurer's at $30. When employed by the Town Corporation, township constables were to be paid at the rate of $1.50

and auditors $4 per day. The assessor was to receive $50 per annum and the collector of taxes, an office soon relegated to the chief constable, $30 a year.[40]

The design adopted by the council for a seal to be affixed to the official documents of the Town Corporation was executed by John Ellis of Toronto at a cost of $24. The hybrid blazon, as contained in By-law no. 19, dated September 28, 1857, entitled "To establish a Common Seal," reads as follows:

> Be it enacted . . . that a Common Seal for the said Town is hereby established and that the same be described as follows, viz.:
>
> In a shield quarterly.
>
> 1st. A ship (azure or blue) representing "Commerce."
>
> 2nd. An Engine. The distinguishing manufacture of the Town.
>
> 3rd. A Garb (Meaning a Wheat Sheaf upon a Golden Field) for Agriculture.
>
> 4th. Gules (for red). An Oak Tree proper, indicative of the original state of the Country; its stability and present prosperity.
>
> Surrounded by, for Crest, "a Beehive," with Motto over it on a Ribbon "Industry."
>
> Supporters, a Deer on Dexter, and Bear on the Sinister side, standing upon a scroll bearing the words, "Commerce," "Manufacture," "Agriculture."
>
> On margin of Seal, "Town of Oakville," (above) "Corporation" (in base).[41]

The seal was destroyed by fire and to date only one paper has come to light bearing its imprint, which is too faint to reproduce. The seal used at the present time has been much simplified for only the oak tree and ship have been retained. Though the result is a less handsome design, the elimination of the engine, "the distinguishing manufacture of the Town," and the wheat sheaf "for Agriculture" were perhaps inevitable as a result of the changing pattern of events during the intervening years.

It so happened that the villages of Oakville and Milton were incorporated as separate municipalities on the same day. These events were pleasing signs of growth but they meant new problems and new responsibilities as well. The editor of the Hamilton *Spectator* commented: "How the spirited inhabitants of the new towns will relish the change has yet to be ascertained. It is more than probable, however, that when they begin to effect improvements, in order to keep pace with other towns, many of them will be apt to discover the difference between the maintenance of a village and a town corporation—that is in pounds, shillings and pence view. But, as Halton has become a county of great importance, it was desirable that at least the County Town should occupy a higher rank; and as for Oakville, its flourishing trade fairly entitles it to take rank among the first ports on Lake Ontario."[42]

II

Except for those dealing with such routine matters as providing for the election of officers and the raising of finances, the by-laws enacted by the Municipal Council of the Town of Oakville fall mainly into two categories: those concerned with the welfare and conduct of the citizens, and those relating to town improvement. A large proportion were by-laws passed after 1850 by the Township Council which the Town Council adopted unaltered or with minor changes, so that the townspeople merely continued under the same system to which they had already become accustomed. The enforcement of these laws was placed in the hands of Chief Constable George Baker, livery stable proprietor and county bailiff, who had the assistance of those county constables resident in Oakville. After two years, however, Baker's services proved unsatisfactory. When his resignation was accepted, the council was careful to lay down in By-law no. 35, dated January 10, 1859, the duties of the office. In return for a salary of $300 per annum, the chief constable was "to see that the By-laws . . . be strictly carried out, . . . to superintend all work on streets, and see that the sidewalks are kept in repair, under the orders of the Committee on Streets and Sidewalks," and to supervise all work "other than mechanical ordered by the Council, when said work is done by the day." "He shall be Pound Keeper and Health Officer of the Town. He shall see that the Town Hall [then nonexistent] is kept in order, attend prisoners in the Lock-up [then under construction], and, when absent on other than Town business, shall have a competent substitute, and pay all charges. He shall, when practicable, attend Magistrates' Court and serve all summons and warrants issued by the same." Several men attempted to carry out these duties without success until the appointment of George J. Sumner, who held the post of chief constable until 1902, thirty-seven years.

George Johnson Sumner was born at Hannahsville, Nelson Township, in 1834. His father, William J. Sumner, was then proprietor of the Grove Inn, and later took over the Oakville House. George Sumner grew up in Oakville, was educated at the common school, and learned the trade of ship's carpenter. Like his father, he was a staunch Tory. Because of his kind, quiet manner and meticulous fairness in all his dealings, he was popular in the community. With advancing years Chief Sumner became one of Oakville's most respected citizens. During most of his life he kept a diary in which he rarely failed to make an entry of comment on the day's happenings. As above forty of these little books are extant, his pertinent observations on a variety of matters will be encountered during the course of this history.

In addition to fulfilling his duties as chief constable, Sumner continued to work at odd times in the shipyards. He also did jobs of house carpentering, painting, and paper-hanging and often assisted his relative, George Ziller the undertaker, in laying out the dead. Sumner weighed grain for Hagaman, and in summer, as agent for the steamers, sold tickets several times a day to passengers at the pier.

In his capacity of chief constable, Sumner's responsibilities were various, the foremost, of course, being that of enforcing the law. Though he was permitted on special occasions to hire a team and waggon to take sentenced persons to the county gaol fifteen miles away, the normal procedure was to use the cheaper railway transportation and travel to Milton via Toronto by rail, a journey of over fifty miles. Sumner was responsible for the care, lighting, and heating of the Town Hall. At all public functions he was present to take tickets at the door, maintain order, and when the building was empty to put out the lights. He was the first to enter and the last to leave the Town Hall, and during winter when balls were frequent could be found there on duty until the small hours of the morning. As he could always be relied upon to sit through the night with the very ill or dying, he frequently went about his day's work after a sleepless night. He superintended all work on roads and sidewalks. In winter the plank sidewalk leading along Dundas Street had to be cleared of snow as far as the station before the arrival of the morning train. After one snowfall in 1868 it took Chief Sumner and thirteen men (at 10¢ an hour) five hours to remove the snow from this walk.

At times Chief Sumner had many drunken sailors as inmates in the Lock-up. One notoriously belligerent sailor he made a point of arresting in the early stages of drunkenness before he caused too much trouble, or got an opportunity to beat his wife. Sumner carried meals from the Canadian Hotel to his "lodgers" in the Lock-up, for which the Town Corporation issued 25c meal tickets. Besides the forcefully detained inmates, there took shelter in the Lock-up increasing numbers of tramps who were provided with a place to sleep. "The Hotel de Sumner," reported the *Argus* in the seventies, "is occupied nightly by tramps. . . . They all express themselves highly pleased with the accommodations given to them and when going away promise that should they ever come this way again they will be sure to call."[43] Though a fervent temperance worker, Sumner showed exceptional tolerance with troublesome drunks and listened patiently to their misfortunes. Only once did he enter in his diary, "Gave a tramp a caning for giving me impudence."

As tax collector, Chief Sumner made out and delivered the tax bills, then collected the taxes from door to door. Repeated visits throughout most of the year were required to get in all the tax money. One evening he wrote, "I have been hunting up dogs and taxes, I get plenty of the former but little of the latter." Some of this work was not congenial to his kindly disposition. When forced to sell the chattels of the poor for taxes, he invariably became "sick of the office of Chief Constable." As Health Officer he periodically inspected dwellings for insanitary practices. As Harbour Master, at a later date, he collected tolls, saw to repairs on the piers, and was frequently out at 2 A.M. to load apples and other produce onto vessels. As Truant Officer, Sumner kept a tolerant eye on the school population, and took its census. In his private capacity as property owner he attended to all repairs to his house including painting and paper-hanging, laid out his vegetable garden, and pruned his fruit trees and berry bushes every spring. Chief Sumner lived with his wife, five sons, and two daughters in the house that is now the home of Walter Moorehouse, no. 33 William Street. In 1855 he had purchased this house built by his father from his brother, William Chisholm Sumner, who went into business at Owen Sound. On an income which averaged between $450 and $500 per annum George J. Sumner raised what John A. Williams in his reminiscences termed "the best family in Oakville—a credit to their parents and the Town."

In By-law no. 15, entitled "To provide against the spread of Contagious and Infectious Diseases," the first council attempted to better the sanitary conditions of the town. It regulated the slaughtering of animals.

> Whereas the Inhabitants of this town have suffered much annoyance from slaughter houses situated therein, and the protection of the public health required the removal of such nuisances,
>
> Be it therefore enacted . . . that no person shall keep, erect, maintain, or use any building or shed within the Town of Oakville for the purpose of slaughtering animals, or dressing, or preparing meat for butchers' stalls.
>
> No person shall kill any animal within the said town without burying the blood and offal of such animal, at least two feet in the ground, and a distance of fifty feet from any dwelling house.

It was not lawful either to hang out the skins or hides of slaughtered animals for drying or curing, the penalty being a fine up to five pounds or imprisonment up to twenty days. A few years later, when the Committee on Police and Public Order became as well the Board of Health, "to promote the Sanitary Condition of the Town" the Health Officer began an inspection of dwellings. Periodic announcements were inserted in the press warning householders to see that their cellars were cleaned, drains opened, privies whitewashed, hog pens cleaned, and all garbage removed from the yards. "A free use of lime is recommended . . . which will be supplied by the council at cost 25¢ per bushel . . . those unable to purchase will be supplied gratis."[44] Householders of those days took to disposing of their garbage by digging a hole in the garden and, when it was full, digging another. Ashes were still piled in back of the house until it became necessary to have them hauled away in the spring. The simple expedient of dumping them in the street led the editor of a local newspaper to comment: "No doubt it is very convenient to dump coal ashes on the street, and thus get rid of it without further trouble or annoyance. Quite a number of people are in the habit of doing so with unfailing regularity. They are not aware that a heap of coal ashes is a dangerous impediment, and spoils the sleighing on that part of the road disfigured by its presence. . . . Many citizens are crying out against this evil, and the council would do well to put a stop to it."[45]

The fever known as ague, always so prevalent in the town, was not considered a problem for the council until the late seventies, when a special committee "on the sanitary condition of the marsh" was formed. After due consideration, this committee reported that to fill the marsh on both sides of the creek was too expensive "and hence should not be entertained"; that to plant willow trees would be inexpensive but that protection of them from cattle and ice jams in the spring would prove difficult. In any case, it was doubtful if the trees "would have any direct effect." The committee concluded: "That the most available plant as a preventative to malaria is the sunflower, it is of thrifty growth and easily cultivated at a very trifling expense; this plant we find has been largely cultivated for Sanitary purposes in many places in the United States and invariably with most satisfactory results."[46] This recommendation was acted upon; the mayor requested by proclamation that sunflower seeds be planted in gardens and all places on both sides of The Sixteen unfrequented by cattle. In the press, Chief Sumner announced the receipt of "a supply of SUNFLOWER SEEDS for gratuitous distribution. The Sanitary Committee urges upon people of this town the importance of at once sowing these seeds extensively, as a remedy for malaria."[47]

At a later date, when the matter of fever was again under discussion in the council, the suggestion was made that other towns had found pouring kerosene on marshes effective. One councilman, a former lake captain, surrounded the point and put a period to the discussion by asserting, "Well, if you want all the world to know we have ague in Oakville, just pour oil on the creek." Around the turn of the century, however, malaria began to lessen and eventually died out.

In accordance with the new Public Health Act a permanent Board of Health was established in 1885, and Dr. J. S. W. Williams was appointed Medical Health Officer. However, Chief Sumner continued his patrols as Health Inspector through the years.

In By-law no. 10, the first council laid down specifications for the quality and weight of bread: ". . . all Bread baked and offered for Sale in the Town of Oakville, shall be made of good wholesome Flour or Meal, and sold by avoidupois weight. . . . The Loaves shall be Quartern Loaves of Four Pounds, and half Quartern Loaves of Two pounds." According to the provisions of By-law no. 13, weights and measures used by "every Merchant, Retailer, Trader, and Dealer in Merchandise" were to "conform to the Standards of this Province," and to secure conformity they were subject to examination twice yearly by the Town Inspector of Weights and Measures. The sale of fresh butchered meat by non-resident peddlers, as regulated by By-law no. 42, made obligatory the obtaining of a licence which was issued only to reliable persons dealing in "sound and good wholesome meat."

It had long been the custom of the townspeople to put the water of Lake Ontario to good use, and on Monday mornings the beach near the harbour was thronged with sailors' wives doing their weekly washing. Judging by the rapidity with which the council tackled the problem of bathing in public, this would seem also to have been common practice. By-law no. 2 reads as follows:

> Whereas, the Inhabitants have suffered much annoyance from persons Bathing in Public Places, and in view of Private Dwellings and it is necessary to prevent the same,
>
> Be it therefore enacted . . . that . . . Bathing in Public Places is hereby prohibited, and also in view of Private Dwellings during daylight.

The penalty for infraction, not less than five nor more than twenty shillings or "imprisonment and hard labour for any period not exceeding eight days," would indicate that severe measures were required to control bathing in the lake. This by-law was repealed in 1876 by no. 114, which prohibited bathing in The Sixteen at any time but permitted it in the lake between the hours of 8 A.M. and 10 P.M. However, bathers were to approach no nearer to the harbour than opposite Thomas Street on the east and Chisholm Street on the west.

For the maintenance of public order, the council passed By-law no. 7, "For the Regulation and Good Government of the Inhabitants of the Town of Oakville." It then became unlawful for any person "to encumber, injure or foul" public property, to be found in a public place in a state of drunkenness, to swear or use obscene language. Neither was it lawful to be found begging, "to beat in an excessive manner or otherwise abuse or illtreat any animal in the public streets or highways . . . to erect or have upon his or her premises . . . anything that may be a public nuisance. Neither shall it be lawful for any person to ring a bell, blow a horn, shout or make any unusual noise in any of the streets . . . fire any gun or firearms, or fire or set off fireballs, squibs, crackers, or other fireworks . . . immoderately to ride or drive any horses or cattle . . . lead or drive them upon any of the sidewalks of this town." Infraction of this law meant payment of fines up to five pounds, or imprisonment with hard labour up to thirty days in the county gaol or the Lock-up at Oakville.

The laws in respect of human conduct, and their enforcement, caused the council and Chief Sumner relatively little anxiety compared with those aimed at regulating the behaviour of the large population of fowl and quadrupeds. In a village it was to be expected that large numbers of domestic animals would be free commoners; but this condition was hardly becoming in a town. The council applied themselves to this lively topic with zest. No longer should the streets be cluttered with a horde of cattle, hogs, sheep, geese, turkeys, ducks, and chickens; By-law no. 8, which runs to three pages, covers the subject in detail. With the exception of milch cows during spring and summer, all roving animals were to be impounded. The charges made for feeding each sheep, goat, goose, turkey, hen, or duck was 10¢; for each horse, ass, or head of horned cattle, 30¢; for each hog, 50¢. Over and above the impounding charges, there were other penalties, ranging from 15¢ for fowls to $8 for stallions, the latter penalty under certain circumstances recoverable before the mayor. Damages caused by the animals were to be made good, the poundkeeper could demand payment for feeding, and, if not redeemed within a stated length of time, the animals might be sold to the highest bidder. A pound was established on the northwest corner of Navy and Randall streets, enclosed with a high board fence, and a poundkeeper was engaged (after two years the chief constable was instructed to act as poundkeeper). Four feet was established as the height of board fences in the town but, if rails were used, the fence must be five feet high. The chief and other constables were to act as fenceviewers; thus the ancient and honourable office of fenceviewer was taken over by the police.

The council, finding itself powerless to enforce the provisions of this by-law, repealed it the following spring. The repeated attacks upon the freedom of Oakville's animals, during the thirty years that followed, would indicate that the council was not in accord with public sentiment. One person who made life difficult for Chief Sumner was an Irishwoman who lived on Dundas Street, north of Palmer Avenue. Molly Menear, a widow who supported herself and two daughters by peddling small articles round the town, was looked upon as somewhat of a "character." She kept a large assortment of animals: from three to eight cattle, two or three brood sows, a large flock of geese which frequented the river, and many chickens. Her handling of livestock drew a compliment from one who knew her: "To-day a man can't run a hundred acre farm and keep as many head of stock as this old lady could do on her town lot 208 by 50 feet wide."[48] Her animals did not always stay on the lot, however, and Molly appeared frequently before the magistrate. "Had Mary Manear up for letting her hogs run at large, fine and costs, $2.25," noted Chief Sumner in 1868. One old sow in particular would squeal unmercifully when Sumner went after her; the neighbourhood boys would sound the alarm, and Molly would run to the corner and give a hog call which could be heard all over town. In the scramble which followed, the sow invariably managed to elude Sumner, much to the Chief Constable's discomfiture and the delight of the younger generation. When John Potter's house was destroyed by fire in 1869, Molly's house also caught and burned to the ground. She then determined to have a stone house and spent years collecting stone from the creek bed, which she carried up the bank in her apron. She finally succeeded in hauling enough stone to build the house that is now no. 127 Dundas Street North (it has since been covered with stucco).

In protest of the custom of cow owners, the *Oakville Express* published the following statistics on animals running at large in the eighties:[49]

	Head of Cattle	*Sheep*	*Hogs*	*Horses*
Ward 1.	60	34	17	35
Ward 2.	31		17	33
Ward 3.	77		41	46
Totals	168	34	75	114

A few years later, when a "cow by-law" was under consideration, letters to the press complained of cows breaking sidewalks, ruining gardens, gazing through windows of dwellings, and befouling the piers to such an extent that an evening stroll to the lighthouse could be undertaken only with considerable caution. On the other hand, there were those who maintained that the "cows keep the streets like a lawn" and when put to vote of the ratepayers, the cow by-law lost by nine votes.[50] The matter of animals running at large was eventually solved not by the council but by the gradual abandoning within the town of the practices of the farm.

As the Hamilton *Spectator* pointed out, now that Oakville was a separate municipality, many improvements would have to be effected, and this meant taxes. The assessed yearly value of property in the town appeared by the assessment roll of 1858 to be $32,349 and, as the expenses for that year amounted to $4,852, it was found necessary to levy a rate of 12¢ on the dollar. The following year the rate dropped to 10¢, then in 1861 to 4¢, and during the next few years fluctuated between 4¢ and 7¢.[51]

Another source of revenue was the sale of various kinds of licences to peddlers, auctioneers, shops where liquor was sold, taverns, and persons holding public exhibitions. The wording of the by-law which covered the latter classification was lifted intact from Trafalgar Township By-law no. 7 passed in 1850. According to Oakville's By-law no. 18 licences costing from $10 to $25 must be obtained from the mayor "before any and every exhibition of wax figures, wild animals, puppet shows, wire dancing, circus riding, or other idle feats which showmen, circus riders, mountebanks or jugglers exhibit." However, a licence for "Vocal or instrumental Concerts, scientific or artistical Lectures" cost only $2. The chief constable or his deputy was to attend all such exhibitions, "whose duty it shall be to preserve order and quiet, and thus render them the protection of the said Town."

Regardless of the petition of the Sons of Temperance, "praying that no License be granted for Saloons," licences were granted to both purveyors of liquor and tavern keepers. The by-laws relative to liquor licences were amended and revised about as frequently as the domestic animal by-laws. For a time the revenue was devoted to the maintenance of streets and sidewalks. At a later date, the more practical method of using money from the general fund was adopted. In 1862 By-law no. 55 to amend By-law no. 1 set up the Public Improvements Fund whereby "all monies received from the Municipality Fund of Upper Canada was to be spent on public improvements such as a Lock-up and Market Building."

The subject of a market building was not a new one in Oakville. "During the last three years," wrote a citizen to the local press, soon after Oakville became incorporated as a town, "few towns, if any, in Canada West have shown so rapid and healthy an increase. It is the duty of the council to do everything in their power to make the place desirable and attractive to Settlers and nothing is better calculated to secure this end than a good market building."[52] The Trafalgar Agricultural Association had been formed in the early thirties[53] and it is reasonable to suppose that before long Oakville had a market day when farmers in the surrounding district could dispose of their produce. In 1852 the Oakville Agricultural Association was formed with George K. Chisholm as president and Robert Balmer as secretary.[54] Exhibitions of "Agricultural produce, farm implements, Live Stock, Domestic Manufactures and the Fine Arts" were held annually in the Temperance Hall. According to a correspondent of the *Spectator*, the fair held late in October of 1855 was a great success, and the hall was crowded with exhibits. "The Fine Arts Department was well represented. Mr. Urquhart and Chisholm and Moore, Druggists, displayed some very nice perfumery." The money for expenses and prizes had largely been donated by public-spirited local merchants, many of whom, as well as the members of the agricultural association, "ate at the hospitium of Mr. J. Williams" at the Oakville House. During the dinner, the prize lists were brought in by newsboys.[55]

Although William Chisholm had set aside for public use the Market Square, George's Square, and the cemetery, there was at that time no corporate body to which property could be transferred. It will be recalled that all unsold land in Oakville, which he lost by foreclosure, was later bought back by his three sons. As soon as the Municipal Council came into existence, steps were taken to secure these blocks for the town. The first to be acquired was the Market Square on the west side of Navy Street, between William and King streets.

With the deed to Market Square in their possession, the council instructed the Committee on Market Buildings to see to the drawing of plans. The large building at first contemplated could not be completed for some time, however, and it was decided to erect immediately "a small brick building of such size and dimensions as will answer for a Lock-up House until the Market buildings are completed, and which can afterwards be converted into a Fire Engine House."[56]

The committee chose the north side of Market Square, at the top of the hill on William Street, as the site for the building which was called by the good English term of Lock-up. It was constructed by Nelson and Snell for the sum of $1,528.02. On the lower floor were cells which were "ready for the reception of prisoners" by February 1, 1859; on the upper floor were situated the Council Chambers. For some years thereafter this building served as a combination Town Hall and Lock-up, both terms being applied to it. Though construction of the larger Market Building went forward, it was not until 1862 that it was ready for use. William Lee, proprietor of the sash and door manufactory on Dundas Street, supplied the plans and superintended the work. The contract for brick and plaster work was let to Joseph and Isaac Boon. The two-storey building, 84 by 36 feet, was completed in the autumn at a total cost of $4,734.52. On the ground floor a centre hall running the entire length of the building separated the market, which was conveniently laid out in stalls, from the two rooms used by the newly formed Oakville Rifles as an armoury.[57] The stalls were offered at public auction and rented to butchers for about $24 a year. By proclamation of the Mayor Tuesdays and Fridays became market days "for the sale of farmers' produce free of charge." The second storey of the building was devoted to an auditorium which was heated by stoves installed by Duncan Chisholm and furnished with chairs obtained from Jaques and Hay, Toronto, for 37½¢ apiece, and boasted a piano. The Market Building (so called until the seventies) was opened to the public on November 27, 1862, with a benefit concert for distressed Lancashire operatives in Britain. Local talent assisted by "several gentlemen from a distance" took part in the programme arranged by the Reverend Robert Shanklin of St. Jude's Church. The hall proved capable of comfortably seating five hundred persons, and its acoustics were deemed "excellent." The programme, heard on two successive evenings, was as follows:

1. Hail Smiling Morn	Oakville Amateurs.
2. Duett-Piano (from Sonambula)	Miss Chisholm and Miss Pettit.
3. Annie of the Vale, Solo and Chorus	Miss Wilson.
4. Solo	Mr. Boswell.
5. Winds Gently Whisper	Messrs. Goldsmith, Boswell, Sugden and Newlands.
6. Merry is the Green Wood	Miss Shortiss.
7. Mark! The Merry Elves	Miss McCorquodale, Miss Scott.
8. Sweet from that on my Dreamy Gaze (from Lurline)	Mr. Goldsmith.
9. Duett from Norma	Miss Scott and Miss McCorquodale.
10. The Englishman	Mr. Sugden.
11. Liberty for Me	Miss Scott.
12. Duett	Messrs. Goldsmith and Sugden.
13. The Emigrant Ship	Mr. Sutherland.
14. Tickling Trio	Messrs. Goldsmith, Boswell and Sugden.[58]

The proceeds from this concert amounted to $100. At a meeting held shortly after, the council passed a resolution: "That the suffering of the unemployed in Great Britain deserves the warmest sympathy from this Province . . . therefore the sum of one hundred dollars is hereby granted from the general funds of this Town for that purpose and that the Mayor do transmit the said amount to the Right Honourable, the Lord Mayor of London."[59]

Most public, and all professional entertainments were held in the Market Building: strawberry teas and bazaars given by the women's auxiliaries of the churches, political rallies, balls, and so forth. In 1867 the townspeople saw a Negro performance (these, according to Sumner, were always well attended), a Panorama to which the Town Corporation sent all the school children, and the play *Ten Nights in a Bar-room,* given by professionals.[60] Two years later, Professor Stone gave a velocipede performance after which he instructed in "learning to ride" at 1¢ a minute.

The Oakville Agricultural Association seems to have given way in the sixties to the Trafalgar Agricultural Society, which held fairs alternately at Oakville and Milton. For two autumn days, the Market Building was surrounded by sheep, hog, and poultry pens. Cattle and horses were confined in pens on the vacant lot at the corner of William and Thomas streets, where St. Jude's Church now stands, the overflow being tethered along William Street. Prize lists of these township fairs published in the newspapers show the exhibits in the "Floral Hall" to have been similar to those at their modern counterparts, the county fairs. In 1868, John Cosley, barber, hairdresser, and editor and publisher of *The Bee* "showed some excellent wigs."[61] According to the poster advertising that year's fair, there was over $600 to be paid out in prizes, ranging from $4 for horses and cattle down to 25¢ for "shell work, wax, feather and hair flowers and small fruits." No. 15 of the "Rules and Regulations" specifies that "Directors are prohibited from wearing their Badges while attending to the animals or articles during the Show." No. 17 rules that "all persons who may feel dissatisfied with the decision of the Judges of our Show, and afterwards abuse them in their absence, will be suspended from the privileges of the Society for a term not exceeding two years, provided a charge be preferred by any of the Society's members and sustained by reliable evidence."[62]

It was in the Market Building that immigrants were housed until they succeeded in securing employment. By the time it was erected, most immigrants were crossing the Atlantic by steamship rather than in sailing vessels, and by 1875 practically all were arriving in Canada by this means. Early in May, 1869, five families, totalling twenty-four adults and children, arrived in Oakville to be followed by others during the next week.[63] They overflowed into the Lock-up, and Chief Sumner was responsible for providing them all with beds and food. Not infrequently, immigrants were victims of fraud, and it may well be that this fate had overtaken these people whose arrival under such distressing circumstances was witnessed by a townsman.

An early settler, prominent in the Congregational Church at Oakville which had foundered on the rocks of finance, made a trip to his homeland. There he visited his brother, a substantial merchant of good standing in one of the smaller towns, who assisted in raising a sum of money to help the Congregationalists at Oakville. At the same time the visitor induced a number of young men and heads of families to come out to Canada to work on his "plantation." Having faith in his integrity because of his brother, these people gave this man their passage money. Their journey to a new home went smoothly but its promoter disappeared before they reached Oakville, leaving them to continue the journey alone. Upon their arrival, the immigrants found the so-called "plantation" to consist of a town lot in Oakville, block no.

62 situated west of The Sixteen on the north side of Colborne Street between Forsyth and Chisholm streets. Though amazed, the owner's wife did what she could for these people; he, having absconded with all their funds, plus the money for the Congregationalists, never again appeared in the district. Forced to make the best of their situation, most of these people remained in Oakville where the names of at least four families are still known today.

The inmates of the Lock-up were provided with four-foot logs for fuel, but usually they were too lazy to cut them into stove lengths. It was far more convenient to place one end of the log in the stove and shove it in as it burned. Chief Sumner worried continually about the hazard of fire, and at nights he would get up to look out of his window from which the Lock-up was visible. One night in October, 1876, when six tramps occupied the Lock-up, it caught fire and burned to the ground. The council then decided to remodel the lower floor of the Market Building for council chambers and to install cells for a jail. During the time these alterations were in progress, Sumner could do nothing about arresting disturbers of the peace, and confided to his diary, "If I had my Lock-up, I would put them in it." When at a later date the Lock-up was rebuilt, it was used primarily for housing tramps who came in great numbers at this period, and Sumner called it the Tramp Room. Persons arrested for crimes were placed in the cells of the Market Building. The term "Town Hall" had begun to be used, but it was not until the council met in the new rooms that the Market Building became in point of fact the Town Hall.

In a town where the buildings were predominantly of frame construction, the fear of fire was omnipresent and very real. The facilities for fighting fire were limited to a little hand pump and a small length of hose which drew water from the wells and cisterns of houses. Merchants continued, each night, to place their cash boxes and small valuables wrapped in a heavy covering under their beds. There was but one place in the town that was really fireproof: the vaults in the Custom House, built of solid brick two and one-half feet thick.[64] The first fire-engine, the little "Cataract," had been purchased in 1854 for £100, raised by special assessment of Oakville ratepayers of ¼*d.* in the pound,[65] and Samuel Jull, David Duff, and G. K. Chisholm had been commissioned to make the purchase. Upon petition of W. F. Romain and others, extra hose was purchased the following year for £50.[66] The Cataract was kept in the old schoolhouse, one end of which was "repaired as a fire-engine house" at a cost of £6.5.9½.[67] The hose, obtained from Perry & Company, Montreal, at a cost of £50, was made of leather riveted every half inch with brass. Henry Gulledge, the saddler, kept it in repair.[68] At a later date John Ross Robertson, who collected and left to the province such a wealth of historical material, wished to secure the little Cataract but it had unfortunately been junked by the Committee on Fire and Water.

By-law no. 11, "To prevent Fires in the Town of Oakville," covers the subject of fire prevention extensively, going into great detail concerning chimneys, partitions carrying stove pipes, candles, lamps and lanterns, smoking in stables and workshops using combustible materials, the burning of rubbish, etc. "No person . . . shall carry fire through any of the Streets, Squares, or Courtyards in said Town, except in some covered vessel or metal Fire pan." It was enacted that each flue in every "House, Shop or Office . . . be well and effectively swept . . . every three months." In fact, many of the provisions were probably well-nigh impossible to enforce. The Standing Committee on Fire and Water went into action and soon reported that forty-five volunteers had been enrolled to form a fire company under the auspices of the council on condition that the engine and hose be put at their disposal, and that they be provided with uniforms. The council then appropriated $50 for this purpose, and within two weeks the "Cataract Fire Engine Company No. 1" was regularly organized. When the alarm of fire was sounded by the bell on St. Jude's Church, the engine was dragged out, attached to the first team or waggon to appear, and rushed to the scene of the fire, where there was never a lack of boys to take turns at the pump handles.

It is remarkable that the worst fires in Oakville's commercial centre started, not in the smaller frame stores, of which there were so many, but in the large, well-built brick buildings. The two fires that proved most disastrous both took place on a spring Sunday, when the stores were closed and the blaze got well under way before being discovered. At two o'clock on the afternoon of a Sunday in March, 1868, the three-storey brick building of Arnott and Barclay situated on the north-east corner of Thomas and Colborne streets caught fire, and, along with the surrounding frame buildings, was completely consumed. For a time it was thought that St. Jude's Church across the way might also go up in flames, but the firemen and townspeople succeeded in keeping the fire from spreading and got it under control before it reached the post office. James Arnott, John Barclay, John A. Williams, Hiram McCraney and Edward Hillmer lost their stocks of merchandise and places of business. The first two mentioned were partially insured; but the others, having no insurance, lost heavily. James C. Morgan, headmaster of the grammar school, who occupied one of the upper flats, lost a piano and his library, valued at $1,500, and W. G. Hewson, clerk, lost all his possessions.[69] The corner was not built up again for some time, and the ruins of the buildings remained for years. Barclay and Hillmer started up in business across Colborne Street, the former buying the corner store in the Romain Block, and Hillmer occupying a frame building to the east, where he had his butcher shop and livery stable.

During a dry spell in October, 1871, Chisholm's bush, which stood in the rear of Colonel G. K. Chisholm's residence between Kerr Street and The Sixteen, caught fire. A wind blowing from the north-west spread the fire so rapidly that for a time the town was in great danger. For five days, the whole district was covered by a dense cloud of smoke; but when the wind finally changed to the north-east the town was saved and the fire burned itself out. This narrow escape caused the council to examine the condition of the fire equipment, which they found to be very "inefficient." Realizing that without a good supply of water the engine was useless, they planned to build brick cisterns or "fire wells" on Colborne Street. Each was to have a capacity of ten thousand gallons, and was to be kept filled by rainwater piped from the eaves of adjacent buildings. Four of these wells were built along Colborne Street at Navy, Thomas, George, and Dunn streets. (Forty years later the fire well at Thomas Street was accidentally uncovered and no one knew what it was.) At the same time, a second fire-engine, the "Phoenix," and a reel mounted on wheels carrying five hundred feet of hose and drawn by hand, were purchased second hand from the City of Toronto at a cost of about $500. A special meeting was called to organize a fire company for the Phoenix, and new uniforms were procured. A few years later the council offered prizes to the first horse or team bringing the engines to a fire, $3 for the Phoenix and $2 for the smaller Cataract, "the said engines to be returned to the engine house free, by parties receiving prizes for the same."[70]

Fifteen years after the buildings of Barclay and Arnott were destroyed occurred the most disastrous fire in the town's history, when the entire business section was very nearly wiped out. Within a few hours' time, the handsome Romain Block and the adjoining stores lay in ashes. In this four-storey building, which occupied one-third of the block (lot A) on the south side of Colborne Street between Navy and Thomas streets, were located a large number of the town's most important commercial enterprises.

The fire brigade was quite powerless to act when the brick house of

Shubel Lewis, built in 1874, caught fire on a February day in 1888. The house, turreted like a castle and impressive if ugly, stood in a thick grove of trees high on the bank overlooking the lake on the west side of the harbour. On the day of the fire the temperature was ten below zero, and icebergs extended so far out into the lake that the fire hose would not reach the open water. The firemen were obliged to stand by while the house burned to the ground. This episode made a great impression on one young volunteer, Alfred Hillmer, a son of Edward Hillmer, who later served as Oakville's fire chief for thirty-seven years.

In 1885 a fire bell was placed on the Town Hall; some time later the building was remodelled to accommodate the fire-engine, and a tower was erected in which the fire hoses could be hung to drain and dry. By the nineties the building had become so shaky that it was condemned until extensive repairs were made. Chief Sumner recorded in his diary, "George Carson is propping up the Town Hall for fear it caves in with a load of Grit Sin." When the Town Hall burned down in December, 1913, many of the town records, including the seal of the municipality, were lost.

Oakville had been an incorporated municipality only a few months when the mayor, George K. Chisholm, proposed that the cemetery on Reynolds Street north of Palmer Avenue (block 43) should be moved, and a new school built on the site. The proposal included a gift by him of a plot of land for a new cemetery, and the letter he wrote to the council reads as follows:

Gentlemen—When I look back for a few years and remember on what scale the improvements of our town were based, and what were then the estimates made of the wants of the inhabitants of that day, I am convinced that the time has arrived when we should lay the foundation for more extensive improvements, in almost every shape for the increasing population of the Town. The subject of education is of the first and most imperative importance. When our present comfortable school house was erected, it was thought sufficient for many years, in two years it was found too small and, to-day it is quite insufficient for the wants of the people. . . . In like manner, when a cemetery was first laid out, it was on the ground now occupied by the school house. A very few years sufficed to show that the site was badly chosen and then it was accordingly removed to what was then supposed a long distance from the Town. It is now found to be in the midst of the people and its removal to a more distant locality appears to be imperative.

After much consideration, I have determined to submit to you my views on these subjects, as follows:

I propose to give the Town a plot of ground of about five acres, situate in front of the second concession, on the bank where the road crosses the Sixteen-Mile Creek, for a public cemetery. The present one to be removed there as soon as practicable, and the site appropriated for the purposes of a Public School to be erected by the Town, one that would be an ornament to the place, and of sufficient dimensions to meet the educational requirements of the Town for many years to come.

On completion of the school house, say in five years, the present lot to be conveyed to me or my heirs free, on payment for the present building as a valuation, or the Town to hold the lot and pay me for the same valuation.

If the proposition be accepted, it is most important, as early as possible to prohibit interments in the present cemetery, and make the necessary improvements without delay to the new ground by stumping and fencing, that it may be opened for the interments early next season.

All expenses incurred for this purpose would be more than repaid by the sale of lots.

I have but one object in view in this matter, which is to place the Council in a position to make improvements which I consider necessary for the prosperity and reputation of our rising town.

Your Obedient Serv't
G. K. Chisholm.[71]

15 March 1858

The council "fully concurred in the necessity of making such changes" and viewed the offer as "not only generous but most opportunely made." They gratefully accepted the ground for a new cemetery. The piece of land under discussion is situated at the northern boundary of the municipality at the point where the 6th Line crosses the Lower Middle Road, now the Queen Elizabeth Way. Here the winding Sixteen forms a point of land surrounded on three sides by steep banks of red clay and shale some seventy-five feet in height, a beautiful spot. The council formed a committee for laying out the new cemetery. The land was surveyed by George C. Tremaine, whose "Map of Halton County, Canada West" had appeared that year. After being stumped the cemetery was surrounded by a white picket fence and a line of hitching posts was placed on the 6th Line. A road was cut through to the southern section, reserved for the use of the Roman Catholics, and along it were planted pines, some of which have survived to the present day. A sale of lots was held at the Town Hall, and those purchased were marked with little white stakes bearing the names of the owners. The removal of remains from the old cemetery on Reynolds Street for re-interment in the new Town Cemetery was immediately begun, though the transfer was not to be completed for more than twenty years. As we have already seen, the plan to build a new schoolhouse on the old site was not carried out. At a later date the Town

Cemetery was so neglected by the Corporation that cattle grazed at will among the tombstones. To keep out the trampling cows many owners of burial plots followed the example of R. K. Chisholm who surrounded the family plot with an iron fence.[72]

To the south of the cemetery along the 6th Line was Slabtown, a community of Irish families who lived in shacks and shanties on the bank of The Sixteen. To the north the Lower Middle Road descended steeply into the valley to cross the river on a newly erected bridge. This portion of the valley of The Sixteen is of particular interest as here is to be found the only section surviving in the township of the ancient Indian trail which circled the head of Lake Ontario.

It has been previously pointed out that the Indians when travelling by land chose the dry level ground under the ridge which in prehistoric times had been the shore of Lake Ontario's predecessor, Lake Iroquois.[73] After the creation of the Province of Upper Canada, the government made sporadic attempts to render this trail passable by bridging The Sixteen and other larger streams in its path. Wilmot clearly shows this trail, which he called the "Old Road from York to the Head of the Lake," on his survey of Trafalgar Township, 1806, and therefore we know its exact location.

As it approached the Sixteen from the east, the Old Road swung away from the deep ravine which today forms the southern limit of the Oakville Golf Course. At the river, it descended the east bank in a southerly direction to cross The Sixteen about 210 yards above the present bridge on the Queen Elizabeth Way. Reaching the far side of of the river, below the sheer shale cliff, the road continued south along the flats, ascended the west bank where it curved north, and returned once more to the level ground below the ridge. After the opening of the Lower Middle Road somewhat to the south of it, the Old Road, running through the land which by then had become private farm land, was officially discontinued. Thereafter it fell into disuse and gradually disappeared except at the point where it crossed the river.

It so happened that William McKenzie King, owner of the land to the north (the south half of lot 16 of the 2nd concession), located the barns of King's Castle near the Old Road, and he is said to have erected and maintained a bridge across the river so that his cattle could reach the pasture on top of the west bank. However, King was probably not aware that his cows crossed The Sixteen at the place where it was forded by countless travellers who followed this link in the long trail which traversed the North American Continent from Quebec in the north to New Orleans in the south. This fact would have interested King who on his voyages round the world on sailing ships had spent some time in New Orleans. The Old Road on the west bank is visible today from the Queen Elizabeth bridge. Trees mask its ascent of the east bank to the north, but an excursion up the river will prove that it still exists exactly where Wilmot placed it on his survey.

When a new bridge was needed at The Sixteen on the Lower Middle Road, the township council resolved to improve the steep approaches which had proved "both expensive and difficult" to maintain. The owners of the adjacent land having agreed, Henry Winter, Deputy Provincial Surveyor, ran a new line (for £2.15) and the £75 contract for building a new bridge and cutting down the approaches was awarded to William M. King.[74] Upon its completion in 1855, this new section of the road was confirmed to the public as part of the "Queen's Highway."[75]

Another bridge built at Cemetery Hill, in 1868, is the focal point for a story in which the political rivalries of the day figure. When tenders for the bridge were invited it was specified that stone for the abutments was to be drawn from the Milton mountain. Estimates were submitted by two contractors, one a Reformer and the other a Tory. The Reformer (he may well have been W. M. King who had recently established a Reform newspaper, the *Oakville Advertiser*) approached G. K. Chisholm for permission to use stone from the bed of The Sixteen on his land south of the bridge. The request was promptly denied. The Tory succeeded in securing both permission to use the stone and the contract. Since his estimate had been based on hauling stone from Milton, the Tory is said to have made a tidy sum on the contract. This may have been the bridge that was later boxed in, the only covered bridge in the district. Among readers of this history there may be some who had their fortunes told by Mrs. Jacklin, the Negro fortune teller who lived at the turn in the road on the west bank. Here teamsters paused to let their horses rest and drink from the spring flowing out of the bank. While gazing into her crystal ball (which curiously resembled a glass insulator such as those used to carry wires on telephone poles) Mrs. Jacklin would reveal the future. Only the fruit trees now growing along the abandoned road bear testimony to her long residence there. The box bridge was no longer needed after the construction of the High Level Bridge, which eliminated the long climb up Cemetery Hill, although it proved dangerously narrow for automotive traffic. It is of interest to note that, when the Queen Elizabeth Way was constructed, the present bridge was built in 1936 by William Whitaker King, of the King Paving Company, a grandson of William McKenzie King.

George's Square had been reserved by William Chisholm, the founder of Oakville, for the use of the townspeople, but it had never been used as a public park. It will be recalled that after Chisholm's losses to his creditors all his interest in the townsite was bought back by his sons and this land belonged to George K. Chisholm, the mayor. In 1859 the council appointed Joseph Milbourne, Jeremiah Hagaman, and W. H. Young a committee to ascertain from the mayor whether George's Square had "ever been conveyed to the town, and, if not . . . if it was the intention to convey same." To this the mayor replied:

> I beg leave, in answer to your inquiries, to state, First: That George's Square has never been conveyed to the town, and is consequently private property.
>
> As to the Second inquiry: Whether it is the intention to convey it to the Town? I beg to say, that an answer could be more appropriately given, when the town expresses a desire to have it so conveyed, and then the consent would, probably, depend upon the use which was intended to make of it; or, if no such expression be given, it would be becoming to wait until it was voluntarily offered by the owner.[76]

And there the matter rested for sixteen years. However, when the subject was again broached, George's Square was conveyed to the Corporation and has since been used as a public park.

Between 1850 and 1857 the streets of Oakville were maintained by statute labour, according to the township law then in force whereby all men between the ages of twenty-one and sixty were liable to perform such labour. Those whose names did not appear on the assessment rolls and those assessed up to £50 were liable for two days. Assessments of between £50 and £150 called for three days' labour and so on up the scale to eleven days for assessments of between £1,600 and £2,000. Commutation was at the same rate as formerly, 2*s*.6*d*. per day.[77] When Oakville withdrew from the township, the municipal council in By-law no. 4 set the amount of statute labour each person was to perform "in accordance with the Statute 16 Victoria, Chapter 182," 1853. The scale set out in this statute was somewhat higher, and as a result, ratepayers were liable for more labour than was required by the township. Being more interested in securing money than labour, the Town Corporation at this time raised the commutation from 2*s*.6*d*. to 3*s*.9*d*. per day. Pathmasters were to notify each person contributing labour as to the number of days he owed, and the time, place, and necessary tools. Since only one pathmaster was appointed for each ward, the proportion of townspeople who preferred commutation must have been large. During the first year, the office of pathmaster in Ward 1 was filled by Pharis Doty, in Ward 2 by David Patterson, and in Ward 3 by W. H. Young.

Colborne Street had been provided with footways in 1849 when plank sidewalks were laid by public subscription along both sides of the street. The following year the Township Council agreed to a special assessment on village property by which £50 was raised and a walk was laid "on the east side of Navy Street to the Pier."[78] In 1851 a township by-law enacted that in Oakville "one-half of the Statute Labour . . . is hereby commuted and ordered to be paid in cash at the rate of two shillings sixpence currency for each day."[79] With this money repairs were made, the walks on Colborne Street extended, and crossways laid at some corners. During 1855 new plank walks were laid to the Temperance Hall, the Roman Catholic and Presbyterian churches, the schoolhouse, and across The Sixteen to the top of the hill beyond the foundry. The total costs amounted to £216.11.6.[80]

Although the Town Council continued to use statute labour for maintaining the streets, a different system was introduced for building and repairing the plank sidewalks. Under By-law no. 27, effective between 1858 and 1871, sidewalks were constructed or repaired "by individual expense, or by local assessment on the frontage of real property benefited thereby." Walks could be built "on any side of any street" only after two-thirds of the property-holders had signed and presented a petition to the council. Those who preferred could construct (within sixty days after the petition had been granted) or repair (within ten days) sidewalks at their own expense, under the supervision of the Standing Committee on Streets and Sidewalks, but otherwise their share of the cost of the walk bordering their property would be collected along with their taxes. The Corporation made itself responsible for the cost of all crossways, and no persons desiring to construct them at their own expense could do so without the permission of the committee, and then only at street corners. All unauthorized crossings were to be removed forthwith, and the builder subjected to a fine of $2. The by-law specified that all walks were to be not less than two feet wide, and the council reserved the right to order the construction of walks on any street "without being petitioned for." When, in future, "a Sidewalk is constructed to the Railway Station, the owners . . . shall be assessed for the construction of a Sidewalk three feet in width, and any greater width considered necessary . . . for the accommodation of the public at large, shall be borne and paid for from the general funds of the Town." That no misunderstanding should arise as to what "shall be considered as streets" these were defined as those "leading north and south of Colborne Street, east from Navy and west from Forsyth streets." The plank walk to the railway station was laid along Dundas Street in 1864 at a cost of $713.80.[81]

Colborne Street, being the most travelled of all the streets, was unquestionably the worst in Oakville and, except in midwinter and midsummer, lay deep in mud. The council passed a resolution in 1861 "that an experiment be made . . . of gravelling with beach gravel on Colborne Street, east from Navy eight feet by sixty-six and three inches deep."[82] To bring 166 loads from the lake shore took three teams six days, at a cost of $17.50, and the labour of eight men at 75¢ each per day amounted to $12, making the total cost $29.50.[83] This first attempt at gravelling the main street proved so successful that six years later the whole length, from the bridge to Reynolds Street, was prepared by Albert Hilliard at a cost of $450.[84] The gravel was laid sixteen feet wide and nine inches deep, and the action of waggon wheels soon spread it over the roadway.

Owing to the prevalence of commutation of statute labour, the work of maintaining the streets passed gradually to hired labour, and the offices of overseers of highways and pathmasters were absorbed by the Committee on Streets and Sidewalks.

The great clouds of dust which damaged the merchants' stocks and kept people away from the shopping district in dry weather made it imperative that Colborne Street be sprinkled. For a time the cost was borne by the shopkeepers, "as is customary in other municipalities," according to the council. Various methods were tried, including using the fire engines; but eventually, after years of bickering, the Corporation assumed the responsibility and in 1890 secured a watering cart for sprinkling the streets of the town at night.

The street allowances had been so completely denuded of trees that for the first forty years Oakville's streets were quite bare. Through the efforts of W. F. Romain, the council in 1868 took up the project of planting Colborne Street and many of the back streets with maple trees. In commendation of this action, the editor of the *Canadian Champion* wrote in the following summer: "Having protected them by a stringent By-law, they soon took root and flourished in the sandy soil of Oakville, and in a few years the town will resemble in its grove-like aspect, the better class of American towns. Nearly all the trees took root and where they did not, the corporation this Spring had them carefully replanted. The cost of each tree, with boxing and planting, we are told, average 40¢."[85]

The first Town Councils of Oakville reflected the fact that the town was preponderately Tory; not until the seventies did the Grits make any headway in the Town Council. Time after time in the general elections the Reform candidate was returned by the county, but Oakville consistently voted Conservative. In one general election in which the mayor of the town, George K. Chisholm, was defeated in the county, only four men in Oakville voted against him. Their identity was known because of the open voting, and these men were decidedly unpopular on account of their politics. In the first election after Confederation, when Chisholm was again defeated, Oakville was the only municipality in the county which gave him a majority. Out of 206 votes cast in the town, only 11 were in support of the Reform candidate. After William McCraney and W. H. Young became the recognized leaders of Oakville's Reformers, the elections for ward councilmen were considerably enlivened. According to Sumner, the election of 1870 "went off all right—only a few knock downs." During the next few years there was "considerable jawing over nothing" in the council; but, upon one occasion, Sumner wrote, "Council met, had a stormy night of it . . . calling the Mayor a liar and a coward. I fear for his Religion."

It is significant that the Reformers came to power in the Town Council when the secret ballot was used for the first time in the town election of 1876.[86] After attending the first council meeting of that year, Sumner wrote, "They are showing their Grit. I expect to get my discharge. I look for no mercy." But what he feared did not at this time come to pass. "The Town will go to the De'l if Politics are not put an end to . . . some very uncalled for words used," he remarked sadly in his diary.

The new Grit council was full of hustle and bustle and plans for improving the town, especially in the matter of lighting the streets. During one heated argument, a Tory councilman exclaimed in exasperation, "This discussion is like shearing a goat—great cry and little wool." The spectacular result was the placing of one lamp in the centre of the bridge across The Sixteen—"a great farce," according to Sumner. Indeed, it was not until five years later that five more lamps were erected on Colborne Street, one at each intersection on alternate sides between the bridge and Dundas Street. The kerosene lamps sat in glass cases mounted on posts and for many years John Ford tended them every day, carrying with him a ladder, rags, and a can of coal oil. Gradually, the lamps were extended along Dundas Street to the railway station and, late in the afternoon, the lamplighter would start on his rounds to tend the thirty-one lamps, arriving at the station about six-thirty. "Fortunately," he told the council, "I have a comfortable sleeping place at the end of Dundas Street." Starting on the return trip about ten o'clock, Ford extinguished the lamps and those citizens who arrived by train after eleven-thirty found their way home in the dark as best they could. John Ford was a rugged individualist who took matters into his own hands and settled them as he saw fit. He became tired of carrying a ladder with him each day, and lowered the lamps, so that he might reach them from the ground, by sawing off the tops of the posts. As Ford was an exceptionally short man, after this reduction the lamps stood little more than five feet off the ground.

The spring rains of 1878 caused what Sumner termed "the largest flood ever seen in this Town." The abutments and the west approach to the bridge across The Sixteen were carried away so that it became necessary to tear the bridge down and build a new one. This project cost $1,500. Constructed of heavy timber, the arched bridge was supported in the centre by a timber crib and, as it sat close to the water, the approaches on each side were quite steep. The bridge was well balanced and could be swung on its axis by a hand lever in a few minutes' time to allow vessels to pass up and down the river. For fifteen years this bridge withstood the floods. When it was found that repairs were impracticable, it was replaced by the steel swing bridge called Aberdeen Bridge.

The last plank sidewalk to be built in Oakville was laid along the 6th Line to the Town Cemetery in 1885. After experiments with tar and cinders proved successful the following year, the laying of wooden sidewalks was discontinued and as the old walks deteriorated many of them were replaced with this material.

In the varied enterprises of these years of initiation and advance, Oakville had been indebted to the leadership of several outstanding men. When, within the space of a year, death came to George K. Chisholm and Justus Williams, the town lost two citizens who had devoted themselves unsparingly to its interests from the time of William Chisholm. The founder had died when Oakville was still in its infancy, and these men, the one his friend and the other his eldest son, had seen the fulfilment of his hopes and plans. The village he had carved out of the forest had, within thirty years, become an important town.

From the time he had settled at Oakville in the early thirties, Justus Williams had taken the lead in religious and educational matters.

Colonel Chisholm had become the political and military leader round whom Tory Oakville had rallied. He had been mayor of Oakville from 1857 to 1862 and again in 1873 and 1874, and councillor each intervening year. Both men were strong upholders of the Tory Loyalist tradition, "Fear God, honour the King," and of the social ethics of Victorianism. They both died in harness; Justus Williams was stricken while attending a meeting at his church and Colonel Chisholm when engaged at the Council Chambers.

Colonel Chisholm's stroke came on April 13, 1874. He was taken in a carriage by his brother R. K. Chisholm to his home, where he died the following day without having regained consciousness. Having organized the local militia and the Masonic Lodge, Colonel Chisholm was buried with military and Masonic honours. His funeral was given a full and respectful description by the *Canadian Champion*:

On Saturday last the remains of the late Lieutenant-Colonel George King Chisholm, of Oakville, were borne to their last resting-place by probably the largest crowd that was ever congregated on a similar occasion in this county; it was estimated that no less than 2,000 persons were present. The deceased having been a distinguished member of the Masonic Order, and at the time of his death the Master of White Oak Lodge, No. 198, Oakville, the members of the craft to the number of 150 were present, among them being Grand Sec'y Harris, D.D.G.M. Mason, and others from Hamilton, Toronto, Milton, Burlington, Georgetown &c. The Freemasons assembled at the hall of the White Oak Lodge, and after forming in the usual order, juniors in front, marched to the late residence of the deceased, where the usual Masonic service was conducted by R.W. Bro. Harris. The bearers were officers of the 20th Battalion, in uniform, most of them also wearing the badge of Masonry. The procession then formed and proceeded to St. Jude's Church, where the Rev. Bro. Worrell, Incumbent of the church, read the appropriate lessons and service, the choir singing funeral hymns. The clergyman, in addition to the surplice of a minister of the Church of England, wore the lambskin apron of a Master Mason, and the collar of Lodge Chaplain. The organist played the "Dead March" as the congregation entered the church, which was densely filled, and a large crowd being compelled, for lack of room, to remain outside. The stores and other places of business were closed as the funeral cortege passed slowly through the town, the flags on shipping and public buildings were at half-mast out of respect for the deceased, and the bell of St. Jude's Church was solemnly tolled during a great portion of the day.

At the conclusion of the service in the church, the procession re-formed and marched to the cemetery, the mourners and Masonic fraternity only entering the "Chisholm lot." The coffin being deposited in the grave, the funeral service of the Church of England was read by the Rev. Worrell, after which the Masonic service was conducted by Bro. Kaitting, Past

Master of the Lodge to which the deceased belonged, assisted by the Grand Secretary and District Deputy Master. After the last sad offices had been paid, the brethren marched back to the Lodge room, where a resolution of condolence was passed. R. W. Bro. Mason then addressed the Lodge, speaking in the highest terms of the deceased. He mentioned that the last correspondence he had with Bro. Chisholm was about a week before his death, and was concerning the claims on the charity of the order of the widow of a deceased Mason. In the death of Col. Chisholm, the county of Halton and particularly the town of Oakville, lost a great friend and public benefactor.[87]

Chief Sumner, who assisted Ziller in laying out the body of Colonel Chisholm, wrote in his diary, "In him I have lost a dear old friend, one whom I loved dearly"; and after the funeral, "All the lodges in the county were represented and . . . it was the largest funeral I ever saw in Oakville. It was a lovely day. It was the first appearance of George Ziller's hearse."

To Justus Williams death came swiftly. While attending a meeting in the vestry of St. Jude's Church on March 29, 1875, he suffered a stroke and died almost immediately. Justus Wright Williams had been president of the Oakville Temperance Society for thirty-one years; treasurer of the township and the town; Justice of the Peace from 1846 if not before; trustee of the school from its establishment and treasurer of the Board of Education of the town. He has been described as "dignified in appearance, standing nearly six feet, of sedate but gentlemanly manner and a true Christian gentleman."

These citizens, who had given the town such long and faithful service, had lived to see changes in the economic status of Oakville become unmistakably apparent. The Port's trade and commerce were being seriously affected by several economic factors, some regional in origin, others general throughout the country; but the full portent of these changes was at this time not yet clear. Though it was declining in importance Oakville had not yet completely relinquished the title of "one of the Principal Shipping Ports on Lake Ontario."

III

SOMBRE YEARS

CHAPTER TEN

THE TURN OF THE TIDE

AS A PORT Oakville had reached its zenith about 1860. Rail communication and changes in agricultural practices were bringing about alterations in the economic pattern which affected either advantageously or adversely almost every community in the county. Many ports of Lake Ontario were affected adversely, and Oakville, the largest of the four ports in Halton County, suffered the most severely.

Wheat had always been one of Oakville's largest exports. During the unprecedented prosperity of the early fifties, Canada had had abundant harvests. Other countries whose crops were short had given high prices for everything the Canadian farmer could produce, and the price of wheat had risen to $2.50 per bushel. Prosperous times brought expansion: the farmers contracted to buy more land while what they tilled was still unpaid for, and the province expended heavily in railway building. As a member of Parliament subsequently observed when looking back upon these years, "We ran into debt individually, municipally and provincially, as if pay day had never been to come."[1] The Crimean War ended, the price of wheat dropped, and the financial crisis of 1857-8 which followed came at a time when frost had destroyed a large percentage of the crops. The farmer was forced to go into debt not only for his seed but for his living, and his only return was from surplus stock. In the districts around Oakville, as elsewhere, the farmer, profiting by this experience, turned his attention to diversified farming, and to supplying the markets created by growing cities near at hand. Other important contributing factors to the fall in the production of wheat were the inroads of insects and disease and, in the older sections of Halton County, depleted soils. Farther north, in the rich newly cleared lands of the agricultural frontier, wheat was still the principal crop; but comparatively little of this grain reached Oakville. Ironically, it was the railway, so loudly hailed in the name of progress, that proved disastrous to Oakville's economy.

Soon after the building of the Great Western Railway along the lake shore, the Grand Trunk Railway was constructed through the interior from Toronto to Sarnia on Lake Huron, in the western district. It passed through Georgetown and Acton in the northern section of the county, Guelph, and Berlin (now Kitchener). The waggon journey to the lake ports was no longer necessary, as farmers could dispose of their grain to buyers at Georgetown, of whom one of the largest was Francis Barclay, brother of John Barclay of Oakville. The north-to-south commerce was thus diverted by the railway to move east and west and the relative positions of inland and lake shore communities were reversed. In the rear of the county the villages along the Grand Trunk Railway forged ahead while in the "front" the ports on Lake Ontario declined. With the disappearance of the water-borne commerce, the harbours of Oakville and Bronte, being situated at the mouths of rivers, continued navigable, but the neglected piers at Wellington Square and Port Nelson soon washed away. Little cross-roads communities along the 7th Line and other thoroughfares leading to the ports wilted, and some even disappeared.

It is possible that, if the projected railway to the interior had succeeded, Oakville's commerce might not have suffered as severely as it did. Nothing came of the Oakville & Arthur Railway, for which a charter was obtained in the fifties.[2] Probably this enterprise would have served only to postpone the evil day, for by the late 1860's the frontier product, wheat, was no longer the keystone of the economy of the province. The agricultural frontier had reached the limits of the fertile land below the Laurentian Shield and the rich soils were fast being depleted by the concentration on wheat as a crop.

Stage-coach lines still ran into the interior of the county. Originally these lines had been established to connect the villages in the north with the Great Western Railway at Oakville. "Daily Stage runs to Stewarttown, thro' Postville, Ashgrove and Hornby. Fare to Milton 87½¢ [seven York shillings], Hamilton 50¢, Toronto 50¢."[3] The extra fare charged for the shorter distance to Milton is an indication of the wretched state of the roads. After losing their planking, the three roads leading to the ports, until recently the main thoroughfares in the county, had been neglected. In 1869 a group of men led by George K. Chisholm petitioned the County Council to gravel these roads. The sectional jealousy which had long been simmering boiled over when a by-law appropriating $100,000 for gravelling the three roads was submitted to the ratepayers in the county, and was defeated in every municipality but Oakville. The maintenance of the roads leading to the ports was considered more of a burden than a benefit and, as one man put it, the best plan seemed to be "to abandon them and allow cattle to roam over them."[4]

Milton had been bypassed by the Grand Trunk Railway, and a charter was obtained in 1871 for the Oakville, Milton and Guelph Railway.[5] As this project was received coldly in Guelph, the charter was allowed to expire in favour of that of the Credit Valley Railway, originating at Toronto and passing through Milton on its way to the western district. As a marketing centre, Toronto was in the ascendancy, drawing to it the commerce of which Oakville had had such a substantial share before the era of the railway. The Queen City was gaining a commercial supremacy in Canada which was soon to be second only to that of Montreal.[6]

Owing to the state of the roads, the old stage-coach lines were discontinued in the early seventies and once again direct transportation between the rear and the front of the county was by waggons and buggies. The alternative was a rail trip to Milton via Toronto, a journey of over fifty miles to reach a destination only fifteen miles from Oakville by road. But this would seem preferable, judging by what the *Atlas* had to say about the county's roads in 1877. "Truth compels us to say that its roads are, as a general thing, only fit for travel in summer, or when covered with snow. At other times the mud is something to be remembered with anything but pleasure by the unfortunate traveller."[7] This isolation of the front of the county from the rear served to intensify the sectional jealousy and rivalry which had existed so long.

The decline in the commerce of the Port of Oakville is readily traced in the Tables of Trade and Navigation of the Province of Canada. In round figures, over 282,000 bushels of wheat were shipped to the United States in 1856 as against 86,000 bushels in 1862, only six years later. That year, the expense of collecting tolls on exports, $1,426, amounted to three times the revenue. In 1863 the number of bushels exported dropped to 44,000, but in 1864, rose slightly to somewhat over 45,000. Between 1865 and 1867 the Port of Oakville disappears from the tables, probably because the export figures were so low they were pooled under the heading of "Other Ports." The tables are not available between Confederation and 1875, in which year some 23,000 bushels of wheat were shipped from Oakville to the United States. During the eighties, however, the amount shipped rarely exceeded one or two schooner loads. The gross revenue of the harbour, which at one time had reached hundreds of thousands of dollars ($625,545 in 1855 for example) dropped by 1875 to under $1,000 and after 1880 never again reached $500.[8]

In the early sixties, when Oakville's warehouses were only partly filled, the owners and captains of vessels, as well as the grain buyers, were caught in the slump. Some captains were part owners only, but those who had put all they possessed into their schooners, mortgaging them for large sums in the expectation of being able to pay off all their debts in two or three seasons, were completely ruined.[9] "It has been a dull fall. Vessels are poor property," wrote Sumner in 1867, and the Town Council sanctioned the revision of schooner assessments, giving as the reason "the depreciation of floating stock."[10] Most of the older captains retired from the lakes to go into business in the town; but there still remained a group of younger, hardier men who refused just yet to be bowed by the inevitable.

On the lakes, the transition from sail to steam was about complete, and there was little demand for new sailing vessels. Being at the mercy of the lake winds, schooners were slow, and their schedules unpredictable; voyages were frequently so long that owners lost money on cargoes. Although steamers were very much more expensive to operate, their voyages were, to a large degree, calculable. Wooden ships were outdated, but in any case the supply of timber in the district surrounding Oakville was practically exhausted, and the master shipbuilders were either turning to the construction of iron ships at other ports or following the timber to the upper lakes.

One of the last vessels to come from the shipyards on The Sixteen was the *White Oak*, built by Duncan Chisholm for his brother, Captain George. By permission of the Town Council, the west side of Market Square adjoining Chisholm's shipyard was used temporarily. This schooner of 200 tons' burden, whose capacity was approximately 14,000 bushels of wheat, was one of the highest priced vessels ever built on the river. Until then, the usual cost of schooners had not risen above $1 per bushel, carrying capacity; but the *White Oak* cost $1.12, and her masts, which had been difficult to secure, had cost $100 apiece.

As an added flourish, the masts were topped with huge acorns gilded with gold leaf.

The launch took place on the first celebration of the creation of the Dominion of Canada, July 1, 1867; and, in spite of the heat, it was witnessed by almost two thousand people. The schooner's name had been kept secret and it was expected that she would be christened *New Dominion*, in honour of Confederation, as were numerous other vessels launched that year. Much to everyone's surprise, Captain Chisholm's ten-year-old daughter, Kate, christened the vessel *White Oak* in honour of the founder of Oakville. Chief Sumner, who had worked on the ship's construction, wrote in his journal that night: "This has been a great day in Oakville. Athletic games, etc. The *White Oak* was launched at 10 o'clock. A great many people were present. Everything went off well considering."

Some days later, flying the white pennant bordered with blue and centred with a red C which had been Captain George's "house flag," the *White Oak* sailed out of Oakville with a cargo of lumber worth $165,000.[11] She had many masters and ended her days in the lumber trade on Lake Huron, around the Bruce Peninsula. When her useful days were over, the *White Oak* was allowed to fall apart at Collins Inlet on the north shore of Georgian Bay, some six hundred miles by water from Oakville.

When the building of wooden ships became a precarious business, the shipbuilders John and Melancthon Simpson moved away to take up the construction of steel ships at Toronto, St. Catharines, and other ports on Lake Ontario. John Potter returned to building dwelling houses and Duncan Chisholm had his tin shop. Ships' carpenters who remained at Oakville found work during the summer along Lake Huron, where wooden vessels were still in demand for the lumber trade. Ships' captains and sailors had also to seek employment at other ports. These men returned to spend the winter months at Oakville and, since they had little to occupy them, there were at times lively goings-on. One of the greatest battles that ever took place in the town was fought one Sunday afternoon near the Victoria House between Protestant sailors and Roman Catholics. The principal weapons were axe-handles and many heads were battered and a few arms broken. Dependent as they were for their livelihood upon large consigners and shipowners, who invariably were Tories, the town's mariners were predominantly Tory, and they exerted their influence to keep the Grits from making headway in Oakville. Before one general election, the Grits rented the Town Hall for a rally. On the appointed evening, the candidate and his supporters were assembled when a band of sailors suddenly rushed in, swinging their fists and shooting off pistols at the feet of their opponents. The Grits were driven down the stairs and out of the Town Hall, their candidate making good his escape by swimming The Sixteen. It is probable that Tory sailors were an important factor in the failure of the Grits to gain a foothold in Oakville until the seventies. Grit influence increased in direct proportion as the mariners decreased in numbers; but their fighting spirit was in no way lessened accordingly, and Tory memories were long indeed, as the following anecdote would indicate.

The story concerns two retired lake captains who had not seen each other for many years until a mutual friend arranged a meeting at Oakville. As Captain X confined his conversational efforts to "yes" and "no," Captain Y became indignant and returned home. Some days later, the friend remonstrated with Captain X, asking why he had so used his old friend who had travelled a long distance to see him, to which Captain X replied that he had done so with good reason. It seems that, fifty-three years before, when both were hurrying home from the lakes to vote in the coming general election, they had met in port and agreed to vote Conservative. It was the day of the open vote, and word soon reached Captain X that Captain Y had gone back on his agreement and voted Grit, a sin for which Captain X never forgave him.

The fleets of sailing ships, which for fifty years had carried the bulk trade of grain and lumber, were vanishing from the lakes. Their masts were thinning along The Sixteen as one after another they disappeared into the "bone yard" or to the bottom of the lakes. In 1871 only eight vessels wintered in the harbour where not many years before dozens could be seen. Some, with their masts removed, were converted into steamers or barges, but the greatest number by far were lost on the lakes. Gradually ribbons of black smoke from steam-driven freighters replaced white sails against blue skies, and the beautiful sailing ships became legend.

The *Royal Oak*, built by the Simpsons and renamed the *Fabiola*, carried coal until she was lost off the Duck Islands when returning from Oswego in 1900. The *Baltic*, in which Captain Robert Wilson had crossed the Atlantic and among whose commanders were Captains John Andrew, Hiram Williams, and others, went ashore when laden with barley in 1894. Her captain, his wife and daughter, and crew of three were rescued by breeches buoy, but the *Baltic* was a total wreck. The *Dauntless*, built in The Sixteen and for many years owned and sailed by Captain Hiram Williams, was used in the lumber trade on Lake Erie, and ended her days as a semaphore vessel in the Detroit River. Old sailors remembered the year when the spring flood carried the *Dauntless* so high onto the bank of The Sixteen that it was necessary to build ways under her and launch her like a new vessel. The *Kate*, another of Captain George Chisholm's schooners, built for him by John Potter, got ashore many times and after three rebuildings ended as the *Wilfrid Plunkett*, which burned at Belleville in 1910.

And there was the *Jessie Drummond*, built in The Sixteen by Captain Arthur Clarkson. In her later days, when she belonged to Captain James Quinn, she was reputed to have been the last sailing vessel to deliver coal to Toronto Harbour about 1900. Having sailed as mate in the *Baltic* under Captain Hiram Williams, Captain Quinn knew the water ways from Duluth to Cape Breton, and was in command of the *Jessie Drummond* when she got ashore near Port Hope. Captain Jimmy and his crew barely escaped with their lives, and he insisted that they attend service the following Sunday at a nearby church. Dressed in their oilskins, the men created quite a stir. After the service, a lady congratulated them upon their narrow escape and welcomed them to the church, whereupon Captain Jimmy drew himself up, bowed most punctiliously, and in his booming voice replied, "Madam, we're damned glad to be here." Not long before his death, he asserted proudly, "I never drifted into port, I always went in sailing."

Captain James Quinn was the eldest son of Michael Quinn, shoemaker, who came from Ireland to Oakville in the forties. In the middle fifties, Michael Quinn built the house on Burnet Street midway between Wilson and Chisholm streets (now no. 60 Burnet Street) where, until not long ago, his sons and daughters continued to live. Tragedy struck the family in 1878 when two sons were lost on the stone hooker *Pinta* which went down in a sudden high wind in plain view off Oakville. The following notice appeared in a local newspaper on November 24:

LOST! LOST!

On Thursday morning, the 20th inst. the scow "Pinta," under command of William Quinn, left Oakville Harbour, laden with stone, for Toronto, and when running down about 4 miles at 10 o'clock A.M. reefing to the then terrible wind the vessel went down, and while sinking it was discovered by Mr. George Schofield, that two of three persons then aboard escaped in a small scow; one of these bodies was recovered [Samson Howell] at Port Dalhousie. The other two still missing may be identified by the description given below.

The bodies of William Quinn, described as having the "Tattoo of a full rigged ship on right arm of some four or five inches in diameter," and Joseph, age eighteen, were never recovered. That of young Howell showed he had frozen to death long before his scow was blown ashore at Port Dalhousie. He was a grandson of one of Trafalgar Township's earliest settlers, Squire Howell, whose house still stands on the 4th Line south of the Dundas Street, overlooking The Sixteen. Soon after the *Pinta* was seen to sink, Chief Constable Sumner and several men drove down the Lake Shore Road east of Oakville, where the masts showed about a mile out in the lake. All day, in a high wind, they raked the bottom of the lake without success. In after years, John A. Williams was inspired to write a long poem on the loss of the *Pinta.*

The stone hookers, of which there were several in and out of Oakville, continued to operate successfully for a number of years after the large vessels had practically disappeared from the lake. At Toronto the demand for building stone was large and as early as 1857 it had become necessary to adopt measures to control the lifting of stone along the lake shore. On the same day that Oakville was incorporated as a municipality, a statute was passed by Parliament entitled "an act for the protection of persons owning Lands on the shore of Lake Ontario, in the Counties of York, Peel and Halton."[12] This statute prohibited the removal of stone from the bed of the lake nearer to the shore than fifty feet beyond the low water mark. None the less, stone hookers continued, as usual, to work close to the shore, posting a man on top of the mast to watch for onlookers. The stone, collected by a rake having two heavy tines set at right angles to a long handle, was taken aboard scows and later transferred to the hookers *Mary Ann, Coral, Pinta, Lillian,* and *Rover* for transporting to Toronto. That hands employed on these vessels were not the most experienced is evidenced by the statement made by Captain John Williams upon the occasion of the celebration at Toronto of his ninetieth birthday. He asserted that in 1867 he had joined the stonehooker *Rover* as cook at ten years of age.[13]

A master mariner of the sixties was Captain Maurice Phelan (or Felan, as it came to be spelled in the simplified manner of the district; Faux became Fox, etc.). Maurice Felan, a native of County Limerick, left Ireland about 1853 to come with his family to Canada West, settling near Wellington Square. He went on the lakes and, after securing his master's papers, commanded the *Three Bells* and other vessels owned by Thompson Smith, which engaged in the lumber trade on Lakes Michigan and Huron. At a later date, Captain Felan was part owner with Duncan Chisholm of the schooner *Victoria.* One November,

Chisholm eagerly explained to Felan that he could obtain four hundred tons of pig iron at the low price of $2.50 per ton if it could at once be transported across the lake from Oswego. Navigation was closed, no lights would be burning on the lake, and no insurance could be procured, but Chisholm persuaded Felan to try and recruit a crew in Toronto. Felan did not succeed in getting a single man although, as he later admitted, he did not try too hard, not being anxious to make the voyage. However, when Chisholm offered to go along, Felan decided to take the risk and induced four other captains at Oakville to act as crew. The ground was covered with snow when the *Victoria* set out for Oswego. The trip across was difficult enough, but the return voyage was worse, as the ship became coated with ice and her rigging froze. When land was sighted, and a tower appeared against the sky-line, Captain Coote inquired what it was. Upon being told by Felan that it was the Toronto Asylum, Coote asserted warmly, "That is where you ought to be." The *Victoria,* coming in under full sail on Christmas Day, was greeted by a large crowd assembled on the dock, and all cheered the fantastic ice-covered ship as she sailed up The Sixteen.[14] When Captain Felan married Maggie Williams, daughter of the hotel proprietor, in 1868, "Several of the boys got rather elevated after the occasion," according to Sumner. After buying the land on the lake shore west of Oakville, a part of the old Kenney farm, in 1871, Captain Felan left the lakes to devote his time to farming.

Another lake captain of this later day was Maurice Fitzgerald, whose father, James Fitzgerald, by trade a tailor, had come from County Cork to Oakville about 1840. When a youth of fifteen, in 1861, Maurice had signed his first articles of agreement with Captain George Gerrie, and sailed away on the *Junius.* In 1871, the year Fitzgerald received his master's papers and his first command, the *Meteor,* he was on his way to Chicago just at the time of its Great Fire. Six years later, his ship left Chicago in company with the ill-fated *Magellan,* under command of Captain Belyea of Bronte. It was not until he reached Oakville that Captain Fitzgerald learned that the *Magellan* had been rammed at night by a steamer, which cut through her amidships, leaving her crew to drown in Lake Michigan. Accidents such as this were not uncommon, and many sailing ships and their crews were lost in collisions with heavy steamships. Fitzgerald also commanded a vessel owned by Thompson Smith, the *Duncan City,* named after the sawmill town near Cheboyagan, in the Straits of Mackinac, where Smith had large interests. This vessel was engaged in the lumber trade between Lakes Huron and Michigan and Chicago. Fitzgerald recalled having seen

Brigham Young and his Mormons camped on the shores of Lake Michigan. At that time, Captain Fitzgerald and his wife lived in the little clapboard cottage which is now the west section of the shop the Town and Countrywoman on Colborne Street East. The *Marcia C. Hall,* called by sailors *"Marshy Haul,"* was Captain Fitzgerald's last command.

Unlike the majority of his contemporaries, Captain Fitzgerald refused to make any compromise with steam. He preferred instead to leave the lakes and go into the coal business. For over twenty years he lived at no. 13 Navy Street South and, sitting on the porch, his captain's cap giving him a jaunty air in spite of the flowing white beard, he was always ready to lay down his newspaper and engage in a chat. That the crews of steamships were sailors he flatly refused to concede. "Mechanics," he would roar, "that's what they are, nothing but damned mechanics. In a fog they get lost and go ashore; they don't know anything about sailing and you can tell them I said so."

Like many other former masters of sailing ships, Captain Fitzgerald lived to a venerable age. In the 1920's there were four retired lake captains who were well along in their eighties: Captains James Andrew, James Dougherty, Maurice Fitzgerald, and Robert Williams; Captain Maurice Felan rates special mention as having attained the age of ninety-five. At that time, all but Captain Williams lived at Oakville.

George Hardy Morden was a lake captain who made the compromise with steam. Having followed the lumber trade to the western district along Lake Erie, he founded the Morden Line of steamers engaged in transporting lumber from the north round Georgian Bay. The 200-ton schooner named the *Dolly Morden* for his daughter was sailed by his sons, but only the youngest of the three, Captain George, remained on the lakes. Captain W. H. Morden went into the coal business at Oakville, and for a number of years served as reeve of the township. His father "was a great one to buy land," according to Reeve Morden whose farm, which had once been tilled by the Reverend George Washington, was part of a thousand acres Captain G. H. Morden had acquired before his death in 1908.

The schooners *"Marshy Haul"* and *Jennie Matthews* called frequently at Oakville to deliver coal. Until the seventies, large lump coal had been used primarily for melting pig iron at the foundry and was brought in bags on the decks of schooners returning from the United States. About 1870 R. K. Chisholm, realizing the advantages of coal as household fuel, brought in a smaller size, probably what is today known as "chestnut," and he is reputed to have been the first person in the town to install a coal stove. This fuel gained rapidly in popularity. In 1873 an advertisement in the *Argus* advises that "parties desiring their winter's supply of coal must leave orders during the present month of September . . . [the advertiser guaranteeing] to fill them before the close of navigation." Within three years coal at the price of $5.25 per ton delivered was coming into general use.[15] In the early seventies the *Argus* carried advertisements for hot-air furnaces; but these were not used much before the eighties, and then were employed mostly for heating larger buildings such as stores. In the late eighties the installation of a furnace was of enough importance to draw the following comment from the *Oakville Star*: "H. Wilson, our Rockbottom grocer . . . has just put in a complete furnace, heating his store and dwelling above. . . . Furnaces are now considered to be superior to any other method of heating."

The decline in the commerce of the port and in the numbers of ships passing in and out of the harbour drastically reduced its revenue to the point where the proprietor, R. K. Chisholm, was unable to keep it in repair. By 1871, the channel had become so clogged with gravel that vessels could not enter the harbour, and were obliged to stand outside the piers. Grain had therefore to be bagged and all produce was hauled either by waggon or scow to the end of the pier for loading.[16]

The charter granted to William Chisholm was still in effect; but the loan of £2,500 advanced by the government remained unpaid. Although R. K. Chisholm was anxious to be rid of the responsibility, the general impression was that there was plenty of money to be made out of the harbour, and a number of men were anxious to secure its control. Chisholm was the target of much recrimination; and after long discussions in the Town Council and at a public meeting held in the Town Hall a deputation went to Ottawa. The matter was placed before the House of Commons by the Member for Halton, and on motion of Sir Francis Hincks the House passed a resolution declaring it expedient for the government to take over the Oakville Harbour and offer it for sale.[17] Before long the following notice was posted about the town:[18]

> Government Sale! Notice is hereby given that on the fifteenth day of November, at 2 o'clock P.M. OAKVILLE HARBOUR! will be sold by Public Auction! at the Town Hall, in the Town of Oakville.
>
> Conditions of Sale will be as follows: The tolls to be collected shall be in accordance with the Schedule of Rates established by the Order in Council of March 1st, A.D. 1872, a copy of which may be seen at my office.

The purchaser to maintain at least ten feet of water in the Harbour and otherwise keep it in proper repair.

The upset price to be $6,000.00 and the purchaser to pay one thousand dollars in cash and the remainder upon the completion of title deeds; and in the settlement of the balance of the purchase money, the net tolls collected, less the expenses incurred since the harbour came into the possession of Government, will be deducted from such balance.

JOHN K. APPELBE,
Oakville October 22, 1872. Auctioneer.

A syndicate formed by a group of local men appointed as their representative at the sale the new owner of the Chisholm brothers' mill, Isaac Warcup. Warcup was outbid by one John T. Shewell, who contracted to pay the government $6,600 for the harbour rights.[19] When, within the year, Shewell met with financial ruin, he transferred "all his right, title and interest" in the harbour to the Town Corporation "for the nominal sum of two hundred and fifty dollars."[20] It was then ordered "that the Dominion Government free itself from any further responsibility in respect of said Harbour, as a mere local work, by surrendering it to the town of Oakville."[21] By Order-in-Council dated November 5, 1874, the harbour was "granted, transferred and conveyed to the corporation of the town of Oakville," and in this ownership it has since remained. Under the terms of the transfer, the Corporation assumed the responsibility of keeping the harbour "at all time hereafter" in a good and sufficient state of repair. A Harbour Committee of three councilmen was appointed, and Chief Constable Sumner was made Harbour Master.

It was not long before the Harbour Committee was faced with the problem of extensive repairs. On March 16, 1876, the harbour sustained serious damage from an east storm which the *Argus* featured, complete with drawings. The views and an abbreviation of the article were reprinted in a Montreal newspaper, and the Harbour Master mounted a set in his scrap-book. From one of these the drawing on page 333 together with the following description of "The Great Storm at Oakville" was taken:

The wind blew with a tremendous force, and the watery billows rolled high. During the storm's height a view from near the pier was grand beyond conception. On the east side of the pier there was a large cone of ice formed, the point of which was about forty feet from the edge of the water; and all along the shore the ice banks extended into the lake for about fifty yards, and they probably reached the bottom of the lake in from four to ten feet of water; and rose above the water from six to twenty feet. Against this barrier of ice the sea broke with awful force, . . .

and incredible as it may look, it is nevertheless a fact that showers of stones were with nearly every wave thrown high above the ice cone, falling and rolling down upon the ice banks, and very many of them going over into the harbour. One gigantic wave threw a number of stones full twenty feet above the ice cone (sixty feet from the water's edge) high in the air . . . a large flat one, being some six inches thick and weighing not less than 120 pounds. Many others of similar size were continually in the air. Friday the wind abated and . . . the sea soon thereafter went down. A beach formed outside the line of ice, and near the pier where formerly there were twelve feet of water it was now dry land—or stones and gravel rather—two or three feet above the water's edge. At the extreme end of the pier where the ice had been washed off, the planks and covering of the pier had been entirely swept away, and many cords of stone were washed out. The tons of solid ice encircling the lighthouse entirely protected it from the fury of the storm.

Oddly enough, the limits of the harbour had never been established and in 1877 William Kingsford, engineer in charge of harbours of the Great Lakes, attempted to discover just what the harbour comprised. Having already published pamphlets on the history of plank roads and Canadian canals, Kingsford was well qualified to conduct this research. Indeed shortly after, at the age of seventy-nine, he applied himself to writing a history of Canada which ran to ten volumes and became a standard work.

In his long report on the Oakville harbour Kingsford admits failure to find any map "setting forth what the harbour is" or any documents which might prove its limits. He recommended that the limits be arrived at by agreement with R. K. Chisholm and this undoubtedly was done.

The years following upon the deeding of the harbour to the Town Corporation were full of trial and tribulation. The very next spring, floods which necessitated replacing the Colborne Street bridge carried away the land end of the pier. Government aid was requested but was promptly denied. Each year thereafter brought new problems of expenditure. The Corporation did its utmost with what was assuming the proportions of a bad bargain.

The problem of outlets for their grain continued to be a serious one for the farmers of Halton, as elsewhere. A large number of them belonged to the Grange, reputed to have been founded by a group of Scottish farmers in the upper reaches of Peel County. The Grange was a secret cult with its own ritual which aimed at the social improvement of the farming class and encouraged co-operative buying and selling. The first meetings are said to have been held about 1867 in the miniature Scottish castle called "The Grange" which stands on a hill a few miles south of the Forks of the Credit. Built shortly before of freestone and granite from nearby quarries, "The Grange," with its tower, is today an impressive if lonely sight in the rock-strewn Caledon Hills. Here were held meetings of the first farmers' co-operative in Ontario; in less than a decade the membership had risen to some 30,000. The local Grange had been organized by farmers who were dissatisfied with the difference between prices paid by Oakville dealers and by those at Oswego. Some accused dealers of selling as number one grade the grain they had bought in as number two, and the weighing also came in for its share of criticism. In 1878 the Grangers decided to set up a warehouse of their own and secured the property on The Sixteen at the foot of William Street, the site of William Chisholm's grain warehouse. Subscribing ten dollars apiece, the farmers formed the Grangers Warehouse Company, and erected a building of 25,000 bushels' capacity. Their business prospered, and soon they were contemplating building their own vessels for shipping to Oswego and eliminating the middleman by selling direct. The society's attempts at conducting a retail grocery business did not meet with outstanding success, however. They rented a large room in the tavern on the northeast corner of Dunn and Colborne streets, in the old days the establishment of Thomas Lloyd but then run by James Young, and set up a co-operative general store. Every Saturday the place was jammed with farmers who, according to custom, sampled the stock before making purchases. Unhappily, no margin had been allowed for sampling, and, when the store showed a deficit of $300 at the end of the first year, it came to an abrupt end.[22]

By the mid eighties, the production of grain the world over seemed to have outrun consumption, and for the Canadian farmer this was a time of crippling competition and vanishing profits. With the opening of the Canadian West, the avalanche of grain which poured upon the central markets of the world forced prices down so that the adoption of mixed farming was becoming inevitable. The increased use of substitutes for barley and malt in making beer had affected the barley trade of Halton County with American breweries, and the McKinley Act of 1890 brought it finally to an end. By this Act, the tariff on grain was raised from ten to thirty cents on a bushel. The farmers in the vicinity of Oakville hastened to ship all that was available before the deadline on November 1. To get the grain to the other side of the lake before midnight on the last day of October, everything that would float was pressed into service by dealers and Grangers. One vessel was so overloaded that she stuck on the bar outside the Oakville harbour but she succeeded in getting free soon enough to join the race to Oswego. Some ships arrived on time; but among those which were too late was a vessel carrying 10,000 bushels of the Grangers' barley. She arrived at twelve-thirty on the morning of November 1 and the Grangers lost heavily when obliged to pay $3,000 duty instead of $1,000. After this experience farmers turned to stock and dairy farming and in 1894 the Grangers sold their warehouse to John Wales, flour and feed merchant at Oakville. Fourteen years later this building became the Oakville Club, which it remains today. In what is now the reception room, the weigh scales once stood and, until recent alterations, the door through which bags of grain were run into the warehouse on a tramway was the front door of the club.

After the collapse of the grain trade, it was not long before the two other warehouses standing along The Sixteen near the bridge were demolished and the materials used for building a barn back in the country. The warehouse at the foot of King Street, built by George Chalmers and used by James Reid, became an ice house; but it eventually disappeared also. Only the stone building at the foot of Robinson Street, which between 1867 and 1887 belonged to P. A. MacDougald, stands at the present time, and it is still known as "MacDougald's Warehouse."

By the turn of the century the day of wooden ships was drawing to a close. Whereas in earlier times twenty or more sailing vessels anchored at one time in The Sixteen, now one entering the harbour to collect a cargo of apples or to deliver coal would create considerable interest. When the *Jennie Matthews* unloaded coal at the yards near the bridge, old sailors would gather around to swap tales. Undoubtedly they chuckled over the story of how the *Jennie Matthews,* built at Port Huron in 1875, got her first cargo, 24,145 bushels of wheat, to the mill at Oakville from Chicago via the Welland Canal. This was one of the largest cargoes to be brought through the canal up to that date; and, being full canal size, the schooner, in order to squeeze through the canal, had to be well dubbed along her sides.[23] It is interesting to find that as early as 1875, the Oakville mill used American wheat, but whether in preference to or in addition to Canadian wheat has not been established.

Though sailing ships were few and far between, the harbour was by no means deserted by lake craft; but the activity now centred around the steamships which continued to call. They collected and delivered passengers and took aboard freight which arrived in considerable quantity at the pier. This freight, light and perishable, contrasted singularly with the heavy bulk cargoes of lumber and wheat which had gone under the hatches of the wind-driven schooners. The thousands of crates of small fruits required careful handling and rapid delivery to the market centres of Toronto, Hamilton, and Montreal. The rise in the cultivation of small fruits, particularly strawberries, in which the district growers had become so successful, and in the manufacture of containers in which they were shipped, coincided with the decline in the commerce in grain. These industries, although somewhat of a compensation, were a meagre substitute for the commerce in lumber and wheat, the loss of which had had so profound an effect upon the town.

II

The combination of economic depression and failing commerce caused the population of Oakville to drop more than 25 per cent within four years. The number of residents shrank from over 2,000 in 1857 to 1,450 by 1861,[24] and this downward trend continued during the decade that followed. In 1871, the population totalled slightly over one thousand, less than half of what it had been fifteen years before. Unlike many other Canadian communities, Oakville seems to have profited little from the prosperity brought by the Civil War. The demand for food supplies was great, but the diversion of commerce away from Oakville by the railway was by then well under way. The boom was over, the bottom had dropped out of property values, and real estate "could be had for a song," as John A. Williams expressed it. Whole families were selling out their holdings in and around the town and were moving to other places, many choosing the forest areas in the south-western district of Canada West, which the building of the railway to Windsor had made more accessible. Undoubtedly, some were lured by the discovery in this area of "rock oil," as petroleum was then called. Those who chose the rear townships began once more to pioneer on the land.

Among those who preferred the more settled section was the Coates family, who located in Aldborough Township not far from Lake Erie. Richard Coates, who accompanied his sons Richard junior and Orpheus and their families, died there, an octogenarian, in 1868; today the village of Rodney spreads over a section of their farm. A number of Oakville men fought in the Civil War as paid substitutes,[25] and some young men set out from Oakville for Australia, either to look for gold or to avail themselves of the opportunities offered by that colony to settlers. Among them was Colonel G. K. Chisholm's son, Peter, who ran away from home never to be heard of thereafter.

The Oakville branch of the Bank of Toronto had closed its doors in 1860, and during the years that followed a number of general merchants dropped out, "like frost-bitten flies," according to Williams. And to the problems of economic depression was added that of the "silver nuisance."

Because it was still being accepted at face value, American silver flooded into Canada after the Civil War. Retailers and the consuming public were quite content to buy their goods with silver at par; therefore, the ultimate loss fell on the larger business men and wholesalers, who accumulated the depreciated currency. A movement was set on foot by business leaders in the large towns whereby the American silver was accepted only at 4 per cent discount[26] and the Oakville industries bought silver for their payrolls at this discount from the merchants.[27] As a man will spend silver twice as readily as he will spend bills, the coins were kept in circulation, but the discount cut down on the merchants' profits. Their tills overflowed with silver, and Williams tells of crawling under the counters every night after closing hour to collect the coins that had fallen onto the floor during the day.

The "silver nuisance" added considerably to the troubles of Chief Sumner as tax collector. Not only did he find it well-nigh impossible to collect the town's taxes, but, when they were paid, he was given silver almost exclusively. Between 1867 and 1871 he complained repeatedly in his diary, "Money hard to get, can get nothing but silver." During the course of only one day, he would take in between two and three hundred dollars in coins as tax money.

Chief Sumner's diary alludes to the change that had come over the town. We see it in such comments as, "Oakville so dull can't even start a fight" or "the Town is going to the dogs" and others of a similar nature. He wrote, when the Oakville House was enlarged in 1869 by the addition of a third storey: "Johnny Williams is getting his Tavern raised one storey. Rather a rough time for it."

For several of the longer estabished merchants, who had dealt extensively in grain, this was a period of business failure. The first to go through bankruptcy was W. F. Romain. In 1869 he lost everything to his creditors, including his home on First Street and all its household furnishings.[28] Reorganizing on a lesser scale, Romain succeeded in continuing for some years longer as general merchant in the town, but he never went back to live in the large house in which he had taken so much pride. Besides the slump in their trade, James Arnott and his son-in-law John Barclay sustained heavy losses in 1868 when fire destroyed their three-storey brick buildings standing side by side on Colborne Street at the north-east corner of Thomas Street. Arnott was advanced in years and retired, but Barclay, after being "sold out," contrived to make a fresh start on a more limited basis. Obadiah Marlatt moved away, selling his brick store to the general merchant, John A. Williams. James P. Gage dissolved partnership with W. E. Hagaman and moved to Iowa where he became prominent as a banker. James Reid also followed the wheat westward, to the new province of Manitoba. After trimming his sails to meet the unfavourable wind, Hagaman in 1872 took into partnership his brother-in-law, Bennett Jull of Orangeville. The firm of Hagaman and Jull reduced their large store by half, leasing the north half to Thomas Patterson, formerly head tailor of the custom-made men's clothing department. His wife was a milliner, and the Pattersons gained a wide reputation, not only in the town but throughout the district, he for his tailoring and Mrs. Patterson for ladies' bonnets and hats. Hagaman and Jull hung on for a time; but finally in 1870 Hagaman moved the business to Ridgetown, Ontario.

Like the merchants, the industries were feeling the effects of Oakville's deteriorating economic status. In 1868 Milbourne's tannery closed down for a time, and the manufactury of soap and patent medicines went out of business, the unoccupied building on the lake shore at the harbour falling into ruin. The Victoria Brewery stopped running in 1870. Four years previously the oil refinery had burned down in a fire that spread flaming oil on the water of The Sixteen as far as the harbour. Under the heading "Great Fire at Oakville" the Hamilton *Spectator,* July 13, 1866, reported that on the preceding morning the Oakville Oil Refinery belonging to R. S. Wood, "one of the largest coal oil refineries in Canada," was completely destroyed. Originating from a defect in a new still of a very large size that had been recently installed, the fire raged throughout the day. Four stills, the huge tanks in the yard, and several wooden buildings in front of the refinery were lost, but the refined oil was saved. No attempt was made to rebuild the refinery, and for years the river bank was strewn with debris.

The greatest misfortune, however, was the failure in 1871 of the town's largest industry, the foundry. Only a few years before, John Doty had contemplated expanding the business by building his own rolling mill on the south side of Colborne Street, opposite the foundry. He had thought that at Oakville he could manufacture at less cost than machinists at Toronto or Hamilton, for he would have the same conveniences of water and rail communication and his expenses would be less than in a city.[29] This plan never materialized. In 1871 William Robertson foreclosed on the mortgage and Doty lost the foundry. Other than water transportation, which had been of paramount importance at the time when it was established, the foundry had derived no special advantages from its location at Oakville. The railway was changing the distribution of industry by concentrating it at points of international contact. Hamilton was just such a point. The junction of the railways running between Canada and the United States, it was becoming the focus of large-scale industry, and thereby replacing Dundas, the pioneer supply base and gateway to the interior. Specialization and concentration were drawing even small industries away from scattered sites where the district provided no special advantages into larger and more central situations.

John Doty moved to Toronto, where he formed a new company and made a success of manufacturing marine engines. For some years this company occupied the brick building on the north-west corner of Front and Bathurst streets, which once had been the home of the Receiver-General of Upper Canada, J. H. Dunn. The house had been built for him in 1835 by Toronto's eminent architect, John G. Howard[30] who will be recalled as the builder and owner of Colborne Lodge and the donor of High Park to the City of Toronto.

As well as the foundry, Doty owned and operated the fleet of miniature steamers known as the Doty Line, which ferried passengers to and from Toronto Island. The little sister paddlewheelers *Mayflower* and *Primrose* were built by him, and it may be mentioned in passing that they are lying in the Oakville harbour at the time of writing, being used as tow barges by a construction company engaged in repairing the harbour. The commodore of the fleet of eleven little ferries which, in the middle eighties, began wintering at Oakville, was a native of the town, Captain Robert Williams, son of the hotel proprietor John Williams. Captain Robert lived in a house which stood facing the lake at the foot of Thomas Street where the Old Post Office Museum is now situated. Moved at a later date, this house now stands as no. 29 King Street. Captain Williams manned the ferry fleet with many Oakville men, former commanders of sailing ships who at this period were hard put to find berths. Among these were Captain George Moulton and Captain Thomas Hinton, master of the *Forest Queen* in 1862 at the age of twenty-one. Captain Hinton's little paddlewheeler *Louella,* which was long regarded as the handsomest ferry on Toronto Bay, made her first trip to the Island in 1882. Propelled by Doty engines, she carried 122 passengers, and held the record for the number of persons saved from drowning by her crew.[31] The *Louella* remained in the Island service until 1934, when she made her last trip.[32]

After foreclosing on the mortgage he held on the Oakville foundry, William Robertson, hardware merchant, leased it to Dayer and Bounsall; but it was not long before they also went under. A hard-headed Scotsman, Robertson considered that it was possible to place the business on a paying basis and in 1877 he sold his hardware business to McIntyre and McGiffin and, entering into partnership with Dayer, went into the foundry. Employing about twenty-five hands, they devoted themselves largely to the manufacture of sinks, cisterns, well and force pumps, which were guaranteed to be frost proof, and several lines of small hardware such as screws, clothes-line reels, and barn-door rollers.[33] In 1880 Robertson converted part of the building into a steam flouring mill, mainly for custom work.[34] He counted on the trade of farmers located in the western section of the township, who could approach his mill by the 6th Line and thereby eliminate the steep hills of The Sixteen. But, as one of his contemporaries expressed it, Robertson "seemed ever to be resisting the inevitable." Competition of the larger centres was too strong, and the manufacturing end of the business soon went into receivership, followed by litigation.[35] The steam flouring mill continued until 1890 when it also shut down. The large two-storey limestone building, after standing empty for some years, was finally demolished. John A. Williams, the merchant, bought the little building which had served as an office and, moving it to the south-east corner of Colborne and Second streets, he converted it into the residence that now stands as no. 9 Second Street.[36]

At a time when the problems of all business enterprise were intensified by continuing depression, only those industries which enjoyed special advantages from their environment managed to survive. Thus the tannery, the carriage manufactories, and the saw and planing mills, unlike the foundry, managed to come through successfully.

As long as timber was available in the district, the steam sawmill on The Sixteen below the bridge continued to turn out lumber. With the growth of the larger cities and the spread of industrialism in the United States and Canada came the demand for more and more lumber, and in the late sixties Thompson Smith was employing eleven sawyers. In 1870 Smith's sawmill was bought by William McCraney, son of Hiram McCraney who operated a sawmill on The Sixteen, and grandson of William who is reputed to have settled on the lake shore before the township was opened.

As mentioned earlier in this history, Hiram McCraney's water sawmill on The Sixteen above the Lower Middle Road went into operation in the 1830's when his son William was yet a child. In 1864, after three years spent in California prospecting for gold, William assumed control of this sawmill.[37] Six years later he bought from Thompson Smith the steam sawmill near the harbour. He had been owner of this mill for only a few weeks when in April, 1870, it and the surrounding lumber yard were reduced to a smoking ruin. To express the sympathy that was felt for McCraney a public meeting was held in the Town Hall.[38] He contrived to rebuild the sawmill immediately and within the year it was valued at $11,000.[39] It continued to turn out boards, shingles, and railway ties at a rate that made it in a few years one of the largest mills in the county.[40] By 1877 McCraney owned another sawmill at Bronte and the following year he sold the Oakville property to Pharis Doty.

A native of the United States and a boiler maker by trade, Pharis Doty had followed his brother John to Oakville and had worked in the foundry. In the sixties he became manager of the sawmill for Thompson Smith[41] who by that time had moved away to Toronto. In 1854 Pharis Doty had bought the land on the south-east corner of Colborne and Brant streets, where he built the roughcast house that stands today as no. 130 Colborne Street West. In 1882 the sawmill again burned to the ground, was rebuilt, and continued under Charles F. Doty, son of Pharis Doty. But timber was becoming scarce in the district and in 1901 C. F. Doty dismantled the machinery, sold it to Robert Fox of Omagh, and the mill was torn down.[42]

It is of interest to note that Thompson Smith had left Oakville in the sixties to take over the sawmill established at Toronto by Richard Tinning, whom we met early in this narrative. It was to his yards at the foot of Bay Street that quantities of timber and lumber cut at William Chisholm's sawmill on The Sixteen and other water mills in the district had been delivered during the 1830's. In 1846, at the foot of York Street, Tinning had set up the first steam sawmill at Toronto and, leasing a tract of land extending north from the bay along York Street to Front Street, he had erected several buildings, in one of which he lived until his death in 1858.[43] When Thompson Smith took over this property, it included Tinning's Wharf. Smith occupied the residence and located his office nearby on the Esplanade south of the Queen's Hotel.[44] Today railway tracks and the Union Station occupy the site of Smith's lumber yard; the Royal York Hotel stands upon the site of the old Queen's Hotel. Employing his talent for developing run-down concerns, Smith built this business into an important enterprise, taking over mills at greater distances as the lumber trade pushed farther north along Lake Huron. We have seen how he engaged a number of Oakville captains to command his vessels. Thompson Smith, who played such a leading part in establishing three of Oakville's industries, the sawmill, the tannery, and the planing mill, died at the age of seventy-six, far from home at Duncan City in the Straits of Mackinac.

After his removal to Toronto, Smith continued for some years as owner of the Oakville tannery. Located as it was in a district where the raising of cattle was steadily increasing, the tannery was almost certain to succeed. When it reopened after the shut-down in 1868, Joseph Milbourne seems to have had no further connection with the business. What the *Canadian Champion* refers to as "the extensive tannery owned by Thompson Smith"[45] was placed in charge of a manager, Charles S. Reid. In 1871 this concern, valued at $20,559, was employing eighteen men.[46] It was about this time that the suicide at the tannery of a young bookkeeper named William Roche created quite a sensation in the town. Roche had formed a romantic attachment for the beautiful daughter of the proprietor of the Canadian Hotel and, when she chose to marry another, he shot himself late one night. For years the spot in the tannery where he was found by the watchman was pointed out as a place of special interest.[47]

By the late seventies, when Christopher Armstrong took over the tannery, it had become one of the largest in the western section of the province. "Christy" Armstrong was a specialist in the processing of patent and "enameled" leathers. He had migrated to Canada from Dublin, Ireland, and after spending a few years in Montreal, had come to Oakville in the sixties to work for Joseph Milbourne.[48] The leather produced was used principally for carriage and buggy tops and for patent leather shoes. In the eighties the firm of Armstrong & Company was formed, with Stafford Marlatt and Captain Maurice Felan as principal stockholders.

Stafford Dean Marlatt was born at Grimsby of Loyalist parentage. His ancestor, Joseph Marlatt, was among the first settlers to obtain a grant of land in Trafalgar Township, drawing lot 1 of the 1st concession north of the Dundas Street. Joseph Marlatt, who died in 1813, lies buried on the farm which is still in the possession of his descendants. Stafford Marlatt was very proud of the fact that his family had supported William Lyon Mackenzie at the time of the Rebellion. Two of his uncles, Samuel Marlatt and David Ghent, were arrested, but the former was acquitted, and the latter released without trial.[49] Stafford claimed for himself the distinction of having driven Mackenzie in his waggon from Grimsby to Dundas upon his return to Canada after the royal pardon. He married into a Reform family, the Trillers. Phillip Triller and his seven daughters are said to have assisted Mackenzie. Hard pressed by the militia when he reached The Sixteen, so the story goes, Mackenzie was hidden in Triller's attic, and, while the soldiers were entertained with wine and smiles by the daughters, the fugitive was let down by means of a rope ladder on the opposite side of the house. Stafford Marlatt came into possession of a large part of the Triller farm on the lake shore west of Bronte, lots 1 and 2 of the 4th concession of Nelson Township to which Triller referred in his petition of 1808, quoted on page 180. After farming there for some years, Marlatt became a general merchant and grain buyer in Bronte, but when he bought an interest in the tannery, he purchased no. 82 William Street, Oakville, from John Barclay and called it "Ferndale." Barclay had occupied this house until after the death of his father-in-law, James Arnott, when he moved across to no. 81 William Street The house of Stafford Marlatt has gone through several stages of alteration since he lived there and now contains apartments.

The continuing deforestation of the land had caused considerable decrease in the flow of water in The Sixteen. By 1870 when Isaac Warcup bought the flouring mill from the Chisholm Brothers, he found that a new dam was necessary to keep the mill running This new dam of about one hundred and seventy feet in length was placed below the entrance to the tunnel running through the hog's back. The level of the impounded water was higher than the tunnel's entrance so that it ran directly into the tunnel from the mill pond. Warcup also remodelled the brick cottage facing the 6th Line on the hill above the mill into a larger residence by adding to it a second storey. The offices of the King Paving Company now occupy this house. Warcup was much interested in perpetual motion and was still at work on the solution of this problem when he died at an advanced age.

The Oakville Carriage Works of Jeremiah Hagaman on Navy Street and the Halton Carriage Works of James Fairfield seemed to do a good business. In 1869 Fairfield took into partnership William Whitaker; the vehicles they manufactured were "warranted free from rattling." At this time appears the name of the new firm of Harper and Helson whose advertising was headed by the graceful drawing reproduced on page 222. Under the name of the Excelsior Carriage Works, this manufactory occupied the brick building on the east side of Dundas Street north of Church Street, which in later times became the aluminum factory. The south section of this building would seem to have been erected about 1860 by Jacob Barnes, maker of well pumps and stumping machines, who was also proprietor of the Halton County Hotel across the way. Upon Barnes's death in the late sixties the building was secured by Harper and Helson who were "prepared to take orders for Buggies, Waggons, Express Waggons, Democrats, Sleighs and Cutters, etc."[50] But this manufactory survived only a short time, and in 1870 the plant was taken over by Robert B. Tait, the first cabinet-maker in Oakville to use steam-power for making furniture. His firm, the Oakville Steam Cabinet Factory, specialized in turning out overmantels and bar-room equipment elaborately ornamented with fretwork. In 1879 William H. Carson, builder and contractor, converted this factory into a planing mill, which he conducted for some thirty years. With bricks salvaged from the Romain Block fire, Carson enlarged the building to the north. At the same time, R. S. Wood's planing mill farther north on Dundas Street continued the manufacture of doors, sash, blinds, and "Superior" washing machines.

After James Reid moved to Manitoba, his building was purchased in 1868 by W. H. Young, cabinet-maker and undertaker, who was soon to find it a great financial burden.[51] In an old bill of Young's we find some expenses in connection with a funeral listed as follows:

To hearse and attendant	$6.50
To 4 pairs of gloves	.60
To grave opening	3.00
To loan of hat bands	.65
To taking burial case to cemetery	.25[52]

On his letterheads Young gave as his address "Union Arcade," a name difficult to explain. It so happens that one of the earliest photographs extant of shops on Colborne Street shows the section of the

Union Arcade which adjoined Young's building on the east.[53] Judging from the size of the trees and the names on signboards above the porches, this photograph, shown as plate 3, was taken about 1869. As the stores shown still stand as nos. 39 and 41 Colborne Street East, it warrants inspection. Notice should be taken of the nicely proportioned roof lines, a characteristic of early frame shops which in this instance has been obliterated by the recent addition of new fronts; of the sixteen large panes with which the show windows were glazed; and of the young trees in their boxings recently planted by the Town Corporation. Unhappily, the trim little St. Jude's Church no longer graces the north-west corner of Thomas Street. In 1878 Young remodelled his premises into two stores, leasing that on the east to W. G. Hewson who had recently become established as a general merchant.

Aaron Mathews, who occupied the shop on the east side of Young, was a native of England. Some years before he had become established in Oakville as general merchant and repairer of clocks and watches. It was he who kept in order the clocks in the Town Hall and schoolhouse.[54] Mathews taught his trade to young William Busby. In 1875, Mathews moved away to Cleveland, Ohio, where he went into the contracting business and laid many miles of cement sidewalks in that city. At Oakville William Busby continued the repairing of watches and clocks, in 1881 building his own store.

The shop next to St. Jude's Church was bought in 1870 by the watch and clock maker, Ezekiel Smith, son of Levi Smith, farmer on the Dundas Street in the township. During the Revolution the Smith family had fled from New Jersey to settle in Grimsby Township; and upon the opening of Trafalgar Township the brothers Isaac, Joseph, and Benjamin Smith drew land as settlers in the western section along the Dundas Street. As they became of age, the younger brothers Absolom and Levi followed, to settle nearby. All became strong Reformers; it was Absolom who sheltered Mackenzie late in the night after he had swum The Sixteen, and provided him with dry clothing. "Zeke" Smith's son Wilbert was also a watch and clock maker and carried on the business established by his father until his death in 1934. At a sale of his effects many interesting relics of former generations came to light, such as clocks with wooden works, strips of hand-loomed carpets which had gained his mother a local reputation, and a child's go-cart of the style used in the sixties or possibly earlier.

In 1868, as already recounted, the Ferrahs, "bakers and confectioners," bought the shop, now nos. 56 and 60, formerly owned by David Duff the cabinet-maker. On its west side they added a little bake shop which was set back some twenty feet from the street and had across its front a strip of lawn. In the huge brick bake ovens situated in the rear of the larger building, Robert Ferrah and his father John continued to bake the bread for which they had become famous and the wedding cakes which they undertook to supply "on the shortest notice."[55] The building retained its porch, so characteristic of an earlier period, for another quarter of a century, when it was removed during the course of alterations.[56]

Among Edward Hillmer's competitors in the butcher business were the three Morrisons, John, James, and Peter. These men were natives of Dunblane in Perthshire, Scotland, and they are reputed never to have relinquished their custom of wearing plaids. The Morrisons were large exporters of live cattle to Scotland. Tariff changes effected in the early seventies by the United States had seriously interfered with the export to that country of dead meat, and Canadian exporters had to look for another market. Shipping dead meat to England proved unsuccessful; and in 1874 an experiment was made by a firm in Glasgow of importing live cattle from Canada. During the first few years, improper handling caused great losses, many of the animals dying on the St. Lawrence even before reaching Montreal. On the ocean steamships they were pitifully overcrowded and, in many instances, sheep sheds were erected above the cattle stalls. Frequently during a storm the livestock was thrown overboard to lighten the vessels. Within a decade, however, improved transportation facilities reduced deaths on the ocean passage to under one per cent,[57] and, once established, the industry assumed enormous proportions. Every year the Morrisons bought two or three hundred head of cattle for shipping to Glasgow. The stock was kept on their farm east of Oakville, where Morrison Road now runs. Their butcher shop adjoined the Romain Block on the east and every July, when the farmers brought their stock to the Morrisons' shop to be weighed, the east end of Colborne Street near the bridge was filled with lowing and milling cattle. The Morrisons' shop was continued for many years by a relative, John McDonald.

Two business enterprises which had been established in Oakville in the middle thirties were at this time taken over by sons of the founders: Henry Gulledge's harness shop and John Urquhart's Medical Hall. After entering upon an apprenticeship with his father, Edmund H. Gulledge had put the finishing touches on his trade by working for a time in Jamestown, New York. In 1871, at the age of nineteen, he returned to Oakville and was accepted as partner by his father; six years later he bought out his father's interest in the business. Besides harness, the only article to which his father had given attention, E. H.

Gulledge sold ready-made boots and shoes and trunks.[58] The photograph (plate 30) shows Gulledge's shop, the old store of W. F. Romain, on the south-east corner of Colborne and Thomas streets. We find him announcing "Ladies boots bought at Gulledge's are always up to the highest temperature of style, fit and fashion and at the lowest zero prices."[59] Young John Urquhart had preferred the life of a sailor; and in 1860, at the age of sixteen, ran away from home to go on the lakes. But before John Urquhart senior died in 1867 ("a very large funeral—twenty-six teams," observed Sumner) he had had the satisfaction of knowing that young John had bowed to his parents' wishes and entered upon a medical career. His first instructor was Dr. John Rolph, a supporter of Mackenzie during the Rebellion. John Urquhart graduated with honours from the University of Toronto and returned to practise at Oakville for a time before going to Edinburgh for a postgraduate course. When he died at the age of ninety, in the house where he was born, Dr. John Urquhart was reputedly the oldest practising physician in the province. Urquhart's and Gulledge's were the oldest concerns in the town when, within a few years of each other, they were discontinued. The chemist's shop had done business for just onto a century, and the harness shop for 104 years. E. H. Gulledge lived to be ninety-six years of age.

Some conception of the cost of living in the sixties and seventies may be had from various account books and old bills of the Oakville merchants.[60] Comparison between the prices of the same commodities shows little fluctuation since the thirties, in some instances none. These prices continued substantially the same until the price slaughtering brought about by depression in the nineties. In 1861 P. A. MacDougald was selling a pound of butter or two dozen eggs for 15¢, the same price these commodities had brought in the thirties. For a half bushel of dried apples he asked $1.13, for a pound of feathers the same as in earlier times, 42¢, and for a nine-pound ham, 72¢, or 8¢ per pound. He sold a hank of bed cord for 25¢, half a dozen "wood cased pencils" for 4¢, a hoop skirt or a velvet trimmed hat for $1.25. A bill of Edward Hillmer's dated 1875 reads:

Beef steak—2½ lbs. @ 12½¢	.31¢
Turkeys—41 lbs. @ 10¢	4.10
Horse and buggy to Bronte	1.00
" " " " Milton	3.00
Team for five days	10.00[61]

About the same time James McDonald took in exchange for his carpentry work 13 pounds of pork at 12½¢ a pound, an advance of 2¢ over the thirties. A lake salmon "as long as your arm," says Williams, could be had for the same price as in earlier days, 25¢, and one "as long as your leg" for between 40¢ and 50¢. Two whitefish, each weighing 3 or 4 pounds, sold for a quarter. Charles Sovereign was provided with a dress coat for which he paid the tailor Thomas Patterson $9.50; a pair of trousers at $3.50 and a silk hat at $2.00 completed his outfit of Sunday best. Those manufacturers who dealt largely with farmers still resorted to barter. As late as 1883 Duncan Chisholm was advertising "farm produce, sheep skins, rags and old iron taken in exchange for iron, tinware and stoves"; and the makers of waggons continued to accept as payment such commodities as wool, beef, and bacon.

In 1871 the only newspaper published in Oakville bore a name which at this period was popular for newspapers all over the province, *The Argus*. This "weekly journal of Politics, News, Literature, and Miscellany," carried at its masthead the quotation, "Argus' head a hundred eyes possessed; and only two at once declined to rest; the others watched." In the offices of the *Argus*, which occupied the second floor of Duncan Chisholm's building, above his tin shop, four men were employed in putting out the weekly. The newspaper was bought in December, 1874, by Edward Bailey, formerly of the Toronto *Globe*, who promptly changed its name to the *Express and County of Halton Advertiser* and devoted much space to advancing the cause of the Clear Grits. As 1874 was election year, Bailey at once set to work on the Tories in the town.

The bitterly contested provincial elections of these years have been likened to a lacrosse match without a referee on the field. "Of course there was no bribery," recalled an old timer, "but when a man was offered $5 for a rooster and then taken down to vote, you were pretty sure how he would vote." The election of 1874 turned out to be one that was long remembered. Daniel Black Chisholm, brother of Duncan Chisholm and barrister of Hamilton, fought the election for the Conservatives against John White of Milton. Chisholm stood for temperance, adopting the slogan, "Save the boys from a drunkard's hell and a drunkard's grave." When news came by telegraph at 1 A.M. that he had been victorious, he was drawn about the town in a boat mounted upon wheels. The parade terminated at the Town Hall, where Chisholm made a speech to the large crowd that had assembled.[62] Two weeks later the victory was fittingly celebrated by a public dinner. On the day before, an ox bedecked with ribbons and streamers was carried through the streets on the shoulders of volunteer firemen. During the night the firemen roasted the ox over a fire built in the ruins of the buildings of Arnott and Barclay at Colborne and Thomas streets. The following day the Town Hall was thronged with people, who sat down to dinner at 1 P.M.; parcels of meat were dispatched to the homes of those unable to come to the hall.[63] The pleasant memories of this momentous occasion were in no way blighted by the unseating of Chisholm for irregularities in the voting. In the by-election that followed, when for the first time the secret ballot was used in the county, the electors returned to the vacant seat in the House of Commons the Grit candidate who also stood for temperance, William McCraney of Oakville.

Bailey, the editor of the *Express*, became so abusive of certain leading Tories that within the year public opinion was roused against him to the extent of burning him in effigy.[64] Nevertheless, Bailey insisted that he would "stick it out." He sold the *Express* but immediately founded the *Standard and Halton and Peel Gazetteer*[65] which carried at its masthead the determined motto, "Hew the Line, and let the Chips fall where they may." Energetically, Bailey set to his "hewing" and among those who were struck by the flying "chips" was that staunch Orangeman, Edward Hillmer. Not long after Bailey had referred to Hillmer as "English Ned" and "Boss of the Bull Pen," a lively odour permeated the offices of the *Standard*, which were located in the east end of the Romain Block over Moses McCraney's store. All work was suspended for several days after the dead skunk was removed from the chimney and as long as Bailey remained in Oakville the name of "cat skinner" clung to him.

These strong political animosities were directly responsible for the reorganization of the Masonic Lodge. In 1868 members of the Fraternity of Freemasons living in and near the town, who were members of lodges in Toronto, Hamilton, and Milton, had obtained the dispensation of the Grand Master to work a lodge in Oakville. Named in honour of Oakville's founder,[66] who had been a member of St. Andrew's Lodge No. 1 at Toronto,[67] White Oak Lodge No. 198 met on "Tuesday on or before full moon."[68] The first officers were George K. Chisholm, Worshipful Master; William Robertson, Senior Warden; John Kaitting, Junior Warden; R. K. Chisholm, secretary-treasurer; Dr. D. D. Wright, Senior Deacon; John Doty, Junior Deacon; James Kelley, Inside Guard, and Captain Peter Lyon, Tyler.[69] After meeting for a time in William Robertson's hardware store the lodge moved to rooms over John Barclay's store in the Romain Block until it was destroyed by fire. Because of the feeling of two members, one a Tory and the other a Grit, it became impossible to secure any new members as each blackballed the proposed names of those belonging to the opposite political party. It finally became necessary in 1882 to surrender the charter and apply for another which the following year was granted under the name of the Oakville Lodge.[70]

William McCraney who served several terms as Member for Halton in the Dominion Parliament was recognized as the leader of Oakville's Grits and W. H. Young as his second in command. After the death of G. K. Chisholm the Conservatives looked for leadership to Duncan Chisholm. On warm summer evenings Captain Duncan could usually be found in his favourite seat beneath the spreading maple which stood before the door of his shop.

Upon Captain Duncan's retirement the building at the south-west corner of Colborne and Dunn streets was acquired by James Kelley's son, Peter, who established a furniture store. The photograph (plate 31) shows it as it then looked. For about seventy years this building has continued as a furniture store, although the recent addition of a "modern" front has greatly altered its appearance. Its next-door neighbour on the west has been a hardware store for an even longer period. After its erection about 1855 by Captain William Wilson, this building was occupied for many years by the general merchant, John McCorkindale. Upon the removal of McCorkindale to Owen Sound in 1878, James Kelley established here a new hardware business[71] which was continued by his son John, and his son-in-law, James McGregor. Since McGregor's time, the business has passed through many hands; but photographs taken fifty years ago show the interior of the store to have been much the same as it is today.

Among the medical profession at this period were several newcomers, the only doctor whom we have already met being Dr. Edwy Ogden. Dr. Ogden was surgeon for the 20th Halton Battalion, and coroner for Oakville and the surrounding district. In earlier times when the office of coroner had been held by justices of the peace William Chisholm had acted as coroner for Oakville, but now medical men were being appointed. In 1875 Dr. Ogden went into partnership with Dr. James J. Johnston, recently assistant physician and surgeon at the New York Lunatic Asylum, but a few months later Dr. Ogden left his practice to the latter and removed to Chicago. At the time of writing Dr. Ogden's house, which remained almost exactly as when he occupied it a century ago, is being demolished. The basement apartment, where all outside walls were stone, consisting of some six rooms opening from a wide centre hall; the surgery lighted by wide french windows; the waiting room with its separate door opening on the north into the garden; the little half-storey bedrooms under the eaves on the upper floor; the large kitchen with its coal range and neither plumbing nor electricity—all remained unchanged to the end.

When making calls Dr. Ogden had frequently been accompanied by young Dr. J. S. W. Williams, who wished to gain experience. Justus Samuel Wright Williams, son of Justus W. Williams, was educated at the Oakville Common and Grammar schools and when he graduated in 1867 from Victoria Medical School returned to practise in his native town. After 1885 when a new law came into force whereby the appointment of Medical Health Officers was required, Dr. Williams occupied this post and that of coroner until his death. During the forty-six years that he practised medicine in the town, his horse and buggy were a familiar sight on the streets and country roads or standing in front of the house built by his father in the early thirties. In later years, Dr. Williams lived in the residence he built east of his birthplace on the south-west corner of Dundas and Colborne streets, which now stands as no. 4 Dundas Street South, having been moved away from Colborne Street not so many years ago.

Another graduate of Victoria Medical School to practise medicine in Oakville was Dr. Thomas J. Sutherland, a son of an early settler in Lambton County. Dr. Sutherland had entered upon his medical career at Creemore, not far from Barrie, in Simcoe County. Dr. Sutherland took up residence in Oakville in 1864, in the brick cottage that is now no. 18 Dundas Street North, the Gilbrea Dairy. He was much interested in traces left by the Indians, and is said to have collected a considerable number of artifacts. After practising for a quarter of a century in the town, Dr. Sutherland died of an illness following an accident.

The dentist, Dr. John Y. Dorland of the Bronte family, had begun his practice in the fifties at Palermo. When he moved to Oakville, he became established in the brick house on Navy Street where not long before Kenney and Howes had manufactured boots and shoes. It is one of the early structures in the town and was at one time the property of Thompson Smith, but nothing specific has been ascertained about its history prior to the 1850's.

Judging from the frequency with which the hotels in Oakville changed hands, it would seem that the business of being a hotel proprietor was more precarious than in former times. The same owners continually changed establishments: John Wray, Joseph and Isaac Boon, Arthur Goring, Thomas and William Walsh, and others. One newcomer, Duncan Olliphant, who sold his farm and in 1870 bought the Royal Exchange Hotel from Joseph Boon, was totally lacking in experience; "a hickory landlord," Sumner dubbed him. The veteran of them all, John Williams, made fewest changes and seemed to prefer the Oakville House to all others. After selling his Canadian Hotel on Navy Street in 1867, Williams had returned to the Oakville House where he remained for eleven years. When he retired in 1878, the owner of the adjacent livery stable, James Dogherty, took possession of the Oakville House. The career of the Halton County Hotel seems to have terminated with the death of its proprietor, Jacob Barnes, in 1868. After some years the building was moved by Hugh Coyne to the south-west corner of George and Colborne streets and remodelled into two stores. Henry Wilson, flour and feed dealer, occupied the east store and Mrs. Moulton, who was famous for her home-made taffy, occupied the west store. Today these are Regan's tobacco shop and the public library respectively. The Victoria House had William Walsh as its proprietor during most of the seventies, and the tavern across the way, conducted in the early days by Thomas Lloyd, was run by George Baker, livery stable owner and the town's first constable. After remodelling the building Baker claimed for his White Oak Hotel "all the modern conveniences second to none" and opened it in grand style on March 1, 1870, with a ball.[72] Some of the rooms were decorated with stuffed birds and animals, the handiwork of his brother, Henry J. Baker. The latter was the local taxidermist whom a newspaper editor distinguished as "one of the best bird stuffers in Ontario."[73] George Baker ran the White Oak Hotel until 1876, when he exchanged establishments with James Young and took over the old Post Inn on the Dundas Street at the 7th Line; there he remained until his death. At the White Oak Hotel, Young was succeeded by one of the Walsh brothers, its last proprietor.

There are indications that the Frontier House on Navy Street ended its career as a hotel and became a private dwelling about 1860. It was leased to various tenants by its owners, the Griggs family, until it became the property of R. S. Appelbe in 1870. Robert Swanton Appelbe, son of Squire Appelbe of Postville, was a solicitor who established himself at Oakville in the sixties, occupying the little house that is now no. 49 Dundas Street North. His wife was a daughter of Thomas Jaffray Robertson, Inspector of Irish Schools until his appointment in 1847 as the first headmaster of the new Normal School founded by Dr. Egerton Ryerson brought him to Toronto. A keen yachtsman, Robertson was one of the small group of men who in 1852 organized the club that two years later became the Royal Canadian Yacht Club. He was elected the first captain (later called commodore) of the club.[74] Upon his death in 1866, Mrs. Robertson made her home with the Appelbes, and forty years later she died on Navy Street at the age of ninety-three.[75] It is also of interest to note that R. S. Appelbe's sister was the wife of Sir Charles A. Hanson, Bart., Lord Mayor of London at the end of World War I. The Appelbe family lived at no. 51 Navy Street South for seventy years; in the not-too-distant past this large house was divided, half of it being moved farther east where it now stands as no. 42 King Street.

During the seventies the railway saw many improvements. Air brakes had been introduced and the average speed increased to seventeen miles per hour with a maximum speed of twenty miles per hour; bells were now used as well as whistles. Conductors who formerly had been indistinguishable from the passengers now wore uniforms. As coal became cheaper, the consumption of wood for fuel declined rapidly, particularly after 1875. By 1873 five trains running each way were stopping daily at Oakville.[76]

Three omnibus services were in operation between the Oakville station and the town in the early seventies: George Baker's, Dogherty's, which was the successor to Holden's, and George Lewis's. In 1871 shortly after Baker opened the White Oak Hotel, Chief Sumner noted in his diary, "George Baker had an oyster supper in honour of his new Omnibus." Three years later Edward Hillmer bought out Lewis, taking over his stable, horses, and bus. Before long, the following news item appeared in the local press: "We notice that Hillmer's 'bus has been undergoing a transformation at the hands of Mr. Whitaker, of Messrs. Fairfield & Co. It is a remarkably good specimen of carriage painting. The two medallion landscapes and the heavy scroll work are very well executed."[77] Six years later Hillmer also bought, for $900, Dogherty's livery stable which was located between the Oakville House and the store of W. H. Young.[78] Edward Hillmer and his family lived at the head of Navy Street on the site of the earliest shipyard on The Sixteen where the disposal plant is now located, and surrounding his house was a small farm with the usual orchard.

With the improvement during the seventies of conditions generally throughout the province, Oakville's circumstances seem to have brightened somewhat. Among the tradesmen were a few newcomers; E. Bethel, jeweller and watch repairer, moved to the town from Toronto, and Henry Wilson and William Joyce set up as general merchants. However, since the wages of clerks were set at $2 a week, there was little opportunity in Oakville for young men just starting out, and the exodus to other places continued.

The most accessible and certainly the most celebrated source of historical data on the town and district is the *Historical Atlas of Halton County* published in 1877 at Toronto by Walker and Miles. In glowing terms it pictures Oakville as a thriving community with the implication that the town was making satisfactory and unaltered progress. The truth of the matter was quite the reverse. In point of fact, the retrogression the town had experienced was a prime reason for the existence of the *Atlas*. It was one of a series of county atlases, and a form of advertising financed by the subscriptions of business firms and individuals who hoped by this means to entice more industry and capital to their particular locality. These publications should therefore be regarded with some degree of scepticism.

Any improvement in local conditions that occurred during the seventies did not last long, as the dark days of the eighties and nineties lay just ahead. It is readily admitted that there was a brighter side in this gloomy period of Oakville's history, for in the last decades of the century Oakville was becoming important as a resort and as the centre for the fruit growing industry. But before approaching the subject of those compensations which the summer season brought to Oakville, let us turn to the activities of the militia and to the troublesome time of the Fenian raids.

III

As was usual in time of peace, the militia of the province had virtually ceased to function. In this the colonies followed Britain, for it is proverbial that the English first engage in a war and then begin to prepare for it. Following the Rebellion merely a list of officers had been kept, and although the annual parade had continued, no one took the matter very seriously. At the time the Gore District was abolished the militia in the county was reorganized into Halton battalions. During the Crimean War when most of the Imperial regiments were withdrawn from Canada, a parliamentary committee reported the militia to be "the main source of defence of the Province, and its successful organization . . . a point of the highest importance."[79] At this time under a commission dated May 28, 1853, Captain George K. Chisholm was gazetted major in the 1st Battalion of Halton.[80] The Militia Act of 1855 authorized the enrolment of two classes of militia, Sedentary, which was still not to be trained, and Active or Volunteer companies, which were trained, paid, and equipped with weapons. On Lieutenant-Colonel Alexander Proudfoot's resignation, Major Chisholm was promoted, December 11, 1857, to the rank of lieutenant-colonel[81] and placed in command of the 1st Battalion of Halton in District no. 7 with headquarters at Oakville. Since it was only "partially organized" with twelve officers in 1857, no returns as to the number of men were made by this battalion to the government but the other five Halton battalions had each enlisted from four hundred and fifty to above six hundred men.[82] The Militia Act proved very successful; the full number of corps were organized and equipped, largely at their own expense, and under instructors from the regular service many attained a creditable degree of proficiency in troop and company drill. In 1859 provision was made for organizing, wherever practicable, volunteer rifle companies which at once proved very popular.

With the outbreak of civil war in the United States, the need for a well-trained militia became increasingly apparent. Late in 1861 the *Trent* affair caused relations with the United States to become strained. A British mail steamer, the *Trent*, was stopped on the high seas by a United States warship and two Confederate commissioners en route to England and France were taken off, an act which was in clear violation of international law. War was expected to break out and the newspapers appealed to the people to arm and to organize. Many new corps were formed, and the forces of the province increased from seven thousand to about thirty thousand within the space of a few weeks. Lieutenant-Colonel Chisholm, "an enthusiastic promoter of volunteer militia," at once organized the Oakville Rifle Volunteer Company with headquarters in the newly completed Market Building. Two rooms on the ground floor were used as an armoury, and drill was held every Friday.[83] As a result of these new duties Chisholm wrote to inform the Town Council that, having accepted command of the Oakville Rifle Volunteer Company and not having the time, aside from his own business, to devote to both offices, he tendered his resignation as mayor.[84] The council, however, replied: ". . . whereas this Council is fully sensible of the sacrifice of time the Mayor is compelled to make in attending to the various matters connected with the Town, and while he has so often been unanimously elected to the office of Mayor, and performed his duties of the office with satisfaction to the people and to the benefit of the Town . . . the Council feels it incumbent on them . . . to request him to withdraw his resignation."[85] Chisholm then wrote that he found that he had "overestimated the sacrifice of time which I would require to make to secure the Rifle Company a permanent organization in the Town" and begged leave to withdraw his resignation. "I shall, therefore, have great pleasure in resuming my seat at your Board."[86]

On January 20, 1862, the Rifle Volunteer Company was again the subject of discussion in the Town Council, when a resolution was moved by the mayor and seconded by John Barclay:

> That when the Empire of which it is our pride and privilege to form an integral part, is adopting the most energetic measures for the defence of our country, it behooves the people of Canada to show by their zealous co-operation, their estimate of the sacrifice Great Britain is now making in men and money to prepare for an emergency, which the present complicated state of affairs of the neighbouring Republic may force upon the British Empire, but more particularly in Canada, as an integral part thereof, and whereas the formation of a Rifle Company for this Town has been duly organized by the proper military authority, and is now in active course of organization and drill, reflecting equal credit on those who had joined such company, thereby expressing their determination to incur the expense, and qualify themselves for active duty when the exigencies of their country require such services, as well as upon the inhabitants of the Town generally, and it is therefore expedient that the inhabitants of the Town should be allowed to contribute towards the expenses of equipping the said company in just proportion to the value of the property possessed by them within the Corporation.
>
> Therefore, Resolved, That the sum of three hundred dollars ($300) be and is hereby appropriated from the general funds of the Town to aid in the clothing and equipment of the 1st. Oakville Rifle Volunteer Company.[87]

This resolution, however, made in the heat of patriotic enthusiasm and expressing such noble sentiments, was "postponed for further consideration" and when examined in the light of cold reality was eventually abandoned by the council.

In April the government of the province supplied the 75 rank and file of the Oakville Rifle Volunteer Company with "Enfield Rifles, Long, complete with Sets of Accoutrements" which were shortly followed by tunics, trousers, and shakoes of rifle (or hunter's) green.[88] Space on the ground floor of the Market Building was enclosed for an armoury and the volunteers were permitted to use the auditorium for three hours' drill two evenings a week.[89]

An event took place in October, 1863, which created so much interest that it was attended by a special reporter of the Hamilton *Spectator* who wrote:

PRESENTATION OF A SWORD TO COLONEL CHISHOLM

One of the most interesting events we have witnessed for a long time took place in the pretty little town of Oakville, on Thursday afternoon last. Some time ago, the officers, non-commissioned officers and men of the First Battalion of Volunteers, Halton, decided to present the Colonel with a suitable testimonial, in token of the high esteem in which they hold him, both as a man and an officer in the militia. The intention was to have presented it last Queen's birthday, but Col. Chisholm being absent in Europe, the event was necessarily postponed. In the meantime a sword was purchased, and on Thursday last, it was duly presented.

The Town Hall, a fine spacious building, and one of the best in the province, was the scene of great animation about five o'clock in the evening. A considerable number . . . of the principal ladies of the place, graced the scene, and lent an additional attraction to the interesting ceremony. . . .

The ceremony commenced by Captain Balmer stepping forward to the edge of the platform, and addressing Col. Chisholm in a few words, explaining the intentions of the donors of the sword.

After thanking the officers and men of the battalion for the "beautifully engrossed" address and the "magnificent present" of the sword, Chisholm complimented them for "filling up the required number of volunteers at the call of the Government, of which I feel proud, as your commanding officer. . . . As efficient preparation for defence is the best security against attack, I would urge all, but more especially young men, to qualify themselves for acting up to the spirit in which the volunteer movement originated throughout the British dominions—'Defence: Not Defiance.' " To the ladies "he desired to be permitted to say that he thought they could greatly encourage the volunteer movement by their influence. The elder ladies could influence their husbands and the younger ones could always ask the question of the intended—'Do you belong to a volunteer company?' "

In the evening upwards of fifty men from all parts of the county "sat down to a sumptuous dinner at the 'Canadian Hotel' prepared by the host, John Williams." The speeches in response to the many toasts, although highly complimentary to the guest of honour, are of little interest to this record, with one exception: Colonel Young of Georgetown referred to "the fratricidal war on the other side of the lines," and pointed to the fact that Canada's long frontier would have to be defended by volunteers. Canadians should not shut their eyes "to the fact that a large army existed in the United States, and that we might, perhaps be menaced by it. We must defend our institutions and defend them to the last."[90]

During 1864 the danger increased. Confederate soldiers who had escaped to Canada perpetrated outrages along the border and in a raid on St. Alban's, Vermont, banks were looted and an innocent bystander killed. The Canadian government formed three Provisional Battalions from the best of the volunteer companies and stationed them along the frontier. The Oakville Company, "formed from the best material Oakville and South Trafalgar could supply," was sent to Chatham. It was expected that the company, 61 rank and file, would be stationed there for some four or six months, but at the end of two months the men returned. Notwithstanding the unexpected arrival there was a large crowd at the station to greet them. "The gallant fellows," wrote a townsman to the Hamilton *Spectator*, "were escorted to the town by the people on foot and in vehicles, which made quite a procession, and the ladies had prepared a strawberry feast, with many other etceteras, to which the boys did ample justice." On the day the men were paid off Colonel Chisholm gave them a barrack-room dinner of which our anonymous scribe wrote: "The writer was one of the invited, and can testify both by sight and participation to the good and substantial food and the hearty, happy manner in which it was eaten. Of course the boards did not *shine* with damask table cloths; neither did they *groan* with the abundance of plate which we read of as decking out the tables of Apsley House when the Duke of Wellington celebrated the battle of Waterloo, but the dishes were white and clean, the meat good and well cooked, excellent bread and potatoes, and each allowance such that those who managed to get through with it had to make an effort. And the pudding—a regular John Bull—thickly spotted with fruit, and for sixty-one men!" In conversing with the men the writer found that although Chatham "has an agueish name" the men had gained on an average of from five to ten pounds in weight and that "the dinner that I enjoyed so much, was only a fair specimen of their dinners generally." Colonel Chisholm complimented the men for their good conduct "which deserved all praise during their time on duty," adding "that they did themselves the greatest credit and had reflected the high honours on him, that he should always be proud of them," and so on.[91] Elsewhere it was stated that "under Col. Chisholm's kindly but firm rule, they behaved themselves so well as to carry away the highest esteem of the people among whom they were quartered."[92] On the Queen's Birthday the ladies of Oakville and Trafalgar presented the Rifle Company with a fine flag, and so ended the first duty of the Oakville Rifles.

During the Civil War it was most convenient for Americans who wished to escape the draft to come to Canada and offer large bounties for substitutes to take their places in the army. According to the reminiscences of John A. Williams, a number of Oakville men offered themselves in this capacity, went across the border, and after being paid deserted from the army. They repeated this procedure several times in different states. Others fought through to the end of the war and a few were killed.

The Civil War came to an end in 1865, but for Canada there was still danger of invasion. With the cessation of hostilities in the United States, a large body of trained soldiers were thrown out of employment and many joined the Fenian Brotherhood. Deciding to turn to advantage the hostile attitude of most Americans toward Great Britain, the Fenians had launched a movement to free Ireland from the "British yoke." An Irish Republic was set up in the United States, but being only on paper it was a republic without territory. The Fenians assumed that as soon as they set foot upon the soil of Canada, the opportunity to rise against their British governors would be welcomed by Canadians. A song that was popular at the time clearly sets forth their sentiments:

> We are a Fenian Brotherhood, skilled in the arts of war,
> And we're going to fight for Ireland, the land that we adore,
> Many battles we have won, along with the boys in blue,
> And we'll go and capture Canada, for we've nothing else to do.[93]

The cause had many sympathizers among the Irish in the province. In Oakville there was a strong feeling in favour of the Fenians, particularly among some half dozen prominent Irishmen, and an uprising in the town was fully expected. It was even suspected that if the invaders reached this section of the country many of the militia would join them. One old-timer claimed that a brass cannon was seized from Fenian sympathizers, and thrown into The Sixteen beside the foundry where, in all probability, it still lies today. Various precautionary measures were taken. William Ward,* who had arrived in Oakville

*In his reminiscences John A. Williams tells us that Ward was descended from a long line of British ribbon designers. When thrown out of employment because plain ribbons became the fashion, Ward had migrated to Canada. His son, Richard, was chosen from among all telegraph operators in Canada to precede Edward, Prince of Wales, and to send despatches which regulated the railway trains upon which he travelled on his visit to Canada in 1860.

shortly before, was installed in the Market Building as caretaker and guard of the armoury. Target practice was held in the field west of Brant Street between Colborne Street and the lake where the hill that rises beside the stream that runs there afforded passersby protection from bullets. On the old McCraney farm on the 4th Line between McCraney's School (later named Pine Grove School) and the railway, earthworks may be seen today which are said to have been thrown up by the militia at this time.

In the spring of 1866 when it was expected that the hosts of Fenians, who for weeks had been assembling upon the Niagara frontier, might come across the lake, the Halton battalions were stationed as a home guard along the lake shore almost to Port Credit. On June 1 the Fenians seized Fort Erie, but the Battle of Ridgeway had been fought and won by the Canadian militia before the Oakville company was mobilized. It was not until June 3 that Lieutenant-Colonel Chisholm and 52 rank and file, whose names are listed in appendix G, arrived at Fort Erie, too late to participate in the fighting. For some weeks they remained on the Niagara frontier to guard against further raids. During the return from Fort Erie, the train on which Chisholm was a passenger came near to being wrecked by an obstruction which had been placed upon the railway track. However, the obstruction was seen as the train slowed down to cross the bridge across The Sixteen and was removed before any damage was caused. Government detectives were put on the case but the culprits were never discovered.

On their return from active duty the eight companies from Halton were organized in September, 1866, as the 20th Halton Battalion of Infantry under the command of Lieutenant-Colonel Chisholm, and it was then that the regimental band was formed. As we have already seen from the news item quoted on page 234, as early as 1851 a substantial sum, realized from the soirée held by the Sons of Temperance, had been used to provide instruments for a town band. There had also been other attempts to organize a band in Oakville but none, as far as is known, was successful, until R. B. Albertson took hold. Albertson had served with the Oakville Rifles at Chatham and Fort Erie where he showed the ability that made him sergeant-major at the age of eighteen. Upon returning from active service he assembled a small group of men which he trained as a band. The day after Christmas, 1866, a ball was held in the Town Hall by volunteers of the Oakville Company in aid of the Band Fund of the battalion. It was attended by one hundred couples.[94] The first performance of the militia band took place at the launching of the *White Oak* on the first Dominion

Day, July 1, 1867. The following year the players succeeded in securing white coats and Glengarries as uniforms. The regimental band of the 20th Halton Battalion lost its leader when Albertson joined the Red River expedition as sergeant of a field band, but two years later he returned to Oakville and to his musical duties there.

The 20th Halton Battalion was brought together for the first time when the companies assembled at Oakville in the spring of 1868 for eight days of training. John Williams' Oakville House was officers' mess and the men were billeted in the Market Building, messing at various hotels in the town. As every company was close to full strength, fifty-five men and N.C.O.'s, nearly five hundred men assembled. Wrote a correspondent to the *Canadian Champion*: "Oakville presented an unusually lively appearance . . . all week it has been 'Tramp, tramp the boys are marching' until the poor fellows were too tired to play wild-cat at night."[95] One of the daily operations was outstandingly successful. Directed by an officer perched high in a tree, the troops deployed, and surrounded and captured a number of "Fenians" which local residents stridently claimed were their laying hens. On Dominion Day, Colonel Durie, Deputy Adjutant-General, accompanied by Colonels R. B. Denison and H. Villiers, held a review. There was no regimental band, as Albertson was absent, and a bugler of the Milton Company led a fife and drum band in which tin whistles substituted for fifes. Colonel Durie was quite profuse in his compliments.[96] Every man looked "every inch a soldier, the march past was excellent." The week ended with a sham battle and a strawberry festival.

The men of the Halton Regiment took a keen interest in fine marksmanship and during this training period it was decided to make the regiment a rifle corps. Part of the expense was voted by the men from their pay.[97]

In 1870 there was great excitement for several weeks when another raid was expected by the Irish-American Fenians but it failed to materialize. In December of that year Colonel Chisholm retired and when the 20th Halton Battalion returned to Oakville for two weeks' training Lieutenant-Colonel John Murray was in command.[98] Again the officers messed at the Oakville House but the men were provided with tents. This was the last camp at Oakville (much to the relief of Chief Sumner who considered the whole proceeding "a lot of nonsense"), as the following spring the militia began training at Niagara-on-the-Lake.[99]

As the Fenian ghost had been finally laid, the council decided that a caretaker was no longer needed in the Town Hall and decreed that

Ward should vacate it. But Ward, having free heat and light together with a substantial income from services rendered at public gatherings, liked his situation and was not easily evicted. The council then agreed that the one responsible for the heating, cleaning, and general maintenance of the Town Hall should also be in attendance at public functions and "that the Chief Constable should occupy such position."[100]

Periodically the council made modest grants to the militia band for playing on special occasions such as the Queen's Birthday. During the summer of 1874 the townspeople were invited by W. F. Romain to attend band concerts on his lawn and P. A. MacDougald, the mayor, followed suit. In 1860 MacDougald had bought the house that today is no. 57 Thomas Street and which he called "Glenorchy." Several times on warm summer evenings the band played on the roof of Duncan Chisholm's store.[101] MacDougald and seventy-six ratepayers petitioned the council "to pass a by-law to make provisions for the purpose of sustaining a band in this town" but when it was found that it would require an immediate outlay of $300 for instruments and $200 a year for a leader, the idea was abandoned. A compromise was reached by granting to the militia band $100 "on condition . . . that they shall play on the Queen's Birthday, Dominion Day and once each week from the 2nd week in June to the 3rd week in Sept., inclusive; the place and number of airs to be decided by the mayor."[102] In 1879 the council renovated a room in the upper storey of the Lock-up for band practice.[103]

The band was in attendance on September 27, 1879, when the 20th Halton Battalion, together with a large number of other militia regiments, was reviewed by the Marquis of Lorne. The band seems to have continued to be associated with the militia until the formation in 1881 of a pipe band by the Halton Battalion, and the brass band then became a citizens' band. A fund was set up into which all members paid a small amount and this was drawn upon to pay the leader. Each player provided his own instrument and money paid to the band for playing on special occasions went into the general fund. It was about this time that Captain Albertson moved to Manitoba and Thomas Howarth took his place as leader of the Oakville Citizens' Band, the name it bears today.

Lieutenant-Colonel William Allan succeeded Lieutenant-Colonel Murray as officer in command of the 20th Halton Battalion in 1881. A Scotsman who had come to Canada with the Argyle and Sutherland Highlanders at the time of the Rebellion, Colonel Allan promptly applied for and received permission to designate his corps as "20th

Halton Battalion, Lorne Rifles."[104] The wearing of tartan trews of Campbell plaid and the diced Glengarry was also authorized, and it was at this time that the pipe band was formed. Thus it was that the Halton Rifles established the Scottish connection which led to its designation in 1931 as "The Lorne Rifles (Scottish)." In the general reorganization in 1936 of all militia units in Canada this regiment was amalgamated with the Peel and Dufferin Regiment and is now designated as The Lorne Scots (Peel, Dufferin and Halton Regiment) which takes great pride in upholding the tradition of fine marksmanship. In the officers' mess a place of honour is given to the likenesses of two early officers who served in the regiment when it was the Gore Militia, Colonel George Chisholm and his brother, Colonel William Chisholm of Oakville, whose immediate forebears roamed Highland glens not far to the north of the Firth of Lorne.

CHAPTER ELEVEN

"BEAUTIFUL OAKVILLE"

BY 1870 Oakville's reputation as a fine summer resort was proving a welcome compensation for the decline in water-borne commerce. "There is not as much activity as formerly in the shipping interest," wrote the editor of the *Canadian Champion* in 1869, "but the presence of the lake adds much to the salubrity of a summer residence at Oakville—indeed we know of no more beautiful or convenient place for the jaded citizens of Toronto or Hamilton, and we have no doubt that yearly more advantage will be taken of its vicinity to those cities."[1] In fact Oakville was soon being called the "Saratoga of Ontario";[2] Saratoga Springs, New York, had long been fashionable amongst the wealthier people of Toronto. Oakville was yearly becoming "more noted for its beauty and picturesqueness," according to our reliable standby, the *Champion*, and during July and August the hotels, of which the Canadian Hotel was the favourite, were usually full. "But such is the rush in Summer that it could be filled twice over if all applications were satisfied."[3] Accommodation could also be had in a number of boarding houses, and many townspeople took summer visitors. In 1877 the *Atlas* stated that some families came from as far away as Texas to spend the summer months at Oakville, and went so far as to predict that "it is highly probable . . . that [Oakville] will grow to be the great summer resort of Canada."[4] But that was before the opening of northern Ontario.

Mrs. Thomas Walsh ran a boarding house which was perhaps the best known of all. In 1883 the Walshes bought the house on the Lake

Shore Road West which had been built by the Reverend George Washington and enlarged by the addition of a mansard roof when it had belonged to Captain Hugh Pullen. The Walshes named their establishment "Rosedale Villa," and every summer it was full to capacity. After the turn of the century Mrs. Walsh and her daughter moved to the house on the south-west corner of Brant and Colborne streets built in the fifties by Pharis Doty. Altogether the Walshes' boarding house was in operation about half a century, many of the same boarders returning year after year.

The prediction made in the early fifties by Judge Beardsley, that one day this area would attract permanent summer residents, came true during the first decade of the twentieth century. Many acres of farm land bordering Lake Ontario were transformed into large estates with sweeping driveways leading to luxurious residences surrounded by broad lawns and landscaped gardens. These estates followed one upon another in close succession until Oakville was being referred to as the "Canadian Newport."

However, by far the greatest number of visitors came by steamer to spend the day. As the mercantile traffic on Lake Ontario declined the pleasure traffic increased. By the 1860's excursionists were coming to Oakville in droves. In the eighties sometimes three or four excursions, a total of from one to three thousand people, arrived in one day.[5] The steamers began these trips in the early spring. During the summer months of 1867 and 1868 the *Rothesay Castle* alone transported one or more excursions almost every day of the week.[6] She had been built in Scotland to be a blockade runner, and after the Civil War she was brought to Canada and used as a lake steamer. Her first appearance at Hamilton in August, 1866, occasioned the *Spectator* to comment on her strange appearance. "She is a Clyde built iron vessel, 197 feet long and only 19 feet wide, her hold is 8½ feet. She is well adapted for the trade she has recently been engaged in—blockade running—being fitted with two powerful oscillating engines, and will run easily 20 miles an hour."[7] A news item of June 3, 1869, describes one of the excursions she brought to Oakville:

> The jubilee of Her Majesty was celebrated in Oakville with the usual demonstration of loyalty, that has so long characterized our noble Town. The foremost among them being a Temperance excursion from Toronto on board the splendid fast sailing steamer *Rothesay Castle*. She arrived... about 12:30 bringing about five hundred Good Templars I.O. of G.T. They were met on the wharf by the Royal Oak Temple, no. 216 of Oakville, numbering over one hundred. . . . It was a splendid sight to see a procession of over six hundred persons, composed almost entirely of young people, who had all declared against the use of intoxicating drinks. . . .

After landing the Toronto Templars were conducted by those of Oakville, to a beautiful grove to the east of the town [Beardsley's Grove], which had been previously fitted up with swings and other amusements, to spend the day. The usual games of running, leaping &c. were indulged in and prizes provided by the town. A competitive game of baseball was played between the Oakville and Toronto clubs, the former winning by 48 to 20.[8]

The *Rothesay Castle* was burned in 1874. After being rebuilt she continued until the nineties, under the name of the *Southern Belle,*[9] to make Oakville a port of call.

In 1876, the year Queen Victoria was proclaimed Empress of India, a 180-foot side-wheeler was launched and christened the *Empress of India.* That same year the *Empress* began bringing daytime excursions to Oakville for a fare of 50¢ per person.[10] A photograph of the harbour taken in the early eighties and reproduced as plate 46 shows her moored alongside the east pier. The *Empress* was later rebuilt and renamed the *Argyle,* and she continued to frequent the Oakville harbour.

Because it was accessible to the harbour, the natural grove of pines known as Chisholm's Grove overlooking the lake on the west bank was a favourite place for picnickers. But R. K. Chisholm sold the property to Shubel Lewis, his father-in-law, who built a house there, and the picnickers were deprived of the only shady spot near the harbour. If excursion boats were to continue to choose Oakville as their objective, some provision would have to be made for the entertainment of their passengers, and the Town Council turned its attention to the matter.

After the rebuff received in 1857 from Colonel George K. Chisholm the council had dropped the matter of having George's Square deeded to the Town Corporation. Sixteen years later Chisholm was again approached and agreed to convey the block to the town. The indenture, dated April 14, 1873, read in part:

Whereas the late Colonel William Chisholm, being then the owner of the land hereinafter conveyed, and the land whereon the town of Oakville is now situated, and being desirous of setting apart a plot of ground for a public free park for the use of the citizens of the said town for purposes of recreation; and having on the map of the said town drawn for the said William Chisholm, caused the said land hereinafter conveyed to be designated as those he intended for such purpose, calling the same "George's Square," by which name said lands have ever since been known.

And whereas the said William Chisholm died without having in any way further given effect to his said desire.

And whereas the party of the first part, son of the said late Colonel William Chisholm, being now the owner of the said land, desiring to

> carry into effect the said wishes of said father, and in order that a public park may be opened thereon for the free use of the citizens of said town, hath agreed . . . to convey the said land . . . for the nominal sum of one dollar to hold forever upon condition that the said parties . . . shall accept and use the same as a free park, under the name of George's Square, and shall within one year from the date hereof fence in the said land, and as soon as possible thereafter construct suitable walks, and grass plots therein, and plant the same suitably with shade trees, and same so fenced, planted and sodded forever after maintain as a free Public Park in reasonable order and condition. . . .[11]

On motion of W. F. Romain the Standing Committee on George's Square and Ornamental Trees was formed and plans were made to "establish a public Park and Pleasure Grounds in the Town of Oakville."[12] The grass was cut, additional trees were planted, and a well was sunk and equipped with an iron pump. The park was surrounded by a picket fence with turnstiles on each of the four sides to exclude four-footed free commoners. Here the town's baseball team, the White Oaks, was soon playing games with Toronto baseball clubs.

Not long after the municipality took over the harbour, the council agreed that it was "desirable that the town should become possessed of that portion of vacant land known as the bank for a public pleasure ground."[13] This was where cordwood had formerly been piled, but by the late seventies steamers were using coal for fuel. Accordingly the owner, R. K. Chisholm, was approached and an agreement reached whereby Chisholm would convey this property to the Corporation in return for the permanent closing of that section of Water Street which ran along the foot of his property from the harbour to King Street; included also in the property acquired by Chisholm was that section of Front Street lying between Navy Street and The Sixteen which the council, back in 1859, had agreed to let Chisholm have the use of "until the same may be required by the town."[14] As originally laid out, Front Street connected with Water Street which lay close along the edge of The Sixteen. Since it led directly from the east pier to the warehouses on the river, Water Street was continually in use during the days when there was great activity in the harbour, but by the seventies it had fallen into disuse. The exchange effected at this time benefited both the parties concerned. Chisholm was enabled to extend his property from the point where Navy Street reaches the harbour to King Street, and the town acquired the lake bank between Navy and Thomas streets for the use of the townspeople.

At once Captain Albertson, leader of the band, applied for permission to build a band stand on the lake bank, but nineteen years passed before the council improved the new park. At the extreme west end of the bank a pole was erected for storm warnings. This pole, with a little house at its foot in which black storm drums of varying shapes were stored, cost the taxpayers $35.50.[15] Chief Sumner was appointed "storm agent" by the government at a salary of $25 a year. The meteorological service, established a few years previously, was expanded at this time to include in its activities daily bulletins of weather probabilities for twenty-four hours ahead. The station at Oakville reported several times a day by telegraph, but since Oakville was so near Toronto its report was found to be of little value, and was soon discontinued.[16] However, Sumner continued to be notified by telegraph when storms were expected, and what drum to hoist. Every spring before the opening of navigation he reeved the halyards on the storm signal and unrove them again upon the arrival of winter. Eventually the storm signal ceased to be used and when it blew down some sixty years later it was not replaced.

A spell of calm cold weather in 1881 caused a thick sheet of ice to form on the lake as far as one could see. On a Saturday afternoon early in February a party of fifteen skaters started from Oakville and went fully fifteen miles across the lake. Before turning back they could plainly see Port Dalhousie on the south shore. For the greater part of the way, they stated, the ice was fully six inches thick, something that the oldest inhabitant could not recall as ever having happened before. During the four days that the ice lasted large crowds assembled to skate on the lake in the moonlight. At Bronte a team of horses harnessed to Morrison & McDonald's meat wagon ran away for a mile on the lake before sensing danger and turning home.[17]

For many years trotting races on the ice, which had long been a popular sport in all parts of the province, were held at Oakville. A mile track was laid out on The Sixteen between the Colborne Street bridge and the mill, and some twenty to thirty horses harnessed to racing cutters competed for the purses awarded to the winners. On several occasions during the two-day meet the thermometer dropped to eight and even fifteen degrees below zero, but the crowd of spectators lining the banks of The Sixteen was not deterred by the cold.[18] The first mention of these races appears in Sumner's diary in 1870. "Had a trotting match in Town to-day. Quite a number of people, and of course had to have a number of fights to make things come out square." Trotting races on the ice are mentioned for the last time in 1902.

Since the deeding of the harbour to the Town Corporation, the council had made heavy expenditures for maintenance. Up to 1886 over $10,000 had been spent, a sum which tolls were insufficient to meet,[19] and that spring worse disaster overtook the harbour.

To those who witnessed the spectacular storm from the north-east, April 8, 1886, was a day long to be remembered. The storm had been in progress for two days when Sumner wrote, "the water is the highest I have ever seen it." Some claimed the waves were thirty feet high. The old timbers in the east pier which had been patched and reinforced for over fifty years gave way, and once breached at the inner end, the pier disintegrated rapidly. During the school lunch hour many children came down to the lake bank in time to see the lighthouse, built in 1837-8, suddenly tumble over into the channel. When the wind abated the pier had disappeared completely and Sumner set red buoys to mark the position of submerged cribs. The harbour was filled with gravel and floating debris and Sumner spent several days salvaging timber from the lake. A temporary scaffolding, erected so that the *Southern Belle* could take aboard and deliver passengers, lasted only a few weeks and thereafter for the entire season all steamer service was suspended.

A special meeting called by the council "to consider what steps should be taken in reference to the Harbour which has been almost totally destroyed by the recent storm" decided upon sending a deputation to Ottawa.[20] It would seem that the deputation succeeded in securing a grant from the government,[21] as the cost of rebuilding the harbour was estimated at $20,000, of which half was raised by debentures. The work, begun the following spring, continued through the entire season until the close of navigation. The new east pier was constructed in the same manner as the original pier, by building the cribs on The Sixteen above the curve and floating them down to the harbour. The new pier was the same length as the first, but as the cribs were sunk inside the old ones, the channel was narrowed by about fifty feet. However, nothing was done about replacing the lighthouse.

At this time the Hamilton Steamboat Company was organized for passenger service between the "Queen City" and the "Ambitious City." The first steamer acquired by the company was the three year old *Mazeppa*, built at Toronto by Oakville's former shipbuilder, Melancthon Simpson.[22] In 1888 the company ordered a steel steamer to be built in England. This vessel sailed the Atlantic to Lake Ontario and was christened *Macassa*, the Indian name of the bay upon which Hamilton is situated; the original English name, Lake Geneva, had been changed by proclamation in 1792 to Burlington Bay.[23] Captain William Zealand, kin to Captain Edward Zealand with whom we have met earlier in this history, was put in command of the steamer *Macassa*.[24] She proved so successful that a larger steamer was brought from England and named *Mojeska*, in honour of the Polish tragedienne the inflections of whose voice when reciting merely the alphabet are reputed to have wrung tears from her audience. For about two years the steamer *Mojeska* called twice daily at Oakville.

When the vessels of the Hamilton Steamboat Company began entering the harbour regularly it became necessary to replace the light. During the summer of 1889 a new lighthouse was built by Henry George, contractor for Port Elgin, at a cost of $960. Construction was begun on April 2, and the new lighthouse was lit for the first time with its improved light on June 4.[25] It stands on the same site today. Another improvement, designed to facilitate the loading and unloading of freight, was the laying along the pier of a small track upon which ran a little trolley.[26]

For some years the vessels of the Hamilton Steamboat Company gave Oakville regular service. After 1888 when the residence of Shubel Lewis on the west bank was reduced to ashes the excursionists and picnickers returned once more to the pine grove, which then became known as Lewis Grove. Allan Kemp, who had opened a boat livery on the inner end of the east pier, ran a ferry across the channel so that excursionists could reach Lewis Grove across the harbour.

Further disaster to the harbour occurred in the spring of 1896. When the ice went out on April 2, a freshet caused the mill dam to break about midnight, and this raised the level of the water north of the Colborne Street bridge more than ten feet. The ice began to break up about three o'clock in the morning, and spectators who lined the bridge were much interested in the assortment of hayricks, pumpkins, huge logs, and a bridge which appeared around the curve in the river. According to the local press, the bridge was identified as having come from the Base Line, and being "well bolted, proved a sturdy sailor." The stone hooker *Lillian* broke from her moorings and was swept into the *White Oak,* causing much damage to the schooner. Before she was carried out into the lake the *Lillian*'s main mast was broken. She was later retrieved from the lake. The stone hooker *Rover* also broke loose, and the Toronto Ferry Company's little *Louella* was "stove in" and filled with water and sank. When the flood subsided the *Louella* and *Rover* lay on their sides on the bank of The Sixteen. Of the two old hulks that sank near the stone warehouse, both of which had passed their days of usefulness, one was later raised. It is probable that the timbers of an old wreck lifted out of the river near the Oakville Club

III. The Lighthouse, 1947

during dredging operations in 1934 were those of the other hulk sunk at this time. They were the subject of much speculation among old-timers before being taken out and deposited in the waters of the lake.

For days the marsh was covered to the height of eight feet with huge cakes of ice.[27] The inner end of the pier was destroyed, and the channel filled with gravel so that again it was impossible for ships to enter or leave the harbour until the channel was dredged. Repairs were made at a cost of $7,500,[28] and a new pavilion, to serve as ticket office and freight shed, was built on the new section of pier at the north end, as it had been found that the former pavilion was too much exposed to the weather.

At long last the Town Council made plans for improving the lake bank on the east side of the harbour. In the spring of 1896, Edgar Bray, engineer and surveyor, was employed to lay it out. Gullies were filled in, knolls removed, the road levelled, and the bank graded down to the beach.[29] After trees were planted and grass seed sown, the new park, named Lakeside Park, looked "twice as large again," according to the local press. When we read that at that time "Lakeside Park comprises some three acres of exceptional beauty stretching along the lake front close to the harbour" we are struck by the changes wrought during the past fifty years. The water of the lake has washed away the wide stony beach and the gently sloping bank by which it was approached, so that now only a fraction of the original Lakeside Park remains. The recent closing of the street, and the addition of the street allowance and the land to the north of it between Navy and Thomas streets, have greatly improved it, but there is little resemblance between the present park and Lakeside Park as it was laid out.

The officials of the Hamilton Steamboat Company who examined the depth of the water in the spring of 1898 were unwilling to risk their large vessels entering the harbour.[30] Arrangements were then made for the double-decked steamer *Greyhound*, built in 1887 by Melancthon Simpson, to call at Oakville. As it turned out this service proved most unsatisfactory; passengers and fruit growers, who waited at the dock for a steamer that frequently failed to appear, became disgusted and resorted to the railway.[31] When it became plain in the spring of 1899 that Oakville would be without regular steamer service, some business men got together and formed the Oakville Navigation Company. Within ten days over $25,000 was subscribed by local men, the majority of them fruit growers. The directors of the company were Allan S. Chisholm, T. C. Hagaman, George Andrew, John McDonald, and W. H. Speers. Hedley Shaw was made president. The company lost no time in purchasing the *White Star,* a steel ship of shallow draught built at Montreal in 1897 for service on the St. Lawrence River. Licensed to carry seven hundred passengers, the *White Star* was "beautifully fitted up, lighted by electricity, steady and comfortable, a first class steamer for the Oakville, Toronto and Lorne Park route."[32] But Chief Sumner, who as Harbour Master and agent for the steamship companies was well acquainted with the situation, wrote, "I hope it will pay the company, but I am afraid of it." For a time it seemed that his fears were justified. The following year the *White Star,* under command of Captain William Boyd, and with W. S. Davis as purser, was chartered for a goodly sum by the Pan American Excursion Company of Buffalo, and the smaller old side-wheeler *Richelieu* was substituted on the Oakville run. But this was the cause of such loud complaints that the next year, with due apologies from the Oakville Navigation Company, the *White Star* was back on her former route and W. S. Davis was made general manager, secretary, and treasurer of the company.

Being of shallow draught the *White Star* could follow closely along the shoreline, and for this reason she became "the most popular excursion boat at Toronto." The large number of church picnics she carried earned her the name of the "Sunday School Boat." As the owner of the pine grove on the west bank was one of the company's directors, this property continued to be used as a picnic ground and was given the name of Harbour Grove. A pavilion was built, a refreshment booth was equipped, swings were set up, and provision was made for ping-pong, tennis, baseball and "every convenience for a day's outing."[33]

In 1903 several cribs were built to form an L at the end of the east pier so that the steamer could land her passengers without entering the harbour. John Potter, then ninety-two years of age, who had helped build the original pier seventy-odd years before, kept a close eye on the work.[34] During this time the *White Star* was undergoing repairs at Toronto and was about to return to service when she caught fire early on the morning of July 11 and burned to the water's edge. A number of persons asleep on board just managed to escape with their lives and a superstitious seaman pointed out that by moving out into the bay with thirteen aboard disaster had been invited. Although she was valued at $40,000 the *White Star* was insured only for the amount of the original subscription, $25,000.[35]

This was the final attempt at regular steamer service at Oakville. Thereafter the fruit growers used the railway and the townspeople were obliged to watch the *Macassa* and *Mojeska* pass at some distance out in the lake. As they reached the half-way point opposite the town they gave the usual friendly salute, the former in her shrill treble and the latter in the low-pitched voice more suitable to the tragedienne whose name she bore. Harbour Grove declined, the owner closed it to the public, and moving the pavilion closer to the lake, rebuilt it into a summer cottage. Soon other cottages appeared to the west and a steam plant in connection with the tannery was built at the foot of the hill on the harbour. For many years the last reminders of the excursion era were the tall pines, but now even those are gone. The encroachment of the tannery on the north, and erosion caused by the water of Lake Ontario on the south, hastened the natural ravages of time. Whatever trees escaped these hazards were uprooted lately, and a large part of the high bank has been removed by modern construction machinery. There is little now to suggest that not long ago there was a pine grove, one of the last natural beauty spots left in the town.

II

The success of fruit growing, which became so important an industry in and around Oakville, is another instance of the importance of environment. In this case the special advantages drawn from environment were geological, the type and quality of the soil. The sand which is so prevalent around Oakville may have originated in an offshore apron or sand bar in Lake Iroquois, the predecessor of Lake Ontario. As read by geologists the story written on the face of The Sixteen's banks is somewhat as follows.

Overlying the bedrock of Precambrian origin, the same rock which forms the Canadian Shield, are deposits laid down by the sea when it spread over the land. In the lower reaches of The Sixteen, where these limestones and grey shales lie exposed close to water level, are found fossils of some of the earliest marine plants and animals. Over a long span of geological time the land rose and the sea receded to a shoreline which seems to have stood somewhere in the neighbourhood of Oakville. The land was then drained by rivers which deposited their loads of sediment in deltas along the shore of the sea. Again the sea crept out of its basin and invaded the land. The deltaic muds were compacted into layers of the red shale which forms the banks of The Sixteen. Over eons of time this inundation of the sea laid down further layers of grey shale and limestone fashioned of shells and billions upon billions of minute sea creatures. With the rising of the land the sea again withdrew, exposing the later rock formation to weathering and erosion. Though they have mostly disappeared, these upper layers of marine limestone and grey shale are still visible on the Niagara escarpment some miles inland and west of Oakville. Near the centre of Halton County stands an outrider of the escarpment which is known as Milton Mountain.

The next geological event was the advance of the glaciers. Of the ice sheets which moved to and fro over Ontario only the last seems to have covered the Oakville area, leaving deposits of boulder clay. As the climate became milder the front of this ice sheet retreated to the east, blocking the St. Lawrence Valley. The floods of water released from the melting glacier formed a lake known to geologists as Lake Iroquois. Having no outlet, this lake was forced to rise to a level high enough to escape through the valleys of the Mohawk and Hudson rivers. The gravelly ridge beyond Oakville's northern boundary, where ran the Old Road to York, was once the shoreline of Lake Iroquois.

The eventual retreat of the ice from the St. Lawrence Valley allowed the waters to escape through this lower outlet and gradually the lake receded from its higher and broader proportions to take the form we know as lake Ontario. Thus the land on which Oakville stands was once the bottom of Lake Iroquois. In the rich soil composed of limestone, red clay, and glacial debris eroded from its shorecliff and mixed with sand by the waters of Lake Iroquois, a luxuriant hardwood forest grew up which contributed a deep layer of vegetable matter.

Strawberries were among the small fruits that were native to many sections bordering Lake Ontario. In *Canada: Past, Present and Future,* W. H. Smith wrote in 1851 that strawberries "grow luxuriantly but they are not so much cultivated as their valuable properties deserve."[36] It was a young Yorkshireman named John Cross, a native of Scarborough, England, who was the first to recognize the possibilities of growing strawberries commercially in Oakville, some say in Canada. The latter assertion is difficult of proof, although the opening sentence of an account which appeared in the *Canadian Champion* after a visit of the editor to Oakville in 1869 might be considered as substantiation:

> On arriving at Oakville station, we found ourselves in the midst of the strawberry bed of Canada. . . . Mr. Cross, formerly millwright, was the first that planted the berry in any quantity and he received the idea, while working on the American side of the Falls, from an American named Burdett, and they formed a partnership in the business, which Mr. Cross now carries on alone. The success of the venture encouraged others, so that now cultivators may be reckoned by the dozen,—The principal of these are J. Hagaman, Capt. [John A.] Chisholm, W. H. Jones, Capt. W. B. Chisholm, E. Skelly, J. T. Howell, A. Mathews and others. The most popular berry is Wilson's *Albany* . . . the *Triomphe de Grande* is also grown, but the Mexican Everbearing, with its fabulous boast of bearing every month receives no countenance among practical men of Oakville. It is regarded as a humbug of the first water.[37]

According to the account anyone wishing to plant a new patch could buy runners for $4 a thousand.

The farm of John Cross lay north of the railway where Cross Avenue now runs. Since the soil here is clay rather than sand, it would seem that he grew his strawberries elsewhere in the vicinity, possibly farther east. There were no commission merchants in Toronto at that time, and he was obliged to accompany each shipment and dispose of it personally at St. Lawrence Market. Wooden and tin pails, the only available containers, proved unsatisfactory for the perishable fruit, so Cross secured samples of quart baskets from the United States. But the shape did not suit him and he set to work to improve upon it. By narrowing the bottom and widening the top he produced the basket with sloping sides which is universally used today. This basket, made of two pieces of wood veneer fastened by two strips of tin punched on a machine, cost less than half a cent to make.[38] Near his home, now no. 43 Cross Avenue, he established a factory east of the 7th Line where baskets were made during the winter season.

Some idea of the extent and value of the strawberry crop in 1869 may be gained from accounts in the *Canadian Champion*:

> Nearly two hundred acres are devoted to strawberries, which have this season yielded enormously, and owing to Oakville being situated on the railway, and having an excellent harbor, fruit is carried off both by land and water in enormous quantities. To show the importance of this interest, we may mention that on Tues. last 400 bushels or 12,800 quarts were shipped for the Toronto and Montreal markets! This, at 10 cents a quart would make nearly $1,200 for one day's shipment. The money made in strawberries will create an impetus to the business, and as the soil and situation of Oakville are all that can be desired, we trust that the pro-

duction of this luscious fruit may bring yearly more and more wealth to the people of Oakville.

Already a society of producers has been organized in Oakville. . . . Hagaman sent away 2,200 quarts from one of his patches in one day, and on Monday week ten tons were sent away. As the season lasts nearly a month, we calculate that nearly 125 tons were gathered; or about one ton to the acre, which at $200 a ton bring into Oakville about $25,000 and some put the figure at $30,000. . . . On visiting the fields we found nearly the whole juvenile population busily engaged in gathering the crimson fruit.[39]

Chief Sumner to whom incidentally the visitor from Milton alluded as "a terror to all evil doers," noted in his diary that the berries at "Cross' strawberry patch" cost 12¢ a quart in 1867. But production increased rapidly (from 1869 to 1870 the acreage jumped from 125 to 300 acres) and within a decade the price dropped to 6¢. Migratory Indians, who flocked to the district during the fruit picking season, and school children helped with the picking at the rate of 1¢ a basket. Strawberry festivals and picnics grew in popularity and were held frequently during the season at the Town Hall by the women's auxiliaries of the churches. By 1877 the average output per day was 300 cases, and the *Atlas of Halton County*, published in that year, calls Oakville "the greatest strawberry growing district in the Dominion."[40] In 1879, a very good season, over 4,000 cases (about 200 tons), were shipped. According to the *Express* "the pleasant resort has the best soil for this berry in the province, and more than $30,000 [worth] were shipped, largely to Toronto and Hamilton."[41] During June and July in the four years (1899 to 1903) that the *White Star* called at Oakville, at 7 A.M., 12 noon, and 6 P.M., hundreds of conveyances loaded with fruit were to be seen hurrying to the harbour. One day's consignment of strawberries alone frequently exceeded forty thousand quarts. At that time the wholesale price was about 5¢ a quart.

An anecdote is still current which appeared in the local *Star* almost fifty years ago. It related how an Italian vendor of bananas was meeting with little success on the wharf at Toronto. He noticed that another pedlar nearby was doing a rushing business and that he was calling "Oakville strawberries, fresh ripe Oakville strawberries." Adapting this to his wares, he announced that he had "Oak-a-villa bananas, nice fresh Oak-a-villa bananas" and was bewildered by the laughter of the people boarding the steamers.[42]

About the time that Cross began manufacturing baskets his neighbour John A. Chisholm, who also cultivated strawberries extensively, commenced making baskets in a shed on his farm near Division

Street.[43] Logs were peeled of their bark by a machine operated by a horsepower, and Chisholm's son, Charles P., developed a paring machine for shaving the wood thin enough for fruit baskets. This "fruit basket manufactury," valued in 1871 at $2,000, employed four men and eight boys who turned out some 300,000 baskets each year during the four months of the winter season that the plant was in operation.[44] John Chisholm senior died in 1874 and in that year his sons William B. and Charles P. bought the Victoria Brewery, then idle for four years, from Francis J. Brown and converted the building into a basket factory.

The career of the former proprietor of the brewery is of sufficient interest to justify digression. In his youth Francis J. Brown, a native of Ringwood, Hants, had gone to sea. He had been attracted to Canada by the discovery of oil near Bothwell in the western district, and just before the first Dominion Day in 1867 he had come to Oakville. After being employed for a time by Henry Hogben as grain buyer for the brewery he became owner of the business in the late sixties. He was a tall, well-built man with the hearty, self-reliant air of one who has spent much of his life on the sea, and became very popular in Oakville. As we know, the Victoria Brewery was a casualty of the depression, and Brown, deciding to return to the sea, went back to England. In 1879 he was commissioned to sail a light-draught paddle-steamer, the *Henry Venn*, from England to Africa, where it was to be used in transporting missionaries up the Niger River to the interior of Africa. Captain Brown had aboard the first native bishop to work in Africa, Bishop Bomper. At some earlier date the Oakville Town Council had presented him with a Canadian flag, and he carried it with him on all his voyages, draped so that all who came aboard his ship passed under it. It is said to have been the first Canadian flag ever flown in Africa.[45] About 1880 Captain Brown was engaged by the Japanese government to sail a converted steamship leased from the British government to Japan. Thereafter he stayed in the Orient for some twenty years, sailing the ships of the Nippon Yusen Kaisha Steamship Company, and opening for trade every port from Vladivostok to India. During this time he shipped home many art objects, ivories, china, bronzes, and the large vases so popular at the period. The first exhibition of his collection was held in 1889 at his residence, now no. 169 Dundas Street North, which he had built in the seventies. This was the beginning of a business founded for his children. In 1896 the family moved to Galt to open the Oriental Bazaar, which is carried on by the family today. When Captain Brown died the flag which had accompanied him on so many voyages draped his coffin; it is highly prized by his family. Mrs. Brown, a descendant of Barnet Griggs, lived to become a centenarian. Many articles that were brought from the Orient by Captain Brown are treasured in Oakville homes today.

The basket factory brought considerable revenue to farmers in the county from the sale of logs. In 1877 nearly three-quarters of a million baskets were manufactured.[46] The log piles along the east bank of The Sixteen in the vicinity of the basket factory extended farther up and down Dundas Street until finally the practice was loudly condemned in letters to the press. It was claimed that horses had suffered injuries, sleighs been overturned, and the public greatly inconvenienced by logs encroaching upon the roadway. The affair caused considerable stir in the Town Council, but in general the opinion was that if log piles were necessary to an industry which afforded the town great benefits, any inconvenience they caused was incidental. And there the matter rested.[47]

At the time the basket factory was moved into the brewery W. B. Chisholm lived in a house situated on the north-east corner of Reynolds and Division streets, although Reynolds Street was not then open this far north, nor would be until well into the seventies. The house was later incorporated in the residence that is now no. 241 Reynolds Street North. In 1881 Chisholm moved his family into the new house he had built on Dundas Street at the south-east corner of Spruce Street, now no. 259 Dundas Street North. It was here that he died, after a series of strokes in 1889. The following year the basket factory was taken over by Pharis Doty & Son.[48] They were succeeded by the Oakville Basket Company, a joint-stock company organized in January, 1892, by men who for years had been the heads of several departments: A. Ion, John and Robert Freestone, Charles Ward, and, as business manager, John C. Ford.[49] On April 29, 1893, the entire factory together with a large quantity of stock on hand was destroyed by a fire that had been deliberately set. Suspicion centred on a brother of the former owners, Robert McKenzie Chisholm, who because of mental illness had recently been confined in the Toronto Asylum but was for some reason released. When interviewed by Chief Sumner he readily admitted to being the "firebug," and was returned to the asylum, where he died soon after.[50]

The basket factory was rebuilt and the building, 34 by 112 feet, sheathed with metal siding, was better suited to the increasing trade. New equipment included a peeler purchased in St. Joseph, Michigan, and two veneering lathes which were capable of producing 5,000 feet of veneer per day. The steam plant was installed by Goldie & McCulloch of Galt. For making strawberry baskets there were thirty iron blocks over which the splints were shaped and clinched with tacks. In one day a single operator could make a maximum of 2,000 of these containers. The "gang" who made fruit and grape baskets could turn out 250,000 per day. Two hours after a log of elm, basswood, soft maple, hickory, or ash entered the veneering room it would be turned into finished baskets.[51]

By the late eighties, the basket factory, together with fruit growing, which was seasonal, and the tannery, were Oakville's principal industries. At about this time Stafford Marlatt bought out Captain Felan's interest in the tannery for his two sons, Wilbur Triller and Cecil Gustavus Marlatt. The latter had recently returned from a short spell of ranching in Texas. The firm of Marlatt & Armstrong continued to make a specialty of patent leathers. Jordan Milbourne, who had worked all his life in the tannery, had started a small tannery of his own across the way (block 105), but lost it by fire and returned to work in the beam house of Marlatt & Armstrong. Here his co-worker was James Hanna, newly arrived from Ireland. It is said that one day Milbourne asked Hanna how he liked Canadian whiskey, to which Hanna replied, "It's full of combustibles." While working with Hanna in the beam house, Milbourne would periodically straighten up and shout, "God save the Queen." But Hanna, who did not share his companion's enthusiasm for Her Majesty, would shout in rejoinder, "God save all un us."

The old building, formerly the distillery, which Thompson Smith converted for the tannery has disappeared except for its foundations. It stood close to the north side of Walker Street where it turns down the hill to the harbour. The lines of the walls may still be traced on block 106, but the building was demolished many years ago, and the structures farther north on the hill along Forsyth Street, which are today identified with the tannery, were built by Marlatt & Armstrong.

In 1892 Wilbur T. Marlatt went into partnership with Julian Sale to establish a small tannery for the manufacture of leather gloves, purses, and novelty leather goods. They took over the large four-storey building at Navy and Colborne streets that had been the general store of Gage & Hagaman. After the raw skins were tanned and dyed they were made into travelling bags, ladies' purses and gloves, silver-trimmed card cases, collar and cuff boxes, and other finished products in great variety, including cricket balls and footballs.[52] These articles supplied the firm that had been established at Toronto in the seventies by Julian Sale, the first concern in that city to deal exclusively in fancy leather goods. After being in operation for about five years the partnership was dissolved and the machinery of the "purse factory," as it was called in the town, moved to Toronto. The making of glove leather was then continued in this building by Marlatt & Armstrong.

III

The addition to Oakville's business that resulted from fruit growing and summer visitors was not enough to restore the town to its former importance. During the last decades of the century, Oakville was at a standstill; the town dozed, the population continued to fall, and to make a living became increasingly difficult. However, these were conditions which Oakville shared with the province as a whole.

Notwithstanding extensive immigration during the sixties and seventies, the province was losing its population almost as rapidly by emigration. Many people were going to the Canadian West; but by far the greater proportion were moving south of the border. The number of persons who left Canada for the United States between 1860 and 1890 has been estimated at one million forty thousand,[53] and to these figures Oakville contributed its share. For instance, according to Dr. Donald Gallie, who practised dentistry in Chicago, there were in that city during the eighties some seventy-five persons who either had come from or were in some way connected with Oakville. The yearly rise in population of the town between 1871 and 1891 was slightly over 3 per cent per one thousand, an increase of one-third or less what one would expect from natural increase. The figures are as follows:

1871	1,710
1875	1,684
1881	1,767
1891	1,823

In 1880 Chief Sumner wrote, "Town going to the dogs—half the people leaving town for other places." During that year the Corporation cared for more than five hundred tramps.

The desire of the younger generation to look farther afield for careers was fostered by the spread of education, the growth of newspapers, and developments in advertising. Sons left home at an early age to seek employment; but, unlike their fathers, the majority no longer wished to learn a trade. The old system of apprenticeship was fast becoming a thing of the past, and the old-country methods of Oakville merchants were considered backward and out of date. In the United States, particularly the middle west, business of all kinds was booming, and numbers of young men were attracted by glowing accounts of money quickly and easily made. The spirit of speculation by which huge fortunes had been and were being made, summed up by the Americans as "get-up-and-git," was absent in Canada. The generation of Canadians who had been schooled in the British tradition founded upon integrity deplored the aggressiveness of the American business man; but, for the younger generation, looking for opportunity, this spirit had appeal.

Judging from letters received by families in Oakville, some of these youths merely traded Canadian for American "slavery." One migrant wrote: "I suppose Oakville is as dull as ever. I am in a hash house, a nice place for a fellow that likes good grub. I am getting three and a half a week and out of that have to pay one dollar for room rent. I work every day in the week from six in the morning until eight at night so you can judge how much time I have to myself."[54] Another Oakville boy, Ted Wilson, who had been working for his uncle, P. A. MacDougald, disappeared and was missing for eight years. His cousin, who had also run away to seek his fortune in the western states, attempted for two years to trace Ted in Colorado, and the reports of this search sent back to Oakville read like a scenario for the type of moving picture film we know as the "western." According to the first rumour, Ted was the gambler who had "gotten into a shooting scrape" in which a policeman was killed, "was taken out of jail and lynched by a mob called the V. G. Committee." The report proved false, and the cousin decided that it must have been Ted who had been playing the fiddle in a dance hall and "had been taken out of town by a couple of out-laws and shot to death for being witness against them in a lawsuit"; or Ted had been killed while prospecting, and so on. Actually he had worked with a surveyor's party in the Rockies, and as helper to a sheep rancher. Some of his wanderings he described in the first letter written to Canada in eight years:

> When I was sixteen years old . . . I was slave to three years apprenticeship to common labour in a grocery store. But to avoid it I have followed my past life, which is much the best. I have been a tramp since that last time I wrote my relatives but now I am doing a good deal better. I tramped all through Mexico for four years . . . sleeping under the shadow of fences. . . . I will go to Canada this winter if possible . . . and until that time I should like to have everyone think I am dead. My experience is worth a good-deal and I may be able to sell some of it some day. Your tramp cousin,
>
> TED.[55]

A third migrant of about the same age wrote without regrets to his uncle as follows: "I suppose Oakville is the same old dead place as it has been ever since I can remember. For my part I can't see how it is that people can live there. I would rather be in states prison in this country than live in the best town in the whole of Canada but I don't suppose that everybody thinks the same as I do. Well, don't get mad at what I have said about poor old Canada."[56]

In the professional, mercantile, industrial, and other fields, many of Oakville's sons and daughters who migrated won outstanding careers. With few exceptions, these have proved difficult to trace, and source material is not readily available. Because of authentic documentation, the accomplishment of the Chisholm brothers is cited as an example of the success attained in the United States by many natives of Oakville. C. P. Chisholm was a mechanic who, it will be recalled, had a number of inventions to his credit, having developed machinery for various purposes in connection with his father's basket factory. His brother John, popularly known as Jack, had sold strawberries at the railway station, carrying a large basket filled with pint boxes; not being permitted to board the trains, he had sold them to passengers through the windows of the cars. While working with their elder brother, William B. Chisholm, at the basket factory, C. P. and John experimented with processing vegetables by evaporation, and soon had in operation five kilns in which finely cut cabbages, potatoes, corn, turnips, peas, and apples were evaporated on a revolving screen over a fire pit. After being packaged in one-pound pasteboard boxes in the building that is now nos. 11 and 13 Inglehart Avenue the vegetables were sold in large quantities to the British government and used by the Royal Navy in all parts of the world for making soup. The two brothers devised much of their own machinery, such as cutters for removing corn from the cob, for slicing cabbage, etc. Their greatest success, however, was the invention of devices to replace the slow and expensive processes of harvesting and podding of peas by hand. At Hamilton, one of the pioneer canning factories employed as many as fifteen hundred pickers, besides a large number of women for shelling peas. A visit to this factory led the brothers to experiment with a machine for extracting peas from the pods. The first machine, built in the barn, was a failure, the percentage of crushed peas being too high. In 1887 the brothers discovered that green peas could be hulled by impacting the pods, at a comparatively gentle velocity, while falling through the air. Their machine, patented first in Germany and later in the United States,[57] extracted the peas undamaged; but the problem of separating peas from pods baffled the Chisholms until help was received from a chance acquaintance John made in the United States.

Though still in its infancy in Canada, the canning industry was making great strides in the United States. Because of the inability of country packers to obtain an adequate supply of hand pickers the packing of green peas was practically confined to the city of Baltimore where Negro labour was plentiful. It was here that John Chisholm, while attending a canning convention, fell into casual conversation with an inventor from Ohio, Robert P. Scott. The two men exchanged hard-luck stories, and it soon became evident that Scott had discovered how to separate peas from pods, and that his invention could eliminate the most serious kink in the Chisholms' machine. Scott and the two Chisholms entered into partnership and were successful in perfecting the viner process. The pea vines were harvested by a threshing machine and hauled to the viner, a machine almost the size of a box car, which was set up on the field under a shed. The vines were fed into it like so much hay; through one opening rolled the peas, graded as to size, and through another opening came the vines for the silo or waste pile. As the invention did away with the labour of hand picking, the pea packing industry was able to transfer to the country districts of the United States, where it spread and grew enormously.

The Chisholm-Scott Company's viners were manufactured at Suspension Bridge, New York, where many Oakville men were employed.

The viners were leased on a royalty basis of 9¢ per dozen cans of peas. John Chisholm, the business manager of the firm, had no use for the "new-fangled method of bookkeeping." He kept the firm's accounts in a small vest-pocket memorandum book. At the end of each year when the partners sat down to divide their earnings, each would state in round figures what his expenses had been. These amounts were deducted, and the profits were equally divided. A quarter or a half million dollars were often thus handled, with the business completed in a few minutes.[58]

As Toronto approached metropolitan status, Oakville was drawn more and more into its orbit, to the increasing disadvantage of the business men of the town. With improved transportation and shipping facilities, the townspeople depended less upon local firms for their needs, particularly in the matter of expensive purchases. In 1880 the store of Timothy Eaton at Toronto developed from a drygoods shop into a departmental store in which a great variety of goods could be purchased at prices with which local merchants were unable to compete. Much of the trade that formerly had come to them now went to Toronto, and "Eaton's" started on the road to becoming the household word it is today. The Oakville merchants were forced to reduce not only the quantity but the quality and variety of their stocks and, as time went on, they turned more and more to supplying the needs of the farmers rather than those of the townspeople.

Merchants were no longer obliged to journey to larger centres to buy their stocks, as wholesalers sent commercial travellers to take orders; "travelling angels," Williams called them. But wholesalers had begun to reduce their credits, a great hardship for the small merchants who still extended credit from one to two years. Moreover, a slow downward trend of prices continued until economic depression became world wide. At one point during the eighties, Oakville merchants were offering thirty pounds of sugar for as little as $1, a fraction over 3¢ per pound.[59] Not until the middle nineties, when population and consumption in Canada again overtook production, did prices begin to rise to a profitable level.

The eighties saw several changes that concerned Oakville in connection with the railways. One was a result of continued depression; financial difficulties led to the amalgamation in 1882 of the Great Western Railway with the Grand Trunk Railway. Two years before, the old wooden trestle across The Sixteen had been replaced by an iron bridge, and the brick piers replaced by stone pillars.[60] And in 1883 Standard Time went into effect throughout North America.

Previously, travellers had been greatly inconvenienced by changes in time from city to city. Between Halifax and Toronto there were no less than five different times and there was also considerable variation in the clocks by which the trains were run. Indeed, lightning calculation on the part of the traveller was required to catch a train before introduction of the Standard Hour system.

It was in 1883 that the Romain Block was destroyed in a fire which came near to wiping out the entire business district. The corner store at Navy Street was occupied by John Barclay, who was, at that time, living in the apartment above. Next were the stores of P. A. MacDougald, the mayor, C. W. Pearce, druggist, and Moses McCraney, general merchant. In the upper storey were located the Masonic Hall, the Orange Hall, the Odd Fellows' Hall (Lodge No. 132, organized in 1874) and the newspaper office of the *Standard*, successor to the *Sentinel*. On the east side of the brick block were Edward Hillmer's butcher shop and livery stable and the express office of his brother Ebenezer who was agent for both the American and the Montreal companies. Then came the Morrisons' butcher shop, S. B. Ganton's book and stationery store, and, at the corner of Thomas Street, the building occupied by the hardware merchants, McIntyre and McGiffin, and the dry-goods merchant, Thomas Patterson.

About eleven o'clock on the night of Sunday, April 17, 1883, John Wesley Wallace, the Negro bell-boy at the Oakville House, was washing dishes when he saw smoke pouring out of the opposite building, and gave the alarm. The fire had started in the office of the *Standard* and, when discovered by John Barclay, was small; but the fire brigade had trouble getting the pump to work, and soon the whole block was in flames. As the fire began in the upper storeys, a large proportion of the stock was removed from the stores; the Barclays themselves had no difficulty in escaping. The fire brigade "did its work gallantly," and large fire wells, installed some years before, supplied the hose with plenty of water; but when the three-storey building collapsed the neighbouring frame buildings began to burn. The Oakville House across the way caught fire no less than seven times; Dr. Sutherland had carried a keg of gun powder into Ganton's store and was about to blow it up in an attempt to stop the spreading of the fire when the flames were finally got under control. From Toronto it looked as if a ship was afire, and a tug was preparing to go to the rescue when a request for help was received from Oakville by telegraph. A special train of two flat cars, engine, and caboose was got ready and a fire engine with a brigade of firemen was sent to Oakville. When the train arrived at 3 A.M. it was found that in the excitement no arrangements had been made to provide horses to draw the engine from the station to the fire; but, in any case, the equipment was not needed. For sending the special train, the Town of Oakville paid the City of Toronto $40.[61]

By 4 A.M. the whole block, with the exception of Ganton's store and the building on the corner of Thomas Street, was laid in ashes. Sumner placed ten men to guard the premises against looting.[62] "The business section is ruined," he wrote. Hillmer's sixteen horses were saved, but he lost several buggies, "provender," household effects, and the building, and again, as seventeen years before, he had no insurance. None of the losers were fully insured, some only half, and others carried none at all; and, although the newspapers reported the loss to be "roughly $40,000," it was nearer $100,000.

Within the year John Barclay rebuilt on the same site at the corner of Navy Street, the Masons occupying the second storey. Gradually the Romain Block was replaced by new buildings, including the Anderson Block in which the Municipal Offices, Council Chambers, and Police Station are located at the present time.

A lively, and inventive, account of this major event came in a clipping from an Indianapolis, Indiana, newspaper to Chief Sumner, who pasted it in his scrap-book. It reads: "Canadian Village burned up—Toronto, Ont. The entire Village of Oakville, on the Lake Shore Road, twenty miles from here, was destroyed by fire to-day. Fire brigades went from here by special train but arrived too late. The village fire department got drunk on two barrels of whiskey rolled out of a drug store in which the fire started. The inhabitants are flocking into Toronto by hundreds." The account is noted as reprinted from a Toronto paper.

The significance of this news item lies in the fact that, at the time of the fire, prohibition reigned in Oakville. This was an experiment which Halton was the first county in the province to make. Those who were unsympathetic towards prohibition of the public sale of intoxicating liquors kept close watch on Oakville and Milton, seizing every opportunity of playing up any untoward incidents to prove their contention that the measure was unsuccessful.

That a large proportion of the population of Oakville and Trafalgar Township were strongly against the use of intoxicating liquors is evidenced by the early formation of temperance societies and the erection at Oakville of the first Temperance Hall in the province. In 1854 the Trafalgar Township Council resolved that "Whereas it is expedient to pass a By-law prohibiting absolutely by Retail the Sale of Wine, Brandy, and other Spirituous Liquors" a vote of the ratepayers should be taken. Voting in the Fourth Ward took place, oddly enough, at the Oakville House, with Robert Balmer as Returning Officer.[63] Although the by-law was lost (by what margin goes unrecorded), the mere fact of its being voted upon at this date is of interest. This was eleven years before the first provincial attempt at prohibition.

From the time that Oakville became a municipality, the licensing of taverns was a subject of considerable contention. The extent of drunkenness in the town was perennially under discussion in the council and the liquor by-laws were continually being repealed, revised, and tightened. In 1865 the Dunkin Act gave the counties the option of prohibiting the sale (but not the importation or possession) of intoxicants, and Halton County voted in favour of a by-law for the adoption of this measure. However, when a grocer appealed against conviction, the by-law, on a technicality, was declared illegal and licences were again issued. Prohibition had lasted only a few months. However, it furnished the Town Corporation with the opportunity of raising by ten dollars the price of tavern licences.

The temperance society was reorganized in 1869 as the Royal Oak Temple no. 216, its members calling themselves Royal Templars. John Cosley's version of the revival of the temperance society as published in his newspaper, *The Bee*, has already been given (see page 263).

As the result of the rising agitation throughout the province for prohibition, the Canada Temperance Act, more popularly known as the Scott Act, was passed in 1878 by the Ontario Legislature. It enacted that, on petition of the voters in a county, the municipalities therein could vote on whether or not they wanted taverns in their communities. An indication of the strength of the temperance movement in Halton County lies in the fact that it was the first county to take the initial step for prohibition, thereby acquiring the name of the "banner county." The provisions of the Scott Act were similar in most respects to those of the Dunkin Act; liquor could be purchased from a licensed purveyor for home consumption only, but could not be sold in taverns.

For three years Oakville held aloof; but on April 19, 1881, when the electors voted on the question of "whisky or no whisky," the new law was carried by a majority of eighty-seven.[64] It is very probable that some voters were influenced by the goings-on at the Canadian Hotel that year. Two women were the proprietors, and the drunken brawls, with which they seemed unable to cope, disturbed the entire neighbourhood. Sumner who lived close by remarked, "Pretty poor considering they are supposed to be ladies," and on the day the new law came into effect he noted: "This has been a very strange day in Oakville. The Scott Act came into force to-day and all the Hotels are closed up, both houses and sheds. People who came into town say they will not come again." And some weeks later he reported the weather as "very dry—I suppose on account of the Scott Act."

The bordering counties of Peel, Wellington, and Wentworth stayed wet and the "rum party" sat smugly by, pointing to Oakville and Milton as horrible examples of the failure of prohibition in the "banner county." There were many drunks in Sumner's Lock-up ("much Scott Act about") and a son of Aaron Mathews, who returned about this time after having been away for some twenty years, found no particular evidence of changed habits—the same drunk was sleeping on the steps of the Oakville House who had been there when he had left the town. Nevertheless in former times, before Oakville went dry, it had been the custom of Chief Sumner to swear in six or eight special constables to handle the numbers of intoxicated persons who attended the fair. After the Scott Act came into force, he required no assistance to manage the few that turned up at the new fair grounds. Many of the hotel keepers, out of spite, closed their waggon sheds and chained up the pump handles so that farmers could not water their horses. These were bitter times, and feeling ran high. Every two years, when the option came up for vote, the local newspapers printed long lists of names, those in favour of renewal and those who stood for the repeal of the law. Terms such as "liar," "scalawag," and "low living scoundrel" were bandied about with great freedom.

The person who suffered the bitterest attacks from the "rum party" was William H. Young, cabinet-maker and undertaker at Oakville, who was appointed police magistrate for Halton County. As son of the first proprietor of the Oakville House, he had been surrounded in his early days by the influence of a tavern, and was a staunch advocate of temperance and prohibition. Young was one of the strongest supporters of the Sons of Temperance in Oakville. In his "Court of Truth and Righteousness" he vigorously and fearlessly enforced every letter of the law, and the clamour against "biased decisions" and his handling of witnesses grew louder and more violent. In 1884 an attempt was made to repeal the law, but it was sustained by the voters. In September Oakville voted 448 to 353 against repeal; "very hot weather, and the Scott Act Election makes it hotter," wrote Sumner. The editor of Milton's *Canadian Champion* wrote reams upon the subject, singling out the magistrate, whom he persistently referred to as "Beak Young," and the inspector (because of a shooting accident) as "our Didn't-know-it-was-loaded Inspector." At one point, when the editor refused to testify concerning a "shebeen" (as cellars and back rooms where liquor was illegally dispensed were called), Young popped him into jail for contempt of court. Thereafter the battle thickened. Shaw, the editor of the *Oakville Star*, who until then had remained absolutely impartial, "skipped down from off the fence on which he has heretofore serenely roosted" to take up Young's defence. The Attorney-General for Ontario was petitioned for an investigation; but, before anything came of it, the electorate in 1888 voted in favour of repeal of the Scott Act for Oakville by a majority of 179.[65]

Young had no hesitation in stating that he was "proud of the constant attention of the liquor press." He collected clippings from newspapers, in particular the *Canadian Champion*, a copy of the petition, and correspondence relating to it between him and the office of the Attorney-General into scrap-books to which he gave the title "The Serpent's Trail," so that these "unintentional compliments" should be "handed down to posterity." His public career continued. In April, 1889, upon the resignation of Robert Balmer, Young was appointed Postmaster. At this time he lived at no. 16 Thomas Street North, which he had purchased from its builder, John A. Williams.[66]

Three years before Balmer's death, the photograph of himself and his wife Elizabeth, daughter of John Terry, shown as plate 47, was taken on the occasion of their golden wedding anniversary, 1895. This quiet and dignified Scotsman, an early comer to the town, had served Oakville meticulously and faithfully for a total of forty-five years. He was Deputy Postmaster for two years, Postmaster for thirty-two years and Town Clerk of the Municipality of the Township of Trafalgar for nine years before becoming Town Clerk of the Municipality of the Town of Oakville, an office which he held until his death. All who knew him remembered Robert Balmer with great respect.

During the first few years that the Scott Act was in force Oakville seems to have been a town without hotels. In 1886, with the backing of the temperance people, James Taylor, harness maker, bought the Canadian Hotel for $5,000, and ran it during the remainder of the dry era. With the repeal of the Scott Act, the hotels took a new lease on life. Most of their proprietors were newcomers. The Victoria House was remodelled by William Wynne, who removed its wide verandah, and its name changed to the Queen's Hotel. Wynne was the owner of several trotting horses that were famous in their day, and two of them are shown in the photograph of the Queen's Hotel (plate 32) which bears the heading "Headquarters for horsemen and bicyclists."[67] The fad for bicycling had reached its height at the time this photograph was taken, with the laying in 1896 of the cinder path from Toronto to Oakville. The cinders were donated by Marlatt & Armstrong and the St. Lawrence Starch Company at Port Credit, and the Toronto Cycling Club paid for the teaming. For a number of years thereafter, the "wheel men" held races to Oakville, and at times the town was full of bicycles.[68]

At the turn of the century the Queen's Hotel closed. Three years later, when the building was remodelled by William Buckle for a meat market, its timbers were found to be placed so close together as to make the structure "strong enough for a railway bridge." It was at this time that the building acquired its brick exterior.

The Oakville House reopened under the proprietorship of Murray Williams, son of Captain Hiram Williams and nephew of the hotel's former proprietor, John Williams. In 1896 Murray Williams bought the Canadian Hotel and soon brought it back to the standard under which it had been maintained by his uncle, the hotel's builder. Under almost a dozen proprietors since its reopening by Sam Flaherty as the International Hotel, this establishment had gone steadily down hill. Murray Williams changed its name to the Murray House and during the forty years he remained proprietor it was a hotel to which visitors returned season after season. Though the waggon sheds are now gone and the fountain no longer plays a stream of water upon which a little white ball rose and fell, the building, which not long ago survived a disastrous fire, is still a hotel, and does business under the name of the Murray. This and the Oakville House remain as the only survivors of Oakville's old-time hostelries, the latter a relic of the town's pioneer days and the former of its most prosperous period.

The new lessee of the Royal Exchange, James Arno, almost completely refitted that establishment in 1888. A special feature of his refurbishing was the new bar with a large mirror surrounded by stuffed birds and animals, one a fox in a crouching position, which undoubtedly came from the hands of Henry Baker. The photograph of the Royal Exchange shown as plate 25, taken about this time, includes one of Hillmer's buses. Having bought out the other two livery stables in the town, Edward Hillmer was by now owner of five buses. They met all trains, including the last at midnight and, upon request, the bus would call at the "respective residences" of train passengers anywhere in town. After losing his stables in the fire of '83, Hillmer had moved across Colborne Street to the livery stables originally occupied by J. Holden, whose bus service was inaugurated on the day the first train came through on the Great Western Railway in the middle fifties. Hillmer's buses became one of Oakville's institutions, and were as much a part of town life, and to be taken equally for granted by the townspeople, as the tannery whistle, the school-bell and the church-bells.

Another familiar feature of town life was the annual fair. The Town Hall was no longer being used as an exhibition hall, as a new building had been erected for this purpose on Reynolds Street on the land which had originally been the old cemetery. Since 1858, when Colonel G. K. Chisholm gave the land on the 6th Line for a new Town Cemetery, no use had been made of block no. 43, which had been set aside in 1835 by William Chisholm for a public cemetery. Although some of the remains had been removed to the new cemetery, many were still interred in the old plot. In 1877 R. K. Chisholm claimed that, as it was not being used for the purpose for which it was given, the land had reverted to him as sole surviving heir of William Chisholm. For a time it looked as if the matter would be taken to court; but eventually an agreement was reached whereby, upon payment of $100, the town would receive a deed to the property on condition that it be used by the Trafalgar Agricultural Association.[69] The council agreed that as the Agricultural Association had "expressed the desire that its annual Exhibition may be permanently established in the Town of Oakville; therefore it is expedient and proper for the Corporation of the Town of Oakville to enlarge the ground, known as the Old Cemetery Lot, by the purchase of such additional land lying adjacent thereto, as may be deemed sufficient to answer the necessary requirements of said annual Exhibition."[70] The block to the north was purchased for $1,100 from James Newlands,[71] the unnamed street running between the two blocks was closed, and all the land thrown into one large square. Subsequently a race track was laid out on the Anderson farm east of Allan Street. The council held a special meeting on October 1, 1880, at which Trafalgar Square was chosen as the name for the new agricultural grounds,[72] and four days later the first fair was held there. It was not until the following January, however, that under Sumner's supervision the remaining sixteen bodies were disinterred for removal to the Town Cemetery,[73] a project which created considerable interest among the townspeople. John A. Williams relates that he was present when some coffins were being lifted and that one, containing the body of a young woman, was almost filled with her hair, which had grown to the foot of the coffin and back again.

The new building, Agricultural Hall, was framed with huge hand-hewn timbers obtained when an old barn back in the township was taken down. The hall was built without a floor so that during the winter it could be used as a skating rink, and was opened to the public with a fancy dress carnival on New Year's Day, 1881.[74]

Queen Victoria's Jubilee took place on June 21, 1887. Upon this great occasion several hundred persons sat down to both dinner and supper in Agricultural Hall. The *Star*'s editor reported the event with his usual verve:

> Ten days ago the most loyal of our citizens began the work of decorating the town . . . and they rested not from their labors until they had both cheeks painted, the hair in curls and a bustle on Tuesday an assured fact. Not since the noble red man, in war paint and feathers, roamed the banks of the Sweet Sixteen has Oakville presented such a scene of dazzling splendor as it did on the morning of the never-to-be-forgotten Jubilee. Colborne street was arched from end to end. Flags fluttered from scores of windows, from the tops of telegraph and telephone poles and from the pinnacle of fame. Almost every place of business had its crescent of evergreens and many-hued streamers, rivalling the rainbow in depth of color and novelty effect. . . . Nature has been lavish in her adornment of our streets and avenues and an artistic touch here and there transforms them into fairy scenes.[75]

The celebration began in the morning with an address at St. Jude's Church. A procession of school children ("a host of innocents," according to the *Star*), headed by the Oakville Band, marched to Agricultural Hall where each child was presented with a medal bearing the head of the Queen. "After partaking of a dinner worthy of Delmonico's," those present heard addresses and then enjoyed a ball game between the White Oaks and teams from Toronto and Hamilton. Between 5 and 7 P.M. supper was served to which "hundreds sat down." In the evening the assembly was entertained by songs, recitations, and "artists in Highland dress" dancing reels, Strathspeys, and hornpipes. With a display of fireworks and a royal salute the event came to an end.[76]

A special feature of the Oakville Fair, as it soon came to be called, was the annual procession of pupils from all the schools in the township. From the Town Hall they marched to Agricultural Hall, where prizes were given to the winners in competitions in singing, map drawing, writing, sewing, etc., as well as horseback riding. The two-day fairs attracted such large crowds that at times Chief Sumner required the assistance of as many as thirteen deputy constables, now that liquor was again on sale.

Besides the ice rink in Agricultural Hall, there was, in the early nineties, the open air rink kept by A. Kemp. The ice on The Sixteen was enclosed and swept clear of snow "from Colborne Street to the old dam." In 1894 it was announced that "a comfortable house for putting on skates is being erected and the ice will be brightly illuminated with electricity." And to these attractions was added that of a brass band the following year.[77]

When first introduced, roller skating was a popular fad, and the rink of Kenney and Howes, opened on the north-west corner of Reynolds and Church streets in 1885, did a thriving business. The admission was five and ten cents; skates were supplied free to the ladies. To the strains of the music of the Oakville Band skaters circled the maple floor.[78] After about ten years enthusiasm waned, the rink ceased to pay, and the building was remodelled on the same site into four dwellings with brick fronts. These stand today as nos. 143 and 145 Church Street and nos. 22 and 24 Reynolds Street North. The flooring in the upper stories came from the skating rink.

Of all the places of entertainment, the most impressive was Commins' Music Hall, built in 1894 on the north-east corner of Colborne and Dundas streets. It was constructed of yellow brick and embellished with terra cotta, and the front entrance was flanked by towers with circular roofs. Each tower was surmounted by three little mushroom turrets, and iron gates "ornamented" the front. The exterior was exceptionally ugly, but the auditorium, according to the local press, was equipped with "upholstered reclining chairs." On the stage, the "charming drop curtain, finished in the most artistic style . . . shows heavy curtains draped at both ends, in the centre of the lagoon with a gondola floating." There were four back-drops to choose from: "a familiar street, an elegant parlour, a lonely and dark kitchen and a natural forest."[79] Soon after the official opening of his Music Hall, Commins presented the Indian poetess, Pauline Johnson, in recitations, Sheridan's "The Rivals" with Leroy Kenney, a native of Oakville who later became famous as an impersonator, and the perennial favourites, "Mrs. Jarley's Wax Works" and "Ten Nights in a Bar-room." But the Music Hall was on too elaborate a scale to be profitable; when it burned to the ground on January 2, 1898, there were murmurs of incendiarism. Thereafter professional entertainments were held, as formerly, in the Town Hall. From the *Oakville Star* comes a description of an amateur performance given in 1888: "A crowded house greeted the presentation of Kardoo in the town hall. . . . When the curtain was raised one of the finest sights to be seen upon earth met the astonished view. Twenty-five handsome young ladies, draped in the emblem of purity, heavily jewelled, and sitting with grace and ease, were presented to the audience. The sight nearly dazed the senses, and made all conscious that it was good to be there. Young men felt like building a temple for each of them, and old bachelors desired to erect two to each—and give the contract without a months delay. The eyes were feasted on beauty, and the ears greeted with pure melody. . . ."

In the early eighties, Oakville had three newspapers, the *Standard,* the *Independent,* and the *Express.* In 1880 the *Standard* had been bought from Edward Bailey by George King, son of William M. King, who published it for three years. Then the presses and other equipment were destroyed in the Romain Block fire, and King moved to the West. For ten years, between 1878 and 1888, the *Independent* was published by C. Rowland Orr; at one point during this period he also published the *Halton New Era,* but little is known of this newspaper. The *New Era* was bought in 1899 by Charles F. Raymond of Guelph, who changed its name to *Raymond's Record.* It was taken over eight years later by William J. Fleuty, also of Guelph, who named it the *Oakville Record;* at that time it was the only Liberal Conservative sheet in the county. After being edited and published for fifteen years by Fleuty, the *Oakville Record* passed through several hands before being taken over in 1930 by George C. Atkins. Atkins bought the *Star* after the death of Arthur S. Forster and merged the two newspapers into the *Oakville Record-Star,* a weekly which is still being published at the present time.

For a short time the *Express* was published by C. Rowland Orr. In 1883 it was bought by J. M. Shaw and his son Campbell, of Elora,[80] who promptly changed the name to the *Oakville Star.* The few extant copies of the *Star* of this period show that the Shaws built it into a newspaper of good standing, and the well-written editorials indicated a breadth of outlook unusual in a small-town newspaper of those times. The special features were well chosen and, altogether, the *Star* possessed a distinction which reflected J. M. Shaw's twenty-five years of newspaper work.

At the time the *Star* began its career, the old rag paper was being replaced by newsprint manufactured from wood pulp, which was cheaper in price but much inferior in quality. The durability of the rag paper used until the eighties largely accounts for the abundance of of newspapers from the earliest days of the province that have survived down to the present time. Although, as we have seen, the *Sentinel* began using a power press in the fifties, the type was still laboriously set by journeymen compositors who were paid according to the amount,

Beautiful ❊ Oakville.

"Nor rural sights alone, but rural sounds,
Exhilarate the spirit and restore
The tone of languid nature."

WM. COWPER.

1897

Published by J. E. COMMINS, Oakville.

A. S. FORSTER, PRINTER, OAKVILLE. J. L. JONES ENG. CO., ENGRAVERS, TORONTO.
J. E. COMMINS, PHOTOGRAPHER

24. Colborne Street looking east from Dunn Street

25. The Royal Exchange Hotel

26. William Busby's store and residence (No. 64 Colborne Street East)

27. The Oakville House

28. Store on the south-west corner of Colborne and Dunn Streets, originally Duncan Chisholm's Tin Shop

29. Dr. John Urquhart's Medical Hall, established 1835 (No. 62 Colborne Street East)

30. Gulledge's Harness Shop on the south-east corner of Colborne and Thomas Streets, originally Romain's store

31. John Kelley's Hardware Store (No. 94 Colborne Street East)

32. The Queen's Hotel, William Wynne, Proprietor

33. W. G. Hewson's Grocery Store (No. 37 Colborne Street East, East Half)

34. William Whitaker & Sons' Carriage Works, Dundas Street North

35. George's Square looking east from Dundas Street

36. Presbyterian Manse, originally the home of John Potter (No. 119 Dundas Street North)

37. Captain F. J. Brown's residence (No. 169 Dundas Street North)

38. Carson's Planing Mill, Dundas Street North

39. Doty's Steam Sawmill on The Sixteen

40. Approach to the railway station

41. Hillmer's Livery Stable, Church Street

42. THE BASKET FACTORY, DUNDAS STREET NORTH

43. THE OLD MILL ON THE SIXTEEN

by measurement, of type set. After the paper had been run off the presses the journeymen returned at night to redistribute the type into their cases, for which they were responsible. The type was referred to by name; as pearl, nonpareil, minion, pica, etc.; today it would be designated as five, six, seven, and twelve point type. Brevier (eight point), so called because it was used in printing breviaries, was the body type most common in the printing of newspapers sixty and seventy years ago. After 1900 on the front page of almost every issue of the *Star* appeared a picture (more frequently than not the likeness of a murderer) which was a line cut made not from a photograph but from a pen and ink drawing. The cuts used by advertisers were from similar engravings; it was not until later that the process for reproducing the photographs themselves came within the price range of small newspapers.

In 1887, at the age of seventeen, Arthur Forster became printer for the Shaws and two years later bought the newspaper. Under Forster, the *Star* changed greatly. He attempted a breezy journalistic style which may be attributed both to his years and to the influence of the era. Though excesses in the use of this style were modified with time, the *Star,* during the forty years that Forster was its editor and publisher, never approached the high journalistic standard it had attained under the Shaws. He himself had no qualms about the direction of his paper. When presented with a copy of the *Oakville Advertiser* dated 1859, published by William M. King (he promised his readers to reprint excerpts from it but failed to do so), Forster commented that "in our estimation journalism has greatly improved since that time, although it is a very creditable sheet."[81] To the personal column headed "Twinklings" and the column containing small news items headed "Constellations," Forster added "The Cradle," "The Altar," and "The Grave." We see by the fashion notes that in 1889 "Eiffel red, or the exact colour which the tower is painted, is very fashionable." Also that "Saigitoo, the medicine man from the Mississaugas of New Credit, . . . son of the well known Indian doctor Maungwudaus," visited Urquhart's Medical Hall with a "full supply of medicines from his father's recipes." The following item headed "Reminiscences" and occasioned by the eighty-third birthday of W. H. Young, is representative of Forster's journalistic style.

Tis midnight! The clock in St. Jude's strikes twelve. Another day is told off and the clock ticks, ticks on with measured pause, moving to another day. The oaks of Oakville bud and leaf, nestle the trilling songster, put on their frost be-dyed hues, and bow beneath their load of snow and proclaim the fact—another year is gone. The ice floes of the Sixteen float out into old Ontario, the blackbird hops from rush to rush, the summer visitor glides up her stream, the cold autumnal winds ruffle the waters . . . and merry youth glides over her surface while the old clock strikes the New Year hour and another year is born. . . .

The Star reaches out the greeting hand as one of those steps across our threshold, while St. Jude's tells off his Three and Eighty years of Oakville life and history. Such an one is our ever alert citizen and friend, W. H. Young. Born in Oakville on the 13th of Dec. 1825 he has seen and known of all her changing scenes through all those fleeting years. The corduroy give place to the busy street, the schoolhouse to the well-ventilated church, the ox team to the railroad, the tallow candle to the electric light, and the straggling hamlet to our beautiful Oakville. He has known to woo and win and wed, to mourn and weep and part. He has lived to strive for what he deemed best, has both failed and often won, but to few is it given to bear the heat and cold, the breezes and the blasts of Three and Eighty seasons, and with frame erect and nimble step attest the fact that Oakville's clime is fair. Greetings to our friend, greetings to the oldest native-born of Oakville. Many happy returns.

In point of fact Young was born at Munn's Corners. Correctness of tone too was questioned by the object of this tribute. Across the top of a clipping of it pasted in his scrap-book, "The Serpent's Trail," Young wrote, "Too much of a *Good Thing.*"

Arthur Forster was a pioneer in agitating for better roads and much of the road improvement in the county may be traced to his hammering away year after year at the subject. Not that bad roads kept the people of Oakville from making long journeys—far from it. In waggons and buggies they started out on expeditions that we in these days of swiftly travelling motor cars would consider a good distance. John A. Williams, who was by now farming in the western district, near Chatham, some 170 miles from Oakville, was visited regularly every year by numerous friends and relatives from his native town who passed by on their way elsewhere or stopped for a few days' visit. It was thus that Williams was able to keep his reminiscences up to date.

These reminiscences, covering a period of more than eighty years, were recorded towards the end of a long life of ninety-two years. Because of their scope and accuracy, they have immeasurably enriched this record. Williams was fond of writing poetry and composing acrostics; and every year each pupil of his Sabbath School class, which he taught for many years at Oakville, received an acrostic at Christmas.

Williams' transition from merchant to farmer took place in 1893. As general merchant, he had done well in Oakville. During the prosperous fifties, when Charles Davis gave up shoemaking to become proprietor of the Halton House, Williams had occupied Davis's store on the northwest corner of George and Colborne streets. The second floor was used as living quarters and in after years Williams wrote: "I used to sit in our dining room window and look over John Moore's tin shop at the brick store which Obadiah Marlatt had built and the rookeries in back of it and calculate what I would do with it. I seemed to feel that I would own it some day." When Marlatt left Oakville in the sixties, Williams bought this building and for a time employed as clerk young William Busby. But Williams found expansion at this time hard going and, after a long and difficult struggle, he concluded that the lot of a farmer was preferable to that of a merchant. In 1893 he sold his business to three brothers, W. A., Nelson, and Frank Robinson; and at the age of sixty-five he took up land in Kent County north of Chatham. With the assistance of his son he cleared it, using the lumber cut from his own timber to build a house in which he placed many possessions that his father Justus Williams had brought with him to Oakville.

After Williams had moved out of the old store at George Street, its original occupant, Charles Davis, who had gotten into trouble for selling liquor without a licence at his temperance inn, returned, in his old age, to shoemaking in the building he had erected in the thirties. After his death in 1880, Charles Bradbury bought the building for a barber shop.

As a lad Charles Bradbury had come to Canada from Lancashire and sailed the lakes on schooners out of Oakville. As he was handy with scissors, his fellow sailors frequently called upon him for hair-cuts, and in this way he learned the barber's trade. Acting upon the suggestion of his friends, Bradbury started a shop in town which became the favourite rendezvous for sailors. Forster delighted in referring to Bradbury as "our Tonsorial artist," but his establishment was much more than a barber shop. He was first in town to supply Toronto newspapers, he had the largest stock of tobacco in Oakville, and he was agent for Parker's Dye Works and for the Allan Steamship Line. In 1885 he installed pool tables, and billiards and pool became "all the rage in town." The council hastened to provide legislation for exacting a licence fee on and "regulating Billiard tables." One lake captain became so devoted to the game that he frequently failed to turn up for dinner; his wife became so exasperated one night that she sent his dinner to the pool room by buggy from a mile down the Lake Shore Road. When Bradbury's property was secured by the Bank of Commerce for a new branch building, the old shop was divided into two sections and moved to William Street; the front section now stands as no. 89 and the rear, which had been the living quarters, is the double house that is nos. 62 and 64 William Street.

Bradbury's barber shop was the headquarters for both political parties. There the federal, provincial, and municipal elections were fought, and lost or won. By the eighties the Reform party had adopted the name Liberal, although to the Oakville Tories its members continued to be Grits. The leadership of the Liberals was assumed by C. G. Marlatt, whose Reform background well fitted him to be president of the Oakville Liberal Club. Marlatt was instrumental in bringing Wilfrid Laurier to speak at a rally held August 13, 1888, in George's Square, at which Sir Richard Cartwright was also present. Though five thousand had been expected, only about fifteen hundred appeared for the speeches. The visitors were entertained at lunch at the Canadian Hotel.

When viewed in the light of later events, Laurier's visit to Oakville is memorable. It was his first big speech in Ontario after having been chosen leader of the Liberal Opposition in Parliament. He became Prime Minister in 1896, and Canada then enjoyed fifteen years of unparalleled prosperity, which was largely attributed to the policies of the Liberal Government, in particular that of intensive immigration. It was during this same period that Oakville's fortunes began gradually to rise. Public utilities were installed and other improvements made in the town at the behest of councils predominantly Grit. Civic pride in the enterprises of the town was not slow to manifest itself. The council sponsored several pamphlets of eulogy of the town, and the hopes for the future are evident in the first of these (1897), *Beautiful Oakville.*

CHAPTER TWELVE

"A SMALL SLEEPY TOWN"

THE LAST TWO DECADES of the nineteenth century were notable for the extensive building of brick churches throughout the towns and villages of Halton and other surrounding counties. No matter how small the community, no matter how numerous the denominations represented therein, the congregations, in face of continued depression, contrived to collect sufficient funds to replace their frame churches with more substantial structures. Within one decade the three Protestant congregations at Oakville built new brick churches.[1] Unhappily, the simplicity of the old white frame structures was discarded in favour of the late Victorian-Gothic.

The first denomination to erect a new building was the Wesleyan Methodist; the congregation's minister, the Reverend Thomas Howard, had gained a reputation for church building. Though there was some opposition at the outset, eventually the Board of Trustees unanimously adopted a resolution to build a new church on the same site. The old building was sold to John A. Williams for $400, with the understanding that the congregation would have the use of it until the new one was completed,[2] and preparations went forward to get the building materials on the ground while the snow of the winter of 1876 lasted. The sand, drawn by volunteer labour, was given by John Alton, and the stone, which cost $4.50 per cord to haul, was the gift of Isaac Warcup. The bricks were purchased by subscription money and cost $8.50 per thousand, delivered. Smith & Gemmall of

Toronto prepared plans and specifications. The stonework, bricklaying, and plastering were done by John Heatley, and the carpentry work by James McDonald.[3]

The laying of the corner-stone took place in the presence of some two thousand persons on July 2, 1877. The ceremony was performed by John McDonald of Toronto, the largest wholesale dry-goods merchant in Canada, known as the "Merchant Prince." In the cavity of the corner-stone was deposited a metal case containing the following documents:

A copy of the *Spectator,* Sept. 27, 1816, published at St. David's, Upper Canada.

A copy of the *Gleaner,* 1818.

A copy of the first edition of the *Christian Guardian,* published by Egerton Ryerson, 1829.

A copy of the *Colonial Advocate*, Sept. 24, 1829 (Wm. L. Mackenzie's newspaper).

An account of the opening of the Grand Trunk Railway of Canada, 1856.

Copies of the minutes of the London, Montreal and Toronto Wesleyan Methodist Conferences, 1876.

A copy of the Oakville *Express*, Toronto *Mail, Weekly Globe* and *Christian Guardian*, all dated 1877.

One specimen of all the silver coins issued from the time Canada had become a dominion, and a copper farthing of the reign of George II, dated 1754.[4]

After the case was lowered into the cavity, McDonald struck the corner-stone three times in the name of the Holy Trinity.[5] The new church, called St. John's Church, was dedicated by the Reverend Dr. Egerton Ryerson on January 13, 1878.

Before it was completed, the building had cost in the neighbourhood of $18,000. Few of the details of the costs are available, but according to James McDonald's account books[6] the carpentry work totalled $3,589.81. John Cowton did the painting, and the upholstered pews, the money for which was raised by the ladies of the congregation, were made in the planing mill of R. S. Wood. Two hot air furnaces were installed. It was not until the year following dedication that a pipe organ, built by Lye & Son, Toronto, was obtained. A receipted bill shows that the "organ blower" received $20 per annum for his services.

Upon completion of the new church the old frame building, which had served as the second church of the Wesleyan Methodists for over twenty-five years, was moved by its owner, John A. Williams, to the north-east corner of Thomas and Colborne streets which had stood vacant for ten years after fire destroyed the buildings of Arnott and Barclay. "The old Methodist Church," noted the local press, "is at its last resting place. . . . We understand it is to be converted into three stores."[7] This plan was put into effect and today the building is nos. 47, 49, and 51 Colborne Street East.

Fortunately, St. John's was large enough to receive the members of the Methodist Episcopal Church when, in 1884, union was effected with the Wesleyans. The Methodist Episcopalians had occupied their church on the west side of the town at John and Wilson streets until 1869 when they built a new place of worship on the east bank of The Sixteen at the north-west corner of Navy and Randall behind the schoolhouse. The first service in the new church took place on January 2, 1870.[8] The sect had its own circuit in which the villages Palermo and Springfield-on-the-Credit (now Erindale) were joined with Oakville. Each week, the two preachers on the circuit alternated in conducting the morning service at one of these churches, the afternoon at another, and the evening at the third. Bishop Carman came to Oakville many times to preach and one of the ministers on the circuit in 1878 was the Reverend J. W. Warne who was soon to go out to India as a missionary. With the union of the Methodist Episcopal and Wesleyan Methodist Churches in Canada, the two congregations united in service for the first time in over fifty years, on June 1, 1884.[9]

After forty-five years of continual use, St. Jude's Anglican Church at Colborne and Thomas Streets, which had begun existence as the Methodist chapel, had become so shaky that plans were laid for a new building. Canon John Bell Worrell had been rector for fifteen years; and, during his incumbency, the congregation had been increased by the addition of a number of British families. Several retired Army and Navy officers who had come to Canada to farm had settled in the vicinity of Oakville, mostly along the Lake Shore Road; among the townspeople they were known as the "English Crowd." Inspired by the success of the Methodists, the Anglicans formed a Building Committee the year St. John's Church was dedicated. "Instead of repairing and adding to the old Church," the committee solicited subscriptions for building a new church.[10] The land on the south-west corner of the intersection of William and Thomas streets was bought, but it was not until five years later, June 13, 1883, that the corner-stone was laid by the Right Worshipful Daniel Spry, Grand Master of the Grand Lodge of A. F. and A. M. of Canada.[11]

To assist in raising money for the building fund, the Women's Guild of St. Jude's Church was formed in 1884, and "every female member of the Congregation" was invited to join.[12] Various entertainments were given, but the most popular were the amateur theatricals of the "English Church Theatre" organized by a young Englishman, Cyril Maude, whose family, in the hope that a few years' farming would alter his determination to become an actor, had sent him to Canada. He worked on the fruit farm of Richard Postans, originally "King's Castle." For rehearsing, Maude and his group secured the barn on Robinson Street in the rear of Ferrah's bakery, recently demolished to make way for the government liquor store. The first performance, "Mrs. Jarley's Wax Works," given in the Town Hall, was a great success, and it was followed by other plays. But the enthusiasm of the group waned when Maude left Oakville to enter upon his outstanding career. He reached his greatest popularity about the time of World War I in the role of "Grumpy." Cyril Maude always had a ready welcome for Oakville friends when they visited him behind the scenes and for many years he continued to send subscriptions to St. Jude's Church.

At the time it was built, the new St. Jude's was said to be in the style of All Saints' Church in Toronto. The bell from the old church, which for half a century had announced services and warned of fires in the community, was hung in the tower. And Richard Coates's organ was brought from the balcony of the old church and installed on the east wall of the chancel, where it continued in use for many years.

After the removal of its spire,[13] the old frame building was sold to Samuel McGiffin who converted it into a hardware store. McGiffin was a son of Captain Samuel McGiffin, a master mariner who had settled at Oakville in the early forties. Another son, Captain John, was commander of the schooner *Jennie Matthews* and of the steamer *Canada,* which ran between Montreal and Chicago, and commodore of the Niagara Navigation Company's steamers which ran between Toronto and Niagara. He lived on Navy Street, at the south-east corner of William Street in the house which is now no. 33 Navy Street South, but which has undergone many stages of alterations since his time. The house of his brother, Sam, the hardware merchant, on the opposite corner, has altered little. In 1873 Sam McGiffin purchased the house built in the thirties by William J. Sumner, now no. 27 Navy Street South.

The church building had been McGiffin's hardware store for several years when doubts arose "as to the power" of the Diocese of Niagara of the Church of England to convey the property to McGiffin. The transfer was then legalized by an Act of Parliament.[14] In 1898 the building was secured by the Merchants Bank, the first chartered bank to come to Oakville. After twelve years, the old building was torn down and the new brick building which is now the Bank of Montreal was built on the site. The architect for the new bank was Robert McGiffin, a nephew of the former owner. Some of the materials from the old church were used to build the office of Hillmer's Ice and Fuel Company, near the railway on Dundas Street; one of the church doors escaped destruction, and exists at the present time.

With the exception of their participation in the activities of St. Jude's Church, the "English Crowd" mostly kept to themselves. One of the first to settle in the district was the Reverend George Evans, an eccentric Irishman who was known as "the Fox-Hunting Clergyman." His estate east of the Town Line, lot 32 of the 3rd concession in Toronto Township, which he named after his ancestral Irish home in County Tyrone, "Gortmerron," was one of the show places in Canada West. He was a crack shot, a hard drinker, and a good horseman; when over seventy he still followed the hounds.[15] He attended St. Jude's Church and, when he died at the age of eighty-five, he was buried in St. Jude's Cemetery. And there were General Jackson and his son, both of whom had been through the Indian Mutiny, who also lived east of the town. On the Lake Shore Road West were Captain Hugh Pullen, R.N. retired, Captain Bunbury, and Major Francis Lloyd, whose little daughter used to drive a donkey-cart into town. Attired in the clothes of the English countryside and walking at the donkey's head swinging their canes, the major and his wife presented a novel sight to the rural population. There were also numbers of young bachelors who, like Maude, worked on farms in the district. It was not unusual to see these men appear in full evening dress at a ball in the Town Hall when, only a few hours before, they had been driving a load of manure along Colborne Street. The class distinctions of Victorian England were rigidly adhered to, and these people kept mostly within their own circle. Few remained in Canada; one by one they sold their farms and returned to England.

At a meeting of the St. Jude's congregation held in 1887, it was decided that a parish hall should be built, and the suggestion of Chistopher Armstrong, that the building "commemorate Her Majesty's Jubilee," was adopted.[16] It was he who gave the window depicting Queen Victoria in her robes of state, which was placed in the parish hall. The new church and parish hall were both dedicated at the same time, on June 3, 1889, by the Bishop of Niagara.[17]

The rectory, situated a mile west of the town, had been enlarged by the addition of a second storey during the occupancy of Canon Worrell. As the rector found living so far from the town a great inconvenience, the present rectory, no. 90 William Street, was purchased. For a time the old rectory was rented and was eventually bought by the occupant. In 1894 the property passed into the hands of Dr. William T. Stuart, who named it after the ancient palace of the Scottish Kings at Edinburgh, "Holyrood."

In 1895, the tower of St. Jude's was raised, and on each corner was placed a small tin spire. A fine view of the surrounding country was to be had from the tower and, during the next few years, the sum of $5.30 went into the church fund from "Tower Views" at 5¢ each.[18]

A note in the handwriting of Canon Worrell is to be found in St. Jude's Burial Register which reads: "J. B. Worrell completed 34½ years ministry at St. Jude's and 56½ years of his service in the Sacred Ministry—*when he resigned*." At that time, 1903, Canon Worrell was eighty-three years of age; and when he died at Oakville he had reached the age of ninety-eight. His son, Clarendon Lamb Worrell, became Bishop of Nova Scotia, the oldest bishopric outside the British Isles, founded in 1797. He was also Primate of all Canada. Another son, John Austin Worrell, was Chancellor of Trinity University. The two rectors who succeeded Canon Worrell were graduates of the university which had trained so many missionaries of the Anglican Church who had come to Canada, Trinity College, Dublin. They, in turn, were succeeded by two graduates of Trinity College, Toronto.

Three years after the resignation of Canon Worrell, the installation in the tower of a clock and chimes was projected. The *Star* carried the following announcement on September 20, 1906: "His Majesty the King has graciously consented to allow his name to be cast on the tenor bell of the new peal for St. Jude's Anglican Church, Oakville. Consent has been received to cast on the bells the names of the Lord Bishop of Niagara, the Governor-General, the Lieutenant-Governor of Ontario, the Mayor, Rector, Church Wardens and Committeemen. The name of Mrs. Walker Smith appears on the bell donated by her. Nine bells have been ordered. Subscriptions for the tenth are coming in. It is expected the bells will be in use on St. Jude's day next." The nine bells, weighing eight tons and made in London, England, by Mears & Steinbeck, were hung and the clock fixed in its place in the tower by October 11. During the following week the try-out of the chimes created much interest in the town. On the 18th Bishop DuMoulin, of the Diocese of Niagara, came for the dedication. The clock, made in London by Benson's, Ludgate Hill, Fleet Street, was not in action until the 26th, when it struck for the first time.[19] Big Ted, as the largest bell was called by the ringer, bears the inscription, "Edward, King and Emperor, A.D. 1906."

Having enlarged their church in the sixties, the members of the Canada Presbyterian Church were in no immediate need of a new building. However, the minister was provided with a manse; not long after the arrival of the Reverend William Meikle, the house of John Potter, known as "Potter's Folly," now no. 119 Dundas Street North, was secured by the congregation for that purpose. At this time the subject of music as an accompaniment to the church services was broached following the decision of the General Assembly that music was permissible. The idea was warmly received by a large number of the congregation, but violently opposed by some of the older members. In 1872, the Session of Elders stated that it "did not desire the introduction of instrumental music in the worship of God in the Sanctuary, nevertheless, knowing that such is the desire of the Canada Presbyterian Church it is hereby agreed to appeal the action."[20] During the two years that the matter rested, the pros and cons were hotly discussed by the congregation. When a vote was taken in 1873 it was found that forty-eight members stood for and only ten against "the use of an instrument of music in the ordinary services of the Congregation," and five later gave way to the wish of the majority. Bowing to the expressed desire of the congregation, the Session decreed that "an organ is permitted to be used in Sabbath School and Church."[21]

The organ stood below the pulpit, and on each side of it were ranged the members of the choir. Declaring he "couldna worship God in a church where they had the devil's instrument, a kistfu' o' whustles," one member left the Church and is said to have "gone over" to the Wesleyan Methodists, who, however, had not only a kistfu' o' whustles, but a flute player to accompany the choir. Perhaps it was he who met John Barclay on his way to church with his small son on the day in June, 1873, when the organ was to be used for the first time. "John," he said, "don't go to the church, there is a devil in there." Needless to say, young Robert Barclay could not reach the church fast enough to catch a glimpse of the devil. John Barclay never lost hope of eliminating the organ, but he did not go to the length of leaving the Church, as did another member who objected to the singing of a voluntary during the taking of the collection.[22]

Sunday services at the Canada Presbyterian Church were held at 10:30 A.M. and 6:30 P.M.[23] The communion service began at 10 A.M. and lasted until 2 P.M., the children being permitted to go home for dinner and then return. Since it was a branch of the Free Church of Scotland, the Canada Presbyterian Church was always referred to by its members as the Kirk. The churches in Ontario united in 1875 with those of the Maritimes and Lower Province, and were thereafter "designated and known as the Presbyterian Church in Canada." The charge at Omagh was no longer joined to the Oakville church and in 1882 the church on the Dundas Street, by then called Knox Sixteen Church, was separated from Oakville.

In 1887 the congregation at Oakville prepared to build a new church, and purchased the property on the south-east corner of Dunn and Colborne streets, where stood the old White Oak Hotel. The corner-stone was laid July 1, 1887, and Knox Church, as the new church was called, was ready for dedication on May 20, 1888.[24] Constructed by James McDonald junior, a son of the builder of the first church, the brick building cost somewhat over $15,000.[25] The interior was lit by "five large, handsome gasoliers and plain gasoliers in brackets at sidewalls."[26] The cost of carpeting was borne by eighteen members, each of whom paid $4. The carriage sheds were moved from the old site and set up along Robinson Street in rear of the church. At the dedication ceremony a member presented to the church an illuminated book containing the names of contributors and accounts in connection with its construction.

The frame church on William Street, which James McDonald had taken in part payment, was remodelled on the same site into three houses: the double house that is now nos. 137 and 139 William Street, and the single house that is no. 141. The White Oak Hotel, which originally was Thomas Lloyd's tavern, was divided into three sections and moved to different parts of the town. (See Appendix I.) Looking at these buildings today one would never suppose that incorporated within them are parts of one of the earliest structures in the town.

The funeral of Captain Robert Wilson, perhaps the oldest member of the Presbyterian Church, was the first to be held at Knox Church. The tribute to Captain Wilson, which Mr. Meikle wrote into the Session Minutes, reads in part:

> He came, with his family, in comparative youth, from Ireland. For many years he was actively engaged in the business of our great Lakes, and became a master mariner. He was highly esteemed by his employers, and by the men that served under him.

He was more than thirty years Elder in our church. In the Session he ever manifested the greatest pleasure to promote the welfare of the people, had most kindly sympathies with all in trouble, and was ever prepared to aid them to the full extent of his abilities and opportunities.[27]

In the same year that the bell and chimes were installed in St. Jude's Church, a bell was hung in the tower of Knox Church. The bell was cast by Meneely & Co. of West Troy, New York, and inscribed with the words, "Presented by Mrs. R. R. Cromarty and Mrs. C. G. Marlatt, 1906."[28] From Chief Sumner's diary we learn that both these large bells were heard for the first time on February 25. Knox Church was remodelled and renovated throughout after World War I; and, in memory of the men who had fallen in the war, the window depicting the Last Supper was given by C. G. Marlatt.

The Negroes in Oakville had succeeded in securing a place of worship in the seventies. As early as the 1830's, ministers of the African Methodist Episcopal Church had come from the United States to preach among that portion of the coloured settlers in Canada who were Methodists. Classes and societies increased so rapidly that an American bishop organized an annual conference; but Canadian ministers found being subject to foreign discipline unsatisfactory. Also, it was unsafe for ministers who were escaped slaves to attend conferences in the United States because of the danger of recapture. In 1856 the Negroes withdrew from the A.M.E. Church of the United States, and met at Chatham, near the village of Dresden, where there was a large settlement headed by the Reverend Josiah Henson, mentioned earlier in this narrative. Adopting the articles as given by John Wesley, they formed an independent church to which was given the name of the British Methodist Episcopal Church. Not long afterwards Samuel Adams, blacksmith, and his father-in-law, the Reverend William Butler, brought their families to settle at Bronte. About 1860, they set to work to organize a church in the village. But it was soon found that there were more Negroes at Oakville, and the congregation secured the use of the old building erected by the Congregationalists on the northwest corner of John and Wilson streets, which had been vacated by the Methodist Episcopal congregation after the opening of their new church on Navy Street. The record book bears the inscription, "British Methodist Episcopal Church of Oakville, organized Dec. 13, 1875" and the "Oakville and Bronte Circuit" is mentioned.[29] It shows that there were sixteen Oakville families, among whom were the Johnsons, Duncans, Strothers, and Hills. There was also Christopher Columbus Lee, for many years butler to R. K. Chisholm. The singing and shouting typical of the Old South made the protracted evangelist meetings very popular; one of the ministers was much sought after by gatherings in Toronto and Hamilton because of his singing of spirituals. To assist in financing their church the Negroes held frequent balls in the Town Hall, and in 1883 the first cake-walk created much interest. "Something new in Town," commented Sumner. In 1887 the congregation purchased the church property; but dissension and estrangement sprang up between the B.M.E. and A.M.E. adherents as to the ownership of the property. Before two years were out, the building burned to the ground, and the outcries of incendiarism probably had some foundation in truth. Finally, the two factions settled their difficulties and the twenty-five members at Oakville and the thirty-eight at Bronte united to build the present church on the north side of Colborne Street, west of Chisholm Street. The corner-stone was laid in 1891, and on January 1 of the following year, the Turner African Methodist Episcopal Church, so named in honour of Bishop Turner, opened for service.[30]

The invasion of Oakville in the early eighties by the Salvation Army is described by John A. Williams in the following words: "A party of Christian people from Toronto visited Oakville in the style of an army and marched through the streets beating drums and speaking and singing at corners of streets, retiring to Church for services. Great revival ensued." According to the Army's publication, *Roll Call*, the first meeting held in the Town Hall was not an outstanding success, "the invading army being composed of an old man who was deaf, a boy and a dog."[31] Within a year, the Methodist Episcopal Church at Navy and Randall, which had stood vacant for about a year after the union of the Methodists, was secured by the Salvation Army for their barracks. Among the first "to take their stand in the Army" were George Busby and Mrs. Thomas Hinton.

Cynthia Greeniaus (Mrs. Hinton), a descendant of the Loyalist family who had been granted land at Sheridan, had been converted at a protracted meeting held in the old Red Schoolhouse nearby. Her father had moved to Oakville in 1852 to work for Thompson Smith, and Cynthia married Captain Thomas Hinton who was sailing lumber out of Oakville for Smith. At the time his wife became interested in Salvation Army work, Captain Hinton was master of the little *Louella* which plied Toronto Bay between the city and the island.

One of the earliest events in the history of the corps, a "War Cry March" to a circus which came to the town, was described in the *Roll Call*. "Bedecked with 'War Crys,' " relates the *Roll Call*, "the faithful few took their stand near the circus grounds. The proprietors became so incensed that they ordered out the elephants and tried to disperse the Salvationists; but the beasts refused to obey their master, and the Army carried on."[32] When George Busby and his wife died of typhoid fever, Sergeant-Major Hinton was left to carry on alone. At times the only representative of the Salvation Army in the town, she went valiantly forth, and there were few indeed to whom "Grandma Hinton's" sweet face, framed by the navy blue Army bonnet, was not familiar. It was she who kept the work alive in the face of discouraging difficulties.

The camp meetings of the Methodists, which in earlier times had taken place only in summer, now took the form of protracted meetings held in the churches any time during the year. They had formerly been conducted by local preachers who gathered from all parts of the district, but the meetings held in co-operation with the Presbyterians in 1888 were conducted by the popular evangelists, Crossley and Hunter. During the five weeks these men remained in Oakville meetings were held both in St. John's Church and Knox Church.[33] Thereafter Crossley and Hunter returned frequently to hold evangelistic meetings in the town.

Except for the changing of the name of the Methodist church to St. John's United Church following the union of Methodist, Presbyterian, and Congregational Churches in Canada effected in 1925, from which Knox Church held aloof, there have been virtually no further changes in the churches at Oakville. Today the places of worship remain the same as those recorded in this section of the town's history. St. Andrew's Roman Catholic Church is the only structure which dates back to the time when Oakville was still in its infancy. Should William Chisholm return today, this is probably the only building he would recognize in the village he founded.

The prospect of the need of a new and larger schoolhouse, which had been discussed at the time Oakville's population was expanding so rapidly, disappeared with the levelling-off of the population. Few changes took place until the passing of the School Law Improvement Act in 1871. As a result of this Act, the name of high school was given to the grammar school and the term public school replaced that of common school; also, the headmaster became principal, and the local superintendent was called school inspector. Of greater importance, the Act required that schoolhouses have a site of not less than half an acre and a playground protected by a fence, and that schoolrooms have walls ten feet high and be adequately heated and ventilated. The amount of floor space per pupil was specified; desks with seats having backs were required, and such necessary apparatus as maps and blackboards. A well, or other means of procuring water, must be provided and "proper and separate offices for both sexes at some distance and suitably enclosed." These are but a few of the many provisions of the School Law Improvement Act. With the enforcement of this legislation, the old log and frame schoolhouses disappeared from the township as they were replaced by new buildings.

The brick building of the Oakville School answered the essential requirements as laid down by the Act; but alterations in the boundaries of the school sections brought more children to the school. The School Inspector, Robert Little, reported: "The High and Public Schools are united, and are taught in the same building. As the County Council have not yet set off the High School Boundaries, and as changes will, in all probability, be made, I have not taken any steps in regard to the accommodation required by the Public School."[34] At this time the school population of Oakville, that is, children between the ages of five and sixteen years, totalled 475. However, Little reported that "irregularity of attendance and absenteeism are alarmingly prevalent."[35] School was conducted during twelve months of the year, and the teaching staff consisted of the Misses Harcus, Mills, and Annie Balmer. J. W. Narroway, graduate of the Toronto Normal School, was appointed principal of the high school in 1877, and Dr. Charles Horace Lusk, who was more interested in teaching than in practising medicine, was appointed Narroway's assistant.[36] P. A. Switzer, graduate of Victoria College, who was headmaster of the public school, succeeded Narroway as principal of the high school in 1874, Lusk continuing as his assistant.[37]

It was at this time that the Town Council raised $4,000 "for the erection of new School Buildings,"[38] or, more correctly, for an addition to the old building. It will be remembered that the schoolhouse stood on the site of the first village cemetery, and when the work was begun, Chief Sumner noted in his diary, "I had fifteen skeletons found in digging the cellar for the schoolhouse buried today." One of these is said to have been the remains of Pat McGuiness, who had lived in the log house on the south-east corner of Navy Street. When Pat died of smallpox, he had been buried in his bed-clothes, ticking and all. At the time the excavations were being made for the addition to the schoolhouse, the feathers of the ticking were found to be as sound as the day they were buried. The bedding was burned, and the body re-interred, as Sumner stated.[39]

The £300 raised in 1850 had been spent on erecting a two-storey building approximately forty-one feet long by twenty-five feet in width with a bell cupola placed on the east end of the roof above the entrance facing east upon Navy Street. This original building now forms the section between the tower and the east block. With the £250 appropriation made in 1854, the building was extended to the west by the addition of a new entrance, hall, and stairway, and a thirty-five foot section of two storeys. The schoolhouse then faced south towards Colborne Street, and the new main entrance is the one used today. In 1874, with the appropriation of $4,000, a wing approximately thirty by forty feet, containing two rooms, was added on the north side, to which access was had from the main hallway on the ground floor and from the landing of the stairway in the upper storey. In front of the main entrance on the south side, a tower was erected which gave added protection from the weather and provided an upstairs room for the library. But at this time the tower ended with its mansard roof, and it was not until about 1900 that the bell was removed from the original cupola and hung in a new one atop the tower.

In 1877 Switzer was succeeded as principal of the high school by Nesbitt James Wellwood,[40] a native of Ireland who had come to Canada in his early youth and been educated at Oshawa, Whitby, and the University of Toronto.[41] Dr. Lusk continued as his assistant, and Henry Husband was made principal of the public school. A son of John Husband, an early settler in Nassagaweya Township[42] Henry Husband had begun teaching at Oakville in 1875.

We see, by the local press, that a Gurney furnace was installed in the schoolhouse in the autumn of 1878;[43] that the following year a well was "put down" and an iron pump installed on the school grounds, at a cost of $26.48.[44] Three years later, the Town Council raised the sum of $2,700 for building a two-storey addition across the east end of the schoolhouse, with entrances on Navy Street. Little reported that "by setting this apart for the High School, a large room was obtained for the public school departments."[45] Some time after 1900 the schoolhouse achieved its present dimensions when the west wing was lengthened to give four more windows on the south side and entrances at this end of the building. In the spring of 1910, the high school was moved to its new building on Reynolds Street, and the old school took the name of Central School. Headmasters of both schools are listed in Appendix H.

The playground had been enlarged by the purchase in 1889, by the Board of Education of Oakville, of block no. 49 in front of the schoolhouse, where George Baker's livery stable had long stood. Church Street was closed between Navy Street and the bank of The Sixteen, the barns were removed, and the office of the livery stable was moved east on Church Street, where it was used in connection with Hillmer's livery stable, as shown in the photograph (plate 41). The names of the livery stable horses, painted above the hooks where their harness hung, are still to be seen on the wall, but this old dwelling-house is now in so dilapidated a state that it will probably have disappeared by the time these words appear in print.

As has been recorded elsewhere in this volume, the first pupil matriculated from the Oakville Grammar School in 1861, the second in 1868, and two more in 1870. There were no matriculants between 1870 and 1882, when there were two, and there was a further gap to 1894, when one more succeeded in passing the examinations.[46] Until 1892, when Chief Sumner was appointed truant officer, the average attendance had never risen above 50 per cent and two years later it attained only 60 per cent. By the spring of 1910 the average attendance had reached 64 per cent of the school population.[47]

A citizen who showed a keen interest in the affairs of the community and particularly in its educational activities was William Busby, who was first elected to the Board of Education about 1883. For a quarter of a century he was chairman of the board and at the time of his death at the age of eighty-two he was its oldest member. William Busby was also interested in beautifying Oakville, and wished to see the community dump improved, but he did not live to see it become the playing field of today. Used for many years as the town dump, the marsh at the bottom of the east bank of the river, north of the Colborne Street bridge, was eventually filled in. In recent years it was covered with top soil, graded, and in recognition of William Busby's activities named Busby Park.

During his long term as Superintendent of Education, Dr. Egerton Ryerson worked steadily to procure libraries for all schools in the province. As early as 1848 he wrote in his annual report: "It is an interesting reflection that there is no portion of our territory so wild or remote, where man has penetrated, that the *library* has not peopled the wilderness around him, with the good and wise of this and other ages. . . . A colonial nation, we inherit the matured literature of England; but in our country as in that, this literature has not extended to the masses. In instituting a general library system, we create, or rather put in circulation, the first really popular literature, beyond that contained in the newspaper and in the books of the Sunday-school."[48]

We have seen, in an earlier section of this history, that by 1865 the library established in connection with the grammar school contained more than six hundred books.

When the Mechanics' Institute disintegrated through lack of support, its library was probably pooled with the school library, which had been placed in the tower of the schoolhouse. With the changes made by Parliament in 1877, in the Act relating to Mechanics' Institutes, came a revival of interest in this movement. It was not long before the Oakville *Standard* announced "a meeting of subscribers to the proposed formation of a Mechanics' Institute" and in 1879 we find the Oakville Institute incorporated with a membership of 172.[49] Under the charter, the yearly subscription was $1. The expenditures of 1880 list the rental of a library and reading-room at $57.50 and payment of salaries $22.08.[50] Although the Institute showed no phenomenal growth during the years that followed, the revenue from its membership, coupled with the government grant and small grants from the Town Council, enabled it to survive. Between 1880 and 1887, the number of books in its library, open only on Saturday afternoons, grew from six hundred to above thirteen hundred.

The special need for these institutes disappeared, however; lectures on chemistry, astronomy, and other kindred subjects failed to attract audiences and, again, interest in the Mechanics' Institutes waned. With the passing of the Free Libraries Act, they gave place to "public libraries," a term which in 1895 was adopted by both free and association libraries. The name of the Oakville Public Library then appears; being an association library, it continued along the same lines as the Institute library. The fee remained unaltered at $1 a year, or 25¢ for three months for summer visitors, and the library was open one day a week. The success of association libraries depended largely upon the interest of a few workers; they were maintained by membership fees, government and municipal grants, and money raised by entertainments. The Oakville Library moved about 1903 from the schoolhouse tower to two rooms over the Bank of Toronto, now the office of the *Record Star*.[51] In 1908, the library moved farther east to its present location at no. 74 Colborne Street which is part of the building that began its existence as John Forman's tavern (see Appendix I). Only a few years ago, during the course of alterations at the library, a sign came to light over a doorway which read "Temperance Hotel."

The Oakville Public Library continued as an association library until 1938, when it became a free public library in charge of a trained librarian, supported by grants from the municipality and the province and by a membership fee of 10¢.

The need for expanding the educational facilities of Oakville was met by the building of the present high school, the Brantwood School on the east side of the town, and, on the west, the Westwood School. The time approaches, however, when provision must be made to replace Central School. It is to be hoped that the old building which has served Oakville as its schoolhouse for more than a century will not be demolished, but adapted to some other purpose useful to the community.

II

Under the leadership of a town council which aimed at the attraction of new industries, the people of Oakville devoted themselves with enthusiasm to town improvements during the first decade of the twentieth century. The installation of electric power, a water and sewage system, and a telephone network, and the laying of cement sidewalks, followed one upon the other in close succession. The opening of the electric railway from Hamilton was thought to promise a boom in real estate, and several surveys were laid out. But of all these material advantages, illumination by electricity seemed to arouse the keenest interest.

It is a curious fact that electric lighting made its initial appearance in Oakville at Harbour Grove upon the occasion of the largest temperance gathering held in Canada up to that date, in 1889. The Royal Templars' Camp, at which all the provinces except Nova Scotia were represented, lasted ten days and was attended by "forty eloquent speakers and three Royal Revival Bands." Seating was arranged for twelve hundred persons, and in the large dining hall erected for the purpose ladies of the W.C.T.U. served meals to the public. Resplendent in gold-braided uniforms complete with epaulettes, gilt swords, and feather-trimmed cocked hats, the Templars continued their meetings well into the evening by electric light. The system was set up by Kay Company of Hamilton. Wires for Edison's incandescent light bulbs were strung through the trees, and the power was supplied by a dynamo run by a steam threshing-machine mounted upon a platform below the bank near the west pier. These were the first electric lights to be seen in Oakville.

A by-law providing for the furnishing of electricity by the municipality was quashed by the ratepayers of Oakville early in 1891. Soon after, however, permission was granted to Charles M. B. Lawrence of Stratford, Ontario, to erect poles to carry the wiring necessary for lighting the streets of the town and the stores and dwellings of subscribers. To provide power Lawrence installed a dynamo in McDonald's planing mill. This plant had been bought in 1887 from the widow of R. S. Wood by James McDonald junior, who had followed in his father's footsteps as carpenter and contractor in the town. As so frequently happens with saw and planing mills, this plant went up in flames within two years, but it was immediately rebuilt by McDonald.[52]

When poles had been erected, a dynamo installed, and the wiring of stores and homes of subscribers completed, the plant was placed in charge of a Scotsman, Robert McGowan. The *Star* announced that the stores of those merchants who were installing electricity would have power by New Year's Day, 1892.[53] The plan was to run the same boilers twenty-four hours a day: to operate the machinery of the planing mill in the day-time, and to run the dynamo for the production of electric energy at night. However, the plan failed, as it was found that running a dynamo with wood fuel was far different from running a planing mill. The boilers ate up the wood so rapidly that it proved impossible to maintain a fire even enough to generate electricity in a steady flow. Abandoning that attempt, Lawrence and McGowan moved the equipment to the old paint factory on the lake shore at the foot of George Street, where coal was used for fuel. It was not until March 7 that Sumner reported in his diary, "Electric lights to-night—they show up well."

The street lights were situated at the intersections along Colborne Street and in front of the churches. They were suspended by a rope from a long arm that reached out over the intersection, and every day each carbon-arc light was lowered for inspection and re-carboned if necessary.

McDonald's planing mill again caught fire in 1893. The residence of Captain Brown across the way was seriously endangered, but after playing the hoses on it for several hours, the firemen succeeded in saving it. The mill however, was a total loss[54] and was never rebuilt. For years its chimney stood on the bank of The Sixteen close to Dundas Street, one of the landmarks of the town. Finally, in the interest of public safety, it was demolished by dynamite in 1911.[55] The two black walnut trees which today flank the entrance walk to the house that was Captain Brown's, no. 169 Dundas Street North, are said to have sprouted from the stumps of those killed by the fire which destroyed McDonald's planing mill.

The electric light plant was bought from the executors of the estate of C. M. B. Lawrence in 1901 by A. B. Wass[56] who supplied power to householders at the rate of 10¢ per 1000 watts.[57] Early in the summer of 1906 the plant failed and the townspeople who had converted to electricity returned to kerosene lamps. In August when a by-law providing for the supplying of electric energy by the municipality was again submitted to the ratepayers it was carried by a majority of 173 votes.[58] The electric light plant was then leased by the Corporation but after two years this system was abandoned. Arrangements were made whereby current was obtained from the Cataract Power Company of Hamilton and when the more powerful street lights went on for the first time on February 22, 1909, Sumner noted carefully: "There are 112 lights of 32 C[andle] P[ower] and 20 of 50 C. P. consuming 5080 watts per hour. If burning 7 hours per night for the year, would cost $3.50 per night. An all night service would cost more." The brick paint factory which had served as the electric light plant was remodelled into a summer cottage known for many years as the Electric Light Cottage. In more recent times it has been called the "Worn Doorstep"; it is now no. 78 Front Street.

At the time the "electric light by-law" was submitted to the ratepayers of Oakville it was accompanied by a second by-law which provided for the installation of a water and sewage system. Both measures were largely due to the exertions of C. G. Marlatt whose tannery, by then the town's largest industry, was badly in need of both power and water. The water and sewage by-law was also carried by a large majority, and plans went forward for the new water-works. In September, 1908, work was begun on the reservoir situated near the lake shore between Kerr and Wilson streets on the west side of the town. At this time was formed the Oakville Water and Light Commission whose first chairman was C. G. Marlatt.

Among the older ratepayers was a group who viewed with suspicion the "extravagances" of the Grit councils. One of them inspected the construction of the reservoir and concluded "the mud hole is a fine place to bury our money." George Sumner, who was no longer Chief Constable, belonged to this group. After thirty-seven years of faithful service to the town in so many capacities Sumner had been summarily dismissed one night without warning or explanation. This injustice he accepted philosophically and with fortitude, but being thus suddenly deprived of work after having lived such a busy life, and at an age when he felt incapable of making a new venture, he was for a time quite lost. However, he occupied himself with his garden and with visits to his children in various sections of the province and the United States.

The water pumped from Lake Ontario passed through the filtration basin into a tall standpipe located in the rear of the schoolhouse at Randall Street. From there it was distributed throughout the town. During the course of laying the water mains on Colborne Street a section of the old corduroy road was uncovered at Allan Street. Several logs were cut through and found to be in a "good state of preservation."[59] Since then in other sections of Colborne Street East, logs have come to light which were believed to have formed part of the corduroy road.

With the installation of a water system and its attendant hydrants for fighting fire came the organization of an official fire brigade. On April 28, 1909, the Oakville Fire Department was organized under the guidance of J. Lister from Georgetown, who became temporary chief. A constitution was drawn up whereby firemen were elected once a year by ballot taken among the members of the brigade, and a set of rules was adopted. Each of the three companies had a captain and his lieutenant, and Alfred Hillmer was placed in charge of the hook and ladder waggon. From the time he was a small boy, Alf, a son of Edward Hillmer, had prided himself on being the first to reach a fire. In October, 1910, the Town Council appointed him Fire Chief, an office he held for thirty-four years. As a young man, Alf had bought cattle at Toronto for his father's butcher shop, and together with his brother, George, had conducted the livery stable after the death of Edward Hillmer. It was Alf who for many years drove the buses, and his horses were used to pull the fire engine. After the fire bell was lost with the destruction of the Town Hall the alarms of fire were sounded by long blasts on the tannery whistle, and the horses regularly kicked out their stalls in their anxiety to get off to the fire. At the close of World War I the municipality obtained a chemical truck from the flying field at Leaside. Four years later, in 1923, the first motorized hose truck was secured and motorization of the Oakville Fire Department was completed with the addition in 1929 of the pumper. When Chief Hillmer died at the age of eighty-one he was succeeded by the present chief who has long been a member of the fire department, Chief Fred Shaw.

The replacing of tar and cinder walks and the remaining plank walks by granolithic, as cement was then called, was undertaken after an experimental piece laid around the north-east corner of Dunn and Colborne streets proved satisfactory. Many of the walks we tread today were laid in 1905 by the Simcoe Paving Company or in 1907 by the Maple Leaf Paving Company. According to the inspector, Chief Sumner, the granolithic walks cost 12½¢ per square foot and most of the town was paved for somewhat under $8,000. All local improvements were paid for by a frontage tax extending over a number of years.[60]

By the early 1900's transportation services had considerably improved. Thirteen trains stopped daily at Oakville and to this service was added the hourly service to Hamilton by radial. The electrically operated Hamilton Radial Railway ran directly into the town. The Radial had been in operation between Hamilton and Burlington, on tracks laid in 1875 along Burlington Beach by the Hamilton and Northwestern Railway, for ten years before it had been extended to Oakville in 1904. The cars ran along Rebecca Street, and until the bridge was built across The Sixteen they terminated at the west side of the river. In January, 1906, the last span of the 634-foot bridge was lowered into place,[61] and thereafter the cars ran along Randall Street to the terminal at Thomas Street which today is the office of the Oakville Public Utilities Commission. The ride from Hamilton was pleasant, and in summer many excursionists who had formerly come by steamer now came to Oakville by the Radial.

Expansion was also taking place in the services of communication. By 1909 Oakville had a new post office, and the one-hundredth telephone had been installed. When first established in the middle eighties by the Bell Telephone Company the telephone exchange was located in the store of the local manager, William Busby. In a corner of his jewelry store a small, primitive exchange switchboard and its associated apparatus was set up and service was available from 8 A.M. to 8 P.M.

on week days, 2 to 4 on Sundays, and 10 to 12 on holidays. Among the subscribers were the tannery, the basket factory, the foundry, the *Star,* and, of course, the railway station. For some years there were less than twenty-five telephones in the town, but gradually a few merchants and hotels were added to the network. About 1886, when a line was constructed to join the Toronto-Hamilton circuit just south of Waterdown, the town was connected with the rapidly developing web of long distance wires. In the two years between 1909 and 1911 the number of telephones increased from one to two hundred, and through the courtesy of the Bank of Toronto a telephone card was printed which listed the numbers of Oakville subscribers on one side and those of Bronte on the reverse. Busby continued as local manager until 1912. The increase in the number of telephones, which reached five hundred by 1915, made a larger building necessary, and the exchange moved to a new building next door. Within the following ten years the number of subscribers ran into four figures.[62]

Since Robert Balmer's day the post office had acquired a new home. For some ten years after W. H. Young became postmaster there had been agitation for a new post office, but it was not until 1903 that the Davis Block was erected and the post office located in the west half, now no. 65A Colborne Street East. The real estate office of W. S. Davis occupied the east half of the building, now no. 65B. The old building which had housed Oakville's second post office for nearly fifty years was moved to the next street and converted into the double house that is now nos. 66 and 68 Church Street. Upon its former site the Lunau Block was built at a later date.

Young's assistant in the post office, Louis V. Cote, succeeded him as postmaster about 1904. A few years later, when Davis required the use of his entire block, Cote erected a new building on the site left vacant by the destruction by fire of Hunter's bakery in 1905. The new building, which housed both post office and Custom House, now nos. 85 and 87, was ready for occupancy in 1910.

Louis V. Cote served as postmaster until his death in 1937, when James James was appointed to the post. As most residents of the town today well know, the fifth and present post office was built by the government on the site of the old Royal Exchange Hotel which was demolished several years earlier. Limestone for the new building came from the valley of the Credit River. The opening ceremony in 1939 was attended by the Postmaster-General.

Ill health had forced R. K. Chisholm to resign his post as Customs Collector in 1894. As deputy he had served for eight years, and as Customs Collector for fifty-two, a total of sixty years in the Custom

House. He was succeeded by Captain Maurice Felan, and the building that is now no. 70 Navy Street South continued as the Custom House until 1910, when the office was moved to rooms above Cote's new post office. Felan was succeeded by other collectors until 1937 when the Custom House, established 103 years before, was closed on April 1. Oakville was no longer a Port of Entry.

In the days before the banking laws of the province were revised Oakville had been most unfortunate in the matter of private banks. After the closing in 1860 of its Oakville branch by the Bank of Toronto, the town had been without banking facilities for a decade. In 1871 a private bank organized by C. Tate Scott moved into the office formerly occupied by the Bank of Toronto in the Custom House.[63] Thirteen years later Scott encountered financial difficulties and the rumour spread that he had "skipped" to the United States. As it happened, he had gone there to see an uncle who had an interest in the bank, and upon his return it was found that Scott had placed the bank's assets in the hands of R. K. Chisholm for the benefit of the depositors. Each depositor lost only the interest on the principal during the winding up of C. Tate Scott & Co.'s affairs.[64] The Corporation suffered no loss, having shortly before transferred the town's account to Andrew & Howarth.[65] Andrew & Howarth's, established in 1881, was also a private bank, and in 1887 a second private bank was established in the town, the bank of C. W. Anderson and Sons. The Merchants Bank of Canada which established an Oakville branch in 1898 was the first chartered bank in the town.

Long remembered by the residents of Oakville and the surrounding district was the month of December, 1902. Within two and one-half weeks the two private banks failed, leaving a trail of misery as the result of the crash. The first inkling of disaster came at noon on the first day of December when the sound of a shot rang out on Colborne Street. Thomas Howarth had committed suicide in his office next to the Oakville House. This tragedy started a run on the private banks which caused them to go under. When on December 18 Anderson's Bank failed, about $200,000 was involved. Nearly everyone in the town was affected by one or other of the failures. The Town Corporation lost all the recently collected tax money, and Knox Church, having accounts in both banks, lost heavily. When the affairs of the Andersons were wound up the five hundred depositors, many of whom had placed their life's savings in the bank, received 2½¢ on the dollar,[66] and Cyrus Anderson and his sons lost all they possessed to the Bank of Hamilton. The assets included the farm east of Allan Street, the large residence called "Grit Anchorage" built in the seventies, now no. 189

Colborne Street East at the north-east corner of Allan Street, and the Anderson Block in which the bank was located. This building is now the Town Clerk's Office, and the Police Station, and the Town Council meets on the second floor in what was once Anderson Hall.

The Bank of Toronto chose to return to Oakville at the time that the confusion following upon these disastrous failures was at its height. On December 22 its Oakville branch opened next door to Anderson's bank in the building that is now no. 26 Colborne Street East.[67] The third chartered bank to establish a branch at Oakville was the Bank of Hamilton, which came in 1910. Thirteen years later this bank was merged with the Canadian Bank of Commerce as the Merchants Bank had been merged the previous year with the Bank of Montreal.

The branch manager appointed to the Bank of Hamilton was the dealer in real estate, W. S. Davis. About 1883, at the age of fourteen, William Sinclair Davis had come from Milton to act as assistant to Balmer in the post office at a wage reputed to be 50¢ a week. During the seventeen years he worked there many outsiders who used the facilities of the post office expressed surprise that more people did not live in such a beautiful section of the country. Impressed by these casual remarks, Davis explored the field of real estate and in 1900 he became established in the business. In the years that followed he succeeded in attracting hundreds of home owners to Halton County and most of the land on which large estates were laid out passed through his hands. When in 1907 James Ryrie of the Toronto jewelry firm purchased land on the lake shore east of Oakville, a part of the original farm of Barnet Griggs, he established a precedent. Within two years Herbert C. Cox of the Canada Life Assurance Company purchased the former Coates property. In close succession others followed to lay out large estates and build spacious summer homes in this "Canadian Newport."

The demand for summer cottages led to the opening in 1905–6 of the Carson and Bacon surveys along Park Avenue in the eastern section of the town known as Orchard Beach. In 1907 the Anderson farm, owned by the Bank of Hamilton after the failure of Anderson's bank, became Brantwood Survey. The farm of John A. Chisholm senior, north of Spruce Street, was laid out in two surveys, Inglehart's Survey in 1909 and Tuxedo Park a year later. When Inglehart bought thirty-seven acres of the farm the sale included the "old soup factory" and its machinery.[68]

The first house to appear in Brantwood Survey was that of William J. Shaw, father of the present Fire Chief, who built at the north-east corner of Allan Street and Sumner Avenue. It was not long before

W. S. Davis was authorized by the Bank of Hamilton to improve Brantwood Survey by grading the streets, laying cement sidewalks, and installing sewers. As it turned out, all these surveys were prematurely developed. A few summer cottages appeared at Orchard Beach, a few houses were built in Tuxedo Park and on the fringes of Brantwood Survey, but the centre of Brantwood Survey remained open fields through which cement sidewalks stretched forlornly.

The name Brantwood, a contraction of Brant's Wood and the counterpart of the contraction of "Brant's Ford" to Brantford, was occasioned by a legend concerning the same Indian warrior, Joseph Brant. According to this legend, Brant, as chief of the Missisaugas, was joint owner of the Indian Reserve at the Sixteen Mile Creek. When visiting the house of Charles Anderson one stormy night, Brant learned of the birth of a son to the Andersons, and offered to present Anderson with two hundred acres of land should the child be given his name. Thus, according to the legend, Joseph Brant Anderson secured his farm bordering on the east the townsite of Oakville.

This legend, though undoubtedly founded upon fact, is not altogether accurate. It is an example of how tales grow and flourish in the absence of confutation, and is yet another proof of the fallibility of tradition. In the first instance, Joseph Brant was not chief of the Missisauga Indians and therefore the lands of the reserve at The Sixteen were not his to bestow. Brant was a Mohawk and chief of the Indians of the Six Nations who were dispossessed of their lands in the Province of New York following the Revolution. As Loyalists they were granted Crown lands along the Grand River in Upper Canada. His exploits in the War of 1812 were referred to in the *Atlas of Halton County* published in 1877 and reiterated in several pamphlets on Oakville, but it must be pointed out that Joseph Brant died at an advanced age in 1807.[69] His youngest son John was appointed his successor at the age of thirteen and it was Captain John Brant who led the Indians of the Six Nations at the battles of Queenston Heights and Beaver Dams.[70] Secondly, records in the archives, both provincial and dominion, and in the Registry Office for Halton County reveal no connection whatsoever between Brant and the Indian Reserve at The Sixteen. If a gift of land was made to Anderson it most likely consisted of lands along the Grand River. Such a gesture was characteristic of Brant who delighted in making gifts of these lands, naïvely ignoring the fact that they belonged not to him but to his people. His generosity resulted in many defective land titles, confusion about which has continued down to the present time.[71]

The search for confirmation of the legend, however, brought to light a diverting narrative which, if involved, is factual and rests firmly upon contemporary documents of unquestionable authenticity. The old Anderson farm lying north of Colborne Street along the east side of Allan Street was originally lot 12 of the 3rd concession of Trafalgar Township. Here we find the only instance in the township of the estate of a rebel being forfeit to the Crown. This land had been granted in 1806 to Samuel Fraser, an American settler of Vaughan Township north of the Town of York. Because the boundary of the Missisauga Indian Reserve encroached upon this lot it was somewhat narrower than the others. This no one seems to have noticed until Fraser complained to the Department of Crown Lands that he had not drawn the full amount of land to which he was entitled by his warrant. In restitution Fraser was granted lot 11 across the road in the 4th concession, another fifty acres.[72] Fraser set to work to carve a farm from the wilderness, and in due course received patents to both lots. In April, 1810, he sold the southern section of lot 12, 3rd concession, about one hundred acres, to Charles Anderson of the Township of Grimsby. Besides Fraser there were on the farm James Gugins, his wife Mary Joset Content (née Bassell), and their four children.[73] With the outbreak of the War of 1812 Gugins joined the volunteer militia, but thereafter was no more heard of, and Content was left to provide as best she could for her children. Fraser went also, but before his departure he executed deeds in the name of Content Gugins, leaving her all his property in Trafalgar Township. Fraser then "joined the enemy."

Content Gugins' father, John Bassell (Bazill), was "Keeper or Crier for the Court of Quarter Sessions and the Home District Court" which met in the Parliament Buildings at York. From the age of sixteen he had served in various regiments of the King, during the Revolution as drum-major in the 1st Battalion of the 84th Regiment of Foot. In consideration of his long service he had received the appointment of court crier.[74] The early actions of the war took place far from the capital, and the Court of Quarter Sessions continued to meet regularly in the Parliament Buildings. According to a minute of the proceedings of this court, John Bassell was granted an increase in salary from £10 to £15 in the spring of 1813. He did not live to benefit from it, however. Immediately below the minute appears the following entry, "In consequence of the Enemy having possession of the Town of York the court could not meet on the 27th of April." Though too old to enroll in the militia John Bassell turned out with the other men to oppose the enemy, and at the blowing up of the powder magazine on the water front he received a serious head injury. He was taken to the home of his daughter in Trafalgar Township where he soon died.[75]

Mary Joset Content Gugins continued to live in the log house on the south side of the concession road (which was later to become the Lake Shore Road) for some years before discovering that by reason of his "absconding" Fraser's lands were forfeit to the Crown. She appealed to Sir Francis Gore, and was allowed to retain lot 11 where she lived with her children and her second husband, Mitchell. It was here that some thirty years later Reverend James Nisbet and his father Thomas built their brick cottage near the lake. The balance of the land, the north section of lot 12, 3rd concession, was advertised under the heading of "Land of Traitors" by the commissioners of forfeited estates, to be sold on May 24, 1819.[76] It was bought for £75 by the owner of the southern section, Charles Anderson.[77]

A native of County Antrim, North of Ireland, Charles Anderson had come to the province in 1788. He married Ann, only daughter of the Loyalist, W. Henry Nelles, and settled east of the Forty Mile Creek where he bought 100 acres on the main road from Niagara to Burlington Bay.[78] This land, lot 8, 2nd concession of Grimsby Township, is now within the Town of Grimsby.[79] Anderson stated in 1795 that he had "built a two story house and other valuable buildings and has fifty acres under culture."[80] Chief Joseph Brant was a frequent visitor to The Forty and usually he stayed with Charles Anderson.[81] In a letter dated July 14, 1798, Brant refers to Anderson as having got a man "to agree to frame my little houses at the Beach."[82] To the son born to him in 1800 Anderson gave the name of Joseph Brant.

Upon the opening of Trafalgar Township for settlement Charles Anderson petitioned for land as a settler, and was granted lot 13, 2nd concession south of the Dundas Street. Situated at the northern boundary of Oakville this land borders the west side of the 7th Line and through its southern section runs the ridge now called the Red Hill below which ran the "Old Road from York to the Head of the Lake." As previously shown, Anderson had acquired all the land bordering the Missisauga Indian Reserve on the east in the 3rd concession and when his son, Joseph Brant Anderson, grew to man's estate, he came to Trafalgar Township about 1826 to work this land. Close to the road, which was little more than a footpath (it was not even then the Lake Shore Road), he built a log cabin for himself and his wife. The story has come down to us of how his sheep were attacked at night by wolves, and while his wife held a lantern, Anderson stopped up the hole in the pen by which they had entered and with his hands choked to death two of the animals.

Charles Anderson left all his land in Trafalgar Township to his son, Joseph Brant, under a will which is herewith quoted in part:

In the name of God Amen—

I Charles Anderson of the Township of Grimsby, County Lincoln, District of Niagara and Province of Upper Canada yeoman, being weak in bodily health, and knowing the uncertainty of the Mortal Life, but of Sound and [illegible] Mind and Memory, thanks be to God for this Same Blessing; Do make this my Last Will and Testament in manner and form following viz.;

I give, Devise and bequeath unto my third son Joseph Brant all that Certain parcel or tract of Land situated in the Township of Trafalgar in the Gore District, known and discribed [*sic*] as Lots number thirteen in the second Concession and twelve in the third Concession of the said Township of Trafalgar four hundred acres more or less. . . . 19 Dec 1829.[83]

J. B. Anderson replaced his log cabin with a frame dwelling in 1836, and when it was destroyed by fire fifty-nine years later it was said to be one of the oldest frame dwellings in the town.[84] The pine cut off the Anderson farm in the seventies was the last timber to go out of the Port of Oakville.

III

Industrially Oakville made little if any headway during the first decade of the twentieth century. Those two old established industries, the tannery and the basket factory, had things mostly their own way. However, Oakville was again becoming well known for its shipbuilding, though the lake craft which slipped from the ways into the waters of The Sixteen were the very antithesis of those of an earlier day. Captain James Andrew was building racing and pleasure yachts for wealthy sportsmen, and the emphasis had shifted from weight, durability, and capacity to lightness of construction for speed. These craft were small in number but their superiority in craftsmanship and performance gained them a wide reputation.

Yachting on Lake Ontario had increased enormously during the seventies. Oakville was chosen as the objective of many Royal Canadian Yacht Club races, and over a summer week-end fifty or more yachts were commonly seen in the harbour. On Saturday nights the yachtsmen built huge bonfires on the wide beach that then bordered the west side of the harbour. At times the town was overrun with yachtsmen, whose behaviour deteriorated as their numbers increased. They were often a drunken disorderly lot who considered it their privilege to create an uproar in whatever port they honoured by their presence, but in general the townspeople were tolerant of the destruction they caused.[85] When yachts built at Oakville began to make a name for themselves round the lakes a spirit of comradeship which before had been non-existent developed between the visiting crews and the inhabitants. As time went on the interest in pleasure sailing grew and the town became proud of the wide reputation Captain Andrew gained for the yachts he built.

A native of Dundonald, Scotland, James Andrew had come as a youth with his family to Oakville. Glowing accounts of the rapidly developing County of Halton received from a cousin at Acton had induced the Andrews to migrate to Canada. During the six weeks they were aboard the vessel *Crown* one child had died and another had been born, to whom was given the middle name of Crown. At Montreal the Andrews boarded the steamer *Magnet*, and when they landed at Oakville they decided to make the town their home. James and his brother, John went on the lakes at an early age, becoming master mariners. About 1861 Captain James Andrew engaged in shipbuilding, travelling over Canada from coast to coast to build schooners on the shores of many waters, gaining a reputation for swift-sailing ships. When the demand for larger vessels ceased he turned to tugs and small steamers such as the little *Sadie*, built in 1885 for the Doty Ferry Company,[86] and the *Thistle*, for the Toronto Ferry Co. Andrew located his shipyard on the west bank of The Sixteen next to Doty's sawmill. The first of his famous yachts was built for C. Armstrong, C. G. Marlatt, and W. T. Marlatt, and when launched on October

44. THE BAND, *circa* 1867

45. MR. AND MRS. JOHN CROSS

46. THE HARBOUR, SHOWING THE STEAMER *Empress of India, circa* 1883

47. Mr. and Mrs. Robert Balmer, 1895

48. Richard Coates,
Senior

49. The spire of St. Andrew's Church

50. The opening of Aberdeen Bridge, 1895

25, 1887, this sloop was christened, in honour of C. G. Marlatt's first wife, the *Aggie*.[87] Remodelled into a cutter by Andrew five years later the *Aggie* held her own against yachts from the drawing boards of the Fifes, Watson and Payne, and others of the famous designers of Scotland and England. In 1895 Andrew built the *Winetta* (renamed the *Merrythought* when rebuilt by Andrew twenty years later) and the year following he built the cutter which became famous in the chronicles of pleasure sailing on Lake Ontario, the *Canada*.

It so happened that the *Canada*'s planking was cut from that timber for which Oakville was once renowned, and which has since been unobtainable, white oak. In the winter of 1895-6 when the Lincoln Park Yacht Club of Chicago challenged the Royal Canadian Yacht Club to a series of races with the *Vencedor*, then in course of construction, a syndicate was formed by members of the Canadian club. An order was placed with William Fife Jr. of Fairlie, Scotland, for the design of a yacht to be built at Oakville by Captain Andrew who was to prepare all the necessary materials during the winter. It was at this time that the rakers from one of the stonehookers discovered some old white oak timber which had sunk of its own weight and lay on the bottom of The Sixteen near the junction of Dundas Street and the 6th Line. In earlier times this had been the location of the shute by which staves were slid from the top of the bank onto the decks of vessels lying in the river below. With derricks mounted on scows the stone rakers raised the timbers which, preserved by the water, were found to be "as good as new." As no squared timber had left the port after the middle forties, these timbers bearing the marks of the adze may have lain in The Sixteen for fifty years, if not longer. Andrew bought them, and after being sawn into planking at Doty's adjacent sawmill they provided all that was required for the new yacht.[88] It took much searching to find all the wood suitable for constructing the yacht, but Andrew collected it piece by piece. One night the inmates of a nearby shanty known as Tramp Castle helped themselves to what had been set aside for the rigging, and used it for firewood. The following day Andrew nailed up the Castle, temporarily ending its career as a haven for tramps.[89]

Though it was well into April before Andrew received the plans for the *Canada*, the yacht was ready for launching June 23, only a few days after the launch of the *Vencedor*, which had been well under way when the challenge was made. Within four days the *Canada* was ready for trials off Oakville with the *Zelma*. Under the command of "the greatest freshwater skipper of his time," Aemilius Jarvis, the *Canada* won the trophy which thereafter was known as the "*Canada's* Cup," still considered the Blue Ribbon of the Great Lakes.[90]

Captain Andrew built many defenders and challengers of the "*Canada's* Cup." The sloops *Beaver*, designed by A. E. Payne of Southampton, England, and *Minota* were launched within six weeks in 1899. The *Beaver* lost the cup to the Americans but the *Invader*, built by Andrew in 1901, brought it back to Canada. The cutter *Strathcona*, another defender of the"*Canada's* Cup," was launched in the presence of a large crowd on May 27, 1903. Set up in England by her designer, Payne, her frames were dismantled, shipped out to Oakville, and reassembled by Andrew. Her sails were made by Ratsey and Co., the famous sailmakers of Cowes on the Isle of Wight. The *Strathcona* was sixty feet long and painted white with a silver waterline and black underbody. Her keel weighed twelve tons. In reporting the launch of the *Strathcona* the *Star* employed the metaphor of a writer who told of the launching of one of the earliest vessels built at Oakville three-quarters of a century before. "The boat glided into the water of The Sixteen like a duck taking the water and rested peacefully there."

In the International Race of 1903 the *Strathcona* was skippered by Jarvis but the *Irondoquoit* won by a very narrow margin, gaining the "*Canada's* Cup" for the Americans.[91] Two years later Andrew launched the *Zoraya* and the *Téméraire*, both designed and framed in Scotland. Fife designed the latter yacht and also the *Crusader* which Andrew built in 1907. These three yachts had also been commissioned for the purpose of competing for international trophies. The record of Andrew's activities falters and we find him building no more yachts until 1914, when he launched the vessel to which was given the Indian name for the Canadian beaver, *Ahmeek*. The year following Andrew sold his shipyard.

All of Captain Andrew's yachts flew the burgees of the R.C.Y.C. and many the ensigns of Commodores, Vice-Commodores, and Rear-Commodores of the club. Although most of his yachts were built from the plans of famous designers, his own *Aggie* won nearly every R.C.Y.C. trophy at least once. She held the club championship for a number of years in succession and her skipper, C. G. Marlatt, was Commodore of the club for a time. The *Aggie* was fifty-seven years old when she was driven ashore in a gale and broke up not far from the old Triller farm west of Bronte, from which her timbers had come. When the H.M.C.S. *Oakville*, the corvette adopted by the town during World

War II, sailed out into the Atlantic on convoy duty she carried the ship's clock from the *Aggie.*

Upon his retirement Captain Andrew continued to live with his sisters at no. 5 William Street, where they had moved in 1891. The west wing of this house had begun as the merchant's shop of the founder of the village in 1828. A day never passed without Captain Andrew and his dog walking several times down Navy Street to view the lake and the harbour.

The buildings used today by Andrew's successors at the shipyard are to be seen in the photograph (plate 50) showing the opening of Aberdeen Bridge in 1894. This bridge was built by William Gibson of Beamsville, who brought stone for the abutments and central pier in barges from the Niagara peninsula across the lake. The removal of the old timber abutments brought to light a number of white oak staves which were collected by several persons who intended to carve them into souvenirs. The total cost of the bridge amounted to $11,000, of which $3,000 was granted by the County Council.[92] Being placed at a higher level above the water than former bridges, the new one was easier of approach. The new Governor-General "cheerfully assented to the name of Aberdeen Bridge"[93] and the official opening on September 18, 1894, was a great day for the town. The bridge was christened with a bottle of champagne by small Maggie McDonald dressed in Aberdeen tartan. Each member of the Town Council was presented with a bouquet of flowers by various young ladies, and the first vehicle to cross the bridge officially was McDonald's Aberdeen carriage. However, several days previously one of the Felan boys had ridden across on horseback and Arthur Kemp, in his anxiety to be the first across, had driven a waggon over the bridge late the night before.[94] The official party boarded the *Aggie*; the bridge, which was easily operated by one man, was swung open; and the yacht sailed up The Sixteen and back. The bridge was then swung back and was officially open to traffic. For the rest of the day the little steamer *Shamrock* of the Toronto ferry fleet was on hand to take citizens on the lake for an outing, and the banquet in the evening held at the International Hotel (as the Canadian Hotel was called for a time) was well attended. At least one child is known to have been christened Aberdeen in honour of the bridge.

The *Star* in 1906 carried a news item to the effect that the store of Thomas Patterson on the south-west corner of Colborne and Thomas streets was being faced with brick and remodelled into a hotel with a fifty-two foot bar.[95] When it changed hands within a few years its name was changed from Hotel Decker to Gibson House. In 1915 a friend of the proprietor, Charles Priestman of Toronto, began walking along the Lake Shore Road once a year on St. Patrick's Day to visit Gibson at Oakville. Not long ago the Gibson House burned to the ground and upon its foundations, which date back to the days when Oakville was a village, rose the modernistic Halton Inn. At the time of writing, Mr. Priestman, at the age of eighty-five, has made his thirty-sixth visit to Oakville on foot.

Turning to one of Oakville's oldest landmarks, the mill, we find that about 1890 it again changed hands. Isaac Warcup, who was feeling his age and wished to retire, sold the mill to Foulds and Shaw. The former was a miller, and Hedley Shaw, who had worked for Warcup for a time, was a clever business man possessed of a flair for organization. He saw that the era of small mills dispersed over the countryside was coming to an end, for transportation was too difficult in a section of the province where wheat was no longer extensively grown. He realized that as the sources of supply lay outside the region, the future of the milling industry in Ontario depended upon the concentration of large mills on the route of freighters coming down from lake-head ports loaded with wheat from the west. Foulds and Shaw sold their mill about 1900 to T. H. Ashbury, and Shaw then proceeded to develop the scheme for which, as he later asserted, he had received "much of the inspiration during his occupation of the old mill, that well known landmark at Oakville."[96] He bought the old foundry building and the machinery Robertson had installed in his flouring mill, which had lain idle for thirteen years. The stone building was demolished in 1903 and large quantities of timbers and other materials were shipped away by water to St. Catharines where Shaw built a new mill.[97] This was the beginning of the Maple Leaf Milling Company founded by Hedley Shaw, a concern which soon established mills at Thorold, Welland, Port Colborne, and out west in Manitoba.[98] At Port Colborne the company built a ten-storey mill for the opening of which in 1911 a special train was run from Toronto. At Oakville it took aboard a large party of townspeople who attended the ceremony.[99] By then the Maple Leaf Milling Company had become the second largest milling company in Canada.

The new owners of the mill at Oakville, T. H. Ashbury & Sons, had come from Blyth, Ontario. They installed modern machinery in the mill which included the largest overshot wheel in Canada. This 37-ton wheel had a diameter of 24 feet and from it was derived 75 horsepower.[100] Ashbury & Sons retained the business for twenty-seven years. The grain elevators they built on the side of the hill above the mill were constructed of tamarac, which is distasteful to rats and mice, and the bins were interlocked so that the grain was carried down to the mill by gravity. With each addition the elevators extended farther down the hill, their ultimate capacity reaching a total of 32,000 bushels. Beside the elevators was a flight of wooden steps, 134, to be exact. This number is engraved on the memory of Mr. Lorne Ashbury. It was his job to receive the grain. No sooner would he get down to the mill than another waggon load of grain would arrive and back up the steps he would go. At the rear of the mill Ashbury built a 30-foot cedar surge tank containing a vertical rack which screened debris from the water before it reached the wheel. Regularly every week his two sons were set to the disagreeable task of cleaning the rack.

To obtain timbers for clothing the dam was both difficult and expensive until Ashbury hit upon the expedient of using the railway ties that were piled at intervals along the tracks. It was a simple matter to have his men collect such ties as were needed and throw them over the railway bridge into The Sixteen, from where they were teamed up to the dam. This arrangement worked admirably until the appearance one year of a representative of the railway. Thereafter Ashbury was obliged to obtain his timber in a more orthodox manner, at a price of 10¢ per tie to the railway.[101]

Ashbury had also to contend with the nuisance of the Irishmen breaking holes in the flume. Every spring when the suckers were running these Irishmen came from the rear of the township to load up with fish, driving their waggons over the oak-stave tube of the flume without the slightest compunction, and breaking holes in it which were expensive to repair. According to the *Express*, in April, 1880, one man had caught more than five hundred suckers,[102] and even thirty years later the fish were to be had in such quantity that they overflowed the waggons, sliding over the tail boards on the ascent up the hill. One year the government received a loud complaint from these men. They stated that because Ashbury had neglected to install a fish ladder in the dam they were obliged to travel a long distance to obtain the fish. Forthwith an inspector arrived. It so happened that he came at a time when the water in The Sixteen was the lowest it had been in years. Ashbury took him up to the dam through the bed of the river, and pointing out the shallowness of the mill pond, remarked that those fish which succeeded in climbing a ladder would surely die. Nothing more was heard of the matter and Ashbury was spared the necessity of installing a fish ladder which would have weakened the structure of the dam. But year after year the Irishmen continued to drive their waggons over the oak tubing of the mill race.[103]

As long as the dam built by Warcup stood, the mill pond was a favourite swimming hole. Today only the north-west shoulder of the dam remains on the flats of The Sixteen below the Town Cemetery. Opposite on the south bank is the entrance to the tunnel, and below the railway bridge some remains of the oak staves of the flume may still be found. After Ashbury sold the mill in 1927 it had several owners. Three years later the building caught fire and only the shell was left. But as long as the north wall stood, the stone bearing the date 1827 was visible in the gable. Now little more than the foundations remain of William Chisholm's mill.

After the dismantling of his father's sawmill on The Sixteen, Charles F. Doty spent some years in the north. Upon returning to Oakville he established a planing mill on the 7th Line north of the railway, where the business is located at the present time. That same year, 1908, Doty went into partnership with W. S. Davis to form the Oakville Pressed Brick Works, situated farther north on the west side of the 7th Line above the Lower Middle Road or Queen Elizabeth Way. The brick kilns stood at the foot of the Red Hill. Bricks had long been made from the good clay found in the district, notably on the old farm of John A. Chisholm, where the mud was stirred in a vat by a horse harnessed to a long pole. After being packed into moulds the bricks were baked in kilns fired with wood, and many of the early brick buildings in the town were built of these bricks.

The first aluminum cooking utensils to be made in Canada were the brand known as the Oakville Aluminium Ware, manufactured locally. When the Ware Manufacturing Company, Limited, began the erection of a factory beside the railway east of the 7th Line in 1910 it was the only factory of the kind in the Dominion.[104] It took a year and a half to build and it was not until September, 1911, that it got into production. Unfortunately the concern expanded too rapidly, and within a few years was forced to seek smaller quarters, in Carson's planing mill on Dundas Street; there the manufacture of aluminum cooking utensils was continued. The building beside the railway was occupied for a short time by the Oak Tire Company but this concern soon disappeared, and thereafter the building stood vacant for many years until at the beginning of World War II it became the factory of the Barringham Rubber Company.

In the spring of 1912 the premises of the Oakville Fruit Growers' Association on the 6th Line south of the railway were acquired by

E. S. Glassco and his brother of Hamilton. Here in the centre of the fruit-growing district they established a fruit-preserving plant under the name of Glassco Company Limited, a concern which continues under the same name today.

For a time the town had three newspapers: Arthur Forster's *Star*, the *Oakville Record* of William Fleuty, and Gerald Mitchell's *News*. Fleuty had bought *Raymond's Record* in 1907, and altered its name to the *Oakville Record*. The same year Mitchell, an apprentice of the *Star*, opened a small job printing plant. On the advice of friends he started a third newspaper, which he called the *News*. After some years, however, ill health and the inability of the town to support three weekly papers compelled Mitchell to move his plant to Hamilton.

The Trafalgar Agricultural Association continued to hold its annual fall fair at Trafalgar Square, but this event had begun to take on a somewhat different aspect. It was becoming less of an agricultural exhibition and more of a horse show. A number of horsemen had chosen to locate in the vicinity: Harry Giddings, owner and trainer of race horses; Harland Smith; and Hugh Wilson, grandson of Captain William Wilson, whose specialty was training Canadian-bred hunters. As a result of Wilson's exertions H. C. Cox had been able to build up a fine stable at "Ennisclare," his estate on the Lake Shore Road east of Oakville. Wilson exhibited his and Cox's horses in many horse shows in Canada and the United States. These horses regularly walked from the ring of Madison Square Gardens in New York City with a majority of the trophies. Bringing hounds from Montreal and Philadelphia, Wilson and Cox also started the Ennisclare Hunt Club, which attracted other clubs to the Oakville Fair. As advertised in 1911, the biggest features were the "Ennisclare Hunt Specials—Prizes for the best hunters and a cup for the members of a recognized Hunt Club in their costume for jumping; Riders all in pink and hounds of the Ennisclare Hunt; Military Event, squadrons of the Mississauga Horse."[105] Harland Smith regularly drove his coach drawn by four horses which in earlier times had carried the Royal Mail through the countryside of England.

About this time the association arrived at the decision that the fair grounds on Reynolds Street were inadequate. Some ten acres of land were purchased on the west side of the town north of the Radial track where a grandstand was erected (by Wilson) and a horse ring laid out. An aeroplane hangar, brought from Beamsville, was used for displaying exhibits of produce and handicrafts. The new fair grounds then became Trafalgar Park, and the old grounds, after being converted into a recreation park, became Victoria Park. In the old Agricultural Hall, now called Victoria Hall, the first moving pictures were shown in the town.

From a purely agricultural fair run by local farmers the Oakville Fair had developed into a horse show financed by wealthy horsemen of Toronto and elsewhere. As it became more of a society event the farmers lost interest, and when many of Wilson's fine horses were destroyed in two disastrous fires the fair rapidly lost momentum. The automobile, improved highways, and the proximity of the Canadian National Exhibition at Toronto, with which no township fair could hope to compete, combined to kill the Oakville Fair. Eventually the new fair grounds were taken over by the Municipal Corporation of the Town of Oakville and converted into a motor park for visiting tourists. The aeroplane hangar was moved to the grounds of the Oakville Club and became a badminton court.

Even at this time Oakville was still "a small sleepy town" almost as well known, according to some, for its old maids and grass widows as it was for its strawberries. In fifty years it had not regained the population it had had at the time of its incorporation as a municipality. Until 1908 the figure was nearly static at between 1,700 and 1,800, but in the three years between 1908 and 1911 the number rose to 2,374, an increase of 574.[106] The life of the inhabitants was as simple as it was leisurely. Many of its characteristics had for generations been typical of towns throughout the western section of Ontario. The preference for old-country ways remained, and American customs, although accepted with perhaps more tolerance than formerly, were still regarded with reserve. Class distinctions were strong, and the geographical barrier of this "stratified society" was The Sixteen. The west side of the town or "over the crik" continued to be regarded, as in earlier times, as the section of the working classes. Householders placed much emphasis upon privacy, and almost invariably surrounded their property with cedar hedges or high vine-covered board fences. In the tangled undergrowth which flourished in the shade of the fences grew tall ferns, Solomon's seal, stars of Bethlehem, lilies of the valley, and day lilies in untended profusion. Nearly every house had its grape arbour, and its narrow porch was screened by festoons of honeysuckle or that indigenous vine so dear to the hearts of early pioneers, the Virginia creeper. Only the more impressive houses displayed on their lawns and along driveways the showy formal pieces planted according to the new fashion with cannas, salvia, and ageratum. The rural custom of winter and summer kitchens was maintained, and during warm weather the average housewife did her washing in wooden tubs outside. Many of the three-score families who owned cows tethered them beside the street or in nearby vacant lots. Others placed their animals in the care of Freddy Quinn, who daily herded his charges outside the town to graze along country roads.

Most social functions still centred around the home and the church. An important adjunct to any household was the upright piano which came in for much use or misuse. However, the organization of group activities had begun. In 1903 the Tennis Club was started by W. S. Davis, Allan S. Chisholm, and others, becoming the Oakville Club five years later, when the Grangers' warehouse at the foot of William Street was remodelled for a club house. Percy A. Bath was elected first president of the Oakville Club which had its formal opening July 10, 1908.[107] The previous July the lawn bowling green had been laid out on the south side of the Town Hall. The first troop of Boy Scouts was organized by Frank Chisholm, son of Captain G. B. Chisholm, in the spring of 1911, and before long the troop had a bugle band which was receiving instruction from Oakville's bandmaster, W. H. Tuck.[108]

The president of the first Boy Scout Council was James C. Morgan, superintendent of the Foresters' Home, whom we met as headmaster of the Oakville Grammar School back in the sixties. Upon leaving the town Morgan had acted for thirty-six years as Superintendent of Education for Simcoe County. Meanwhile the local court of the fraternal insurance society, the Independent Order of Foresters, had been organized in 1899 with twelve charter members. When the society selected Oakville as the location of its orphans' home Morgan returned as superintendent. The orphaned children of Foresters throughout Canada, the United States, and the British Isles were cared for in the home which for a few years occupied the former residence of G. K. Chisholm, "The Retreat," at the head of Forsyth Street. The Morgans lived next door at no. 43 Bond Street, the house built by John Doty. Soon the Foresters purchased the tract of land running from Bond Street north along Kerr Street, where a new home was erected, and the children had the benefit of gardening and fruit farming. During World War II the property was secured by the Canadian Army, and is now the Central Command Headquarters.

The Girl Guide movement did not take hold as readily as the Boy Scouts. Though formed not long after the Boy Scouts the Guides were not particularly successful. However, when reorganized about 1923 the Girl Guides built up a strong organization in Oakville.

During the first decade of the century the life of the townspeople was regulated to a great extent by the sound of the tannery whistle. At its bidding they rose in the morning, started and ceased work, ate their dinners, and now and then rushed to a fire. Many other things they had known all their lives and took for granted: the rumble of farmers' waggons as they drove to the hitching posts in the shade of the maple trees on Colborne Street; the clouds of dust rising behind the bus as it passed many times a day on its way to the station; the morass of mud in the streets in wet weather; the loads of stinking hides that jolted slowly on their way to the tannery; the unskinned carcasses dripping blood onto the sawdust-covered floor of butcher shops after slaughtering day. Many of the shops were conducted in traditional ways, and over the years changed little. The shops that they frequented as children hold precedence in the memories of the present generation. Foremost of all was that paradise for the child with only a penny to spend, Phoebe Baker's. In front of her shop stood the last sagging porch in the town, unquestionably a public menace but allowed to collapse with age because no one had the temerity to approach Phoebe on the subject of its removal. A former school teacher and daughter of George Baker, keeper of the livery stable, Phoebe was handicapped by having the use of only one arm. The stuffed peacock in the window, displaying a handsome tail dimmed with dust, must certainly have been the work of her uncle, the taxidermist. A myriad of knick-knacks, toys, and odds and ends of every conceivable description crammed the interior of Phoebe's shop. It mattered little that moths had ravaged the hair of the china dolls; and the layers of dust that hid the wondrous collection merely served to enhance its interest. Across the main street was the shop of the wife of Captain Moulton, where a little paper cornucopia of Mrs. Moulton's famous taffy or licorice "shoe strings" could be had for a penny. A few doors away the drug store of Dr. Urquhart still retained the atmosphere and appearance of an old country apothecary's shop. On shelves behind the heavily panelled counters were ranged the same little jars bearing the names of drugs that his father had brought with him from England. Next to Urquhart's were the Ferrahs' who had become famous for their home-made ice cream. The little bake-shop on the west side of their building had been destroyed in a fire which had swept away all the buildings on the south side of Colborne Street from the Ferrahs' residence to Thomas Street. But within a few years the Ferrahs had erected on its site a brick building in which they installed the first soda fountain in the town. When W. A. Ferrah, the last of the family, died, the eighty-year-old firm, conducted by three generations of Ferrahs, came to an end.

The stores of William G. Hewson and John Barclay in the western end of the shopping district were now conducted by their sons. In 1895 James L. Hewson took over his father's business, and after he moved to the opposite side of Colborne Street he built up a reputation for quality by carrying only the best brands of groceries. James Hewson was actively interested in municipal affairs, a characteristic also possessed by his son-in-law, James Black, under whose name the business continues at the present time. By 1889, when Robert Barclay took over his father's business, the merchandise handled was confined to the type of dry goods most in demand by the farmers in the district. Upon his retirement, "Bob" Barclay relinquished a business that he and his father had conducted for seventy years.

E. H. Gulledge who had lost his building in the same fire that destroyed all the buildings from Thomas Street to the Ferrahs' was now located on the spot where his father had set up in business in 1835. Adjoining his shoe store on the west, and set somewhat below the street level, was the harness shop. The customer descended several steps into a shop from the walls and ceiling of which hung saddles, harness, whips, and all the many items of equipment required in the driving of horses.

But the era of the horse and buggy was drawing to a close. Automobiles were appearing on the streets of the town. Murray Williams, proprietor of the Murray House, and Allan Chisholm, son of R. K. Chisholm, were the first to own automobiles[109] which they used only for pleasure driving. The regulation governing the driving of motorcars appeared in the *Star* in 1903. Through towns and villages these vehicles were to be driven not faster than ten miles per hour, and the limit on highways was fixed at fifteen. At all times drivers must slow down for teams and buggies and in the case of frightened horses come to a complete stop. The automobile was strictly a fair-weather vehicle, and only on warm summer days did ladies don veils and dusters for a drive on dusty gravel roads in the open touring car, resplendent with brass fittings. The drive to Toronto by the Lake Shore Road, with its narrow bridges and steep hills which required careful negotiation, was a good day's journey. A return trip the same day was attempted by only the hardier souls. The carriage manufactory of William Whitaker on Dundas Street eventually became a garage, as did the livery stable of the Hillmers. During World War I motor buses replaced the old horse-drawn buses, and these survivals of the era of stage-coaches became merely a memory. The livery stable which had occupied the same site for some eighty years continued in use as a garage until destroyed by fire in the 1930's.

With the rapid increase in the use of the automobile as a means of travel, and the ensuing improvement of the provincial highways, the town's popularity as a summer resort grew by leaps and bounds. Oakville's proximity to Hamilton and Toronto ultimately led to its becoming the dormitory for a large number of city business men. As the daily commuters multiplied, the permanent population started once more to show an upward curve, and Oakville entered upon the fourth phase of its existence, industrialization.

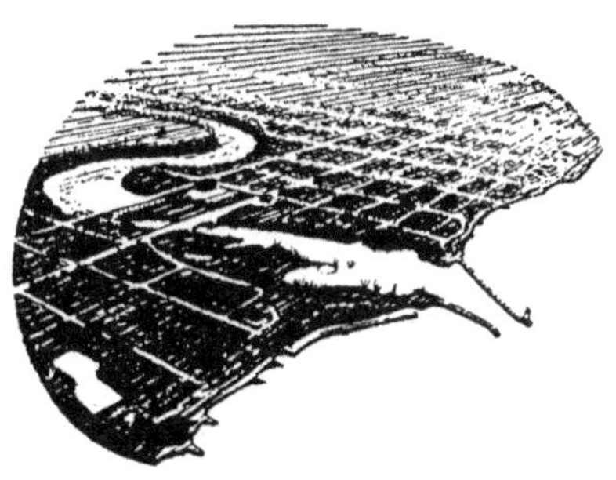

EPILOGUE

THE HISTORY OF OAKVILLE is closely bound up with the development of transportation. In every instance, changes in the means of transportation either advanced or retarded the progress of the town. At the outset, the necessity for getting to market the staves, timber, and surplus produce of the district was the reason for the existence of the harbour and the village by which it was surrounded. While Oakville's commerce was dependent upon water and waggon transportation it thrived in proportion to the extension of roads into the interior. When waggon haulage was facilitated by the plank road, the building of wooden ships reached its peak, and the population of Oakville doubled within three years. The era of iron and steam, with its railways, brought about the disruption of the town's economy through the diversion of commerce from north and south to east and west. The long period of regression and lethargy that followed ended only when the advent of the automobile and the construction of highways placed the town in the main stream of traffic running east and west. The first of these highways brought regular bus service, more summer residents, and more commuters, and three decades later, with the Queen Elizabeth Way, came industrialization.

The new phase began with the laying on the Lake Shore Road of Canada's first major road pavement, the Toronto-Hamilton Highway which ran through Oakville's business section on Colborne Street. When its last section, the seven-mile stretch between Clarksons and Oakville, was completed, the new highway was opened to traffic on December 7, 1915. Thereafter a great stream of international traffic poured into the province year after year. Oakville now began to feel the pressure of city influences together with those of an American tendency brought by multitudes of tourists motoring through the town en route to the north country. Gasoline pumps loomed outside the stores of retail merchants, quick lunch counters appeared, advertising became increasingly important, and Colborne Street began to lose the Victorian aspect it had worn for so long. The old shops facing upon a broad expanse of pavement bare of trees gradually underwent exterior remodelling which made them counterparts of those across the border. With the invasion of city influences, the residential sections of Oakville also began to change. As old board fences collapsed and tall hedges died they were not replaced, and the tangled undergrowth was cleared away. Gardens thus opened to the street lost their mysterious nooks and corners, acquiring instead neat lawns and formal plantings. When the most desirable tracts of farm land on the lake shore east of the town were taken up by large estates, a similar development started along the highway west of the town. The owners of these new estates were in residence only during the summer.

According to urban standards, Oakville was "dead." But the older inhabitants and those who for that reason had been attracted to it were content that it should remain a small residential town. The few industries managed to achieve a limited degree of success. The old basket factory, taken over at the beginning of World War I by J. M. Wallace, burned down in 1920, and the plant was then moved to its present location beside the railway. And the aluminum factory continued to make kitchen utensils in the old brick building on Dundas Street North. But it was the tannery of Marlatt & Armstrong that was by far the town's most important industry.

The leather, which had been manufactured for the carriage trade, was now used for upholstering the seats and covering the tops of automobiles, and the firm's specialty, patent leather, was still extensively used for shoes. The tannery was one of the largest plants of its kind in Canada, and it continued to expand, with new buildings being added along the west bank of The Sixteen. Then one day in the middle twenties the news that the tannery had failed burst over the town with the suddenness of a bomb. For the first time in seventy years the fires in the boilers went out. It was the silencing of the tannery whistle, more than any other circumstance, that proved a constant reminder of the failure of this establishment. The silence marked the end not only of the town's largest and oldest existing industry, but of an era. The smells and smoke to which the townspeople had long since become resigned, the hundreds of hides stretched on the frames and laid in the tannery yards to dry in the sun, the shining *Aggie* swinging at her moorings in the harbour, C. G. Marlatt riding in his open touring car along Colborne Street several times a day, and a thousand other details associated with the little empire that was the tannery, all disappeared. Involved in the crash was the house Marlatt had built on Dunn Street South in 1899 at a cost, according to the *Star*, of $8,000, and the garden spreading over five of the six lots in the block. The house is now a funeral parlour, and a number of houses occupy the garden. The auxiliary tannery at Navy and Colborne streets was purchased by James R. Kendall, who continued the manufacture of glove and other leathers in the building erected by Gage & Hagaman. After serving as store and factory for ninety-three years, this building was destroyed by fire in 1948.

In earlier times Oakville had been in the orbit of Hamilton, but with the rise of the automobile the town became more closely allied to Toronto. Increasing numbers of summer residents began maintaining homes in the town the year round, going daily to business in the city twenty miles away. Oakville was the spiritual home of these commuters. They took an active part in the social and religious life of the community, but none in its municipal affairs. The Town Council continued to consist of tradesmen and retail merchants whose interests were centred locally. As the town gradually assumed the proportions of a dormitory, Torontonians tended to regard it as a suburb despite the fact that Oakville rejected this conception of itself. By 1921 the resident population stood at 3,289 and a decade later, though it had reached only 3,857, large numbers of persons lived on its outskirts who were identified with Oakville.

Just before the beginning of World War II the four-lane highway named in honour of the Queen was opened between Toronto and Hamilton. This highway more or less parallels the Lake Shore Road, but bypasses towns and cities on the older road. In the vicinity of Oakville the Queen Elizabeth Way passes along what had formerly been known as the Lower Middle Road, the northern boundary of the town. Except that it attracted more commuters to the town, this highway brought no major changes until the end of the war. It was then that Oakville entered upon its newest phase of development, industrialism.

With the expansion of the Canadian industrial economy and the decentralization of industry which followed upon the close of World War II the industrialization of Oakville was inevitable. The town is in a key position between the two largest urban markets in Ontario. It is easy of access by rail and road. It offers to industries the opportunity of acquiring enough land to allow for future expansion, and to employees it offers better living conditions than do the cities. And this is considered a good area from which to draw labour.

At the end of the War the tannery buildings, which for years had stood vacant, filled up with manufacturing firms. The building where aluminum kitchen-ware had first been made, which had stood idle for an even longer period than the tannery, was taken over by a manufacturer of rubber-coated fabrics and vulcanized rubber clothing. As building materials once more became available, new plants appeared within the town, the largest centring on the north near the railway and the Queen Elizabeth Way. The opening of a street through what was once the farm of John Cross, and named in his honour, made possible the extension of the industrial area westward. The various manufacturing concerns now located in Oakville are engaged in making a great variety of products. These include paint, varnish, pigments, materials and equipment for porcelain enamelling, patent medicines, cosmetics and their containers, fruit syrups for soda fountains, soil pipes, commercial and industrial refrigerating and air conditioning units, fluorescent light bulbs, lampshades, wardrobes, laminated paper products, patent doors, insecticides, tools, dies, charts for recording instruments, electrotyping, and wax engraving. In the manufacture of some of these products, plastics are extensively used, and the firm engaged in turning out rubber-coated fabrics has expanded into this field. The manufacture of glove leather, aluminum kitchen utensils, and various types of baskets continues as in earlier times. The veteran of all the industries, the basket factory, may be considered the heaviest of them all; the products listed above come under the category of light industry. In recent years this firm has branched out into the making of wood products such as sheets of plywood and skewers. It is of interest to note that only a few hundred yards from where vegetables were dried over a wood fire some eighty years ago the same process is being carried on by modern methods of dehydration.

With the influx of industry, which began in 1946, the population of the town began to rise steadily, increasing at the rate of between 400 and 500 yearly. In 1948 the population figure topped 5,000. At the time of writing it exceeds 6,500 and continues to climb. Most of the available space within the town has been absorbed by mushroom building, including the farm of G. K. Chisholm on the west side of The Sixteen. This is now the Forster Survey, almost a community in itself. Adjoining it is the rapidly expanding Ortona Barracks, Headquarters of the Central Command, Canadian Army. Large estates along the

Lake Shore Road are being subdivided into lots for small houses. With the exception of the addition of Brantwood Survey, however, the limits of the Municipal Corporation remain the same as they were when Oakville became separated from Trafalgar Township in 1857.

Oakville is no longer a purely residential town. It is fast acquiring all the attributes of other industrial towns in close proximity to larger centres. As it did a century ago with the coming of the railway, the commercial area is once more moving eastward. No longer confined to the main thoroughfare, it is spreading out also into the residential sections on the north and south. New street lights have been installed recently, and the congestion of traffic somewhat eased by the widening of the eastern approach and the placing of parking meters along each curb. Retail merchants continue to increase, and the addition of "modern" fronts makes difficult the identification of the older buildings. There is a variety of specialty shops and chain stores, and the town now boasts a supermarket. The banks have expanded in size and increased in number, and additions to the churches are being planned. The electric carillon of Knox Church now competes with the chimes of St. Jude's. The high school has been considerably enlarged, as have Brantwood School on the east and Westwood School across the river. Central School stands relatively unchanged, but its days seem numbered. The new fifty-bed Oakville-Trafalgar Memorial Hospital is the last word in planning and equipment. Each week two newspapers published in the town appear on the news-stands. The town sports are now under the supervision of an athletic director. At Victoria Park, which is devoted to baseball, and Busby Park, where softball is played, games take place at night under powerful electric lighting. Following upon a series of mild winters when there was little if any ice for skating, a new community centre was opened. This centre includes an arena where skating on artificial ice is provided throughout the year, and a public auditorium. There are two cinema theatres in the town, and Victoria Hall, where in days gone by the first flickering moving pictures were shown, is now largely devoted to the social activities of high-school students.

Needless to say the facilities of the town and all public services were inadequate to meet this rapid expansion, and the Town Council wrestled with the problems of relieving the strain on public utilities. The systems for providing water and disposing of waste, the fire department, electric and telephone services were expanded. Pressure on the post office was somewhat relieved by the institution of a mail delivery which made necessary the numbering of buildings and houses. Both these innovations proved most unpopular among older residents, who were thus deprived of the pleasure of visiting with their friends when calling for their mail at the post office. These are but a few of the problems that have faced the Town Council, and while many remain unsolved, new ones continually arise.

As the tendency towards both living and working in Oakville becomes stronger, the pendulum now swings back to the days before improved transportation turned Oakville into more or less of a dormitory. With the return of men from the armed forces (and it may be mentioned in passing that during both world wars Oakville had more men in the armed forces than any other town with the same population in Canada) the complexion of the Town Council began to alter. An interest in the municipal affairs of the community became apparent among relative newcomers, whether engaged in business in Toronto, or in local industry.

Besides the man-made changes within the town there are those wrought by the waters of Lake Ontario along the lake front. Several years of unprecedentedly high water during the 1940's caused great havoc at the entrance of the harbour. In a short space of time the aspect of the harbour became so altered by the disappearance of old landmarks as to be almost unrecognizable. The destruction began when the water broke through the centre of the east pier, which thereafter disintegrated rapidly. Before long the wide beach extending from the foot of the hill to the pier, along which ran the communicating road, disappeared completely, taking with it a dwelling-house, the pavilion, and a number of trees. A broad expanse of open water then lay between the foot of the hill and the remaining section of the pier, and the lighthouse stood in splendid isolation, as may be seen by the photograph opposite page 382. Gradually the broad grassy slope of Lakeside Park became eroded by the water, and the ancient oak which had stood guard over the mouth of The Sixteen for centuries vanished. Neither materials, labour, nor funds were available to retard this havoc during wartime, and it was not until 1947 that the Dominion Government took steps to save the harbour from total destruction. To form a turning basin within the harbour a new steel and concrete breakwater was constructed at an angle from the base of the hill to the lighthouse. During the summer that this work was in progress the lighthouse stood on the west pier. Within the space of a few minutes it had been lifted from its foundations, placed upon a barge, and after being moored overnight in the river, set on this temporary location. Upon completion of the breakwater the lighthouse was returned to its new foundation some ten feet south of its original site on the old timber pier which paralleled the west pier. At the time of writing, it stands at the entrance to the harbour, its green light now powered by electricity.

This long chronicle now draws to a close. During the course of its unfolding we have seen the outcome of the several plans of William Chisholm; how the foremost plan succeeded and Oakville became a port of considerable importance; how after some thirty years, with the coming of the railway, commerce faltered and fell away, never to return. We have seen the collapse of the secondary plan, to put to use the water-power in The Sixteen for the purposes of manufacturing and thus make Oakville an industrial town. And we have seen how, after the passage of more than a century, the hopes of the founder are being realized. What William Chisholm failed to accomplish with water-power has come to pass with the use of electricity, and manufacturing now flourishes in Oakville. By 1941 the number of industries had increased to eight and the recent census shows an increase to fifty-five within the last decade. But this apparently is only the beginning. In the autumn of 1951 came the announcement that a large tract of land in Trafalgar Township situated only a short distance east of Oakville had been acquired by the Ford Motor Company of Canada. In a building covering thirty-two acres of floor space, to be the largest industrial building in the Dominion, will be assembled all the Ford cars and trucks made in Canada. The anticipated number of employees of Ford Oakville is reported to be in the neighbourhood of five thousand. Already other manufacturing concerns are following in the wake of this huge enterprise.

What this will mean for Oakville is a question to which no one may foresee the answer. Even before the Ford plan was made public, one heard on all sides that within the near future Oakville would become a a city. This is a prophecy with a familiar ring. It may be remembered that the advent of the railway nearly a century ago caused a widespread impression that Oakville's growth would continue unchecked. "What in the world is to prevent this place growing to be an important City?" asked a nameless visitor in a letter to the local press in 1855. "It must, there is nothing to prevent it."

The harbour, though little used by commercial shipping, has lost none of its popularity among owners of pleasure craft. It continues also to perform one of its initial functions, that of a harbour of refuge. The recent announcement by the Canadian Government of its intention to carry forward the St. Lawrence Seaway has implications for Oakville. When this project becomes reality and large ships from many countries pass through Lake Ontario, Oakville may regain some of its former importance as a port.

Meanwhile the Sixteen Mile Creek, the erstwhile Nesaugayonk of the red man, now a negative factor in the schemes of white men, flows quietly through its lower reaches within the town of Oakville to the deep waters of Lake Ontario.

APPENDIXES

APPENDIX A

Extract from the Reminiscences of John A. Williams

"There is a tradition of a great battle having been fought in ancient times near the Sixteen River between rival tribes. The island by the mill, at that time was much more prominent than now, the Indians had raised corn on it and muskrats were plentiful around its borders, but after the woods above were cut off the spring floods tore away much. Dr. Sutherland fixed the scene of the battle ground somewhere above the railroad station on account of the number of arrowheads and other Indian relics that have been found in that locality. But on account of George Crookfinger having told Col. William Chisholm that a great Chief was buried on the spot where C. W. Coote's house now stands and having been present myself at the time the large pine stump was taken out and the mound dug away and having seen the kettle and other relics as they were taken out I fancied there might have been a battle near there. I was only ten or twelve at the time. Whether there was a battle where I locate it is unknown but the fact remains that a mound existed at the place where Dunn Street joins the river and was excavated by the order of Col. Wm. Chisholm. The relics taken from it are perhaps in possession of his descendants—if not destroyed in the fire which occurred many years ago destroying the old Chisholm residence on the east corner of Colborne and Thomas streets."

Artifacts continue to appear on the land situated along the west bank of the river south of the railway, and it seems likely that the battle referred to extended over the whole area. C. W. Coote's house where the pine tree stood is now no. 39 Dunn Street North, and the mound, excavated about 1840, was close by. Evidently the relics found there were destroyed in the manner suggested by Williams.

APPENDIX B

Justus Williams' Remedies*

Pills. 1 part opium, 2 parts camphor mixed together with flour and a little peppermint water or spirits

Vinegar & Redpepper for scarlet fever

For a Metic or vomit

Boil slipperyjohn Bark to a jelly
Strain, and cool it to one quart
add ½ oz of metic tartar, 1 oz salsoda, 1 spoonful Lodlum, 1 Do of vinegar and 1 of Honey. Shake them well and they will be fit for use. 1 spoonful for a Grown person, 1 teaspoonful for a Child.

To make Rheumatic drops

Take 1 gal of Alcohol or fourth proof Brandy
1 lb of Gummyrrh
1 oz of Cayenne pepper
Pulverize the two latter & put the whole into a stone jug, sit it into a kettle of cold water put it over the fire and Boil it 10 or 15 minutes.

To Make Composition powder

Take 2 lb of Bayberry, or Black birch bark
1 lb of Hemlock 1 lb of Ginger 2 oz Cloves
2 oz Cayenne pepper. let the whole be pulverized and thoroughly mixed. One teaspoonful is a dose. This medicine is good for colds, & an almost infallible cure for bowel complaints of every kind and may be given with safety without regard to age or condition.

Ague

Take ½ pt fourth proof Brandy
1 piece of Allum as large as a walnut
½ or ¾ lb loaf sugar
3 nutmegs and ½ oz peruviom bark
¼ oz oil lemon
Grate and mix them together then add two quarts boiling water, let it stand until it is cold then take ¾ gill once in every four hours when the ague is off.

*These remedies are written in the back of Justus Williams' shop ledger, dated 1830–6.

APPENDIX C

QUARTERLY REPORT OF THE OAKVILLE COMMON SCHOOL FROM DEC. 12TH 1836 TO MARCH 12TH 1837; SHEWING THE PROGRESS, ATTENDANCE, &C OF THE PUPILS RECEIVING INSTRUCTION THEREIN*

Pupils' names	*Period of attendance*	*Absence ½ days*	*whole*	*General observations*
Edward Case	3 Mths	6	1	Has done very well
Jane Tassie	3 "	14	3	do — do sickness the cause of absence
Jos Prekore [Precours]	3 "	17	1	Might do better, improving however
Jos. Kenny	3 "	4	8	Both of these boys have done
Chas Kenny	3 "	5	7	pretty well
Jno Williams	3 "	8	10	Improving steadily, very fast in ciphering
A Williams	3 "	4	10	Do do
Jas Magill	3 "	11	17	Doing pretty well
A Diamond	3 "	13	23	Has improved very rapidly
A Crooks	3 "	8	21	Do
Thos Hatton	3 "	15	11	Pretty well, doing well in figures
Geo. Griggs	2¾ "	0	20	Has done very well
Jas Busk	3 "	3	13	Pretty well
H Cronkrite	3 "	4	17	These boys have done well, still
Wm Cronkrite	3 "	3	20	there is a want of *life* and *exertion*
Chas Thomas	1½ "	5	37	Has improved very fast in reading
R Lloyd	3 "	8	23	Too irregular an attendant to improve much
Bridg[t] Sweeny	3 "	5	37	Considering her irregularity, has done well
Louis Basnich [Bisnois]	3 "	18	6	Very well
Jno H Terry	3 "	9	17	A want of inclination and other things retard him
Jon[n] Lane	3 "	5	20	Did very well
Alex[r] Griggs	3 "	4	27	A variety of causes prevent this boy's improvement, a *total* want of application and inclination
M Robinson	3 "	8	8	Improving very rapidly
Wm Bissett	3 "	5	10	Has done tolerably well
Ralph Bissett	3 "	4	9	Do do
Easther Leach	2¾ "	0	18	Pretty well

*John A. Williams, who preserved this report found in his father's papers, and who was eight years of age when it was written (sixth in the list above), stated that it was the first report of William Tassie, schoolmaster.

Pupils' names	*Period of attendance*	*Absence ½ days*	*whole*	*General observations*
Chas Leach	2¾ "	0	19	Do —
George Hinton	2 Mths	0	2	Very well but might have done better
Edwd Hinton	2 "	0	1	Do
Jno Young	1¾ "	1	5	Improved very much
A Butts	1½ "	0	22	Do — his absence &c draw-back
Anne Lebar	1¼ "	0	14	So so
Andrew Lebar	1 "	0	3	Progress very rapid especially in writing & figures
Ja^{s} Lebar	1 "	0	3	Do — Do

APPENDIX D

Registry of Ownership of Vessels Registered at the Custom House, Port of Oakville*

Name	Description	Where she belongs	Tons	Where built	Builder	Master
Amelia	Schooner	Oakville	105½	Oakville 1836	Jacob Randall	Hiram Williams
Champion	“	“	114	“ 1852	Melancthon Simpson	“ “
Peerless	“	“	172	Bronte 1853	“ “	John Belyea
Lily	“	“	141	“ 1854	John “	Sam'l Williams
Sultan	“	“	111	Oakville “	Chas. Wm. Thomas	Sam'l Kingston
John Potter	“	“	116	“ “	—	Francis Crooks
Three Bells	“	“	221	“ “	John Simpson	Wm. Wilson
Belle	“	“	32	“ 1856	Melancthon “	Sam'l Kingston
Canadian	“	“	160	“ “	“ “	Fransis Crooks
Coquette	“	“	176	“ 1857	“ “	G. B. Chisholm
Royal Albert	“	“ (sunk 1868)	165	“ 1858	John “	Robert Coote
Victoria	“	“	238	“ 1862	Duncan Chisholm	
Monarch, 3 masted	“	“	348	“ 1863	“ “	
Sea Gull	“	“	238	“ 1864	John Simpson	
Kate	“	“	100	“ 1866	W. J. Miller	
Smith & Post	“	“	255	“ “	John Potter†	
Dauntless	“	“	179	“ 1867	“ “	
White Oak	“	“	213	“ “	Duncan Chisholm	
Wood Duck	“	“	77	Bronte 1868	Hiram Cronkrite	

*From the Public Archives of Canada, MSS Department.

†Other vessels said to have been built by John Potter are the *Chieftain, MarcoPolo, Royal Oak, Oddfellow*, and *Henrietta P. Murray*.

APPENDIX E

Masters of Sailing Vessels out of Oakville

Edward Andrew
James Andrew
John Andrew
Nicholas Boylan
Duncan Chisholm
George Brock Chisholm
Robert Coote
William Coote
Arthur Clarkson
Francis Crooks
James Dougherty
Maurice Felan
Maurice Fitzgerald
John Gallie
George Gerrie
Henry Hinton
Thomas Hinton
Francis Jackman
John Jeffery
Samuel Kingston
William Lawson
Peter Lyon
Alexander Martin
George Morgan
Duncan McCorquodale
James McCorquodale
Peter McCorquodale
Robert McCorquodale
John McGiffin
Samuel McGiffin
James McKnight
John Moore
George H. Morden
George Moulton
John Murray
James Quinn
Jacob Randall
C. J. Schofield
William Street
Stephen Waggoner
Hiram Williams
Robert Williams
Samuel Williams
William Williams
George Wilson
Robert Wilson
William Wilson

APPENDIX F

An Act to Incorporate the Town of Oakville*

[Assented to 27th May, 1857.]

Whereas from the rapidly increasing population of the Village of Oakville, in the County of Halton, and from its being one of the principal Shipping Ports on Lake Ontario, it is necessary to confer upon the said Village the power of Municipal Government: Therefore, Her Majesty, by and with the advice and consent of the Legislative Council and Assembly of Canada, enacts as follows:

I. From and after the passing of this Act, the inhabitants of the Town of Oakville shall be a body corporate apart from the Township of Trafalgar in which the said Town is situate, and as such shall have perpetual succession and a Common Seal with such powers as are now by law conferred upon Incorporated Towns in Upper Canada; and the powers of such Corporation shall be exercised by, through and in the name of the municipality of the Town of Oakville.

II. The said Town of Oakville shall comprise and consist of the following lots and parcels of land, that is to say: Lots Numbers twelve, thirteen, fourteen, fifteen and sixteen and the gore adjoining lot sixteen in the third concession of Trafalgar, and lots eleven, twelve, thirteen, fourteen, fifteen, sixteen, and the gore, and lot seventeen in the broken front or fourth concession of the said Township of Trafalgar.

III. The said Town of Oakville shall be divided into three wards in the manner following, that is to say:

Ward number one shall comprise all that portion of the Town west of Navy street, with the entire portion lying on the west side of the Sixteen Mile Creek.

Ward number two shall comprise all that portion of the Town east of Navy street and south of Colborne street.

Ward number three shall comprise all that portion of the Town east of Navy street and north of Colborne street.

IV. Immediately after the passing of this Act it shall be lawful for the Governor of this Province to appoint a Returning Officer for the said Town of Oakville, which Returning Officer shall appoint the time and place for holding the first election in each ward of the said Town, of which appointment, and of the names of the Deputy Returning Officers for the several Wards he shall give notice, by posting the same at least ten days before the election in three or more public places in each of the Wards of the said Town.

V. The duties of the Returning Officer and Deputy Returning Officers, and the qualifications of the voters and the persons elected as Councillors at such first election, shall be as prescribed by law with respect to Townships in Upper Canada.

**Statutes of Canada*, 1857, c. 93.

VI. The Collector or Township Clerk of the Township of Trafalgar, or other person having legal custody of the Collector's Roll for the year one thousand eight hundred and fifty-six, shall furnish to each Deputy Returning Officer a true copy of the said Roll so far as the same relates to voters resident within the limits of each of such Wards, and so far as such Roll contains the names of the male freeholders and householders rated upon such Roll in respect of real property lying within such limits, with the amount of the assessed value of such real property for which they shall be respectively rated on such Roll, which copy shall be verified upon oath or in such manner as is now required by law .

VII. The said Returning Officer and Deputy Returning Officers before holding the said elections, shall take the same oath or affirmation as is now required by law for Returning Officers and Deputy Returning Officers in Towns in Upper Canada.

VIII. Elections of Councillors of the said Town of Oakville after the year one thousand eight hundred and fifty-seven, shall be held in conformity with the statutory provisions in respect of the several Incorporated Towns of Upper Canada.

IX. The several persons who shall be elected or appointed under this Act shall take the same oaths of office and of qualification as are now required by law.

X. The said Councillors to be elected under this Act for the said Town, shall be organized in the same manner and in the same way as in any other Incorporated Town in Upper Canada, and have, use and exercise the same powers and privileges as any other Incorporated Town in Upper Canada, and the first meeting of the said Council shall be held in the School House in the said Town, at eleven o'clock on the first Saturday after the day on which the Election of Councillors shall have been held.

XI. Any Councillor elected to serve in the Township Council of the said Township of Trafalgar, for the present year, and residing within the above prescribed limits of the said Town, shall, immediately on the appointment of a Returning Officer for the said Town as provided by this Act, cease to be such Councillor, and the duly qualified electors of the Wards in which the said Town is situate, shall thereupon proceed to elect a new Councillor or Councillors, as the case may be, to serve in the Council of the said Township for the remainder of the year, as in the case of death or resignation provided for by the Municipal laws in Upper Canada.

XII. The Officers of the said Council of the Township of Trafalgar shall not proceed to collect any rate or assessment imposed by the said Council for the present year, within the limits of the said Town, but the amount which may be required for the purposes of the said Town within the present year, shall be based on the assessment of the Township assessor or assessors for the present year, and shall be collected by the Officer or Officers to be appointed by the said Town Council for that purpose;

Provided always that nothing herein contained shall affect any School rates or School section for the present year.

XIII. The Clerk of the said Township shall, and he is hereby required to furnish to the Clerk to be appointed by the Council of the said Town, on demand made by him therefor, a true copy of the Assessment Roll for the present year, so far as the same shall contain the rateable property assessed within the said Town, and the names of the owners or occupiers thereof.

XIV. The expenses of any assessment imposed for the present year, so far as the same shall relate to assessments made within the limits of the said Town, and the expenses of furnishing any documents, or copies of papers or writings, by the Clerk or other Officer of the Council of the said Township hereinbefore referred to, or required to be furnished, shall be borne and paid by the said Town Council to the said Township Council, or otherwise as the said Township Council shall require.

XV. From and after the passing of this Act the said Town shall cease to form part of the said Township of Trafalgar, and shall, to all intents and purposes, form a separate and independent Municipality, with all the privileges and rights of an Incorporated Town in Upper Canada, but nothing herein contained shall affect or be construed to affect any taxes imposed for the payment of debt contracted by the Township of Trafalgar, but the said Town shall pay to the Treasurer of the said Township of Trafalgar in each and every year until such existing debt be fully paid and discharged, the same amount which was collected within the present described limits of the said Town, towards the payment of such debt for the year one thousand eight hundred and fifty-six, and the same shall be a debt against the said Town.

XVI. All Acts and parts of Acts and provisions of law or of parliament, and all Acts, By-Laws, Rules and Regulations of any Township Meeting, County Council, or Township Council in Upper Canada, in force in Upper Canada immediately before the time when this Act shall come into force, in so far as the same may be inconsistent with or contradictory to the provisions of this Act, shall be and are hereby repealed, and shall cease to be in force from and after the day when this Act shall come into force.

XVII. This Act shall be deemed a Public Act.

APPENDIX G

VOLUNTEER MILITIA 1865–66: PAY-LIST OF 1ST OAKVILLE RIFLE COMPY—LT. COL. GEO. CHISHOLM AT OAKVILLE*

Pay Serg't
David Johnson

Sergeants
James Wilson
R. B. Albertson
W. G. Hewson

Corporals
R. D. Bigger
W. H. Speers
Wm. Litchfield

Privates
Thompson Bigger
P. L. Chisholm
Charles P. Chisholm
Thomas Dowdle
Richard Dowdle
Sam'l Deer
Richard Dowdle, Jun'r
W. T. Duff
D. Chisholm
(left Co. before completing drill)
Rob Chisholm
W. E. Cullingsworth
Joseph Clark
George Busby
Thomas Fletcher
J. A. Chisholm
Oliver Fish
Wm. Ford

Privates
John W. Ford
Robert Hinton
James Hall
Wm. Moulton
Philo Noble
Thomas Osborne
Thomas Pepper
Robert Patterson
John Pickering
Wm. Pepper
Isaac Obee
Bennett Reed
(undecipherable)
George Slater
Henry Upham
Wm. Ward
W. A. Young
Edgar Skelley
John Freestone
Chas. Molman
Edmund Leach
A. M. Mason
James Kelley
Lewis Kemp
Harry A. Ward
Egerton Freeman
Rob't H. Evans
R. O. Bigger
John Mellash
James Breet

Dated Oakville 29 May, 1866
Total 53 men
(Drill 3 hours duration)

*Public Archives of Canada.

APPENDIX H

Headmasters of the Oakville Schools

Grammar School

1854–6	Arthur Cole Verner, Trinity College, Dublin
1857–64	William Oliver, University of Toronto
1865–6	W. B. Fleming, University of Toronto
1867–8	James Choppin Morgan, University of Toronto
1869–70	John Pepper, University of Toronto
1871–3	Rev. William Lumsden, Victoria College*
1874–7	P. A. Switzer
1877–1905	Nesbitt J. Wellwood
1905–10	John T. Lillie
1910–14	L. J. Williams
1914–24	William B. Wyndham
1924–47	Robert H. Archibald

Common School

1854–6	Arthur Cole Verner
1857–62	Daniel Benjamin Chisholm
1863–4	Charles H. Lusk, M.D.
1865	S. B. Ganton
1866	James Choppin Morgan
1867–8	W. W. Bredin
1869–70	J. W. Narroway
1871–2	Charles H. Lusk, M.D.
1873	P. A. Switzer
1874–5	W. Galbraith
1876–1902	Henry Husband
1903–5	— McGill
1906–7	George Graham
1908–39	R. Frank Sanderson

*From 1873 to 1900 Charles H. Lusk, M.D., was assistant to the principal. According to the School Law Improvement Act of 1871 changes were made in the following terms: headmaster became principal, common school became public school, grammar school became high school, and local superintendent became school inspector.

APPENDIX I

Older Buildings on Colborne Street East

North side

Nos. 19–23	1827	North-west section of frame building erected for inn by William Young for its owner, William Chisholm.
	1836	Two-storey addition built across the front by new owner, William J. Sumner.
	1869	Third storey added by John Williams. This inn has always retained its original name, the Oakville House.
No. 37	1855 c.	Brick building erected by James Reid.
	1868	Bought by W. H. Young, cabinet-maker.
	1878	Remodelled into two stores, Young occupying the west half and William G. Hewson, general merchant, the east half.
	1924	Savoy Café, J. W. Ming.
No. 39		An early store.
No. 41		Another early store.
	1870–1934	Occupied by Ezekiel Smith followed by his son Wilbert Smith.
Nos. 47–51	1850	Erected on the south-east corner of Dunn and Randall streets as the Wesleyan Methodist Church.
	1878	Moved to Colborne Street when present church was built and remodelled into three stores.
Nos. 64–69	1881	Erected by William Busby, jeweller and watch-maker.
	1885 c.–1915	Exchange of Bell Telephone Company.
No. 75A,B,C	1834 c.	Frame building erected and occupied by Joshua Van Allen, tailor.
	1845 c.	Occupied by John Moore, tinsmith, followed by his son Cyrus and grandson Harry, also tinsmiths, for about seventy-five years.
No. 77	1856	Brick building erected by Obadiah Marlatt, general merchant at Post's Corners (Postville).
	1865 c.–1893	Occupied by John A. Williams, general merchant.
	1893–5 c.	Occupied by William, Nelson, and Frank Robinson, clothiers.
No. 81	1834 c.	Frame building erected by William Creighton, general merchant.
	1869–1905	Occupied by Charles Coote, general merchant.
	1879	Building faced with brick.

Nos. 85–87	1834	Site of dwelling house of Michael Butler, shipwright, and his wife Ann.
	1850's–73	Bakery and boarding house.
	1873	Bakery purchased by James Hunter from his daughter, Annie Butler.
	1905	Destroyed by fire.
	1910	Present building erected for fourth post office.
No. 91		Site of an early building; originally two stores which stood opposite on the south-west corner of Dunn Street, occupied by Duncan Chisholm, tinsmith and dealer in stoves, and Mrs. Mary Wilson, baker and confectioner.
	1855	Moved to present site and remodelled into one store.
	1855–68	Occupied by John and Robert Ferrah, bakers and confectioners.
	1952	Building demolished.
No. 99	1843 c.	Erected for dwelling and blacksmith's shop by Howard.
	1860	Remodelled into hotel, the Victoria House.
	1888 c.	Renovated and renamed the Queen's Hotel.
	1900	Queen's Hotel closed.
	1903	Remodelled and faced with brick by William Buckle, butcher.
	1952	Building demolished.
No. 115		Section of the White Oak Hotel moved to this site from the south-east corner of Dunn Street when the Presbyterian Church was built in 1888. The White Oak Hotel was originally Lloyd's tavern and another section of it, possibly the oldest, was moved to the lake shore at the foot of Allan Street where it was incorporated within the house now owned by Wm. O. Gibson, no. 176 King Street.

South side

No. 38		A third section of the White Oak Hotel.
Nos. 58–60	1835	Frame building erected by George Brown, merchant at Milton.
	1841–68	Occupied by David Duff, cabinet-maker.
	1868–1912	Occupied by John and Robert Ferrah, bakers, followed by W. A. Ferrah.
	1912–35	The Ferrahs continued to bake their bread in ovens in the rear of this building, but sold it in their new store built next door on the west side.

No. 62	1840 c.	Medical Hall and dwelling of John Urquhart, apothecary.
	1875–1933	Continued as such by his son, Dr. John Urquhart.
No. 68	1835	Site of original shop of Henry Gulledge, saddler and harness maker.
	1875–1933	Present store occupied by his son, E. H. Gulledge.
Nos. 72–74	1834	Erected by John Forman as a temperance inn on the south-west corner of Randall and Dundas streets.
	1860's	Halton County Hotel.
	1870 c.	Moved to present site, remodelled into two stores. West store occupied by Henry Wilson, flour and feed merchant, east store occupied by Mrs. Moulton.
	1926	Renovated and brick facing added.
No. 86		An early building, probably used in conjunction with the Royal Exchange Hotel which stood on the west, the site of the post office.
	1850	The *Oakville Weekly Sun* published and printed here.
	1870's	James Kelley's blacksmith shop.
No. 94	1855	Brick building erected by Captain William Wilson upon the site of James Steele's saddler's shop which had probably been destroyed by fire. Incorporated within the present building are the foundations of the earlier structure. The little casement windows glazed with small panes and the cellar stairway which once opened to the outside daylight are now under the centre section of this building.
	1855–78	Occupied by John McCorkindale, general merchant.
	1878	James Kelley established a hardware business which was carried on by his son, John, his son-in-law, James McGregor, and various other proprietors.
No. 100	1856	Brick building erected by Duncan Chisholm, tinsmith and dealer in stoves.
	1878	Peter Kelley established a furniture business which was carried on by his daughters until recent times.
No. 114	1833	Frame dwelling-house erected by Justus W. Williams. His merchant's shop stood on the east side on the site of No. 118.
	1880's	Faced with brick.
	1951	Original fireplaces, doors, and stairway remain.

ADDENDUM

to

"*OAKVILLE AND THE SIXTEEN*"

Since the original printing of OAKVILLE AND THE SIXTEEN in 1953 changes in several street names and a new street-numbering system have caused confusion in identifying some of the locations mentioned.

It is believed that this addendum, prepared by Frances Ahern for the Oakville Historical Society will make even more enjoyable the reading of this excellent book.

Page	Street-numbering used in "Oakville and the Sixteen"	Present street-numbering and changed street names
33	5 William St.	115 William St.
52	55 Navy St. North	Dem. 1965: apartment site
53	63 Navy St. South	19 Navy St.
	54 Front St.	176 Front St.
	15 Dundas St. South	83 Trafalgar Road
	Samuel Lawson	280 Lawson St.
63	81 Colborne St. E.	215 Lakeshore Rd. E.
	Williams - shop	266-270 Lakeshore Rd. E.
64	56-60 Colborne St.	Dem. 1969: now 176 Lakeshore Rd. E.
70	John Terry	Dem. 1964: s.w. corner Brookfield & Lakeshore W.
73	27 Navy St. South	65 Navy St.
	33 William St.	145 William St.
75	153 Colborne St. E.	321 Lakeshore Rd. E.
	157 " " "	Dem. 1965
	69 Robinson St.	Dem. 1950's: n.w. cor. George & Robinson Sts.
83	62 Colborne St. E.	182 Lakeshore Rd. E.
100	Foot of Brant St.	126 Bath St.
126	George Griggs	1028 Lakeshore Rd. E.
	"Half-way House"	1475 " " "
160	55 Navy St. North	Dem. 1965: apartment site
185	McCraney homestead	549 Lakeshore Rd. W.
	Hiram McCraney	nr. "Country Squire", Q.E.W.
186	Culham farms - Sixth Line	Dem. 1970: housing development
192	"Post's Inn" - 7th Line	Dem. 1965: s.w. cor. Trafalgar Rd. & Hwy. #5
195	34 (35) Division St.	293 MacDonald Road
206	167 Colborne St. E.	321 Lakeshore Rd. E.
	171 " " "	Dem. 1965
207	226 Colborne St. E.	410 Lakeshore Rd. E.
212	81 William St.	215 William St.
216	113 Dundas St. North	235 Trafalgar Road
	119 " " "	243 " "
220	23 King St.	41 Navy St.
	187 Dundas St. North	311 Trafalgar Road
	41 Navy St. South	45 Navy St.
	204 Colborne St. E.	390 Lakeshore Road E.
	9 Thomas St. South	65 Thomas St.
221	31 Front St.	143 Front St.
	46 George St.	44 George St.
223	13 Navy St. South	85 Navy St.
224	94 Colborne St. E.	234 Lakeshore Rd. E.
	98 " " "	240 " " "
	77 " " "	209 " " "
225	37 " " "	145-9 " " "
	14 Second St.	88 Second St.
	266 Colborne St. E.	410 Lakeshore Road E.
	277 Dundas St. North	407 Trafalgar Road
227	17 Reynolds St. South	75 Reynolds St.
	145 William St.	307 William St.
	W.F. Romain	40 First St.
	63 First St.	31 " "
	10 " "	72 " "
	66 Navy St. South	4 Navy St.
228	70 " " "	8 " "
	15 Bond St.	Dem. 1969: n.e. cor. Queen Mary Dr. & Bond St.
	43 Bond St.	Dem. 1963: n.w. cor. Queen Mary Dr. & Bond St.
	William Cantley	126 Bath St.
	60 Church St.	Dem. 1968: opposite present Post Office
	63 " "	Dem. 1957: site of " " "
	18 Dundas St. North	Dem. 1958: n.w. cor. Church St. & Trafalgar Road
230	28 Chisholm St.	132 Chisholm St.

Page	Street-numbering used in "Oakville and the Sixteen"	Present street-numbering and changed street names
235	Judge Beardsley	1028 Lakeshore Road E.
	"The Grove"	76 Alexander Drive
236	49 Robinson St. ("south")	Dem. 1954: n.e. cor. Robinson & Thomas
240	18 Dundas St. North	Dem. 1958: n.w. cor. Church St. & Trafalgar Road
	84 Church St.	Dem. 1968: now parking lot
241	12 Navy St. South	86 Navy St.
	18 " " "	Dem. 1969: s.w. cor. Navy & Robinson Sts.
242	66 Navy St. South	4 Navy St.
243	70 " " "	8 " "
244	49 Dunn St. South	31 Dunn St.
245	63 Church St.	Dem. 1957: site of present Post Office
246	75 A,B,C Colborne St. E.	Dem. 1950's: now 207 Lakeshore Rd. E.
248	James Wesley Hill Farm	457 Ninth Line
250	70 Robinson St.	Dem. 1960's: s.w. cor. George & Robinson Sts.
	60 Colborne St. E.	Dem. 1950's: s.w. cor. Chisholm St. & Lakeshore Road W.
251	26 & 28 Navy St. South	68 & 70 Navy St.
	182 Dundas St. North	302 Trafalgar Road
252	13 Navy St. South	85 Navy St.
	Dundas St. at Division St.	Trafalgar Road at MacDonald Road
253	"Royal Exchange Hotel"	Dem: 216 etc. Lakeshore Road E.
254	51 Navy St. South	29 Navy St.
255	"Railway Station Hotel"	Dem. 1935: approx. 466 Trafalgar Road
258	86 Colborne St.	Dem. 1960's: now 218 Lakeshore Road E.
261	"King's Castle"	1126 Sixth Line
267	William St.	295, 297, 299 William St.
269	92 Park Avenue	10 Park Avenue
271	14 Dunn St. North	Dem. 1970: n.e. cor. Dunn & Church Sts.
272	"Retreat", Lakeshore Road W.	417 Lakeshore Road W.
285	150 King St.	312 King St.
306	33 William St.	145 William St.
311	127 Dundas St. North	247 Trafalgar Road
339	60 Burnet St.	38 Burnet St.
342	13 Navy St. South	85 Navy St.
352	29 King St.	191 King St.
	9 Second St.	93 Second St.
353	for "south-east" read:	south-west cor. Lakeshore Rd. W. & Brant St.
	130 Colborne St. W.	130 Lakeshore Road W.
355	82 William St.	214 William St.
	81 William St.	215 William St.
357	39 & 41 Colborne St. E.	149 & 155 Lakeshore Road E.
	56 & 60 " " "	Dem. 1969: now 176 Lakeshore Road E.
363	4 Dundas St. South	Dem. 1960's: now Loblaw parking lot
	18 " " North	Dem. 1950's: n.w. cor. Church St. & Trafalgar Road
	"brick house, Navy St."	86 Navy St.
364	s.w. cor. George & Colborne	196-202 Lakeshore Road E.
	49 Dundas St. North	159 Trafalgar Road
365	51 Navy St. South	29 Navy St.
	42 King St.	154 King St.
374	57 Thomas St.	29 Thomas St.
377	"Rosedale Villa"	417 Lakeshore Road West
	s.w. cor. Brant & Colborne	130 Lakeshore Road West
387	43 Cross Avenue	217 Cross Avenue
389	169 Dundas St. North	289 Trafalgar Road
390	241 Reynolds St. North	315-317 MacDonald Road
	259 Dundas St. North	385 Trafalgar Road
395	11 & 13 Inglehart Avenue	403 & 405 Inglehart Avenue
401	16 Thomas St. North	120 Thomas St.
405	143 & 145 Church St.	305 & 309 Church St.
	22 & 24 Reynolds St. North	128 & 132 Reynolds St.
410	89 William St.	225 William St.
	62 & 64 William St.	186 & 188 William St.

Page	Street-numbering used in "Oakville and the Sixteen"	Present street-numbering and changed street names
413	47, 49 & 51 Colborne St. E.	165, 167 & 169 Lakeshore Road E.
414	33 Navy St. South	53 Navy St.
	27 " " "	65 " "
416	90 William St.	226 William St.
417	119 Dundas St. North	243 Trafalgar Road
418	137, 139 & 141 William St.	295, 297 & 299 William St.
425	74 Colborne St.	198 Lakeshore Road E.
428	169 Dundas St. North	289 Trafalgar Road
	78 Front St.	212 Front St.
431	65 A & B Colborne St. E.	187 & 189 Lakeshore Road E.
	66 & 68 Church St.	192 & 194 Church St.
	85 & 87 Colborne St.	219 Lakeshore Road E.
432	70 Navy St. South	4 Navy St.
432-3	189 Colborne St. E.	Dem. 1960's: n.e. cor. Allan St. & Lakeshore Road E.
433	26 Colborne St. E.	132 Lakeshore Road E.
441	5 William St.	115 William St.
447	43 Bond St.	Dem. 1960's: n.w. cor. Bond St. & Queen Mary Drive
448	"Phoebe Baker"	171 Lakeshore Road E.
	"Mrs. Moulton's"	196 " " "
	Dr. Urquhart	182 " " "
	Ferrah's Bakery	174 " " "
449	J.L. Hewson - Grocery	142 " " "
	Robt. Barclay - Drygoods	126 " " "
	E.H. Gulledge	190 " " "
459	39 Dunn St.	149 Dunn St.
	North Side	
470	19-23 Colborne St. E.	125 Lakeshore Road E.
	37 " " "	145 " " "
	39 " " "	149 " " "
	41 " " "	155 " " "
	47-51 " " "	165-169 " " "
	64-69 " " "	193-195 " " "
	75A,B,C " " "	207 " " "
	77 " " "	209 " " "
	81 " " "	215 " " "
471	85-87 " " "	219 " " "
	91 " " "	Dem. 1952: now 229 Lakeshore Road E.
	99 " " "	239 Lakeshore Road E.
	115 " " "	265-267 " " "
	South Side	
	38 " " "	150 Lakeshore Road E.
	58-60 " " "	Dem. 1969: now 176 Lakeshore Road E.
472	62 " " "	182 Lakeshore Road E.
	68 " " "	190 " " "
	72-74 " " "	196-202 " " "
	86 " " "	218 " " "
	94 " " "	234 " " "
	100 " " "	240 " " "
	114 " " "	266-270 " " "

NOTES

THE SOURCES of this history were not easily found. The material was gathered almost everywhere but in Oakville itself. Municipal records prior to 1914 had vanished in the Town Hall fire. Except for Walker and Miles' *Illustrated Atlas of Halton County* (Toronto, 1877), published sources are virtually non-existent. Therefore the search had to be carried far afield. Beginning in Toronto and Hamilton it eventually extended across the province, to distant places in the United States, and to Nova Scotia, Ireland, and Scotland. Particularly rewarding in source material were odd copies of contemporary newspapers scattered far and wide. Unfortunately no copy of the *Oakville Observer* came to light, only a reprint in the Upper Canada column of the *Montreal Gazette*.

It was the author's good fortune to come across important records. These have since been placed in safe keeping and are available to historians. In the Ontario Archives catalogued under Trafalgar Township Papers are to be found the Township Assessment Rolls, 1823–99, Record Book, 1844–66, Account Book, 1850–72, and the Denominational Census of 1840 and 1841. Charles Sovereign's Journals, 1834–84, also were placed there by Mrs. A. O. Flumerfelt of Bronte, and the Minutes the Nelson Circuit of the Wesleyan Methodist Church were deposited in the Victoria College Library.

That annotation may be reduced to a minimum, reference to authorities has been omitted in the following instances: (1) Transfers of property—all dates of conveyances and names of grantors and grantees were secured from the Abstract Index and its related documents at the Registry Office for Halton County. (2) Locations of merchants, industries, residents, tenants, etc.—these were obtained from the assessment rolls of Trafalgar Township to 1856 inclusive, and thereafter from those of the Town of Oakville; from the map of Halton County of 1858 and the Map of Oakville of 1863. (3) Names of inhabitants and their children, their place and date of birth, dates of migration, death, etc.—these were secured from the census of Trafalgar Township of 1841 and 1851; from the censuses of the Town of Oakville, 1861 *et seq.*; and from gravestones, obituary notices, and church records.

"Oakville newspapers" refers to undated clippings found in scrap-books in the possession of various persons.

Prologue (pp. 3–13)

1. *Patriot*, Toronto, July 5, 1833.
2. *Indian Treaties and Surrenders* (Ottawa, 1892), vol. I, p. 40.
3. Public Archives of Canada, MS map of Great Lakes region and Northern British colonies 1756-7, original in Ministère de la Guerre, Paris; MS map of Lake Ontario signed D. B. Crown Point July 31, 1760, original in Haldimand Papers, British Museum.
4. Ontario, Department of Lands and Forests, Division of Maps and Surveys, "Surveyors' Letters—Augustus Jones," p. 103.
5. Ontario Archives, Certificate of Thomas Merritt, Deputy Surveyor of Woods, June 18, 1806.
6. Henry Scadding, *Toronto of Old* (Toronto, 1873), p. 418.
7. Ontario Archives, Report of Samuel Wilmot, 1806.
8. Percy J. Robinson, *Toronto during the French Régime* (Toronto, 1933), p. 4.

9. Ontario, Department of Lands and Forests, Division of Maps and Surveys, Samuel Wilmot's Field Notes of Survey of Trafalgar Township, 1806.

10. Ontario Archives, Trafalgar Township Papers, Certificates of Settlement Duties.

11. Ontario Archives, Crown Lands Papers, June 20, 1806.

12. *Ninth Report of the Bureau of Archives for the Province of Ontario*, 1912, p. 20.

13. Ontario Archives, Crown Lands Papers, G. Hillier to T. Ridout, April 2, 1819.

14. *Indian Treaties and Surrenders*, p. 51.

15. Ontario Archives, Robinson Papers, Agreement between Wm. Chisholm and David McDougall, 1822.

16. *Gore Gazette*, Ancaster, Dec. 24, 1827.

17. Ontario Archives, Crown Lands Papers, Chisholm to Hillier, Jan. 9, 1824.

18. *Journals of the House of Assembly*, 1826-7, app., Report of Gore District Buildings.

19. P.A.C., Upper Canada Sundries, Sept. 18, 1826.

20. P.A.C., Upper Canada State Papers, 1827, vol. 14, p. 116.

21. *Ibid*., pp. 115–16.

22. *Upper Canada Gazette*, July 17, 1827.

23. Ontario Archives, Trafalgar Township Papers, Lot 13, 3rd concession, S.D.S.

24. Ontario Archives, Crown Lands Papers, Indian Reserves in Upper Canada, 1842.

25. *Journals of the House of Assembly*, 1828, app., Report on the Petition of Wm. Chisholm.

26. *Ibid.*

27. *Ibid.*

28. *Statutes of Upper Canada, Local and Private*, 9 Geo. IV, c. 20, 1828.

29. R. B. Sullivan, *Lecture Delivered before the Mechanics' Institute, Hamilton* (Hamilton, 1848).

30. Walker and Miles, *Illustrated Atlas of Halton County* (Toronto, 1877), p. 81.

31. Letter addressed by Lord Selkirk to George Chisholm, York, Dec. 22, 1803, in the possession of F. H. Chisholm.

Chapter one (pp. 17–50)

1. Basil Hall, *Travels in America* (London, 1829), vol. I, p. 237.

2. *Western Mercury*, Hamilton, Aug. 18, 1831, description of Oakville harbour.

3. John A. Williams, Reminiscences, in possession of Mrs. Sydney Williams, Eberts, Ont.

4. *Journals of the House of Assembly*. At this period the authority for building harbours and incorporating joint-stock companies lay with the House of Assembly. These statements have been made only after carefully checking the *Journals* and are, as far as the writer has been able to ascertain, entirely correct.

5. *Montreal Gazette*, April 26, 1836.

6. Joseph Pickering, *Inquiries of an Emigrant* (London, 1831), pp. 100, 105. On p. 156 appears the following: "It is generally asserted and believed that the water in the lakes rises annually for seven years and then gradually sinks that number alternately." As this statement is made by other writers of the period it seems likely that the idea originated with the Indians who passed it on to the settlers.

7. Sir Richard Bonnycastle, *Canada and the Canadians, in 1846* (London, 1846), vol. I, p. 9.

8. Ontario, Department of Lands and Forests, Division of Maps and Surveys, Plan of Oakville, 1833, by H. J. Castle.

9. Public Archives of Canada, Upper Canada Sundries, Chisholm to Colborne, April 9, 1832.

10. *Journals of the House of Assembly*, 1832-3, app., p. 208.

11. John Nicholson, *Operative Mechanic* (London, 1853), p. 311.

12. John Mactaggart, *Three Years in Canada* (London, 1829), vol. I, p. 296.
13. *Journals of the House of Assembly*, 1830, app., p. 195, "Sundry Sums expended by William Chisholm for the improvement of the Oakville Harbour, 1828-29."
14. P.A.C., Upper Canada Sundries, May 17, 1831.
15. Charles Tomlinson, ed., *Cyclopaedia of Useful Arts, Mechanical and Chemical* (London, 1852), vol. I, p. 522.
16. *Canada, Sessional Papers*, XIII, 1854-5, app. GG.
17. *Journals of the House of Assembly*, 1833-4, app., p. 82.
18. George Sumner, Diary, in the possession of Mr. George Doty.
19. *Journals of the House of Assembly*, 1832-3, app., p. 125.
20. Mortgage, J. H. Dunn to William Chisholm, March 26, 1831, in possession of E. A. Chisholm. This instrument is engrossed on a large piece of parchment nearly three feet square, a very handsome document.
21. *Colonial Advocate*, Toronto, Sept. 22, 1831.
22. *Western Mercury*, Oct. 6, 1831.
23. *Ibid.*
24. *Ibid.*, Aug. 18, 1831.
25. W. H. Smith, *Canada: past, present and future* (Toronto, 1851), vol. I, p. 259.
26. Pickering, *op. cit.*, p. 100.
27. Mactaggart, *op. cit.*, vol. II, p. 105.
28. Pickering, *op. cit.*, p. 158.
29. *Patriot*, Toronto, July 5, 1833.
30. Ontario Historical Society, *Papers and Records*, vol. XXIII, p. 356.
31. Mr. Lorne Ashbury, who with his father ran the mill for over twenty-five years, testifies to the fact that in the east gable was a stone bearing the date 1827 which disappeared after the building was destroyed by fire.
32. Tomlinson, *op. cit.*, vol. I, p. 177.
33. Trafalgar Township Assessment Roll, 1833.
34. Charles Sovereign, Account Book, 1834-84.
35. Pickering, *op. cit.*, p. 80.
36. *Gore Gazette*, Ancaster, Oct. 6, 1827.
37. *Ibid.*, April 6, 1829.
38. Ontario Archives, Trafalgar Township Papers, Lots 9 & 12, 3rd concession S.D.S.
39. D. G. Creighton, *The Commercial Empire of the St. Lawrence* (Toronto, 1937), p. 259.
40. Mactaggart, *op. cit.*, vol. I, p. 245.
41. *Ibid.*, pp. 95, 245.
42. D. D. Calvin, *A Saga of the St. Lawrence* (Toronto, 1945), pp. 63–73.
43. Bonnycastle, *op. cit.*, vol. I, p. 70.
44. *Ibid.*, pp. 71–2.
45. *History of York County* (Toronto, 1885), p. 159; Registry Office, York County, Abstract Index.
46. Smith, *op. cit.*, vol. II, p. 413.
47. Calvin, *op. cit.*, pp. 83–5.
48. Oakville newspaper, 1910.
49. Williams, Reminiscences.
50. William Howes, Reminiscences, *Oakville Star*, 1911.
51. Newspaper clipping, 1901, quoting Benjamin Waldbrook, in possession of Mr. James Waldbrook.
52. Howes, Reminiscences.
53. Walker and Miles, *Historical Atlas of Halton County* (Toronto, 1877), p. 83.
54. Castle's plan of Oakville, 1833.
55. *Gore Gazette*, Aug. 16, 1828.
56. *Ibid.*
57. Chisholm Papers, Account Book, Dec., 1829–Oct., 1830.
58. *Gore Balance*, Hamilton, May 27, 1830.

59. Chisholm Papers, Account Book, Dec., 1829–Oct., 1830.
60. *Western Mercury*, May 19, 1831.
61. A. W. Havighurst, *Long Ships Passing* (New York, 1945), p. 65.
62. *Montreal Gazette*, Aug. 29, 1835.
63. *Journals of the House of Assembly*, 1831, app., p. 195.
64. *Colonial Advocate*, Sept. 22, 1831.
65. Castle's plan of Oakville, 1833.
66. Chisholm Papers, Account Book, Dec., 1829–Oct., 1830.
67. *Ibid.*
68. *Colonial Advocate*, Sept. 22, 1831.
69. *Western Mercury*, Aug. 18, 1831.
70. Sir Richard Bonnycastle, *The Canadas, in 1841* (London, 1842), p. 163.
71. *Western Mercury*, Aug. 11, 1831.
72. *Ibid.*, Dec. 8, 1831.
73. *Niagara Reporter*, quoted in the *Montreal Gazette*, Sept. 24, 1836.
74. *British Colonist*, Toronto, Nov. 15, 1838.
75. The author of "Schooner Days" in the *Toronto Evening Telegram*, Mr. C. H. J. Snider, kindly gave this information.
76. *Spectator*, Hamilton, July 21, 1852, obituary of Captain Nicholas Boylan.
77. Alexander Muir, memoir, courtesy of Mr. C. H. J. Snider.
78. *Western Mercury*, Hamilton, April 24, 1834.
79. *Ibid.*, Aug. 18, 1834.
80. *Patriot*, July 5, 1833.
81. Ontario Archives, "Indian Reserves in Upper Canada, 1842," p. 165.
82. Registry Office, Halton County, Abstract Index, Trafalgar Township, Lot 16, 3rd and 4th concessions.
83. P.A.C., Map Division, Public Works Plan no. 121, Oakville (not dated).
84. Castle's plan of Oakville, 1833.
85. *Patriot*, July 11, 1834.
86. *Ibid.*, Aug. 16, 1833.
87. *Montreal Gazette*, 1833.
88. Chisholm Papers, "Report on the Oakville Harbour," April 25, 1877, by William Kingsford.
89. Henry Scadding, *Toronto of Old* (Toronto, 1873), p. 342.
90. *Ibid.*
91. *Christian Guardian*, Toronto, Feb. 14, 1838.
92. A. R. Thomas, *Descendants of William Thomas of Hardwick, Mass.* (1891).
93. P.A.C., Upper Canada Land Petitions, C 1817-22, no. 53.
94. Ferdinand Brock Tupper, *Family Records* (Guernsey, 1835), p. 111.
95. P.A.C., Upper Canada Land Petitions, B 10, Part 1, 1804-23.
96. Provincial Secretary's Office, Original Grants, Book HE, p. 107.
97. E. A. Cruickshank, ed., *Documentary History of the Campaign upon the Niagara Frontier in the Year 1812* (Lundy's Lane Historical Society, 1903), vol. IV, p. 221.
98. *Ibid.*, vol. III, p. 228.
99. Thomas Wright, *History of Ireland* (n.d.), vol. III, p. 69.
100. *Minutes of the Municipal Council of the Town of Oakville*, 1873, p. 16.
101. *Journals of the House of Assembly*, 1831-2, app., p. 209.
102. *Ibid.*
103. E. A. Talbot, *Five Years' Residence in the Canadas* (London, 1823), vol. I, p. 151.
104. Mactaggart, *op. cit.*, vol. II, p. 310.
105. P.A.C., Series Q, vol. 283; Scadding, *op. cit.*, p. 371; *The Oracle* quoted in John Ross Robertson, *Landmarks of Toronto* (Toronto, 1894), vol. VI, pp. 315, 333.
106. P.A.C., U.C. State Papers, H, no. 19, pp. 87–91.
107. Memoir of Eliza Lucas Matthewman, 1844-1933, in possession of Mrs. P. C. Sutton.
108. *U. E. Loyalist*, Sept. 29, 1827.
109. *Ibid.*

110. *Western Mercury*, March 10, 1831; *Journals of the House of Assembly*, 1830-1, app., p. 233, Gore District accounts.
111. Thomas Rolph, *Statistical Account of Upper Canada* (Dundas, U.C., 1836), p. 218.
112. P.A.C., Upper Canada Sundries, Chisholm to Colborne, April 9, 1832.
113. *Western Mercury*, Aug. 23, 1832.
114. Trafalgar Township By-law no. 226, June 20, 1859.
115. Rolph, *op. cit.*, p. 218.

Chapter two (pp. 51–90)

1. Ontario Archives, Educational Papers, Annual Report of the Local Sup't, Trafalgar Township, 1852. Dates of erection of schoolhouses given.
2. Public Archives of Canada, Land Book N, p. 87.
3. Sir Richard Bonnycastle, *The Canadas in 1841* (London, 1842), vol. I, p. 163.
4. *Journals of the House of Assembly*, 1840, Appendix, p. 43, Reports on Public Departments.
5. Chisholm Papers, Account Book, Dec. 1829–Oct. 1830.
6. G. W. Warr, *Canada as it is* (London, 1847), p. 50.
7. P.A.C., Census of Trafalgar Township, 1841.
8. Rev. T. Radcliff, ed., *Authentic Letters from Upper Canada; with an account of Canadian field sports, by T. W. Magrath, Esq.* (Dublin, 1833), p. 229.
9. *Ibid.*, p. 234.
10. *Ibid.*, p. 230–1.
11. Warr, *op. cit.*, p. 48.
12. *Oakville Star*, 1911, recollections of William Howes.
13. Chisholm Papers, bill of W. F. Romain, 1847.
14. Warr, *op. cit.*, p. 46.
15. William Panton's memoirs, MS in possession of author.
16. George Stimpson, *A Book about a Thousand Things* (New York, 1946), p. 501.
17. E. A. Talbot, *Five Years' Residence in the Canadas* (London, 1824), vol. I, p. 209.
18. *Ibid.*, p. 217.
19. Anna Brownell Jameson, *Winter Studies and Summer Rambles in Canada* (London, 1838), p. 64.
20. Census of Trafalgar Township, 1841.
21. *Gore Gazette*, Ancaster, Aug. 18, 1828.
22. Chisholm Papers, Account Book, Dec. 1829–Oct. 1830.
23. *Correspondent and Advocate*, Toronto, April 4, 1836.
24. H. A. Innis and A. R. M. Lower, eds., *Select Documents in Canadian Economic History 1783–1885* (Toronto, 1933), p. 370, note.
25. *Correspondent and Advocate*, Toronto, April 4, 1836.
26. *Kingston Chronicle* quoted in the *Montreal Gazette*, March 26, 1833.
27. *Genealogy of the Williams Family* (1847); Census of Trafalgar Township, 1841.
28. John A. Williams, Reminiscences.
29. *Christian Guardian*, Toronto, June 1, 1833.
30. Walker and Miles, *Illustrated Atlas of Halton County* (Toronto, 1877), p. 78.
31. Census of Trafalgar Township, 1841.
32. Peter Jarvis, *Diary*, published privately by T. R. Jarvis, Oakville.
33. P.A.C., "Registry of Ownership of Vessels registered at the Custom House, Port of Oakville," undated.
34. Chisholm Papers, Deed from William Chisholm to Alexander Proudfoot, 1836.
35. Stanley Mills, *The Davis and Gage Families* (Hamilton, 1926); *Stoney Creek*, pamphlet published by the Women's Wentworth Historical Society.
36. Trafalgar Township Assessment Rolls; Census, 1841.

37. Ontario Archives, Charles Sovereign's Journal, 1834–84, Nov. 1, 1842.
38. *Hamilton Free Press*, Nov. 12, 1836.
39. *Oakville Observer*, quoted in the *Montreal Gazette*, March 10, 1836.
40. Archives of the Court House, Montreal, "Repertoire of Henry Griffith, Notary Public," no. 8309, July 9, 1829.
41. Information supplied by Allan Gulledge, Oakville.
42. Charles Sovereign, Journal.
43. *Patriot*, Toronto, Nov. 13, 1840.
44. Chisholm Papers, Account Book, Dec. 1829–Oct. 1830.
45. *Gore Gazette*, Dec. 27, 1828.
46. Information supplied by Miss Agnes Balmer, granddaughter of John Terry.
47. *British Colonist*, Toronto, March 13, 1838.
48. Newspaper clipping *circa* 1916, article by "Rob Roy," pen name of John D. McGregor, on the history of Trafalgar Township, scrap-book of the late Mrs. John Byers.
49. Recollections of Mrs. John Fleming, *née* Lucy Young, *circa* 1900, in possession of the late Mrs. John Byers; Minutes of the Court of Quarter Sessions of the Home District, tavern licences granted.
50. *Mercury*, Hamilton, Aug. 18, 1831.
51. *Ibid.*, Sept. 18, 1831.
52. P.A.C., Upper Canada Land Petitions, 1819, S, no. 12, 201–3.
53. *Ibid.*, endorsement.
54. *Hamilton Free Press*, Sept. 18, 1832.
55. *Gore Gazette*, December issues, 1828.
56. Deeds, William Chisholm to William J. Sumner, 22 Oct. 1831; Wm. J. Sumner to William Chisholm Sumner, 23 Aug. 1839.
57. Benjamin Shenston, Book of Remembrance, 1833, MS, University of Toronto Library.
58. Joseph Pickering, *Inquiries of an Emigrant* (London, 1831), p. 73; Chisholm Papers, bills of Wm. Chisholm, 1842.
59. *Oakville Observer*, quoted in the *Montreal Gazette*, March 10, 1836.
60. *Christian Guardian*, Jan. 7, 1837.
61. *Oakville Observer, op. cit.*
62. Jameson, *op. cit.*, pp. 64–5.
63. Williams, Reminiscences.
64. Diamond Memorial Tablet, St. Jude's Church, Oakville.
65. *Oakville Record-Star*, 1941, obituary of Joel Mackinder.
66. *Oakville Observer, op. cit.*
67. Chisholm Papers, bills.
68. Williams, Reminiscences.
69. Census of Trafalgar Township, 1841; Assessment Rolls.
70. R. D. Wadsworth, *The Temperance Manual* (Montreal, 1847), p. 5.
71. *Oakville*, pamphlet, 1912, p. 31; *Beautiful Oakville*, pamphlet, 1897; *Oakville Star*, 1911.
72. Williams, Reminiscences.
73. *Patriot*, May 23, 1834.
74. *British Colonist*, Jan. 4, 1840.
75. *Christian Guardian*, Oct. 23, 1839.
76. *Oakville Star*, 1903, 60th anniversary of the Temperance Hall.
77. Wadsworth, *op. cit.*, pp. 24, 25, 53.
78. *Western Mercury*, Hamilton, July 13, 1832.
79. H. I. Cowan, *British Emigration to British North America, 1783–1837* (Toronto, 1928), p. 223.
80. *Ibid.*, p. 220.
81. John Mactaggart, *Three Years in Canada* (London, 1829), vol. II, p. 304.
82. Cowan, *op. cit.*, p. 217.
83. Innis and Lower, *Select Documents*, pp. 108–9.
84. Cowan, *op. cit.*, p. 218.
85. *Western Mercury*, June 28, 1832.
86. *Ibid.*

87. *Colonial Advocate*, Toronto, Aug. 13, 1832.
88. Shenston, *op. cit.*
89. *Western Mercury*, March 6, 1833.
90. P.A.C., Upper Canada Sundries, Aug. 2, 1834.
91. *Oakville Star*, 1903. Letter quoted in full.
92. Chisholm Papers, Commission Sir John Colborne to William Chisholm, Aug. 19, 1834.
93. *Oakville Star*, 1903, letter referred to in note 91.
94. P.A.C., Upper Canada Sundries, Aug. 28, 1834.
95. *Ibid.*, April 24, 1835.
96. Dr. John Urquhart, sketch of his father's life in possession of Mrs. S. A. B. McCleary.
97. Williams, Reminiscences.
98. *Journals of the House of Assembly*, 1839, App., Customs Returns.
99. Chisholm Papers, Appointment by William Chisholm of R. K. Chisholm, March 1, 1838.
100. *Journals of the House of Assembly*, 1843, App., vol. III (B.B.).
101. Williams, Reminiscences.
102. D. C. Masters, *The Rise of Toronto* (Toronto, 1947), pp. 13, 56.
103. *Patriot*, Feb. 23, 1836.
104. Census of Trafalgar Township, 1841.
105. *Oakville Observer, op. cit.*
106. Registry Office of Halton County, Abstract Index, Trafalgar Township, lots 13, 14, 15, 16, 3rd. concession S.D.S.
107. *Montreal Gazette*, April 26, 1836.
108. "Map of the Property of Wm. Chisholm Esq. at the Mouth of the Sixteen Mile Creek, Township of Trafalgar U. C., 1837, Edward B. Palmer."
109. *Transactions of the Royal Society of Canada*, vol. XXXI, 1937, pp. 131–52, W. S. Wallace, "Forsyth, Richardson and Company in the Fur Trade"; data obtained through the courtesy of Mr. A. J. H. Richardson, Ottawa.
110. W. S. Wallace, *Dictionary of Canadian Biography* (Toronto, 1945).
111. *Montreal Gazette*, Aug. 4, 1847.
112. *Municipality of the Town of Oakville, Council Minutes*, Oct. 29, 1877, p. 49.
113. Registry Office of Halton County, Abstract Index.
114. *Journals of the House of Assembly*, 1840, App., p. 40.
115. Statutes of Canada, 3 Vict. c. 32, Local and Private, 1840.
116. Statutes of Upper Canada and the Province of Canada.

Chapter three (pp. 91–115)

S. D. Clark, *Church and Sect in Canada* (Toronto, 1948) has been used as a general reference book in connection with the first section of this chapter.

1. Anson Green, *Life and Times* (Toronto, 1877), p. 64.
2. W. J. D. Waddilove, ed., *The Stewart Missions* (London, 1838), pp. 174–89.
3. Inhabitants of Trafalgar Township to Robert Gourlay, 1817, answer to question no. 3. Letter in possession of the late Mrs. Wright-Orr, found in the papers of her father, Dr. D. D. Wright.
4. Green, *op. cit.*, pp. 90–1.
5. *Ibid.*, p. 86.
6. Minutes of the Nelson Circuit (Wesleyan Methodist), MS, Victoria College Library.
7. *Ibid.*
8. John Carroll, *Case and His Cotemporaries* (Toronto, 1871), vol. II, pp. 249–53.
9. *Canadian Champion*, Milton, July 29, 1869, letter of Justus Williams.
10. Nelson Circuit Minutes.
11. *Canadian Champion*, July 29, 1869.
12. John A. Williams, Reminiscences, copies of accounts re building of Oakville chapel.

13. *Christian Guardian*, Feb. 12, 1890, letter of Rev. S. C. Philp.
14. *Ibid.*, Aug. 16, 1835.
15. Green, *op. cit.*, p. 239.
16. *Directory of Halton County*, 1869–70.
17. Public Archives of Canada, Census of Trafalgar Township, 1851.
18. *Ibid.*
19. *Oakville Observer*, quoted in the *Montreal Gazette*, March 10, 1836.
20. Carroll, *op. cit.*, vol. III, pp. 477–8.
21. *Ibid.*, p. 25.
22. *Ibid.*, p. 143.
23. Nelson Circuit Minutes.
24. *Canadian Champion*, July 29, 1869.
25. *Christian Guardian*, Feb. 12, 1890, letter of Rev. S. C. Philp.
26. *Ibid.*
27. *Ibid.*
28. S. E. Sanderson, *Methodism in Canada* (Toronto, 1910), vol. II, p. 166; W. S. Savage, "Address delivered on the occasion of the Fiftieth Anniversary of St. John's Church, Oakville, Jan. 13, 1928," MS in possession of Miss Ellena Savage.
29. *Christian Guardian*, Feb. 12, 1890, letter of Rev. S. C. Philp.
30. Williams, Reminiscences.
31. William Gregg, *History of the Presbyterian Church in the Dominion of Canada* (Toronto, 1885), p. 534.
32. *Oakville Observer*, quoted in the *Montreal Gazette*, March 10, 1836.
33. *Toronto Albion*, quoted in the *Montreal Gazette*, April 12, 1836.
34. Innes Addison, *Matriculation Albums of the University of Glasgow, 1728–1858*, vol. I, p. 239. Rev. Robert Murray's name does not appear on records of the Church of Scotland at the Church Offices, Edinburgh, therefore he apparently was not sent out by that organization. A search of the records of Scottish universities revealed but one Robert Murray at this period, and he came from Ireland. Though unable to offer conclusive proof, the author believes this to be the man appointed to Oakville.
35. Minutes of the Presbytery of Armagh, 1797–1816, 1825–32.
36. *Ibid.*
37. Archives of the Archdiocese of Toronto, Rev. W. J. O'Grady to Bishop Macdonnell, Oct. 20, 1830.
38. Archives of the Diocese of Hamilton.
39. Archives of the Archdiocese of Toronto, A Register of Baptisms performed by the Rev. Edward Gordon, 1830–33.
40. Archives of the Archdiocese of Toronto, Rev. W. J. O'Grady to Bishop Macdonnell, Jan. 9, 1831.
41. *Journals of the House of Assembly*, 1836, App., vol. II, p. 25, no. 102.
42. St. Andrew's Church, Oakville, Records, Historical Sketch, anonymous, 1890; Theobald Spetz, *Diamond Jubilee of the Diocese of Hamilton* (1916), p. 253.
43. Dean Harris, *The Catholic Church in the Niagara Peninsula* (Toronto, 1895), p. 264.
44. *Oakville Record*, clipping, *circa* 1910.
45. Historical Sketch, 1890, *op. cit.*; Spetz, *op. cit.*, p. 253.
46. Archives of the Archdiocese of Toronto, May 30, 1843.
47. *Ibid.*, March 8, 1842.
48. *Stewart Missions*, 1838–9, p. 56.
49. *Ibid.*, 1840, p. 71.
50. *Ibid.*
51. *Burlington*, pamphlet, 1927, p. 6.
52. Synod Office, Diocese of Niagara, Deed, March 24, 1842. When deeds of land were executed in 1840 between Justus Williams and others, lots C and F became confused. The error, undetected at the time the property was sold to the Church of England in Canada, was not rectified until 1869 when the titles were cleared by the execution of new deeds by the several parties concerned.
53. Ontario Archives, Strachan Letter Books, 1843–66; 1844–9.

54. *History of the Diocese of Niagara to 1950* (Hamilton, 1950), p. 36.
55. Census of Trafalgar Township, 1841.
56. Registry Office, Halton County, Abstract Index.
57. John Lovell, *Canada Dirctory,* 1851; Census of Trafalgar Township, 1841.
58. Williams, Reminiscences.
59. *Ibid.*
60. George Sumner, Diary.
61. Nelson Circuit Minutes.
62. Ontario Archives, Denominational Census of Trafalgar Township, 1840, 1841.
63. J. G. Hodgins, ed., *Documentary History of Education* (Toronto, 1897), vol. IV.
64. Legislative Library, Educational Reports, MS Report Gore District Grammar School, 1828.
65. Hodgins, *op. cit.*, p. 160.
66. Williams, Reminiscences.
67. *Journals of the Legislative Assembly, Province of Canada,* 1850, app., Educational Reports.
68. Williams, Reminiscences.
69. *Oakville Observer*, quoted in the *Montreal Gazette*, March 10, 1836.
70. E. J. Hathaway, *Jesse Ketchum and His Times* (Toronto, 1929), p. 330.
71. P.A.C., Provincial Secretary's Office, letter re Palermo Grammar School, 1850; *Journal of Education*, 1850, vol. III, p. 12.
72. Waterloo Historical Society, *Transactions,* 1915, p. 20, James Kerr, "Recollections of my Schooldays at Tassie's."
73. Census of Trafalgar Township, 1841.
74. *Ibid.*, shows both mills in production. They were situated at the end of Mill Street which runs from highway no. 25 to the Twelve Mile Creek south of the railway.
75. *Educational Reports, 1820–50,* Report on the Public Departments of the Province, 1839, Report of the Committee on Education, app. G, p. 356.
76. *Ibid.*
77. Record Book, Trafalgar Township, 1844; Assessment Rolls.
78. P.A.C., P.S.O. Letters no. 2273, Dec., 1841.
79. Hodgins, *op. cit.*, p. 301.
80. *British Colonist*, Toronto, May 25, 1842.
81. *Ibid.*
82. Hodgins, *op. cit.*, p. 265.
83. *Ibid.*, p. 212; *Canadian Mercantile Almanac*, 1844.
84. A. Shortt and A. G. Doughty, eds., *Canada and Its Provinces* (Toronto, 1914), vol. XVIII, p. 302.
85. P.A.C., P.S.O., Letters no. 2273, Dec., 1841.
86. W. S. Wallace, *History of the University of Toronto* (Toronto, 1927), p. 51.
87. John Ross Robertson, *Landmarks of Toronto* (Toronto, 1896), vol. II, p. 749.
88. Henry Scadding, *Toronto of Old* (Toronto, 1873), p. 373.

Chapter four (pp. 116–132)

1. Walter Havighurst, *Long Ships Passing* (New York, 1945), p. 122.
2. *Western Mercury*, Hamilton, Aug. 25, 1831.
3. *Ibid.*, Aug. 23, 1832.
4. *Ibid.*, Dec. 27, 1832.
5. *Ibid.*, Oct. 10, 1833.
6. *Ibid.*, Jan. 10, 1833.
7. Chisholm Papers.
8. *Montreal Gazette*, Sept. 28, 1833.
9. *Western Mercury*, April 3, 1834.
10. *Patriot*, Toronto, April 18, 1834.
11. *Courier of Upper Canada*, Oct. 21, 1834.

12. Henry Scadding, *Toronto of Old* (Toronto, 1873), p. 575; J. R. Robertson, *Landmarks of Toronto* (Toronto, 1896), vol. II, p. 857.
13. Scadding, *op. cit.*, p. 561–2.
14. Havighurst, *op. cit.*, p. 223.
15. Sir Richard Bonnycastle, *The Canadas, in 1841* (London, 1842), vol. 1, p. 138.
16. Chisholm Papers; Robertson, *Landmarks*, vol. II, pp. 614, 984; *Western Mercury*, May 5, 1834.
17. *Courier of Upper Canada*, Oct. 21, 1834.
18. Robertson, *Landmarks*, vol. II, p. 906.
19. *Journals of the House of Assembly*, 1836, app., vol. III, no. 146.
20. *Oakville Observer*, quoted in the *Montreal Gazette*, March 10, 1836.
21. *Journals of the House of Assembly*, 1836, app., vol. III, no. 146.
22. *Cobourg Star*, quoted in the *Montreal Gazette*, April 19, 1836.
23. *Journals of the House of Assembly*, 1837, app., no. 27.
24. *Ibid.*, 1839, app., vol. II, part 1, p. 159.
25. *Dundas Post*, quoted in the *Montreal Gazette*, July 5, 1836.
26. *Journals of the House of Assembly*, 1839, app., vol. II, part 1, p. 159.
27. Chisholm Papers; Robertson, *Landmarks*, vol. II, pp. 614, 984.
28. *British Colonist*, Toronto, April 26, 1838.
29. Robertson, *Landmarks*, vol. II, p. 906.
30. *Ibid.*, p. 984.
31. *Directory of the Home District*, 1837.
32. *Hamilton Gazette*, quoted in the *Montreal Gazette*, April 14, 1836; *Hamilton Free Press*, Aug. 18, 1836.
33. A. Shortt and A. G. Doughty, eds., *Canada and Its Provinces*, vol. X, p. 499.
34. Robertson, *Landmarks*, vol. II, p. 864.
35. *Toronto Courier*, quoted in the *Montreal Gazette*, April 7, 1836.
36. *Journals of the House of Assembly*, 1836–7, p. 525.
37. *Upper Canada Gazette*, April 6, 1837, quoted in Robertson, *Landmarks*, vol. II, p. 864.
38. *Journals of the House of Assembly*, 1839, app., vol. II, p. 306.
39. *Ibid.*, 1841, app. (V).
40. *Ibid.*, 1849, app. (B.B.), no. VI.
41. *Ibid.*, 1839, app., vol. II, p. 306.
42. *British Colonist*, April 26, 1838.
43. *Canada and Its Provinces*, vol. X, p. 499.
44. *Ibid.*, p. 538.
45. Joseph Pickering, *Inquiries of an Emigrant* (London, 1831), p. 77.
46. *Western Mercury*, March 10, 1831.
47. *Ibid.*
48. *Ibid.*, May 16, 1833.
49. Scadding, *op. cit.*, p. 49.
50. Robertson, *Landmarks*, vol. I, p. 380.
51. Sir Richard Bonnycastle, *Canada and the Canadians in 1846* (London, 1846), vol. I, p. 209.
52. Griggs Papers in possession of Miss Jean Moore, Rochester.
53. Trafalgar Township Assessment Rolls.
54. Anna Brownell Jameson, *Winter Sketches and Summer Rambles in Canada* (London, 1838), vol. I, p. 61.
55. The statement found in the *Historical Atlas of Halton County*, Walker and Miles (Toronto, 1877), p. 81, that the Trafalgar Post Office was established 1820 at Post's Corners is open to question. According to the township census, 1841, the first postmaster, Alexander Proudfoot, migrated to Upper Canada in 1820. The earliest assessment roll, 1823, shows his shop located on the south-west corner of the Dundas Street at the 9th Line. Peter Jarvis' *Diary* (see below) together with other sources locate the Trafalgar Post Office in the place of business of the postmaster, a custom which yet prevails in rural districts. *The Journals of the Legislative Assembly, Province of Canada*, 1846, app. (F.) lists this post office as having been established "previous to 1828," but it does not appear on the list

of post offices in the province in the *Journals of the House of Assembly*, 1821, p. 62. The date of its establishment would seem to be *circa* 1822. The store ended its days as a sheep pen, but the house still stands.

56. Peter Robinson Jarvis, *Diary* published privately by T. R. Jarvis, Oakville.
57. *Journals of the Legislative Assembly, Province of Canada*, 1846, app. (F.).
58. Chisholm Papers, Commission of Postmaster, Thomas Allan Stayner, Postmaster General to William Chisholm, Oct. 6, 1835.
59. Chisholm Papers, examples of letters, postage prepaid and collect.
60. *Directory of the Home District*, 1837; *Toronto Almanac and Royal Calendar*, 1839.
61. *Journals of the Legislative Assembly*, 1846, app. (F.).
62. Commission, Oct. 6, 1835.
63. *Journals of the Legislative Assembly*, 1846, app. (F.).
64. *Oakville Observer*, quoted in the *Montreal Gazette*, March 10, 1836.
65. *Gore Gazette*, Ancaster, 1827.
66. *Oakville Star*, June 21, 1906, comments re copy of *Observer* found in papers of "the late Mr. Crickmore, Q.C."
67. *Gore Balance*, Hamilton, Dec. 16, 1830.

Chapter five (pp. 133–174)

1. Public Archives of Canada, Upper Canada Land Petitions, 1793–95, C. Bundle, no. 96, Petition of George Chisholm, March 25, 1793.
2. Ontario Archives, Upper Canada Land Book F, 1804–6, pp. 299, 303.
3. *Indian Treaties and Surrenders* (Ottawa, 1905), vol. I, p. 22.
4. *Journals of the House of Assembly*; Minutes of the Court of Quarter Sessions of the Home District.
5. P.A.C., Upper Canada Sundries, S Series, April 1, 1817.
6. Oakville newspaper, Feb. 9, 1872, obituary of Col. George Chisholm.
7. *Wentworth Landmarks* (Hamilton, 1897), p. 90.
8. Ontario Archives, "Prince Regent's Land Grants to Flank Co's, Militia U. C., War 1812–14."
9. See William Wood, ed., *Select British Documents of the Canadian War of 1812*, Publications of the Champlain Society, XIII (Toronto, 1920), vol. I, pp. 546–56, "Diary of William McCay of the Township of Nelson."
10. Alexander Clark Casselman, *Richardson's War of 1812* (Toronto, 1902), p. 56.
11. E. A. Cruickshank, ed., *Documentary History of the Campaign upon the Niagara Frontier in 1812* (Lundy's Lane Historical Society, 1903), Part III, p. 77, Woodruff to Thorburn.
12. P.A.C., C Series, 1812–14, several entries.
13. Chisholm Papers, Commission General Roger Sheaffe to William Chisholm, Dec. 25, 1812.
14. Robert Gourlay, *Letters to Resident Landowners* (Kingston, 1818), p. 21.
15. Inhabitants of Trafalgar Township to Robert Gourlay, 1817, answer no. 31. The original letter, found in the papers of Dr. D. D. Wright by his daughter, the late Mrs. Wright-Orr, was lost, but a copy came into the hands of the author. Some answers to the thirty-three questions Gourlay published in his *Statistical Account of Upper Canada* (London, 1822), but many were omitted either in full or in part. This letter contains much valuable new material, hitherto unpublished, relative to Trafalgar Township. A transcription has been placed in the Ontario Archives.
16. Gilbert C. Patterson, *Land Settlement in Upper Canada* (Sixteenth Report of the Department of Archives, Province of Ontario, Toronto, 1921), pp. 132–3.
17. Chisholm Papers, G. Hillier to the Presiding Council, dated Government House, Oct. 30, 1826: "Sirs—I am commanded by His Excellency the Lt. Governor to bring under the consideration of the Honble. Executive Council that referring to the application of Mr. Wm. Johnson Kerr for the usual allowance of Land in consideration of his services during the late war and to the decision of the Executive Council thereon, His Excellency thinks it just to Captains William

Chisholm and John Clark to express to the Council that he has received from the conducts of these Gentlemen and from the sentiments which they have repeatedly and publicly avowed, a sufficient assurance to induce him to recommend the removal of the restriction with respect to their Lands which former communications with His Majesty's Government has imposed. . . . G. HILLIER."

James Baby to Col. Nathaniel Coffin, dated Executive Council Chamber at York, Oct. 30, 1826: "To his Excellency Sir Peregrine Maitland . . . respecting the claims of Captains William Chisholm and John Clark to grants of Land for Services in the Militia during the late War with the United States of America, Cheerfully concur in your Excellency's view of their cases, and respectfully recommend that they be respectfully granted the quota of Land allowed to Officers of their Rank. The council will with equal readiness acquiesce in the extension of the same indulgence to other Persons. . . ."

18. Chisholm Papers; *Journals of the House of Assembly*, 1820.
19. 56 Geo. III, c. 19, 1816.
20. *Examiner*, Toronto, May 13, 1840.
21. *Ibid.*
22. *Ibid.*
23. *Western Mercury*, Hamilton, Dec. 12, 1831.
24. D. D. Calvin, *A Saga of the St. Lawrence* (Toronto, 1945), p. 112.
25. *Ibid.*
26. *Gore Gazette*, Ancaster, Dec. 24, 1827.
27. *Journals of the House of Assembly*, 1823.
28. C. W. Carruthers, *Retrospect of Thirty-six Years in Canada West* (Hamilton, 1861), p. 242.
29. *Gore Gazette*, Dec. 24, 1829.
30. Chisholm Papers, Commission Deputy Postmaster Daniel Sutherland to William Chisholm, Jan. 25, 1825.
31. Chisholm Papers.
32. *Gore Balance*, Hamilton, Sept. 30, 1830.
33. *Ibid.*, Oct. 14, 1830.
34. *Ibid.*, Oct. 28, 1830.
35. Egerton Ryerson, pamphlet on education, undated.
36. *Correspondent and Advocate*, Toronto, July 27, 1836.
37. *Western Mercury*, Oct. 6, 1831.
38. *Colonial Advocate*, Toronto, Sept. 22, 1831.
39. *Journals of the House of Assembly*, 1831, app., p. 173.
40. *Patriot*, Toronto, Dec. 17, 1833.
41. *Montreal Gazette*, Feb. 23, 1836.
42. John A. Williams, Reminiscences.
43. D. C. Masters, *The Rise of Toronto* (Toronto, 1947), p. 27.
44. Charles Lindsey, *The Life and Times of William Lyon Mackenzie* (Toronto, 1862), p. 108.
45. *Constitution*, Toronto, Aug. 16, 1837.
46. Chisholm Papers, Sir John Colborne to the Inhabitants of Oakville and Trafalgar Township, March 24, 1836.
47. *The Toronto Almanac and Royal Calendar of Upper Canada*, 1839.
48. P.A.C., Upper Canada Sundries, May 6, 1836.
49. *Patriot*, Dec. 17, 1836.
50. *Ibid.*, July 22, 1836.
51. *Canadian Correspondent*, Toronto, Sept. 3, 1833.
52. *Ibid.*
53. *Patriot*, July 8, 1834.
54. C. C. Taylor, *Toronto "Called Back"* (Toronto, 1886), p. 60.
55. *Patriot*, April 3, 1840.
56. Sir Richard Bonnycastle, *The Canadas, in 1841* (London, 1842), vol. I, p. 175.
57. Joseph Pickering, *Inquiries of an Emigrant* (London, 1831), p. 119.
58. *Journals of the House of Assembly*, 1839, Gore District Accounts.

59. Pickering, *op. cit.*, p. 119.
60. *Patriot*, 1838, vol. IX.
61. Masters, *The Rise of Toronto*, p. 34.
62. Henry Scadding, *Toronto of Old* (Toronto, 1873), pp. 136–7.
63. *Patriot*, Nov. 16, 1838.
64. *Ibid.*, Jan. 24, 1840.
65. *British Colonist*, Toronto, July 26, 1838.
66. *Ibid.*, July 31, 1839.
67. *Ibid.*
68. *Ibid.*
69. *Ibid.*, March 3, 1841.
70. *Ibid.*, March 31, 1841.
71. J. G. Hodgins, *Documentary History of Education* (Toronto, 1908), vol. I, p. 184.
72. *Examiner*, Feb. 19, 1840.
73. Walker and Miles, *Illustrated Atlas of Halton County* (Toronto, 1877), p. 83.
74. 48 Geo. III, c. 1.
75. Chisholm Papers, Commission Sir Francis Gore to William Chisholm, May 8, 1816.
76. *Ibid.*, Sir Peregrine Maitland to William Chisholm, Aug. 12, 1824.
77. Descendants of John Chisholm (Mrs. T. W. Kirby, Portland, Oregon, Cameron Hughson, Toronto, and Miss Helen Bishop, Owen Sound) verify the fact that the monument stood on his land though records at Lincoln County Registry Office show no conveyance of land to the Government. Indeed the second monument's cornerstone had been laid for three years before part of lot 2, originally granted to John Chisholm, and the adjoining section of lot 3, Niagara Township, was purchased by the Government. Absolute proof would require a survey of lot 2.
78. *The Northern Traveller* (New York, 1828), p. 70.
79. *Gore Balance*, vol. I, no. 6, 1830.
80. P.A.C., Paylist of Officers, 2nd Regiment of Gore Militia, March 16, 1838.
81. Chisholm Papers, Commission Sir John Colborne to William Chisholm, May 26, 1831.
82. P.A.C. Paylist, 2nd Gore.
83. P.A.C., Upper Canada Sundries, Nov. 24, 1835.
84. Ontario Historical Society, *Papers and Records*, vol. XVII, Coventry, "Contemporary Account of the Rebellion."
85. *Toronto Almanac and Royal Calendar of Upper Canada*, 1839, p. 86.
86. Sir Francis Bond Head, *A Narrative of the Rebellion In Upper Canada* (London, 1839), p. 332.
87. *Ibid.*
88. *Ibid.*
89. *Christian Guardian*, Dec. 13, 1837.
90. York Pioneer Society, *Report for 1948*, p. 15, T. A. Reed, ed., "Extracts from the Diary of a Loyalist, 1837."
91. Lindsey, *Life of Mackenzie*, p. 105.
92. *Ibid.*, p. 105–9.
93. Smith Papers in possession of Mr. Reginald Smith, William Chisholm to Hiram Smith, Dec. 23, 1837.
94. *Ibid.*, "Muster Roll and Returns of 2nd Gore Militia, Company 1, Head Quarters Chippawa, 26th Dec 1837."
95. *Ibid.*, Hiram Smith to Hannah Smith, Dec. 28, 1837.
96. *Ibid.*, Hannah Smith to Hiram Smith, Dec. 31, 1837.
97. *Ibid.*, Hiram Smith to Hannah Smith, Dec. 30, 1837.
98. Rear-Admiral Drew, *A Narrative of the Capture and Destruction of the Steamer Caroline* (London, 1864), p. 6.
99. Gould's *Stenographic Reporter*, vol. XI, 1841, "The Trial of Alexander McLeod."
100. Smith Papers, Hiram Smith to Hannah Smith, Jan. 4, 1838.

101. *British Colonist*, Feb. 15, 1838.
102. Lorne Pierce, *William Kirby: The Portrait of a Tory Loyalist* (Toronto, 1929), p. 37.
103. Charles Durand, *Reminiscences of the Rebellion of 1837* (Toronto, 1898), p. 336.
104. P.A.C., Upper Canada Land Petitions, C Bundle, Chisholm to Macaulay, Dec. 9, 1938 (enclosure).
105. *Christian Guardian*, Jan. 30, 1839.
106. *Correspondent and Advocate*, July 2, 1835, "Magistrates of the Gore District appointed under a Commission of the Peace, dated 2 April 1833"; Fothergill's *Toronto Almanac*, 1839, pp. 198, 218.
107. *Patriot*, Sept. 22, 1839.
108. *Ibid.*
109. *Ibid.*
110. *Journals of the House of Assembly*, 1839–40, app., vol. I, p. 30,**.
111. *Patriot*, Aug. 7, 1840.
112. *Ibid.*, Nov. 24, 1840.
113. Ontario Archives, "Subscription List of the 2nd Regiment of Gore Militia, towards the General Fund for the Re-construction of the Monument at Queenston Heights, to the memory of the late Major-General Sir Isaac Brock, Nov. 1, 1840."
114. P.A.C., Upper Canada Land Petitions, 1831–7, C Bundle no. 174, Petition of William Chisholm, March 25, 1837.
115. Ontario Department of Lands and Forests, Division of Maps and Surveys, Letterbook, "Surveyor-General's Letters written 1827–1840," Macaulay to Rankin, 1837.
116. Ontario Historical Society, *Papers and Records*, vol. XXVII, p. 497, "Surveyor Charles Rankin's Exploration of the Pioneer Road, Garafraxa to Owen Sound, 1837."
117. *Ibid.*
118. Mabel Dunham, *Grand River* (Toronto, 1945), p. 284.
119. W. H. Smith, *Canada: past, present and future* (Toronto, 1851), vol. II, p. 110.
120. *Journals of the House of Assembly*, 1839, app., vol. II, p. 810.
121. Adam Shortt, *Lord Sydenham* (Makers of Canada Series, Toronto, 1908), pp. 266–8.
122. *Journal Express*, Hamilton, Sept. 12, 1840.
123. *Patriot*, Sept. 23, 1840.
124. *Ibid.*
125. *Ibid.*, Oct. 13, 1840.
126. *Ibid.*
127. *Ibid.*, Dec. 11, 1840.
128. *Owen Sound Daily Sun-Times*, Oct. 7, 1940, Centennial issue, reprint of history by William Wye Smith published 1861 when editor of the paper.
129. *Journals of the House of Assembly, Province of Canada*, 1841, app., vol. I (M.M.).
130. Chisholm Papers, Bills proving that this reference is to Hinchinbrook Township, Frontenac County, then being settled under relatively the same plan as the Owen Sound development.
131. *Ibid.*, William Chisholm to John Davidson, Commissioner of Crown Lands, Sept. 13, 1841.
132. *Ibid.*, Bills at Garafraxa, 1841.
133. J. M. Dent, *The Last Forty Years* (Toronto, 1881), p. 84.
134. Henry J. Morgan, *Celebrated Canadians* (Quebec, 1865), p. 395.
135. R. B. Sullivan, *Lecture Delivered before the Mechanics' Institute, Hamilton* (Hamilton, 1848).
136. E. L. Marsh, *History of Grey County* (Owen Sound, 1931), pp. 180–1.
137. *Owen Sound Daily Sun-Times*, *op. cit.*, reprint of history by A. M. Stephens who worked with Rankin; Registry Office, Grey County, Abstract Index of Sydenham Township.
138. Dunham, *op. cit.*

139. Smith, *op. cit.*, p. 115.
140. John Lovell, *Canada Directory*, 1857.
141. Old Post Office Museum, Oakville, William Miller to John Miller, May 12, 1842.
142. *British Colonist*, May 11, 1842.
143. Osgoode Hall, Surrogate Clerk's Office, Will of William Chisholm, March 27, 1841.
144. Registry Office, Halton County, Abstracts of lots 13, 14, 15, 16 of the 3rd concession, lots 13, 14, 15, 16 of the Broken Front, Trafalgar Township.

Chapter six (pp. 177–221)

1. *Niagara Reporter* quoted in the *Montreal Gazette,* Sept. 25, 1836.
2. *Journal of the Gore District Council, 1849*, app., p. 68.
3. *Ibid.*
4. Public Archives of Canada, Upper Canada Land Petitions, T, 1806–8, Jan. 5, 1808.
5. Ontario Archives, Trafalgar Township Assessment Roll, 1823.
6. Inhabitants of the Township of Trafalgar to Robert Gourlay, 1817 (see chapter v, note 15).
7. Trafalgar Township Assessment Rolls, 1823 *et sequitur.*
8. *Ibid.*
9. *Ibid.,* 1827.
10. *Minutes of the Gore District Council,* 1840–9, 1850–2.
11. Bruce McCausland, "The Vanished Village," magazine article (scrap-book, undated).
12. *Patriot,* Toronto, Oct, 29, 1840.
13. Registry Office for Halton County, Trafalgar Township Abstract Index; Trafalgar Township Assessment Rolls; *Minutes of the Presbytery of Hamilton and Toronto, 1844–57; Streetsville Review* and other newspapers, various issues containing advertisements.
14. *Journals of the Legislative Assembly, Province of Canada,* 1847, app. (Q.Q.).
15. *Ibid.*
16. *Hamilton Gazette* quoted in the *Montreal Gazette,* March 16, 1836.
17. *Streetsville Review,* April 10, 1857.
18. W. S. Wallace, *Dictionary of Canadian Biography* (Toronto, 1945).
19. Records of Knox Church, Oakville.
20. P.A.C. Upper Canada Land Petitions, 1806–7, M Bundle 8, no. 42.
21. Ontario Archives, Trafalgar Township Papers, lot 19, 4th concession S.D.S., Crown lease, Sept. 29, 1807.
22. W. S. Savage, "The Early Days," MS in possession of Miss Ellena Savage.
23. St. Jude's Church, Burial Register.
24. This sawmill appears for the first time on the Trafalgar Township Assessment Roll of 1839 but some rolls immediately preceding this date are missing.
25. P.A.C., Census of Trafalgar Township, 1851.
26. Trafalgar Township Assessment Roll, 1839.
27. P.A.C., Upper Canada Land Petitions, H Bundle, 1806–7, no. 8.
28. P.A.C., Upper Canada Land Book G, p. 129.
29. John Ross Robertson, *Landmarks of Toronto* (Toronto, 1894), vol. I, pp. 17-18.
30. Toronto Public Library, MS Collection, Dictionary of Quetton St. George.
31. Trafalgar Township Assessment Roll, 1828.
32. Trafalgar Township Census, 1851.
33. John A. Williams, Reminiscences, copies of bills re construction of Methodist chapel.
34. Order-in-Council, June 17, 1806.
35. Trafalgar Township Census, 1851.
36. P.A.C., Upper Canada Land Petitions, L 1801 Bundle 5, no. 15.
37. Robertson, *Landmarks of Toronto,* vol. I, p. 342.

38. *Ibid.*, p. 310.
39. *Journals of the House of Assembly,* March 4, 1803.
40. Minutes of the Court Quarter Sessions of the Home District, Jan. 23, 1813.
41. Savage, "The Early Days."
42. D. D. Calvin, *A Saga of the St. Lawrence* (Toronto, 1945), pp. 58–9.
43. *Streetsville Review,* Nov. 4, 1848.
44. A. H. E. Jacobs, *Bread and Man*: *Ciba Symposium* (pamphlet, Ciba Co., Montreal), Dec., 1946, vol. VIII, no. 9, pp. 480–3.
45. George Winter Warr, *Canada as it is* (London, 1847), p. 82.
46. Census of Trafalgar Township, 1841.
47. P.A.C., Upper Canada Land Petitions, 1804–6, P. 7, no. 2.
48. Minutes of the Court of Quarter Sessions of the Home District, Jan. 13, 1816.
49. *Ibid.,* 1809, 1814.
50. *Ibid,* 1814.
51. *Ibid.*, 1813.
52. The impression that the name of Post's Corners derived from the post office is erroneous. The spot was known by that name before the Trafalgar Post Office was located there. In the *Journal of the Municipal Council of the District of Gore,* 1849, p. 114, we find, "commonly called Post's or the Seventh Line Road." Two years later W. H. Smith in *Canada*: *past, present and future* (1851), vol. I, p. 261, wrote, "At the point of junction, where the plank road crosses Dundas street, is the Trafalgar post-office, and close by is a steam saw mill; but the place is more generally known from being the site of 'Post's tavern,' the usual stopping place of stages travelling the road." Tremaine's Map of the County of Halton, 1858, shows the corners as "Postsville."
53. 9 Vict., c. 98, May 18, 1846.
54. *Spectator,* Hamilton, Dec. 7, 1850.
55. Trafalgar Township By-law no. 15, Feb. 13, 1850.
56. W. H. Smith, *Canada*: *past, present and future,* vol. I, p. 259.
57. *Ibid.*; *Spectator,* Dec. 7, 1850.
58. *Journal of the Proceedings of the Municipal Council of the District of Gore* (Hamilton, 1849), p. 114.
59. *Spectator,* Dec. 7, 1850.
60. *Ibid.*
61. *Journal of the Proceedings of the Municipal Council of the District of Gore,* 1840–9, p. 68.
62. *Journal of the Board of Agriculture,* 1851–8, p. 526.
63. John A. Williams, Reminiscences.
64. Ontario Archives, Trafalgar Township Papers, lot 12, 2nd S.D.S.
65. *Ibid.*
66. *Journal of the Legislative Assembly, Province of Canada,* 1845–6, app. (A).
67. Registry Office for Halton County, Abstract Index; Trafalgar Township Assessment Rolls.
68. Port Hope *Guide,* March 15, 1859, quoted in E. C. Guillet, *Early Life in Upper Canada* (Toronto, 1933), p. 539.
69. *Journal of the Municipal Council of the Township of Trafalgar,* 1856, p. 7.
70. *Journal of the Municipal Council of the County of Halton,* 1858, By-law no. 20.
71. *Tackabury's Atlas of Canada,* 1875, p. 47.
72. *Ibid.*
73. *Sentinel,* Oakville, Dec. 14, 1855.
74. *Streetsville Review,* April 9, 1853.
75. *Canadian Champion,* Milton, July 25, 1867.
76. George C. Tremaine, Map of Halton County, 1858.
77. *Sentinel,* Dec. 14, 1855.
78. *Globe*, Toronto, Dec. 14, 1855.
79. Cobourg *Star,* Jan. 10, 1855, quoted in Guillet's *Early Life in Upper Canada,* p. 572.

80. Halton *Journal,* Milton, Dec. 6, 1855.
81. *Sentinel,* Oct. 7, 1856.
82. Burial Register, Knox Church, Oakville.
83. Trafalgar Township Assessment Rolls.
84. *Oakville Star,* Oct. 19, 1893.
85. *Streetsville Review,* March 21, 1857.
86. 18 Vict., c. 192, 1855.
87. *Sentinel,* Dec. 11, 1855.
88. *Journal of the Legislative Assembly, Province of Canada,* 1843, app. (A.A.).
89. P.A.C., Upper Canada Sundries, 1841–3, no. 24919, Sept. 23, 1842.
90. *Journal of the Legislative Assembly,* 1844, app. (I.I.).
91. P.A.C., Upper Canada State Book H, p. 615.
92. P.A.C., Upper Canada State Book K, p. 198.
93. P.A.C., Upper Canada State Book I, p. 491.
94. *Oakville Weekly Sun,* Aug. 20, 1850.
95. P.A.C., Upper Canada State Book K, p. 198.
96. *Journal of the Legislative Assembly,* 1846, app. (I.I.); *Ibid.,* 1853, app. (B).
97. Chisholm Papers, Account Book, March, 1852–Oct., 1855, p. 134.
98. Chisholm Papers, Dissolution of Partnership between John Doty and Abiather Ashley Hibberd, Nov. 19, 1855.
99. *Sentinel,* quoted in the *Streetsville Review,* May 2, 1854.
100. John Lovell, ed., *Canada Directory,* 1857–8.
101. *Sentinel,* Sept. 11, 1857.
102. Isabella Bishop, *The Englishwoman in America* (London, 1856), p. 193.
103. P.A.C., Census of the Town of Oakville, 1861.
104. *Canadian Champion,* Jan. 7, 1864.
105. *Ibid.*
106. Ontario Archives, Land Book J, p. 530.
107. P.A.C., Upper Canada Land Petitions, 1804–6, P. 7, no. 2; Henry Scadding, *Toronto of Old* (Toronto, 1874), p. 96.
108. Registry Office for Halton County, Abstract Index; George Walton, *A Commercial Directory and Register* (Toronto, 1837), p. 105.
109. Ontario Archives, Register of Prisoners committed to the Home District Gaol beginning Jan. 1838, no. 319.
110. P.A.C., Upper Canada Sundries, Petition of J. Milbourne, 1839.
111. Charles Lindsey, *Life and Times of Wm. Lyon Mackenzie* (Toronto, 1862), vol. II, p. 380.
112. *British Colonist,* Toronto, Aug. 16, 1838.
113. *Ibid.,* Nov. 3, 1838.
114. *Examiner,* Toronto, Feb. 5, 1840.
115. *Journal of the Legislative Assembly,* 1853, app. (B.).
116. P.A.C., Census of the Town of Oakville, 1861.
117. Trafalgar Township Assessment Rolls; *Gazetteer of Ontario,* 1869.
118. Williams, Reminiscences.
119. Trafalgar Township Census, 1851; Lovell's *Canada Directory,* supplement, 1853.
120. Map of the Town of Oakville, 1863.
121. *Sentinel,* Dec. 21, 1855.
122. P.A.C., Census of the Town of Oakville, 1861.
123. Henry Morgan, *Canadian Men and Women of Our Time* (Toronto, 1912).
124. *Ibid.*
125. *Canadian Champion,* July 15, 1869.
126. *History of Toronto and County of York, Ontario* (Toronto, 1885), vol. II, p. 141.
127. Ontario Historical Society, *Papers and Records,* vol. III, p. 171.
128. *British Colonist,* May 26, 1841.
129. *Canadian Biographical Dictionary and Portrait Gallery of Eminent Self-made Men* (Toronto, 1885), Ontario vol. I, p. 723; *Globe,* July 15, 1893.

130. Oakville newspaper, obituary of W. E. Hagaman.
131. Charles Sovereign, Journal.
132. P.A.C., Registry of Ownership of Vessels registered at the Port of Oakville, undated.
133. *Journal of the Legislative Assembly,* 1854, app. (A.).
134. *Toronto Evening Telegram,* July 7, 1945, C. H. J. Snider's column, "Schooner Days."
135. Oil painting of the *Coquette* in possession of Mrs. Irven Fell.
136. Walter Havighurst, *The Long Ships Passing* (New York, 1945), p. 75.
137. Chisholm Papers, Agreement between R .K. Chisholm and Captain Peter Lyon, Feb. 11, 1852.
138. Williams, Reminiscences.
139. *Journal of the Municipal Council of the Township of Trafalgar,* 1854, p. 210.
140. *Oakville Record-Star,* 1941, obituary of Joel Mackinder.
141. *Sentinel,* Sept. 11, 1857.
142. G. A. Cuthbertson, *Freshwater,* (Toronto, 1931), p. 240.
143. *Milwaukee News,* undated clipping in possession of Mr. George Ingleby, Toronto.
144. Cuthbertson, *op. cit.*; Savage, *op. cit.*; "Schooner Days," *Toronto Evening Telegram,* June 30, 1945.
145. *Spectator,* July 21, 1852.
146. Trafalgar Township Census, 1841; information received from Miss Dorothy Wilson, Toronto.
147. Diaries of John Moore in possession of Miss Jean Moore, Rochester.
148. *Oakville Weekly Sun,* Sept. 5, 1850.

Chapter seven (pp. 222–265)

1. W. H. Smith, *Canadian Gazetteer* (Toronto, 1846).
2. Public Archives of Canada, Census of Trafalgar Township, 1851.
3. *Sentinel,* Oakville, Sept. 11, 1857.
4. *Ibid.,* Dec. 11, 1855.
5. *Ibid.*
6. *Ibid.*
7. 1851 Census.
8. Chisholm Papers, Account Book, March, 1852, to Oct., 1855, p. 104.
9. *Ibid.*
10. Toronto Public Library, Banting Collection, Pim Papers.
11. *Canadian Champion,* Milton, May 20, 1869, announcement of sale of Romain's household effects by Wm. Wass, auctioner.
12. *Sentinel,* Sept. 11, 1857.
13. Susanna Moodie, *Life in the Clearings Versus the Bush* (London, 1853), p. 52.
14. *Ibid.,* p. 293.
15. *Sentinel,* Sept. 11, 1857.
16. *Ibid.*
17. *Oakville Weekly Sun,* Sept. 7, 1850.
18. *Ibid.*
19. Chisholm Papers.
20. *Sentinel,* Sept. 11, 1857.
21. *Canadian Champion,* June 18, 1862.
22. *Ibid.,* June 3, 1869.
23. George J. Sumner, diaries.
24. *Gazetteer of the County of Halton,* 1869.
25. Newspaper clipping in possession of Mrs. Marion Capewell, Haddonfield, New Jersey.
26. *Sentinel,* Sept. 11, 1857.
27. *Ibid.*

28. W. S. Savage, Address delivered on occasion of the Fiftieth Anniversary of St. John's Church, Oakville, Jan. 13, 1928.
29. *Canadian Sons of Temperance,* March 11, 1851, quoted in the *Express,* Oakville, March 26, 1880.
30. Lorenzo Sabine, *Loyalists of the American Revolution* (Boston, 1864), vol. I, pp. 222–3.
31. P.A.C., Upper Canada Land Petitions, B. 3, Part 1 (1791–1820), no. 31; *Twentieth Report of the Department of Public Records and Archives of Ontario,* pp. 128, 172.
32. William Riddell, *The Legal Profession in Upper Canada* (Toronto, 1916), p. 25.
33. *The Express,* Hamilton, Oct. 28, 1837.
34. *Oakville Weekly Sun,* July 20, 1850.
35. *Streetsville Review,* April 9, 1853.
36. *Sentinel,* April 7, 1854.
37. *Ibid.*, Sept. 11, 1857.
38. *Ibid.,* Dec. 18, 1855.
39. P.A.C., Provincial Secretary's Office, Letter no. 17452, 1847.
40. *Ibid.,* Letter no. 17701, 1847.
41. *Journals of the Legislative Assembly, Province of Canada,* 1848–9, app. (A), no. 27.
42. *Sentinel,* Dec. 21, 1855.
43. Earl Chapin May, *The Canning Clan* (New York, 1938), pp. 1–13.
44. George Nasmith, *Timothy Eaton* (Toronto, 1923), pp. 72–3.
45. *Canadian Champion,* July 8, 1869.
46. Census, Town of Oakville, 1861.
47. *Sentinel,* April 7, 1854.
48. *Ibid.,* Oct. 7, 1856.
49. *Journals of the Legislative Assembly, Province of Canada,* 1846, app. (I.I.); Customs returns, 1851.
50. P.A.C., State Book K, p. 198.
51. *Journals of the Legislative Assembly, Province of Canada,* 1846, app. (I.I.).
52. *Journals of the Legislative Assembly,* 1853, app. (B.).
53. P.A.C., State Book P., p. 136.
54. *Ibid.,* p. 332
55. Chisholm Papers.
56. *Journals of the Legislative Assembly,* 1857, app., accounts of ports.
57. Archives of the Bank of Toronto.
58. *Halton Journal,* Milton, July 31, 1857.
59. Trafalgar Township Account Book, 1850–72, June 20th, 1859; *Council Minutes of the Municipality of the County of Halton,* 1859; *ibid.*, Town of Oakville.
60. C. C. Taylor, *Toronto "Called Back"* (Toronto, 1886), p. 208.
61. *Sentinel,* Dec. 21, 1855.
62. Oakville newspaper clipping, obituary of Edward Hillmer.
63. *Sentinel,* Dec. 14, 1855.
64. W. H. Young, autobiographical sketch in possession of Mrs. P. C. Sutton.
65. *Streetsville Review,* Oct. 13, 1853.
66. *Oakville Weekly Sun,* Sept. 7, 1850.
67. *Sentinel,* April 7, 1854.
68. *Ibid.*
69. Ontario Archives, Trafalgar Township Papers, lot 9, 3rd concession S.D.S.
70. *Oakville Weekly Sun,* Aug. 20, 1850.
71. Charles Sovereign, Journal.
72. *Journal of the Board of Agriculture,* 1851–8.
73. *Ibid.*
74. *Sentinel,* April 7, 1854.
75. *Ibid.,* Dec. 21, 1855.
76. *Gazetteer of the County of Halton,* 1869–70.

77. *Journal of the Board of Agriculture,* 1851–8.
78. *Sentinel,* Jan. 10, 1857.
79. Census, Town of Oakville, 1871.
80. *Spectator,* July 23, 1856.
81. *Oakville Star,* 1908, obituary of William Litchfield.
82. *County of Halton Directory,* 1869–70.
83. Map of Oakville, 1863; *Spectator,* July 13, 1866.
84. *Ibid.; Gazetteer of Halton County,* 1869–70; Census, Town of Oakville, 1871.
85. Ontario Archives, Report of Archdeacon A. N. Bethune of Archidiaconal Tour of the Gore and Wellington Districts, December–January, 1847–8.
86. *Spectator,* March 1, 1854.
87. *Christian Guardian,* 1851, reprinted in an Oakville newspaper.
88. Trafalgar Township Record Book, 1844–74.
89. *Minutes of the Municipal Council, Town of Oakville,* liquor licences; gazetteer lists.
90. *Streetsville Review,* Dec. 23, 1853.
91. Trafalgar Township Account Book, 1850–74 liquor licences.
92. *Streetsville Review,* Dec. 23, 1853.
93. *Sentinel,* Dec. 17, 1855.
94. *Oakville Record-Star,* 1935.
95. *Minutes of the Municipal Council, Town of Oakville,* 1857, p. 64.
96. George J. Sumner, Diary.
97. P.A.C., Provincial Secretary's Office, Letters no. 7324, 7601, 1843–4.
98. *Sentinel,* various issues during 1850's.
99. *Journals of the Legislative Assembly, Province of Canada,* 1852, app. (E.E.).
100. *Ibid.,* 1853, app. (V.).
101. *Ibid.,* 1856, app., Mail contracts.
102. *Sentinel,* Oct. 7, 1856.
103. Map of Halton County, 1858.
104. *Sentinel,* Dec. 21, 1855.
105. *Ibid.*
106. *Journals of the Legislative Assembly, Province of Canada,* 1857, app. (no. 49).
107. Map of Oakville, 1863; Registry Office for Halton County, Abstract Index, Town of Oakville.
108. Census of Trafalgar Township, 1851.
109. *Oakville Star,* 1905.
110. *Oakville Weekly Sun,* Sept. 7, 1850.
111. *Spectator,* March 24, 1858.
112. Chisholm Papers, Prospectus of *Sentinel,* Nov. 22, 1853.
113. *Spectator,* Nov. 7, 1855.
114. *Sentinel,* April 4, 1854.
115. Canadian Press Association, *A History of Canadian Journalism* (Toronto, 1908), p. 7.
116. P.A.C., Upper Canada Land Petitions, C 1817–22, nos. 23, 53.
117. *Ibid.*
118. Chisholm Papers, W. M. King, to R. K. Chisholm, Nov. 10, 1845.
119. *Minutes of the Town Council,* 1860, printed by the *Advertiser.*
120. *Ontario Gazetteer,* 1869.
121. *Canadian Champion,* July 5, 1869.
122. *Souvenir Booklet of Burlington the Beautiful,* 1867–1927, p. 7.
123. *Canadian Champion,* April 16, 1868.
124. *Ibid.*
125. John A. Williams, Reminiscences.
126. *British Colonist,* Toronto, June 7, 1853.
127. W. H. Smith, *Canada: past, present and future* (Toronto, 1851), vol. I, p. 260.
128. *Christian Guardian,* Sept. 15, 1847.

129. John Lovell, ed., *Canada Directory,* 1851.
130. Chisholm Papers, Statement of Imports and Exports at Oakville Harbour, 1853.
131. *Ibid.,* Account Book, March, 1852 to Oct., 1855, p. 9.
132. *Ibid.,* p. 257.
133. D. D. Calvin, *A Saga of the St. Lawrence* (Toronto, 1945), p. 143.
134. *Ibid.,* p. 118.
135. John Ross Robertson, *Landmarks of Toronto* (Toronto, 1894), vol. II, p. 889.
136. Calvin, *op. cit.,* p. 122.

Chapter eight (pp. 266–288)

1. Sir Richard Bonnycastle, *Canada and the Canadians, in 1846* (London, 1846), vol. II, p. 37.
2. A. Macmurchy and T. A. Reed, *Our Royal Town of York* (Toronto, 1929), pp. 18–20.
3. Knox Church records, Session Minutes, Canada Presbyterian Church, 1853-95, p. 250.
4. *Ibid.,* p. 163.
5. *County of Halton Directory,* 1869-70.
6. *Minutes of the Synod, Canada Presbyterian Church,* 1868, app.
7. *Ibid.*
8. *Ibid.*
9. Session Minutes, *op. cit.,* p. 191.
10. Ontario Archives, Trafalgar Township Papers, lot 11, 4th concession S.D.S.; Census, Town of Oakville, 1861.
11. *Oakville Star,* Nov. 15, 1928, obituary of Thomas Nisbet.
12. *Minutes of the Municipal Council,* Town of Oakville, 1868.
13. *Canadian Champion,* Oct. 8, 1868.
14. J. E. Sanderson, *Methodism in Canada* (Toronto, 1910), vol. II, p. 166; W. S. Savage, Address delivered on the occasion of the Fiftieth Anniversary of St. John's Church, Oakville, Jan. 13, 1928.
15. *Wesleyan Methodist Almanac,* 1844.
16. Minutes of the Nelson Circuit, 1832–94.
17. *Ibid.*
18. *County of Halton Directory,* 1869–70.
19. *Christian Guardian,* Dec. 9, 1857, notice of the reopening of the church.
20. *Ibid.,* Feb. 12, 1890, letter of Rev. Samuel C. Philp; Minutes of the Nelson Circuit.
21. Registry Office of Halton County, Abstract Index.
22. *Sentinel,* May 15, 1857.
23. Sanderson, *op. cit.,* vol. II, p. 27.
24. *Ibid.,* p. 125.
25. Ontario Archives, Trafalgar Township Papers, lot 19, 4th concession S.D.S., Crown Lease, Sept. 29, 1807.
26. Map of Halton County, 1858, George C. Tremaine.
27. St. Augustine's Church, Dundas, Baptismal and Marriage Registers.
28. Census, Town of Oakville, 1861.
29. *County of Halton Directory,* 1869–70.
30. Ontario Archives, Strachan Letter Book, 1844–79. July 3, 1844.
31. *Transactions of the Royal Society of Canada,* Series III, 1938, vol. XXXII, section II, p. 57, J. J. Talman, "Clergy of the Church of England in Upper Canada."
32. Ontario Archives, Report of Archdeacon A. N. Bethune of Archidiaconal Tour of the Gore and Wellington Districts, December-January, 1847–8.
33. Ontario Archives, Petition re consecration of St. Jude's Church, Oakville, 1849.
34. St. Jude's Church Records, Dedication of Bishop Strachan, July 1, 1849.
35. Henry Scadding, *Toronto of Old* (Toronto, 1873), p. 336.

36. Ontario Archives, Trafalgar Township Papers, lot 8, 3rd concession S.D.S., petition of Richard Coates, 1824.
37. Scadding, *Toronto of Old,* p. 202.
38. Ontario Archives, Crown Land Papers, Account Book, 1836–55.
39. *Journal of the Board of Agriculture,* 1851–8, p. 583.
40. Coates Papers in possession of Mr. E. G. Lusty, Rodnev, Ont.
41. *Journal of the Municipal Council of the Township of Trafalgar,* April Session, 1850, p. 17.
42. Trafalgar Township By-law no. 26, Feb. 10. 1851; Trafalgar Township Account Book, 1850–74.
43. Chisholm Papers, Account Book, March, 1852, to Oct., 1855, school accounts.
44. Ontario Archives, Educational Papers, Annual Report of Local Superintendent, Trafalgar Township, 1852.
45. Trafalgar Township Account Book, 1850–74.
46. *Journal of Education for Upper Canada,* vol. IV, p. 74, Report of Rev. John Porteus.
47. *Ontario Educational Report for 1853,* p. 62.
48. Ontario Archives, Educational Papers, G. K. Chisholm to Dr. E. Ryerson, Dec. 16, 1853.
49. Trafalgar Township By-law no. 62, Feb. 13, 1854.
50. These conclusions have been drawn only after close examination of the interior and exterior construction of Central School, and a study of old drawings and photographs, keeping in view the building practices at various periods and the amounts of money appropriated.
51. P.A.C., State Book N, p. 110.
52. Trafalgar Township Account Book, 1850–74.
53. *Minutes of the Municipal Council of the County of Halton,* 1855, p. 27.
54. *Ontario Educational Report,* 1858; *Ibid.,* 1860, p. 80; *Minutes of the Municipal Council of the Town of Oakville,* 1858, p. 123.
55. *Sentinel,* Dec. 2, 1855.
56. Ontario Archives, Educational Papers, 1850–94, Common School Reports.
57. *Ibid.*
58. *Council Minutes, Town of Oakville,* 1858, p. 67.
59. *Canada Sessional Papers,* 1869, vol. II (no. 3), p. 60.
60. *Ontario Educational Report,* 1861, p. 203.
61. *Ibid.,* p. 204.
62. Ontario Archives, *Catalogue of Books in the Oakville Grammar School,* 1865.
63. *Canadian Champion,* July 2, 1868.
64. *Ontario Educational Report.*
65. 4 & 5 Vict., c. 18, s. 11.
66. Census, Town of Oakville, 1861.
67. *Ontario Educational Report,* 1860, p. 56; *ibid.,* 1862.
68. *County of Halton Directory,* 1869–70.
69. Scadding, *Toronto of Old,* p. 94.
70. Henry Morgan, *Canadian Men and Women of Our Time* (Toronto, 1898).
71. Harvey Cushing, *The Life of Sir William Osler* (Oxford, 1925), vol. I, pp. 41–6.
72. Ontario Archives, *Oakville Mechanics' Institute,* 1853.
73. *Ibid.*
74. Ontario Archives, Department of Education Papers, G. K. Chisholm to Dr. Ryerson, Dec. 16, 1853.
75. *Canada Sessional Papers,* 1881, vol. XIII, part IV (no. 46), pp. 5–9.

Chapter nine (pp. 289–329)

1. George Walton, *A Commercial Directory and Register* (Toronto, 1837). Unfortunately the Minutes of the Court of Quarter Sessions of the Peace of the Gore District, 1816-40, have not come to light. The earliest assessment rolls of the Town of Oakville are dated 1866 and 1873, others having been destroyed in the Town Hall fire.

2. *Journals of the Municipal Council of the District of Gore, 1842–1849*, p. 70.
3. Charles Sovereign, Journal; *Globe*, Toronto, April 4, 1850.
4. *Minutes of the Municipal Council of the Township of Trafalgar*, 1855, p. 4.
5. Trafalgar Township Record Book, 1844-74.
6. *Ibid.*
7. *Ibid.*; Sovereign's Journal.
8. Record Book, *op. cit.*
9. *Ibid.*
10. *Journals of the Municipal Council, Gore District, op. cit.*
11. Trafalgar Township By-law no. 19, Nov. 13, 1850.
12. *Journal of the Municipality of the Township of Trafalgar*, 1850, p. 4.
13. *Ibid.*, p. 19.
14. Trafalgar Township By-law no. 12, Jan. 21, 1850.
15. *Ibid.*, no. 19, Nov. 13, 1850.
16. *Canadian Biographical Dictionary and Portrait Gallery of Eminent Self-made Men* (Toronto, 1880), p. 409.
17. *Journals of the House of Assembly*, 1836, app., vol. I, p. 10, no. 52.
18. Public Archives of Canada, Pay List of the 2nd Regiment of Gore Militia.
19. P.A.C., Series C 769, 1840-42, Royal Canadian Rifles, p. 99.
20. *Journals of the Legislative Assembly, Province of Canada*, 1843, app. (V); Commission on parchment in possession of E. A. Chisholm.
21. *Hamilton Gazette*, March 12, 1849.
22. *Ibid.*
23. Ontario Archives, G. K. Chisholm to J. S. Macdonald, March 16, 1850.
24. *Journals of the Legislative Assembly, Province of Canada*, 1851, app., accounts.
25. Susanna Moodie, *Life in the Clearings Versus the Bush* (London, 1853), p. 47.
26. 16 Vict., c. 218.
27. *Spectator*, Feb. 4, 1854.
28. *Sentinel*, Oakville, April 4, 1854.
29. *Spectator*, Jan. 13, 1855.
30. *Ibid.*, Feb. 2, 1860.
31. John Lovell, *Canada Directory*, 1857-8.
32. P.A.C., Census, Town of Oakville, 1861.
33. *Journal of the Legislative Assembly, Province of Canada*, 1857, p. 27.
34. *Statutes of Canada*, 1857, c. 93.
35. *Ibid.*
36. *Minutes, By-laws and Accounts of the Town Council of the Town of Oakville*, 1857, p. 4.
37. *Ibid.*
38. *Ibid.*, p. 33.
39. Trafalgar Township By-law no. 204, May 11, 1857.
40. Town of Oakville By-law no. 20, Oct. 7, 1857.
41. *Minutes, By-laws*, etc., Town of Oakville, 1857, p. 52.
42. *Spectator*, July 11, 1857.
43. *Argus*, Oakville, 1876.
44. Oakville newspaper clipping.
45. *Ibid.*
46. *Council Minutes, Town of Oakville*, 1878, p. 24.
47. Oakville newspaper clipping.
48. Alfred Hillmer, recollections in possession of Miss Mary Hillmer.
49. *Oakville Express*, 1880.
50. *Oakville Star*, clipping.
51. Numerous By-laws relative to assessment in the Town of Oakville.
52. *Sentinel*, Sept. 11, 1857.
53. Ontario Historical Society, *Papers and Records*, vol. XXVII, James J. Talman, "Agricultural Societies in Upper Canada."
54. *Sentinel*, Oct. 7, 1856.
55. *Spectator*, Nov. 7, 1855.
56. *Council Minutes*, 1857, p. 20.

57. *Spectator*, Jan. 7, 1864.
58. Chisholm Papers, Programme of Concert held at opening of Town Hall.
59. *Council Minutes*, 1863, p. 295.
60. George J. Sumner, Diary.
61. *Canadian Champion*, Oct. 22, 1868.
62. Advertising Poster, Trafalgar Agricultural Association's Fair, Aug. 1868, in possession of L. H. Cornwall.
63. George J. Sumner, Diary.
64. Various persons gave valuable papers into the hands of R. K. Chisholm to place in his vault for safe-keeping. This collection, the bulk of which had remained untouched in packets tied with red tape, included R. K. Chisholm's private papers and is referred to in this history as the Chisholm Papers.
65. Trafalgar Township By-law no. 67, March 8, 1854; Trafalgar Township Account Book, 1850-72.
66. *Journal of the Municipal Council of the Township of Trafalgar*, 1855, p. 11.
67. Traf. Twp. Account Book, 1850-72.
68. *Ibid.*
69. *Canadian Champion*, March 5, 1868.
70. *Council Minutes*, 1886, p. 106.
71. *Ibid.*, 1858, p. 67.
72. Chisholm Papers, correspondence re fencing burial plot.
73. P.A.C., Map of the central part of the Province of Upper Canada, 1 May 1819; Joliet's map, 1674, reproduced in Percy J. Robinson's *Toronto during the French Regime* (Toronto, 1933), p. 21.
74. Trafalgar Township By-law no. 83, Sept. 11, 1855.
75. *Journal of the Municipal Council of the Township of Trafalgar*, 1855, p. 10.
76. *Council Minutes, Town of Oakville*, 1859, p. 145.
77. Trafalgar Township By-law no. 34, April 8, 1851.
78. *Ibid.*, no. 10, Feb. 13, 1850.
79. *Ibid.*, no. 33, April 8, 1851.
80. Traf. Twp. Account Book, 1850-72; Chisholm Papers, Report of Justus Williams, Township Treasurer, 1856.
81. *Council Minutes, Town of Oakville*, 1864, p. 361.
82. *Ibid.*, 1867, p. 26.
83. *Ibid.*, p. 29.
84. *Ibid.*
85. *Canadian Champion*, July 7, 1869.
86. George J. Sumner, Diary.
87. *Canadian Champion*, April 23, 1874.

Chapter ten (pp. 333–375)

1. *Debates in the Parliament of Canada on Confederation*, 1865, p. 742.
2. 18 Vict., c. 192, 1855.
3. John Lovell, ed., *Canada Directory*, 1857-8.
4. *Canadian Champion*, Milton, March 24, 1870.
5. *Historical Atlas of Halton County*, Walker and Miles (Toronto, 1877), p. 78.
6. See D. C. Masters, *The Rise of Toronto* (Toronto, 1947).
7. *Historical Atlas*, p. 76.
8. *Minutes of the Municipal Council of the Town of Oakville*, Harbour Master's Reports, 1870's and 1880's.
9. John A. Williams, Reminiscences.
10. *Council Minutes*, 1867.
11. George Sumner, Diary.
12. *Statutes, Local and Private*, no. 75, c. 85, 1857.
13. *Toronto Evening Telegram*, March 23, 1946, C. H. J. Snider's column, "Schooner Days."
14. *Toronto Star Weekly*, Sept. 6, 1924.
15. Sumner, Diary.

16. *Council Minutes*, 1871.
17. *Journal of the House of Commons*, 1871, p. 102.
18. Chisholm Papers, Notice of Sale of Harbour, 1872.
19. *Council Minutes*, 1874, p. 62.
20. *Ibid.*
21. *Ibid.*
22. Williams, Reminiscences.
23. *Oakville Express*, June 17, 1875.
24. Public Archives of Canada, Census of the Town of Oakville, 1861.

British Canadians	904
French Canadians	9
Born in England	126
Born in Ireland	240
Born in Scotland	79
Born in United States	69
Miscellaneous	23
	1,450

25. Williams, Reminiscences.
26. *Canadian Historical Review*, vol. XXXIX, March, 1948, p. 30, J. M. S. Careless, "The Toronto *Globe* and Agrarian Ralicalism."
27. Williams, Reminiscences.
28. *Canadian Champion*, May 20, 1869.
29. *Ibid.*, July 15, 1869.
30. John Ross Robertson, *Landmarks of Toronto* (Toronto, 1894), vol. I, p. 264.
31. *Ibid.*, vol. II, pp. 958–60.
32. *Toronto Daily Star*, 1934.
33. *Historical Atlas*, p. 82.
34. *Oakville Express*, Feb. 6, 1880.
35. Sumner, Diary.
36. Williams, Reminiscences.
37. Trafalgar Township Assessment Roll, 1864.
38. Sumner, Diary.
39. Census of the Town of Oakville, 1871.
40. *Historical Atlas*, p. 82 .
41. *Gazetteer of Ontario*, 1869.
42. *Oakville Star*, Feb. 21, 1901.
43. *History of York County* (Toronto, 1885), vol. I, p. 159.
44. Registry Office, York County, Abstract Index.
45. *Canadian Champion*, July 6, 1869.
46. Census, Town of Oakville, 1871.
47. Williams, Reminiscences; information from the late Wilbur T. Marlatt.
48. Obituary notice of C. Armstrong, Oakville newspaper.
49. Charles Lindsey, *The Life and Times of Wm. Lyon Mackenzie* (Toronto, 1862), p. 393.
50. *Directory of Halton County*, 1869.
51. William H. Young, autobiographical sketch in possession of Mrs. P. C. Sutton.
52. Chisholm Papers, bills of W. H. Young.
53. *Directory of Halton County*, 1869; *Oakville Express*, 1875; *Oakville Star*, 1888; letterheads, 1900.
54. Council Minutes, 1860's, accounts.
55. *Argus*, Oakville, Sept. 26, 1873.
56. *Oakville Star*, 1896.
57. H. A. Innis and A. R. M. Lower, eds., *Select Documents in Canadian Economic History, 1783-1885* (Toronto, 1933), pp. 554–5.
58. *The Canadian Album* (Toronto, 1898), vol. I, p. 372.
59. *Oakville Star*, 1903.
60. Chisholm Papers, miscellaneous bills of Oakville merchants,

61. *Ibid.*, bills of Edward Hillmer.
62. Sumner, Diary.
63. *Ibid.*
64. *Ibid.*
65. *Standard*, Oakville, March 23, 1883.
66. *Oakville Express*, 1870.
67. John Ross Robertson, *The History of Freemasonry in Canada* (Toronto, 1899), vol. II, p. 255.
68. *Gazetteer of Ontario*, 1869.
69. *Canadian Champion*, March 12, 1869.
70. *Oakville Star*, April 5, 1929.
71. *Standard*, Oakville, Oct. 24, 1883.
72. Sumner, Diary.
73. *Canadian Champion*, Jan. 27, 1870.
74. C. H. J. Snider, *Annals of the R.C.Y.C.* (Toronto, 1937), p. 37.
75. *Oakville Star*, June 14, 1906.
76. *Council Minutes*, 1873, p. 22; *Express*, 1873.
77. Oakville newspaper, 1874.
78. Sumner, Diary.
79. *Journals of the Legislative Assembly, Province of Canada*, 1854-5, vol. XIII, no. 1, app. XX.
80. *Streetsville Review*, June 7, 1853.
81. John Lovell, *Canada Directory*, 1857-8.
82. *Journals of the Legislative Assembly, Province of Canada*, 1857, app. no. 3.
83. *Spectator*, Hamilton, Jan. 7, 1862.
84. *Council Minutes*, 1862, p. 267.
85. *Ibid.*
86. *Ibid.*, p. 268.
87. *Ibid.*, p. 263.
88. *Sessional Papers*, 1863, no. 15.
89. *Council Minutes*, 1862, p. 289.
90. *Spectator*, Hamilton, Nov. 5, 1863.
91. *Ibid.*, July 12, 1865.
92. *Historical Atlas*, p. 87.
93. Captain John A. Macdonald, *Troublous Times in Canada* (Toronto, 1877), p. 16.
94. *Canadian Champion*, Jan. 3, 1867.
95. *Ibid.*, Oct. 14, 1869.
96. William Panton, Recollections, MS in possession of author.
97. Regimental History Book, Peel, Dufferin and Halton Regiment.
98. *Ibid.*
99. Sumner, Diary; *Canadian Champion*, 1871.
100. *Council Minutes*, 1871, p. 67.
101. Sumner, Diary.
102. *Council Minutes*, 1874, pp. 14, 27.
103. *Ibid.*, 1879, p. 10.
104. General Order, Nov. 2, 1881.

Chapter eleven (pp. 376–410)

1. *Canadian Champion*, Milton, July 7, 1869.
2. *Oakville*, pamphlet, 1905.
3. *Canadian Champion*, July 7, 1869.
4. *Historical Atlas of Halton County* (Toronto, 1877), p. 81.
5. George Sumner, Diary.
6. *Ibid.*
7. *Spectator*, Hamilton, Aug. 25, 1866.
8. *Canadian Champion*, June 3, 1869.
9. John Ross Robertson, *Landmarks of Toronto* (Toronto, 1894), vol. II, p. 922.

10. *Ibid.*, pp. 240, 940.
11. Chisholm Papers, Indenture between George King Chisholm and the Municipal Council of the Town of Oakville, April 14, 1873; *Council Minutes*, 1873, p. 16.
12. *Council Minutes*, 1873, p. 18.
13. *Ibid.*, 1877, p. 14.
14. By-law no. 118, Town of Oakville, April 16, 1877; *Council Minutes*, 1859, p. 133.
15. *Council Minutes*, 1877, p. 18.
16. Sumner, Diary.
17. *Spectator*, Feb. 7, 1881; Sumner, Diary.
18. Sumner, Diary.
19. *Council Minutes*, 1886, p. 96.
20. *Ibid.*, p. 94.
21. *The Council Minutes of the Municipality of the Town of Oakville* which are extant begin 1857 and end 1886.
22. Robertson, *Landmarks of Toronto*, vol. II, pp. 932, 952.
23. John Ross Robertson, ed., *The Diary of Mrs. Simcoe* (Toronto, 1911), p. 304.
24. Robertson, *Landmarks of Toronto*, vol. II, p. 932.
25. Sumner, Diary.
26. *Ibid.*
27. *Oakville Star*, 1896; Sumner, Diary.
28. *Ibid.*
29. *Ibid.*
30. *Ibid.*
31. *Ibid.*
32. *Garden of Canada*, pamphlet, 1902.
33. *Ibid.*
34. *Oakville Star*, 1903.
35. *Ibid.*
36. W. H. Smith, *Canada: Past, Present and Future* (Toronto, 1851), vol. II, p. 103.
37. *Canadian Champion*, July 15, 1869.
38. *Ibid.*
39. *Ibid.*, July 7, 1869.
40. *Historical Atlas*, p. 82.
41. *Express*, Oakville, Feb. 6, 1880.
42. *Oakville Star*, 1903.
43. Map of Oakville, 1863.
44. Census, Town of Oakville, 1871.
45. Information given by Miss Minnie Brown, Galt.
46. *Historical Atlas*, p. 82.
47. *Oakville Star*, 1880's.
48. *Ibid.*, Oct. 19, 1893.
49. *Ibid.*
50. Sumner, Diary.
51. *Oakville Star*, Oct. 19, 1893; *Picturesque Oakville*, pamphlet, 1904–5.
52. *Globe*, Toronto, July 15, 1893.
53. H. A. Innis and A. R. M. Lower, eds., *Select Documents in Canadian Economic History, 1783-1885* (Toronto, 1933), p. 632.
54. Chisholm Papers, letters.
55. *Ibid.*, Ted Wilson to R. K. Chisholm, undated.
56. *Ibid.*, letters.
57. *Ibid.*, Letters Patent No. 42584, Berlin, March 6, 1888; U.S. Patent No. 421,244.
58. *In the Supreme Court of the United States, C. P. & J. A. Chisholm & Robert P. Scott versus Zachariah Johnson* (Washington, D.C. 1902), pp. 6–7; *Baltimore*, March, 1936, "History of Canning House Machinery Plant Crowded with Trade Romance," pp. 13–16.
59. Sumner, Diary.

60. *Ibid.*
61. *Council Minutes*, 1883, p. 134.
62. *Spectator*, April 19, 1883; Sumner, Diary; Williams, Reminiscences.
63. Trafalgar Township By-law no. 63, Feb. 13, 1854.
64. Sumner, Diary.
65. *Ibid.*
66. Williams, Reminiscences.
67. *Beautiful Oakville*, pamphlet, 1897.
68. *Oakville Star*, 1896.
69. *Council Minutes*, numerous entries, 1877-9.
70. *Ibid.*, 1879, p. 34.
71. Town of Oakville By-law no. 126, Jan. 12, 1880.
72. Sumner, Diary.
73. *Ibid.*
74. *Ibid.*
75. Oakville newspaper, 1887.
76. *Ibid.*
77. *Oakville Star*, 1895.
78. *Ibid.*
79. *Ibid.*
80. *Oakville*, pamphlet, 1912, p. 31.
81. *Oakville Star*, 1889.
82. Sumner, Diary.

Chapter twelve (pp. 411–50)

1. *Express*, Oakville, April 11, 1878, "Population of the Town of Oakville according to Religious Belief":

Canada Methodists	519
Episcopal	540
Presbyterians	374
British Episcopal Methodists	43
Episcopal Methodists	56
Roman Catholics	297
Baptists	6
Church of Christ	8
Total	1,843
Dogs	99
Cattle	139
Sheep	37
Hogs	111
Horses	92
Ratepayers	584

2. W. S. Savage, "Address delivered on the occasion of the Fiftieth Anniversary of St. John's Church, Oakville, January 13th, 1928"; John A. Williams, Reminiscences.
3. *Ibid.*
4. *Express*, 1887.
5. *Ibid.*
6. James McDonald's account books on loan to author.
7. Clipping from Oakville newspaper.
8. George Sumner, Diary.
9. *Ibid.*
10. St. Jude's Church, Minute Book, 1878-91.
11. Records relating to St. Jude's Church, Synod Office, Diocese of Niagara.
12. Minute Book, 1878-91.
13. Sumner, Diary.
14. 52 Vict., c. 96.

15. W. Perkins Bull, *From Strachan to Owen* (Toronto, 1937), p. 246.
16. Minute Book, 1878-91.
17. Document of Consecration, Synod Office, Diocese of Niagara.
18. Minute Book, 1878-91.
19. Sumner, Diary.
20. Minutes of the Session, Canada Presbyterian Church, Oakville, 1853-95, p. 119.
21. *Ibid.*, p. 121.
22. *Ibid.*, p. 233.
23. *Standard*, Oakville, Oct. 28, 1875.
24. Minutes of the Session, p. 222.
25. *Oakville Star*, 1888.
26. *Ibid.*
27. Minutes of the Session, June 8, 1888.
28. *Oakville Star*, Feb. 22, 1906.
29. Register of the British Episcopal Methodist Church, 1875-1909.
30. Sumner, Diary.
31. *Roll Call*, 1893, undated, scrap-book of Cynthia Hinton in possession of the late Mrs. George Harker.
32. *Ibid.*
33. Minutes of the Session, p. 212.
34. *Ontario Educational Report*, 1871, app., p. 64.
35. *Minutes of the Municipal Council of the County of Halton*, 1872, p. 28.
36. *Ontario Educational Report*, 1894.
37. *Minutes of the Municipal Council of the Town of Oakville*, 1874, p. 102.
38. Town of Oakville By-law no. 101, Oct. 1, 1874.
39. Information from the late Mr. Alfred Hillmer.
40. *Ontario Educational Report*, 1894.
41. *Globe*, Toronto, July 15, 1893.
42. *Nassagaweya Centennial, 1850-1950*, p. 30.
43. *Standard*, Oct. 24, 1878.
44. *Express*, Feb. 13, 1880.
45. *Ontario Educational Report*, 1882.
46. *Ibid.*, various years.
47. *Ibid.*
48. *Journals of Education in Upper Canada*, 1848, p. 81.
49. *Sessional Papers*, 1881, vol. XLIII, part 4 (no. 46), p. 144.
50. *Ibid.*
51. *Oakville Star*, 1903.
52. Sumner, Diary.
53. *Oakville Star*, Dec. 24, 1891.
54. *Ibid.*, Oct. 19, 1893.
55. *Ibid.*, 1911.
56. *Ibid.*, May 2, 1901.
57. *Picturesque Oakville*, pamphlet, 1904.
58. Sumner, Diary.
59. *Oakville Star*, Nov. 20, 1908.
60. *Oakville*, pamphlet, 1912, p. 6.
61. Sumner, Diary.
62. Data from the Bell Telephone Company of Canada.
63. *Standard*, March 23, 1883.
64. Williams, Reminiscences.
65. *Council Minutes*; Sumner, Diary.
66. Clippings from local newspapers, W. S. Davis scrap-book.
67. Sumner, Diary.
68. *Oakville Star*, 1904.
69. W. L. Stone, *Life of Joseph Brant* (Albany, 1864), vol. II, p. 501.
70. *Ibid.*, pp. 509, 516.
71. Mable Dunham, *Grand River* (Toronto, 1945), numerous references.
72. Public Archives of Canada, Land Book G, p. 114.

73. P.A.C., Upper Canada Sundries, Petition of Mary Gugins, Jan., 1816.
74. *Ibid.*
75. *Ibid.*
76. *Journals of the House of Assembly*, 1830, app., p. 148.
77. P.A.C., Land Book C, July 4, 1796.
78. Lincoln County Registry Office, North Grimsby Township, Abstract Index, lot 2, concession 2.
79. P.A.C., Land Book C, July 4, 1796.
80. *Annals of the Forty 1783-1818*, Grimsby Historical Society (1950), p. 36.
81. *Ibid.*, p. 32.
82. *Ibid.*
83. Halton County Registry Office, Will of Charles Anderson, Dec. 19, 1829.
84. *Oakville Star*, 1895.
85. Sumner, Diary.
86. John Ross Robertson, *Landmarks of Toronto* (Toronto, 1896), vol. II, p. 960.
87. The names of the designers and the years in which Captain Andrew's yachts were built were obtained from *Lloyd's Register of Yachts*, 1909-10; the launch dates were obtained from George Sumner's Diary.
88. Information from Mr. Charles F. Doty.
89. *Oakville Star*, 1896.
90. *Clubs and Yachts of the Great Lakes* (Toronto, 1908); C. H. J. Snider, *Annals of the Royal Canadian Yacht Club, 1852-1937* (Toronto, 1937).
91. *Oakville Star*, June 4, 1903.
92. Town of Oakville By-law no. 210, April 16, 1894.
93. *Oakville Star*, 1894.
94. Sumner, Diary.
95. *Oakville Star*, June 7, 1906.
96. *Ibid.*, 1911.
97. *Ibid.*, 1903.
98. Libbi Cruickshank, "The Financial Policy of the Maple Leaf Milling Company, Ltd., 1915-1924, Sarnia, Ont.," Queens University, B.Com. Thesis, 1927.
99. *Oakville Star*, 1911.
100. *Ibid.*
101. Information from Mr. Lorne Ashbury.
102. *Express*, April 10, 1880.
103. Information from Mr. Lorne Ashbury.
104. *Oakville*, pamphlet, 1912, p. 47.
105. *Oakville Star*, 1911.
106. Population figures, Town of Oakville.

1861—1,450	1891—1,823
1871—1,710	1908—1,800
1881—1,767	1911—2,374

107. Sumner, Diary.
108. *Oakville*, pamphlet, 1912, p. 24.
109. Sumner, Diary.

INDEX

www.ingramcontent.com/pod-product-compliance
Lightning Source LLC
LaVergne TN
LVHW010446080826
844660LV00027B/1222

* 9 7 8 1 4 8 7 5 7 9 0 5 0 *